PEARSON CUSTOM BUSINESS RESOURCES

Compiled by

Operations Management
Elizabethtown College

Pearson Learning Solutions

New York Boston San Francisco
London Toronto Sydney Tokyo Singapore Madrid
Mexico City Munich Paris Cape Town Hong Kong Montreal

Senior Vice President, Editorial and Marketing: Patrick F. Boles
Editor: Ana Díaz-Caneja
Development Editor: Abbey Lee Briggs
Operations Manager: Eric M. Kenney
Production Manager: Jennifer Berry
Art Director: Renée Sartell
Cover Designer: Renée Sartell

Cover Art: Courtesy of EyeWire/Getty Images and PhotoDisc/Getty Images. Photodisc, "Globe surrounded by business people on computer monitors," courtesy of Photodisc/Getty Images. Dave Cutler (Artist), "Man Dropping Coins Into Glass Jar," courtesy of David Cutler/Images.com. Dave Cutler (Artist), "Three Coins in Glass Jar," courtesy of David Cutler/Images.com. Dean Turner, "Stock Vector: Global Finance" Courtesy of Dean Turner/iStockphoto. Hal Bergman, "Refinery Silhouette" Courtesy of Hal Bergman/iStockphoto. Dan Barnes, "Cargo Container Ship Aerial View" Courtesy of Dan Barnes/iStockphoto. Franc Podgorsek, "Stock Numbers" Courtesy of Franc Podgorsek/iStockphoto. "Customer in Line at Grocery Store" Courtesy of Digital Vision Photography/Veer Inc. Owaki-Kulla, "Pumping Gas" Courtesy of Flirt Photography/Veer Inc. Lynn Johnson, "Yunnan Province, People's Republic of China" Courtesy of Lynn Johnson/Getty Images, Inc. Thomas Bendy, "Student Typing" Courtesy of Thomas Bendy/iStockphoto.

This special edition published in cooperation with Pearson Learning Solutions.

Printed in the United States of America.

Please visit our web site at *www.pearsoncustom.com.*

Attention bookstores: For permission to return any unsold stock, contact us at *pe-uscustomreturns@pearson.com.*

Pearson Learning Solutions, 501 Boylston Street, Suite 900, Boston, MA 02116
A Pearson Education Company
www.pearsoned.com

PEARSON

ISBN 10: 0-558-71799-3
ISBN 13: 978-0-558-71799-5

Editorial Advisory Board

Contents

Operations and Productivity

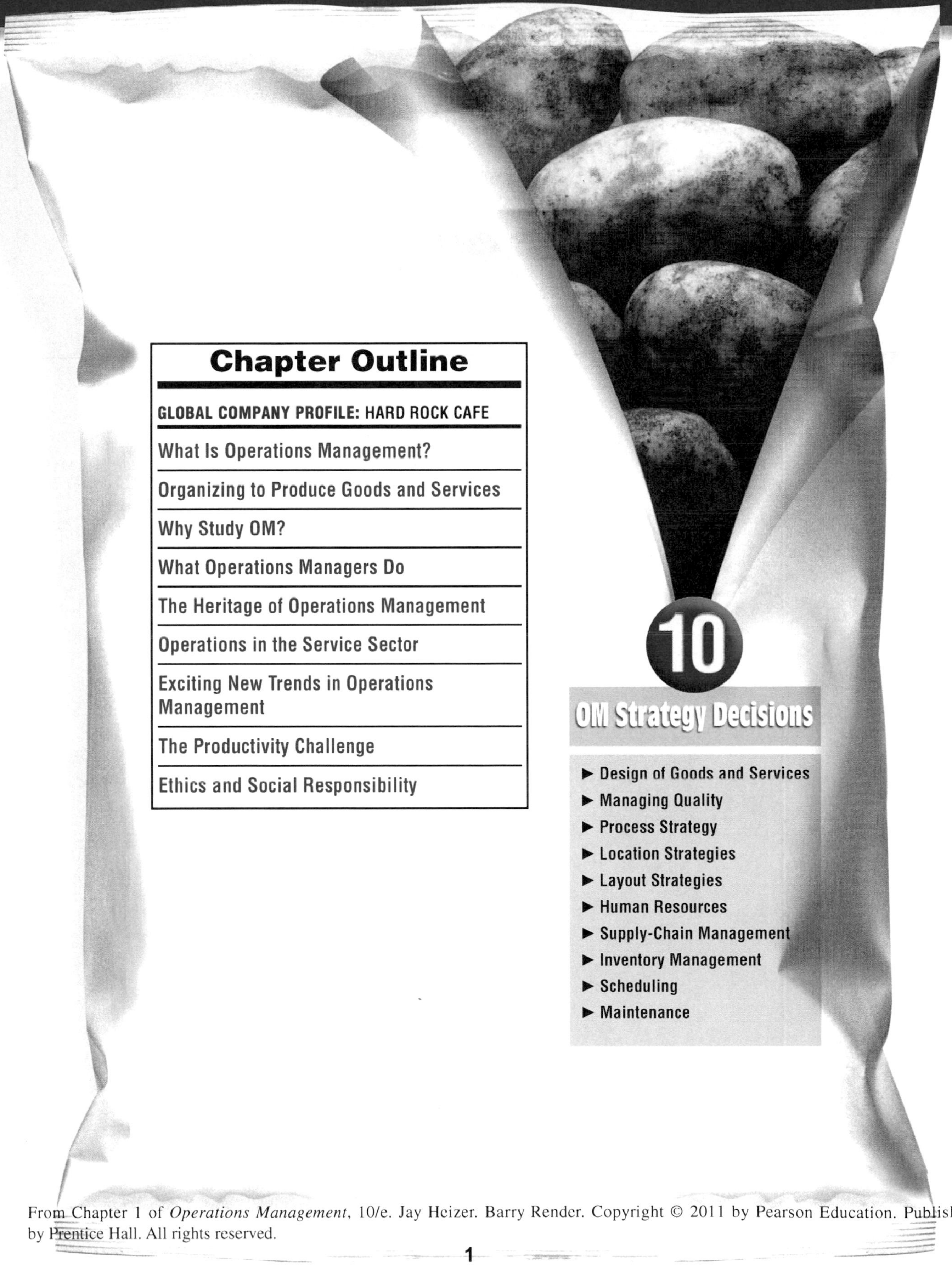

Chapter Outline

10

OM Strategy Decisions

- Design of Goods and Services
- Managing Quality
- Process Strategy
- Location Strategies
- Layout Strategies
- Human Resources
- Supply-Chain Management
- Inventory Management
- Scheduling
- Maintenance

OPERATIONS MANAGEMENT AT HARD ROCK CAFE

Operations managers throughout the world are producing products every day to provide for the well-being of society. These products take on a multitude of forms. They may be washing machines at Whirlpool, motion pictures at Dreamworks, rides at Disney World, or food at Hard Rock Cafe. These firms produce thousands of complex products every day—to be delivered as the customer ordered them, when the customers wants them, and where the customer wants them. Hard Rock does this for over 35 million guests worldwide every year. This is a challenging task, and the operations manager's job,

Hard Rock Cafe in Orlando, Florida, prepares over 3,500 meals each day. Seating more than 1,500 people, it is one of the largest restaurants in the world. But Hard Rock's operations managers serve the hot food hot and the cold food cold.

Andre Jenny/Alamy Images

Operations managers are interested in the attractiveness of the layout, but they must be sure that the facility contributes to the efficient movement of people and material with the necessary controls to ensure that proper portions are served.

Hard Rock Café

Hard Rock Café

Lots of work goes into designing, testing, and costing meals. Then suppliers deliver quality products on time, every time, for well-trained cooks to prepare quality meals. But none of that matters unless an enthusiastic wait staff, such as the one shown here, is doing its job.

whether at Whirlpool, Dreamworks, Disney, or Hard Rock, is demanding.

Orlando-based Hard Rock Cafe opened its first restaurant in London in 1971, making it over 39 years old and the granddaddy of theme restaurants. Although other theme restaurants have come and gone, Hard Rock is still going strong, with 129 restaurants in more than 40 countries—and new restaurants opening each year. Hard Rock made its name with rock music memorabilia, having started when Eric Clapton, a regular customer, marked his favorite bar stool by hanging his guitar on the wall in the London cafe. Now Hard Rock has millions of dollars invested in memorabilia. To keep customers coming back time and again, Hard Rock creates value in the form of good food and entertainment.

The operations managers at Hard Rock Cafe at Universal Studios in Orlando provide more than 3,500 custom products, in this case meals, every day. These products are designed, tested, and then analyzed for cost of ingredients, labor requirements, and customer satisfaction. On approval, menu items are put into production—and then only if the ingredients are available from qualified suppliers. The production process, from receiving, to cold storage, to grilling or baking or frying,

Hard Rock Café

Efficient kitchen layouts, motivated personnel, tight schedules, and the right ingredients at the right place at the right time are required to delight the customer.

and a dozen other steps, is designed and maintained to yield a quality meal. Operations managers, using the best people they can recruit and train, also prepare effective employee schedules and design efficient layouts.

Managers who successfully design and deliver goods and services throughout the world understand operations. In this text, we look not only at how Hard Rock's managers create value but also how operations managers in other services, as well as in manufacturing, do so. Operations management is demanding, challenging, and exciting. It affects our lives every day. Ultimately, operations managers determine how well we live.

Learning Objectives

LO1: Define operations management

LO2: Explain the distinction between goods and services

LO3: Explain the difference between production and productivity

LO4: Compute single-factor productivity

LO5: Compute multifactor productivity

LO6: Identify the critical variables in enhancing productivity

AUTHOR COMMENT Let's begin by defining what this course is about.

WHAT IS OPERATIONS MANAGEMENT?

LO1: Define operations management

Operations management (OM) is a discipline that applies to restaurants like Hard Rock Cafe as well as to factories like Ford and Whirlpool. The techniques of OM apply throughout the world to virtually all productive enterprises. It doesn't matter if the application is in an office, a hospital, a restaurant, a department store, or a factory—the production of goods and services requires operations management. And the *efficient* production of goods and services requires effective applications of the concepts, tools, and techniques of OM that we introduce in this text.

VIDEO 1.1 Operations Management at Hard Rock

VIDEO 1.2 Operations Management at Frito-Lay

As we progress through this text, we will discover how to manage operations in a changing global economy. An array of informative examples, charts, text discussions, and pictures illustrates concepts and provides information. We will see how operations managers create the goods and services that enrich our lives.

In this chapter, we first define *operations management*, explaining its heritage and exploring the exciting role operations managers play in a huge variety of organizations. Then we discuss production and productivity in both goods- and service-producing firms. This is followed by a discussion of operations in the service sector and the challenge of managing an effective and efficient production system.

Production
The creation of goods and services.

Operations management (OM)
Activities that relate to the creation of goods and services through the transformation of inputs to outputs.

Production is the creation of goods and services. **Operations management (OM)** is the set of activities that creates value in the form of goods and services by transforming inputs into outputs. Activities creating goods and services take place in all organizations. In manufacturing firms, the production activities that create goods are usually quite obvious. In them, we can see the creation of a tangible product such as a Sony TV or a Harley-Davidson motorcycle.

In an organization that does not create a tangible good or product, the production function may be less obvious. We often call these activities *services*. The services may be "hidden" from the public and even from the customer. The product may take such forms as the transfer of funds from a savings account to a checking account, the transplant of a liver, the filling of an empty seat on an airplane, or the education of a student. Regardless of whether the end product is a good or service, the production activities that go on in the organization are often referred to as operations, or *operations management*.

AUTHOR COMMENT Operations is one of the three functions that every organization performs.

ORGANIZING TO PRODUCE GOODS AND SERVICES

To create goods and services, all organizations perform three functions (see Figure 1). These functions are the necessary ingredients not only for production but also for an organization's survival. They are:

1. *Marketing*, which generates the demand, or at least takes the order for a product or service (nothing happens until there is a sale).
2. *Production/operations*, which creates the product.
3. *Finance/accounting*, which tracks how well the organization is doing, pays the bills, and collects the money.

Universities, churches or synagogues, and businesses all perform these functions. Even a volunteer group such as the Boy Scouts of America is organized to perform these three basic functions. Figure 1 shows how a bank, an airline, and a manufacturing firm organize themselves to perform these functions. The blue-shaded areas of Figure 1 show the operations functions in these firms.

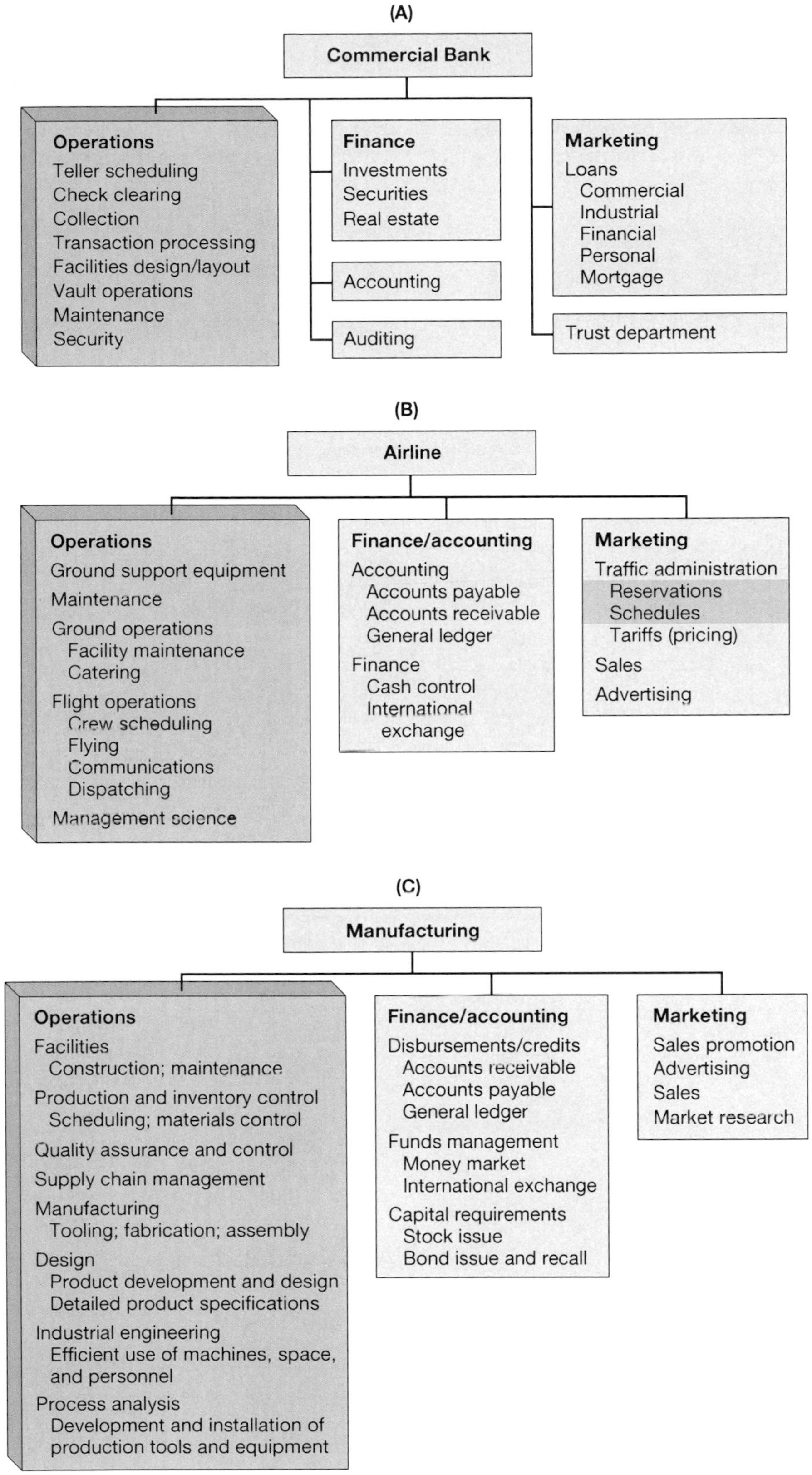

◀ **FIGURE 1**

Organization Charts for Two Service Organizations and One Manufacturing Organization

(A) A bank, (B) an airline, and (C) a manufacturing organization. The blue areas are OM activities.

AUTHOR COMMENT The areas in blue indicate the significant role that OM plays in both manufacturing and service firms.

AUTHOR COMMENT
Good OM managers are scarce and, as a result, career opportunities and pay are excellent.

WHY STUDY OM?

We study OM for four reasons:

1. OM is one of the three major functions of any organization, and it is integrally related to all the other business functions. All organizations market (sell), finance (account), and produce (operate), and it is important to know how the OM activity functions. Therefore, we study *how people organize themselves for productive enterprise*.
2. We study OM because we want to know *how goods and services are produced*. The production function is the segment of our society that creates the products and services we use.
3. We study OM to *understand what operations managers do*. Regardless of your job in an organization, you can perform better if you understand what operation managers do. In addition, understanding OM will help you explore the numerous and lucrative career opportunities in the field.
4. We study OM *because it is such a costly part of an organization*. A large percentage of the revenue of most firms is spent in the OM function. Indeed, OM provides a major opportunity for an organization to improve its profitability and enhance its service to society. Example 1 considers how a firm might increase its profitability via the production function.

EXAMPLE 1

Examining the options for increasing contribution

Fisher Technologies is a small firm that must double its dollar contribution to fixed cost and profit in order to be profitable enough to purchase the next generation of production equipment. Management has determined that if the firm fails to increase contribution, its bank will not make the loan and the equipment cannot be purchased. If the firm cannot purchase the equipment, the limitations of the old equipment will force Fisher to go out of business and, in doing so, put its employees out of work and discontinue producing goods and services for its customers.

APPROACH ▶ Table 1 shows a simple profit-and-loss statement and three strategic options (marketing, finance/accounting, and operations) for the firm. The first option is a *marketing option*, where good marketing management may increase sales by 50%. By increasing sales by 50%, contribution will in turn increase 71%. But increasing sales 50% may be difficult; it may even be impossible.

▶ TABLE 1
Options for Increasing Contribution

		Marketing Option[a]	*Finance/Accounting Option*[b]	*OM Option*[c]
	Current	**Increase Sales Revenue 50%**	**Reduce Finance Costs 50%**	**Reduce Production Costs 20%**
Sales	$100,000	$150,000	$100,000	$100,000
Costs of goods	–80,000	–120,000	–80,000	–64,000
Gross margin	20,000	30,000	20,000	36,000
Finance costs	–6,000	–6,000	–3,000	–6,000
Subtotal	14,000	24,000	17,000	30,000
Taxes at 25%	–3,500	–6,000	–4,250	–7,500
Contribution[d]	$ 10,500	$ 18,000	$ 12,750	$ 22,500

[a]Increasing sales 50% increases contribution by $7,500, or 71% (7,500/10,500).
[b]Reducing finance costs 50% increases contribution by $2,250, or 21% (2,250/10,500)
[c]Reducing production costs 20% increases contribution by $12,000, or 114% (12,000/10,500).
[d]Contribution to fixed cost (excluding finance costs) and profit.

The second option is a *finance/accounting option*, where finance costs are cut in half through good financial management. But even a reduction of 50% is still inadequate for generating the necessary increase in contribution. Contribution is increased by only 21%.

The third option is an *OM option*, where management reduces production costs by 20% and increases contribution by 114%.

SOLUTION ▶ Given the conditions of our brief example, Fisher Technologies has increased contribution from $10,500 to $22,500. It may now have a bank willing to lend it additional funds.

INSIGHT ▶ The OM option not only yields the greatest improvement in contribution but also may be the only feasible option. Increasing sales by 50% and decreasing finance cost by 50% may both be virtually impossible. Reducing operations cost by 20% may be difficult but feasible.

LEARNING EXERCISE ▶ What is the impact of only a 15% decrease in costs in the OM option? [Answer: A $19,500 contribution; an 86% increase.]

Example 1 underscores the importance of an effective operations activity of a firm. Development of increasingly effective operations is the approach taken by many companies as they face growing global competition.

WHAT OPERATIONS MANAGERS DO

AUTHOR COMMENT An operations manager must successfully address the 10 decisions around which this text is organized.

All good managers perform the basic functions of the management process. The **management process** consists of *planning*, *organizing*, *staffing*, *leading*, and *controlling*. Operations managers apply this management process to the decisions they make in the OM function. The 10 major decisions of OM are shown in Table 2. Successfully addressing each of these decisions requires planning, organizing, staffing, leading, and controlling. Typical issues relevant to these decisions are also shown.

Management process The application of planning, organizing, staffing, leading, and controlling to the achievement of objectives.

Where Are the OM Jobs? How does one get started on a career in operations? The 10 OM decisions identified in Table 2 are made by individuals who work in the disciplines shown in the blue areas of Figure 1. Competent business students who know their accounting, statistics, finance, and OM have an opportunity to assume entry-level positions in all of these areas. As you read this text, identify disciplines that can assist you in making these decisions. Then take courses in those

◀ TABLE 2
Ten Critical Decisions of Operations Management

Ten Decision Areas	Issues
1. Design of goods and services	What good or service should we offer? How should we design these products?
2. Managing quality	How do we define the quality? Who is responsible for quality?
3. Process and capacity design	What process and what capacity will these products require? What equipment and technology is necessary for these processes?
4. Location strategy	Where should we put the facility? On what criteria should we base the location decision?
5. Layout strategy	How should we arrange the facility? How large must the facility be to meet our plan?
6. Human resources and job design	How do we provide a reasonable work environment? How much can we expect our employees to produce?
7. Supply-chain management	Should we make or buy this component? Who should be our suppliers and how can we integrate them into our strategy?
8. Inventory, material requirements planning, and JIT (just-in-time)	How much inventory of each item should we have? When do we reorder?
9. Intermediate and short-term scheduling	Are we better off keeping people on the payroll during slowdowns? Which job do we perform next?
10. Maintenance	How do we build reliability into our processes? Who is responsible for maintenance?

AUTHOR COMMENT Current OM emphasis on quality and supply chain has increased job opportunities in these 10 areas.

Operations Management Positions	
SEARCH JOBS	
Date	Job Title
1/15	**Plant Manager** Division of Fortune 1000 company seeks plant manager for plant located in the upper Hudson Valley area. This plant manufacturers loading dock equipment for commercial markets. The candidate must be experienced in plant management including expertise in production planning, purchasing, and inventory management. Good written and oral communication skills are a must, along with excellent application of skills in managing people.
2/23	**Operations Analyst** Expanding national coffee shop: top 10 "Best Places to Work" wants junior level systems analyst to join our excellent store improvement team. Business or I.E. degree, work methods, labor standards, ergonomics, cost accounting knowledge a plus. This is a hands-on job and excellent opportunity for a team player with good people skills. West coast location. Some travel required.
3/18	**Quality Manager** Several openings exist in our small package processing facilities in the Northeast, Florida, and Southern California for quality managers. These highly visible positions require extensive use of statistical tools to monitor all aspects of service, timeliness, and workload measurement. The work involves (1) a combination of hands-on applications and detailed analysis using databases and spreadsheets. (2) process audits to identify areas for improvement and (3) management of implementation of changes. Positions involve night hours and weekends. Send resume.
4/6	**Supply Chain Manager and Planner** Responsibilities entail negotiating contracts and establishing long-term relationships with suppliers. We will rely on the selected candidate to maintain accuracy in the purchasing system, invoices, and product returns. A bachelor's degree and up to 2 years related experience are required. Working knowledge of MRP, ability to use feedback to master scheduling and suppliers and consolidate orders for best price and delivery are necessary. Proficiency in all PC Windows applications, particularly Excel and Word, is essential. Knowledge of Oracle business systems I is a plus. Effective verbal and written communication skills are essential.
5/14	**Process Improvement Consultants** An expanding consulting firm is seeking consultants to design and implement lean production and cycle time reduction plans in both service and manufacturing processes. Our firm is currently working with an international bank to improve its back office operations, as well as with several manufacturing firms. A business degree required; APICS certification a plus.

▲ **FIGURE 2** **Many Opportunities Exist for Operations Managers**

areas. The more background an OM student has in accounting, statistics, information systems, and mathematics, the more job opportunities will be available. About 40% of *all* jobs are in OM.

The following professional organizations provide various certifications that may enhance your education and be of help in your career:

- APICS, the Association for Operations Management (**www.apics.org**)
- American Society for Quality (ASQ) (**www.asq.org**)
- Institute for Supply Management (ISM) (**www.ism.ws**)
- Project Management Institute (PMI) (**www.pmi.org**)
- Council of Supply Chain Management Professionals (**www.cscmp.org**)

Figure 2 shows some recent job opportunities.

THE HERITAGE OF OPERATIONS MANAGEMENT

The field of OM is relatively young, but its history is rich and interesting. Our lives and the OM discipline have been enhanced by the innovations and contributions of numerous individuals. We now introduce a few of these people, and we provide a summary of significant events in operations management in Figure 3.

From the Collections of Henry Ford Museum & Greenfield Village

Cost Focus		Quality Focus	Customization Focus
Early Concepts 1776–1880 Labor Specialization (Smith, Babbage) Standardized Parts (Whitney) **Scientific Management Era 1880–1910** Gantt Charts (Gantt) Motion & Time Studies (Gilbreth) Process Analysis (Taylor) Queuing Theory (Erlang)	**Mass Production Era 1910–1980** Moving Assembly Line (Ford/Sorensen) Statistical Sampling (Shewhart) Economic Order Quantity (Harris) Linear Programming PERT/CPM (DuPont) Material Requirements Planning (MRP)	**Lean Production Era 1980–1995** Just-in-Time (JIT) Computer-Aided Design (CAD) Electronic Data Interchange (EDI) Total Quality Management (TQM) Baldrige Award Empowerment Kanbans	**Mass Customization Era 1995–2015** Globalization Internet/E-Commerce Enterprise Resource Planning International Quality Standards (ISO) Finite Scheduling Supply-Chain Management Mass Customization Build-to-Order Sustainability

▲ **FIGURE 3 Significant Events in Operations Management**

Eli Whitney (1800) is credited for the early popularization of interchangeable parts, which was achieved through standardization and quality control. Through a contract he signed with the U.S. government for 10,000 muskets, he was able to command a premium price because of their interchangeable parts.

Frederick W. Taylor (1881), known as the father of scientific management, contributed to personnel selection, planning and scheduling, motion study, and the now popular field of ergonomics. One of his major contributions was his belief that management should be much more resourceful and aggressive in the improvement of work methods. Taylor and his colleagues, Henry L. Gantt and Frank and Lillian Gilbreth, were among the first to systematically seek the best way to produce.

Another of Taylor's contributions was the belief that management should assume more responsibility for:

1. Matching employees to the right job.
2. Providing the proper training.
3. Providing proper work methods and tools.
4. Establishing legitimate incentives for work to be accomplished.

By 1913, Henry Ford and Charles Sorensen combined what they knew about standardized parts with the quasi-assembly lines of the meatpacking and mail-order industries and added the revolutionary concept of the assembly line, where men stood still and material moved.

Quality control is another historically significant contribution to the field of OM. Walter Shewhart (1924) combined his knowledge of statistics with the need for quality control and provided the foundations for statistical sampling in quality control. W. Edwards Deming (1950) believed, as did Frederick Taylor, that management must do more to improve the work environment and processes so that quality can be improved.

Operations management will continue to progress with contributions from other disciplines, including *industrial engineering* and *management science*. These disciplines, along with statistics, management, and economics, contribute to improved models and decision making.

Innovations from the *physical sciences* (biology, anatomy, chemistry, physics) have also contributed to advances in OM. These innovations include new adhesives, faster integrated circuits, gamma rays to sanitize food products, and higher-quality glass for LCD and plasma TVs. Innovation in products and processes often depends on advances in the physical sciences.

Especially important contributions to OM have come from *information technology*, which we define as the systematic processing of data to yield information. Information technology—with wireless links, Internet, and e-commerce—is reducing costs and accelerating communication.

Decisions in operations management require individuals who are well versed in management science, in information technology, and often in one of the biological or physical sciences. In this text, we look at the diverse ways a student can prepare for a career in operations management.

AUTHOR COMMENT
Services are especially important because almost 80% of all jobs are in service firms.

OPERATIONS IN THE SERVICE SECTOR

Manufacturers produce a tangible product, while service products are often intangible. But many products are a combination of a good and a service, which complicates the definition of a service. Even the U.S. government has trouble generating a consistent definition. Because definitions vary, much of the data and statistics generated about the service sector are inconsistent. However, we define **services** as including repair and maintenance, government, food and lodging, transportation, insurance, trade, financial, real estate, education, legal, medical, entertainment, and other professional occupations.[1]

Services
Economic activities that typically produce an intangible product (such as education, entertainment, lodging, government, financial, and health services).

Differences Between Goods and Services

Let's examine some of the differences between goods and services:

- Services are usually *intangible* (for example, your purchase of a ride in an empty airline seat between two cities) as opposed to a tangible good.
- Services are often *produced and consumed simultaneously*; there is no stored inventory. For instance, the beauty salon produces a haircut that is "consumed" simultaneously, or the doctor produces an operation that is "consumed" as it is produced. We have not yet figured out how to inventory haircuts or appendectomies.
- Services are often *unique*. Your mix of financial coverage, such as investments and insurance policies, may not be the same as anyone else's, just as the medical procedure or a haircut produced for you is not exactly like anyone else's.
- Services have *high customer interaction*. Services are often difficult to standardize, automate, and make as efficient as we would like because customer interaction demands uniqueness. In fact, in many cases this uniqueness is what the customer is paying for; therefore, the operations manager must ensure that the product is designed (i.e., customized) so that it can be delivered in the required unique manner.
- Services have *inconsistent product definition*. Product definition may be rigorous, as in the case of an auto insurance policy, but inconsistent because policyholders change cars and mature.
- Services are often *knowledge based*, as in the case of educational, medical, and legal services, and therefore hard to automate.
- Services are frequently *dispersed*. Dispersion occurs because services are frequently brought to the client/customer via a local office, a retail outlet, or even a house call.

LO2: Explain the distinction between goods and services

The activities of the operations function are often very similar for both goods and services. For instance, both goods and services must have quality standards established, and both must be designed and processed on a schedule in a facility where human resources are employed.

Having made the distinction between goods and services, we should point out that in many cases, the distinction is not clear-cut. In reality, almost all services and almost all goods are a mixture of a service and a tangible product. Even services such as consulting may require a tangible report. Similarly, the sale of most goods includes a service. For instance, many products

[1]This definition is similar to the categories used by the U.S. Bureau of Labor Statistics.

have the service components of financing and delivery (e.g., automobile sales). Many also require after-sale training and maintenance (e.g., office copiers and machinery). "Service" activities may also be an integral part of production. Human resource activities, logistics, accounting, training, field service, and repair are all service activities, but they take place within a manufacturing organization. Very few services are "pure," meaning they have no tangible component. Counseling may be one of the exceptions.

Growth of Services

Services constitute the largest economic sector in postindustrial societies. Until about 1900, most Americans were employed in agriculture. Increased agricultural productivity allowed people to leave the farm and seek employment in the city. Similarly, manufacturing employment has decreased in the past 30 years. The changes in manufacturing and service employment, in millions, are shown in Figure 4(a). Interestingly, as Figure 4(b) indicates, the number of people employed in manufacturing has decreased since 1950, but each person is now producing almost 20 times more than in 1950. Services became the dominant employer in the early 1920s, with manufacturing employment peaking at about 32% in 1950. The huge productivity increases in agriculture and manufacturing have allowed more of our economic resources to be devoted to services, as shown in Figure 4(c). Consequently, much of the world can now enjoy the pleasures of education, health services, entertainment, and myriad other things that we call services. Examples of firms and percentage of employment in the U.S. **service sector** are shown in Table 3. Table 3 also provides employment percentages for the nonservice sectors of manufacturing, construction, agriculture, and mining on the bottom four lines.

Service sector
The segment of the economy that includes trade, financial, lodging, education, legal, medical, and other professional occupations.

Service Pay

Although there is a common perception that service industries are low paying, in fact, many service jobs pay very well. Operations managers in the maintenance facility of an airline are very well paid, as are the operations managers who supervise computer services to the financial community. About 42% of all service workers receive wages above the national average. However, the service-sector average is driven down because 14 of the U.S. Department of Commerce categories of the 33 service industries do indeed pay below the all-private industry average. Of these, retail trade, which pays only 61% of the national private industry average, is large. But even considering the retail sector, the average wage of all service workers is about 96% of the average of all private industries.

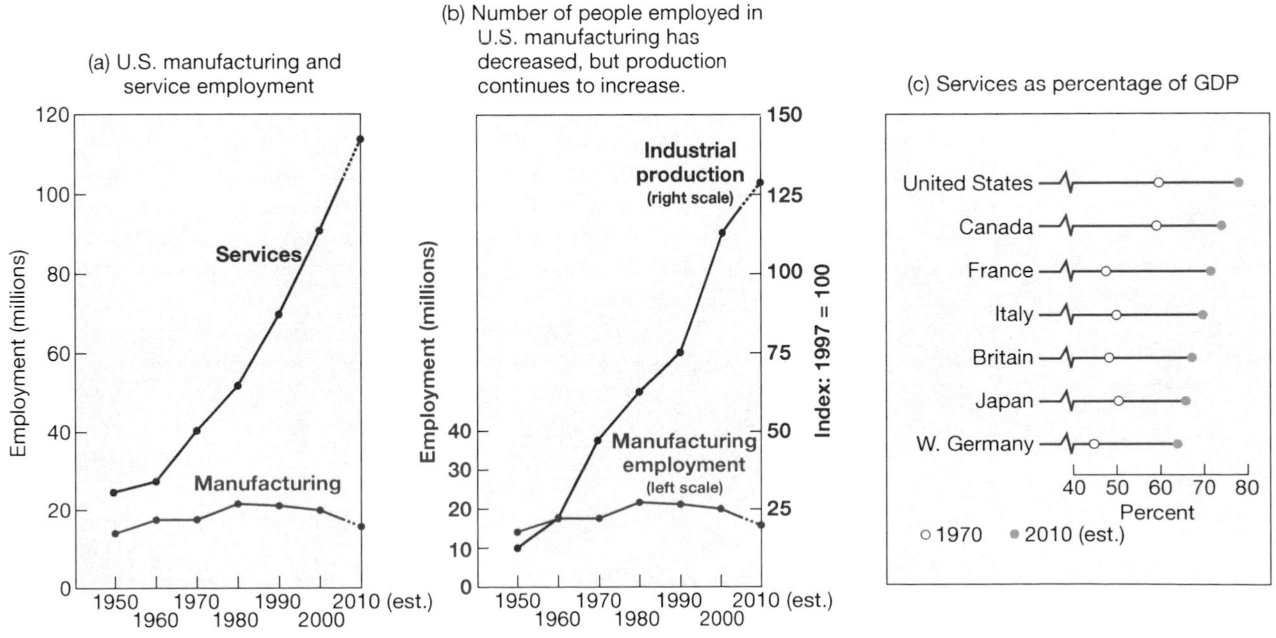

▲ **FIGURE 4 Development of the Service Economy and Manufacturing Productivity**

Sources: U.S. Bureau of Labor Statistics; Federal Reserve Board, Industrial Production and Capacity Utilization (2009); and Statistical Abstract of the United States (2008).

▶ **TABLE 3**
Examples of Organizations in Each Sector

Sources: Statistical Abstract of the United States (2008), Table 600, and Bureau of Labor Statistics, 2008.

AUTHOR COMMENT
Service jobs with their operations component are growing as a percentage of all jobs.

Sector	Example	Percent of All Jobs	
Service Sector			
Education, Legal, Medical, Other	San Diego Zoo, Arnold Palmer Hospital	25.8	78.8
Trade (retail, wholesale)	Walgreen's, Wal-Mart, Nordstrom	14.4	
Utilities, Transportation	Pacific Gas & Electric, American Airlines	5.2	
Professional and Business Services	Snelling and Snelling, Waste Management, Inc.	10.7	
Finance, Information, Real Estate	Citicorp, American Express, Prudential, Aetna	9.6	
Food, Lodging, Entertainment	Olive Garden, Motel 6, Walt Disney	8.5	
Public Administration	U.S., State of Alabama, Cook County	4.6	
Manufacturing Sector	General Electric, Ford, U.S. Steel, Intel		11.2
Construction Sector	Bechtel, McDermott		8.1
Agriculture	King Ranch		1.4
Mining Sector	Homestake Mining		.5
Grand Total			100.0

AUTHOR COMMENT
One of the reasons OM is such an exciting discipline is that an operations manager is confronted with ever-changing issues, from technology to sustainability.

EXCITING NEW TRENDS IN OPERATIONS MANAGEMENT

OM managers operate in an exciting and dynamic environment. This environment is the result of a variety of challenging forces, from globalization of world trade to the transfer of ideas, products, and money at electronic speeds. The direction now being taken by OM—where it has been and where it is going—is shown in Figure 5. Let's look at some of these challenges:

- *Ethics:* Operations managers' roles of buying from suppliers, transforming resources into finished goods, and delivering to customers places them at critical junctures where they must frequently make ethical decisions.
- *Global focus:* The rapid decline in communication and transportation costs has made markets global. Similarly, resources in the form of capital, materials, talent, and labor are now also global. As a result, countries throughout the world are contributing to globalization as they vie for economic growth. Operations managers are rapidly responding with creative designs, efficient production, and quality goods.
- *Rapid product development:* Rapid international communication of news, entertainment, and lifestyles is dramatically chopping away at the life span of products. Operations managers are responding with management structures, technology, and alliances (partnerships) that are more responsive and effective.
- *Environmentally sensitive production:* Operation managers' continuing battle to improve productivity is increasingly concerned with designing products and processes that are ecologically sustainable. That means designing products and packaging that minimize resource use, are biodegradable, can be recycled, and are generally environmentally friendly.
- *Mass customization:* Once managers recognize the world as the marketplace, the cultural and individual differences become quite obvious. In a world where consumers are increasingly aware of innovation and options, substantial pressure is placed on firms to respond. And operations managers are responding with creative product designs and flexible production processes that cater to the individual whims of consumers. The goal is to produce customized products, whenever and wherever needed.
- *Empowered employees:* The knowledge explosion and more technical workplace have combined to require more competence in the workplace. Operations managers are responding by moving more decision making to individual workers.
- *Supply-chain partnering:* Shorter product life cycles, demanding customers, and fast changes in technology, material, and processes require supply-chain partners to be more in tune with the needs of end users. And because suppliers can contribute unique expertise, operations managers are outsourcing and building long-term partnerships with critical players in the supply chain.
- *Just-in-time performance:* Inventory requires financial resources and impedes response to rapid changes in the marketplace. These forces push operations managers to viciously cut inventories at every level, from raw materials to finished goods.

These trends are part of the exciting OM challenges that are discussed in this text.

Traditional Approach	Reasons for Change	Current Challenges
Ethics and regulation not at the forefront	*Public concern over pollution, corruption, child labor, etc.*	High ethical and social responsibility; increased legal and professional standards
Local, regional, national focus	*Growth of reliable, low-cost communication and transportation*	Global focus; international collaboration
Lengthy product development	*Shorter life cycles; growth of global communication; CAD; Internet*	Rapid product development; design collaboration
Low-cost production, with little concern for environment; free resources (air, water) ignored	*Public sensitivity to environment; ISO 14000 standard; increasing disposal costs*	Environmentally sensitive production; green manufacturing; sustainability
Low-cost standard products	*Rise of consumerism; increased affluence; individualism*	Mass customization
Emphasis on specialized, often manual tasks	*Recognizing the importance of the employee's total contribution; knowledge society*	Empowered employees; enriched jobs
"In-house" production; low-bid purchasing	*Rapid technology change; increasing competitive forces*	Supply-chain partnering; joint ventures; alliances
Large lot production	*Shorter product life; increasing need to reduce inventory*	Just-in-time performance; lean; continuous improvement

▲ **FIGURE 5** **Changing Challenges for the Operations Manager**

THE PRODUCTIVITY CHALLENGE

AUTHOR COMMENT Why is productivity important? Because it determines our standard of living.

The creation of goods and services requires changing resources into goods and services. The more efficiently we make this change, the more productive we are and the more value is added to the good or service provided. **Productivity** is the ratio of outputs (goods and services) divided by the inputs (resources, such as labor and capital) (see Figure 6). The operations manager's job is to enhance (improve) this ratio of outputs to inputs. Improving productivity means improving efficiency.[2]

Productivity
The ratio of outputs (goods and services) divided by one or more inputs (such as labor, capital, or management).

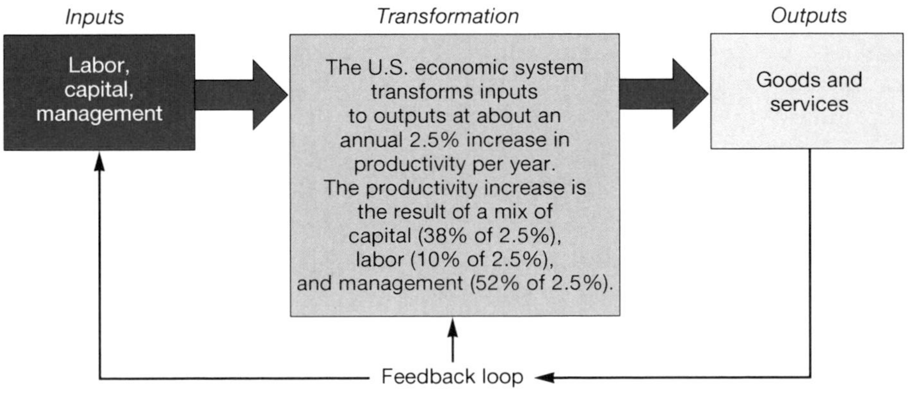

◄ **FIGURE 6**
The Economic System Adds Value by Transforming Inputs to Outputs
An effective feedback loop evaluates performance against a strategy or standard. It also evaluates customer satisfaction and sends signals to managers controlling the inputs and transformation process.

[2]*Efficiency* means doing the job well—with a minimum of resources and waste. Note the distinction between being *efficient*, which implies doing the job well, and *effective*, which means doing the right thing. A job well done—say, by applying the 10 decisions of operations management—helps us be *efficient*; developing and using the correct strategy helps us be *effective*.

OM in Action ► Improving Productivity at Starbucks

"This is a game of seconds . . ." says Silva Peterson, whom Starbucks has put in charge of saving seconds. Her team of 10 analysts is constantly asking themselves: "How can we shave time off this?"

Peterson's analysis suggested that there were some obvious opportunities. First, stop requiring signatures on credit-card purchases under $25. This sliced 8 seconds off the transaction time at the cash register.

Then analysts noticed that Starbucks's largest cold beverage, the Venti size, required two bending and digging motions to scoop up enough ice. The scoop was too small. Redesign of the scoop provided the proper amount in one motion and cut 14 seconds off the average time of one minute.

Third were new espresso machines; with the push of a button, the machines grind coffee beans and brew. This allowed the server, called a "barista" in Starbucks's vocabulary, to do other things. The savings: about 12 seconds per espresso shot.

As a result, operations improvements at Starbucks outlets have increased the average yearly volume by nearly $200,000, to about $940,000 in the past 6 years. This is a 27% improvement in productivity—about 4.5% per year. In the service industry, a 4.5% per year increase is very tasty.

Sources: The Wall Street Journal (August 4, 2009): A1, A10 and (April 12, 2005): B2:B7; *Industrial Engineer* (January 2006): 66; and **www.finfacts.com**, October 6, 2005.

This improvement can be achieved in two ways: reducing inputs while keeping output constant or increasing output while keeping inputs constant. Both represent an improvement in productivity. In an economic sense, inputs are labor, capital, and management, which are integrated into a production system. Management creates this production system, which provides the conversion of inputs to outputs. Outputs are goods and services, including such diverse items as guns, butter, education, improved judicial systems, and ski resorts. *Production* is the making of goods and services. High production may imply only that more people are working and that employment levels are high (low unemployment), but it does not imply high *productivity*.

LO3: Explain the difference between production and productivity

Measurement of productivity is an excellent way to evaluate a country's ability to provide an improving standard of living for its people. *Only through increases in productivity can the standard of living improve.* Moreover, only through increases in productivity can labor, capital, and management receive additional payments. If returns to labor, capital, or management are increased without increased productivity, prices rise. On the other hand, downward pressure is placed on prices when productivity increases, because more is being produced with the same resources.

The benefits of increased productivity are illustrated in the *OM in Action* box "Improving Productivity at Starbucks."

For well over a century (from about 1869), the U.S. has been able to increase productivity at an average rate of almost 2.5% per year. Such growth has doubled U.S. wealth every 30 years. The manufacturing sector, although a decreasing portion of the U.S. economy, has recently seen annual productivity increases exceeding 4%, and the service sector, with increases of almost 1%, has also shown some improvement. The combination has moved U.S. annual productivity growth in this early part of the 21st century slightly above the 2.5% range for the economy as a whole.[3]

In this text, we examine how to improve productivity through operations management. Productivity is a significant issue for the world and one that the operations manager is uniquely qualified to address.

LO4: Compute single-factor productivity

Productivity Measurement

The measurement of productivity can be quite direct. Such is the case when productivity is measured by labor-hours per ton of a specific type of steel. Although labor-hours is a common measure of input, other measures such as capital (dollars invested), materials (tons of ore), or energy (kilowatts of electricity) can be used.[4] An example of this can be summarized in the following equation:

$$\text{Productivity} = \frac{\text{Units produced}}{\text{Input used}} \tag{1}$$

[3]U.S. Dept. of Labor, July 2009: www.bls.gov/ipc/prodybar.html

[4]The quality and time period are assumed to remain constant.

For example, if units produced = 1,000 and labor-hours used is 250, then:

$$\text{Productivity} = \frac{\text{Units produced}}{\text{Labor-hours used}} = \frac{1{,}000}{250} = 4 \text{ units per labor-hour}$$

The use of just one resource input to measure productivity, as shown in Equation (1), is known as **single-factor productivity**. However, a broader view of productivity is **multifactor productivity**, which includes all inputs (e.g., capital, labor, material, energy). Multifactor productivity is also known as *total factor productivity*. Multifactor productivity is calculated by combining the input units as shown here:

$$\text{Productivity} = \frac{\text{Output}}{\text{Labor} + \text{Material} + \text{Energy} + \text{Capital} + \text{Miscellaneous}} \qquad (2)$$

To aid in the computation of multifactor productivity, the individual inputs (the denominator) can be expressed in dollars and summed as shown in Example 2.

Single-factor productivity
Indicates the ratio of one resource (input) to the goods and services produced (outputs).

Multifactor productivity
Indicates the ratio of many or all resources (inputs) to the goods and services produced (outputs).

EXAMPLE 2

Computing single-factor and multifactor gains in productivity

Collins Title wants to evaluate its labor and multifactor productivity with a new computerized title-search system. The company has a staff of four, each working 8 hours per day (for a payroll cost of $640/day) and overhead expenses of $400 per day. Collins processes and closes on 8 titles each day. The new computerized title-search system will allow the processing of 14 titles per day. Although the staff, their work hours, and pay are the same, the overhead expenses are now $800 per day.

APPROACH ▶ Collins uses Equation (1) to compute labor productivity and Equation (2) to compute multifactor productivity.

SOLUTION: ▶

$$\text{Labor productivity with the old system: } \frac{8 \text{ titles per day}}{32 \text{ labor-hours}} = .25 \text{ titles per labor-hour}$$

$$\text{Labor productivity with the new system: } \frac{14 \text{ titles per day}}{32 \text{ labor-hours}} = .4375 \text{ titles per labor-hour}$$

$$\text{Multifactor productivity with the old system: } \frac{8 \text{ titles per day}}{\$640 + 400} = .0077 \text{ titles per dollar}$$

$$\text{Multifactor productivity with the new system: } \frac{14 \text{ titles per day}}{\$640 + 800} = .0097 \text{ titles per dollar}$$

Labor productivity has increased from .25 to .4375. The change is $(.4375 - .25)/.25 = 0.75$, or a 75% increase in labor productivity. Multifactor productivity has increased from .0077 to .0097. This change is $(.0097 - .0077)/.0077 = 0.26$, or a 26% increase in multifactor productivity.

INSIGHT ▶ Both the labor (single-factor) and multifactor productivity measures show an increase in productivity. However, the multifactor measure provides a better picture of the increase because it includes all the costs connected with the increase in output.

LEARNING EXERCISE ▶ If the overhead goes to $960 (rather than $800), what is the multifactor productivity? [Answer: .00875.]

RELATED PROBLEMS ▶ 1.1, 1.2, 1.5, 1.6, 1.7, 1.8, 1.9, 1.11, 1.12, 1.14, 1.15

LO5: Compute multifactor productivity

Use of productivity measures aids managers in determining how well they are doing. But results from the two measures can be expected to vary. If labor productivity growth is entirely the result of capital spending, measuring just labor distorts the results. Multifactor productivity is usually better, but more complicated. Labor productivity is the more popular measure. The multifactor-productivity measures provide better information about the trade-offs among factors, but substantial measurement problems remain. Some of these measurement problems are:

1. *Quality* may change while the quantity of inputs and outputs remains constant. Compare an HDTV of this decade with a black-and-white TV of the 1950s. Both are TVs, but few people would deny that the quality has improved. The unit of measure—a TV—is the same, but the quality has changed.
2. *External elements* may cause an increase or a decrease in productivity for which the system under study may not be directly responsible. A more reliable electric power service may

greatly improve production, thereby improving the firm's productivity because of this support system rather than because of managerial decisions made within the firm.

3. *Precise units of measure* may be lacking. Not all automobiles require the same inputs: Some cars are subcompacts, others are 911 Turbo Porsches.

Productivity measurement is particularly difficult in the service sector, where the end product can be hard to define. For example, economic statistics ignore the quality of your haircut, the outcome of a court case, or service at a retail store. In some cases, adjustments are made for the quality of the product sold but *not* the quality of the sales presentation or the advantage of a broader product selection. Productivity measurements require specific inputs and outputs, but a free economy is producing worth—what people want—which includes convenience, speed, and safety. Traditional measures of outputs may be a very poor measure of these other measures of worth. Note the quality-measurement problems in a law office, where each case is different, altering the accuracy of the measure "cases per labor-hour" or "cases per employee."

Productivity Variables

Productivity variables
The three factors critical to productivity improvement—labor, capital, and the art and science of management.

As we saw in Figure 6, productivity increases are dependent on three **productivity variables**:

1. *Labor*, which contributes about 10% of the annual increase.
2. *Capital*, which contributes about 38% of the annual increase.
3. *Management*, which contributes about 52% of the annual increase.

These three factors are critical to improved productivity. They represent the broad areas in which managers can take action to improve productivity.

LO6: Identify the critical variables in enhancing productivity

Labor Improvement in the contribution of labor to productivity is the result of a healthier, better-educated, and better-nourished labor force. Some increase may also be attributed to a shorter workweek. Historically, about 10% of the annual improvement in productivity is attributed to improvement in the quality of labor. Three key variables for improved labor productivity are:

1. Basic education appropriate for an effective labor force.
2. Diet of the labor force.
3. Social overhead that makes labor available, such as transportation and sanitation.

Illiteracy and poor diets are a major impediment to productivity, costing countries up to 20% of their productivity. Infrastructure that yields clean drinking water and sanitation is also an opportunity for improved productivity, as well as an opportunity for better health, in much of the world.

In developed nations, the challenge becomes *maintaining and enhancing the skills of labor* in the midst of rapidly expanding technology and knowledge. Recent data suggest that the average American 17-year-old knows significantly less mathematics than the average Japanese at the same age, and about half cannot answer the questions in Figure 7. Moreover, more than 38% of American job applicants tested for basic skills were deficient in reading, writing, or math.[5]

FIGURE 7 ▶
About Half of the 17-Year-Olds in the U.S. Cannot Correctly Answer Questions of This Type

AUTHOR COMMENT
Perhaps as many as 25% of U.S. workers lack the basic skills needed for their current job.

6 yds

4 yds

What is the area of this rectangle?

______ 4 square yds
______ 6 square yds
______ 10 square yds
______ 20 square yds
______ 24 square yds

If $9y + 3 = 6y + 15$ then $y =$

______ 1   ______ 4
______ 2   ______ 6

Which of the following is true about 84% of 100?

______ It is greater than 100
______ It is less than 100
______ It is equal to 100

[5]"Can't Read, Can't Count," *Scientific American* (October 2001): 24; and "Economic Time Bomb: U.S. Teens Are among Worst at Math," *The Wall Street Journal* (December 7, 2004): B1.

Overcoming shortcomings in the quality of labor while other countries have a better labor force is a major challenge. Perhaps improvements can be found not only through increasing competence of labor but also via *better utilized labor with a stronger commitment.* Training, motivation, team building, and human resource strategies, as well as improved education, may be among the many techniques that will contribute to increased labor productivity. Improvements in labor productivity are possible; however, they can be expected to be increasingly difficult and expensive.

Capital Human beings are tool-using animals. Capital investment provides those tools. Capital investment has increased in the U.S. every year except during a few very severe recession periods. Annual capital investment in the U.S. has increased at an annual rate of 1.5% after allowances for depreciation.

Inflation and taxes increase the cost of capital, making capital investment increasingly expensive. When the capital invested per employee drops, we can expect a drop in productivity. Using labor rather than capital may reduce unemployment in the short run, but it also makes economies less productive and therefore lowers wages in the long run. Capital investment is often a necessary, but seldom a sufficient ingredient in the battle for increased productivity.

The trade-off between capital and labor is continually in flux. The higher the cost of capital, the more projects requiring capital are "squeezed out": they are not pursued because the potential return on investment for a given risk has been reduced. Managers adjust their investment plans to changes in capital cost.

Management Management is a factor of production and an economic resource. Management is responsible for ensuring that labor and capital are effectively used to increase productivity. Management accounts for over half of the annual increase in productivity. This increase includes improvements made through the use of knowledge and the application of technology.

Using knowledge and technology is critical in postindustrial societies. Consequently, postindustrial societies are also known as knowledge societies. **Knowledge societies** are those in which much of the labor force has migrated from manual work to technical and information-processing tasks requiring ongoing education. The required education and training are important high-cost items that are the responsibility of operations managers as they build organizations and workforces. The expanding knowledge base of contemporary society requires that managers use *technology and knowledge effectively.*

Knowledge society
A society in which much of the labor force has migrated from manual work to work based on knowledge.

More effective use of capital also contributes to productivity. It falls to the operations manager, as a productivity catalyst, to select the best new capital investments as well as to improve the productivity of existing investments.

TEK Image/Photo Researchers, Inc.

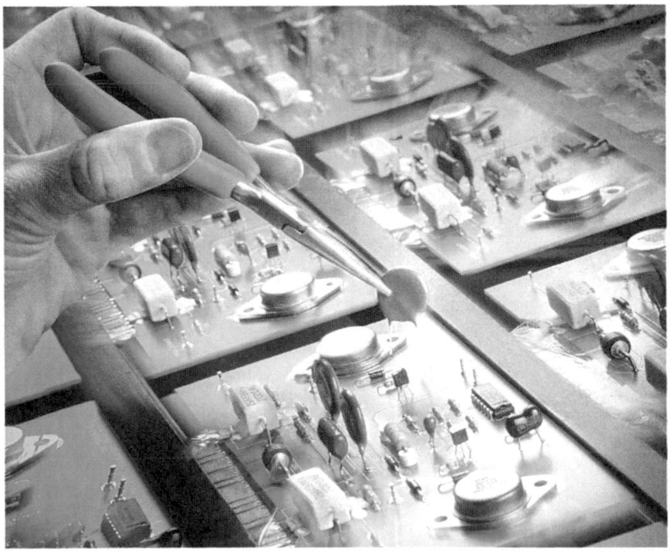

John McLean/Photo Researchers, Inc.

The effective use of capital often means finding the proper trade-off between investment in capital assets (automation, left) and human assets (a manual process, right). While there are risks connected with any investment, the cost of capital and physical investments is fairly clear-cut, but the cost of employees has many hidden costs including fringe benefits, social insurance, and legal constraints on hiring, employment, and termination.

Siemens, the multi-billion-dollar German conglomerate, has long been known for its apprentice programs in its home country. Because education is often the key to efficient operations in a technological society, Siemens has spread its apprentice-training programs to its U.S. plants. These programs are laying the foundation for the highly skilled workforce that is essential for global competitiveness.

Siemens press picture, Courtesy of Siemens AG, Munich/Berlin

The productivity challenge is difficult. A country cannot be a world-class competitor with second-class inputs. Poorly educated labor, inadequate capital, and dated technology are second-class inputs. High productivity and high-quality outputs require high-quality inputs, including good operations managers.

Productivity and the Service Sector

The service sector provides a special challenge to the accurate measurement of productivity and productivity improvement. The traditional analytical framework of economic theory is based primarily on goods-producing activities. Consequently, most published economic data relate to goods production. But the data do indicate that, as our contemporary service economy has increased in size, we have had slower growth in productivity.

Productivity of the service sector has proven difficult to improve because service-sector work is:

1. Typically labor intensive (for example, counseling, teaching).
2. Frequently focused on unique individual attributes or desires (for example, investment advice).
3. Often an intellectual task performed by professionals (for example, medical diagnosis).
4. Often difficult to mechanize and automate (for example, a haircut).
5. Often difficult to evaluate for quality (for example, performance of a law firm).

The more intellectual and personal the task, the more difficult it is to achieve increases in productivity. Low-productivity improvement in the service sector is also attributable to the growth of low-productivity activities in the service sector. These include activities not previously a part of the measured economy, such as child care, food preparation, house cleaning, and laundry service. These activities have moved out of the home and into the measured economy as more and more women have joined the workforce. Inclusion of these activities has probably resulted in lower measured productivity for the service sector, although, in fact, actual productivity has probably increased because these activities are now more efficiently produced than previously.

However, in spite of the difficulty of improving productivity in the service sector, improvements are being made. And this text presents a multitude of ways to make these improvements. Indeed, what can be done when management pays attention to how work actually gets done is astonishing!

Although the evidence indicates that all industrialized countries have the same problem with service productivity, the U.S. remains the world leader in overall productivity *and* service productivity. Retailing is twice as productive in the U.S. as in Japan, where laws protect shopkeepers from discount chains. The U.S. telephone industry is at least twice as productive as Germany's. The U.S. banking system is also 33% more efficient than Germany's banking oligopolies. However, because productivity is central to the operations manager's job and because the service sector is so large, we take special note in this text of how to improve productivity in the service sector. (See, for instance, the *OM in Action* box "Taco Bell Improves Productivity and Goes Green to Lower Costs.")

OM in Action ► Taco Bell Improves Productivity and Goes Green to Lower Costs

Founded in 1962 by Glenn Bell, Taco Bell seeks competitive advantage via low cost. Like many other services, Taco Bell relies on its operations management to improve productivity and reduce cost.

Its menu and meals are designed to be easy to prepare. Taco Bell has shifted a substantial portion of food preparation to suppliers who could perform food processing more efficiently than a stand-alone restaurant. Ground beef is precooked prior to arrival and then reheated, as are many dishes that arrive in plastic boil bags for easy sanitary reheating. Similarly, tortillas arrive already fried and onions prediced. Efficient layout and automation has cut to 8 seconds the time needed to prepare tacos and burritos and has cut time in the drive-thru lines by one minute. These advances have been combined with training and empowerment to increase the span of management from one supervisor for 5 restaurants to one supervisor for 30 or more.

Operations managers at Taco Bell believe they have cut in-store labor by 15 hours per day and reduced floor space by more than 50%. The result is a store that can handle twice the volume with half the labor.

In 2010, Taco Bell will have completed the rollout of its new Grill-to-Order kitchens by installing water- and energy-savings grills that conserve 300 million gallons of water and 200 million KwH of electricity each year. This "green"-inspired cooking method also saves the company's 5,600 restaurants $17 million per year.

Effective operations management has resulted in productivity increases that support Taco Bell's low-cost strategy. Taco Bell is now the fast-food low-cost leader with a 73% share of the Mexican fast-food market.

Sources: Energy Business Journal (May 12, 2008): 111; *Harvard Business Review* (July/August 2008): 118; and J. Hueter and W. Swart, *Interfaces* (January–February 1998): 75–91.

ETHICS AND SOCIAL RESPONSIBILITY

AUTHOR COMMENT
Ethics must drive all of a manager's decisions.

Operations managers are subjected to constant changes and challenges. The systems they build to convert resources into goods and services are complex. The physical and social environment changes, as do laws and values. These changes present a variety of challenges that come from the conflicting perspectives of stakeholders such as customers, distributors, suppliers, owners, lenders, and employees. These stakeholders, as well as government agencies at various levels, require constant monitoring and thoughtful responses.

Identifying ethical and socially responsible responses while building productive systems is not always clear-cut. Among the many ethical challenges facing operations managers are:

- Efficiently developing and producing safe, quality products.
- Maintaining a sustainable environment.
- Providing a safe workplace.
- Honoring stakeholder commitments.

Managers must do all of this in an ethical and socially responsible way while meeting the demands of the marketplace. If operations managers have a *moral awareness and focus on increasing productivity* in a system where all stakeholders have a voice, then many of the ethical challenges will be successfully addressed. The organization will use fewer resources, the employees will be committed, the market will be satisfied, and the ethical climate will be enhanced.

CHAPTER SUMMARY

Operations, marketing, and finance/accounting are the three functions basic to all organizations. The operations function creates goods and services. Much of the progress of operations management has been made in the twentieth century, but since the beginning of time, humankind has been attempting to improve its material well-being. Operations managers are key players in the battle to improve productivity.

As societies become increasingly affluent, more of their resources are devoted to services. In the U.S., more than three-quarters of the workforce is employed in the service sector. Productivity improvements are difficult to achieve, but operations managers are the primary vehicle for making improvements.

Key Terms

Production
Operations management (OM)
Management process
Services
Service sector
Productivity
Single-factor productivity
Multifactor productivity
Productivity variables
Knowledge society

Ethical Dilemma

Major corporations with overseas subcontractors (such as IKEA in Bangladesh, Unilever in India, and Nike in China) have been criticized, often with substantial negative publicity, when children as young as 10 have been found working in the subcontractor's facilities. The standard response is to perform an audit and then enhance controls so it does not happen again. In one such case, a 10-year-old was terminated. Shortly thereafter, the family, without the 10-year-old's contribution to the family income, lost its modest home, and the 10-year-old was left to scrounge in the local dump for scraps of metal. Was the decision to hire the 10-year-old ethical? Was the decision to terminate the 10-year-old ethical?

Discussion Questions

1. Why should one study operations management?
2. Identify four people who have contributed to the theory and techniques of operations management.
3. Briefly describe the contributions of the four individuals identified in the preceding question.
4. Figure 1 outlines the operations, finance/accounting, and marketing functions of three organizations. Prepare a chart similar to Figure 1 outlining the same functions for one of the following:
   a. a newspaper
   b. a drugstore
   c. a college library
   d. a summer camp
   e. a small costume-jewelry factory
5. Answer Question 4 for some other organization, perhaps an organization where you have worked.
6. What are the three basic functions of a firm?
7. Name the 10 decision areas of operations management.
8. Name four areas that are significant to improving labor productivity.
9. The U.S., and indeed much of the world, has been described as a "knowledge society." How does this affect productivity measurement and the comparison of productivity between the U.S. and other countries?
10. What are the measurement problems that occur when one attempts to measure productivity?
11. Mass customization and rapid product development were identified as current trends in modern manufacturing operations. What is the relationship, if any, between these trends? Can you cite any examples?
12. What are the five reasons productivity is difficult to improve in the service sector?
13. Describe some of the actions taken by Taco Bell to increase productivity that have resulted in Taco Bell's ability to serve "twice the volume with half the labor."

Solved Problems **Virtual Office Hours help is available at www.MyOMLab.com**

▼ SOLVED PROBLEM 1.1

Productivity can be measured in a variety of ways, such as by labor, capital, energy, material usage, and so on. At Modern Lumber, Inc., Art Binley, president and producer of apple crates sold to growers, has been able, with his current equipment, to produce 240 crates per 100 logs. He currently purchases 100 logs per day, and each log requires 3 labor-hours to process. He believes that he can hire a professional buyer who can buy a better-quality log at the same cost. If this is the case, he can increase his production to 260 crates per 100 logs. His labor-hours will increase by 8 hours per day.

What will be the impact on productivity (measured in crates per labor-hour) if the buyer is hired?

▼ SOLUTION

(a) $$\text{Current labor productivity} = \frac{240 \text{ crates}}{100 \text{ logs} \times 3 \text{ hours/log}} = \frac{240}{300} = .8 \text{ crates per labor-hour}$$

(b) $$\text{Labor productivity with buyer} = \frac{260 \text{ crates}}{(100 \text{ logs} \times 3 \text{ hours/log}) + 8 \text{ hours}} = \frac{260}{308} = .844 \text{ crates per labor-hour}$$

Using current productivity (.80 from [a]) as a base, the increase will be 5.5% (.844/.8 = 1.055, or a 5.5% increase).

▼ SOLVED PROBLEM 1.2

Art Binley has decided to look at his productivity from a multifactor (total factor productivity) perspective (refer to Solved Problem 1.1). To do so, he has determined his labor, capital, energy, and material usage and decided to use dollars as the common denominator. His total labor-hours are now 300 per day and will increase to 308 per day. His capital and energy costs will remain constant at \$350 and \$150 per day, respectively. Material costs for the 100 logs per day are \$1,000 and will remain the same. Because he pays an average of \$10 per hour (with fringes), Binley determines his productivity increase as follows:

▼ SOLUTION

	Current System		System with Professional Buyer	
Labor:	300 hrs. @10 =	3,000	308 hrs. @10 =	\$3,080
Material:	100 logs/day	1,000		1,000
Capital:		350		350
Energy:		150		150
Total Cost:		\$4,500		\$4,580

Multifactor productivity of current system:
= 240 crates/4,500 = .0533 crates/dollar

Multifactor productivity of proposed system:
= 260 crates/4,580 = .0568 crates/dollar

Using current productivity (.0533) as a base, the increase will be .066. That is, .0568/.0533 = 1.066, or a 6.6% increase.

Problems*

• **1.1** John Lucy makes wooden boxes in which to ship motorcycles. John and his three employees invest a total of 40 hours per day making the 120 boxes.
a) What is their productivity?
b) John and his employees have discussed redesigning the process to improve efficiency. If they can increase the rate to 125 per day, what will be their new productivity?
c) What will be their unit *increase* in productivity per hour?
d) What will be their percentage change in productivity? Px

• **1.2** Riverside Metal Works produces cast bronze valves on a 10-person assembly line. On a recent day, 160 valves were produced during an 8-hour shift.
a) Calculate the labor productivity of the line.
b) The manager at Riverside changed the layout and was able to increase production to 180 units per 8-hour shift. What is the new labor productivity per labor-hour?
c) What is the percentage of productivity increase? Px

• **1.3** This year, Benson, Inc., will produce 57,600 hot water heaters at its plant in Yulee, Florida, in order to meet expected global demand. To accomplish this, each laborer at the Yulee plant will work 160 hours per month. If the labor productivity at the plant is 0.15 hot water heaters per labor-hour, how many laborers are employed at the plant?

• **1.4** As a library or Internet assignment, find the U.S. productivity rate (increase) last year for the (a) national economy, (b) manufacturing sector, and (c) service sector.

• **1.5** Lori produces "Final Exam Care Packages" for resale by her sorority. She is currently working a total of 5 hours per day to produce 100 care packages.
a) What is Lori's productivity?
b) Lori thinks that by redesigning the package, she can increase her total productivity to 133 care packages per day. What will be her new productivity?
c) What will be the percentage increase in productivity if Lori makes the change? Px

•• **1.6** Eric Johnson makes billiard balls in his New England plant. With recent increases in his costs, he has a newfound interest in efficiency. Eric is interested in determining the productivity of his organization. He would like to know if his organization is maintaining the manufacturing average of 3% increase in productivity. He has the following data representing a month from last year and an equivalent month this year:

	Last Year	Now
Units produced	1,000	1,000
Labor (hours)	300	275
Resin (pounds)	50	45
Capital invested (\$)	10,000	11,000
Energy (BTU)	3,000	2,850

Show the productivity percentage change for each category and then determine the improvement for labor-hours, the typical standard for comparison. Px

•• **1.7** Eric Johnson (using data from Problem 1.6) determines his costs to be as follows:
- *Labor:* \$10 per hour
- *Resin:* \$5 per pound
- *Capital expense:* 1% per month of investment
- *Energy:* \$.50 per BTU.

Show the percent change in productivity for one month last year versus one month this year, on a multifactor basis with dollars as the common denominator. Px

**Note:* Px means the problem may be solved with POM for Windows and/or Excel OM.

• **1.8** Kleen Karpet cleaned 65 rugs in October, consuming the following resources:

Labor:	520 hours at \$13 per hour
Solvent:	100 gallons at \$5 per gallon
Machine rental:	20 days at \$50 per day

a) What is the labor productivity per dollar?
b) What is the multifactor productivity? PX

•• **1.9** David Upton is president of Upton Manufacturing, a producer of Go-Kart tires. Upton makes 1,000 tires per day with the following resources:

Labor:	400 hours per day @ \$12.50 per hour
Raw material:	20,000 pounds per day @ \$1 per pound
Energy:	\$5,000 per day
Capital costs:	\$10,000 per day

a) What is the labor productivity per labor-hour for these tires at Upton Manufacturing?
b) What is the multifactor productivity for these tires at Upton Manufacturing?
c) What is the percent change in multifactor productivity if Upton can reduce the energy bill by \$1,000 per day without cutting production or changing any other inputs? PX

•• **1.10** Sawyer's, a local bakery, is worried about increased costs—particularly energy. Last year's records can provide a fairly good estimate of the parameters for this year. Judy Sawyer, the owner, does not believe things have changed much, but she did invest an additional \$3,000 for modifications to the bakery's ovens to make them more energy efficient. The modifications were supposed to make the ovens at least 15% more efficient. Sawyer has asked you to check the energy savings of the new ovens and also to look over other measures of the bakery's productivity to see if the modifications were beneficial. You have the following data to work with:

	Last Year	Now
Production (dozen)	1,500	1,500
Labor (hours)	350	325
Capital investment (\$)	15,000	18,000
Energy (BTU)	3,000	2,750

PX

Taras Vyshnya/Shutterstock

•• **1.11** Cunningham Performance Auto, Inc., modifies 375 autos per year. The manager, Peter Cunningham, is interested in obtaining a measure of overall performance. He has asked you to provide him with a multifactor measure of last year's performance as a benchmark for future comparison. You have assembled the following data. Resource inputs were: labor, 10,000 hours; 500 suspension and engine modification kits; and energy, 100,000 kilowatt-hours. Average labor cost last year was \$20 per hour, kits cost \$1,000 each, and energy costs were \$3 per kilowatt-hour. What do you tell Mr. Cunningham? PX

•• **1.12** Lake Charles Seafood makes 500 wooden packing boxes for fresh seafood per day, working in two 10-hour shifts. Due to increased demand, plant managers have decided to operate three 8-hour shifts instead. The plant is now able to produce 650 boxes per day.
a) Calculate the company's productivity before the change in work rules and after the change.
b) What is the percentage increase in productivity?
c) If production is increased to 700 boxes per day, what is the new productivity? PX

••• **1.13** Charles Lackey operates a bakery in Idaho Falls, Idaho. Because of its excellent product and excellent location, demand has increased by 25% in the last year. On far too many occasions, customers have not been able to purchase the bread of their choice. Because of the size of the store, no new ovens can be added. At a staff meeting, one employee suggested ways to load the ovens differently so that more loaves of bread can be baked at one time. This new process will require that the ovens be loaded by hand, requiring additional manpower. This is the only thing to be changed. If the bakery makes 1,500 loaves per month with a labor productivity of 2.344 loaves per labor-hour, how many workers will Lackey need to add? (*Hint:* Each worker works 160 hours per month.)

•• **1.14** Refer to Problem 1.13. The pay will be \$8 per hour for employees. Charles Lackey can also improve the yield by purchasing a new blender. The new blender will mean an increase in his investment. This added investment has a cost of \$100 per month, but he will achieve the same output (an increase to 1,875) as the change in labor-hours. Which is the better decision?
a) Show the productivity change, in loaves per dollar, with an increase in labor cost (from 640 to 800 hours).
b) Show the new productivity, in loaves per dollar, with only an increase in investment (\$100 per month more).
c) Show the percent productivity change for labor and investment.

••• **1.15** Refer to Problems 1.13 and 1.14. If Charles Lackey's utility costs remain constant at \$500 per month, labor at \$8 per hour, and cost of ingredients at \$0.35 per loaf, but Charles does not purchase the blender suggested in Problem 1.14, what will the productivity of the bakery be? What will be the percent increase or decrease?

•• **1.16** In December, General Motors produced 6,600 customized vans at its plant in Detroit. The labor productivity at this plant is known to have been 0.10 vans per labor-hour during that month. 300 laborers were employed at the plant that month.
a) How many hours did the average laborer work that month?
b) If productivity can be increased to 0.11 vans per hour, how many hours would the average laborer work that month?

•• **1.17** Natalie Attired runs a small job shop where garments are made. The job shop employs eight workers. Each worker is paid \$10 per hour. During the first week of March, each worker worked 45 hours. Together, they produced a batch of 132 garments. Of these garments, 52 were "seconds" (meaning that they were flawed). The seconds were sold for \$90 each at a factory outlet store. The remaining 80 garments were sold to retail outlets at a price of \$198 per garment. What was the labor productivity, in dollars per labor-hour, at this job shop during the first week of March?

▶ **Refer to myomlab for these additional homework problems: 1.18–1.19**

Case Studies

► National Air Express

National Air is a competitive air-express firm with offices around the country. Frank Smith, the Chattanooga, Tennessee, station manager, is preparing his quarterly budget report, which will be presented at the Southeast regional meeting next week. He is very concerned about adding capital expense to the operation when business has not increased appreciably. This has been the worst first quarter he can remember: snowstorms, earthquakes, and bitter cold. He has asked Martha Lewis, field services supervisor, to help him review the available data and offer possible solutions.

Service Methods

National Air offers door-to-door overnight air-express delivery within the U.S. Smith and Lewis manage a fleet of 24 trucks to handle freight in the Chattanooga area. Routes are assigned by area, usually delineated by zip code boundaries, major streets, or key geographical features, such as the Tennessee River. Pickups are generally handled between 3:00 P.M. and 6:00 P.M., Monday through Friday. Driver routes are a combination of regularly scheduled daily stops and pickups that the customer calls in as needed. These call-in pickups are dispatched by radio to the driver. Most call-in customers want as late a pickup as possible, just before closing (usually at 5:00 P.M.).

When the driver arrives at each pickup location, he or she provides supplies as necessary (an envelope or box if requested) and must receive a completed air waybill for each package. Because the industry is extremely competitive, a professional, courteous driver is essential to retaining customers. Therefore, Smith has always been concerned that drivers not rush a customer to complete his or her package and paperwork.

Budget Considerations

Smith and Lewis have found that they have been unable to meet their customers' requests for a scheduled pickup on many occasions in the past quarter. Although, on average, drivers are not handling any more business, they are unable on some days to arrive at each location on time. Smith does not think he can justify increasing costs by $1,200 per week for additional trucks and drivers while productivity (measured in shipments per truck/day) has remained flat. The company has established itself as the low-cost operator in the industry but has at the same time committed itself to offering quality service and value for its customers.

Discussion Questions

1. Is the productivity measure of shipments per day per truck still useful? Are there alternatives that might be effective?
2. What, if anything, can be done to reduce the daily variability in pickup call-ins? Can the driver be expected to be at several locations at once at 5:00 P.M.?
3. How should package pickup performance be measured? Are standards useful in an environment that is affected by the weather, traffic, and other random variables? Are other companies having similar problems?

Source: Adapted from a case by Phil Pugliese under the supervision of Professor Marilyn M. Helms, University of Tennessee at Chattanooga. Reprinted by permission.

► Frito-Lay: Operations Management in Manufacturing

Video Case

Frito-Lay, the massive Dallas-based subsidiary of PepsiCo, has 38 plants and 48,000 employees in North America. Seven of Frito-Lay's 41 brands exceed $1 billion in sales: Fritos, Lay's Cheetos, Ruffles, Tostitos, Doritos, and Walker's Potato Chips. Operations is the focus of the firm—from designing products for new markets, to meeting changing consumer preferences, to adjusting to rising commodity costs, to subtle issues involving flavors and preservatives—OM is under constant cost, time, quality, and market pressure. Here is a look at how the 10 decisions of OM are applied at this food processor.

In the food industry, product development kitchens experiment with new products, submit them to focus groups, and perform test marketing. Once the product specifications have been set, processes capable of meeting those specifications, and the necessary quality standards are created. At Frito-Lay, quality begins at the farm, with onsite inspection of the potatoes used in Ruffles and the corn used in Fritos. Quality continues throughout the manufacturing process, with visual inspections and with statistical process control of product variables such as oil, moisture, seasoning, salt, thickness, and weight. Additional quality evaluations are conducted throughout shipment, receipt, production, packaging, and delivery.

The production process at Frito-Lay is designed for large volumes and small variety, using expensive special-purpose equipment, and with swift movement of material through the facility. Product-focused facilities, such as Frito-Lay's, typically have high capital costs, tight schedules, and rapid processing. Frito-Lay's facilities are located regionally to aid in the rapid delivery of products because freshness is a critical issue. Sanitary issues and necessarily fast processing of products put a premium on an efficient layout. Production lines are designed for balanced throughput and high utilization. Cross-trained workers, who handle a variety of production lines, have promotion paths identified for their particular skill set. The company rewards employees with medical, retirement, and education plans. Its turnover is very low.

The supply chain is integral to success in the food industry; vendors must be chosen with great care. Moreover, the finished food product is highly dependent on perishable raw materials. Consequently, the supply chain brings raw material (potatoes, corn, etc.) to the plant securely and rapidly to meet tight production schedules. For instance, from the time that potatoes are picked in St. Augustine, Florida, until they are unloaded at the Orlando plant, processed, packaged, and shipped from the plant is under 12 hours. The requirement for fresh product requires on-time, just-in-time deliveries combined with both low raw material and finished goods inventories. The continuous-flow nature of the specialized equipment in the production process permits little work-in-process inventory. The plants usually run 24/7. This means that there are four shifts of employees each week.

Tight scheduling to ensure the proper mix of fresh finished goods on automated equipment requires reliable systems and effective maintenance. Frito-Lay's workforce is trained to recognize problems early, and professional maintenance personnel are available on every shift. Downtime is very costly and can lead to late deliveries, making maintenance a high priority.

Discussion Questions*

1. From your knowledge of production processes and from the case and the video, identify how each of the 10 decisions of OM is applied at Frito-Lay.
2. How would you determine the productivity of the production process at Frito-Lay?
3. How are the 10 decisions of OM different when applied by the operations manager of a production process such as Frito-Lay versus a service organization such as Hard Rock Cafe (see the Hard Rock Cafe video case below)?

*You may wish to view the video that accompanies this case before addressing these questions.

Source: Professors Beverly Amer (Northern Arizona University), Barry Render (Rollins College), and Jay Heizer (Texas Lutheran University).

▶ Hard Rock Cafe: Operations Management in Services — Video Case

In its 39 years of existence, Hard Rock has grown from a modest London pub to a global power managing 129 cafes, 12 hotels/casinos, live music venues, and a huge annual Rockfest concert. This puts Hard Rock firmly in the service industry—a sector that employs over 75% of the people in the U.S. Hard Rock moved its world headquarters to Orlando, Florida, in 1988 and has expanded to more than 40 locations throughout the U.S., serving over 100,000 meals each day. Hard Rock chefs are modifying the menu from classic American—burgers and chicken wings—to include higher-end items such as stuffed veal chops and lobster tails. Just as taste in music changes over time, so does Hard Rock Cafe, with new menus, layouts, memorabilia, services, and strategies.

At Orlando's Universal Studios, a traditional tourist destination, Hard Rock Cafe serves over 3,500 meals each day. The cafe employs about 400 people. Most are employed in the restaurant, but some work in the retail shop. Retail is now a standard and increasingly prominent feature in Hard Rock Cafes (since close to 48% of revenue comes from this source). Cafe employees include kitchen and wait staff, hostesses, and bartenders. Hard Rock employees are not only competent in their job skills but are also passionate about music and have engaging personalities. Cafe staff is scheduled down to 15-minute intervals to meet seasonal and daily demand changes in the tourist environment of Orlando. Surveys are done on a regular basis to evaluate quality of food and service at the cafe. Scores are rated on a 1 to 7 scale, and if the score is not a 7, the food or service is a failure.

Hard Rock is adding a new emphasis on live music and is redesigning its restaurants to accommodate the changing tastes. Since Eric Clapton hung his guitar on the wall to mark his favorite bar stool, Hard Rock has become the world's leading collector and exhibitor of rock 'n' roll memorabilia, with changing exhibits at its cafes throughout the world. The collection includes 1,000's of pieces, valued at $40 million. In keeping with the times, Hard Rock also maintains a Web site, **www.hardrock.com**, which receives over 100,000 hits per week, and a weekly cable television program on VH-1. Hard Rock's brand recognition, at 92%, is one of the highest in the world.

Discussion Questions*

1. From your knowledge of restaurants, from the video, from the *Global Company Profile* that opens this chapter, and from the case itself, identify how each of the 10 decisions of operations management is applied at Hard Rock Cafe.
2. How would you determine the productivity of the kitchen staff and wait staff at Hard Rock?
3. How are the 10 decisions of OM different when applied to the operations manager of a service operation such as Hard Rock versus an automobile company such as Ford Motor Company?

*You may wish to view the video that accompanies this case before addressing these questions.

▶ **Additional Case Study:** Visit **www.myomlab.com** or **www.pearsonhighered.com/heizer** for this free case study:
Zychol Chemicals Corp.: The production manager must prepare a productivity report, which includes multifactor analysis.

Bibliography

Broedner, P., S. Kinkel, and G. Lay. "Productivity Effects of Outsourcing." *International Journal of Operations and Production Management* 29, no. 2 (2009): 127.

Hounshell, D. A. *From the American System to Mass Production 1800–1932: The Development of Manufacturing.* Baltimore: Johns Hopkins University Press, 1985.

Lewis, William W. *The Power of Productivity.* Chicago: University of Chicago Press, 2004.

Maroto, A., and L. Rubalcaba. "Services Productivity Revisited." *The Service Industries Journal* 28, no. 3 (April 2008): 337.

Sahay, B. S. "Multi-factor Productivity Measurement Model for Service Organization." *International Journal of Productivity and Performance Management* 54, no. 1–2 (2005): 7–23.

San, G., T. Huang, and L. Huang. "Does Labor Quality Matter on Productivity Growth?" *Total Quality Management and Business Excellence* 19, no. 10 (October 2008): 1043.

Sprague, Linda G. "Evolution of the Field of Operations Management," *Journal of Operations Management* 25, no. 2 (March 2007): 219–238.

Tangen, S. "Demystifying Productivity and Performance." *International Journal of Productivity and Performance Measurement* 54, no. 1–2 (2005): 34–47.

Taylor, F. W. *The Principles of Scientific Management.* New York: Harper & Brothers, 1911.

van Biema, Michael, and Bruce Greenwald. "Managing Our Way to Higher Service-Sector Productivity." *Harvard Business Review* 75, no. 4 (July–August 1997): 87–95.

Wren, Daniel A. *The Evolution of Management Thought,* New York: Wiley, 1994.

Rapid Review

Main Heading	Review Material	myomlab
WHAT IS OPERATIONS MANAGEMENT?	■ **Production**—The creation of goods and services. ■ **Operations management (OM)**—Activities that relate to the creation of goods and services through the transformation of inputs to outputs.	**VIDEOS 1.1 and 1.2** OM at Hard Rock OM at Frito-Lay
ORGANIZING TO PRODUCE GOODS AND SERVICES	All organizations perform three functions to create goods and services: 1. *Marketing*, which generates demand 2. *Production/operations*, which creates the product 3. *Finance/accounting*, which tracks how well the organization is doing, pays the bills, and collects the money	
WHY STUDY OM?	We study OM for four reasons: 1. To learn how people organize themselves for productive enterprise 2. To learn how goods and services are produced 3. To understand what operations managers do 4. Because OM is a costly part of an organization	
WHAT OPERATIONS MANAGERS DO	■ **Management process**—The application of planning, organizing, staffing, leading, and controlling to achieve objectives. Ten major OM decisions are required of operations managers: 1. Design of goods and services 2. Managing quality 3. Process and capacity design 4. Location strategy 5. Layout strategy 6. Human resources, job design, and work measurement 7. Supply-chain management 8. Inventory, material requirements planning, and JIT (just-in-time) 9. Intermediate and short-term scheduling 10. Maintenance About 40% of *all* jobs are in OM. Operations managers possess job titles such as plant manager, quality manager, process improvement consultant, and operations analyst.	
THE HERITAGE OF OPERATIONS MANAGEMENT	Significant events in modern OM can be classified into five eras: 1. Early concepts (1776–1880)—Labor specialization (Smith, Babbage), standardized parts (Whitney) 2. Scientific management (1880–1910)—Gantt charts (Gantt), motion and time studies (Gilbreth), process analysis (Taylor), queuing theory (Erlang) 3. Mass production (1910–1980)—Assembly line (Ford/Sorensen), statistical sampling (Shewhart), economic order quantity (Harris), linear programming (Dantzig), PERT/CPM (DuPont), material requirements planning 4. Lean production (1980–1995)—Just-in-time, computer-aided design, electronic data interchange, total quality management, Baldrige Award, empowerment, kanbans 5. Mass customization (1995–present)—Globalization, Internet/e-commerce, enterprise resource planning, international quality standards, finite scheduling, supply-chain management, mass customization, build-to-order, sustainability	
OPERATIONS IN THE SERVICE SECTOR	■ **Services**—Economic activities that typically produce an intangible product (such as education, entertainment, lodging, government, financial, and health services). Almost all services and almost all goods are a mixture of a service and a tangible product. ■ **Service sector**—The segment of the economy that includes trade, financial, lodging, education, legal, medical, and other professional occupations. Services now constitute the largest economic sector in postindustrial societies. The huge productivity increases in agriculture and manufacturing have allowed more of our economic resources to be devoted to services. Many service jobs pay very well.	
EXCITING NEW TRENDS IN OPERATIONS MANAGEMENT	Some of the current challenges for operations managers include: • High ethical and social responsibility; increased legal and professional standards • Global focus; international collaboration • Rapid product development; design collaboration • Environmentally sensitive production; green manufacturing; sustainability • Mass customization • Empowered employees; enriched jobs • Supply-chain partnering; joint ventures; alliances • Just-in-time performance; lean; continuous improvement	

Rapid Review *continued*

Main Heading	Review Material	myomlab
THE PRODUCTIVITY CHALLENGE	■ **Productivity**—The ratio of outputs (goods and services) divided by one or more inputs (such as labor, capital, or management). High production means producing many units, while high productivity means producing units efficiently. Only through increases in productivity can the standard of living of a country improve. U.S. productivity has averaged 2.5% per year for over a century. $$\text{Productivity} = \frac{\text{Units produced}}{\text{Input used}} \quad (1)$$ ■ **Single-factor productivity**—Indicates the ratio of one resource (input) to the goods and services produced (outputs). ■ **Multifactor productivity (total factor productivity)**—Indicates the ratio of many or all resources (inputs) to the goods and services produced (outputs). Multifactor Productivity $$= \frac{\text{Output}}{\text{Labor} + \text{Material} + \text{Energy} + \text{Capital} + \text{Miscellaneous}} \quad (2)$$ Measurement problems with productivity include: (1) the quality may change, (2) external elements may interfere, and (3) precise units of measure may be lacking. ■ **Productivity variables**—The three factors critical to productivity improvement are labor (10%), capital (38%), and management (52%). ■ **Knowledge society**—A society in which much of the labor force has migrated from manual work to work based on knowledge.	Problems: 1.1–1.17 Virtual Office Hours for Solved Problems: 1.1, 1.2
ETHICS AND SOCIAL RESPONSIBILITY	Among the many ethical challenges facing operations managers are (1) efficiently developing and producing safe, quality products; (2) maintaining a clean environment; (3) providing a safe workplace; and (4) honoring stakeholder commitments.	

Self Test

■ **Before taking the self-test,** refer to the learning objectives listed at the beginning of the chapter and the key terms listed at the end of the chapter.

LO1. Productivity increases when:
- **a)** inputs increase while outputs remain the same.
- **b)** inputs decrease while outputs remain the same.
- **c)** outputs decrease while inputs remain the same.
- **d)** inputs and outputs increase proportionately.
- **e)** inputs increase at the same rate as outputs.

LO2. Services often:
- **a)** are tangible. **b)** are standardized.
- **c)** are knowledge based. **d)** are low in customer interaction.
- **e)** have consistent product definition.

LO3. Productivity:
- **a)** can use many factors as the numerator.
- **b)** is the same thing as production.
- **c)** increases at about 0.5% per year.
- **d)** is dependent upon labor, management, and capital.
- **e)** is the same thing as effectiveness.

LO4. Single-factor productivity:
- **a)** remains constant. **b)** is never constant.
- **c)** usually uses labor as a factor. **d)** seldom uses labor as a factor.
- **e)** uses management as a factor.

LO5. Multi-factor productivity:
- **a)** remains constant.
- **b)** is never constant.
- **c)** usually uses substitutes as common variables for the factors of production.
- **d)** seldom uses labor as a factor.
- **e)** always uses management as a factor.

LO6. Productivity increases each year in the United States are a result of three factors:
- **a)** labor, capital, management
- **b)** engineering, labor, capital
- **c)** engineering, capital, quality control
- **d)** engineering, labor, data processing
- **e)** engineering, capital, data processing

Answers: LO1. b; LO2. c; LO3. d; LO4. c; LO5. c; LO6. a.

Solutions to Even-Numbered Problems

1.2 **(a)** 2 valves/hr.
(b) 2.25 valves/hr.
(c) 12.5%

1.4 Varies by site and source.

1.6 Productivity of labor: 9.3%
Productivity of resin: 11.1%
Productivity of capital: –10.0%
Productivity of energy: 6.1%

1.8 **(a)** .0096 rugs/labor-dollar
(b) .00787 rugs/dollar

1.10 Productivity of capital dropped; labor and energy productivity increased.

1.12 **(a)** Before: 25 boxes/hr.
After: 27.08 boxes/hr.
(b) Increase: 8.3%
(c) 29.167 boxes/hr.

1.14 **(a)** .293 loaves/dollar
(b) .359 loaves/dollar
(c) Labor change: 0%; Investment change: 22.5%

1.16 **(a)** 220 hours per laborer; 66,000 labor hours
(b) 200 hours per laborer

Linear Programming: Model Formulation and Graphical Solution

Objectives of a business frequently are to maximize profit or minimize cost.

Many major decisions faced by a manager of a business focus on the best way to achieve the objectives of the firm, subject to the restrictions placed on the manager by the operating environment. These restrictions can take the form of limited resources, such as time, labor, energy, material, or money; or they can be in the form of restrictive guidelines, such as a recipe for making cereal or engineering specifications. One of the most frequent objectives of business firms is to gain the most profit possible or, in other words, to *maximize* profit. The objective of individual organizational units within a firm (such as a production or packaging department) is often to *minimize* cost. When a manager attempts to solve a general type of problem by seeking an objective that is subject to restrictions, the management science technique called **linear programming** is frequently used.

__Linear programming__ is a model that consists of linear relationships representing a firm's decision(s), given an objective and resource constraints.

There are three steps in applying the linear programming technique. First, the problem must be identified as being solvable by linear programming. Second, the unstructured problem must be formulated as a mathematical model. Third, the model must be solved by using established mathematical techniques. The linear programming technique derives its name from the fact that the functional relationships in the mathematical model are *linear*, and the solution technique consists of predetermined mathematical steps—that is, a *program*. In this chapter we will concern ourselves with the formulation of the mathematical model that represents the problem and then with solving this model by using a graph.

Model Formulation

A linear programming model consists of certain common components and characteristics. The model components include decision variables, an objective function, and model constraints, which consist of decision variables and parameters. **Decision variables** are mathematical symbols that represent levels of activity by the firm. For example, an electrical manufacturing firm desires to produce x_1 radios, x_2 toasters, and x_3 clocks, where x_1, x_2, and x_3 are symbols representing unknown variable quantities of each item. The final values of x_1, x_2, and x_3, as determined by the firm, constitute a *decision* (e.g., the equation $x_1 = 100$ radios is a decision by the firm to produce 100 radios).

__Decision variables__ are mathematical symbols that represent levels of activity.

The **objective function** is a linear mathematical relationship that describes the objective of the firm in terms of the decision variables. The objective function always consists of either *maximizing* or *minimizing* some value (e.g., maximize the profit or minimize the cost of producing radios).

The __objective function__ is a linear relationship that reflects the objective of an operation.

The **model constraints** are also linear relationships of the decision variables; they represent the restrictions placed on the firm by the operating environment. The restrictions can be in the form of limited resources or restrictive guidelines. For example, only 40 hours of labor may be available to produce radios during production. The actual numeric values in the objective function and the constraints, such as the 40 hours of available labor, are **parameters**.

A __constraint__ is a linear relationship that represents a restriction on decision making.

__Parameters__ are numerical values that are included in the objective functions and constraints.

The next section presents an example of how a linear programming model is formulated. Although this example is simplified, it is realistic and represents the type of problem to which linear programming can be applied. In the example, the model components are distinctly identified and described. By carefully studying this example, you can become familiar with the process of formulating linear programming models.

A Maximization Model Example

Beaver Creek Pottery Company is a small crafts operation run by a Native American tribal council. The company employs skilled artisans to produce clay bowls and mugs with authentic Native American designs and colors. The two primary resources used by the

Time Out *for George B. Dantzig*

Linear programming, as it is known today, was conceived in 1947 by George B. Dantzig while he was the head of the Air Force Statistical Control's Combat Analysis Branch at the Pentagon. The military referred to its plans for training, supplying, and deploying combat units as "programs." When Dantzig analyzed Air Force planning problems, he realized that they could be formulated as a system of linear inequalities—hence his original name for the technique, "programming in a linear structure," which was later shortened to "linear programming."

company are special pottery clay and skilled labor. Given these limited resources, the company desires to know how many bowls and mugs to produce each day in order to maximize profit. This is generally referred to as a *product mix* problem type. This scenario is illustrated in Figure 1.

Figure 1

Beaver Creek Pottery Company

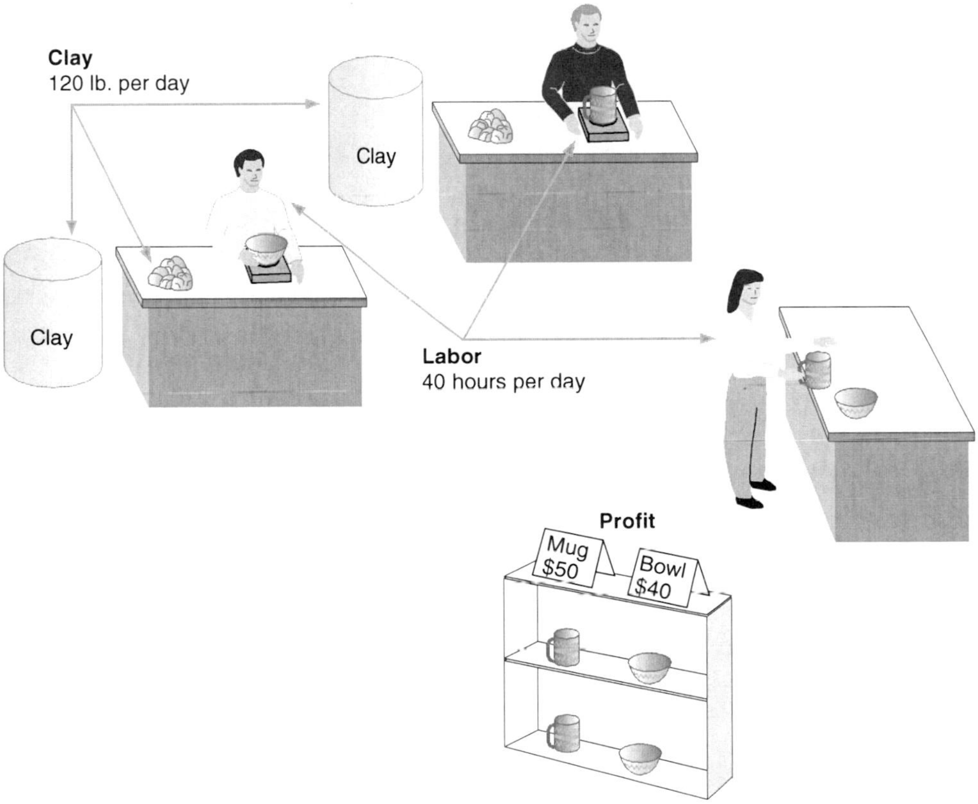

The two products have the following resource requirements for production and profit per item produced (i.e., the model parameters):

	Resource Requirements		
Product	Labor (hr./unit)	Clay (lb./unit)	Profit ($/unit)
Bowl	1	4	40
Mug	2	3	50

A linear programming model consists of decision variables, an objective function, and constraints.

There are 40 hours of labor and 120 pounds of clay available each day for production. We will formulate this problem as a linear programming model by defining each component of the model separately and then combining the components into a single model. The steps in this formulation process are summarized as follows:

> ### *Summary of LP Model Formulation Steps*
>
> ***Step 1: Define the decision variables***
>
> How many bowls and mugs to produce
>
> ***Step 2: Define the objective function***
>
> Maximize profit
>
> ***Step 3: Define the constraints***
>
> The resources (clay and labor) available

Decision Variables

The decision confronting management in this problem is how many bowls and mugs to produce. The two decision variables represent the number of bowls and mugs to be produced on a daily basis. The quantities to be produced can be represented symbolically as

$$x_1 = \text{number of bowls to produce}$$
$$x_2 = \text{number of mugs to produce}$$

The Objective Function

The objective of the company is to maximize total profit. The company's profit is the sum of the individual profits gained from each bowl and mug. Profit derived from bowls is determined by multiplying the unit profit of each bowl, \$40, by the number of bowls produced, x_1. Likewise, profit derived from mugs is derived from the unit profit of a mug, \$50, multiplied by the number of mugs produced, x_2. Thus, total profit, which we will define symbolically as Z, can be expressed mathematically as $\$40x_1 + \$50x_2$. By placing the term *maximize* in front of the profit function, we express the objective of the firm—to maximize total profit:

$$\text{maximize } Z = \$40x_1 + 50x_2$$

where

$$Z = \text{total profit per day}$$
$$\$40x_1 = \text{profit from bowls}$$
$$\$50x_2 = \text{profit from mugs}$$

Model Constraints

In this problem two resources are used for production—labor and clay—both of which are limited. Production of bowls and mugs requires both labor and clay. For each bowl produced, 1 hour of labor is required. Therefore, the labor used for the production of bowls is $1x_1$ hours. Similarly, each mug requires 2 hours of labor; thus, the labor used to produce mugs every day is $2x_2$ hours. The total labor used by the company is the sum of the individual amounts of labor used for each product:

$$1x_1 + 2x_2$$

However, the amount of labor represented by $1x_1 + 2x_2$ is limited to 40 hours per day; thus, the complete labor constraint is

$$1x_1 + 2x_2 \leq 40 \text{ hr.}$$

The "less than or equal to" ($\leq$) inequality is employed instead of an equality ($=$) because the 40 hours of labor is a maximum limitation that *can be used*, not an amount that *must be used*. This constraint allows the company some flexibility; the company is not restricted to using exactly 40 hours but can use whatever amount is necessary to maximize profit, up to and including 40 hours. This means that it is possible to have idle, or excess, capacity (i.e., some of the 40 hours may not be used).

The constraint for clay is formulated in the same way as the labor constraint. Because each bowl requires 4 pounds of clay, the amount of clay used daily for the production of bowls is $4x_1$ pounds; and because each mug requires 3 pounds of clay, the amount of clay used daily for mugs is $3x_2$. Given that the amount of clay available for production each day is 120 pounds, the material constraint can be formulated as

$$4x_1 + 3x_2 \leq 120 \text{ lb.}$$

Nonnegativity constraints restrict the decision variables to zero or positive values.

A final restriction is that the number of bowls and mugs produced must be either zero or a positive value because it is impossible to produce negative items. These restrictions are referred to as **nonnegativity constraints** and are expressed mathematically as

$$x_1 \geq 0, x_2 \geq 0$$

The complete linear programming model for this problem can now be summarized as follows:

$$\begin{aligned} \text{maximize } Z &= \$40x_1 + 50x_2 \\ \text{subject to} & \\ 1x_1 + 2x_2 &\leq 40 \\ 4x_1 + 3x_2 &\leq 120 \\ x_1, x_2 &\geq 0 \end{aligned}$$

The solution of this model will result in numeric values for x_1 and x_2 that will maximize total profit, Z. As *one possible* solution, consider $x_1 = 5$ bowls and $x_2 = 10$ mugs. First, we will substitute this hypothetical solution into each of the constraints in order to make sure that the solution does not require more resources than the constraints show are available:

$$\begin{aligned} 1(5) + 2(10) &\leq 40 \\ 25 &\leq 40 \end{aligned}$$

and

$$\begin{aligned} 4(5) + 3(10) &\leq 120 \\ 50 &\leq 120 \end{aligned}$$

*A **feasible solution** does not violate any of the constraints.*

Because neither of the constraints is violated by this hypothetical solution, we say the solution is **feasible** (i.e., it is possible). Substituting these solution values in the objective function gives $Z = 40(5) + 50(10) = \$700$. However, for the time being, we do not have any way of knowing whether \$700 is the *maximum* profit.

Now consider a solution of $x_1 = 10$ bowls and $x_2 = 20$ mugs. This solution results in a profit of

$$\begin{aligned} Z &= \$40(10) + 50(20) \\ &= 400 + 1{,}000 \\ &= \$1{,}400 \end{aligned}$$

*An **infeasible problem** violates at least one of the constraints.*

Although this is certainly a better solution in terms of profit, it is **infeasible** (i.e., not possible) because it violates the resource constraint for labor:

$$1(10) + 2(20) \leq 40$$
$$50 \not\leq 40$$

The solution to this problem must maximize profit without violating the constraints. The solution that achieves this objective is $x_1 = 24$ bowls and $x_2 = 8$ mugs, with a corresponding profit of \$1,360. The determination of this solution is shown using the graphical solution approach in the following section.

Graphical Solutions of Linear Programming Models

Graphical solutions are limited to linear programming problems with only two decision variables.

Following the formulation of a mathematical model, the next stage in the application of linear programming to a decision-making problem is to find the solution of the model. A common solution approach is to solve algebraically the set of mathematical relationships that form the model either manually or using a computer program, thus determining the values for the decision variables. However, because the relationships are *linear*, some models and solutions can be illustrated *graphically*.

The graphical method is realistically limited to models with only two decision variables, which can be represented on a graph of two dimensions. Models with three decision variables can be graphed in three dimensions, but the process is quite cumbersome, and models of four or more decision variables cannot be graphed at all.

The graphical method provides a picture of how a solution is obtained for a linear programming problem.

Although the graphical method is limited as a solution approach, it is very useful at this point in our presentation of linear programming in that it gives a picture of how a solution is derived. Graphs can provide a clearer understanding of how the computer and mathematical solution approaches presented in subsequent chapters work and, thus, a better understanding of the solutions.

Graphical Solution of a Maximization Model

The product mix model will be used to demonstrate the graphical interpretation of a linear programming problem. Recall that the problem describes Beaver Creek Pottery Company's attempt to decide how many bowls and mugs to produce daily, given limited amounts of labor and clay. The complete linear programming model was formulated as

$$\begin{aligned}
&\text{maximize } Z = \$40x_1 + 50x_2\\
&\text{subject to}\\
&\quad x_1 + 2x_2 \leq 40 \text{ hr. of labor}\\
&\quad 4x_1 + 3x_2 \leq 120 \text{ lb. of clay}\\
&\quad x_1, x_2 \geq 0\\
&\text{where}\\
&\quad x_1 = \text{number of bowls produced}\\
&\quad x_2 = \text{number of mugs produced}
\end{aligned}$$

Figure 2 is a set of coordinates for the decision variables x_1 and x_2, on which the graph of our model will be drawn. Note that only the positive quadrant is drawn (i.e., the quadrant where x_1 and x_2 will always be positive) because of the nonnegativity constraints, $x_1 \geq 0$ and $x_2 \geq 0$.

Management Science Application

Operational Cost Control at Kellogg

Kellogg is the world's largest cereal producer and a leading producer of convenience foods, with worldwide sales in 1999 of almost $7 billion. The company started with a single product, Kellogg's Corn Flakes, in 1906 and over the years developed a product line of other cereals, including Rice Krispies and Corn Pops, and convenience foods such as Pop-Tarts and Nutri-Grain cereal bars. Kellogg operates 5 plants in the United States and Canada and 7 distribution centers, and it contracts with 15 co-packers to produce or pack some of the Kellogg products. Kellogg must coordinate the production, packaging, inventory, and distribution of roughly 80 cereal products alone at these various facilities.

For more than a decade Kellogg has been using a large-scale linear programming model called the Kellogg Planning System (KPS) to plan its weekly production, inventory, and distribution decisions. The model decision variables include the amount of each product produced in a production process at each plant, the units of product packaged, the amount of inventory held, and the shipments of products to other plants and distribution centers. Model constraints include production processing time, packaging capacity, balancing constraints that make sure that all products produced are also packaged during the week, inventory balancing constraints, and inventory safety stock requirements. The model objective is cost minimization. Kellogg has also developed a tactical version of this basic operational linear programming model for long-range planning for 12 to 24 months into the future. The KPS model is credited with saving Kellogg $4.5 million in reduced production, inventory, and distribution costs in 1995, and it is estimated that KPS has saved Kellogg many more millions of dollars since the mid-1990s. The tactical version of KPS recently helped the company consolidate production capacity with estimated projected savings of almost $40 million.

Peter Yates/Corbis/Bettmann

Source: G. Brown, J. Keegan, B. Vigus, and K. Wood, "The Kellogg Company Optimizes Production, Inventory, and Distribution," *Interfaces* 31, no. 6 (November–December 2001): 1–15.

Figure 2
Coordinates for graphical analysis

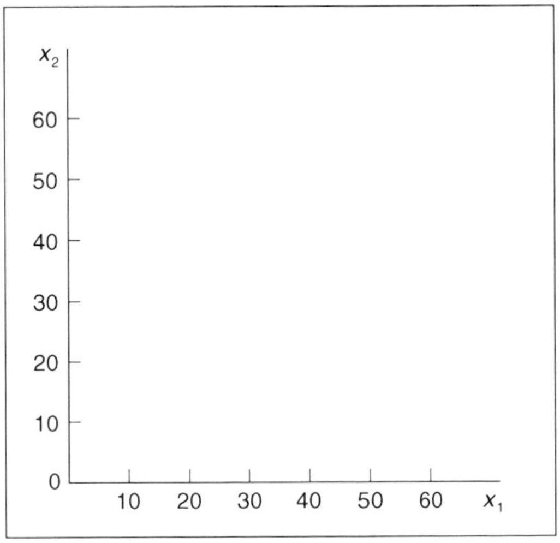

Constraint lines are plotted as equations.

The first step in drawing the graph of the model is to plot the constraints on the graph. This is done by treating both constraints as equations (or straight lines) and plotting each line on the graph. Let's consider the labor constraint line first:

$$x_1 + 2x_2 = 40$$

A simple procedure for plotting this line is to determine two points that are on the line and then draw a straight line through the points. One point can be found by letting $x_1 = 0$ and solving for x_2:

$$(0) + 2x_2 = 40$$
$$x_2 = 20$$

Thus, one point is at the coordinates $x_1 = 0$ and $x_2 = 20$. A second point can be found by letting $x_2 = 0$ and solving for x_1:

$$x_1 + 2(0) = 40$$
$$x_1 = 40$$

Now we have a second point, $x_1 = 40, x_2 = 0$. The line on the graph representing this equation is drawn by connecting these two points, as shown in Figure 3. However, this is only the graph of the constraint *line* and does not reflect the entire constraint, which also includes the values that are less than or equal to ($\leq$) this line. The *area* representing the entire constraint is shown in Figure 4.

Figure 3

Graph of the labor constraint line

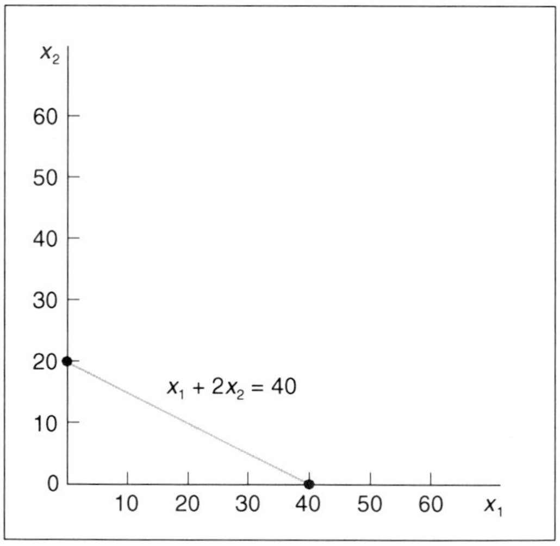

To test the correctness of the constraint area, we check any two points—one inside the constraint area and one outside. For example, check point *A* in Figure 4, which is at the intersection of $x_1 = 10$ and $x_2 = 10$. Substituting these values into the following labor constraint,

$$10 + 2(10) \leq 40$$
$$30 \leq 40 \text{ hr.}$$

Figure 4
The labor constraint area

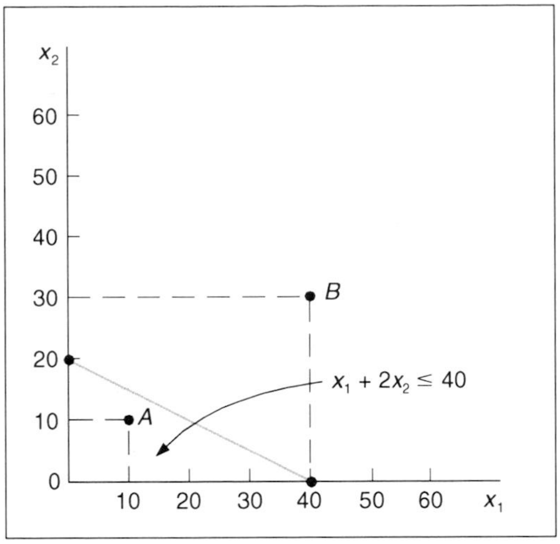

shows that point A is indeed within the constraint area, as these values for x_1 and x_2 yield a quantity that does not exceed the limit of 40 hours. Next, we check point B at $x_1 = 40$ and $x_2 = 30$:

$$\begin{aligned} 40 + 2(30) &\leq 40 \\ 100 &\nleq 40 \text{ hr.} \end{aligned}$$

Point B is obviously outside the constraint area because the values for x_1 and x_2 yield a quantity (100) that exceeds the limit of 40 hours.

We draw the line for the clay constraint the same way as the one for the labor constraint—by finding two points on the constraint line and connecting them with a straight line. First, let $x_1 = 0$ and solve for x_2:

$$\begin{aligned} 4(0) + 3x_2 &= 120 \\ x_2 &= 40 \end{aligned}$$

Performing this operation results in a point, $x_1 = 0, x_2 = 40$. Next, we let $x_2 = 0$ and then solve for x_1:

$$\begin{aligned} 4x_1 + 3(0) &= 120 \\ x_1 &= 30 \end{aligned}$$

This operation yields a second point, $x_1 = 30, x_2 = 0$. Plotting these points on the graph and connecting them with a line gives the constraint line and area for clay, as shown in Figure 5.

Combining the two individual graphs for both labor and clay (Figures 4 and 5) produces a graph of the model constraints, as shown in Figure 6. The shaded area in Figure 6 is the area that is common to both model constraints. Therefore, this is the only area on the graph that contains points (i.e., values for x_1 and x_2) that will satisfy both constraints simultaneously. For example, consider the points R, S, and T in Figure 7. Point R satisfies both constraints; thus, we say it is a *feasible* solution point. Point S satisfies the clay constraint ($4x_1 + 3x_2 \leq 120$) but exceeds the labor constraint; thus, it is infeasible. Point T satisfies neither constraint; thus, it is also infeasible.

Figure 5
The constraint area for clay

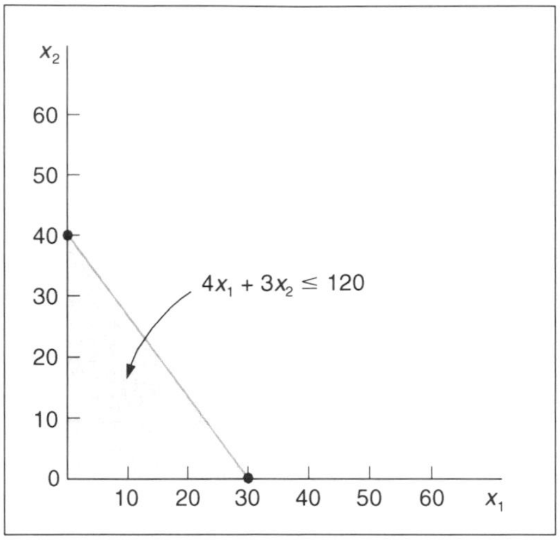

Figure 6
Graph of both model constraints

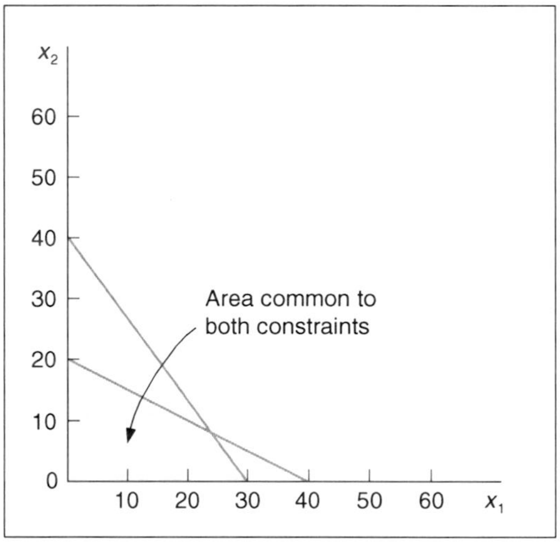

The feasible solution area is an area on the graph that is bounded by the constraint equations.

The shaded area in Figure 7 is referred to as the *feasible solution area* because all the points in this area satisfy both constraints. Some point within this feasible solution area will result in *maximum profit* for Beaver Creek Pottery Company. The next step in the graphical solution approach is to locate this point.

The Optimal Solution Point

The second step in the graphical solution method is to locate the point in the feasible solution area that will result in the greatest total profit. To begin the solution analysis, we first plot the objective function line for an *arbitrarily* selected level of profit. For example, if we say profit, Z, is \$800, the objective function is

$$\$800 = 40x_1 + 50x_2$$

Plotting this line just as we plotted the constraint lines results in the graph shown in Figure 8. Every point on this line is in the feasible solution area and will result in a profit

Figure 7
The feasible solution area constraints

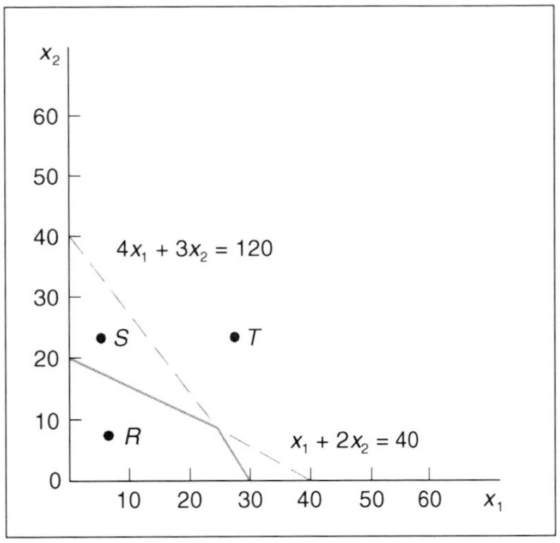

of \$800 (i.e., every combination of x_1 and x_2 on this line will give a Z value of \$800). However, let us see whether an even greater profit will still provide a feasible solution. For example, consider profits of \$1,200 and \$1,600, as shown in Figure 9.

Figure 8
Objective function line for $Z = \$800$

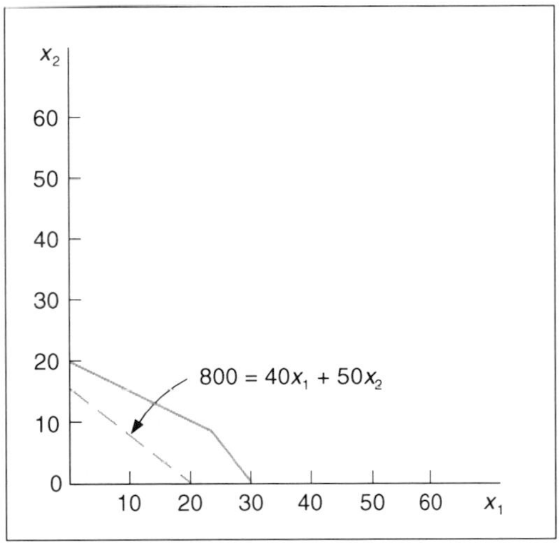

A portion of the objective function line for a profit of \$1,200 is outside the feasible solution area, but part of the line remains within the feasible area. Therefore, this profit line indicates that there are feasible solution points that give a profit greater than \$800. Now let us increase profit again, to \$1,600. This profit line, also shown in Figure 9, is completely outside the feasible solution area. The fact that no points on this line are feasible indicates that a profit of \$1,600 is not possible.

Because a profit of \$1,600 is too great for the constraint limitations, as shown in Figure 9, the question of the maximum profit value remains. We can see from Figure 9 that profit increases as the objective function line moves away from the origin (i.e., the point $x_1 = 0$, $x_2 = 0$). Given this characteristic, the maximum profit will be attained at the point where the objective function line is farthest from the origin *and* is still touching a point in the feasible solution area. This point is shown as point B in Figure 10.

Figure 9
Alternative objective function lines for profits, Z, of \$800, \$1,200, and \$1,600

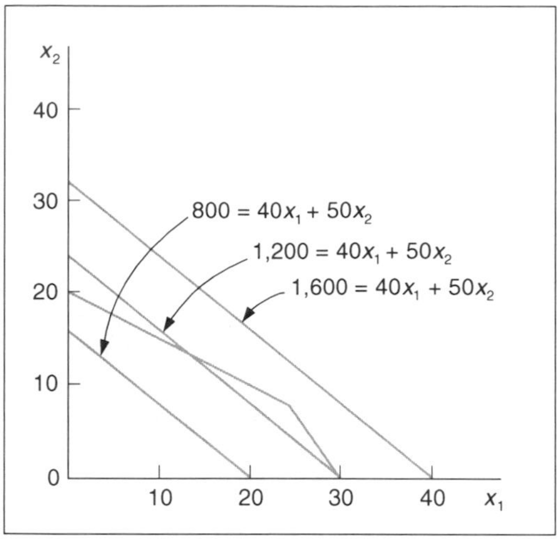

Figure 10
Identification of optimal solution point

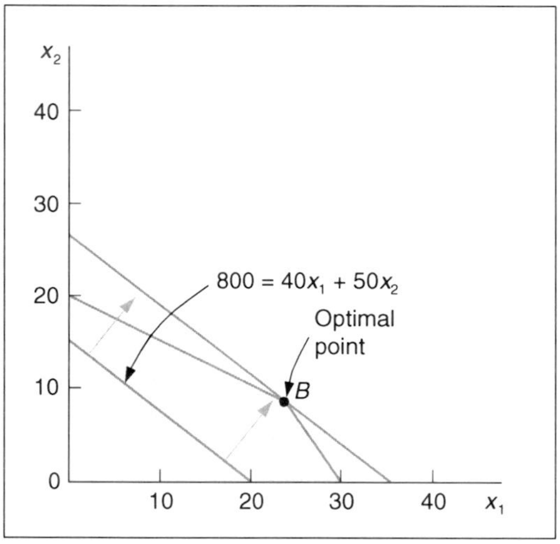

The ***optimal solution*** *is the best feasible solution.*

To find point B, we place a straightedge parallel to the objective function line $\$800 = 40x_1 + 50x_2$ in Figure 10 and move it outward from the origin as far as we can without losing contact with the feasible solution area. Point B is referred to as the **optimal** (i.e., best) **solution.**

The Solution Values

The third step in the graphical solution approach is to solve for the values of x_1 and x_2 once the optimal solution point has been found. It is possible to determine the x_1 and x_2 coordinates of point B in Figure 10 directly from the graph, as shown in Figure 11. The graphical coordinates corresponding to point B in Figure 11 are $x_1 = 24$ and $x_2 = 8$. This is the optimal solution for the decision variables in the problem. However, unless an absolutely accurate graph is drawn, it is frequently difficult to determine the correct solution directly from the graph. A more exact approach is to determine the solution values mathematically once the optimal point on the graph has been determined. The mathematical approach for determining the solution is described in the following pages. First, however, we will consider a few characteristics of the solution.

Figure 11
Optimal solution coordinates

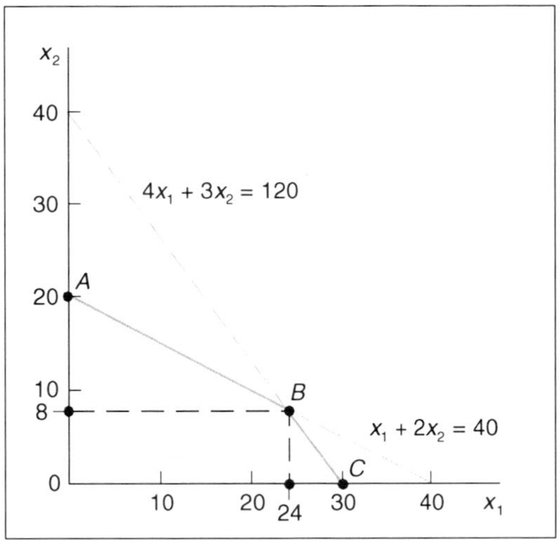

The optimal solution point is the last point the objective function touches as it leaves the feasible solution area.

In Figure 10, as the objective function was increased, the last point it touched in the feasible solution area was on the boundary of the feasible solution area. The solution point is always on this boundary because the boundary contains the points farthest from the origin (i.e., the points corresponding to the greatest profit). This characteristic of linear programming problems reduces the number of possible solution points considerably, from all points in the solution area to just those points on the boundary. However, the number of possible solution points is reduced even more by another characteristic of linear programming problems.

The solution point will be on the boundary of the feasible solution area and at one of the *corners* of the boundary where two constraint lines intersect. (The graphical axes, you will recall, are also constraints because $x_1 \geq 0$ and $x_2 \geq 0$.) These corners (points *A*, *B*, and *C* in Figure 11) are protrusions, or *extremes*, in the feasible solution area; they are called **extreme points.** It has been proven mathematically that the optimal solution in a linear programming model will always occur at an extreme point. Therefore, in our sample problem the possible solution points are limited to the three extreme points, *A*, *B*, and *C*. The optimal extreme point is the extreme point the objective function touches last as it leaves the feasible solution area, as shown in Figure 10.

__Extreme points__ are corner points on the boundary of the feasible solution area.

Constraint equations are solved simultaneously at the optimal extreme point to determine the variable solution values.

From the graph shown in Figure 10, we know that the optimal solution point is *B*. Because point *B* is formed by the intersection of two constraint lines, as shown in Figure 11, these two lines are *equal* at point *B*. Thus, the values of x_1 and x_2 at that intersection can be found by solving the two equations *simultaneously*.

First, we convert both equations to functions of x_1:

$$x_1 + 2x_2 = 40$$
$$x_1 = 40 - 2x_2$$

and

$$4x_1 + 3x_2 = 120$$
$$4x_1 = 120 - 3x_2$$
$$x_1 = 30 - (3x_2/4)$$

Now we let x_1 in the first equation equal x_1 in the second equation,

$$40 - 2x_2 = 30 - (3x_2/4)$$

and solve for x_2:

$$5x_2/4 = 10$$
$$x_2 = 8$$

Substituting $x_2 = 8$ into either one of the original equations gives a value for x_1:

$$x_1 = 40 - 2x_2$$
$$x_1 = 40 - 2(8)$$
$$= 24$$

Thus, the optimal solution at point B in Figure 11 is $x_1 = 24$ and $x_2 = 8$. Substituting these values into the objective function gives the maximum profit,

$$Z = \$40x_1 + 50x_2$$
$$Z = \$40(24) + 50(8)$$
$$= \$1{,}360$$

In terms of the original problem, the solution indicates that if the pottery company produces 24 bowls and 8 mugs, it will receive $1,360, the maximum daily profit possible (given the resource constraints).

Given that the optimal solution will be at one of the extreme corner points, A, B, or C, we can also find the solution by testing each of the three points to see which results in the greatest profit, rather than by graphing the objective function and seeing which point it last touches as it moves out of the feasible solution area. Figure 12 shows the solution values for all three points, A, B, and C, and the amount of profit, Z, at each point.

Figure 12
Solutions at all corner points

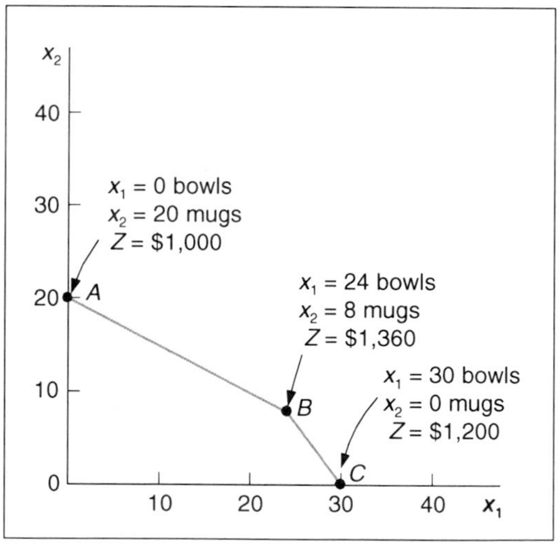

As indicated in the discussion of Figure 10, point B is the optimal solution point because it is the last point the objective function touches before it leaves the solution area. In other words, the objective function determines which extreme point is optimal. This is because the objective function designates the profit that will accrue from each combination of x_1 and x_2 values at the extreme points. If the objective function had had different coefficients (i.e., different x_1 and x_2 profit values), one of the extreme points other than B might have been optimal.

Let's assume for a moment that the profit for a bowl is \$70 instead of \$40, and the profit for a mug is \$20 instead of \$50. These values result in a new objective function, $Z = \$70x_1 + 20x_2$. If the model constraints for labor or clay are not changed, the feasible solution area remains the same, as shown in Figure 13. However, the location of the objective function in Figure 13 is different from that of the original objective function in Figure 10. The reason for this change is that the new profit coefficients give the linear objective function a new *slope*.

Figure 13
The optimal solution with $Z = 70x_1 + 20x_2$

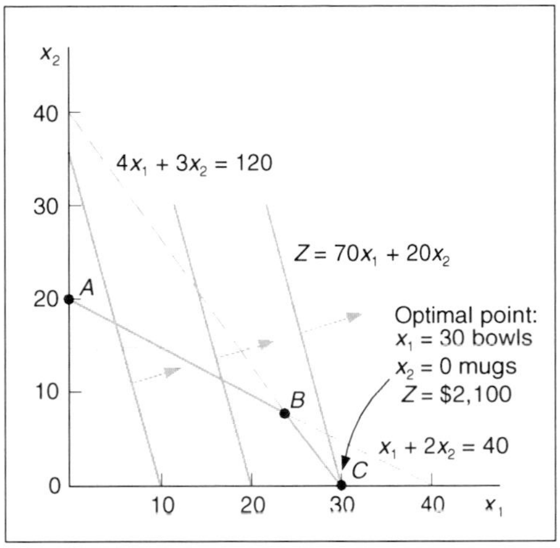

The ***slope*** *is computed as the "rise" over the "run."*

The **slope** can be determined by transforming the objective function into the general equation for a straight line, $y = a + bx$, where y is the dependent variable, a is the y intercept, b is the slope, and x is the independent variable. For our sample objective function, x_2 is the dependent variable corresponding to y (i.e., it is on the vertical axis), and x_1 is the independent variable. Thus, the objective function can be transformed into the general equation of a line as follows:

$$\begin{aligned} Z &= 70x_1 + 20x_2 \\ 20x_2 &= Z - 70x_1 \\ \underset{\underset{y}{\uparrow}}{x_2} &= \underset{\underset{a}{\uparrow}}{\frac{Z}{20}} - \underset{\underset{b}{\uparrow}}{\frac{7}{2}}x_1 \end{aligned}$$

This transformation identifies the slope of the new objective function as $-7/2$ (the minus sign indicates that the line slopes downward). In contrast, the slope of the original objective function was $-4/5$.

If we move this new objective function out through the feasible solution area, the last extreme point it touches is point C. Simultaneously solving the constraint lines at point C results in the following solution:

$$\begin{aligned} x_1 &= 30 \\ 4x_1 + 3x_2 &= 120 \end{aligned}$$

and

$$\begin{aligned} x_2 &= 40 - (4x_1/3) \\ x_2 &= 40 - 4(30)/3 \\ x_2 &= 0 \end{aligned}$$

Thus, the optimal solution at point C in Figure 13 is $x_1 = 30$ bowls, $x_2 = 0$ mugs, and $Z = \$2,100$ profit. Altering the objective function coefficients results in a new solution.

This brief example of the effects of altering the objective function highlights two useful points. First, the optimal extreme point is determined by the objective function, and an extreme point on one axis of the graph is as likely to be the optimal solution as is an extreme point on a different axis. Second, the solution is sensitive to the values of the coefficients in the objective function. If the objective function coefficients are changed, as in our example, the solution may change. Likewise, if the constraint coefficients are changed, the solution space and solution points may change also. This information can be of consequence to the decision maker trying to determine how much of a product to produce.

Multiple optimal solutions can occur when the objective function is parallel to a constraint line.

It should be noted that some problems do not have a single extreme point solution. For example, when the objective function line parallels one of the constraint lines, an entire line segment is bounded by two adjacent corner points that are optimal; there is no single extreme point on the objective function line. In this situation there are **multiple optimal solutions.** This and other irregular types of solution outcomes in linear programming are discussed at the end of this chapter.

Slack Variables

Once the optimal solution was found at point *B* in Figure 12, simultaneous equations were solved to determine the values of x_1 and x_2. Recall that the solution occurs at an extreme point where constraint equation lines intersect with each other or with the axis. Thus, the model constraints are considered as *equations* (=) rather than $\leq$ or $\geq$ inequalities.

A slack variable is added to a $\leq$ constraint to convert it to an equation (=).

There is a standard procedure for transforming $\leq$ inequality constraints into equations. This transformation is achieved by adding a new variable, called a **slack variable,** to each constraint. For the pottery company example, the model constraints are

$$\begin{aligned} x_1 + 2x_2 &\leq 40 \text{ hr. of labor} \\ 4x_1 + 3x_2 &\leq 120 \text{ lb. of clay} \end{aligned}$$

*A **slack variable** represents unused resources.*

The addition of a unique slack variable, s_1, to the labor constraint and s_2 to the constraint for clay results in the following equations:

$$\begin{aligned} x_1 + 2x_2 + s_1 &= 40 \text{ hr. of labor} \\ 4x_1 + 3x_2 + s_2 &= 120 \text{ lb. of clay} \end{aligned}$$

The slack variables in these equations, s_1 and s_2, will take on any value necessary to make the left-hand side of the equation equal to the right-hand side. For example, consider a hypothetical solution of $x_1 = 5$ and $x_2 = 10$. Substituting these values into the foregoing equations yields

$$\begin{aligned} x_1 + 2x_2 + s_1 &= 40 \text{ hr. of labor} \\ 5 + 2(10) + s_1 &= 40 \text{ hr. of labor} \\ s_1 &= 15 \text{ hr. of labor} \end{aligned}$$

and

$$\begin{aligned} 4x_1 + 3x_2 + s_2 &= 120 \text{ lb. of clay} \\ 4(5) + 3(10) + s_2 &= 120 \text{ lb. of clay} \\ s_2 &= 70 \text{ lb. of clay} \end{aligned}$$

In this example, $x_1 = 5$ bowls and $x_2 = 10$ mugs represent a solution that does not make use of the total available amount of labor and clay. In the labor constraint, 5 bowls and 10 mugs require only 25 hours of labor. This leaves 15 hours that are not used. Thus, s_1 represents the amount of *unused* labor, or slack.

In the clay constraint, 5 bowls and 10 mugs require only 50 pounds of clay. This leaves 70 pounds of clay unused. Thus, s_2 represents the amount of *unused* clay. In general, slack variables represent the amount of *unused resources*.

The ultimate instance of unused resources occurs at the origin, where $x_1 = 0$ and $x_2 = 0$. Substituting these values into the equations yields

$$\begin{aligned} x_1 + 2x_2 + s_1 &= 40 \\ 0 + 2(0) + s_1 &= 40 \\ s_1 &= 40 \text{ hr. of labor} \end{aligned}$$

and

$$\begin{aligned} 4x_1 + 3x_2 + s_2 &= 120 \\ 4(0) + 3(0) + s_2 &= 120 \\ s_2 &= 120 \text{ lb. of clay} \end{aligned}$$

Because no production takes place at the origin, all the resources are unused; thus, the slack variables equal the total available amounts of each resource: $s_1 = 40$ hours of labor and $s_2 = 120$ pounds of clay.

What is the effect of these new slack variables on the objective function? The objective function for our example represents the profit gained from the production of bowls and mugs,

$$Z = \$40x_1 + \$50x_2$$

A slack variable contributes nothing to the objective function value.

The coefficient \$40 is the contribution to profit of each bowl; \$50 is the contribution to profit of each mug. What, then, do the slack variables s_1 and s_2 contribute? They contribute *nothing* to profit because they represent unused resources. Profit is made only after the resources are put to use in making bowls and mugs. Using slack variables, we can write the objective function as

$$\text{maximize } Z = \$40x_1 + \$50x_2 + 0s_1 + 0s_2$$

As in the case of decision variables (x_1 and x_2), slack variables can have only nonnegative values because negative resources are not possible. Therefore, for this model formulation, x_1, x_2, s_1, and $s_2 \geq 0$.

The complete linear programming model can be written in what is referred to as *standard form* with slack variables as follows:

$$\begin{aligned} &\text{maximize } Z = \$40x_1 + \$50x_2 + 0s_1 + 0s_2 \\ &\text{subject to} \\ &\qquad x_1 + 2x_2 + s_1 = 40 \\ &\qquad 4x_1 + 3x_2 + s_2 = 120 \\ &\qquad x_1, x_2, s_1, s_2 \geq 0 \end{aligned}$$

The solution values, including the slack at each solution point, are summarized as follows:

Solution Summary with Slack

Point	Solution Values	Z	Slack
A	$x_1 = 0$ bowls, $x_2 = 20$ mugs	\$1,000	$s_1 = 0$ hr.; $s_2 = 60$ lb.
B	$x_1 = 24$ bowls, $x_2 = 8$ mugs	\$1,360	$s_1 = 0$ hr.; $s_2 = 0$ lb.
C	$x_1 = 30$ bowls, $x_2 = 0$ mugs	\$1,200	$s_1 = 10$ hr.; $s_2 = 0$ lb.

Figure 14 shows the graphical solution of this example, with slack variables included at each solution point.

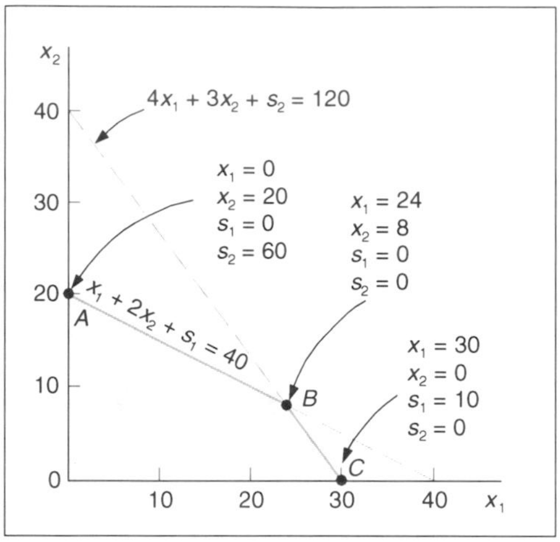

Figure 14
Solutions at points *A*, *B*, and *C* with slack

Management Science Application

Improving Customer Service at Amazon.com

Amazon.com started as an Internet book retailer in 1995 and 10 years later was a Fortune 500 company with annual sales of more than $7 billion. Amazon.com is now an Internet retailer that offers new and used products in a variety of categories including music and video, consumer electronics, food, clothing, furniture, and appliances. From 2001 through 2003 Amazon.com achieved the highest score ever recorded in any service industry by the American Customer Satisfaction Index. The company's success is partly a result of its strong customer service operations. Customer service is provided through features on the Web site or via telephone or e-mail. Customer service representatives are available at internally or externally managed contact centers 24 hours a day. Because of its sales growth and the seasonality of its sales (which generally decline in the summer), Amazon must make accurate decisions about the capacity of its contact centers, including the number of customer service representatives to hire and train at its internally managed centers, and the volume of voice calls and e-mails to allocate to external service providers (referred to as *cosourcers*). The service times for calls and e-mails are categorized depending on the product type, the customer type, and the purchase type. Amazon's objective is to process calls and e-mails at target service levels for different categories; for voice calls the target is that a specific percentage of callers wait no more than a specific time, and for e-mails the target is that a percentage of them receive a response within some time period. Amazon uses a linear programming model to optimize its capacity decisions at its customer service contact centers. The approach provides a minimum-cost capacity plan that provides the number of representatives to hire and train at Amazon's own centers and the volume of contacts to allocate to each cosourcer each week for a given planning horizon. Objective function costs include the number of normal and overtime hours, the number of new representatives hired and transferred, and the cost of contracting with cosourcers. There are several categories of constraints related to the number of voice calls and e-mails and for normal and overtime hours at both the internally managed contact centers and at cosourcers. For a 1-year (52-week) planning horizon the linear programming model consists of approximately 134,000 constraints and almost 16,000 variables.

REUTERS/Dylan Martinez/Landov

Source: M. Keblis and M. Chen, "Improving Customer Service Operations at Amazon.com," *Interfaces* 36, no. 5 (September–October 2006): 433–45.

Summary of the Graphical Solution Steps

The steps for solving a graphical linear programming model are summarized here:

1. Plot the model constraints as equations on the graph; then, considering the inequalities of the constraints, indicate the feasible solution area.
2. Plot the objective function; then, move this line out from the origin to locate the optimal solution point.
3. Solve simultaneous equations at the solution point to find the optimal solution values.

Or

2. Solve simultaneous equations at each corner point to find the solution values at each point.
3. Substitute these values into the objective function to find the set of values that results in the maximum Z value.

A Minimization Model Example

As mentioned at the beginning of this chapter, there are two types of linear programming problems: maximization problems (like the Beaver Creek Pottery Company example) and minimization problems. A minimization problem is formulated the same basic way as a maximization problem, except for a few minor differences. The following sample problem will demonstrate the formulation of a minimization model.

A farmer is preparing to plant a crop in the spring and needs to fertilize a field. There are two brands of fertilizer to choose from, Super-gro and Crop-quick. Each brand yields a specific amount of nitrogen and phosphate per bag, as follows:

	Chemical Contribution	
Brand	NITROGEN (LB./BAG)	PHOSPHATE (LB./BAG)
Super-gro	2	4
Crop-quick	4	3

The farmer's field requires at least 16 pounds of nitrogen and at least 24 pounds of phosphate. Super-gro costs $6 per bag, and Crop-quick costs $3. The farmer wants to know how many bags of each brand to purchase in order to minimize the total cost of fertilizing. This scenario is illustrated in Figure 15.

The steps in the linear programming model formulation process are summarized as follows:

Summary of LP Model Formulation Steps

Step 1: Define the decision variables

How many bags of Super-gro and Crop-quick to buy

Step 2: Define the objective function

Minimize cost

Step 3: Define the constraints

The field requirements for nitrogen and phosphate

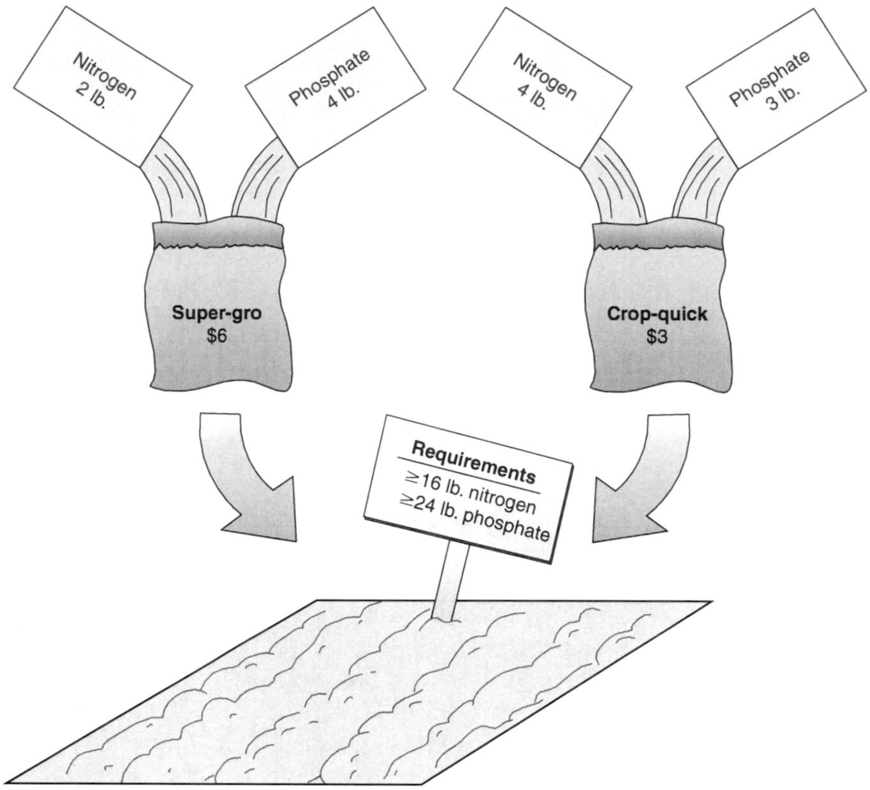

Figure 15
Fertilizing farmer's field

Decision Variables

This problem contains two decision variables, representing the number of bags of each brand of fertilizer to purchase:

$$x_1 = \text{bags of Super-gro}$$
$$x_2 = \text{bags of Crop-quick}$$

The Objective Function

The farmer's objective is to minimize the total cost of fertilizing. The total cost is the sum of the individual costs of each type of fertilizer purchased. The objective function that represents total cost is expressed as

$$\text{minimize } Z = \$6x_1 + 3x_2$$

where

$$\$6x_1 = \text{cost of bags of Super-gro}$$
$$\$3x_2 = \text{cost of bags of Crop-quick}$$

Model Constraints

The requirements for nitrogen and phosphate represent the constraints of the model. Each bag of fertilizer contributes a number of pounds of nitrogen and phosphate to the field. The constraint for nitrogen is

$$2x_1 + 4x_2 \geq 16 \text{ lb.}$$

where

$$2x_1 = \text{the nitrogen contribution (lb.) per bag of Super-gro}$$
$$4x_2 = \text{the nitrogen contribution (lb.) per bag of Crop-quick}$$

Rather than a ≤ (less than or equal to) inequality, as used in the Beaver Creek Pottery Company model, this constraint requires a ≥ (greater than or equal to) inequality. This is because the nitrogen content for the field is a minimum requirement specifying that at least 16 pounds of nitrogen be deposited on the farmer's field. If a minimum cost solution results in more than 16 pounds of nitrogen on the field, that is acceptable; however, the amount cannot be less than 16 pounds.

The constraint for phosphate is constructed like the constraint for nitrogen:

$$4x_1 + 3x_2 \geq 24 \text{ lb.}$$

The three types of linear programming constraints are ≤, =, and ≥.

With this example we have shown two of the three types of linear programming model constraints, ≤ and ≥. The third type is an exact equality, =. This type specifies that a constraint requirement must be exact. For example, if the farmer had said that the phosphate requirement for the field was exactly 24 pounds, the constraint would have been

$$4x_1 + 3x_2 = 24 \text{ lb.}$$

As in our maximization model, there are also nonnegativity constraints in this problem to indicate that negative bags of fertilizer cannot be purchased:

$$x_1, x_2 \geq 0$$

The complete model formulation for this minimization problem is

$$\begin{aligned} &\text{minimize } Z = \$6x_1 + 3x_2 \\ &\text{subject to} \\ &2x_1 + 4x_2 \geq 16 \text{ lb. of nitrogen} \\ &4x_1 + 3x_2 \geq 24 \text{ lb. of phosphate} \\ &\quad x_1, x_2 \geq 0 \end{aligned}$$

Graphical Solution of a Minimization Model

We follow the same basic steps in the graphical solution of a minimization model as in a maximization model. The fertilizer example will be used to demonstrate the graphical solution of a minimization model.

The first step is to graph the equations of the two model constraints, as shown in Figure 16. Next, the feasible solution area is chosen, to reflect the ≥ inequalities in the constraints, as shown in Figure 17.

Figure 16
Constraint lines for fertilizer model

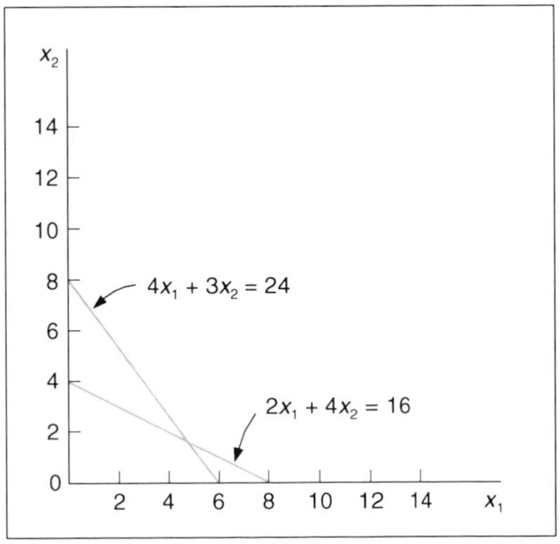

Figure 17
Feasible solution area

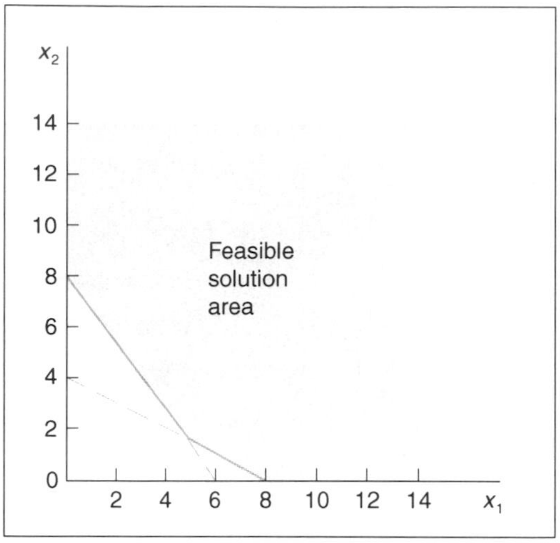

The optimal solution of a minimization problem is at the extreme point closest to the origin.

After the feasible solution area has been determined, the second step in the graphical solution approach is to locate the optimal point. Recall that in a maximization problem, the optimal solution is on the boundary of the feasible solution area that contains the point(s) farthest from the origin. The optimal solution point in a minimization problem is also on the boundary of the feasible solution area; however, the boundary contains the point(s) *closest* to the origin (zero being the lowest cost possible).

As in a maximization problem, the optimal solution is located at one of the extreme points of the boundary. In this case the corner points represent extremities in the boundary of the feasible solution area that are *closest* to the origin. Figure 18 shows the three corner points—*A*, *B*, and *C*—and the objective function line.

As the objective function edges *toward* the origin, the last point it touches in the feasible solution area is *A*. In other words, point *A* is the closest the objective function can get to the origin without encompassing infeasible points. Thus, it corresponds to the lowest cost that can be attained.

Figure 18
The optimal solution point

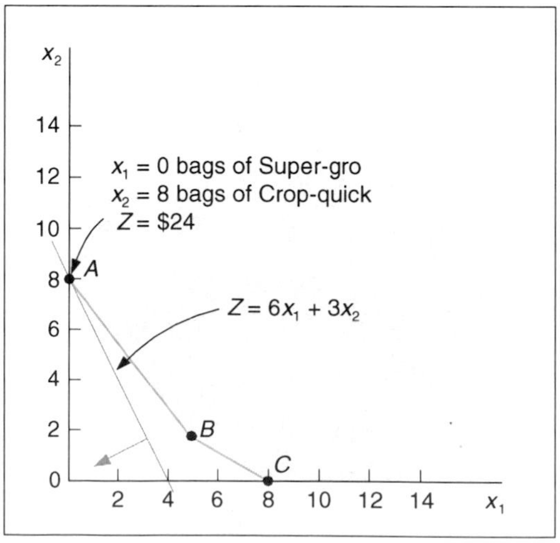

Management Science Application

Determining Optimal Fertilizer Mixes at Soquimich (South America)

Soquimich, a Chilean fertilizer manufacturer, is the leading producer and distributor of specialty fertilizers in the world, with revenues of almost US$0.5 billion in more than 80 countries. Soquimich produces four main specialty fertilizers and more than 200 fertilizer blends, depending on the needs of its customers. Farmers want the company to quickly recommend optimal fertilizer blends that will provide the appropriate quantity of ingredients for their particular crop at the lowest possible cost. A farmer will provide a company sales representative with information about previous crop yields and his or her target yields and then company representatives will visit the farm to obtain soil samples, which are analyzed in the company labs. A report is generated, which indicates the soil requirements for nutrients, including nitrogen, phosphorus, potassium, boron, magnesium, sulfur, and zinc. Given these soil requirements, company experts determine an optimal fertilizer blend, using a linear programming model that includes constraints for the nutrient quantities required by the soil (for a particular crop) and an objective function that minimizes production costs. Previously the company determined fertilizer blend recommendations by using a time-consuming manual procedure conducted by experts. The linear programming model enables the company to provide accurate, quick, low-cost (discounted) estimates to its customers, which has helped the company gain new customers and increase its market share.

Peter Beck/CORBIS-NY

Source: A. M. Angel, L. A. Taladriz, and R. Weber, "Soquimich Uses a System Based on Mixed-Integer Linear Programming and Expert Systems to Improve Customer Service," *Interfaces* 33, no. 4 (July–August 2003): 41–52.

The final step in the graphical solution approach is to solve for the values of x_1 and x_2 at point A. Because point A is on the x_2 axis, $x_1 = 0$; thus,

$$\begin{aligned} 4(0) + 3x_2 &= 24 \\ x_2 &= 8 \end{aligned}$$

Given that the optimal solution is $x_1 = 0, x_2 = 8$, the minimum cost, Z, is

$$\begin{aligned} Z &= \$6x_1 + \$3x_2 \\ Z &= 6(0) + 3(8) \\ &= \$24 \end{aligned}$$

This means the farmer should not purchase any Super-gro but, instead, should purchase eight bags of Crop-quick, at a total cost of $24.

Surplus Variables

Greater-than or equal-to constraints cannot be converted to equations by adding slack variables, as with $\leq$ constraints. Recall our fertilizer model, formulated as

$$\begin{aligned} &\text{minimize } Z = \$6x_1 + \$3x_2 \\ &\text{subject to} \\ &\qquad 2x_1 + 4x_2 \geq 16 \text{ lb. of nitrogen} \\ &\qquad 4x_1 + 3x_2 \geq 24 \text{ lb. of phosphate} \\ &\qquad x_1, x_2 \geq 0 \end{aligned}$$

where
x_1 = bags of Super-gro fertilizer
x_2 = bags of Crop-quick fertilizer
Z = farmer's total cost ($) of purchasing fertilizer

A surplus variable is subtracted from a ≥ constraint to convert it to an equation (=).

*A **surplus variable** represents an excess above a constraint requirement level.*

Because this problem has ≥ constraints as opposed to the ≤ constraints of the Beaver Creek Pottery Company maximization example, the constraints are converted to equations a little differently.

Instead of adding a slack variable as we did with a ≥ constraint, we subtract a **surplus variable.** Whereas a slack variable is added and reflects unused resources, a surplus variable is subtracted and reflects the excess above a minimum resource requirement level. Like a slack variable, a surplus variable is represented symbolically by s_1 and must be nonnegative.

For the nitrogen constraint, the subtraction of a surplus variable gives

$$2x_1 + 4x_2 - s_1 = 16$$

The surplus variable s_1 transforms the nitrogen constraint into an equation.

As an example, consider the hypothetical solution

$$x_1 = 0$$
$$x_2 = 10$$

Substituting these values into the previous equation yields

$$\begin{aligned} 2(0) + 4(10) - s_1 &= 16 \\ -s_1 &= 16 - 40 \\ s_1 &= 24 \text{ lb. of nitrogen} \end{aligned}$$

In this equation s_1 can be interpreted as the *extra* amount of nitrogen above the minimum requirement of 16 pounds that would be obtained by purchasing 10 bags of Crop-quick fertilizer.

In a similar manner, the constraint for phosphate is converted to an equation by subtracting a surplus variable, s_2:

$$4x_1 + 3x_2 - s_2 = 24$$

Figure 19
Graph of the fertilizer example

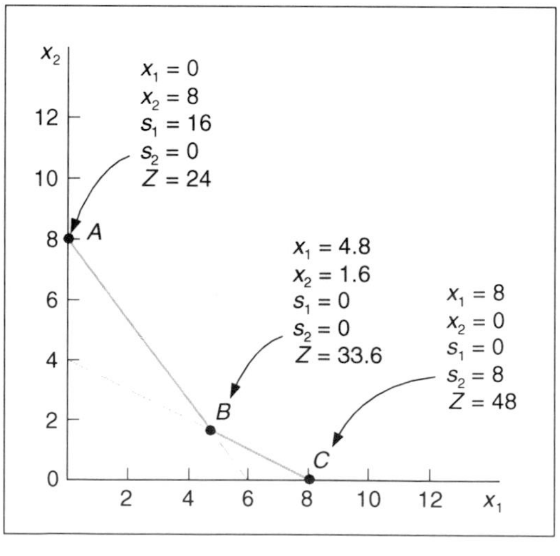

As is the case with slack variables, surplus variables contribute nothing to the overall cost of a model. For example, putting additional nitrogen or phosphate on the field will not affect the farmer's cost; the only thing affecting cost is the number of bags of fertilizer purchased. As such, the standard form of this linear programming model is summarized as

$$\begin{aligned}
&\text{minimize } Z = \$6x_1 + 3x_2 + 0s_1 + 0s_2\\
&\text{subject to}\\
&\qquad 2x_1 + 4x_2 - s_1 = 16\\
&\qquad 4x_1 + 3x_2 - s_2 = 24\\
&\qquad x_1, x_2, s_1, s_2 \geq 0
\end{aligned}$$

Figure 19 shows the graphical solutions for our example, with surplus variables included at each solution point.

Irregular Types of Linear Programming Problems

For some linear programming models, the general rules do not always apply.

The basic forms of typical maximization and minimization problems have been shown in this chapter. However, there are several special types of atypical linear programming problems. Although these special cases do not occur frequently, they will be described so that you can recognize them when they arise. These special types include problems with more than one optimal solution, infeasible problems, and problems with unbounded solutions.

Multiple Optimal Solutions

Consider the Beaver Creek Pottery Company example, with the objective function changed from $Z = 40x_1 + 50x_2$ to $Z = 40x_1 + 30x_2$:

$$\begin{aligned}
&\text{maximize } Z = 40x_1 + 30x_2\\
&\text{subject to}\\
&\quad x_1 + 2x_2 \leq 40 \text{ hr. of labor}\\
&\quad 4x_1 + 3x_2 \leq 120 \text{ lb. of clay}\\
&\quad x_1, x_2 \geq 0\\
&\text{where}\\
&\quad x_1 = \text{bowls produced}\\
&\quad x_2 = \text{mugs produced}
\end{aligned}$$

The graph of this model is shown in Figure 20. The slight change in the objective function makes it now *parallel* to the constraint line, $4x_1 + 3x_2 = 120$. Both lines now have the same slope of $-4/3$. Therefore, as the objective function edge moves outward from the origin, it touches the whole line segment BC rather than a single extreme corner point before it leaves the feasible solution area. This means that every point along this line segment is optimal (i.e., each point results in the same profit of $Z = \$1{,}200$). The endpoints of this line segment, B and C, are typically referred to as the **alternate optimal solutions.** It is understood that these points represent the endpoints of a range of optimal solutions.

__Alternate optimal solutions__ are at the endpoints of the constraint line segment that the objective function parallels.

The pottery company, therefore, has several options in deciding on the number of bowls and mugs to produce. Multiple optimal solutions can benefit the decision maker because the number of decision options is enlarged. The multiple optimal solutions (along the line segment BC in Figure 20) allow the decision maker greater flexibility. For example, in the

Multiple optimal solutions provide greater flexibility to the decision maker.

Figure 20

Graph of the Beaver Creek Pottery Company example with multiple optimal solutions

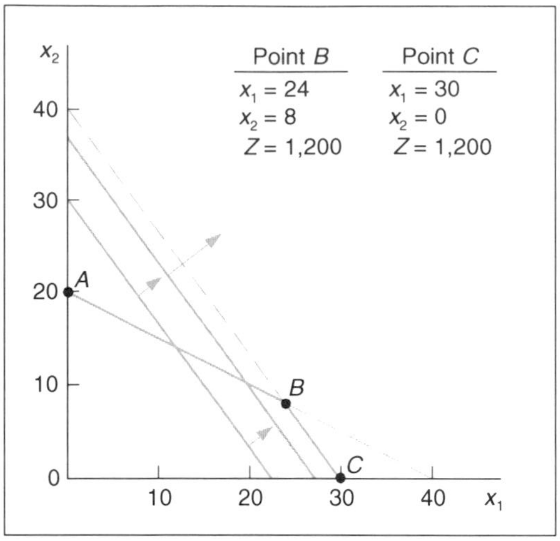

case of Beaver Creek Pottery Company, it may be easier to sell bowls than mugs; thus, the solution at point *C*, where only bowls are produced, would be more desirable than the solution at point *B*, where a mix of bowls and mugs is produced.

An Infeasible Problem

In some cases a linear programming problem has no feasible solution area; thus, there is no solution to the problem. An example of an infeasible problem is formulated next and depicted graphically in Figure 21:

$$\begin{aligned} \text{maximize } Z &= 5x_1 + 3x_2 \\ \text{subject to} & \\ 4x_1 + 2x_2 &\leq 8 \\ x_1 &\geq 4 \\ x_2 &\geq 6 \\ x_1, x_2 &\geq 0 \end{aligned}$$

Figure 21

Graph of an infeasible problem

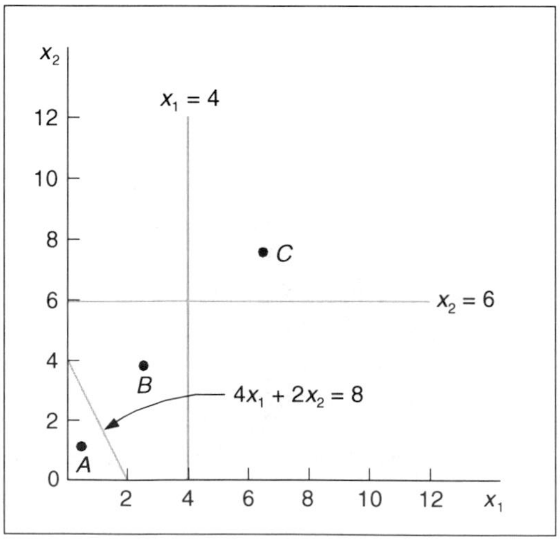

An ***infeasible problem*** *has no feasible solution area; every possible solution point violates one or more constraints.*

Point A in Figure 21 satisfies only the constraint $4x_1 + 2x_2 \leq 8$, whereas point C satisfies only the constraints $x_1 \geq 4$ and $x_2 \geq 6$. Point B satisfies none of the constraints. The three constraints do not overlap to form a feasible solution area. Because no point satisfies all three constraints simultaneously, there is no solution to the problem. Infeasible problems do not typically occur, but when they do, they are usually a result of errors in defining the problem or in formulating the linear programming model.

An Unbounded Problem

*In an **unbounded problem** the objective function can increase indefinitely without reaching a maximum value.*

In some problems the feasible solution area formed by the model constraints is not closed. In these cases it is possible for the objective function to increase indefinitely without ever reaching a maximum value because it never reaches the boundary of the feasible solution area.

An example of this type of problem is formulated next and shown graphically in Figure 22:

$$\text{maximize } Z = 4x_1 + 2x_2$$

subject to

$$x_1 \geq 4$$
$$x_2 \leq 2$$
$$x_1, x_2 \geq 0$$

Figure 22
An unbounded problem

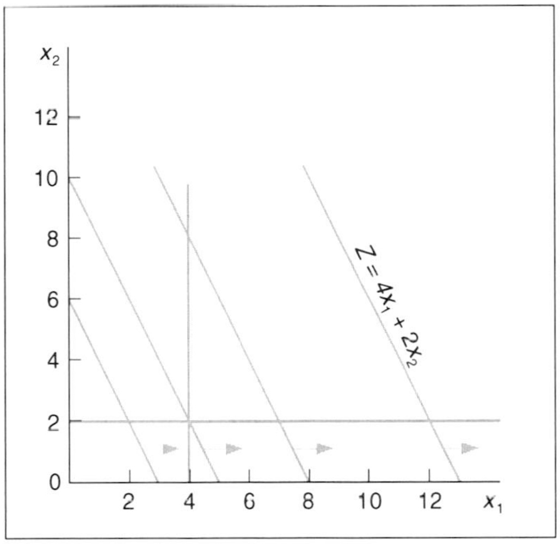

The solution space is not completely closed in.

In Figure 22 the objective function is shown to increase without bound; thus, a solution is never reached.

Unlimited profits are not possible in the real world; an unbounded solution, like an infeasible solution, typically reflects an error in defining the problem or in formulating the model.

Characteristics of Linear Programming Problems

The components of a linear programming model are an objective function, decision variables, and constraints.

Now that we have had the opportunity to construct several linear programming models, let's review the characteristics that identify a linear programming problem.

A linear programming problem requires a choice between alternative courses of action (i.e., a decision). The decision is represented in the model by decision variables. A typical choice task for a business firm is deciding how much of several different products to produce, as in the Beaver Creek Pottery Company example presented earlier in this chapter. Identifying the choice task and defining the decision variables is usually the first step in the formulation process because it is quite difficult to construct the objective function and constraints without first identifying the decision variables.

The problem encompasses an objective that the decision maker wants to achieve. The two most frequently encountered objectives for a business are maximizing profit and minimizing cost.

A third characteristic of a linear programming problem is that restrictions exist, making unlimited achievement of the objective function impossible. In a business firm these restrictions often take the form of limited resources, such as labor or material; however, the sample models in this chapter exhibit a variety of problem restrictions. These restrictions, as well as the objective, must be definable by mathematical functional relationships that are linear. Defining these relationships is typically the most difficult part of the formulation process.

Properties of Linear Programming Models

In addition to encompassing only linear relationships, a linear programming model also has several other implicit properties, which have been exhibited consistently throughout the examples in this chapter. The term *linear* not only means that the functions in the models are graphed as a straight line; it also means that the relationships exhibit **proportionality**. In other words, the rate of change, or slope, of the function is constant; therefore, changes of a given size in the value of a decision variable will result in exactly the same relative changes in the functional value.

__Proportionality__ means the slope of a constraint or objective function line is constant.

Linear programming also requires that the objective function terms and the constraint terms be **additive**. For example, in the Beaver Creek Pottery Company model, the total profit (Z) must equal the sum of profits earned from making bowls ($\$40x_1$) and mugs ($\$50x_2$). Also, the total resources used must equal the sum of the resources used for each activity in a constraint (e.g., labor).

The terms in the objective function or constraints are __additive__.

Another property of linear programming models is that the solution values (of the decision variables) cannot be restricted to integer values; the decision variables can take on any fractional value. Thus, the variables are said to be *continuous* or **divisible**, as opposed to *integer* or *discrete*. For example, although decision variables representing bowls or mugs or airplanes or automobiles should realistically have integer (whole number) solutions, the solution methods for linear programming will not necessarily provide such solutions. This is a property that will be discussed further as solution methods are presented in subsequent chapters.

The values of decision variables are continuous or __divisible__.

The final property of linear programming models is that the values of all the model parameters are assumed to be constant and known with **certainty**. In real situations, however, model parameters are frequently uncertain because they reflect the future as well as the present, and future conditions are rarely known with certainty.

All model parameters are assumed to be known with __certainty__.

To summarize, a linear programming model has the following general properties: linearity, proportionality, additivity, divisibility, and certainty.

Summary

The two example problems in this chapter were formulated as linear programming models in order to demonstrate the modeling process. These problems were similar in that they concerned achieving some objective subject to a set of restrictions or requirements. Linear programming models exhibit certain common characteristics:

- An objective function to be maximized or minimized
- A set of constraints
- Decision variables for measuring the level of activity
- Linearity among all constraint relationships and the objective function

The graphical approach to the solution of linear programming problems is not a very efficient means of solving problems. For one thing, drawing accurate graphs is tedious. Moreover, the graphical approach is limited to models with only two decision variables. However, the analysis of the graphical approach provides valuable insight into linear programming problems and their solutions.

In the graphical approach, once the feasible solution area and the optimal solution point have been determined from the graph, simultaneous equations are solved to determine the values of x_1 and x_2 at the solution point.

References

Baumol, W. J. *Economic Theory and Operations Analysis*, 4th ed. Upper Saddle River, NJ: Prentice Hall, 1977.

Charnes, A., and Cooper, W. W. *Management Models and Industrial Applications of Linear Programming*. New York: John Wiley & Sons, 1961.

Dantzig, G. B. *Linear Programming and Extensions*. Princeton, NJ: Princeton University Press, 1963.

Gass, S. *Linear Programming*, 4th ed. New York: McGraw-Hill, 1975.

Hadley, G. *Linear Programming*. Reading, MA: Addison-Wesley, 1962.

Hillier, F. S., and Lieberman, G. J. *Introduction to Operations Research*, 4th ed. San Francisco: Holden-Day, 1986.

Llewellyn, R. W. *Linear Programming*. New York: Holt, Rinehart and Winston, 1964.

Taha, H. A. *Operations Research, an Introduction*, 4th ed. New York: Macmillan, 1987.

Wagner, H. M. *Principles of Operations Research*, 2nd ed. Upper Saddle River, NJ: Prentice Hall, 1975.

Example Problem Solutions

As a prelude to the problems, this section presents example solutions to two linear programming problems.

Problem Statement

Moore's Meatpacking Company produces a hot dog mixture in 1,000-pound batches. The mixture contains two ingredients—chicken and beef. The cost per pound of each of these ingredients is as follows:

Ingredient	Cost/lb.
Chicken	\$3
Beef	\$5

Each batch has the following recipe requirements:

a. At least 500 pounds of chicken
b. At least 200 pounds of beef

The ratio of chicken to beef must be at least 2 to 1. The company wants to know the optimal mixture of ingredients that will minimize cost. Formulate a linear programming model for this problem.

Solution

Step 1: Identify Decision Variables

Recall that the problem should not be "swallowed whole." Identify each part of the model separately, starting with the decision variables:

$$\begin{aligned} x_1 &= \text{lb. of chicken} \\ x_2 &= \text{lb. of beef} \end{aligned}$$

Step 2: Formulate the Objective Function

$$\text{minimize } Z = \$3x_1 + \$5x_2$$

where

$$\begin{aligned} Z &= \text{cost per 1,000-lb batch} \\ \$3x_1 &= \text{cost of chicken} \\ \$5x_2 &= \text{cost of beef} \end{aligned}$$

Step 3: Establish Model Constraints

The constraints of this problem are embodied in the recipe restrictions and (not to be overlooked) the fact that each batch must consist of 1,000 pounds of mixture:

$$\begin{aligned} x_1 + x_2 &= 1{,}000 \text{ lb.} \\ x_1 &\geq 500 \text{ lb. of chicken} \\ x_2 &\geq 200 \text{ lb. of beef} \\ x_1/x_2 &\geq 2/1 \text{ or } x_1 - 2x_2 \geq 0 \end{aligned}$$

and

$$x_1, x_2 \geq 0$$

The Model

$$\begin{aligned} &\text{minimize } Z = \$3x_1 + \$5x_2 \\ &\text{subject to} \\ &\quad x_1 + x_2 = 1{,}000 \\ &\quad x_1 \geq 500 \\ &\quad x_2 \geq 200 \\ &\quad x_1 - 2x_2 \geq 0 \\ &\quad x_1, x_2 \geq 0 \end{aligned}$$

Problem Statement

Solve the following linear programming model graphically:

$$\begin{aligned} &\text{maximize } Z = 4x_1 + 5x_2 \\ &\text{subject to} \\ &\quad x_1 + 2x_2 \leq 10 \\ &\quad 6x_1 + 6x_2 \leq 36 \\ &\quad x_1 \leq 4 \\ &\quad x_1, x_2 \geq 0 \end{aligned}$$

Solution

Step 1: Plot the Constraint Lines as Equations

A simple method for plotting constraint lines is to set one of the constraint variables equal to zero and solve for the other variable to establish a point on one of the axes. The three constraint lines are graphed in the following figure:

The constraint equations

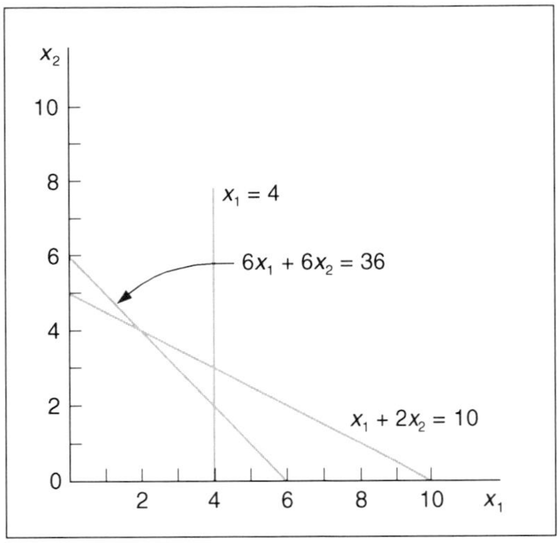

Step 2: Determine the Feasible Solution Area

The feasible solution area is determined by identifying the space that jointly satisfies the ≤ conditions of all three constraints, as shown in the following figure:

The feasible solution space and extreme points

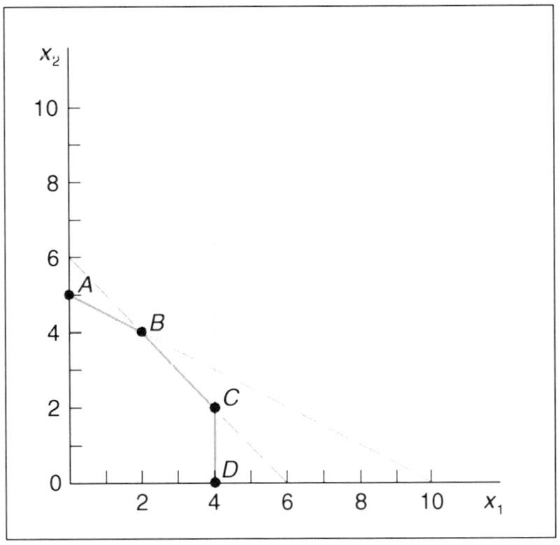

Step 3: Determine the Solution Points

The solution at point A can be determined by noting that the constraint line intersects the x_2 axis at 5; thus, $x_2 = 5, x_1 = 0$, and $Z = 25$. The solution at point D on the other axis can be determined similarly; the constraint intersects the axis at $x_1 = 4, x_2 = 0$, and $Z = 16$.

The values at points B and C must be found by solving simultaneous equations. Note that point B is formed by the intersection of the lines $x_1 + 2x_2 = 10$ and $6x_1 + 6x_2 = 36$. First, convert both of these equations to functions of x_1:

$$x_1 + 2x_2 = 10$$
$$x_1 = 10 - 2x_2$$

and

$$6x_1 + 6x_2 = 36$$
$$6x_1 = 36 - 6x_2$$
$$x_1 = 6 - x_2$$

Now set the equations equal and solve for x_2:

$$10 - 2x_2 = 6 - x_2$$
$$-x_2 = -4$$
$$x_2 = 4$$

Substituting $x_2 = 4$ into either of the two equations gives a value for x_1:

$$x_1 = 6 - x_2$$
$$x_1 = 6 - (4)$$
$$x_1 = 2$$

Thus, at point B, $x_1 = 2, x_2 = 4$, and $Z = 28$.

At point C, $x_1 = 4$. Substituting $x_1 = 4$ into the equation $x_1 = 6 - x_2$ gives a value for x_2:

$$4 = 6 - x_2$$
$$x_2 = 2$$

Thus, $x_1 = 4, x_2 = 2$, and $Z = 26$.

Step 4: Determine the Optimal Solution

The optimal solution is at point B, where $x_1 = 2, x_2 = 4$, and $Z = 28$. The optimal solution and solutions at the other extreme points are summarized in the following figure:

Optimal solution point

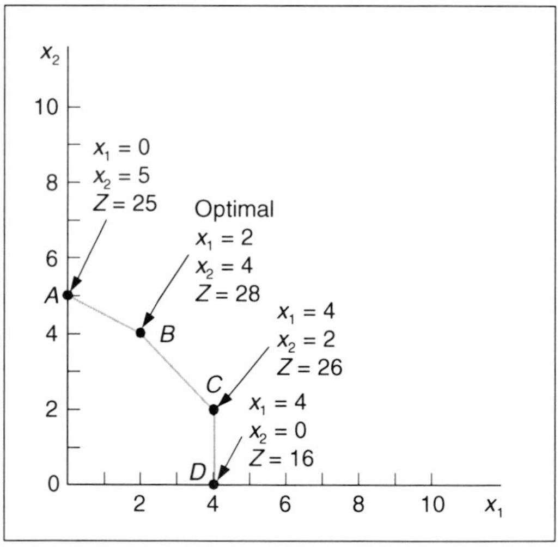

Problems

1. When Marie McCoy wakes up Saturday morning, she remembers that she promised the PTA she would make some cakes and/or homemade bread for its bake sale that afternoon. However, she does not have time to go to the store to get ingredients, and she has only a short time to bake things in her oven. Because cakes and breads require different baking temperatures, she

cannot bake them simultaneously, and she has only 3 hours available to bake. A cake requires 3 cups of flour, and a loaf of bread requires 8 cups; Marie has 20 cups of flour. A cake requires 45 minutes to bake, and a loaf of bread requires 30 minutes. The PTA will sell a cake for \$10 and a loaf of bread for \$6. Marie wants to decide how many cakes and loaves of bread she should make.

a. Formulate a linear programming model for this problem.
b. Solve this model by using graphical analysis.

2. A company produces two products that are processed on two assembly lines. Assembly line 1 has 100 available hours, and assembly line 2 has 42 available hours. Each product requires 10 hours of processing time on line 1, while on line 2 product 1 requires 7 hours and product 2 requires 3 hours. The profit for product 1 is \$6 per unit, and the profit for product 2 is \$4 per unit.
   a. Formulate a linear programming model for this problem.
   b. Solve this model by using graphical analysis.

3. The Munchies Cereal Company makes a cereal from several ingredients. Two of the ingredients, oats and rice, provide vitamins A and B. The company wants to know how many ounces of oats and rice it should include in each box of cereal to meet the minimum requirements of 48 milligrams of vitamin A and 12 milligrams of vitamin B while minimizing cost. An ounce of oats contributes 8 milligrams of vitamin A and 1 milligram of vitamin B, whereas an ounce of rice contributes 6 milligrams of A and 2 milligrams of B. An ounce of oats costs \$0.05, and an ounce of rice costs \$0.03.
   a. Formulate a linear programming model for this problem.
   b. Solve this model by using graphical analysis.

4. What would be the effect on the optimal solution in Problem 3 if the cost of rice increased from \$0.03 per ounce to \$0.06 per ounce?

5. The Kalo Fertilizer Company makes a fertilizer using two chemicals that provide nitrogen, phosphate, and potassium. A pound of ingredient 1 contributes 10 ounces of nitrogen and 6 ounces of phosphate, while a pound of ingredient 2 contributes 2 ounces of nitrogen, 6 ounces of phosphate, and 1 ounce of potassium. Ingredient 1 costs \$3 per pound, and ingredient 2 costs \$5 per pound. The company wants to know how many pounds of each chemical ingredient to put into a bag of fertilizer to meet the minimum requirements of 20 ounces of nitrogen, 36 ounces of phosphate, and 2 ounces of potassium while minimizing cost.
   a. Formulate a linear programming model for this problem.
   b. Solve this model by using graphical analysis.

6. The Pinewood Furniture Company produces chairs and tables from two resources—labor and wood. The company has 80 hours of labor and 36 board-ft. of wood available each day. Demand for chairs is limited to 6 per day. Each chair requires 8 hours of labor and 2 board-ft. of wood, whereas a table requires 10 hours of labor and 6 board-ft. of wood. The profit derived from each chair is \$400 and from each table, \$100. The company wants to determine the number of chairs and tables to produce each day in order to maximize profit.
   a. Formulate a linear programming model for this problem.
   b. Solve this model by using graphical analysis.

7. In Problem 6, how much labor and wood will be unused if the optimal numbers of chairs and tables are produced?

8. In Problem 6, explain the effect on the optimal solution of changing the profit on a table from \$100 to \$500.

9. The Crumb and Custard Bakery makes coffee cakes and Danish pastries in large pans. The main ingredients are flour and sugar. There are 25 pounds of flour and 16 pounds of sugar available, and

the demand for coffee cakes is 5. Five pounds of flour and 2 pounds of sugar are required to make a pan of coffee cakes, and 5 pounds of flour and 4 pounds of sugar are required to make a pan of Danish. A pan of coffee cakes has a profit of $1, and a pan of Danish has a profit of $5. Determine the number of pans of cakes and Danish to produce each day so that profit will be maximized.

a. Formulate a linear programming model for this problem.
b. Solve this model by using graphical analysis.

10. In Problem 9, how much flour and sugar will be left unused if the optimal numbers of cakes and Danish are baked?

11. Solve the following linear programming model graphically:

$$\text{maximize } Z = 3x_1 + 6x_2$$

subject to

$$3x_1 + 2x_2 \leq 18$$
$$x_1 + x_2 \geq 5$$
$$x_1 \leq 4$$
$$x_1, x_2 \geq 0$$

12. The Elixer Drug Company produces a drug from two ingredients. Each ingredient contains the same three antibiotics, in different proportions. One gram of ingredient 1 contributes 3 units, and 1 gram of ingredient 2 contributes 1 unit of antibiotic 1; the drug requires 6 units. At least 4 units of antibiotic 2 are required, and the ingredients contribute 1 unit each per gram. At least 12 units of antibiotic 3 are required; a gram of ingredient 1 contributes 2 units, and a gram of ingredient 2 contributes 6 units. The cost for a gram of ingredient 1 is $80, and the cost for a gram of ingredient 2 is $50. The company wants to formulate a linear programming model to determine the number of grams of each ingredient that must go into the drug in order to meet the antibiotic requirements at the minimum cost.

a. Formulate a linear programming model for this problem.
b. Solve this model by using graphical analysis.

13. A jewelry store makes necklaces and bracelets from gold and platinum. The store has 18 ounces of gold and 20 ounces of platinum. Each necklace requires 3 ounces of gold and 2 ounces of platinum, whereas each bracelet requires 2 ounces of gold and 4 ounces of platinum. The demand for bracelets is no more than four. A necklace earns $300 in profit and a bracelet, $400. The store wants to determine the number of necklaces and bracelets to make in order to maximize profit.

a. Formulate a linear programming model for this problem.
b. Solve this model by using graphical analysis.

14. In Problem 13, explain the effect on the optimal solution of increasing the profit on a bracelet from $400 to $600. What will be the effect of changing the platinum requirement for a necklace from 2 ounces to 3 ounces?

15. In Problem 13:

a. The maximum demand for bracelets is four. If the store produces the optimal number of bracelets and necklaces, will the maximum demand for bracelets be met? If not, by how much will it be missed?
b. What profit for a necklace would result in no bracelets being produced, and what would be the optimal solution for this profit?

16. A clothier makes coats and slacks. The two resources required are wool cloth and labor. The clothier has 150 square yards of wool and 200 hours of labor available. Each coat requires 3 square yards

of wool and 10 hours of labor, whereas each pair of slacks requires 5 square yards of wool and 4 hours of labor. The profit for a coat is $50, and the profit for slacks is $40. The clothier wants to determine the number of coats and pairs of slacks to make so that profit will be maximized.

a. Formulate a linear programming model for this problem.
b. Solve this model by using graphical analysis.

17. In Problem 16, what would be the effect on the optimal solution if the available labor was increased from 200 to 240 hours?

18. Solve the following linear programming model graphically:

$$\text{maximize } Z = 1.5x_1 + x_2$$

subject to

$$x_1 \le 4$$
$$x_2 \le 6$$
$$x_1 + x_2 \le 5$$
$$x_1, x_2 \ge 0$$

19. Transform the model in Problem 18 into standard form and indicate the value of the slack variables at each corner point solution.

20. Solve the following linear programming model graphically:

$$\text{maximize } Z = 5x_1 + 8x_2$$

subject to

$$3x_1 + 5x_2 \le 50$$
$$2x_1 + 4x_2 \le 40$$
$$x_1 \le 8$$
$$x_2 \le 10$$
$$x_1, x_2 \ge 0$$

21. Transform the model in Problem 20 into standard form and indicate the value of the slack variables at each corner point solution.

22. Solve the following linear programming model graphically:

$$\text{maximize } Z = 6.5x_1 + 10x_2$$

subject to

$$2x_1 + 4x_2 \le 40$$
$$x_1 + x_2 \le 15$$
$$x_1 \ge 8$$
$$x_1, x_2 \ge 0$$

23. In Problem 22, if the constraint $x_1 \ge 8$ is changed to $x_1 \le 8$, what effect does this have on the feasible solution space and the optimal solution?

24. Universal Claims Processors processes insurance claims for large national insurance companies. Most claim processing is done by a large pool of computer operators, some of whom are permanent and some of whom are temporary. A permanent operator can process 16 claims per day, whereas a temporary operator can process 12 per day, and on average the company processes

at least 450 claims each day. The company has 40 computer workstations. A permanent operator generates about 0.5 claim with errors each day, whereas a temporary operator averages about 1.4 defective claims per day. The company wants to limit claims with errors to 25 per day. A permanent operator is paid $64 per day, and a temporary operator is paid $42 per day. The company wants to determine the number of permanent and temporary operators to hire in order to minimize costs.

a. Formulate a linear programming model for this problem.
b. Solve this model by using graphical analysis.

25. In Problem 24, explain the effect on the optimal solution of changing the daily pay for a permanent claims processor from $64 to $54. Explain the effect of changing the daily pay for a temporary claims processor from $42 to $36.

26. In Problem 24, what would be the effect on the optimal solution if Universal Claims Processors decided not to try to limit the number of defective claims each day?

27. In Problem 24, explain the effect on the optimal solution if the minimum number of claims the firm processes each day increased from 450 to at least 650.

28. Solve the following linear programming model graphically:

$$\begin{aligned} \text{minimize } Z &= 8x_1 + 6x_2 \\ \text{subject to} & \\ 4x_1 + 2x_2 &\geq 20 \\ -6x_1 + 4x_2 &\leq 12 \\ x_1 + x_2 &\geq 6 \\ x_1, x_2 &\geq 0 \end{aligned}$$

29. Solve the following linear programming model graphically:

$$\begin{aligned} \text{minimize } Z &= 3x_1 + 6x_2 \\ \text{subject to} & \\ 3x_1 + 2x_2 &\leq 18 \\ x_1 + x_2 &\geq 5 \\ x_1 &\leq 4 \\ x_2 &\leq 7 \\ x_2/x_1 &\leq 7/8 \\ x_1, x_2 &\geq 0 \end{aligned}$$

30. In Problem 29, what would be the effect on the solution if the constraint $x_2 \leq 7$ was changed to $x_2 \geq 7$?

31. Solve the following linear programming model graphically:

$$\begin{aligned} \text{minimize } Z &= 5x_1 + x_2 \\ \text{subject to} & \\ 3x_1 + 4x_2 &= 24 \\ x_1 &\leq 6 \\ x_1 + 3x_2 &\leq 12 \\ x_1, x_2 &\geq 0 \end{aligned}$$

32. Solve the following linear programming model graphically:

$$\text{maximize } Z = 3x_1 + 2x_2$$

subject to

$$2x_1 + 4x_2 \leq 22$$
$$-x_1 + 4x_2 \leq 10$$
$$4x_1 - 2x_2 \leq 14$$
$$x_1 - 3x_2 \leq 1$$
$$x_1, x_2 \geq 0$$

33. Solve the following linear programming model graphically:

$$\text{minimize } Z = 8x_1 + 2x_2$$

subject to

$$2x_1 - 6x_2 \leq 12$$
$$5x_1 + 4x_2 \geq 40$$
$$x_1 + 2x_2 \geq 12$$
$$x_2 \leq 6$$
$$x_1, x_2 \geq 0$$

34. Gillian's Restaurant has an ice-cream counter where it sells two main products, ice cream and frozen yogurt, each in a variety of flavors. The restaurant makes one order for ice cream and yogurt each week, and the store has enough freezer space for 115 gallons total of both products. A gallon of frozen yogurt costs \$0.75 and a gallon of ice cream costs \$0.93, and the restaurant budgets \$90 each week for these products. The manager estimates that each week the restaurant sells at least twice as much ice cream as frozen yogurt. Profit per gallon of ice cream is \$4.15, and profit per gallon of yogurt is \$3.60.
    a. Formulate a linear programming model for this problem.
    b. Solve this model by using graphical analysis.

35. In Problem 34, how much additional profit would the restaurant realize each week if it increased its freezer capacity to accommodate 20 extra gallons total of ice cream and yogurt?

36. Copperfield Mining Company owns two mines, each of which produces three grades of ore—high, medium, and low. The company has a contract to supply a smelting company with at least 12 tons of high-grade ore, 8 tons of medium-grade ore, and 24 tons of low-grade ore. Each mine produces a certain amount of each type of ore during each hour that it operates. Mine 1 produces 6 tons of high-grade ore, 2 tons of medium-grade ore, and 4 tons of low-grade ore per hour. Mine 2 produces 2, 2, and 12 tons, respectively, of high-, medium-, and low-grade ore per hour. It costs Copperfield \$200 per hour to mine each ton of ore from mine 1, and it costs \$160 per hour to mine each ton of ore from mine 2. The company wants to determine the number of hours it needs to operate each mine so that its contractual obligations can be met at the lowest cost.
    a. Formulate a linear programming model for this problem.
    b. Solve this model by using graphical analysis.

37. A canning company produces two sizes of cans—regular and large. The cans are produced in 10,000-can lots. The cans are processed through a stamping operation and a coating operation. The company has 30 days available for both stamping and coating. A lot of regular-size cans requires 2 days to stamp and 4 days to coat, whereas a lot of large cans requires 4 days to stamp and 2 days to coat. A lot of regular-size cans earns \$800 profit, and a lot of large-size cans earns \$900 profit. In

order to fulfill its obligations under a shipping contract, the company must produce at least nine lots. The company wants to determine the number of lots to produce of each size can (x_1 and x_2) in order to maximize profit.

a. Formulate a linear programming model for this problem.
b. Solve this model by using graphical analysis.

38. A manufacturing firm produces two products. Each product must undergo an assembly process and a finishing process. It is then transferred to the warehouse, which has space for only a limited number of items. The firm has 80 hours available for assembly and 112 hours for finishing, and it can store a maximum of 10 units in the warehouse. Each unit of product 1 has a profit of $30 and requires 4 hours to assemble and 14 hours to finish. Each unit of product 2 has a profit of $70 and requires 10 hours to assemble and 8 hours to finish. The firm wants to determine the quantity of each product to produce in order to maximize profit.
    a. Formulate a linear programming model for this problem.
    b. Solve this model by using graphical analysis.

39. Assume that the objective function in Problem 38 has been changed from $Z = 30x_1 + 70x_2$ to $Z = 90x_1 + 70x_2$. Determine the slope of each objective function and discuss what effect these slopes have on the optimal solution.

40. The Valley Wine Company produces two kinds of wine—Valley Nectar and Valley Red. The wines are produced from 64 tons of grapes the company has acquired this season. A 1,000-gallon batch of Nectar requires 4 tons of grapes, and a batch of Red requires 8 tons. However, production is limited by the availability of only 50 cubic yards of storage space for aging and 120 hours of processing time. A batch of each type of wine requires 5 cubic yards of storage space. The processing time for a batch of Nectar is 15 hours, and the processing time for a batch of Red is 8 hours. Demand for each type of wine is limited to seven batches. The profit for a batch of Nectar is $9,000, and the profit for a batch of Red is $12,000. The company wants to determine the number of 1,000-gallon batches of Nectar (x_1) and Red (x_2) to produce in order to maximize profit.
    a. Formulate a linear programming model for this problem.
    b. Solve this model by using graphical analysis.

41. In Problem 40:
    a. How much processing time will be left unused at the optimal solution?
    b. What would be the effect on the optimal solution of increasing the available storage space from 50 to 60 cubic yards?

42. Kroeger supermarket sells its own brand of canned peas as well as several national brands. The store makes a profit of $0.28 per can for its own peas and a profit of $0.19 for any of the national brands. The store has 6 square feet of shelf space available for canned peas, and each can of peas takes up 9 square inches of that space. Point-of-sale records show that each week the store never sells more than half as many cans of its own brand as it does of the national brands. The store wants to know how many cans of its own brand of peas and how many cans of the national brands to stock each week on the allocated shelf space in order to maximize profit.
    a. Formulate a linear programming model for this problem.
    b. Solve this model by using graphical analysis.

43. In Problem 42, if Kroeger discounts the price of its own brand of peas, the store will sell at least 1.5 times as much of the national brands as its own brand, but its profit margin on its own brand will be reduced to $0.23 per can. What effect will the discount have on the optimal solution?

44. Shirtstop makes T-shirts with logos and sells them in its chain of retail stores. It contracts with two different plants—one in Puerto Rico and one in The Bahamas. The shirts from the plant in Puerto Rico cost $0.46 apiece, and 9% of them are defective and can't be sold. The shirts from The

Bahamas cost only $0.35 each, but they have an 18% defective rate. Shirtstop needs 3,500 shirts. To retain its relationship with the two plants, it wants to order at least 1,000 shirts from each. It would also like at least 88% of the shirts it receives to be salable.

a. Formulate a linear programming model for this problem.
b. Solve this model by using graphical analysis.

45. In Problem 44:
    a. Suppose Shirtstop decided it wanted to minimize the defective shirts while keeping costs below $2,000. Reformulate the problem with these changes and solve graphically.
    b. How many fewer defective items were achieved with the model in (a) than with the model in Problem 44?

46. Angela and Bob Ray keep a large garden in which they grow cabbage, tomatoes, and onions to make two kinds of relish—chow-chow and tomato. The chow-chow is made primarily of cabbage, whereas the tomato relish has more tomatoes than does the chow-chow. Both relishes include onions, and negligible amounts of bell peppers and spices. A jar of chow-chow contains 8 ounces of cabbage, 3 ounces of tomatoes, and 3 ounces of onions, whereas a jar of tomato relish contains 6 ounces of tomatoes, 6 ounces of cabbage, and 2 ounces of onions. The Rays grow 120 pounds of cabbage, 90 pounds of tomatoes, and 45 pounds of onions each summer. The Rays can produce no more than 24 dozen jars of relish. They make $2.25 in profit from a jar of chow-chow and $1.95 in profit from a jar of tomato relish. The Rays want to know how many jars of each kind of relish to produce to generate the most profit.
    a. Formulate a linear programming model for this problem.
    b. Solve this model graphically.

47. In Problem 46, the Rays have checked their sales records for the past 5 years and have found that they sell at least 50% more chow-chow than tomato relish. How will this additional information affect their model and solution?

48. A California grower has a 50-acre farm on which to plant strawberries and tomatoes. The grower has available 300 hours of labor per week and 800 tons of fertilizer, and he has contracted for shipping space for a maximum of 26 acres' worth of strawberries and 37 acres' worth of tomatoes. An acre of strawberries requires 10 hours of labor and 8 tons of fertilizer, whereas an acre of tomatoes requires 3 hours of labor and 20 tons of fertilizer. The profit from an acre of strawberries is $400, and the profit from an acre of tomatoes is $300. The farmer wants to know the number of acres of strawberries and tomatoes to plant to maximize profit.
    a. Formulate a linear programming model for this problem.
    b. Solve this model by using graphical analysis.

49. In Problem 48, if the amount of fertilizer required for each acre of strawberries was determined to be 20 tons instead of 8 tons, what would be the effect on the optimal solution?

50. The admissions office at Tech wants to determine how many in-state and how many out-of-state students to accept for next fall's entering freshman class. Tuition for an in-state student is $7,600 per year, whereas out-of-state tuition is $22,500 per year. A total of 12,800 in-state and 8,100 out-of-state freshmen have applied for next fall, and Tech does not want to accept more than 3,500 students. However, because Tech is a state institution, the state mandates that it can accept no more than 40% out-of-state students. From past experience the admissions office knows that 12% of in-state students and 24% of out-of-state students will drop out during their first year. Tech wants to maximize total tuition while limiting the total attrition to 600 first-year students.
    a. Formulate a linear programming model for this problem.
    b. Solve this model by using graphical analysis.

51. Janet Lopez is establishing an investment portfolio that will include stock and bond funds. She has $720,000 to invest, and she does not want the portfolio to include more than 65% stocks. The average annual return for the stock fund she plans to invest in is 18%, whereas the average annual return for the bond fund is 6%. She further estimates that the most she could lose in the next year in the stock fund is 22%, whereas the most she could lose in the bond fund is 5%. To reduce her risk, she wants to limit her potential maximum losses to $100,000.
    a. Formulate a linear programming model for this problem.
    b. Solve this model by using graphical analysis.

52. Professor Smith teaches two sections of business statistics, which combined will result in 120 final exams to be graded. Professor Smith has two graduate assistants, Brad and Sarah, who will grade the final exams. There is a 3-day period between the time the exam is administered and when final grades must be posted. During this period Brad has 12 hours available and Sarah has 10 hours available to grade the exams. It takes Brad an average of 7.2 minutes to grade an exam, and it takes Sarah 12 minutes to grade an exam; however, Brad's exams will have errors that will require Professor Smith to ultimately regrade 10% of the exams, while only 6% of Sarah's exams will require regrading. Professor Smith wants to know how many exams to assign to each graduate assistant to grade in order to minimize the number of exams to regrade.
    a. Formulate a linear programming model for this problem.
    b. Solve this model by using graphical analysis.

53. In Problem 52, if Professor Smith could hire Brad or Sarah to work 1 additional hour, which should she choose? What would be the effect of hiring the selected graduate assistant for 1 additional hour?

54. Starbright Coffee Shop at the Galleria Mall serves two coffee blends it brews on a daily basis, Pomona and Coastal. Each is a blend of three high-quality coffees from Colombia, Kenya, and Indonesia. The coffee shop has 10 pounds of each of these coffees available each day. Each pound of coffee will produce sixteen 16-ounce cups of coffee. The shop has enough brewing capacity to brew 30 gallons of these two coffee blends each day. Pomona is a blend of 20% Colombian, 35% Kenyan, and 45% Indonesian, while Coastal is a blend of 60% Colombian, 10% Kenyan, and 30% Indonesian. The shop sells 1.5 times more Pomona than Coastal each day. Pomona sells for $2.05 per cup, and Coastal sells for $1.85 per cup. The manager wants to know how many cups of each blend to sell each day in order to maximize sales.
    a. Formulate a linear programming model for this problem.
    b. Solve this model by using graphical analysis.

55. In Problem 54:
    a. If Starbright Coffee Shop could get 1 more pound of coffee, which one should it be? What would be the effect on sales of getting 1 more pound of this coffee? Would it benefit the shop to increase its brewing capacity from 30 gallons to 40 gallons?
    b. If the shop spent $20 per day on advertising that would increase the relative demand for Pomona to twice that of Coastal, should it be done?

56. Solve the following linear programming model graphically and explain the solution result:

$$\text{minimize } Z = \$3{,}000x_1 + 1{,}000x_2$$

subject to

$$60x_1 + 20x_2 \geq 1{,}200$$
$$10x_1 + 10x_2 \geq 400$$
$$40x_1 + 160x_2 \geq 2{,}400$$
$$x_1, x_2 \geq 0$$

57. Solve the following linear programming model graphically and explain the solution result:

$$\text{maximize } Z = 60x_1 + 90x_2$$

subject to

$$60x_1 + 30x_2 \leq 1{,}500$$
$$100x_1 + 100x_2 \geq 6{,}000$$
$$x_2 \geq 30$$
$$x_1, x_2 \geq 0$$

58. Solve the following linear programming model graphically and explain the solution result:

$$\text{maximize } Z = 110x_1 + 75x_2$$

subject to

$$2x_1 + x_2 \geq 40$$
$$-6x_1 + 8x_2 \leq 120$$
$$70x_1 + 105x_2 \geq 2{,}100$$
$$x_1, x_2 \geq 0$$

Case Problem

METROPOLITAN POLICE PATROL

The Metropolitan Police Department was recently criticized in the local media for not responding to police calls in the downtown area rapidly enough. In several recent cases, alarms had sounded for break-ins, but by the time the police car arrived, the perpetrators had left, and in one instance a store owner had been shot. Sergeant Joe Davis was assigned by the chief as head of a task force to find a way to determine the optimal patrol area (dimensions) for their cars that would minimize the average time it took to respond to a call in the downtown area.

Sergeant Davis solicited help from Angela Maris, an analyst in the operations area for the police department. Together they began to work through the problem.

Joe noted to Angela that normal patrol sectors are laid out in rectangles, with each rectangle including a number of city blocks. For illustrative purposes he defined the dimensions of the sector as x in the horizontal direction and as y in the vertical direction. He explained to Angela that cars traveled in straight lines either horizontally or vertically and turned at right angles. Travel in a horizontal direction must be accompanied by travel in a vertical direction, and the total distance traveled is the sum of the horizontal and vertical segments. He further noted that past research on police patrolling in urban areas had shown that the average distance traveled by a patrol car responding to a call in either direction was one-third of the dimensions of the sector, or $x/3$ and $y/3$. He also explained that the travel time it took to respond to a call (assuming that a car left immediately upon receiving the call) is simply the average distance traveled divided by the average travel speed.

Angela told Joe that now that she understood how average travel time to a call was determined, she could see that it was closely related to the size of the patrol area. She asked Joe if there were any restrictions on the size of the area sectors that cars patrolled. He responded that for their city, the department believed that the perimeter of a patrol sector should not be less than 5 miles or exceed 12 miles. He noted several policy issues and staffing constraints that required these specifications. Angela wanted to know if any additional restrictions existed, and Joe indicated that the distance in the vertical direction must be at least 50% more than the horizontal distance for the sector. He explained that laying out sectors in that manner meant that the patrol areas would have a greater tendency to overlap different residential, income, and retail areas than if they ran the other way. He said that these areas were layered from north to south in the city, so if a sector area was laid out east to west, all of it would tend to be in one demographic layer.

Angela indicated that she had almost enough information to develop a model, except that she also needed to know the average travel speed the patrol cars could travel. Joe told her that cars moving vertically traveled an average of 15 miles per hour, whereas cars traveled horizontally an average of 20 miles per hour. He said that the difference was due to different traffic flows.

Develop a linear programming model for this problem and solve it by using the graphical method.

Case Problem

"The Possibility" Restaurant

Angela Fox and Zooey Caulfield were food and nutrition majors at State University, as well as close friends and roommates. Upon graduation Angela and Zooey decided to open a French restaurant in Draperton, the small town where the university was located. There were no other French restaurants in Draperton, and the possibility of doing something new and somewhat risky intrigued the two friends. They purchased an old Victorian home just off Main Street for their new restaurant, which they named "The Possibility."

Angela and Zooey knew in advance that at least initially they could not offer a full, varied menu of dishes. They had no idea what their local customers' tastes in French cuisine would be, so they decided to serve only two full-course meals each night, one with beef and the other with fish. Their chef, Pierre, was confident he could make each dish so exciting and unique that two meals would be sufficient, at least until they could assess which menu items were most popular. Pierre indicated that with each meal he could experiment with different appetizers, soups, salads, vegetable dishes, and desserts until they were able to identify a full selection of menu items.

The next problem for Angela and Zooey was to determine how many meals to prepare for each night so they could shop for ingredients and set up the work schedule. They could not afford too much waste. They estimated that they would sell a maximum of 60 meals each night. Each fish dinner, including all accompaniments, requires 15 minutes to prepare, and each beef dinner takes twice as long. There is a total of 20 hours of kitchen staff labor available each day. Angela and Zooey believe that because of the health consciousness of their potential clientele, they will sell at least three fish dinners for every two beef dinners. However, they also believe that at least 10% of their customers will order beef dinners. The profit from each fish dinner will be approximately \$12, and the profit from a beef dinner will be about \$16.

Formulate a linear programming model for Angela and Zooey that will help them estimate the number of meals they should prepare each night and solve this model graphically.

If Angela and Zooey increased the menu price on the fish dinner so that the profit for both dinners was the same, what effect would that have on their solution? Suppose Angela and Zooey reconsidered the demand for beef dinners and decided that at least 20% of their customers would purchase beef dinners. What effect would this have on their meal preparation plan?

Case Problem

Annabelle Invests in the Market

Annabelle Sizemore has cashed in some treasury bonds and a life insurance policy that her parents had accumulated over the years for her. She has also saved some money in certificates of deposit and savings bonds during the 10 years since she graduated from college. As a result, she has \$120,000 available to invest. Given the recent rise in the stock market, she feels that she should invest all of this amount there. She has researched the market and has decided that she wants to invest in an index fund tied to S&P stocks and in an Internet stock fund. However, she is very concerned about the volatility of Internet stocks. Therefore, she wants to balance her risk to some degree.

She has decided to select an index fund from Shield Securities and an Internet stock fund from Madison Funds, Inc. She has also decided that the proportion of the dollar amount she invests in the index fund relative to the Internet fund should be at least one-third but that she should not invest more than twice the amount in the Internet fund that she invests in the index fund. The price per share of the index fund is \$175, whereas the price per share of the Internet fund is \$208. The average annual return during the last 3 years for the index fund has been 17%, and for the Internet stock fund it has been 28%. She anticipates that both mutual funds will realize the same average returns for the coming year that they have in the recent past; however, at the end of the year she is likely to reevaluate her investment strategy anyway. Thus, she wants to develop an investment strategy that will maximize her return for the coming year.

Formulate a linear programming model for Annabelle that will indicate how much money she should invest in each fund and solve this model by using the graphical method.

Suppose Annabelle decides to change her risk-balancing formula by eliminating the restriction that the proportion of the amount she invests in the index fund to the amount that she invests in the Internet fund must be at least one-third. What will the effect be on her solution? Suppose instead that she eliminates the restriction that the proportion of money she invests in the Internet fund relative to the stock fund not exceed a ratio of 2 to 1. How will this affect her solution?

If Annabelle can get \$1 more to invest, how will that affect her solution? \$2 more? \$3 more? What can you say about her return on her investment strategy, given these successive changes?

Solutions to Selected Odd-Numbered Problems

1. $x_1 = 4, x_2 = 0, Z = 40$
3. (a) min. $Z = .05x_1 + .03x_2$; s.t. $8x_1 + 6x_2 \geq 48$, $x_1 + 2x_2 \geq 12$, $x_i \geq 0$; (b) $x_1 = 0, x_2 = 8, Z = 0.24$
5. (a) min. $Z = 3x_1 + 5x_2$; s.t. $10x_1 + 2x_2 \geq 20$, $6x_1 + 6x_2 \geq 36$, $x_2 \geq 2$, $x_i \geq 0$; (b) $x_1 = 4, x_2 = 2, Z = 22$
7. No labor, 4.8 lb. wood
9. (a) max. $Z = x_1 + 5x_2$; s.t. $5x_1 + 5x_2 \leq 25$, $2x_1 + 4x_2 \leq 16$, $x_1 \leq 5$, $x_1, x_2 \geq 0$; (b) $x_1 = 0, x_2 = 4, Z = 20$
11. $x_1 = 0, x_2 = 9, Z = 54$
13. (a) max. $Z = 300x_1 + 400x_2$; s.t. $3x_1 + 2x_2 \leq 18$, $2x_1 + 4x_2 \leq 20$, $x_2 \leq 4$, $x_1, x_2 \geq 0$; (b) $x_1 = 4, x_2 = 3, Z = 2{,}400$
15. (a) maximum demand is not achieved by one bracelet; (b) \$600
17. $x_1 = 15.8, x_2 = 20.5, Z = 1{,}610$
19. A: $s_1 = 4, s_2 = 1, s_3 = 0$; B: $s_1 = 0, s_2 = 5, s_3 = 0$; C: $s_1 = 0, s_2 = 6, s_3 = 1$
21. A: $s_1 = 0, s_2 = 0, s_3 = 8, s_4 = 0$; B: $s_1 = 0, s_2 = 3.2, s_3 = 0, s_4 = 4.8$; C: $s_1 = 26, s_2 = 24, s_3 = 0, s_4 = 10$
23. changes the optimal solution
25. $x_1 = 28.125, x_2 = 0, Z = \$1{,}671.95$; no effect
27. infeasible solution
29. $x_1 = 4, x_2 = 1, Z = 18$
31. $x_1 = 4.8, x_2 = 2.4, Z = 26.4$
33. $x_1 = 3.2, x_2 = 6, Z = 37.6$
35. no additional profit
37. (a) max. $Z = 800x_1 + 900x_2$; s.t. $2x_1 + 4x_2 \leq 30$, $4x_1 + 2x_2 \leq 30$, $x_1 + x_2 \geq 9$, $x_i \geq 0$; (b) $x_1 = 5, x_2 = 5, Z = 8{,}500$
39. $x_1 = 5.3, x_2 = 4.7, Z = 806$
41. (a) 12 hr.; (b) new solution: $x_1 = 5.09, x_2 = 5.45, Z = 111.27$
43. $x_1 = 38.4, x_2 = 57.6, Z = 19.78$; profit reduced
45. (a) min. $Z = .09x_1 + .18x_2$, s.t. $.46x_1 + .35x_2 \leq 2{,}000$, $x_1 \geq 1{,}000$, $x_2 \geq 1{,}000$, $.91x_1 - .82x_2 = 3{,}500$, $x_1 \geq 0, x_2 \geq 0$; (b) 32 fewer defects
47. $x_1 = 160, x_2 = 106.67, Z = 568$
49. $x_1 = 25.71, x_2 = 14.29, Z = 14{,}571$
51. (a) max. $Z = .18x_1 + .06x_2$, s.t. $x_1 + x_2 \leq 720{,}000$, $x_1/(x_1 + x_2) \leq .65$, $.22x_1 + .05x_2 \leq 100{,}000$, $x_1, x_2 \geq 0$; (b) $x_1 = 376{,}470.59$, $x_2 = 343{,}526.41, Z = 88{,}376.47$
53. one more hour for Sarah would reduce the regraded exams from 10 to 9.8; another hour for Brad has no effect
55. only more Colombian would affect the solution; 1 lb of Colombian would increase sales to \$463.20; increasing the brewing capacity has no effect; extra advertising increases sales
57. infeasible

Linear Programming: Computer Solution and Sensitivity Analysis

Graphing can provide valuable insight into linear programming and linear programming solutions in general. However, the fact that this solution method is limited to problems with only two decision variables restricts its usefulness as a *general* solution technique.

In this chapter we will show how linear programming problems can be solved using several personal computer software packages. We will also describe how to use a computer solution result to experiment with a linear programming model to see what effect parameter changes have on the optimal solution, referred to as *sensitivity analysis*.

Computer Solution

*The **simplex method** is a procedure involving a set of mathematical steps to solve linear programming problems.*

When linear programming was first developed in the 1940s, virtually the only way to solve a problem was by using a lengthy manual mathematical solution procedure called the **simplex method**. However, during the next six decades, as computer technology evolved, the computer was used more and more to solve linear programming models. The mathematical steps of the simplex method were simply programmed in prewritten software packages designed for the solution of linear programming problems. The ability to solve linear programming problems quickly and cheaply on the computer, regardless of the size of the problem, popularized linear programming and expanded its use by businesses. There are currently dozens of software packages with linear programming capabilities. Many of these are general-purpose management science or quantitative methods packages with linear programming modules, among many other modules for other techniques. There are also numerous software packages that are devoted exclusively to linear programming and its derivatives. These packages are generally cheap, efficient, and easy to use.

As a result of the easy and low-cost availability of personal computers and linear programming software, the simplex method has become less of a focus in the teaching of linear programming. Thus, at this point in our presentation of linear programming, we focus exclusively on computer solution. However, knowledge of the simplex method is useful in gaining an overall, in-depth understanding of linear programming for those who are interested in this degree of understanding. As noted, computer solution itself is based on the simplex method. Thus, while we present linear programming in the text in a manner that does not require use of the simplex method, we also provide in-depth coverage of this topic on the companion Web site for this text.

In the next few sections we demonstrate how to solve linear programming problems by using Excel spreadsheets and QM for Windows, a typical general-purpose quantitative methods software package.

Excel Spreadsheets

Excel can be used to solve linear programming problems, although the data input requirements can be more time-consuming and tedious than with a software package like QM for Windows that is specifically designed for the purpose. A spreadsheet requires that column and row headings for the specific model be set up and that constraint and objective function formulas be input in their entirety, as opposed to just the model parameters, as with QM for Windows. However, this is also an advantage of spreadsheets, in that it enables the problem to be set up in an attractive format for reporting and presentation purposes. In addition, once a spreadsheet is set up for one problem, it can often be used as a template for others. Exhibit 1 shows an Excel spreadsheet set up for the Beaver Creek Pottery Company.

Exhibit 1

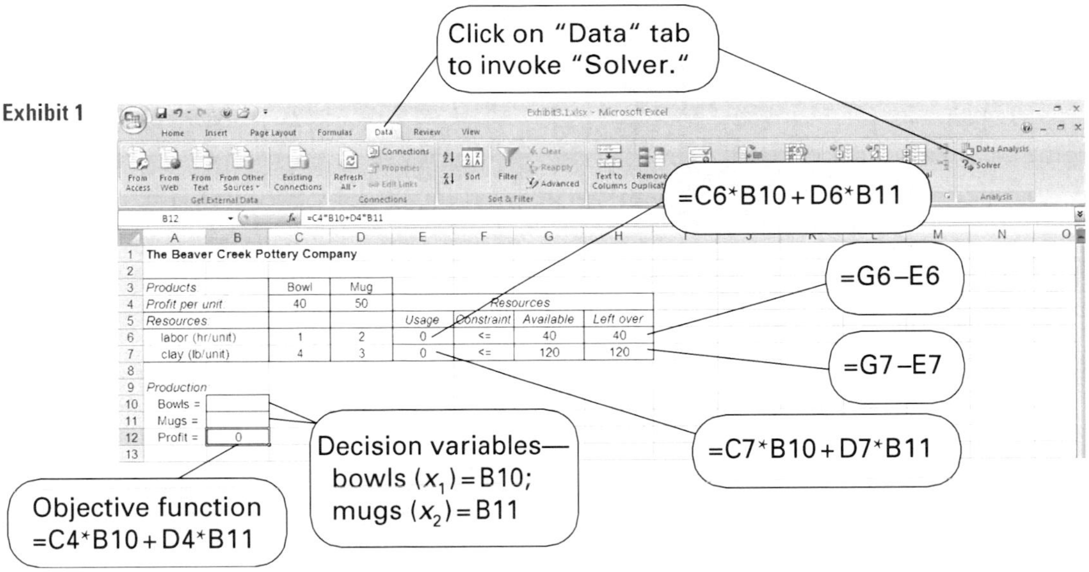

The values for bowls and mugs and for profit are contained in cells B10, B11, and B12, respectively. These cells are currently empty because the model has not yet been solved. The objective function for profit, =**C4*B10+D4*B11**, is embedded in cell B12 shown in bar. This formula is essentially the same as $Z = 40x_1 + 50x_2$, where B10 and B11 represent x_1 and x_2, and B12 equals Z. The objective function coefficients, 40 and 50, are in cells C4 and D4. Similar formulas for the constraints for labor and clay are embedded in cells E6 and E7. For example, in cell E6 we input the formula =**C6*B10+D6*B11**. The <= signs in cells F6 and F7 are for cosmetic purposes only; they have no real effect.

To solve this problem, first click on the "Data" tab on the toolbar at the top of the screen and then click on "Solver" on the far right side of the Data toolbar. The window Solver Parameters will appear, as shown in Exhibit 2. Initially all the windows on this screen are blank, and we must input the objective function cell, the cells representing the decision variables, and the cells that make up the model constraints.

When inputting the Solver parameters as shown in Exhibit 2, we first input the "target cell" that contains our objective function, which is B12 for our example. (Excel automatically inserts the $ sign next to cell addresses; you should not type it in.) Next we indicate that we want to maximize the target cell by clicking on "Max." We achieve our objective by changing cells B10 and B11, which represent our model decision variables. The designation "B10:B11" means all the cells between B10 and B11, inclusive. We next input our model constraints by clicking on "Add," which will access the screen shown in Exhibit 3.

Exhibit 3 shows our labor constraint. Cell E6 contains the constraint formula for labor (=**C6*B10+D6*B11**), whereas cell G6 contains the labor hours available (i.e., 40). We continue to add constraints until the model is complete. Note that we could have input our constraints by adding a single constraint formula, **E6:E7** <= **G6:G7**, which means that the

Exhibit 2

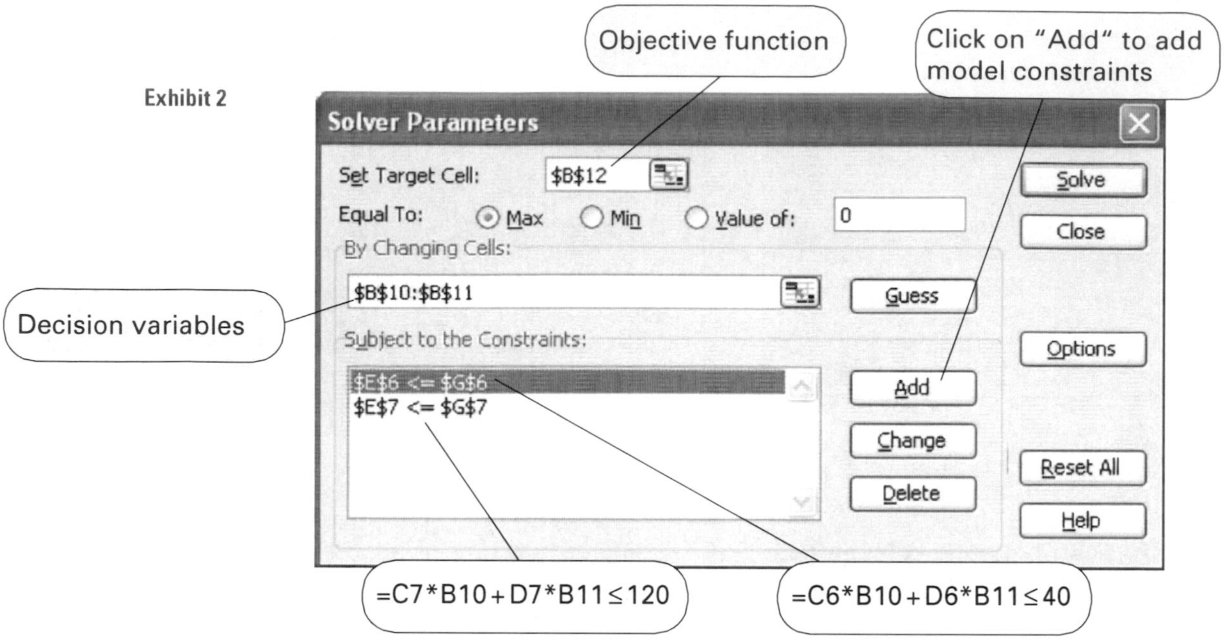

Exhibit 3

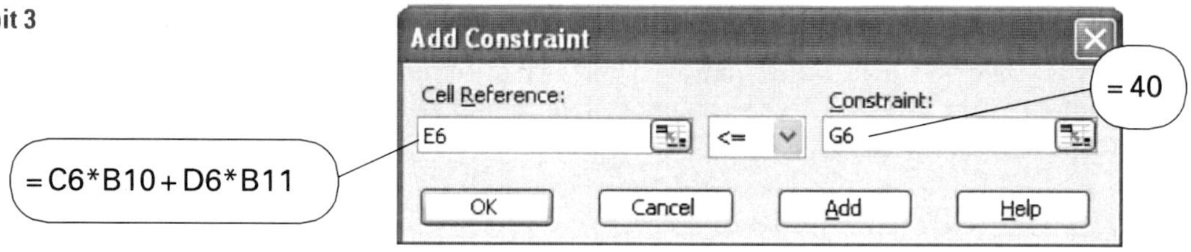

constraints in cells E6 and E7 are less than or equal to the values in cells G6 and G7, respectively. It is also not necessary to input the nonnegativity constraints for our decision variables, **B10:B11** >= **0**. This can be done in the Options screen, as explained next.

Click on "OK" on the Add Constraint window after all constraints have been added. This will return us to the Solver Parameters screen. There is one more necessary step before proceeding to solve the problem. Select "Options" from the Solver Parameters screen and then when the Solver Options screen appears, as shown in Exhibit 4, click on "Assume Linear Model." This will ensure that Solver uses the simplex procedure to solve the model and not some other numeric method (which Excel has available). This is not too important for now, but later it will ensure that we get the right reports for sensitivity analysis, a topic we will take up next. Notice that the Solver Options screen also enables you to establish the nonnegativity conditions by clicking on "Assume Non-Negative." Click on "OK" to return to Solver.

Once the complete model is input, click on "Solve" in the upper-right corner of the Solver Parameters screen (Exhibit 2). First, a screen will appear, titled Solver Results, which will provide you with the opportunity to select the reports you want and then when you click on "OK," the solution screen shown in Exhibit 5 will appear.

If there had been any extra, or *slack*, left over for labor or clay, it would have appeared in column H on our spreadsheet, under the heading "Left Over." In this case there are no slack resources left over.

Exhibit 4

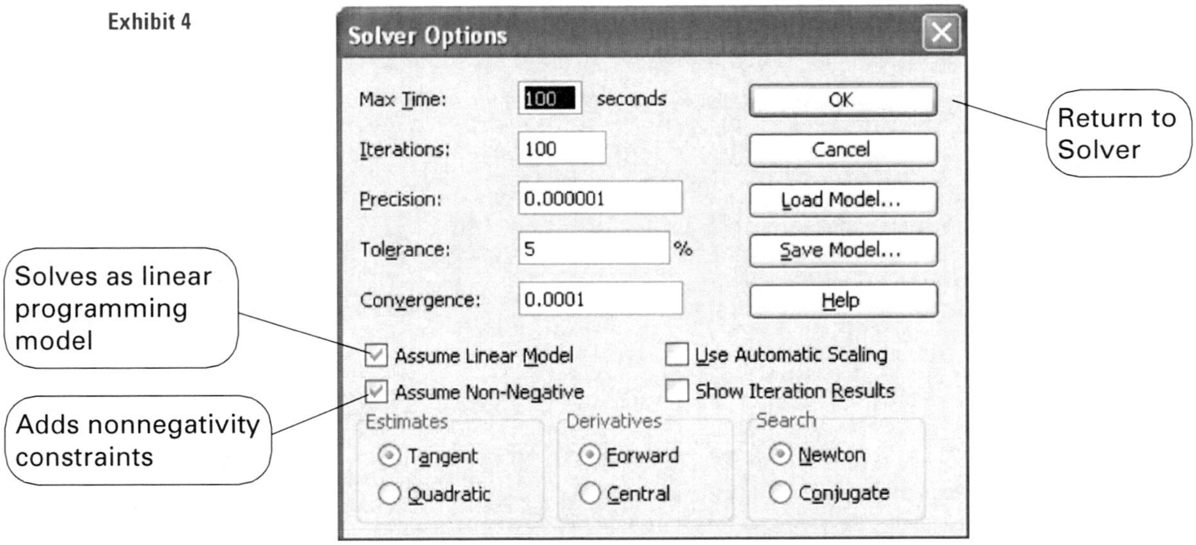

Exhibit 5

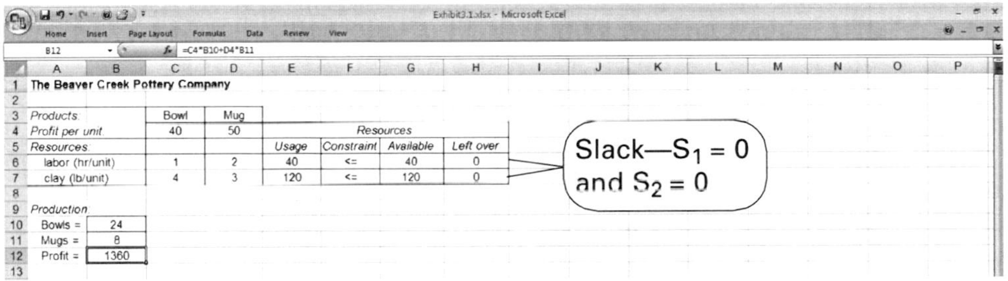

We can also generate several reports that summarize the model results. When you click on "OK" from the Solver screen, an intermediate screen will appear before the original spreadsheet, with the solution results. This screen is titled Solver Results, and it provides an opportunity for you to select several reports, including the answer report, shown in Exhibit 6. This report provides a summary of the solution results.

Exhibit 6

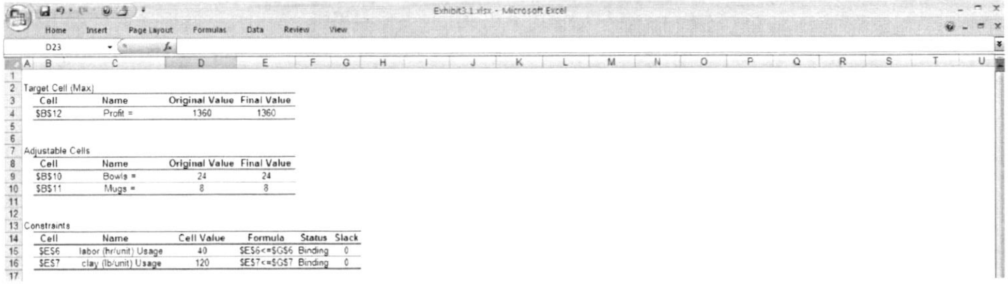

QM for Windows

Before demonstrating how to use QM for Windows, we must first make a few comments about the proper form that constraints must be in before a linear programming model can be solved with QM for Windows. All the variables in the constraint have appeared to the left of the

Management Science Application

Optimizing Production Quantities at GE Plastics

GE Plastics is a $5 billion global business that supplies plastics and raw materials from plants around the world to companies such as automotive, appliance, computer, and medical equipment companies. Among its seven major divisions, the High Performance Polymers (HPP) division is the fastest growing. HPP is a very heat tolerant polymer that is used in the manufacture of microwave cookware, fire helmets, utensils, and aircraft. HPP has a supply chain that consists of two levels of manufacturing plants and distribution channels that is similar to those in all GE Plastics divisions. First-level plants convert feedstocks into resins and then ship them to finishing plants, where they are combined with additives to produce different grades of end products. The products are then shipped to GE Polymerland (a commercial front for GE plastics), which distributes them to customers. Each physical plant has multiple plant lines that operate as independent manufacturing facilities. HPP has 8 resin plant lines that feed 21 finishing plant lines, which produce 24 grades of HPP products. HPP uses a linear programming model to optimize production along this supply chain of manufacturing plant lines and distribution channels. The linear programming model objective function maximizes the total contribution margin, which consists of revenues minus the sum of manufacturing, additive, and distribution costs, subject to demand, manufacturing capacity, and flow constraints. The decision variables are the amount of each resin produced at each resin plant line that will be used at each finishing plant line and the amount of each product at each finishing plant line. The company uses the model to develop a four-year planning horizon by solving 4 single-year models; each single-year LP model has 3,100 variables and 1,100 constraints. The model is solved within an Excel framework, using LINGO, a commercial optimization solver.

Mike Simons/Getty Images

Source: R. Tyagi, P. Kalish, K. Akbay, and G. Munshaw, "GE Plastics Optimizes the Two-Echelon Global Fulfillment Network at Its High Performance Polumers Division," *Interface* 34, no. 5 (September–October 2004); 359–66.

inequality, and all numerical values have been on the right-hand side of the inequality. For example, in the pottery company model, the constraint for labor is

$$x_1 + 2x_2 \leq 40$$

The value, 40, is referred to as the constraint quantity, or *right-hand-side*, value.

The standard form for a linear programming problem requires constraints to be in this form, with variables on the left side and numeric values to the right of the inequality or equality sign. This is a necessary condition to input problems into some computer programs, and specifically QM for Windows, for linear programming solution.

Consider a model requirement that states that the production of product 3 (x_3) must be as much as or more than the production of products 1 (x_1) and 2 (x_2). The model constraint for this requirement is formulated as

$$x_3 \geq x_1 + x_2$$

This constraint is not in proper form and could not be input into QM for Windows as it is. It must first be converted to

$$x_3 - x_1 - x_2 \geq 0$$

This constraint can now be input for computer solution.

Next consider a problem requirement that the ratio of the production of product 1 (x_1) to the production of products 2 (x_2) and 3 (x_3) must be at least 2 to 1. The model constraint for this requirement is formulated as

$$\frac{x_1}{x_2 + x_3} \geq 2$$

Fractional relationships between variables in constraints must be eliminated.

Although this constraint does meet the condition that variables be on the left side of the inequality and numeric values on the right, it is not in proper form. The fractional relationship of the variables, $x_1/(x_2 + x_3)$, cannot be input into the most commonly used linear programming computer programs in that form. It must be converted to

$$x_1 \geq 2(x_2 + x_3)$$

and then,

$$x_1 - 2x_2 - 2x_3 \geq 0$$

We will demonstrate how to use QM for Windows by solving our Beaver Creek Pottery Company example. The linear programming module in QM for Windows is accessed by clicking on "Module" at the top of the initial window. This will bring down a menu with all the program modules available in QM for Windows, as shown in Exhibit 7. By clicking on "Linear Programming," a window for this program will come up on the screen, and by clicking on "File" and then "New," a screen for inputting problem dimensions will appear. Exhibit 8 shows the data entry screen with the model type and the number of constraints and decision variables for our Beaver Creek Pottery Company example.

Exhibit 7

Exhibit 9 shows the data table for our example, with the model parameters, including the objective function and constraint coefficients, and the constraint quantity values. Notice that we also customized the row headings for the constraints by typing in "Labor (hrs)" and "Clay (lbs)." Once the model parameters have been input, click on "Solve" to get the model solution, as shown in Exhibit 10. It is not necessary to put the model into standard form by adding slack variables.

*The **marginal value** is the dollar amount one would be willing to pay for one additional resource unit.*

Notice the values 16 and 6 under the column labeled "Dual" for the "Labor" and "Clay" rows. These dual values are the **marginal values** of labor and clay in our problem. This is useful information that is provided in addition to the normal model solution values when you solve a linear programming model. We talk about dual values in more detail later in this chapter, but for now it is sufficient to say that the marginal value is the maximum dollar

Exhibit 8

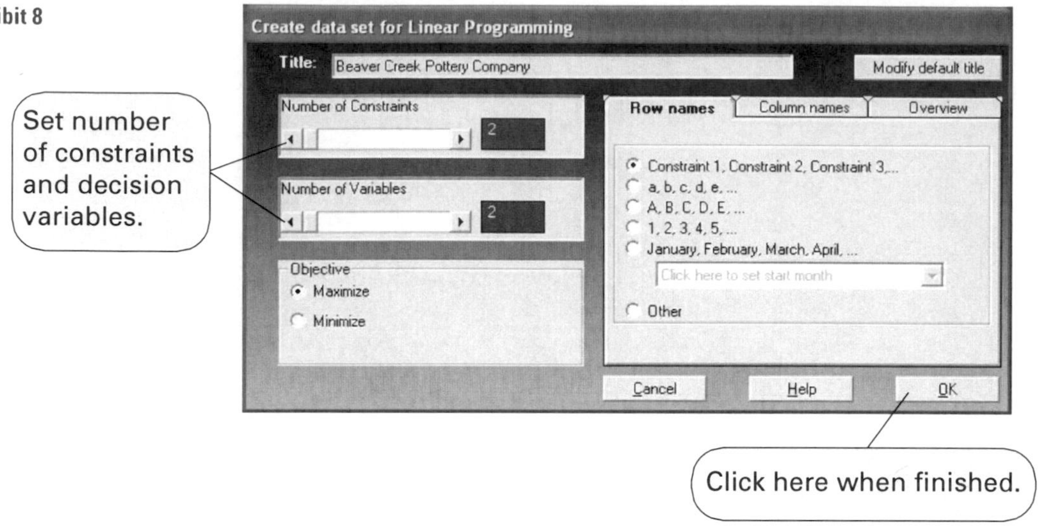

Exhibit 9

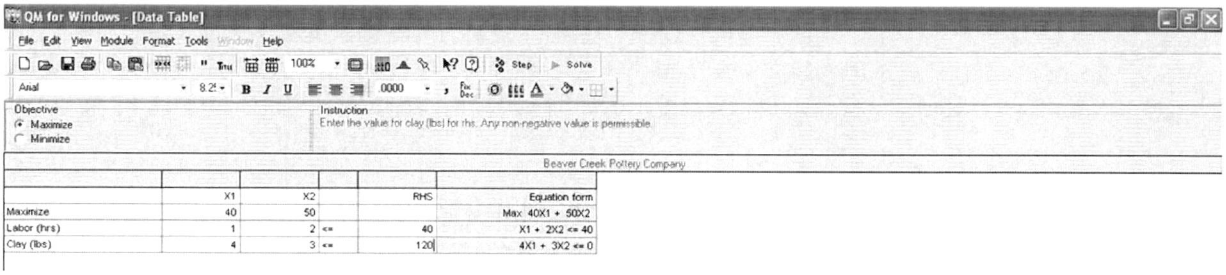

Exhibit 10

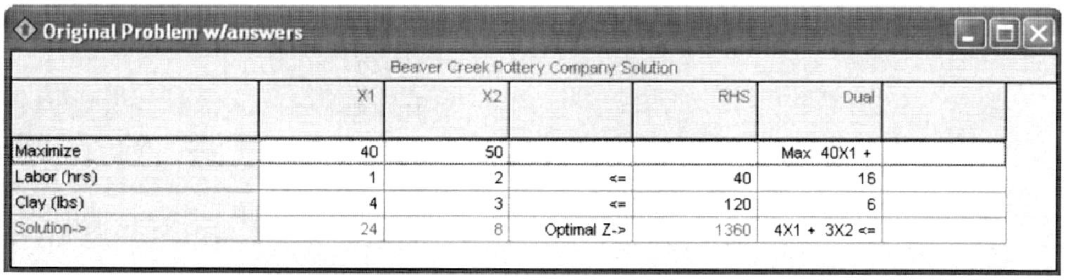

amount the company would be willing to pay for one additional unit of a resource. For example, the dual value of 16 for the labor constraint means that if 1 additional hour of labor could be obtained by the company, it would increase profit by $16. Likewise, if 1 additional pound of clay could be obtained, it would increase profit by $6. Thus, the company would be willing to pay up to $16 for 1 more hour of labor and up to $6 for 1 more pound of clay. The dual value is not the purchase price of one of these resources; it is the maximum amount the company would pay to get more of the resource. These dual values are helpful to the company in making decisions about acquiring additional resources.

QM for Windows provides solution results in several different formats, including a graphical solution by clicking on "Window" and then selecting "Graph." Exhibit 11 shows the graphical solution for our Beaver Creek Pottery Company example.

Exhibit 11

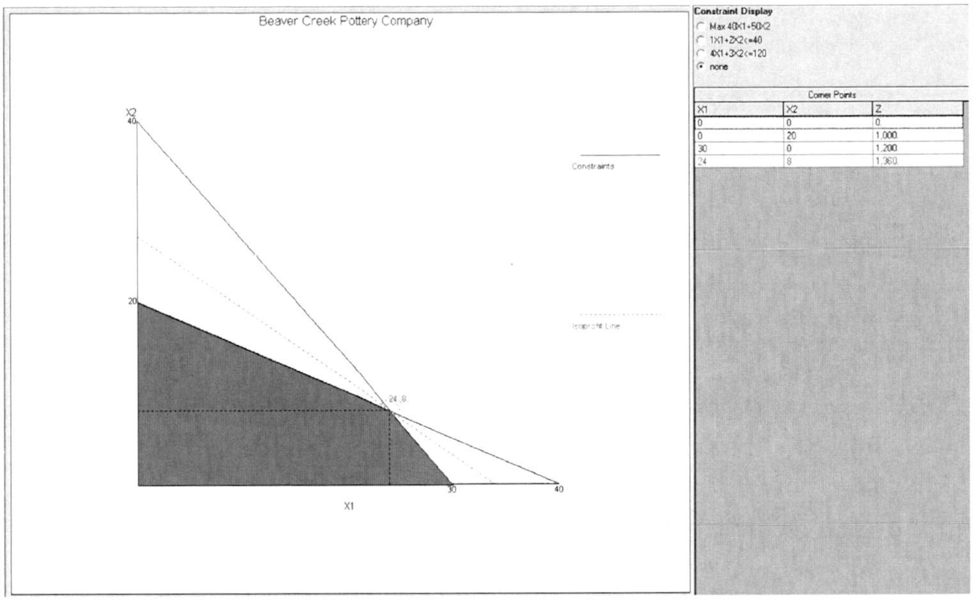

Sensitivity Analysis

Sensitivity analysis is the analysis of the effect of parameter changes on the optimal solution.

In basic linear programming models it is implicitly assumed that the *parameters* of the model are known with certainty. These parameters include the objective function coefficients, such as profit per bowl; model constraint quantity values, such as available hours of labor; and constraint coefficients, such as pounds of clay per bowl. In the examples presented so far, the models have been formulated as if these parameters are known exactly or with certainty. However, rarely does a manager know all these parameters exactly. In reality, the model parameters are simply estimates (or "best guesses") that are subject to change. For this reason, it is of interest to the manager to see what effect a change in a parameter will have on the solution to the model. Changes may be either reactions to anticipated uncertainties in the parameters or reactions to information. The analysis of parameter changes and their effects on the model solution is known as **sensitivity analysis**.

The most obvious way to ascertain the effect of a change in the parameter of a model is to make the change in the original model, *re-solve* the model, and compare the solution results with the original. However, as we will demonstrate in this chapter, in some cases the effect of changes on the model can be determined without solving the problem again.

Changes in Objective Function Coefficients

The first model parameter change we will analyze is a change in an objective function coefficient. We will use our now-familiar Beaver Creek Pottery Company example to illustrate this change:

$$\begin{aligned} \text{maximize } Z &= \$40x_1 + 50x_2 \\ \text{subject to} & \\ x_1 + 2x_2 &\leq 40 \text{ hr. of labor} \\ 4x_1 + 3x_2 &\leq 120 \text{ lb. of clay} \\ x_1, x_2 &\geq 0 \end{aligned}$$

The graphical solution for this problem is shown in Figure 1.

Figure 1
Optimal solution point

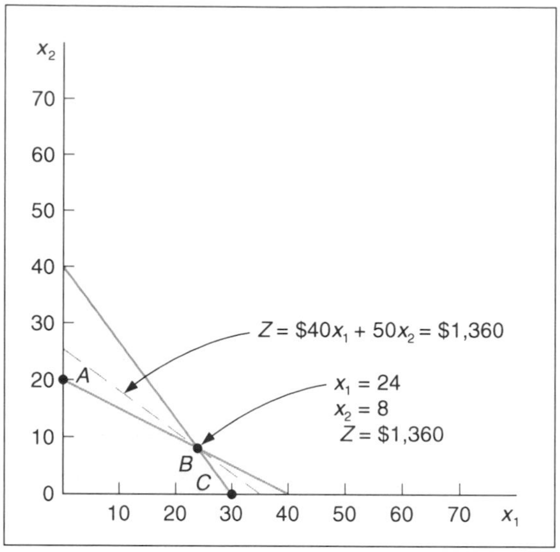

In Figure 1 the optimal solution point is shown to be at point B ($x_1 = 24$ and $x_2 = 8$), which is the last point the objective function, denoted by the dashed line, touches as it leaves the feasible solution area. However, what if we changed the profit of a bowl, x_1, from \$40 to \$100? How would that affect the solution identified in Figure 1? This change is shown in Figure 2.

Figure 2
Changing the objective function x_1 coefficient

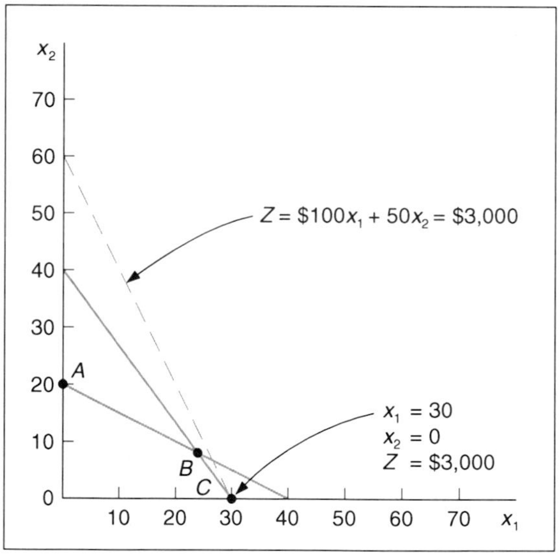

Increasing profit for a bowl (i.e., the x_1 coefficient) from \$40 to \$100 makes the objective function line steeper, so much so that the optimal solution point changes from point B to point C. Alternatively, if we increased the profit for a mug, the x_2 coefficient, from \$50 to \$100, the objective function line would become flatter, to the extent that point A would become optimal, with

$$x_1 = 0, x_2 = 20, \text{and } Z = \$2,000$$

This is shown in Figure 3.

Figure 3
Changing the objective function x_2 coefficient

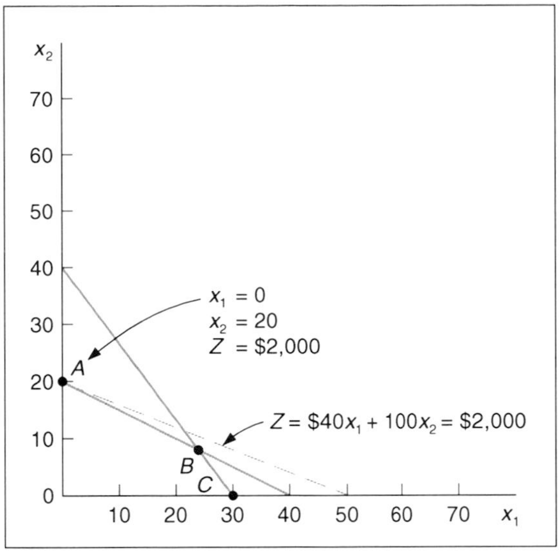

The ***sensitivity range*** *for an objective coefficient is the range of values over which the current optimal solution point will remain optimal.*

The objective of sensitivity analysis in this case is to determine the range of values for a specific objective function coefficient over which the optimal solution point, x_1 and x_2, will remain optimal. For example, the coefficient of x_1 in the objective function is originally \$40, but at some value greater than \$40, point *C* will become optimal, and at some value less than \$40, point *A* will become optimal. The focus of sensitivity analysis is to determine those two values, referred to as the *sensitivity range* for the x_1 coefficient, which we will designate as c_1.

For our simple example, we can look at the graph in Figure 1 and determine the sensitivity range for the x_1 coefficient. The slope of the objective function is currently $-4/5$, determined as follows:

$$Z = 40x_1 + 50x_2$$

or

$$50x_2 - Z - 40x_1$$

and

$$x_2 = \frac{Z}{50} - \frac{4x_1}{5}$$

The objective function is now in the form of the equation of a straight line, $y = a + bx$, where the intercept, a, equals $Z/50$ and the slope, b, is $-4/5$.

If the slope of the objective function increases to $-4/3$, the objective function line becomes exactly parallel to the constraint line,

$$4x_1 + 3x_2 = 120$$

and point *C* becomes optimal (along with *B*). The slope of this constraint line is $-4/3$, so we ask ourselves what objective function coefficient for x_1 will make the objective function slope equal $-4/3$? The answer is determined as follows, where c_1 is the objective function coefficient for x_1:

$$\frac{-c_1}{50} = \frac{-4}{3}$$
$$-3c_1 = -200$$
$$c_1 = \$66.67$$

If the coefficient of x_1 is 66.67, then the objective function will have a slope of $-66.67/50$ or $-4/3$. This is illustrated in Figure 4(a).

Management Science Application

Grape Juice Management at Welch's

With annual sales over $550 million, Welch's is one of the world's largest grape-processing companies. Founded in 1869 by Dr. Thomas B. Welch, it processes raw grapes (nearly 300,000 tons per year) into juice, jellies, and frozen concentrates. Welch's is owned by the National Grape Cooperative Association (NGCA), which has a membership of 1,400 growers. Welch's is NGCA's production, distribution, and marketing organization. Welch's operates its grape-processing plants near its growers. Because of the dynamic nature of product demand and customer service, Welch's holds finished goods inventory as a buffer and maintains a large raw materials inventory, stored as grape juice in refrigerated tank farms. Packaging operations at each plant draw juice from the tank farms during the year as needed. The value of the stored grape juice often exceeds $50 million. Harvest yields and grape quality vary among localities. In order to maintain national quality and consistency in its products, Welch's transfers juices between plants and adjusts product recipes. To do this Welch's uses a spreadsheet-based linear programming model. The juice logistics model (JLM) encompasses 324 decision variables and 361 constraints to minimize the combined costs of transporting grape juice between plants and the product recipes at each plant and the carrying cost of storing grape juice. The model decision variables include the grape juice shipped to customers for different product groups, the grape juice transferred between plants, and inventory levels at each plant. Constraints are for recipe requirements, inventories, and grape juice usage and transfers. During the first year the linear programming model was used, it saved Welch's between $130,000 and $170,000 in carrying costs alone by showing Welch's it did not need to purchase extra grapes that were then available. The model has enabled Welch's management to make quick decisions regarding inventories, purchasing grapes, and adjusting product recipes when grape harvests are higher or lower than expected and when demand changes, resulting in significant cost savings.

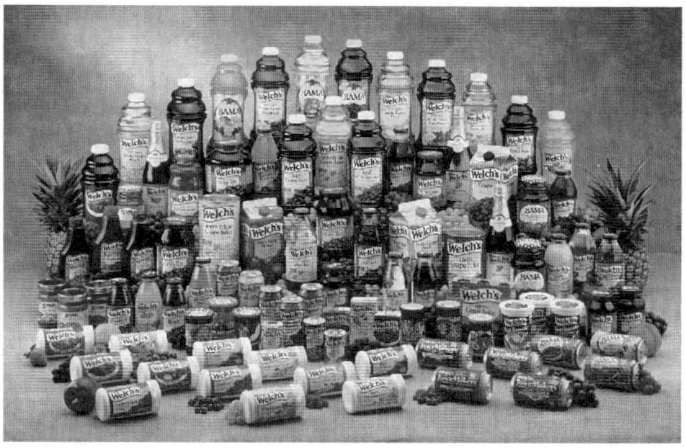

Welch Foods Inc

Source: E. W. Schuster and S. J. Allen, "Raw Material Management at Welch's, Inc.," *Interfaces* 28, no. 5 (September–October 1998): 13–24.

Figure 4
Determining the sensitivity range for c_1

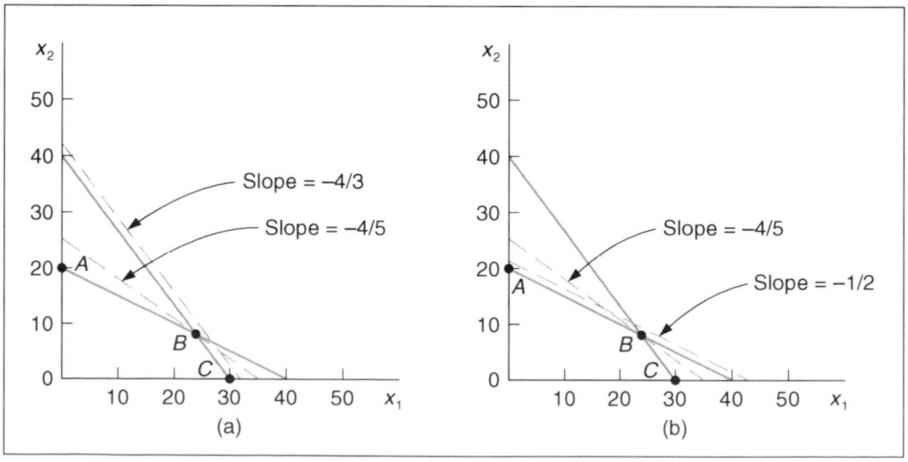

We have determined that the upper limit of the sensitivity range for c_1, the x_1 coefficient, is 66.67. If profit for a bowl increases to exactly \$66.67, the solution points will be both *B* and *C*. If the profit for a bowl is more than \$66.67, point *C* will be the optimal solution point.

The lower limit for the sensitivity range can be determined by observing Figure 4(b). In this case, if the objective function line slope decreases (becomes flatter) from $-4/5$ to the same slope as the constraint line,

$$x_1 + 2x_2 = 40$$

then point *A* becomes optimal (along with *B*). The slope of this constraint line is $-1/2$, that is, $x_2 = 20 - (1/2)x_1$. In order to have an objective function slope of $-1/2$, the profit for a bowl would have to decrease to \$25, as follows:

$$\frac{-c_1}{50} = \frac{-1}{2}$$
$$-2c_1 = -50$$
$$c_1 = \$25$$

This is the lower limit of the sensitivity range for the x_1 coefficient.

The complete sensitivity range for the x_1 coefficient can be expressed as

$$25 \leq c_1 \leq 66.67$$

This means that the profit for a bowl can vary anywhere between \$25.00 and \$66.67, and the optimal solution point, $x_1 = 24$ and $x_2 = 8$, will not change. Of course, the total profit, or *Z* value, will change, depending on whatever value c_1 actually is.

For the manager this is useful information. Changing the production schedule in terms of how many items are produced can have a number of ramifications in an operation. Packaging, logistical, and marketing requirements for the product might need to be altered. However, with the preceding sensitivity range, the manager knows how much the profit, and hence the selling price and costs, can be altered without resulting in a change in production.

Performing the same type of graphical analysis will provide the sensitivity range for the x_2 objective function coefficient, c_2. This range is $30 \leq c_2 \leq 80$. This means that the profit for a mug can vary between \$30 and \$80, and the optimal solution point, *B*, will not change. However, for this case and the range for c_1, the sensitivity range generally applies only if one coefficient is varied and the other held constant. Thus, when we say that profit for a mug can vary between \$30 and \$80, this is true only if c_1 remains constant.

Simultaneous changes can be made in the objective function coefficients as long as the changes taken together do not change the optimal solution point. However, determining the effect of these simultaneous changes is overly complex and time-consuming using graphical analysis. In fact, using graphical analysis is a tedious way to perform sensitivity analysis in general, and it is impossible when the linear programming model contains three or more variables, thus requiring a three-dimensional graph. However, Excel and QM for Windows provide sensitivity analysis for linear programming problems as part of their standard solution output. Determining the effect of simultaneous changes in model parameters and performing sensitivity analysis in general are much easier and more practical using the computer. Later in this chapter we will show the sensitivity analysis output for Excel and QM for Windows.

However, before moving on to computer-generated sensitivity analysis, we want to look at one more aspect of the sensitivity ranges for objective function coefficients. Recall that the model for our fertilizer minimization model is

$$\text{minimize } Z = \$6x_1 + 3x_2$$
subject to
$$2x_1 + 4x_2 \geq 16$$
$$4x_1 + 3x_2 \geq 24$$
$$x_1, x_2 \geq 0$$

Figure 5
Fertilizer example: sensitivity range for c_1

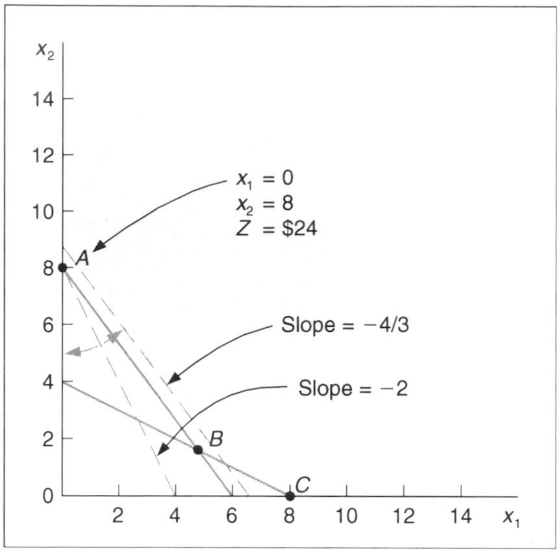

and the solution shown graphically in Figure 5 is $x_1 = 0, x_2 = 8$, and $Z = 24$.

The sensitivity ranges for the objective function coefficients are

$$4 \leq c_1 \leq \infty$$
$$0 \leq c_2 \leq 4.5$$

Notice that the upper bound for the x_1 coefficient range is infinity. The reason for this upper limit can be seen in the graphical solution of the problem shown in Figure 5.

As the objective function coefficient for x_1 decreases from \$6, the objective function slope of -2 decreases, and the objective function line gets flatter. When the coefficient, c_1, equals \$4, then the slope of the objective function is $-4/3$, which is the same as the constraint line, $4x_1 + 3x_2 = 24$. This makes point B optimal (as well as A). Thus, the lower limit of the sensitivity range for c_1 is \$4. However, notice that as c_1 increases from \$6, the objective function simply becomes steeper and steeper as it rotates toward the x_2 axis of the graph. The objective function will not come into contact with another feasible solution point. Thus, no matter how much we increase cost for Super-gro fertilizer (x_1), point A will always be optimal.

Objective Function Coefficient Ranges with the Computer

When we provided the Excel spreadsheet solution for the Beaver Creek Pottery Company example earlier in this chapter, we did not include sensitivity analysis. However, Excel will also generate a sensitivity report that provides the sensitivity ranges for the objective function coefficients. When you click on "Solve" from the Solver Parameters window, you will momentarily go to a Solver Results screen, shown in Exhibit 12, which provides you with an opportunity to select different reports before proceeding to the solution. This is how we selected our answer report earlier. The sensitivity report for our Beaver Creek Pottery Company example is shown in Exhibit 13. However, note that if you have not already clicked on "Assume Linear Model" from the Solver Options screen, as we earlier warned, Excel will not generate this version of the sensitivity report.

Notice that the sensitivity ranges for the objective function coefficients (40 and 50) are not provided as an upper and lower limit but instead show an allowable increase and an allowable decrease. For example, for the coefficient \$40 for bowls (B10), the allowable

Exhibit 12

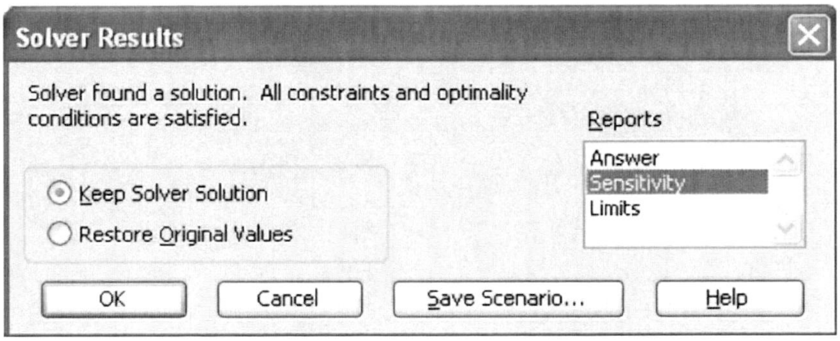

Exhibit 13

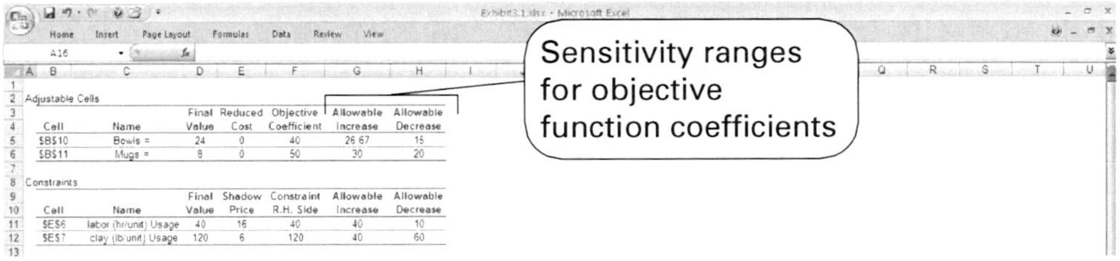

Adjustable Cells

Cell	Name	Final Value	Reduced Cost	Objective Coefficient	Allowable Increase	Allowable Decrease
B10	Bowls =	24	0	40	26.67	15
B11	Mugs =	8	0	50	30	20

Constraints

Cell	Name	Final Value	Shadow Price	Constraint R.H. Side	Allowable Increase	Allowable Decrease
E6	labor (hr/unit) Usage	40	16	40	40	10
E7	clay (lb/unit) Usage	120	6	120	40	60

increase of 26.667 results in an upper limit of 66.667, whereas the allowable decrease of 15 results in a lower limit of 25.

The sensitivity ranges for the objective function coefficients for our example are presented in QM for Windows in Exhibit 14. Notice that this output provides the upper and lower limits of the sensitivity ranges for both variables, x_1 and x_2.

Exhibit 14

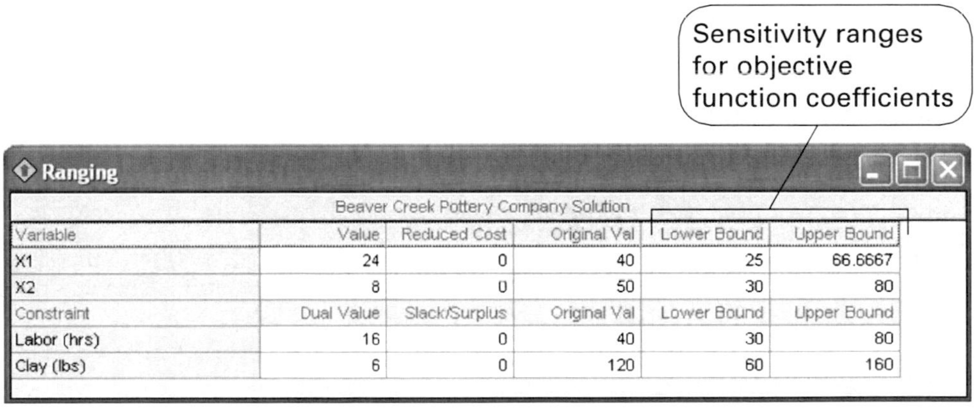

Beaver Creek Pottery Company Solution

Variable	Value	Reduced Cost	Original Val	Lower Bound	Upper Bound
X1	24	0	40	25	66.6667
X2	8	0	50	30	80
Constraint	Dual Value	Slack/Surplus	Original Val	Lower Bound	Upper Bound
Labor (hrs)	16	0	40	30	80
Clay (lbs)	6	0	120	60	160

Changes in Constraint Quantity Values

The second type of sensitivity analysis we will discuss is the sensitivity ranges for the constraint quantity values—that is, the values to the right of the inequality signs in the constraints. For our Beaver Creek Pottery Company model,

$$\begin{aligned} \text{maximize } Z &= \$40x_1 + 50x_2 \\ \text{subject to} & \\ x_1 + 2x_2 + s_1 &= 40 \text{ (labor, hr.)} \\ 4x_1 + 3x_2 + s_2 &= 120 \text{ (clay, lb.)} \\ x_1, x_2 &\geq 0 \end{aligned}$$

the constraint quantity values are 40 and 120.

Consider a change in which the manager of the pottery company can increase the labor hours from 40 to 60. The effect of this change in the model is graphically displayed in Figure 6.

Figure 6
Increasing the labor constraint quantity

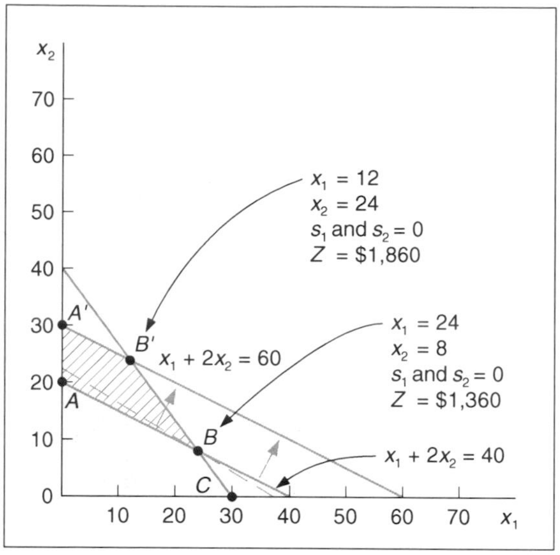

The sensitivity range for a right-hand-side value is the range of values over which the quantity values can change without changing the solution variable mix, including slack variables.

Increasing the available labor hours from 40 to 60 causes the feasible solution space to change. It was originally *OABC*, and now it is *OA′B′C*. *B′* is the new optimal solution, instead of *B*. However, the important consideration in this type of sensitivity analysis is that the solution *mix* (or variables that do not have zero values), including slack variables, did not change, even though the values of x_1 and x_2 did change (from $x_1 = 24, x_2 = 8$ to $x_1 = 12, x_2 = 24$). The focus of sensitivity analysis for constraint quantity values is to determine the range over which the constraint quantity values can change without changing the solution variable mix, specifically including the slack variables.

If the quantity value for the labor constraint is increased from 40 to 80 hours, the new solution space is *OA′C*, and a new solution variable mix occurs at *A′*, as shown in Figure 7(a). Whereas at the original optimal point, *B*, both x_1 and x_2 are in the solution, at the new optimal point, *A′*, only x_2 is produced (i.e., $x_1 = 0, x_2 = 40, s_1 = 0, s_2 = 0$).

Figure 7
Determining the sensitivity range for labor quantity

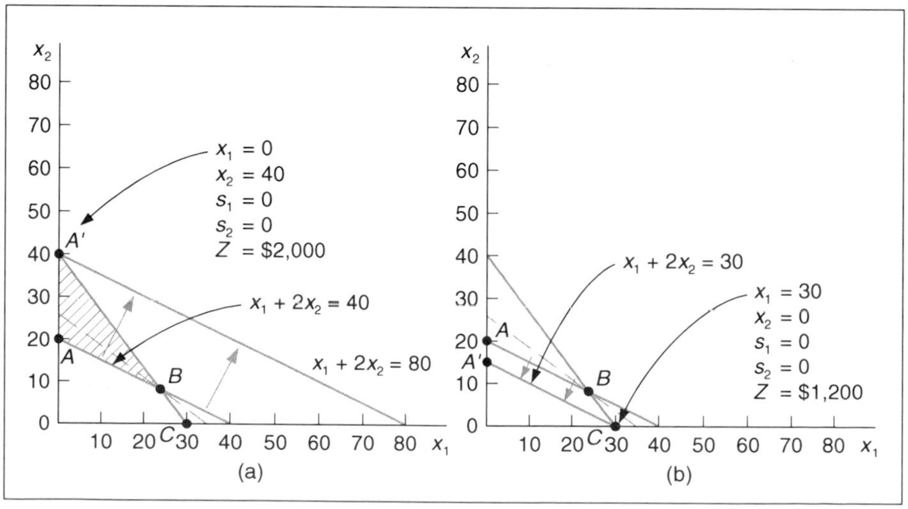

Thus, the upper limit of the sensitivity range for the quantity value for the first constraint, which we will refer to as q_1, is 80 hours. At this value the solution mix changes such that bowls are no longer produced. Furthermore, as q_1 increases past 80 hours, s_1 increases (i.e., slack hours are created). Similarly, if the value for q_1 is decreased to 30 hours, the new feasible solution space is $OA'C$, as shown in Figure 7(b). The new optimal point is at C, where no mugs (x_2) are produced. The new solution is $x_1 = 30, x_2 = 0, s_1 = 0, s_2 = 0$, and $Z = \$1{,}200$. Again, the variable mix is changed. Summarizing, the sensitivity range for the constraint quantity value for labor hours is

$$30 \leq q_1 \leq 80 \text{ hr.}$$

The sensitivity range for clay can be determined graphically in a similar manner. If the quantity value for the clay constraint, $4x_1 + 3x_2 \leq 120$, is increased from 120 to 160, shown in Figure 8(a), then a new solution space, OAC', results, with a new optimal point, C'. Alternatively, if the quantity value is decreased from 120 to 60, as shown in Figure 8(b), the new solution space is OAC', and the new optimal point is A ($x_1 = 0, x_2 = 20, s_1 = 0, s_2 = 0, Z = \$800$).

Summarizing, the sensitivity ranges for q_1 and q_2 are

$$30 \leq q_1 \leq 80 \text{ hr.}$$
$$60 \leq q_2 \leq 160 \text{ lb.}$$

Figure 8
Determining the sensitivity range for clay quantity

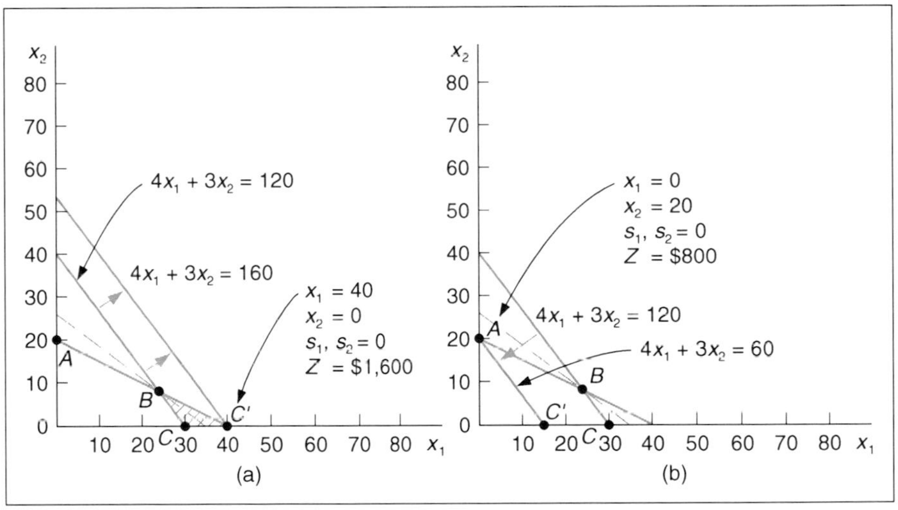

As was the case with the sensitivity ranges for the objective function coefficient, these sensitivity ranges are valid for only one q_i value. All other q_i values are assumed to be held constant. However, simultaneous changes can occur, as long as they do not change the variable mix.

These ranges for constraint quantity values provide useful information for the manager, especially regarding production scheduling and planning. If resources are reduced at the pottery company, then at some point one of the products will no longer be produced, and the support facilities and apparatus for that production will not be needed, or extra hours of resources will be created that are not needed. A similar result, albeit a better one, will occur if resources are increased because profit will be more than with a reduction in resources.

Constraint Quantity Value Ranges with Excel and QM for Windows

Previously we showed how to generate the sensitivity report for Excel, resulting in Exhibit 13. This report is shown again in Exhibit 15, with the sensitivity ranges for the constraint quantity values highlighted. As mentioned previously, the ranges are expressed in terms of an allowable increase and decrease instead of upper and lower limits.

Exhibit 15

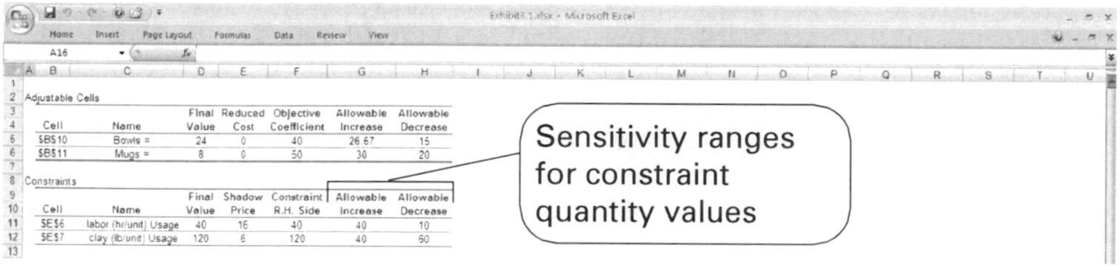

Adjustable Cells

Cell	Name	Final Value	Reduced Cost	Objective Coefficient	Allowable Increase	Allowable Decrease
B10	Bowls =	24	0	40	26.67	15
B11	Mugs =	8	0	50	30	20

Constraints

Cell	Name	Final Value	Shadow Price	Constraint R.H. Side	Allowable Increase	Allowable Decrease
E6	labor (hr/unit) Usage	40	16	40	40	10
E7	clay (lb/unit) Usage	120	6	120	40	60

The sensitivity ranges for the constraint quantity values with QM for Windows can be observed in Exhibit 16.

Exhibit 16

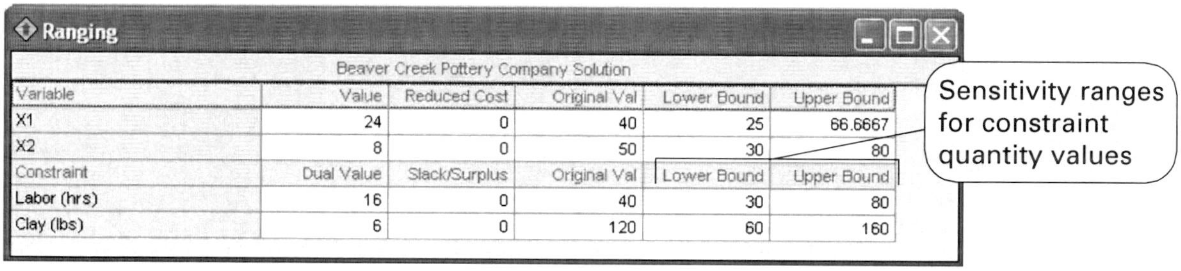

Ranging — Beaver Creek Pottery Company Solution

Variable	Value	Reduced Cost	Original Val	Lower Bound	Upper Bound
X1	24	0	40	25	66.6667
X2	8	0	50	30	80
Constraint	**Dual Value**	**Slack/Surplus**	**Original Val**	**Lower Bound**	**Upper Bound**
Labor (hrs)	16	0	40	30	80
Clay (lbs)	6	0	120	60	160

Other Forms of Sensitivity Analysis

Excel and QM for Windows provide sensitivity analysis ranges for objective function coefficients and constraint quantity values as part of the standard solution output. However, there are other forms of sensitivity analysis, including changing individual constraint parameters, adding new constraints, and adding new variables.

Other forms of sensitivity analysis include changing constraint parameter values, adding new constraints, and adding new variables.

For instance, in our Beaver Creek Pottery Company example, if a new, less-experienced artisan was hired to make pottery, it might take this individual 1.33 hours to produce a bowl instead of 1 hour. Thus, the labor constraint would change from $x_1 + 2x_2 \leq 40$ to $1.33x_1 + 2x_2 \leq 40$. This change is illustrated in Figure 9.

Note that a change in the coefficient for x_1 in the labor constraint rotates the constraint line, changing the solution space from *OABC* to *OAC*. It also results in a new optimal solution point, *C*, where $x_1 = 30, x_2 = 0$, and $Z = \$1{,}200$. Then 1.33 hours would be the logical upper limit for this constraint coefficient. However, as we pointed out, this type of sensitivity analysis for constraint variable coefficients is not typically provided in the standard linear programming computer output. As a result, the most logical way to ascertain the effect of this type of change is simply to run the computer program with different values.

Other types of sensitivity analyses are to add a new constraint to the model or to add a new variable. For example, suppose the Beaver Creek Pottery Company added a third constraint for packaging its pottery, as follows:

$$0.20x_1 + 0.10x_2 \leq 5 \text{ hr.}$$

Figure 9
Changing the x_1 coefficient in the labor constraint

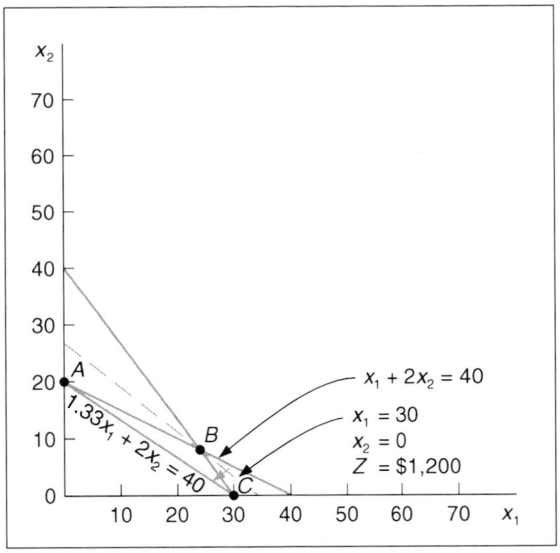

This would require the model to be solved again with the new constraint. This new constraint does, in fact, change the optimal solution, as shown in the Excel spreadsheet in Exhibit 17. This spreadsheet requires a new row (8) added to the original spreadsheet (first shown in Exhibit 1) with our new constraint parameter values, and a new constraint, E8 ≤ G8, added to Solver. In the original model, the solution (shown in Exhibit 5) was 24 bowls and 8 mugs, with a profit of $1,360. With the new constraint for packaging added, the solution is now 20 bowls and 10 mugs, with a profit of $1,300.

Exhibit 17

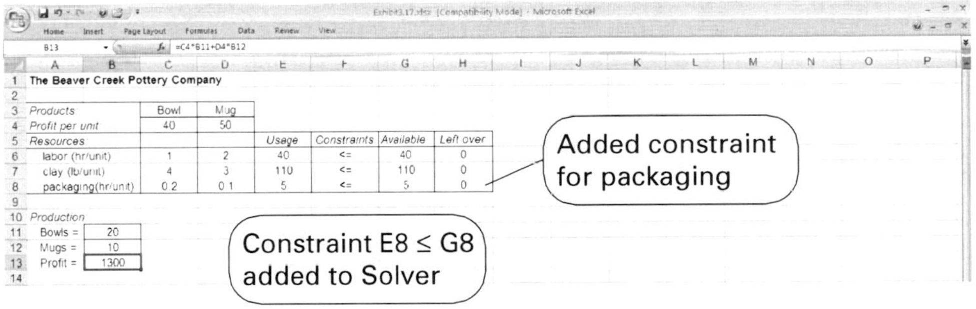

If a new variable is added to the model, this would also require that the model be solved again to determine the effect of the change. For example, suppose the pottery company was contemplating producing a third product, cups, requiring 1.2 hours of labor and 2 lbs. of clay. It can secure no additional resources, and the profit for a cup is estimated to be $30. This change is reflected in the following model reformulation:

$$
\begin{aligned}
&\text{maximize } Z = \$40x_1 + 50x_2 + 30x_3\\
&\text{subject to}\\
&x_1 + 2x_2 + 1.2x_3 \le 40 \text{ (labor, hr.)}\\
&4x_1 + 3x_2 + 2x_3 \le 120 \text{ (clay, lb.)}\\
&x_1, x_2, x_3 \ge 0
\end{aligned}
$$

Solving this new formulation with the computer will show that this prospective change will have no effect on the original solution—that is, the model is not sensitive to this change.

The estimated profit from cups was not enough to offset the production of bowls and mugs, and the solution remained the same.

Shadow Prices

We briefly discussed dual values (also called *shadow prices*) earlier in this chapter, in our discussion of QM for Windows. You will recall that a dual value was defined as the marginal value of one additional unit of resource. We need to mention shadow prices again at this point in our discussion of sensitivity analysis because decisions are often made regarding resources by considering the marginal value of resources in conjunction with their sensitivity ranges.

Consider again the Excel sensitivity report for the Beaver Creek Pottery Company example shown in Exhibit 18.

Exhibit 18

Adjustable Cells

Cell	Name	Final Value	Reduced Cost	Objective Coefficient	Allowable Increase	Allowable Decrease
B10	Bowls =	24	0	40	26.67	15
B11	Mugs =	8	0	50	30	20

Constraints

Cell	Name	Final Value	Shadow Price	Constraint R.H. Side	Allowable Increase	Allowable Decrease
E6	labor (hr/unit) Usage	40	16	40	40	10
E7	clay (lb/unit) Usage	120	6	120	40	60

Shadow prices (dual values)

The shadow price (or marginal value) for labor is $16 per hour, and the shadow price for clay is $6 per pound. This means that for every additional hour of labor that can be obtained, profit will increase by $16. If the manager of the pottery company can secure more labor at $16 per hour, how much more can be obtained before the optimal solution mix will change and the current shadow price is no longer valid? The answer is at the upper limit of the sensitivity range for the labor constraint value. A maximum of 80 hours of labor can be used before the optimal solution mix changes. Thus, the manager can secure 40 more hours, the allowable increase shown in the Excel sensitivity output for the labor constraint. If 40 extra hours of labor can be obtained, what is its total value? The answer is ($16/hr.)(40 hr.) = $640. In other words, profit is increased by $640 if 40 extra hours of labor can be obtained. This is shown in the Excel output in Exhibit 19, where increasing the labor constraint from 40 to 80 hours has increased profit from $1,360 to $2,000, or $640.

Exhibit 19

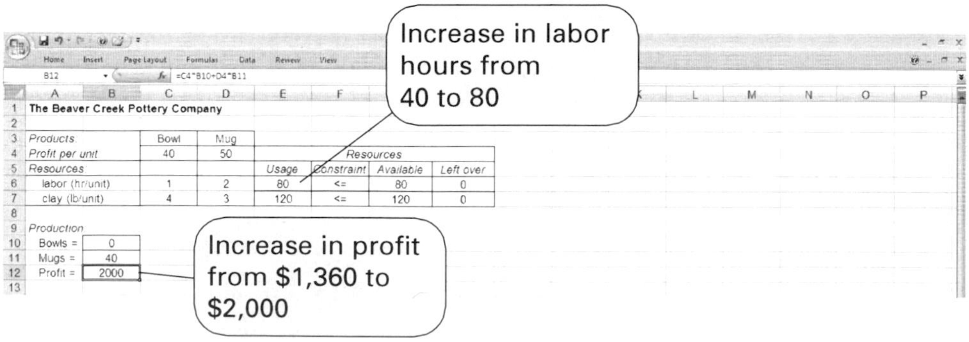

Looking back to Figure 8(a), this is the solution point at C′. Increasing the labor hours to more than 80 hours (the upper limit of the sensitivity range) will not result in an additional increase in profit or a new solution; it will result only in slack hours of labor.

Alternatively, what would be the effect on profit if one of the Native American artisans was sick one day during the week, and the available labor hours decreased from 40 to 32? Profit in this case would decrease by $16 per hour, or a total amount of $128. Thus, total profit would fall from $1,360 to $1,232.

Similarly, if the pottery company could obtain only 100 pounds of clay instead of its normal weekly allotment of 120 pounds, what would be the effect on profit? Profit would decrease by $6 per pound for 20 pounds, or a total of $120. This would result in an overall reduction in profit from $1,360 to $1,240.

The sensitivity range for a constraint quantity value is also the range over which the shadow price is valid.

Thus, another piece of information that is provided by the sensitivity ranges for the constraint quantity values is the range over which the shadow price remains valid. When q_i increases past the upper limit of the sensitivity range or decreases below the lower limit, the shadow price will change, specifically because slack (or surplus) will be created. Therefore, the sensitivity range for the constraint quantity value is the range over which the shadow price is valid.

The shadow price of $16 for 1 hour of labor is not necessarily what the manager would *pay* for an hour of labor. This depends on how the objective function is defined. In the Beaver Creek Pottery Company example, we are assuming that all the resources available, 40 hours of labor and 120 pounds of clay, are already paid for. Even if the company does not use all the resources, it still must pay for them. These are *sunk* costs. Therefore, the individual profit values in the objective function for each product are not affected by how much of a resource is actually used; the total profit is independent of the resources used. In this case, the shadow prices are the maximum amounts the manager would pay for additional units of resource. The manager would pay up to $16 for 1 extra hour of labor and up to $6 for an extra pound of clay.

Alternatively, if each hour of labor and each pound of clay were purchased separately, and thus were not sunk costs, profit would be a function of the cost of the resources. In this case, the shadow price would be the additional amount, over and above the original cost of the resource, that would be paid for one more unit of the resource.

Summary

This chapter has focused primarily on the computer solution of linear programming problems. This required us first to show how a linear programming model is put into standard form, with the addition of slack variables or the subtraction of surplus variables. Computer solution also enabled us to consider the topic of sensitivity analysis, the analysis of the effect of model parameter changes on the solution of a linear programming model.

References

See the references at the end of this chapter.

Example Problem Solution

This example demonstrates the transformation of a linear programming model into standard form, sensitivity analysis, computer solution, and shadow prices.

Problem Statement

The Xecko Tool Company is considering bidding on a job for two airplane wing parts. Each wing part must be processed through three manufacturing stages—stamping, drilling, and finishing—for which the company has limited available hours. The linear programming model to determine how many of part 1 (x_1) and part 2 (x_2) the company should produce in order to maximize its profit is as follows:

$$\text{maximize } Z = \$650x_1 + 910x_2$$
subject to
$$4x_1 + 7.5x_2 \leq 105 \text{ (stamping, hr.)}$$
$$6.2x_1 + 4.9x_2 \leq 90 \text{ (drilling, hr.)}$$
$$9.1x_1 + 4.1x_2 \leq 110 \text{ (finishing, hr.)}$$
$$x_1, x_2 \geq 0$$

A. Solve the model graphically.
B. Indicate how much slack resource is available at the optimal solution point.
C. Determine the sensitivity ranges for the profit for wing part 1 and the stamping hours available.
D. Solve this model by using Excel.

Solution

A.

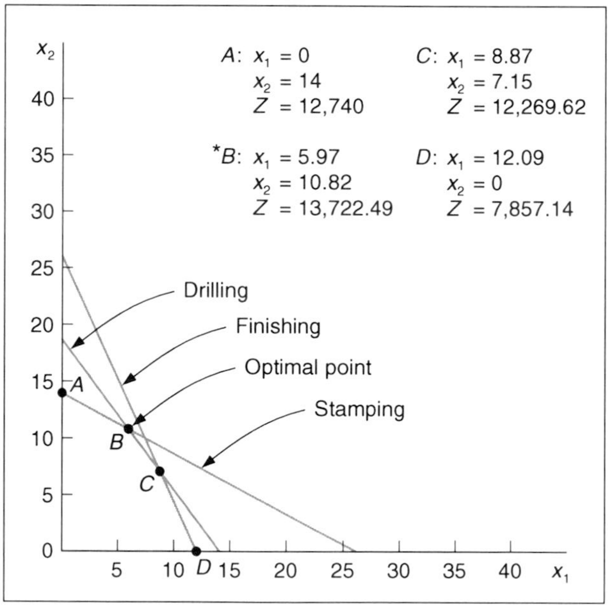

B. The slack at point B, where $x_1 = 5.97$ and $x_2 = 10.82$, is computed as follows:

$$4(5.97) + 7.5(10.82) + s_1 = 105 \text{ (stamping, hr.)}$$
$$s_1 = 0 \text{ hr.}$$
$$6.2(5.97) + 4.9(10.82) + s_2 = 90 \text{ (drilling, hr.)}$$
$$s_2 = 0 \text{ hr.}$$
$$9.1(5.97) + 4.1(10.82) + s_3 = 110 \text{ (finishing, hr.)}$$
$$s_3 = 11.35 \text{ hr.}$$

C. The sensitivity range for the profit for part 1 is determined by observing the graph of the model and computing how much the slope of the objective function must increase to make the optimal point move from *B* to *C*. This is the upper limit of the range and is determined by computing the value of c_1 that will make the slope of the objective function equal with the slope of the constraint line for drilling, $6.2x_1 + 4.9x_2 = 90$:

$$\frac{-c_1}{910} = \frac{-6.2}{4.9}$$
$$c_1 = 1{,}151.43$$

The lower limit is determined by computing the value of c_1 that will equate the slope of the objective function with the slope of the constraint line for stamping, $4x_1 + 7.5x_2 = 105$:

$$\frac{-c_1}{910} = \frac{-4}{7.5}$$
$$c_1 = 485.33$$

Summarizing,

$$485.33 \leq c_1 \leq 1{,}151.43$$

The upper limit of the range for stamping hours is determined by first computing the value for q_1 that would move the solution point from *B* to where the drilling constraint intersects with the x_2 axis, where $x_1 = 0$ and $x_2 = 18.37$:

$$4(0) + 7.5(18.37) = q_1$$
$$q_1 = 137.76$$

The lower limit of the sensitivity range occurs where the optimal point *B* moves to *C*, where $x_1 = 8.87$ and $x_2 = 7.15$:

$$4(8.87) + 7.5(7.15) = q_1$$
$$q_1 = 89.10$$

Summarizing, $89.10 \leq q_1 \leq 137.76$.

D. The Excel spreadsheet solution to this example problem is as follows:

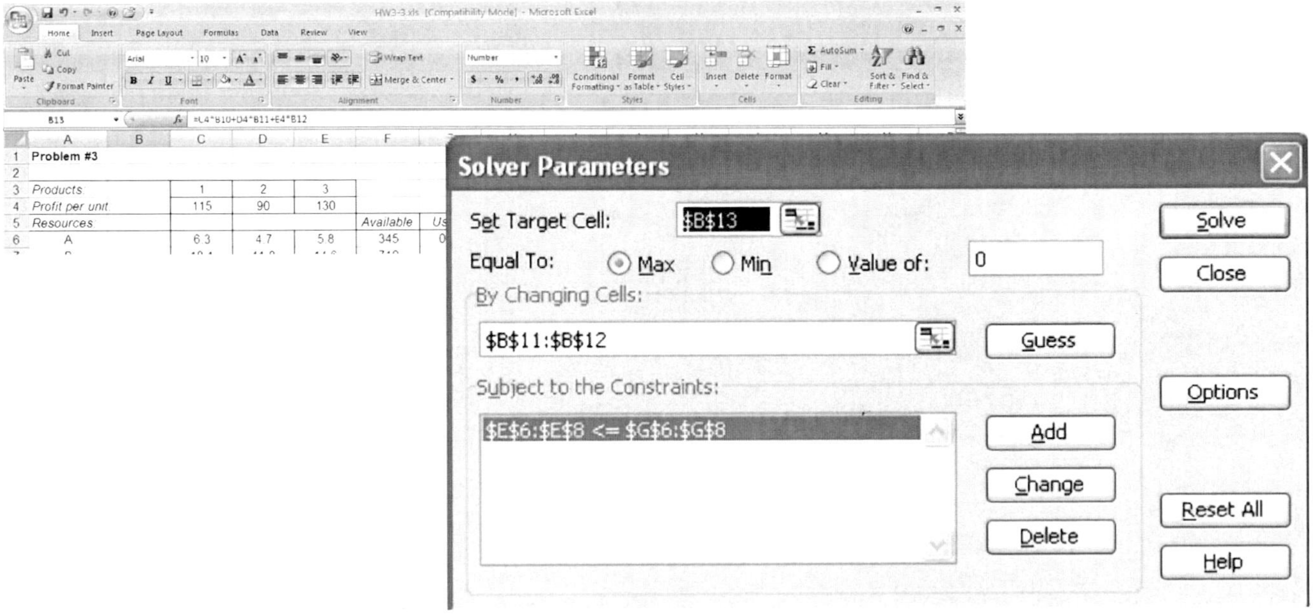

Problems

1. Given the following QM for Windows computer solution of a linear programming model, graph the problem and identify the solution point, including variable values and slack, from the computer output:

Original Problem w/answers

Problem 1 Solution

	X1	X2		RHS	Dual
Maximize	50	90			Max 50X1 +
Constraint 1	6.5	14.4	<=	650	4.2017
Constraint 2	12	15.6	<=	780	1.8908
Constraint 3	8	5	<=	400	0
Solution->	15.2941	38.2353	Optimal Z->	4,205.882	8X1 + 5X2 <=

Linear Programming Results

Problem 1 Solution

Variable	Status	Value
X1	Basic	15.2941
X2	Basic	38.2353
slack 1	NONBasic	0
slack 2	NONBasic	0
slack 3	Basic	86.4706
Optimal Value (Z)		4,205.882

2. Explain the primary differences between a software package such as QM for Windows and Excel spreadsheets for solving linear programming problems.

3. Given the following Excel spreadsheet for a linear programming model and Solver window, indicate the formula for cell B13 and fill in the Solver window with the appropriate information to solve the problem:

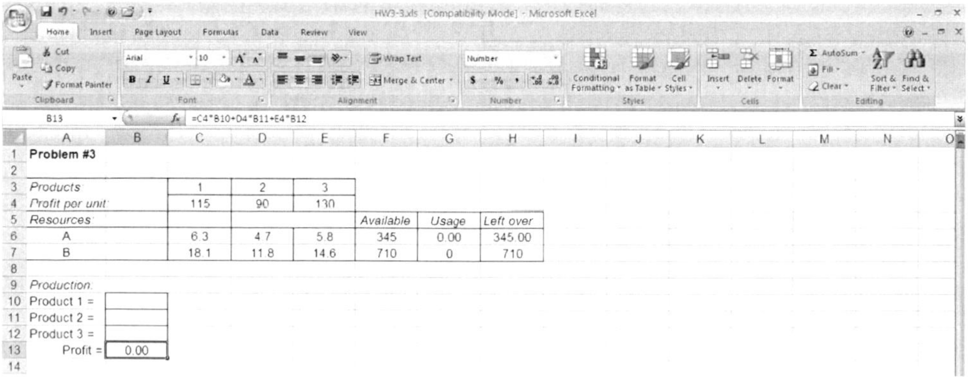

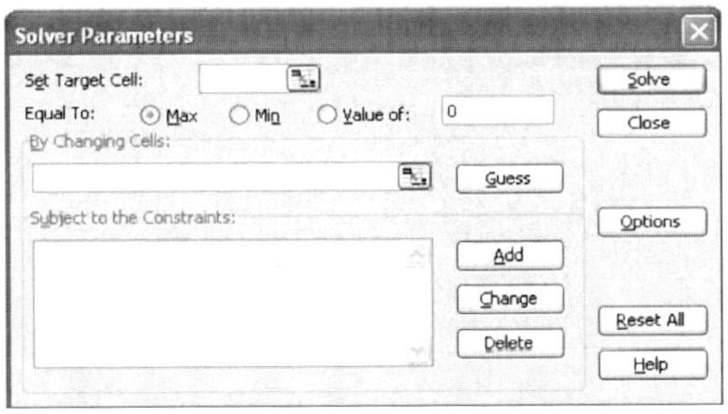

4. Solve the following model using Excel.

$$\begin{aligned} \text{maximize } Z &= 3x_1 + 6x_2 \ (\$, \text{profit}) \\ \text{subject to} & \\ 3x_1 + 2x_2 &\leq 18 \ (\text{units, resource 1}) \\ x_1 + x_2 &\geq 5 \ (\text{units, resource 2}) \\ x_1 &\leq 4 \ (\text{units, resource 3}) \\ x_1, x_2 &\geq 0 \end{aligned}$$

5. The following model was solved graphically:

$$\begin{aligned} \text{maximize } Z &= 5x_1 + 8x_2 \ (\$, \text{profit}) \\ \text{subject to} & \\ 3x_1 + 5x_2 &\leq 50 \ (\text{units, resource 1}) \\ 2x_1 + 4x_2 &\leq 40 \ (\text{units, resource 2}) \\ x_1 &\leq 8 \ (\text{units, resource 3}) \\ x_2 &\leq 10 \ (\text{units, resource 4}) \\ x_1, x_2 &\geq 0 \end{aligned}$$

Given the following Excel spreadsheet for this model, indicate the formulas in cells F6, F7, F8, F9, G6, G7, G8, G9, and B14, and fill in the Solver window with the necessary information to solve the model. Solve the model using Excel.

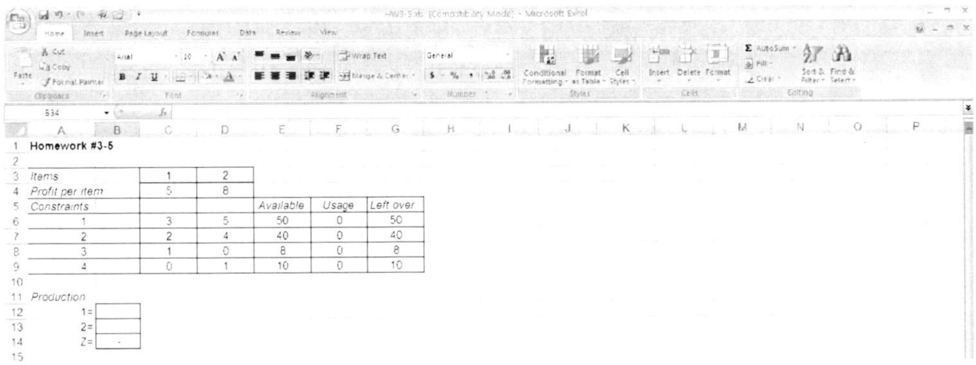

	A	B	C	D	E	F	G
1	Homework #3-5						
2							
3	Items		1	2			
4	Profit per item		5	8			
5	Constraints				Available	Usage	Left over
6		1	3	5	50	0	50
7		2	2	4	40	0	40
8		3	1	0	8	0	8
9		4	0	1	10	0	10
10							
11	Production						
12	1=						
13	2=						
14	Z=	-					
15							

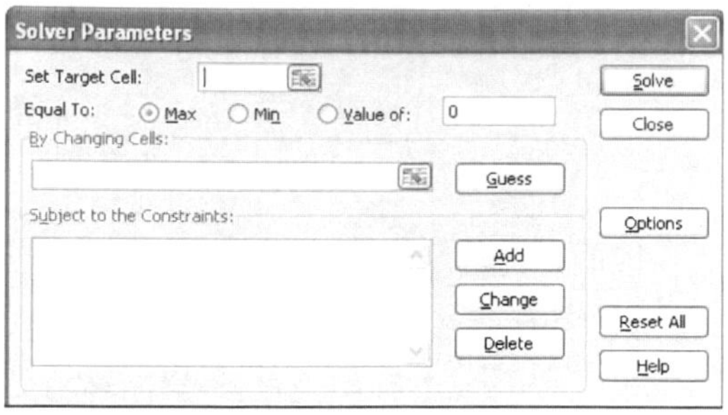

6. Given the following graph of a linear programming model with a single constraint and the objective function maximize $Z = 30x_1 + 50x_2$, determine the optimal solution point:

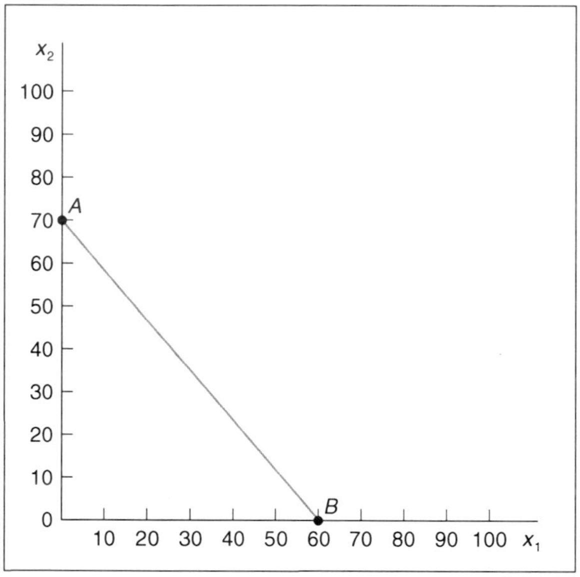

Determine the values by which c_1 and c_2 must decrease or increase in order to change the current solution point to the other extreme point.

7. Southern Sporting Goods Company makes basketballs and footballs. Each product is produced from two resources—rubber and leather. The resource requirements for each product and the total resources available are as follows:

	Resource Requirements per Unit	
Product	Rubber (lb.)	Leather (ft.^{2})
Basketball	3	4
Football	2	5
Total resources available	500 lb.	800 ft.^{2}

Each basketball produced results in a profit of $12, and each football earns $16 in profit.

a. Formulate a linear programming model to determine the number of basketballs and footballs to produce in order to maximize profit.
b. Transform this model into standard form.

8. Solve the model formulated in Problem 7 for Southern Sporting Goods Company graphically.
   a. Identify the amount of unused resources (i.e., slack) at each of the graphical extreme points.
   b. What would be the effect on the optimal solution if the profit for a basketball changed from \$12 to \$13? What would be the effect if the profit for a football changed from \$16 to \$15?
   c. What would be the effect on the optimal solution if 500 additional pounds of rubber could be obtained? What would be the effect if 500 additional square feet of leather could be obtained?

9. For the linear programming model for Southern Sporting Goods Company, formulated in Problem 7 and solved graphically in Problem 8:
   a. Determine the sensitivity ranges for the objective function coefficients and constraint quantity values, using graphical analysis.
   b. Verify the sensitivity ranges determined in (a) by using the computer.
   c. Using the computer, determine the shadow prices for the resources and explain their meaning.

10. A company produces two products, A and B, which have profits of \$9 and \$7, respectively. Each unit of product must be processed on two assembly lines, where the required production times are as follows.

	Hours/Unit	
Product	Line 1	Line 2
A	12	4
B	4	8
Total hours	60	40

   a. Formulate a linear programming model to determine the optimal product mix that will maximize profit.
   b. Transform this model into standard form.

11. Solve Problem 10 graphically.
   a. Identify the amount of unused resources (i.e., slack) at each of the graphical extreme points.
   b. What would be the effect on the optimal solution if the production time on line 1 was reduced to 40 hours?
   c. What would be the effect on the optimal solution if the profit for product B was increased from \$7 to \$15? to \$20?

12. For the linear programming model formulated in Problem 10 and solved graphically in Problem 11:
   a. Determine the sensitivity ranges for the objective function coefficients, using graphical analysis.
   b. Verify the sensitivity ranges determined in (a) by using the computer.
   c. Using the computer, determine the shadow prices for additional hours of production time on line 1 and line 2 and indicate whether the company would prefer additional line 1 or line 2 hours.

13. Irwin Textile Mills produces two types of cotton cloth—denim and corduroy. Corduroy is a heavier grade of cotton cloth and, as such, requires 7.5 pounds of raw cotton per yard, whereas denim requires 5 pounds of raw cotton per yard. A yard of corduroy requires 3.2 hours of processing time; a yard of denim requires 3.0 hours. Although the demand for denim is practically unlimited, the maximum demand for corduroy is 510 yards per month. The manufacturer has 6,500 pounds of

cotton and 3,000 hours of processing time available each month. The manufacturer makes a profit of $2.25 per yard of denim and $3.10 per yard of corduroy. The manufacturer wants to know how many yards of each type of cloth to produce to maximize profit.

a. Formulate a linear programming model for this problem.
b. Transform this model into standard form.

14. Solve the model formulated in Problem 13 for Irwin Textile Mills graphically.
    a. How much extra cotton and processing time are left over at the optimal solution? Is the demand for corduroy met?
    b. What is the effect on the optimal solution if the profit per yard of denim is increased from $2.25 to $3.00? What is the effect if the profit per yard of corduroy is increased from $3.10 to $4.00?
    c. What would be the effect on the optimal solution if Irwin Mills could obtain only 6,000 pounds of cotton per month?

15. Solve the linear programming model formulated in Problem 13 for Irwin Mills by using the computer.
    a. If Irwin Mills can obtain additional cotton or processing time, but not both, which should it select? How much? Explain your answer.
    b. Identify the sensitivity ranges for the objective function coefficients and for the constraint quantity values. Then explain the sensitivity range for the demand for corduroy.

16. United Aluminum Company of Cincinnati produces three grades (high, medium, and low) of aluminum at two mills. Each mill has a different production capacity (in tons per day) for each grade, as follows:

Aluminum Grade	**Mill** 1	2
High	6	2
Medium	2	2
Low	4	10

The company has contracted with a manufacturing firm to supply at least 12 tons of high-grade aluminum, 8 tons of medium-grade aluminum, and 5 tons of low-grade aluminum. It costs United $6,000 per day to operate mill 1 and $7,000 per day to operate mill 2. The company wants to know the number of days to operate each mill in order to meet the contract at the minimum cost.

Formulate a linear programming model for this problem.

17. Solve the linear programming model formulated in Problem 16 for United Aluminum Company graphically.
    a. How much extra (i.e., surplus) high-, medium-, and low-grade aluminum does the company produce at the optimal solution?
    b. What would be the effect on the optimal solution if the cost of operating mill 1 increased from $6,000 to $7,500 per day?
    c. What would be the effect on the optimal solution if the company could supply only 10 tons of high-grade aluminum?

18. Solve the linear programming model formulated in Problem 16 for United Aluminum Company by using the computer.
    a. Identify and explain the shadow prices for each of the aluminum grade contract requirements.
    b. Identify the sensitivity ranges for the objective function coefficients and the constraint quantity values.

c. Would the solution values change if the contract requirements for high-grade aluminum were increased from 12 tons to 20 tons? If yes, what would the new solution values be?

19. The Bradley family owns 410 acres of farmland in North Carolina on which they grow corn and tobacco. Each acre of corn costs $105 to plant, cultivate, and harvest; each acre of tobacco costs $210. The Bradleys have a budget of $52,500 for next year. The government limits the number of acres of tobacco that can be planted to 100. The profit from each acre of corn is $300; the profit from each acre of tobacco is $520. The Bradleys want to know how many acres of each crop to plant in order to maximize their profit.

    Formulate a linear programming model for this problem.

20. Solve the linear programming model formulated in Problem 19 for the Bradley family farm graphically.
    a. How many acres of farmland will not be cultivated at the optimal solution? Do the Bradleys use the entire 100-acre tobacco allotment?
    b. What would the profit for corn have to be for the Bradleys to plant only corn?
    c. If the Bradleys can obtain an additional 100 acres of land, will the number of acres of corn and tobacco they plan to grow change?
    d. If the Bradleys decide not to cultivate a 50-acre section as part of a crop recovery program, how will it affect their crop plans?

21. Solve the linear programming model formulated in Problem 19 for the Bradley farm by using the computer.
    a. The Bradleys have an opportunity to lease some extra land from a neighbor. The neighbor is offering the land to them for $110 per acre. Should the Bradleys lease the land at that price? What is the maximum price the Bradleys should pay their neighbor for the land, and how much land should they lease at that price?
    b. The Bradleys are considering taking out a loan to increase their budget. For each dollar they borrow, how much additional profit would they make? If they borrowed an additional $1,000, would the number of acres of corn and tobacco they plant change?

22. The manager of a Burger Doodle franchise wants to determine how many sausage biscuits and ham biscuits to prepare each morning for breakfast customers. The two types of biscuits require the following resources:

Biscuit	**Labor (hr.)**	**Sausage (lb.)**	**Ham (lb.)**	**Flour (lb.)**
Sausage	0.010	0.10	—	0.04
Ham	0.024	—	0.15	0.04

    The franchise has 6 hours of labor available each morning. The manager has a contract with a local grocer for 30 pounds of sausage and 30 pounds of ham each morning. The manager also purchases 16 pounds of flour. The profit for a sausage biscuit is $0.60; the profit for a ham biscuit is $0.50. The manager wants to know the number of each type of biscuit to prepare each morning in order to maximize profit.

    Formulate a linear programming model for this problem.

23. Solve the linear programming model formulated in Problem 22 for the Burger Doodle restaurant graphically.
    a. How much extra sausage and ham is left over at the optimal solution point? Is there any idle labor time?
    b. What would the solution be if the profit for a ham biscuit were increased from $0.50 to $0.60?

c. What would be the effect on the optimal solution if the manager could obtain 2 more pounds of flour?

24. Solve the linear programming model developed in Problem 22 for the Burger Doodle restaurant by using the computer.
    a. Identify and explain the shadow prices for each of the resource constraints.
    b. Which of the resources constraints profit the most?
    c. Identify the sensitivity ranges for the profit of a sausage biscuit and the amount of sausage available. Explain these sensitivity ranges.

25. Rucklehouse Public Relations has been contracted to do a survey following an election primary in New Hampshire. The firm must assign interviewers to conduct the survey by telephone or in person. One person can conduct 80 telephone interviews or 40 personal interviews in a single day. The following criteria have been established by the firm to ensure a representative survey:
    - At least 3,000 interviews must be conducted.
    - At least 1,000 interviews must be by telephone.
    - At least 800 interviews must be personal.

    An interviewer conducts only one type of interview each day. The cost is \$50 per day for a telephone interviewer and \$70 per day for a personal interviewer. The firm wants to know the minimum number of interviewers to hire in order to minimize the total cost of the survey.

    Formulate a linear programming model for this problem.

26. Solve the linear programming model formulated in Problem 25 for Rucklehouse Public Relations graphically.
    a. Determine the sensitivity ranges for the daily cost of a telephone interviewer and the number of personal interviews required.
    b. Does the firm conduct any more telephone and personal interviews than are required, and if so, how many more?
    c. What would be the effect on the optimal solution if the firm was required by the client to increase the number of personal interviews conducted from 800 to a total of 1,200?

27. Solve the linear programming model formulated in Problem 25 for Rucklehouse Public Relations by using the computer.
    a. If the firm could reduce the minimum interview requirement for either telephone or personal interviews, which should the firm select? How much would a reduction of one interview in the requirement you selected reduce total cost? Solve the model again, using the computer, with the reduction of this one interview in the constraint requirement to verify your answer.
    b. Identify the sensitivity ranges for the cost of a personal interview and the number of total interviews required.

28. The Bluegrass Distillery produces custom-blended whiskey. A particular blend consists of rye and bourbon whiskey. The company has received an order for a minimum of 400 gallons of the custom blend. The customer specified that the order must contain at least 40% rye and not more than 250 gallons of bourbon. The customer also specified that the blend should be mixed in the ratio of two parts rye to one part bourbon. The distillery can produce 500 gallons per week, regardless of the blend. The production manager wants to complete the order in 1 week. The blend is sold for \$5 per gallon.

    The distillery company's cost per gallon is \$2 for rye and \$1 for bourbon. The company wants to determine the blend mix that will meet customer requirements and maximize profits.

    Formulate a linear programming model for this problem.

29. Solve the linear programming model formulated in Problem 28 for the Bluegrass Distillery graphically.
    a. Indicate the slack and surplus available at the optimal solution point and explain their meanings.
    b. What increase in the objective function coefficients in this model would change the optimal solution point? Explain your answer.

30. Solve the linear programming model formulated in Problem 28 for the Bluegrass Distillery by using the computer.
    a. Identify the sensitivity ranges for the objective function coefficients and explain what the upper and lower limits are.
    b. How much would it be worth to the distillery to obtain additional production capacity?
    c. If the customer decided to change the blend requirement for its custom-made whiskey to a mix of three parts rye to one part bourbon, how would this change the optimal solution?

31. Alexis Harrington received an inheritance of \$95,000, and she is considering two speculative investments—the purchase of land and the purchase of cattle. Each investment would be for 1 year. Under the present (normal) economic conditions, each dollar invested in land will return the principal plus 20% of the principal; each dollar invested in cattle will return the principal plus 30%. However, both investments are relatively risky. If economic conditions were to deteriorate, there is an 18% chance she would lose everything she invested in land and a 30% chance she would lose everything she invested in cattle. Alexis does not want to lose more than \$20,000 (on average). She wants to know how much to invest in each alternative to maximize the cash value of the investments at the end of 1 year.

    Formulate a linear programming model for this problem.

32. Solve the linear programming model formulated in Problem 31 for Alexis Harrington graphically.
    a. How much would the return for cattle have to increase in order for Alexis to invest only in cattle?
    b. Should all of Alexis's inheritance be invested according to the optimal solution?
    c. How much "profit" would the optimal solution earn Alexis over and above her investment?

33. Solve the linear programming model formulated in Problem 31 for Alexis Harrington by using the computer.
    a. If Alexis decided to invest some of her own savings along with the money from her inheritance, what return would she realize for each dollar of her own money that she invested? How much of her own savings could she invest before this return would change?
    b. If the risk of losing the investment in land increased to 30%, how would this change the optimal investment mix?

34. Transform the following linear programming model into standard form and solve by using the computer:

$$\text{maximize } Z = 140x_1 + 205x_2 + 190x_3$$

subject to

$$10x_1 + 15x_2 + 8x_3 \leq 610$$

$$\frac{x_1}{x_2} \leq 3$$

$$x_1 \geq 0.4\,(x_1 + x_2 + x_3)$$

$$x_2 \geq x_3$$

$$x_1, x_2, x_3 \geq 0$$

35. Chemco Corporation produces a chemical mixture for a specific customer in 1,000-pound batches. The mixture contains three ingredients—zinc, mercury, and potassium. The mixture must conform to formula specifications that are supplied by the customer. The company wants to know the amount of each ingredient it needs to put in the mixture that will meet all the requirements of the mix and minimize total cost.

    The customer has supplied the following formula specifications for each batch of mixture:

    - The mixture must contain at least 200 pounds of mercury.
    - The mixture must contain at least 300 pounds of zinc.
    - The mixture must contain at least 100 pounds of potassium.
    - The ratio of potassium to the other two ingredients cannot exceed 1 to 4.

    The cost per pound of mercury is \$400; the cost per pound of zinc, \$180; and the cost per pound of potassium, \$90.

    a. Formulate a linear programming model for this problem.
    b. Solve the model formulated in (a) by using the computer.

36. The following linear programming model formulation is used for the production of four different products, with two different manufacturing processes and two different material requirements:

$$
\begin{aligned}
&\text{maximize } Z = \$50x_1 + 58x_2 + 46x_3 + 62x_4\\
&\text{subject to}\\
&4x_1 + 3.5x_2 + 4.6x_3 + 3.9x_4 \leq 600 \text{ hr. (process 1)}\\
&2.1x_1 + 2.6x_2 + 3.5x_3 + 1.9x_4 \leq 500 \text{ hr. (process 2)}\\
&15x_1 + 23x_2 + 18x_3 + 25x_4 \leq 3{,}600 \text{ lb. (material A)}\\
&8x_1 + 12.6x_2 + 9.7x_3 + 10.5x_4 \leq 1{,}700 \text{ lb. (material B)}\\
&\frac{x_1 + x_2}{x_1 + x_2 + x_3 + x_4} \geq .60\\
&x_1, x_2, x_3, x_4 \geq 0
\end{aligned}
$$

    a. Solve this problem by using the computer.
    b. Identify the sensitivity ranges for the objective function coefficients and the constraint quantity values.
    c. Which is the most valuable resource to the firm?
    d. One of the four products is not produced in the optimal solution. How much would the profit for this product have to be for it to be produced?

37. Island Publishing Company publishes two types of magazines on a monthly basis: a restaurant and entertainment guide and a real estate guide. The company distributes the magazines free to businesses, hotels, and stores on Hilton Head Island in South Carolina. The company's profits come exclusively from the paid advertising in the magazines. Each of the restaurant and entertainment guides distributed generates \$0.50 per magazine in advertising revenue, whereas the real estate guide generates \$0.75 per magazine. The real estate magazine is a more sophisticated publication that includes color photos, and accordingly it costs \$0.25 per magazine to print, compared with only \$0.17 for the restaurant and entertainment guide. The publishing company has a printing budget of \$4,000 per month. There is enough rack space to distribute at most 18,000 magazines each month. In order to entice businesses to place advertisements, Island Publishing promises to distribute at least 8,000 copies of each magazine. The company wants to determine the number of copies of each magazine it should print each month in order to maximize advertising revenue.

    Formulate a linear programming model for this problem.

38. Solve the linear programming model formulation in Problem 37 for Island Publishing Company graphically.
    a. Determine the sensitivity range for the advertising revenue generated by the real estate guide.
    b. Does the company spend all of its printing budget? If not, how much slack is left over?
    c. What would be the effect on the optimal solution if the local real estate agents insisted that 12,000 copies of the real estate guide be distributed instead of the current 8,000 copies, or they would withdraw their advertising?

39. Solve the linear programming model formulated in Problem 37 for Island Publishing Company by using the computer.
    a. How much would it be worth to Island Publishing Company to obtain enough additional rack space to distribute 18,500 copies instead of the current 18,000 copies? 20,000 copies?
    b. How much would it be worth to Island Publishing to reduce the requirement to distribute the entertainment guide from 8,000 to 7,000 copies?

40. Mega-Mart, a discount store chain, is to build a new store in Rock Springs. The parcel of land the company has purchased is large enough to accommodate a store with 140,000 square feet of floor space. Based on marketing and demographic surveys of the area and historical data from its other stores, Mega-Mart estimates its annual profit per square foot for each of the store's departments to be as shown in the following table:

Department	Profit per ft.^{2}
Men's clothing	$4.25
Women's clothing	5.10
Children's clothing	4.50
Toys	5.20
Housewares	4.10
Electronics	4.90
Auto supplies	3.80

Each department must have at least 15,000 square feet of floor space, and no department can have more than 20% of the total retail floor space. Men's, women's, and children's clothing plus housewares keep all their stock on the retail floor; however, toys, electronics, and auto supplies keep some items (such as bicycles, televisions, and tires) in inventory. Thus, 10% of the total retail floor space devoted to these three departments must be set aside outside the retail area for stocking inventory. Mega-Mart wants to know the floor space that should be devoted to each department in order to maximize profit.
    a. Formulate a linear programming model for this problem.
    b. Solve this model by using the computer.

41. a. In Problem 40 Mega-Mart is considering purchasing a parcel of land adjacent to the current site on which it plans to build its store. The cost of the parcel is $190,000, and it would enable Mega-Mart to increase the size of its store to 160,000 square feet. Discuss whether Mega-Mart should purchase the land and increase the planned size of the store.
    b. Suppose that the profit per square foot will decline in all departments by 20% if the store size increases to 160,000 square feet. (If the stock does not turn over as fast, increasing inventory costs will reduce profit.) How might this affect Mega-Mart's decision in (a)?

42. The Food Max grocery store sells three brands of milk in half-gallon cartons—its own brand, a local dairy brand, and a national brand. The profit from its own brand is $0.97 per carton, the profit from the local dairy brand is $0.83 per carton, and the profit from the national brand is $0.69 per

carton. The total refrigerated shelf space allotted to half-gallon cartons of milk is 36 square feet per week. A half-gallon carton takes up 16 square inches of shelf space. The store manager knows that each week Food Max always sells more of the national brand than of the local dairy brand and its own brand combined and at least three times as much of the national brand as its own brand. In addition, the local dairy can supply only 10 dozen cartons per week. The store manager wants to know how many half-gallon cartons of each brand to stock each week in order to maximize profit.

a. Formulate a linear programming model for this problem.
b. Solve this model by using the computer.

43. a. If Food Max in Problem 42 could increase its shelf space for half-gallon cartons of milk, how much would profit increase per carton?
b. If Food Max could get the local dairy to increase the amount of milk it could supply each week, would it increase profit?
c. Food Max is considering discounting its own brand in order to increase sales. If it were to do so, it would decrease the profit margin for its own brand to $0.86 per carton, but it would cut the demand for the national brand relative to its own brand in half. Discuss whether the store should implement the price discount.

44. John Hoke owns Hoke's Spokes, a bicycle shop. Most of John's bicycle sales are customer orders; however, he also stocks bicycles for walk-in customers. He stocks three types of bicycles—road-racing, cross-country, and mountain. A road-racing bike costs $1,200, a cross-country bike costs $1,700, and a mountain bike costs $900. He sells road-racing bikes for $1,800, cross-country bikes for $2,100, and mountain bikes for $1,200. He has $12,000 available this month to purchase bikes. Each bike must be assembled; a road-racing bike requires 8 hours to assemble, a cross-country bike requires 12 hours, and a mountain bike requires 16 hours. He estimates that he and his employees have 120 hours available to assemble bikes. He has enough space in his store to order 20 bikes this month. Based on past sales, John wants to stock at least twice as many mountain bikes as the other two combined because mountain bikes sell better.

Formulate a linear programming model for this problem.

45. Solve the linear programming model formulated in Problem 44 for Hoke's Spokes by using the computer.
a. Should John Hoke try to increase his budget for purchasing bikes, increase space to stock bikes, or increase labor hours to assemble bikes? Why?
b. If John hired an additional worker for 30 hours at $10 per hour, how much additional profit would he make, if any?
c. If John purchased a cheaper cross-country bike for $1,200 and sold it for $1,900, would this affect the original solution?

46. Metro Food Services Company delivers fresh sandwiches each morning to vending machines throughout the city. The company makes three kinds of sandwiches—ham and cheese, bologna, and chicken salad. A ham and cheese sandwich requires a worker 0.45 minutes to assemble, a bologna sandwich requires 0.41 minutes, and a chicken salad sandwich requires 0.50 minutes to make. The company has 960 available minutes each night for sandwich assembly. Vending machine capacity is available for 2,000 sandwiches each day. The profit for a ham and cheese sandwich is $0.35, the profit for a bologna sandwich is $0.42, and the profit for a chicken salad sandwich is $0.37. The company knows from past sales records that its customers buy as many ham and cheese sandwiches as the other two sandwiches combined, if not more so, but customers need a variety of sandwiches available, so Metro stocks at least 200 of each. Metro management wants to know how many of each sandwich it should stock to maximize profit.

Formulate a linear programming model for this problem.

47. Solve the linear programming model formulated in Problem 46 for Metro Food Services Company by using the computer.
    a. If Metro Food Services could hire another worker and increase its available assembly time by 480 minutes or increase its vending machine capacity by 100 sandwiches, which should it do? Why? How much additional profit would your decision result in?
    b. What would the effect be on the optimal solution if the requirement that at least 200 sandwiches of each kind be stocked was eliminated? Compare the profit between the optimal solution and this solution. Which solution would you recommend?
    c. What would the effect be on the optimal solution if the profit for a ham and cheese sandwich was increased to \$0.40? to \$0.45?

48. Mountain Laurel Vineyards produces three kinds of wine—Mountain Blanc, Mountain Red, and Mountain Blush. The company has 17 tons of grapes available to produce wine this season. A cask of Blanc requires 0.21 ton of grapes, a cask of Red requires 0.24 ton, and a cask of Blush requires 0.18 ton. The vineyard has enough storage space in its aging room to store 80 casks of wine.

    The vineyard has 2,500 hours of production capacity, and it requires 12 hours to produce a cask of Blanc, 14.5 hours to produce a cask of Red, and 16 hours to produce a cask of Blush. From past sales the vineyard knows that demand for the Blush will be no more than half of the sales of the other two wines combined. The profit for a cask of Blanc is \$7,500, the profit for a cask of Red is \$8,200, and the profit for a cask of Blush is \$10,500.

    Formulate a linear programming model for this problem.

49. Solve the linear programming model formulated in Problem 48 for Mountain Laurel Vineyards by using the computer.
    a. If the vineyard determined that the profit from Red was \$7,600 instead of \$8,200, how would that affect the optimal solution?
    b. If the vineyard could secure one additional unit of any of the resources used in the production of wine, which one should it select?
    c. If the vineyard could obtain 0.5 ton more of grapes, 500 more hours of production capacity, or enough storage capacity to store 4 more casks of wine, which should it choose?
    d. All three wines are produced in the optimal solution. How little would the profit for Blanc have to be for it to no longer be produced?

50. Exeter Mines produces iron ore at four different mines; however, the ores extracted at each mine are different in their iron content. Mine 1 produces magnetite ore, which has a 70% iron content; mine 2 produces limonite ore, which has a 60% iron content; mine 3 produces pyrite ore, which has a 50% iron content; and mine 4 produces taconite ore, which has only a 30% iron content. Exeter has three customers that produce steel—Armco, Best, and Corcom. Armco needs 400 tons of pure (100%) iron, Best requires 250 tons of pure iron, and Corcom requires 290 tons. It costs \$37 to extract and process 1 ton of magnetite ore at mine 1, \$46 to produce 1 ton of limonite ore at mine 2, \$50 per ton of pyrite ore at mine 3, and \$42 per ton of taconite ore at mine 4. Exeter can extract 350 tons of ore at mine 1; 530 tons at mine 2; 610 tons at mine 3; and 490 tons at mine 4. The company wants to know how much ore to produce at each mine in order to minimize cost and meet its customers' demand for pure (100%) iron.

    Formulate a linear programming model for this problem.

51. Solve the linear programming model formulated in Problem 50 for Exeter Mines by using the computer.
    a. Do any of the mines have slack capacity? If yes, which one(s)?
    b. If Exeter Mines could increase production capacity at any one of its mines, which should it be? Why?

c. If Exeter decided to increase capacity at the mine identified in (b), how much could it increase capacity before the optimal solution point (i.e., the optimal set of variables) would change?
d. If Exeter determined that it could increase production capacity at mine 1 from 350 tons to 500 tons, at an increase in production costs to $43 per ton, should it do so?

52. Given the following linear programming model:

$$\text{minimize } Z = 8.2x_1 + 7.0x_2 + 6.5x_3 + 9.0x_4$$

subject to

$$6x_1 + 2x_2 + 5x_3 + 7x_4 \geq 820$$

$$\frac{x_1}{x_1 + x_2 + x_3 + x_4} \geq 0.3$$

$$\frac{x_2 + x_3}{x_1 + x_4} \leq 0.2$$

$$x_3 \geq x_1 + x_4$$

$$x_1, x_2, x_3, x_4 \geq 0$$

transform the model into standard form and solve by using the computer.

53. Marie McCoy has committed to the local PTA to make some items for a bake sale on Saturday. She has decided to make some combination of chocolate cakes, loaves of white bread, custard pies, and sugar cookies. Thursday evening she went to the store and purchased 20 pounds of flour, 10 pounds of sugar, and 3 dozen eggs, which are the three main ingredients in all the baked goods she is thinking about making. The following table shows how much of each of the main ingredients is required for each baked good:

	Ingredient			
	Flour (cups)	Sugar (cups)	Eggs	Baking Time (min.)
Cake	2.5	2	2	45
Bread	9	0.25	0	35
Pie	1.3	1	5	50
Cookies	2.5	1	2	16

There are 18.5 cups in a 5 pound bag of flour and 12 cups in a 5 pound bag of sugar. Marie plans to get up and start baking on Friday morning after her kids leave for school and finish before they return after soccer practice (8 hours). She knows that the PTA will sell a chocolate cake for $12, a loaf of bread for $8, a custard pie for $10, and a batch of cookies for $6. Marie wants to decide how many of each type of baked good she should make in order for the PTA to make the most money possible.

Formulate a linear programming model for this problem.

54. Solve the linear programming model formulated in Problem 53 for Marie McCoy.
a. Are any of the ingredients left over?
b. If Marie could get more of any ingredient, which should it be? Why?
c. If Marie could get 6 more eggs, 20 more cups of flour, or 30 more minutes of oven time, which should she choose? Why?
d. The solution values for this problem should logically be integers. If the solution values are not integers, discuss how Marie should decide how many of each item to bake. How do total sales for this integer solution compare with those in the original, noninteger solution?

55. The Wisham family lives on a farm in South Georgia on which it produces a variety of crops and livestock, including pecans. It has 5 acres of pecan trees that yield approximately 1,000 pounds of unshelled pecans per acre each year. The family uses all of its pecan harvest to produce pecan pies, cookies, 1-pound bags of shelled pecans, and 5-pound bags of unshelled pecans, which it sells in town at the local farmers' market. The family sells pies for \$5, packages of a dozen cookies for \$3, bags of shelled pecans for \$7, and bags of unshelled pecans for \$16. A shelled pecan is half the weight of an unshelled pecan. It requires 4 ounces of shelled pecans to make a pie, and 6 ounces of shelled pecans to make a dozen cookies. The pies and cookies are baked in the family oven, and there are 120 hours of baking time available. It takes 55 minutes to bake a batch of 4 pies and 15 minutes to bake a batch of 2 dozen cookies. It requires family members 6 minutes to shell the pecans for a pie and package it, 4 minutes to shell the pecans for cookies and to package them, 10 minutes to shell the pecans for a 1 lb. bag of shelled pecans and package them, and 1 minute to package a bag of unshelled pecans; and there are 300 hours available from family members for shelling and packaging. The Wisham family wants to know how many pecan pies, dozens of cookies, and bags of shelled and unshelled pecans to produce in order to maximize its sales revenues.

    Formulate a linear programming model for this problem.

56. Solve the linear programming model formulated in Problem 55 for the Wisham family farm using the computer.
    a. Are there any extra (slack) resources available?
    b. If the Wishman family could obtain additional resources, which one would be of most value to them? How much would they be willing to pay for this resource? Why?
    c. If the family could obtain an additional 500 pounds of pecans or 30 hours of oven time, which should they choose?
    d. The family is thinking about buying a bigger oven for \$3,000. If they do so, they could make a batch of 5 pies or a batch 3 dozen cookies at one time. Should they buy the oven? Explain your answer.

57. During the winter WeeMow Lawn Service contracts with customers for cutting lawns starting in the spring. WeeMow provides service to residential and commercial customers. The service has identified 50 possible residential customers and 15 potential commercial customers it has contacted. WeeMow services a customer once every 2 weeks during the growing season. A residential lawn on average takes 1.2 hours to cut, and a commercial property requires 5 hours to cut; the service's available work time is 8 hours, 6 days per week. The profit for a residential lawn is \$23, and the profit for a commercial property is \$61. The service has established a weekly budget of \$350 for management, gas, and other materials, plus equipment repair. A residential lawn averages \$12 in management, gas, material, and repair costs, and a commercial property averages \$20 in costs. WeeMow wants to know how many residential and commercial jobs it should contract for from among its potential customers in order to maximize profits.
    a. Formulate a linear programming model for this problem.
    b. Solve this model graphically.

58. Solve the liner programming model for WeeMow Lawn Service in Problem 57 using the computer.
    a. Which resources constrain how many jobs the service can contract for?
    b. If WeeMow could increase its weekly budget by \$50 per week, or increase its workday to 9 hours, which would be more profitable?
    c. The solution to this problem should logically be integer, that is, whole jobs; however, the optimal solution is not integer. How would you suggest that WeeMow address this discrepancy? Do you think there is a way to handle this problem with the computer program you are using to solve this problem?

Case Problem

Mossaic Tiles, Ltd.

Gilbert Moss and Angela Pasaic spent several summers during their college years working at archaeological sites in the Southwest. While at those digs, they learned how to make ceramic tiles from local artisans. After college they made use of their college experiences to start a tile manufacturing firm called Mossaic Tiles, Ltd. They opened their plant in New Mexico, where they would have convenient access to a special clay they intend to use to make a clay derivative for their tiles. Their manufacturing operation consists of a few relatively simple but precarious steps, including molding the tiles, baking, and glazing.

Gilbert and Angela plan to produce two basic types of tile for use in home bathrooms, kitchens, sunrooms, and laundry rooms. The two types of tile are a larger, single-colored tile and a smaller, patterned tile. In the manufacturing process, the color or pattern is added before a tile is glazed. Either a single color is sprayed over the top of a baked set of tiles or a stenciled pattern is sprayed on the top of a baked set of tiles.

The tiles are produced in batches of 100. The first step is to pour the clay derivative into specially constructed molds. It takes 18 minutes to mold a batch of 100 larger tiles and 15 minutes to prepare a mold for a batch of 100 smaller tiles. The company has 60 hours available each week for molding. After the tiles are molded, they are baked in a kiln: 0.27 hour for a batch of 100 larger tiles and 0.58 hour for a batch of 100 smaller tiles. The company has 105 hours available each week for baking. After baking, the tiles are either colored or patterned and glazed. This process takes 0.16 hour for a batch of 100 larger tiles and 0.20 hour for a batch of 100 smaller tiles. Forty hours are available each week for the glazing process. Each batch of 100 large tiles requires 32.8 pounds of the clay derivative to produce, whereas each batch of smaller tiles requires 20 pounds. The company has 6,000 pounds of the clay derivative available each week.

Mossaic Tiles earns a profit of $190 for each batch of 100 of the larger tiles and $240 for each batch of 100 smaller patterned tiles. Angela and Gilbert want to know how many batches of each type of tile to produce each week to maximize profit. In addition, they have some questions about resource usage they would like answered.

A. Formulate a linear programming model for Mossaic Tiles, Ltd., and determine the mix of tiles it should manufacture each week.
B. Transform the model into standard form.
C. Solve the linear programming model graphically.
D. Determine the resources left over and not used at the optimal solution point.
E. Determine the sensitivity ranges for the objective function coefficients and constraint quantity values by using the graphical solution of the model.
F. For artistic reasons, Gilbert and Angela prefer to produce the smaller, patterned tiles. They also believe that in the long run, the smaller tiles will be a more successful product. What must the profit be for the smaller tiles in order for the company to produce only the smaller tiles?
G. Solve the linear programming model by using the computer and verify the sensitivity ranges computed in (E).
H. Mossaic believes it may be able to reduce the time required for molding to 16 minutes for a batch of larger tiles and 12 minutes for a batch of smaller tiles. How will this affect the solution?
I. The company that provides Mossaic with clay has indicated that it can deliver an additional 100 pounds each week. Should Mossaic agree to this offer?
J. Mossaic is considering adding capacity to one of its kilns to provide 20 additional glazing hours per week, at a cost of $90,000. Should it make the investment?
K. The kiln for glazing had to be shut down for 3 hours, reducing the available kiln hours from 40 to 37. What effect will this have on the solution?

Case Problem

"The Possibility" Restaurant—Continued

Angela Fox and Zooey Caulfield opened a French restaurant called "The Possibility." Initially, Angela and Zooey could not offer a full, varied menu, so their chef, Pierre, prepared two full-course dinners with beef and fish each evening. In the case problem, Angela and Zooey wanted to develop a linear programming model to help determine the number of beef and fish meals they should prepare each night. Solve Zooey and Angela's linear programming model by using the computer.

A. Angela and Zooey are considering investing in some advertising to increase the maximum number of meals they serve. They estimate that if they spend $30 per day on a newspaper ad, it will increase the maximum number of meals they serve per day from 60 to 70. Should they make the investment?
B. Zooey and Angela are concerned about the reliability of some of their kitchen staff. They estimate that on some evenings they could have a staff reduction of as much as 5 hours. How would this affect their profit level?

C. The final question they would like to explore is raising the price of the fish dinner. Angela believes the price for a fish dinner is a little low and that it could be closer to the price of a beef dinner without affecting customer demand. However, Zooey has noted that Pierre has already made plans based on the number of dinners recommended by the linear programming solution. Angela has suggested a price increase that will increase profit for the fish dinner to $14. Would this be acceptable to Pierre, and how much additional profit would be realized?

Case Problem

JULIA'S FOOD BOOTH

Julia Robertson is a senior at Tech, and she's investigating different ways to finance her final year at school. She is considering leasing a food booth outside the Tech stadium at home football games. Tech sells out every home game, and Julia knows, from attending the games herself, that everyone eats a lot of food. She has to pay $1,000 per game for a booth, and the booths are not very large. Vendors can sell either food or drinks on Tech property, but not both. Only the Tech athletic department concession stands can sell both inside the stadium. She thinks slices of cheese pizza, hot dogs, and barbecue sandwiches are the most popular food items among fans and so these are the items she would sell.

Most food items are sold during the hour before the game starts and during half time; thus it will not be possible for Julia to prepare the food while she is selling it. She must prepare the food ahead of time and then store it in a warming oven. For $600 she can lease a warming oven for the six-game home season. The oven has 16 shelves, and each shelf is 3 feet by 4 feet. She plans to fill the oven with the three food items before the game and then again before half time.

Julia has negotiated with a local pizza delivery company to deliver 14-inch cheese pizzas twice each game—2 hours before the game and right after the opening kickoff. Each pizza will cost her $6 and will include 8 slices. She estimates it will cost her $0.45 for each hot dog and $0.90 for each barbecue sandwich if she makes the barbecue herself the night before. She measured a hot dog and found it takes up about 16 square inches of space, whereas a barbecue sandwich takes up about 25 square inches. She plans to sell a slice of pizza and a hot dog for $1.50 apiece and a barbecue sandwich for $2.25. She has $1,500 in cash available to purchase and prepare the food items for the first home game; for the remaining five games she will purchase her ingredients with money she has made from the previous game.

Julia has talked to some students and vendors who have sold food at previous football games at Tech as well as at other universities. From this she has discovered that she can expect to sell at least as many slices of pizza as hot dogs and barbecue sandwiches combined. She also anticipates that she will probably sell at least twice as many hot dogs as barbecue sandwiches. She believes that she will sell everything she can stock and develop a customer base for the season if she follows these general guidelines for demand.

If Julia clears at least $1,000 in profit for each game after paying all her expenses, she believes it will be worth leasing the booth.

A. Formulate and solve a linear programming model for Julia that will help you advise her if she should lease the booth.

B. If Julia were to borrow some more money from a friend before the first game to purchase more ingredients, could she increase her profit? If so, how much should she borrow and how much additional profit would she make? What factor constrains her from borrowing even more money than this amount (indicated in your answer to the previous question)?

C. When Julia looked at the solution in (A), she realized that it would be physically difficult for her to prepare all the hot dogs and barbecue sandwiches indicated in this solution. She believes she can hire a friend of hers to help her for $100 per game. Based on the results in (A) and (B), is this something you think she could reasonably do and should do?

D. Julia seems to be basing her analysis on the assumption that everything will go as she plans. What are some of the uncertain factors in the model that could go wrong and adversely affect Julia's analysis? Given these uncertainties and the results in (A), (B), and (C), what do you recommend that Julia do?

References

Baumol, W. J. *Economic Theory and Operations Analysis*, 4th ed. Upper Saddle River, NJ: Prentice Hall, 1977.

Charnes, A., and Cooper, W. W. *Management Models and Industrial Applications of Linear Programming*. New York: John Wiley & Sons, 1961.

Dantzig, G. B. *Linear Programming and Extensions*. Princeton, NJ: Princeton University Press, 1963.

Gass, S. *Linear Programming*, 4th ed. New York: McGraw-Hill, 1975.

Hadley, G. *Linear Programming*. Reading, MA: Addison-Wesley, 1962.

Hillier, F. S., and Lieberman, G. J. *Introduction to Operations Research*, 4th ed. San Francisco: Holden-Day, 1986.

Llewellyn, R. W. *Linear Programming*. New York: Holt, Rinehart and Winston, 1964.

Taha, H. A. *Operations Research, an Introduction*, 4th ed. New York: Macmillan, 1987.

Wagner, H. M. *Principles of Operations Research*, 2nd ed. Upper Saddle River, NJ: Prentice Hall, 1975.

Solutions to Selected Odd-Numbered Problems

3. Cells: B10:B12; Constraints: B10:B12 ≥ 0, G6 $\leq$ F6, G7 $\leq$ F7; Profit: = B10*C4+B11*D4+B12*E4; Target cell = B13.

5. F6 = C6*B12 + D6*B13, F7 = C7*B12 + D7*B13, G6 = E6 − F6 G7 = E7 − F7, B14 = C4*B12 + D4*B13, $x_1 = 8, x_2 = 5.2, Z = 81.6$

7. (a and b) max. $Z = 12x_1 + 16x_2 + 0s_1 + 0s_2$; s.t. $3x_1 + 2x_2 + s_1 = 500$, $4x_1 + 5x_2 + s_2 = 800$, $x_i \geq 0$, $s_i \geq 0$

9. (a and b) $-\infty \leq c_1 \leq 12.8$, $15 \leq c_2 \leq \infty$, $320 \leq q_1 \leq \infty$, $0 \leq q_2 \leq 1{,}250$; (c) \$0, \$3.20

11. (a) $x_1 = 4, x_2 = 3, Z = 57$, A: $s_1 = 40, s_2 = 0$, B: $s_1 = 0, s_2 = 0$, C: $s_1 = 0, s_2 = 20$; (b) $x_1 = 2, x_2 = 4$; (c) solution point same for profit = \$15, new solution $x_1 = 0, x_2 = 5, Z = 100$ for profit = \$20

13. (a and b) max. $Z = 2.25x_1 + 3.10x_2 + 0s_1 + 0s_2 + 0s_3$; s.t. $5.0x_1 + 7.5x_2 + s_1 = 6{,}500$, $3.0x_1 + 3.2x_2 + s_2 = 3{,}000$, $x_2 + s_3 = 510$, $x_i \geq 0$, $s_j \geq 0$

15. (a) Additional processing time, \$0.75/hr.; (b) $0 \leq c_1 \leq 2.906$, $2.4 \leq c_2 \leq \infty$, $6{,}015 \leq q_1 \leq \infty$, $1{,}632 \leq q_2 \leq 3{,}237$, $0 \leq q_3 \leq 692.308$

17. (a) $x_1 = 4, x_2 = 0, s_1 = 12, s_2 = 0, s_3 = 11, Z = 24{,}000$; (b) $x_1 = 1$, $x_2 = 3, Z = 28{,}500$; (c) C still optimal

19. (a and b) max. $Z = 300x_1 + 520x_2$; s.t. $x_1 + x_2 = 410$, $105x_1 + 210x_2 = 52{,}500$, $x_2 = 100$, $x_i \geq 0$

21. (a) no, max. price = \$80; (b) \$2.095

23. (a) $x_1 = 300, x_2 = 100, s_1 = 0$ lb., $s_2 = 15$ lb., $s_4 = 0.6$ hr., $Z = 230$; (b) $c_1 = \$0.60, x_1 = 257, x_2 = 143, Z = 240$; (c) $x_1 = 300, x_2 = 125$, $Z = 242.50$

25. (a and b) min. $Z = 50x_1 + 70x_2$; s.t. $80x_1 + 40x_2 = 3{,}000$, $80x_1 = 1{,}000$, $40x_2 = 800$, x_i

27. (a) personal interviews, \$0.625/interview; (b) $25 \leq c_2 \leq \infty$, $1{,}800 \leq q_1 \leq \infty$

29. (a) $x_1 = 333.3, x_2 = 166.7, s_1 = 100$ gal., $s_2 = 133.3$ gal., $s_3 = 83.3$ gal., $s_4 = 100$ gal., $Z = 1{,}666$; (b) any values of c

31. max. $Z = 1.20x_1 + 1.30x_2$; s.t. $x_1 + x_2 \leq 95{,}000$, $.18x_1 + .30x_2 \leq 20{,}000$, $x_i \geq 0$

33. (a) 5%, \$16,111.11; (b) $x_1 = 0, x_2 = 66{,}666.7, Z = 86{,}666.67$

35. (a and b) min. $Z = 400x_1 + 180x_2 + 90x_3$; s.t. $x_1 \geq 200$, $x_2 \geq 300$, $x_3 \geq 100$, $4x_3 - x_1 - x_2 \leq 0$, $x_1 + x_2 + x_3 = 1{,}000$, $x_i \geq 0$; (c) $x_1 = 200, x_2 = 600, x_3 = 200, Z = 206{,}000$

37. max. $Z = 0.50x_1 + 0.75x_2$; s.t. $0.17x_1 + 0.25x_2 \leq 4{,}000$, $x_1 + x_2 \leq 18{,}000$, $x_1 \geq 8{,}000$, $x_2 \geq 8{,}000$, $x_1, x_2 \geq 0$; (b) max. $Z = 0.50x_1 + 0.75x_2$; $0.17x_1 + 0.25x_2 = 4{,}000$, $x_1 + x_2 = 18{,}000$, $x_1 = 8{,}000$, $x_2 = 8{,}000$, $x_i \geq 0$

39. $x_1 = 8{,}000, x_2 = 10{,}000, Z = 11{,}500$; (a) \$375; increase, $x_1 = 8{,}000$, $x_2 = 10{,}500, Z = \$11{,}875$; $x_1 = 8{,}000, x_2 = 10{,}560, Z = \$11{,}920$

41. (a) purchase land; (b) not purchase land

43. (a) \$0.78, 360 cartons; (b) \$0; (c) $x_1 = 108, x_2 = 54, x_3 = 162$, $Z = 249.48$, no discount

45. $x_1 = 3, x_3 = 6, Z = 3{,}600$; (a) more assembly hr.; (b) additional profit = \$600; (c) no effect

47. $x_1 = 1{,}000, x_2 = 800, x_3 = 200, Z = 760$; (a) increase by 100, \$38 in additional profit; (b) $x_1 = 1{,}000, x_2 = 1{,}000, Z = 770$; (c) $Z = 810$; $x_1 = 1{,}600, x_2 = 200, x_3 = 200$

49. $x_1 = 20, x_2 = 33.33, x_3 = 26.67, Z = \$703{,}333.4$

51. $x_{13} = 350, x_{21} = 158.33, x_{22} = 296.67, x_{23} = 75, x_{31} = 610, x_{42} = 240, Z = \$77{,}910$

53. max. $Z = 12x_1 + 8x_2 + 10x_3 + 6x_4$; s.t. $2x_1 + 9x_2 + 1.3x_3 + 2.5x_4 \leq 74$; $2x_1 + .25x_2 + x_3 + x_4 \leq 24$; $2x_1 + 5x_3 + 2x_4 \leq 36$; $45x_1 + 35x_2 + 50x_3 + 16x_4 \leq 480$, $x_i \geq 0$

55. max. $Z = \$5x_1 + 3x_2 + 7x_3 + 16x_4$; s.t. $8x_1 + 12x_2 + 32x_3 + 80x_4 \leq 80{,}000$, $\frac{55x_1}{4} + \frac{15x_2}{2} \leq 7{,}200$, $6x_1 + 4x_2 + 10x_3 + 1x_4 \leq 18{,}000$

57. (a) max. $Z = \$23x_1 + 61x_2$; s.t. $1.2x_1 + 5x_2 \leq 96$, $12x_1 + 20x_2 \leq 700$, $x_1 \leq 50$, $x_2 \leq 15$; (b) $x_1 = 43.89, x_2 = 8.67, Z = \$1{,}538.11$

Linear Programming: Modeling Examples

Linear Programming: Modeling Examples

In this chapter, more complex examples of model formulation are presented. These examples have been selected to illustrate some of the more popular application areas of linear programming. They also provide guidelines for model formulation for a variety of problems and computer solutions with Excel and QM for Windows.

You will notice as you go through each example that the model formulation is presented in a systematic format. First, decision variables are identified, then the objective function is formulated, and finally the model constraints are developed. Model formulation can be difficult and complicated, and it is usually beneficial to follow this set of steps in which you identify a specific model component at each step instead of trying to "see" the whole formulation after the first reading.

A Product Mix Example

Quick-Screen is a clothing manufacturing company that specializes in producing commemorative shirts immediately following major sporting events such as the World Series, Super Bowl, and Final Four. The company has been contracted to produce a standard set of shirts for the winning team, either State University or Tech, following a college football bowl game on New Year's Day. The items produced include two sweatshirts, one with silk-screen printing on the front and one with print on both sides, and two T-shirts of the same configuration. The company has to complete all production within 72 hours after the game, at which time a trailer truck will pick up the shirts. The company will work around the clock. The truck has enough capacity to accommodate 1,200 standard-size boxes. A standard-size box holds 12 T-shirts, and a box of 12 sweatshirts is three times the size of a standard box. The company has budgeted $25,000 for the production run. It has 500 dozen blank sweatshirts and T-shirts each in stock, ready for production. This scenario is illustrated in Figure 1.

The resource requirements, unit costs, and profit per dozen for each type of shirt are shown in the following table:

	Processing Time (hr.) per Dozen	Cost per Dozen	Profit per Dozen
Sweatshirt—F	0.10	$36	$ 90
Sweatshirt—B/F	0.25	48	125
T-shirt—F	0.08	25	45
T-shirt—B/F	0.21	35	65

The company wants to know how many dozen (boxes) of each type of shirt to produce in order to maximize profit.

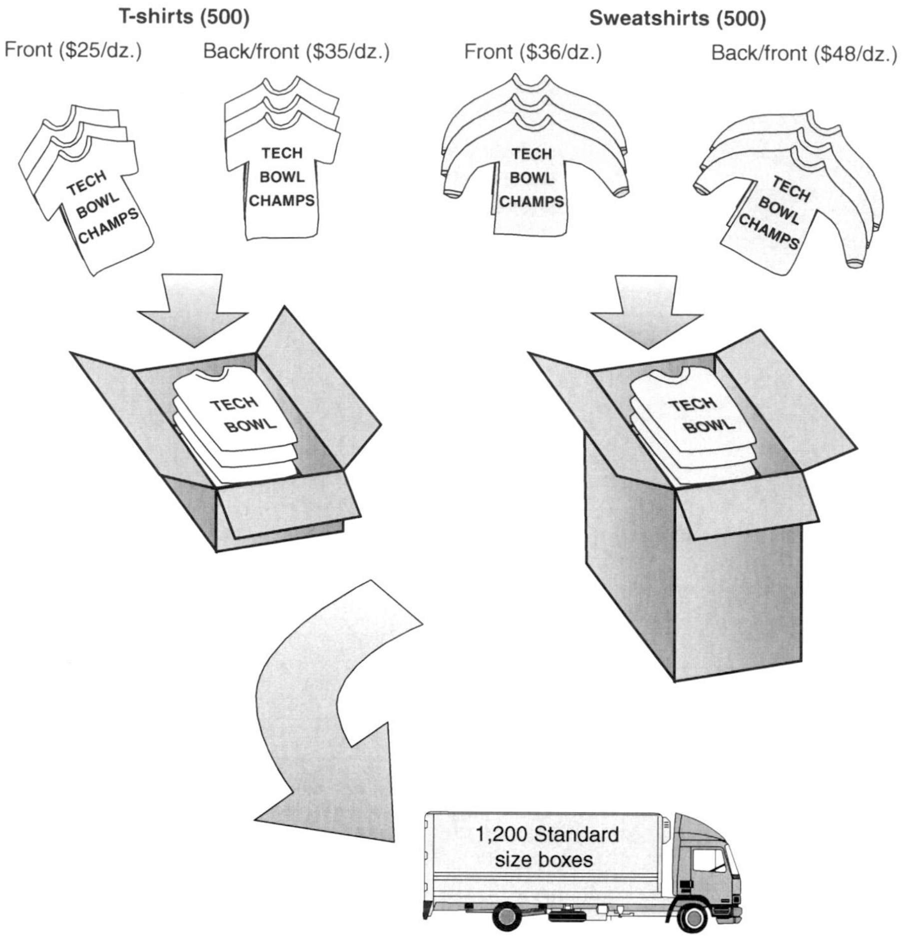

Figure 1 Quick-Screen Shirts

Following is a review of the model formulation steps for this problem:

Summary of Linear Programming Model Formulation Steps

Step 1: Define the decision variables

How many (dozens of) T-shirts and sweatshirts of each type to produce

Step 2: Define the objective function

Maximize profit

Step 3: Define the constraints

The resources available, including processing time, blank shirts, budget, and shipping capacity

Decision Variables

This problem contains four decision variables, representing the number of dozens (boxes) of each type of shirt to produce:

x_1 = sweatshirts, front printing
x_2 = sweatshirts, back and front printing

x_3 = T-shirts, front printing
x_4 = T-shirts, back and front printing

The Objective Function

The company's objective is to maximize profit. The total profit is the sum of the individual profits gained from each type of shirt. The objective function is expressed as

$$\text{maximize } Z = \$90x_1 + 125x_2 + 45x_3 + 65x_4$$

Model Constraints

The first constraint is for processing time. The total available processing time is the 72-hour period between the end of the game and the truck pickup:

$$0.10x_1 + 0.25x_2 + 0.08x_3 + 0.21x_4 \leq 72 \text{ hr}$$

The second constraint is for the available shipping capacity, which is 1,200 standard-size boxes. A box of sweatshirts is three times the size of a standard-size box. Thus, each box of sweatshirts is equivalent in size to three boxes of T-shirts. This relative size differential is expressed in the following constraint:

$$3x_1 + 3x_2 + x_3 + x_4 \leq 1{,}200 \text{ boxes}$$

The third constraint is for the cost budget. The total budget available for production is $25,000:

$$\$36x_1 + 48x_2 + 25x_3 + 35x_4 \leq \$25{,}000$$

The last two constraints reflect the available blank sweatshirts and T-shirts the company has in storage:

$$x_1 + x_2 \leq 500 \text{ dozen sweatshirts}$$
$$x_3 + x_4 \leq 500 \text{ dozen T-shirts}$$

Model Summary

The linear programming model for Quick-Screen is summarized as follows:

This model can be input as shown for computer solution.

$$\begin{aligned}
\text{maximize } Z &= 90x_1 + 125x_2 + 45x_3 + 65x_4 \\
\text{subject to} & \\
0.10x_1 + 0.25x_2 + 0.08x_3 + 0.21x_4 &\leq 72 \\
3x_1 + 3x_2 + x_3 + x_4 &\leq 1{,}200 \\
36x_1 + 48x_2 + 25x_3 + 35x_4 &\leq 25{,}000 \\
x_1 + x_2 &\leq 500 \\
x_3 + x_4 &\leq 500 \\
x_1, x_2, x_3, x_4 &\geq 0
\end{aligned}$$

Computer Solution with Excel

The Excel spreadsheet solution for this product mix example is shown in Exhibit 1. The decision variables are located in cells **B14:B17**. The profit is computed in cell B18, and the

Exhibit 1

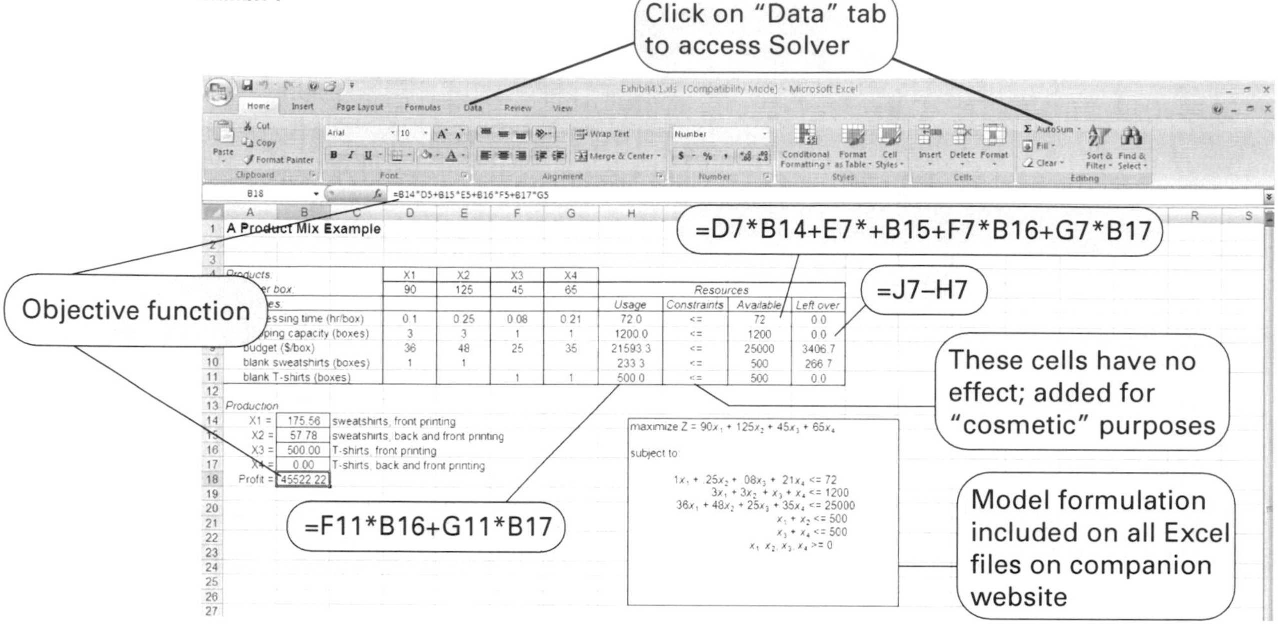

formula for profit, =**B14*D5+B15*E5+B16*F5+B17*G5**, is shown on the formula bar at the top of the spreadsheet. The constraint formulas are embedded in cells H7 through H11, under the column titled "Usage." For example, the constraint formula for processing time in cell H7 is =**D7*B14+E7*B15+F7*B16+G7*B17**. Cells H8 through H11 have similar formulas.

Cells K7 through K11 contain the formulas for the leftover resources, or slack. For example, cell K7 contains the formula =**J7–H7**. These formulas for leftover resources enable us to demonstrate a spreadsheet operation that can save you time in developing the spreadsheet model. First, enter the formula for leftover resources, =**J7–H7**, in cell K7, as we have already shown. Next, using the right mouse button, click on "Copy." Then cover cells K8:K11 with the cursor (by holding the left mouse button down). Click the right mouse button again and then click on "Paste." This will automatically insert the correct formulas for leftover resources in cells K8 through K11 so that you do not have to type them all in individually. This copying operation can be used when the variables in the formula are all in the same row or column. The copying operation simply increases the row number for each cell that the formulas are copied into (i.e., J8 and H8, J9 and H9, J10 and H10, and J11 and H11).

Also, note the model formulation in the box in the lower right-hand corner of the spreadsheet in Exhibit 1. The model formulations for the remaining linear programming models in this chapter are included on the Excel files on the companion website accompanying this text.

The Solver window for this model is shown in Exhibit 2. Notice that we were able to insert all five constraint formulas with one line in the "Subject to the Constraints:" window. We used the constraint **H7:H11 <= J7:J11**, which means that all the constraint usage values computed in cells H7 through H11 are less than the corresponding available resource values computed in cells J7 through J11.

Exhibit 2

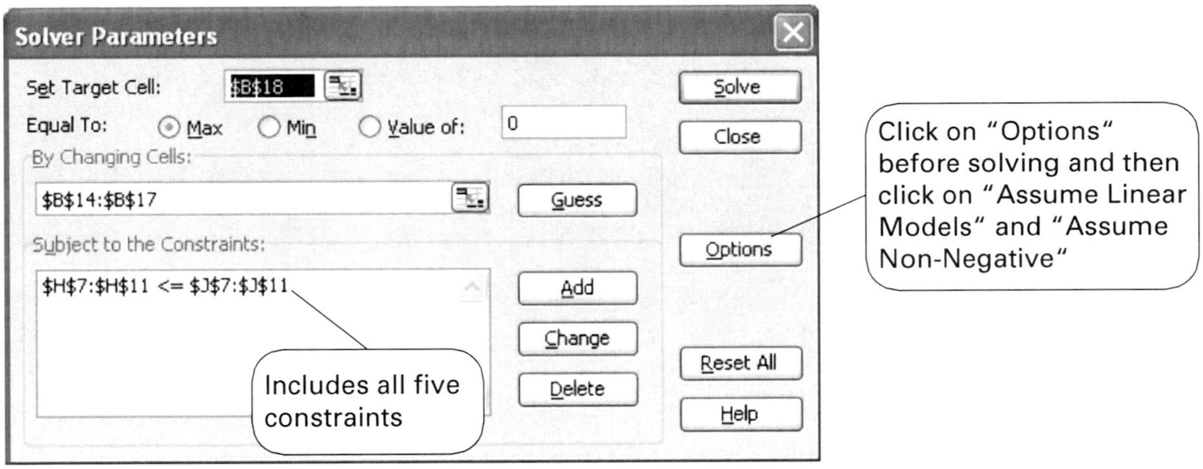

Computer Solution with QM for Windows

The QM for Windows solution for this problem is shown in Exhibits 3 and 4.

Exhibit 3

Original Problem w/answers

Product Mix Example Solution

	X1	X2	X3	X4		RHS	Dual
Maximize	90	125	45	65			Max 90X1 + 125X2 + 45X3 + 65X4
Processing time (hrs)	.1	.25	.08	.21	<=	72	233.3333
Shipping capacity (boxes)	3	3	1	1	<=	1,200	22.2222
Budget ($)	36	48	25	35	<=	25,000	0
Blank sweats (dozens)	1	1	0	0	<=	500	0
Blank T's (dozens)	0	0	1	1	<=	500	4.1111
Solution->	175.5556	57.7778	500	0	Optimal Z->	45,522.22	X3 + X4 <= 500

Exhibit 4

Ranging

Product Mix Example Solution

Variable	Value	Reduced Cost	Original Val	Lower Bound	Upper Bound
X1	175.5556	0	90	50	101.9231
X2	57.7778	0	125	113.0769	138.2143
X3	500	0	45	40.8889	Infinity
X4	0	10.3333	65	-Infinity	75.3333
Constraint	**Dual Value**	**Slack/Surplus**	**Original Val**	**Lower Bound**	**Upper Bound**
Processing time (hrs)	233.3333	0	72	63.3333	98.3333
Shipping capacity (boxes)	22.2222	0	1,200	884	1,460
Budget ($)	0	3,406.666	25,000	21,593.33	Infinity
Blank sweats (dozens)	0	266.6667	500	233.3333	Infinity
Blank T's (dozens)	4.1111	0	500	0	685.7144

Solution Analysis

The model solution is

$$x_1 = 175.56 \text{ boxes of front-only sweatshirts}$$
$$x_2 = 57.78 \text{ boxes of front and back sweatshirts}$$
$$x_3 = 500 \text{ boxes of front-only T-shirts}$$
$$Z = \$45{,}522.22 \text{ profit}$$

The manager of Quick-Screen might have to round off the solution to send whole boxes—for example, 175 boxes of front-only sweatshirts, 57 of front and back sweatshirts, and 500 of front-only T-shirts. This would result in a profit of $45,375.00, which is only $147.22 less than the optimal profit value of $45,522.22.

After formulating and solving this model, Quick-Screen might decide that it needs to produce and ship at least some of each type of shirt. Management could evaluate this possibility by adding four constraints that establish minimum levels of production for each type of shirt, including front and back T-shirts, x_4, none of which are produced in the current solution. The manager might also like to experiment with the constraints to see the effect on the solution of adding resources. For example, the dual value for processing time shows profit would increase by $233.33 per hour (up to 98.33 hours, the upper limit of the sensitivity range for this constraint quality value). Although the 72-hour limit seems pretty strict, it might be possible to reduce individual processing times and achieve the same result.

A Diet Example

Breathtakers, a health and fitness center, operates a morning fitness program for senior citizens. The program includes aerobic exercise, either swimming or step exercise, followed by a healthy breakfast in the dining room. Breathtakers' dietitian wants to develop a breakfast that will be high in calories, calcium, protein, and fiber, which are especially important to senior citizens, but low in fat and cholesterol. She also wants to minimize cost. She has selected the following possible food items, whose individual nutrient contributions and cost from which to develop a standard breakfast menu are shown in the following table:

Breakfast Food	Calories	Fat (g)	Cholesterol (mg)	Iron (mg)	Calcium (mg)	Protein (g)	Fiber (g)	Cost
1. Bran cereal (cup)	90	0	0	6	20	3	5	$0.18
2. Dry cereal (cup)	110	2	0	4	48	4	2	0.22
3. Oatmeal (cup)	100	2	0	2	12	5	3	0.10
4. Oat bran (cup)	90	2	0	3	8	6	4	0.12
5. Egg	75	5	270	1	30	7	0	0.10
6. Bacon (slice)	35	3	8	0	0	2	0	0.09
7. Orange	65	0	0	1	52	1	1	0.40
8. Milk—2% (cup)	100	4	12	0	250	9	0	0.16
9. Orange juice (cup)	120	0	0	0	3	1	0	0.50
10. Wheat toast (slice)	65	1	0	1	26	3	3	0.07

The dietitian wants the breakfast to include at least 420 calories, 5 milligrams of iron, 400 milligrams of calcium, 20 grams of protein, and 12 grams of fiber. Furthermore, she wants to limit fat to no more than 20 grams and cholesterol to 30 milligrams.

Decision Variables

This problem includes 10 decision variables, representing the number of standard units of each food item that can be included in each breakfast:

x_1 = cups of bran cereal
x_2 = cups of dry cereal
x_3 = cups of oatmeal
x_4 = cups of oat bran
x_5 = eggs
x_6 = slices of bacon

$$x_7 = \text{oranges}$$
$$x_8 = \text{cups of milk}$$
$$x_9 = \text{cups of orange juice}$$
$$x_{10} = \text{slices of wheat toast}$$

The Objective Function

The dietitian's objective is to minimize the cost of a breakfast. The total cost is the sum of the individual costs of each food item:

$$\text{minimize } Z = \$0.18x_1 + 0.22x_2 + 0.10x_3 + 0.12x_4 + 0.10x_5 + 0.09x_6 + 0.40x_7 + 0.16x_8 + 0.50x_9 + 0.07x_{10}$$

Model Constraints

The constraints are the requirements for the nutrition items:

$$90x_1 + 110x_2 + 100x_3 + 90x_4 + 75x_5 + 35x_6 + 65x_7 + 100x_8 + 120x_9 + 65x_{10} \geq 420 \text{ calories}$$
$$2x_2 + 2x_3 + 2x_4 + 5x_5 + 3x_6 + 4x_8 + x_{10} \leq 20 \text{ g of fat}$$
$$270x_5 + 8x_6 + 12x_8 \leq 30 \text{ mg of cholesterol}$$
$$6x_1 + 4x_2 + 2x_3 + 3x_4 + x_5 + x_7 + x_{10} \geq 5 \text{ mg of iron}$$
$$20x_1 + 48x_2 + 12x_3 + 8x_4 + 30x_5 + 52x_7 + 250x_8 + 3x_9 + 26x_{10} \geq 400 \text{ mg of calcium}$$
$$3x_1 + 4x_2 + 5x_3 + 6x_4 + 7x_5 + 2x_6 + x_7 + 9x_8 + x_9 + 3x_{10} \geq 20 \text{ g of protein}$$
$$5x_1 + 2x_2 + 3x_3 + 4x_4 + x_7 + 3x_{10} \geq 12 \text{ g of fiber}$$

Model Summary

The linear programming model for this problem can be summarized as follows:

$$\text{minimize } Z = 0.18x_1 + 0.22x_2 + 0.10x_3 + 0.12x_4 + 0.10x_5 + 0.09x_6 + 0.40x_7 + 0.16x_8 + 0.50x_9 + 0.07x_{10}$$

subject to

$$90x_1 + 110x_2 + 100x_3 + 90x_4 + 75x_5 + 35x_6 + 65x_7 + 100x_8 + 120x_9 + 65x_{10} \geq 420$$
$$2x_2 + 2x_3 + 2x_4 + 5x_5 + 3x_6 + 4x_8 + x_{10} \leq 20$$
$$270x_5 + 8x_6 + 12x_8 \leq 30$$
$$6x_1 + 4x_2 + 2x_3 + 3x_4 + x_5 + x_7 + x_{10} \geq 5$$
$$20x_1 + 48x_2 + 12x_3 + 8x_4 + 30x_5 + 52x_7 + 250x_8 + 3x_9 + 26x_{10} \geq 400$$
$$3x_1 + 4x_2 + 5x_3 + 6x_4 + 7x_5 + 2x_6 + x_7 + 9x_8 + x_9 + 3x_{10} \geq 20$$
$$5x_1 + 2x_2 + 3x_3 + 4x_4 + x_7 + 3x_{10} \geq 12$$
$$x_i \geq 0$$

Computer Solution with Excel

The solution to our diet example using an Excel spreadsheet is shown in Exhibit 5. The decision variables (i.e., "servings" of each menu item) for our problem are contained in cells **C5:C14** inclusive, and the constraint formulas are in cells F15 through L15. Cells F17 through L17 contain the constraint (right-hand-side) values. For example, cell F15 contains the constraint formula for calories, =**SUMPRODUCT(C5:C14,F5:F14)**. Then when the Solver Parameters screen is accessed, the constraint **F15>=F17** will be added in. This constraint formula in cell F15 could have been constructed by multiplying each of the values in column C by each of the corresponding column F cell values. The equivalent constraint formula in

Exhibit 5

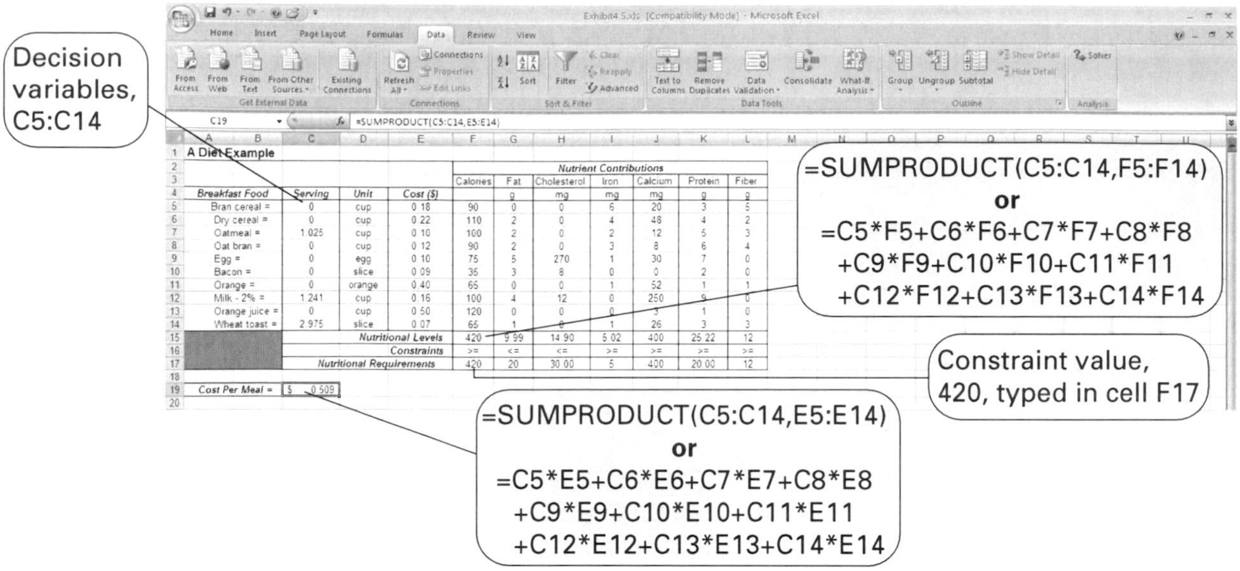

cell F15 to our SUMPRODUCT formula is **=C5*F5+C6*F6+C7*F7+C8*F8+C9*F9+C10*F10+C11*F11+C12*F12+C13*F13+C14*F14**.

The objective function formula is contained in cell C19, =**SUMPRODUCT(C5:C14,E5:E14)**. In this case the objective function value is also computed by using the Excel SUMPRODUCT command rather than by individually multiplying each cell value in column C by each cell value in column E and then summing them. This would be a tedious formula to type into cell C19. Alternatively, the SUMPRODUCT() formula multiplies all the values in cells C5 through C14 by all the corresponding values in cells E5 through E14 and then sums them.

The Solver dialog box for this problem is shown in Exhibit 6. Notice that the constraint box on this screen is not large enough to show all the constraints in the problem.

Solution Analysis

The solution is

$$\begin{aligned} x_3 &= 1.025 \text{ cups of oatmeal} \\ x_8 &= 1.241 \text{ cups of milk} \\ x_{10} &= 2.975 \text{ slices of wheat toast} \\ Z &= \$0.509 \text{ cost per meal} \end{aligned}$$

The result of this simplified version of a real menu planning model is interesting in that it suggests a very practical breakfast menu. This would be a healthy breakfast for anyone.

This model includes a daily minimum requirement of only 420 calories. The recommended daily calorie requirement for an adult is approximately 2,000 calories. Thus, the breakfast requirement is only about 21% of normal daily adult needs. In this model the dietitian must have felt a low-calorie breakfast was needed because the senior citizens had high-calorie lunches and dinners. An alternative approach to a healthy diet is a high-calorie breakfast followed by low-calorie, light meals and snacks the rest of the day. However, in this model, as the calorie requirements are increased above 420, the model simply

Exhibit 6

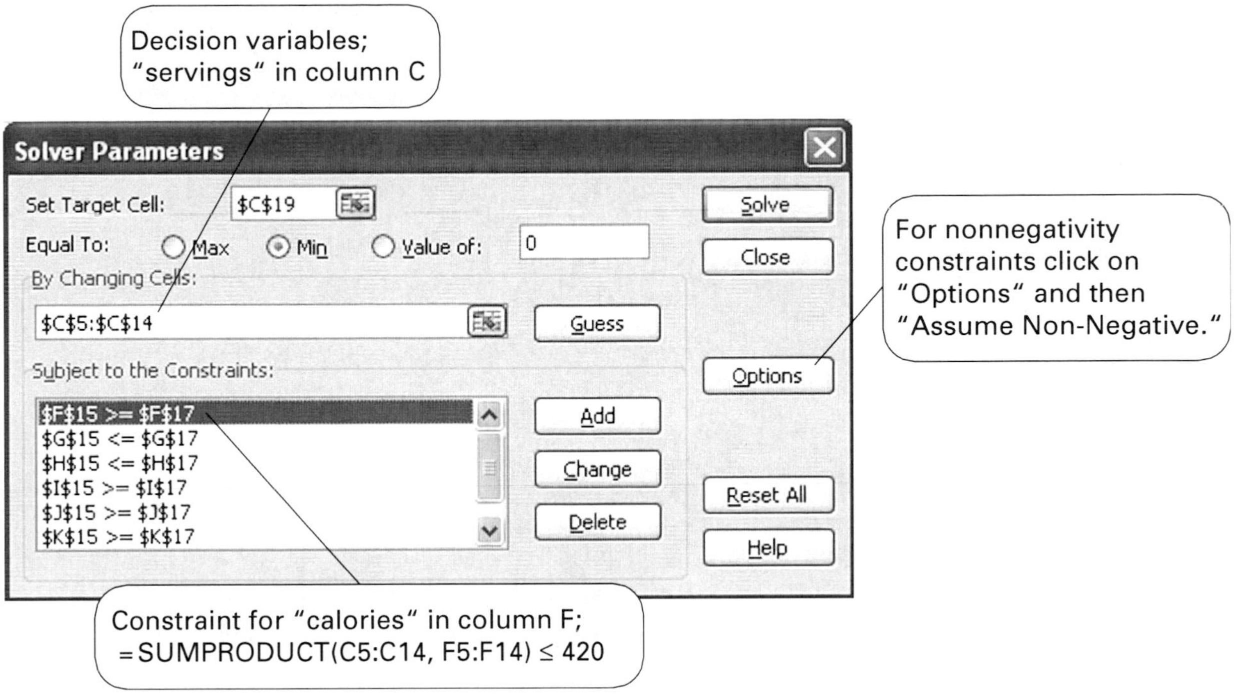

increases the cups of oatmeal. For example, a 700-calorie requirement results in about 5 or 6 cups of oatmeal—not a very appetizing breakfast. This difficulty can be alleviated by establishing upper limits on the servings for each food item and solving the model again with a higher calorie requirement.

An Investment Example

Kathleen Allen, an individual investor, has $70,000 to divide among several investments. The alternative investments are municipal bonds with an 8.5% annual return, certificates of deposit with a 5% return, treasury bills with a 6.5% return, and a growth stock fund with a 13% annual return. The investments are all evaluated after 1 year. However, each investment alternative has a different perceived risk to the investor; thus, it is advisable to diversify. Kathleen wants to know how much to invest in each alternative in order to maximize the return.

The following guidelines have been established for diversifying the investments and lessening the risk perceived by the investor:

1. No more than 20% of the total investment should be in municipal bonds.
2. The amount invested in certificates of deposit should not exceed the amount invested in the other three alternatives.
3. At least 30% of the investment should be in treasury bills and certificates of deposit.
4. To be safe, more should be invested in CDs and treasury bills than in municipal bonds and the growth stock fund, by a ratio of at least 1.2 to 1.

Kathleen wants to invest the entire $70,000.

Decision Variables

Four decision variables represent the monetary amount invested in each investment alternative:

$$
\begin{aligned}
x_1 &= \text{amount (\$) invested in municipal bonds} \\
x_2 &= \text{amount (\$) invested in certificates of deposit} \\
x_3 &= \text{amount (\$) invested in treasury bills} \\
x_4 &= \text{amount (\$) invested in growth stock fund}
\end{aligned}
$$

The Objective Function

The objective of the investor is to maximize the total return from the investment in the four alternatives. The total return is the sum of the individual returns from each alternative. Thus, the objective function is expressed as

$$\text{maximize } Z = \$0.085x_1 + 0.05x_2 + 0.065x_3 + 0.130x_4$$

where

$$
\begin{aligned}
Z &= \text{total return from all investments} \\
0.085x_1 &= \text{return from the investment in municipal bonds} \\
0.05x_2 &= \text{return from the investment in certificates of deposit} \\
0.065x_3 &= \text{return from the investment in treasury bills} \\
0.130x_4 &= \text{return from the investment in growth stock fund}
\end{aligned}
$$

Model Constraints

In this problem the constraints are the guidelines established for diversifying the total investment. Each guideline is transformed into a mathematical constraint separately.

The first guideline states that no more than 20% of the total investment should be in municipal bonds. The total investment is \$70,000; 20% of \$70,000 is \$14,000. Thus, this constraint is

$$x_1 \leq \$14{,}000$$

The second guideline indicates that the amount invested in certificates of deposit should not exceed the amount invested in the other three alternatives. Because the investment in certificates of deposit is x_2 and the amount invested in the other alternatives is $x_1 + x_3 + x_4$, the constraint is

$$x_2 \leq x_1 + x_3 + x_4$$

Standard form requires all variables to be to the left of the inequality and numeric values to the right.

This constraint is not in *standard form* for a computer solution. In standard form, all the variables would be on the left-hand side of the inequality ($\leq$), and all the numeric values would be on the right side. This type of constraint can be used in Excel just as it is shown here; however, for solution with QM for Windows, all constraints must be in standard form. We will go ahead and convert this constraint and others in this model to standard form, but when we solve this model with Excel, we will explain how the model constraints could be used in their original (nonstandard) form. To convert this constraint to standard form, $x_1 + x_3 + x_4$ must be subtracted from both sides of the $\leq$ sign to put this constraint in proper form:

$$x_2 - x_1 - x_3 - x_4 \leq 0$$

The third guideline specifies that at least 30% of the investment should be in treasury bills and certificates of deposit. Because 30% of \$70,000 is \$21,000 and the amount invested in certificates of deposit and treasury bills is represented by $x_2 + x_3$, the constraint is

$$x_2 + x_3 \geq \$21{,}000$$

The fourth guideline states that the ratio of the amount invested in certificates of deposit and treasury bills to the amount invested in municipal bonds and the growth stock fund should be at least 1.2 to 1:

$$[(x_2 + x_3)/(x_1 + x_4)] \geq 1.2$$

Standard form requires that fractional relationships between variables be eliminated.

This constraint is not in standard linear programming form because of the fractional relationship of the decision variables, $(x_2 + x_3)/(x_1 + x_4)$. It is converted as follows:

$$x_2 + x_3 \geq 1.2\,(x_1 + x_4)$$
$$-1.2x_1 + x_2 + x_3 - 1.2x_4 \geq 0$$

Finally, the investor wants to invest the entire \$70,000 in the four alternatives. Thus, the sum of all the investments in the four alternatives must *equal* \$70,000:

$$x_1 + x_2 + x_3 + x_4 = \$70{,}000$$

Model Summary

The complete linear programming model for this problem can be summarized as

$$\text{maximize } Z = \$0.085x_1 + 0.05x_2 + 0.065x_3 + 0.130x_4$$
subject to

$$\begin{aligned} x_1 &\leq 14{,}000 \\ x_2 - x_1 - x_3 - x_4 &\leq 0 \\ x_2 + x_3 &\geq 21{,}000 \\ -1.2x_1 + x_2 + x_3 - 1.2x_4 &\geq 0 \\ x_1 + x_2 + x_3 + x_4 &= 70{,}000 \\ x_1, x_2, x_3, x_4 &\geq 0 \end{aligned}$$

Computer Solution with Excel

The Excel spreadsheet solution for the investment example is shown in Exhibit 7, and its Solver window is shown in Exhibit 8. The spreadsheet is set up very similarly to the

Exhibit 7

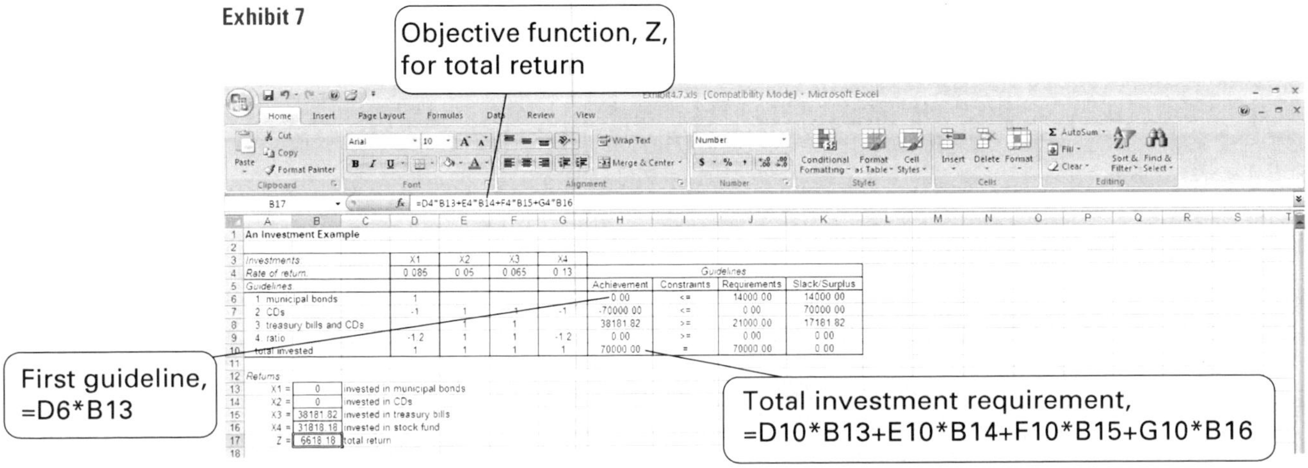

Exhibit 8

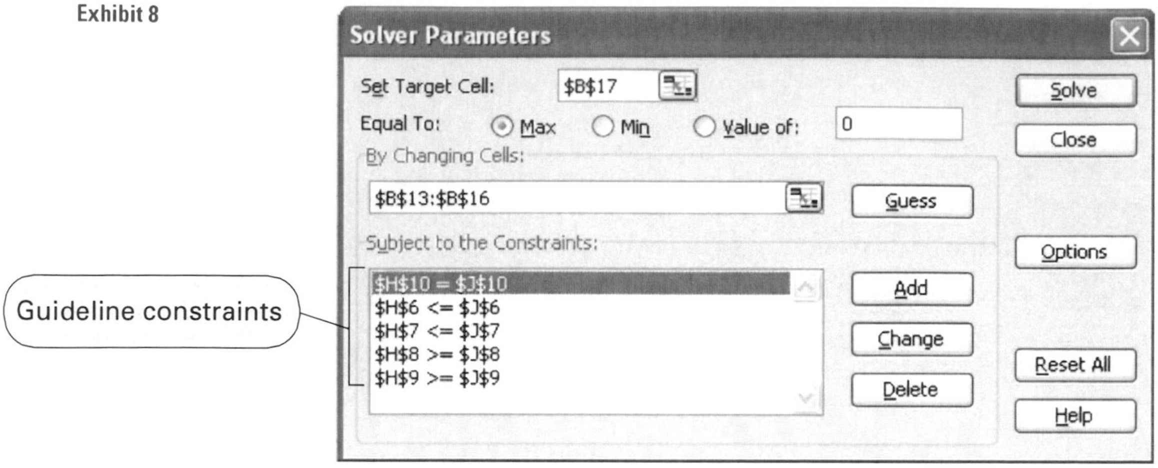

spreadsheet for our product mix example in Exhibit 1. The decision variables are located in cells **B13:B16**. The total return (Z) is computed in cell B17, and the formula for Z is shown on the formula bar at the top of the spreadsheet. The constraint formulas for the investment guidelines are embedded in cells H6 through H10. For example, the first guideline formula, in cell H6, is =**D6*B13**, and the second guideline formula, in cell H7, is =**D7*B13+E7*B14+F7*B15+G7*B16**. (Note that it would probably have been easier just to type the guideline formulas directly into cells H6 through H10 rather than create the array of constraint coefficients in **D6:G10**; however, for demonstration purposes, we wanted to show all the parameter values.)

As mentioned earlier, it is not necessary to convert the original model constraints into standard form to solve this model using Excel. For example, the constraint for certificates of deposit, $x_2 \leq x_1 + x_3 + x_4$, could be entered in the spreadsheet in row 7 in Exhibit 7 as follows. The value 1, the coefficient for x_2, could be entered in cell E7, =**E7*B14** could be entered in cell J7, and the remainder of the constraint to the right side of the inequality could be entered as =**B13+B15+B16** in cell H7. In the Solver window this constraint is entered as it originally was, **H7<=J7**. The fourth guideline constraint could be entered in its original form similarly.

Solution Analysis

The solution is

$$x_3 = \$38{,}181.82 \text{ invested in treasury bonds}$$
$$x_4 = \$31{,}818.18 \text{ invested in a growth stock fund}$$
$$Z = \$6{,}818.18$$

The sensitivity report for our Excel spreadsheet solution to this problem is shown in Exhibit 9.

Notice that the dual (shadow price) value for constraint 5 (i.e., the sum of the investments must equal $70,000) is 0.095. This indicates that for each additional $1 Kathleen Allen invests (above $70,000), according to the existing investment guidelines she has established, she could expect a return of 9.5%. The sensitivity ranges show that there is no upper bound on the amount she could invest and still receive this return.

An interesting variation of the problem is to not specify that the entire amount available (in this case, $70,000) must be invested. This changes the constraints for the first and third guidelines and the constraint that requires that the entire $70,000 be invested.

Recall that the first guideline is "no more than 20% of the total investment should be in municipal bonds." The total investment is no longer exactly $70,000 but the sum of all four

Exhibit 9

Adjustable Cells

Cell	Name	Final Value	Reduced Cost	Objective Coefficient	Allowable Increase	Allowable Decrease
B13	X1 =	0	-0.045	0.085	0.045	1E+30
B14	X2 =	0	-0.015	0.050	0.015	1E+30
B15	X3 =	38181.82	0	0.065	0.065	0.015
B16	X4 =	31818.18	0	0.13	45354.805	0.045

Constraints

Cell	Name	Final Value	Shadow Price	Constraint R.H. Side	Allowable Increase	Allowable Decrease
H6	1. municipal bonds Achievement	0.00	0.000	14000	1E+30	14000
H7	2. CDs Achievement	-70000.00	0.000	0	1E+30	70000
H8	3. treasury bills and CDs Achievement	38181.82	0.000	21000	17181.82	1E+30
H9	4. ratio Achievement	0.00	-0.030	0	70000	37800
H10	total invested Achievement	70000.00	0.095	70000	1E+30	31500

Shadow price for the amount available to invest

investments, $x_1 + x_2 + x_3 + x_4$. The constraint showing that the amount invested in municipal bonds, x_1, as a percentage (or ratio) of this total cannot exceed 20% is written as

$$\frac{x_1}{x_1 + x_2 + x_3 + x_4} \leq 0.20$$

Rewriting this constraint in a form more consistent with a linear programming solution (to eliminate the fractional relationship between variables) results in

$$x_1 \leq 0.2(x_1 + x_2 + x_3 + x_4)$$

and

$$0.8x_1 - 0.2x_2 - 0.2x_3 - 0.2x_4 \leq 0$$

The constraint for the third guideline, which stipulates that at least 30% of the total investment $(x_1 + x_2 + x_3 + x_4)$ should be in treasury bills and CDs $(x_2 + x_3)$, is formulated similarly as

$$\frac{x_2 + x_3}{x_1 + x_2 + x_3 + x_4} \geq 0.30$$

and

$$-0.3x_1 + 0.7x_2 + 0.7x_3 - 0.3x_4 \geq 0$$

Because the entire $70,000 does not have to be invested, the last constraint becomes

$$x_1 + x_2 + x_3 + x_4 \leq 70{,}000$$

The complete linear programming model is summarized as

$$\begin{aligned}
\text{maximize } Z = \$0.085x_1 + 0.05x_2 + 0.065x_3 + 0.130x_4 \\
\text{subject to} \\
0.8x_1 - 0.2x_2 - 0.2x_3 - 0.2x_4 &\leq 0 \\
x_2 - x_1 - x_3 - x_4 &\leq 0 \\
-0.3x_1 + 0.7x_2 + 0.7x_3 - 0.3x_4 &\geq 0 \\
-1.2x_1 + x_2 + x_3 - 1.2x_4 &\geq 0 \\
x_1 + x_2 + x_3 + x_4 &\leq 70{,}000 \\
x_1, x_2, x_3, x_4 &\geq 0
\end{aligned}$$

Management Science Application

A Linear Programming Model for Optimal Portfolio Selection at Prudential Securities, Inc.

In the secondary mortgage market, government agencies purchase mortgage loans from the original mortgage lenders and pool them to create mortgage-backed securities (MBSs). These securities are traded in capital markets along with other fixed-income securities, such as treasury and corporate bonds. The total size of this market for MBSs is well over $1 trillion. There are a number of types of MBSs. The market for MBSs is maintained by a network of dealers, including Prudential Securities, Inc. This firm and others like it underwrite and issue new market-based securities. This market is somewhat more complex than standard bond investments, such as treasury or corporate securities, because the principal on mortgages is returned gradually over the life of the security rather than in a lump sum at the end. In addition, cash flows fluctuate because of the homeowner's right to prepay mortgages. In order to deal with these complexities, Prudential Securities has developed and implemented a number of management science models to reduce investment risk and properly value securities for its investors. One such model employs linear programming to design an optimal securities portfolio to meet various investors' criteria under different interest rate environments. The linear programming model determines the amount to invest in different MBSs to meet a client's objectives for portfolio performance. Constraints might include maximum and minimum percentages (of the total portfolio investment) that could be invested in any one or more securities, the duration of the securities, the amount to be invested, and the amount of the different securities available. This linear programming model and other management science models are used hundreds of times each day at Prudential Securities by traders, salespeople, and clients. The models allow the firm to participate successfully in the mortgage market. Prudential's secondary market trading in MBSs typically exceeds $5 billion per week.

Source: Y. Ben-Dow, L. Hayre, and V. Pica, "Mortgage Valuation Models at Prudential Securities," *Interfaces* 22, no. 1 (January–February 1992): 55–71.

The solution to this altered model is exactly the same as the solution to our original model, wherein the entire $70,000 must be invested. This is logical because only positive returns are achieved from investing, and thus the investor would leave no money not invested. However, if losses could be realized from some investments, then it might be a good idea to construct the model so that the entire amount would not have to be invested.

A Marketing Example

The Biggs Department Store chain has hired an advertising firm to determine the types and amount of advertising it should invest in for its stores. The three types of advertising available are television and radio commercials and newspaper ads. The retail chain desires to know the number of each type of advertisement it should purchase in order to maximize exposure. It is estimated that each ad or commercial will reach the following potential audience and cost the following amount:

	Exposure (people/ad or commercial)	Cost
Television commercial	20,000	\$15,000
Radio commercial	12,000	6,000
Newspaper ad	9,000	4,000

The company must consider the following resource constraints:

1. The budget limit for advertising is \$100,000.
2. The television station has time available for 4 commercials.
3. The radio station has time available for 10 commercials.
4. The newspaper has space available for 7 ads.
5. The advertising agency has time and staff available for producing no more than a total of 15 commercials and/or ads.

Decision Variables

This model consists of three decision variables that represent the number of each type of advertising produced:

$$x_1 = \text{number of television commercials}$$
$$x_2 = \text{number of radio commercials}$$
$$x_3 = \text{number of newspaper ads}$$

The Objective Function

The objective of this problem is different from the objectives in the previous examples, in which only profit was to be maximized (or cost minimized). In this problem, profit is not to be maximized; instead, audience exposure is to be maximized. Thus, this objective function demonstrates that although a linear programming model must either maximize or minimize some objective, the objective itself can be in terms of any type of activity or valuation.

For this problem the objective audience exposure is determined by summing the audience exposure gained from each type of advertising:

$$\text{maximize } Z = 20{,}000x_1 + 12{,}000x_2 + 9{,}000x_3$$

where

$$Z = \text{total level of audience exposure}$$
$$20{,}000x_1 = \text{estimated number of people reached by television commercials}$$
$$12{,}000x_2 = \text{estimated number of people reached by radio commercials}$$
$$9{,}000x_3 = \text{estimated number of people reached by newspaper ads}$$

Model Constraints

The first constraint in this model reflects the limited budget of \$100,000 allocated for advertisement:

$$\$15{,}000x_1 + 6{,}000x_2 + 4{,}000x_3 \leq \$100{,}000$$

where

$$\begin{aligned}\$15{,}000x_1 &= \text{amount spent for television advertising}\\ 6{,}000x_2 &= \text{amount spent for radio advertising}\\ 4{,}000x_3 &= \text{amount spent for newspaper advertising}\end{aligned}$$

The next three constraints represent the fact that television and radio commercials are limited to 4 and 10, respectively, and newspaper ads are limited to 7:

$$\begin{aligned}x_1 &\leq 4 \text{ television commercials}\\ x_2 &\leq 10 \text{ radio commercials}\\ x_3 &\leq 7 \text{ newspaper ads}\end{aligned}$$

The final constraint specifies that the total number of commercials and ads cannot exceed 15 because of the limitations of the advertising firm:

$$x_1 + x_2 + x_3 \leq 15 \text{ commercials and ads}$$

Model Summary

The complete linear programming model for this problem is summarized as

$$\begin{aligned}\text{maximize } Z &= 20{,}000x_1 + 12{,}000x_2 + 9{,}000x_3\\ \text{subject to}&\\ \$15{,}000x_1 + 6{,}000x_2 + 4{,}000x_3 &\leq \$100{,}000\\ x_1 &\leq 4\\ x_2 &\leq 10\\ x_3 &\leq 7\\ x_1 + x_2 + x_3 &\leq 15\\ x_1, x_2, x_3 &\geq 0\end{aligned}$$

Computer Solution with Excel

The solution to our marketing example using Excel is shown in Exhibit 10. The model decision variables are contained in cells **D6:D8**. The formula for the objective function in

Exhibit 10

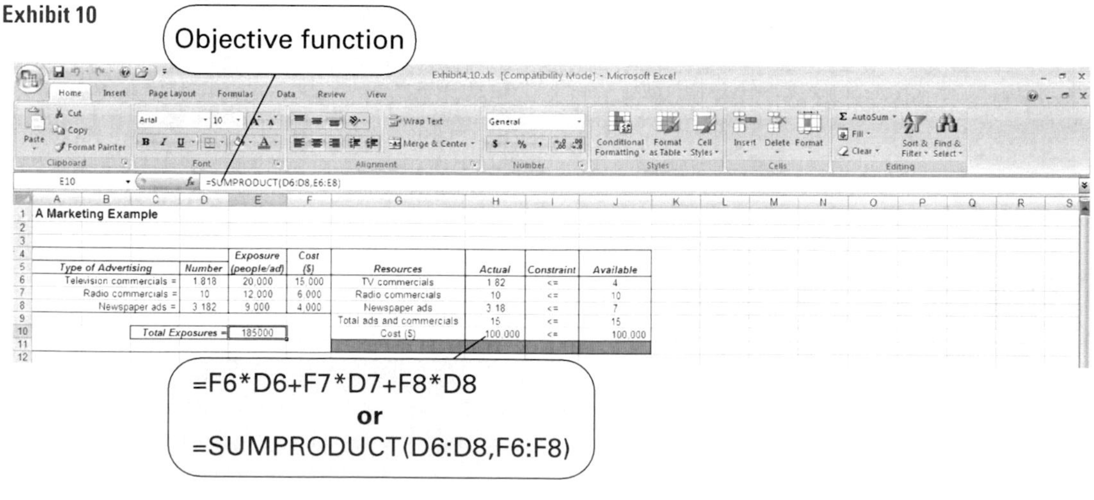

Exhibit 11

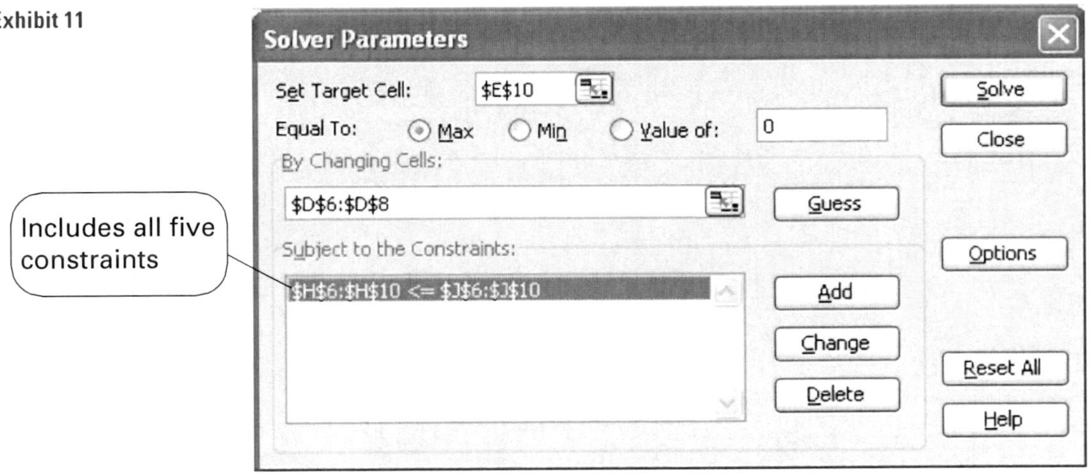

cell E10 is shown on the formula bar at the top of the screen. When Solver is accessed, as shown in Exhibit 11, it is necessary to use only one formula to enter the model constraints: **H6:H10** <= **J6:J10**.

Solution Analysis

The solution shows

$$\begin{aligned} x_1 &= 1.818 \text{ television commercials} \\ x_2 &= 10 \text{ radio commercials} \\ x_3 &= 3.182 \text{ newspaper ads} \\ Z &= 185{,}000 \text{ audience exposure} \end{aligned}$$

This is a case where a non-integer solution can create difficulties. It is not realistic to round 1.818 television commercials to 2 television commercials, with 10 radio commercials and 3 newspaper ads. Some quick arithmetic with the budget constraint shows that such a solution will exceed the $100,000 budget limitation, although by only $2,000. Thus, the store must either increase its advertising or plan for 1 television commercial, 10 radio commercials, and 3 newspaper ads. The audience exposure for this solution will be 167,000 people, or 18,000 fewer than the optimal number, almost a 10% decrease. There may, in fact, be a better solution than this "rounded-down" solution.

The integer linear programming technique, which restricts solutions to integer values, should be used. Although we will discuss the topic of integer programming in more detail for now we can derive an integer solution by using Excel with a simple change when we input our constraints in the Solver window. We specify that our variable cells, **D6:D8**, are integers in the Change Constraint window, as shown in Exhibits 12 and 13. This will result in the spreadsheet solution in Exhibit 14 when the problem is solved, which you will notice is better (i.e., 17,000 more total exposures) than the rounded-down solution.

A Transportation Example

The Zephyr Television Company ships televisions from three warehouses to three retail stores on a monthly basis. Each warehouse has a fixed supply per month, and each store has a fixed demand per month. The manufacturer wants to know the number of television sets to ship from each warehouse to each store in order to minimize the total cost of transportation.

Exhibit 12

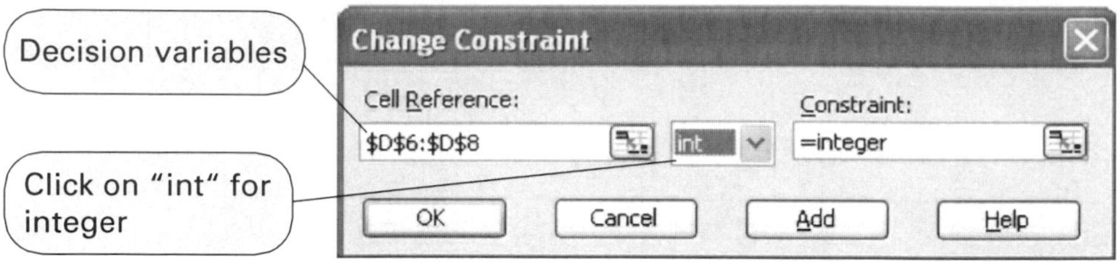

Exhibit 13

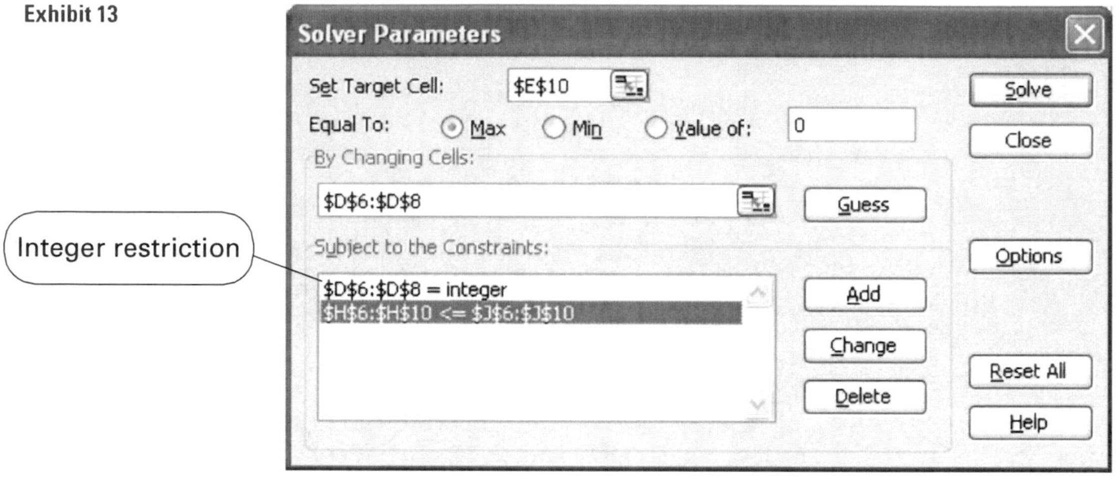

Exhibit 14

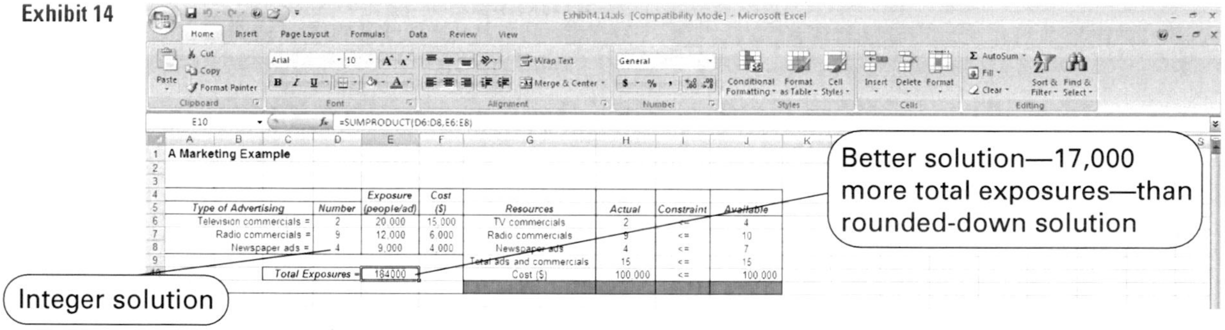

Each warehouse has the following supply of televisions available for shipment each month:

Warehouse	***Supply (sets)***
1. Cincinnati	300
2. Atlanta	200
3. Pittsburgh	200
	700

Each retail store has the following monthly demand for television sets:

Store	***Demand (sets)***
A. New York	150
B. Dallas	250
C. Detroit	200
	600

Costs of transporting television sets from the warehouses to the retail stores vary as a result of differences in modes of transportation and distances. The shipping cost per television set for each route is as follows:

From Warehouse	To Store A	B	C
1	\$16	\$18	\$11
2	14	12	13
3	13	15	17

Decision Variables

The model for this problem consists of nine decision variables, representing the number of television sets transported from each of the three warehouses to each of the three stores:

$$x_{ij} = \text{number of television sets shipped from warehouse } i \text{ to store } j$$
$$\text{where } i = 1, 2, 3, \text{ and } j = \text{A, B, C}$$

*A **double-subscripted** variable is simply another form of variable name.*

The variable x_{ij} is referred to as a **double-subscripted variable.** The subscript, whether double or single, simply gives a "name" to the variable (i.e., distinguishes it from other decision variables). For example, the decision variable x_{3A} represents the number of television sets shipped from warehouse 3 in Pittsburgh to store A in New York.

The Objective Function

The objective function of the television manufacturer is to minimize the total transportation costs for all shipments. Thus, the objective function is the sum of the individual shipping costs from each warehouse to each store:

$$\text{minimize } Z = \$16x_{1A} + 18x_{1B} + 11x_{1C} + 14x_{2A} + 12x_{2B} + 13x_{2C} + 13x_{3A} + 15x_{3B} + 17x_{3C}$$

Model Constraints

The constraints in this model are the number of television sets available at each warehouse and the number of sets demanded at each store. There are six constraints—one for each warehouse's supply and one for each store's demand. For example, warehouse 1 in Cincinnati is able to supply 300 television sets to any of the three retail stores. Because the number shipped to the three stores is the sum of x_{1A}, x_{1B}, and x_{1C}, the constraint for warehouse 1 is

$$x_{1A} + x_{1B} + x_{1C} \leq 300$$

*In a **"balanced" transportation model,** supply equals demand such that all constraints are equalities; in an **"unbalanced" transportation model,** supply does not equal demand, and one set of constraints is ≤.*

This constraint is a $\leq$ inequality for two reasons. First, no more than 300 television sets can be shipped because that is the maximum available at the warehouse. Second, fewer than 300 can be shipped because 300 are not needed to meet the total demand of 600. That is, total demand is less than total supply, which equals 700. To meet the total demand at the three stores, all that can be supplied by the three warehouses is not needed. Thus, the other two supply constraints for warehouses 2 and 3 are also inequalities:

$$x_{2A} + x_{2B} + x_{2C} \leq 200$$
$$x_{3A} + x_{3B} + x_{3C} \leq 200$$

The three demand constraints are developed in the same way as the supply constraints, except that the variables summed are the number of television sets supplied from each of the three warehouses. Thus, the number shipped to one store is the sum of the shipments from the three warehouses. They are equalities because all demands can be met:

$$x_{1A} + x_{2A} + x_{3A} = 150$$
$$x_{1B} + x_{2B} + x_{3B} = 250$$
$$x_{1C} + x_{2C} + x_{3C} = 200$$

Model Summary

The complete linear programming model for this problem is summarized as follows:

minimize $Z = \$16x_{1A} + 18x_{1B} + 11x_{1C} + 14x_{2A} + 12x_{2B} + 13x_{2C} + 13x_{3A} + 15x_{3B} + 17x_{3C}$
subject to

$$x_{1A} + x_{1B} + x_{1C} \leq 300$$
$$x_{2A} + x_{2B} + x_{2C} \leq 200$$
$$x_{3A} + x_{3B} + x_{3C} \leq 200$$
$$x_{1A} + x_{2A} + x_{3A} = 150$$
$$x_{1B} + x_{2B} + x_{3B} = 250$$
$$x_{1C} + x_{2C} + x_{3C} = 200$$
$$x_{ij} \geq 0$$

Computer Solution with Excel

The computer solution for this model was achieved using Excel and is shown in Exhibit 15. Notice that the objective function contained in cell C11 is shown on the formula bar at

Exhibit 15

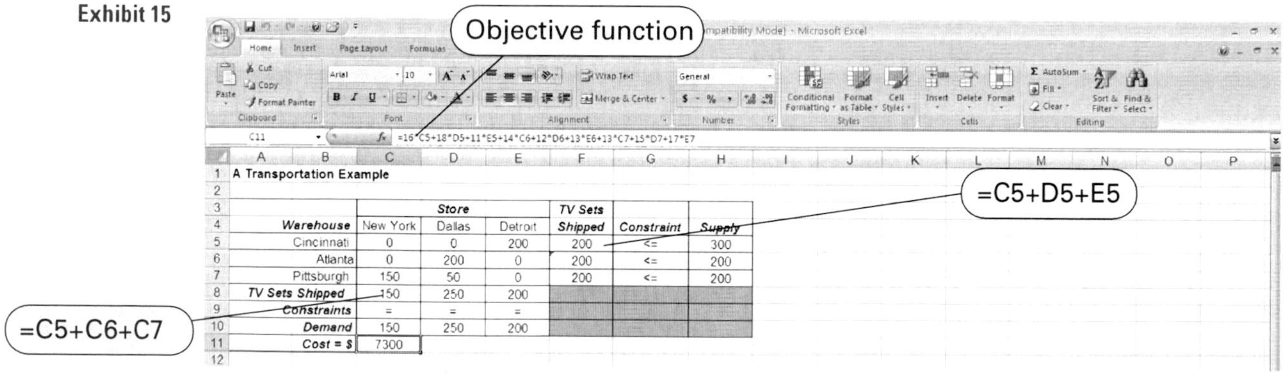

the top of the screen. The constraints for supply are included in cells F5, F6, and F7, whereas the demand constraints are in cells C8, D8, and E8. Thus, a typical supply constraint for Cincinnati would be **C5+D5+E5≤H5**. The Solver window is shown in Exhibit 16.

Exhibit 16

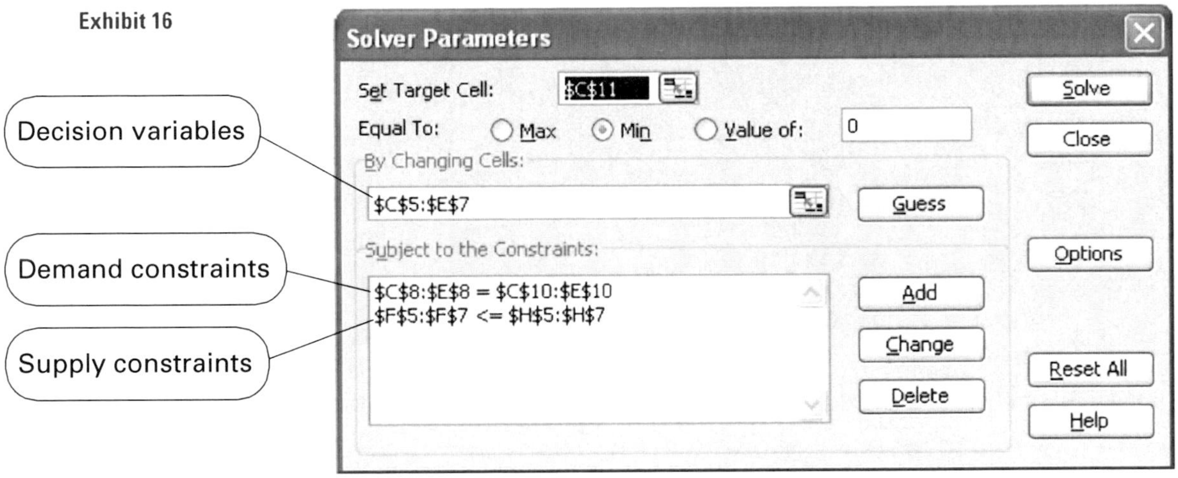

Solution Analysis

The solution is

$$\begin{aligned} x_{1C} &= 200 \text{ TVs shipped from Cincinnati to Detroit} \\ x_{2B} &= 200 \text{ TVs shipped from Atlanta to Dallas} \\ x_{3A} &= 150 \text{ TVs shipped from Pittsburgh to New York} \\ x_{3B} &= 50 \text{ TVs shipped from Pittsburgh to Dallas} \\ Z &= \$7{,}300 \text{ shipping cost} \end{aligned}$$

Note that the surplus for the first constraint, which is the supply at the Cincinnati warehouse, equals 100 TVs. This means that 100 TVs are left in the Cincinnati warehouse, which has inventory and storage implications for the manager.

This is an example of a type of linear programming model known as a *transportation problem*. Notice that all the solution values are integer values. This is always the case with transportation problems because of the unique characteristic that all the coefficient parameter values are ones and zeros.

A Blend Example

A petroleum company produces three grades of motor oil—super, premium, and extra—from three components. The company wants to determine the optimal mix of the three components in each grade of motor oil that will maximize profit. The maximum quantities available of each component and their cost per barrel are as follows:

Component	Maximum Barrels Available/Day	Cost/Barrel
1	4,500	$12
2	2,700	10
3	3,500	14

To ensure the appropriate blend, each grade has certain general specifications. Each grade must have a minimum amount of component 1 plus a combination of other components, as follows:

Grade	Component Specifications	Selling Price/Barrel
Super	At least 50% of 1	$23
	Not more than 30% of 2	
Premium	At least 40% of 1	20
	Not more than 25% of 3	
Extra	At least 60% of 1	18
	At least 10% of 2	

The company wants to produce at least 3,000 barrels of each grade of motor oil.

Decision Variables

The decision variables for this problem must specify the quantity of each of the three components used in each grade of motor oil. This requires nine decision variables, as follows: x_{ij} = barrels of component i used in motor oil grade j per day, where $i = 1, 2, 3$ and $j = s$ (super), p (premium), e (extra). For example, the amount of component 1 in super motor oil is x_{1s}. The total amount of each grade of motor oil will be

$$\begin{aligned} \text{super:} &\quad x_{1s} + x_{2s} + x_{3s} \\ \text{premium:} &\quad x_{1p} + x_{2p} + x_{3p} \\ \text{extra:} &\quad x_{1e} + x_{2e} + x_{3e} \end{aligned}$$

The Objective Function

"Profit" is maximized in the objective function by subtracting cost from revenue.

The company's objective is to maximize profit. This requires that the cost of each barrel be subtracted from the revenue obtained from each barrel. Revenue is determined by multiplying the selling price of each grade of motor oil by the total barrels of each grade produced. Cost is achieved by multiplying the cost of each component by the total barrels of each component used:

$$\begin{aligned} \text{maximize } Z = {} & \$23(x_{1s} + x_{2s} + x_{3s}) + 20(x_{1p} + x_{2p} + x_{3p}) + 18(x_{1e} + x_{2e} + x_{3e}) \\ & - 12(x_{1s} + x_{1p} + x_{1e}) - 10(x_{2s} + x_{2p} + x_{2e}) - 14(x_{3s} + x_{3p} + x_{3e}) \end{aligned}$$

Combining terms results in the following objective function:

$$\text{maximize } Z = 11x_{1s} + 13x_{2s} + 9x_{3s} + 8x_{1p} + 10x_{2p} + 6x_{3p} + 6x_{1e} + 8x_{2e} + 4x_{3e}$$

Model Constraints

This problem has several sets of constraints. The first set reflects the limited amount of each component available on a daily basis:

$$\begin{aligned} x_{1s} + x_{1p} + x_{1e} &\leq 4{,}500 \text{ bbl.} \\ x_{2s} + x_{2p} + x_{2e} &\leq 2{,}700 \text{ bbl.} \\ x_{3s} + x_{3p} + x_{3e} &\leq 3{,}500 \text{ bbl.} \end{aligned}$$

The next group of constraints is for the blend specifications for each grade of motor oil. The first specification is that super contain at least 50% of component 1, which is expressed as

$$\frac{x_{1s}}{x_{1s} + x_{2s} + x_{3s}} \geq 0.50$$

Standard form requires that fractional relationships between variables be eliminated.

This constraint says that the ratio of component 1 in super to the total amount of super produced, $x_{1s} + x_{2s} + x_{3s}$, must be at least 50%. Rewriting this constraint in a form more consistent with linear programming solution results in

$$x_{1s} \geq 0.50(x_{1s} + x_{2s} + x_{3s})$$

and

$$0.50x_{1s} - 0.50x_{2s} - 0.50x_{3s} \geq 0$$

This is the general form a linear programming constraint must be in before you can enter it for computer solution. All variables are on the left-hand side of the inequality, and only numeric values are on the right-hand side.

The constraint for the other blend specification for super grade, not more than 30% of component 2, is developed in the same way:

$$\frac{x_{2s}}{x_{1s} + x_{2s} + x_{3s}} \leq 0.30$$

and

$$0.70x_{2s} - 0.30x_{1s} - 0.30x_{3s} \leq 0$$

The two blend specifications for premium motor oil are

$$0.60x_{1p} - 0.40x_{2p} - 0.40x_{3p} \geq 0$$
$$0.75x_{3p} - 0.25x_{1p} - 0.25x_{2p} \leq 0$$

The two blend specifications for extra motor oil are

$$0.40x_{1e} - 0.60x_{2e} - 0.60x_{3e} \geq 0$$
$$0.90x_{2e} - 0.10x_{1e} - 0.10x_{3e} \geq 0$$

The final set of constraints reflects the requirement that at least 3,000 barrels of each grade be produced:

$$x_{1s} + x_{2s} + x_{3s} \geq 3{,}000 \text{ bbl.}$$
$$x_{1p} + x_{2p} + x_{3p} \geq 3{,}000 \text{ bbl.}$$
$$x_{1e} + x_{2e} + x_{3e} \geq 3{,}000 \text{ bbl.}$$

Model Summary

The complete linear programming model for this problem is summarized as follows:

maximize $Z = 11x_{1s} + 13x_{2s} + 9x_{3s} + 8x_{1p} + 10x_{2p} + 6x_{3p} + 6x_{1e} + 8x_{2e} + 4x_{3e}$

subject to

$$x_{1s} + x_{1p} + x_{1e} \leq 4{,}500$$
$$x_{2s} + x_{2p} + x_{2e} \leq 2{,}700$$
$$x_{3s} + x_{3p} + x_{3e} \leq 3{,}500$$
$$0.50x_{1s} - 0.50x_{2s} - 0.50x_{3s} \geq 0$$
$$0.70x_{2s} - 0.30x_{1s} - 0.30x_{3s} \leq 0$$

$$0.60x_{1p} - 0.40x_{2p} - 0.40x_{3p} \geq 0$$
$$0.75x_{3p} - 0.25x_{1p} - 0.25x_{2p} \leq 0$$
$$0.40x_{1e} - 0.60x_{2e} - 0.60x_{3e} \geq 0$$
$$0.90x_{2e} - 0.10x_{1e} - 0.10x_{3e} \geq 0$$
$$x_{1s} + x_{2s} + x_{3s} \geq 3{,}000$$
$$x_{1p} + x_{2p} + x_{3p} \geq 3{,}000$$
$$x_{1e} + x_{2e} + x_{3e} \geq 3{,}000$$
$$x_{ij} \geq 0$$

Computer Solution with Excel

The Excel spreadsheet solution for this blend example is shown in Exhibit 17. Solver is shown in Exhibit 18. The decision variables are located in cells **B7:B15** in Exhibit 17. The total profit

Exhibit 17

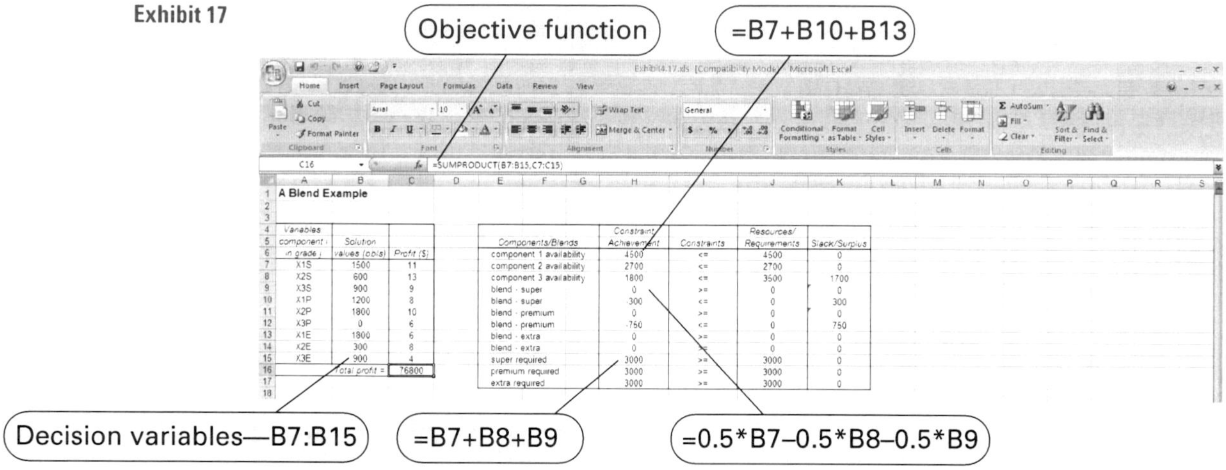

Exhibit 18

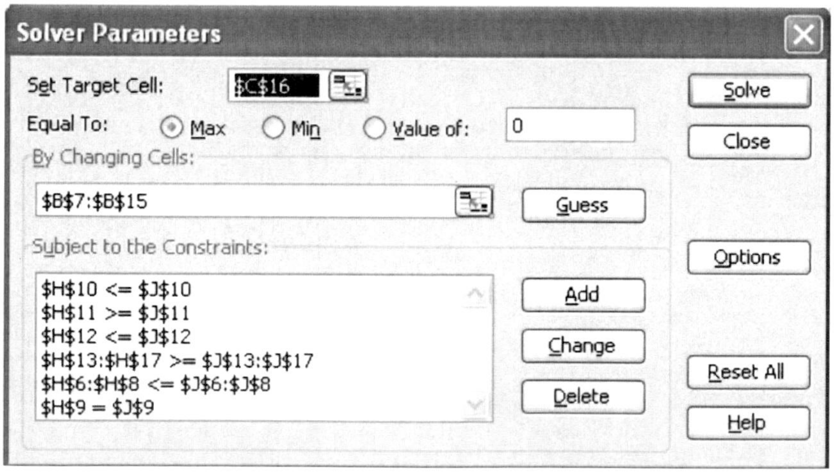

is computed in cell C16, using the formula **=SUMPRODUCT(B7:B15,C7:C15)**, which is also shown on the formula bar at the top of the spreadsheet. The constraint formulas are embedded in cells H6 through H17. Notice that we did not develop an array of constraint coefficients on the spreadsheet for this model; instead, we typed the constraint formulas directly into cells H6:H17, which seemed easier. For example, the constraint formula in cell H6 is

=B7+B10+B13, and the constraint formula in cell H9 is **=.5*B7–.5*B8–.5*B9**. The remaining cells in column H have similar constraint formulas.

Solution Analysis

The solution is

$$
\begin{aligned}
x_{1s} &= 1{,}500 \text{ bbl.}\\
x_{2s} &= 600 \text{ bbl.}\\
x_{3s} &= 900 \text{ bbl.}\\
x_{1p} &= 1{,}200 \text{ bbl.}\\
x_{2p} &= 1{,}800 \text{ bbl.}\\
x_{1e} &= 1{,}800 \text{ bbl.}\\
x_{2e} &= 300 \text{ bbl.}\\
x_{3e} &= 900 \text{ bbl.}\\
Z &= \$76{,}800
\end{aligned}
$$

Summarizing these results, 3,000 barrels of super grade, premium, and extra are produced. Also, 4,500 barrels of component 1, and 2,700 barrels of component 2, and 1,800 barrels of component 3 are used. (This problem also contains multiple optimal solutions.)

Recall that the ***shadow price*** *is the marginal economic value of one additional unit of a resource.*

Exhibit 19 shows the sensitivity report for our Excel solution of the blend problem. Notice that the **shadow price** for component 1 is $20. This indicates that component 1 is by far the most critical resource for increasing profit. For every additional barrel of

Exhibit 19

Adjustable Cells

Cell	Name	Final Value	Reduced Cost	Objective Coefficient	Allowable Increase	Allowable Decrease
B7	X1S values (bbls)	1500	0	11	1E+30	3
B8	X2S values (bbls)	600	0	13	0	0
B9	X3S values (bbls)	900	0	9	0	0
B10	X1P values (bbls)	1200	0	8	3	1E+30
B11	X2P values (bbls)	1800	0	10	2	0
B12	X3P values (bbls)	0	0	6	0	1E+30
B13	X1E values (bbls)	1800	0	6	3	1E+30
B14	X2E values (bbls)	300	0	8	0	1E+30
B15	X3E values (bbls)	900	0	4	22.67	0

Constraints

Cell	Name	Final Value	Shadow Price	Constraint R.H. Side	Allowable Increase	Allowable Decrease
H13	blend - extra Achievement	0	-18	0	1.1E-05	8.5E+02
H14	blend - extra Achievement	0	0	0	6.0E+02	3.0E+02
H15	super required Achievement	3000	0	3000	2.2E-05	1.0E+30
H16	premium required Achievement	3000	-1	3000	2.7E-05	8.3E+02
H17	extra required Achievement	3000	-7	3000	1.8E-05	3.0E+03
H12	blend - premium Achievement	-750	0	0	1.0E+30	7.5E+02
H11	blend - premium Achievement	0	-18	0	1.1E-05	6.0E+02
H9	blend - super Achievement	0	-18	0	1.1E-05	8.5E+02
H10	blend - super Achievement	-300	0	0	1.0E+30	3.0E+02
H6	component 1 availability Achievement	4500	20	4500	1.7E+03	1.1E-05
H7	component 2 availability Achievement	2700	4	2700	3.0E+02	6.0E+02
H8	component 3 availability Achievement	1800	0	3500	1.0E+30	1.7E+03

The shadow price for component 1 is $20.

The upper limit for the sensitivity range for component 1 is 4500 + 1700 = 6200.

component 1 that can be acquired, profit will increase by \$20. For example, if the current available amount of component 1 was increased from 4,500 barrels to 4,501 barrels, profit would increase from \$76,800 to \$76,820. (This dual price is valid up to 6,200 barrels of component 1, the upper limit for the sensitivity range for this constraint quantity value.)

In the refinery industry, different grade stocks of oil and gasoline are available based on the makeup and quality of the crude oil that is received. Thus, as crude oil properties change, it is necessary to change blend requirements. Component availability changes as well. The general structure of this model can be used on a daily basis to plan production based on component availability and blend specification changes.

A Multiperiod Scheduling Example

PM Computer Services assembles its own brand of personal computers from component parts it purchases overseas and domestically. PM sells most of its computers locally to different departments at State University as well as to individuals and businesses in the immediate geographic region.

PM has enough regular production capacity to produce 160 computers per week. It can produce an additional 50 computers with overtime. The cost of assembling, inspecting, and packaging a computer during regular time is \$190. Overtime production of a computer costs \$260. Furthermore, it costs \$10 per computer per week to hold a computer in inventory for future delivery. PM wants to meet all customer orders, with no shortages, to provide quality service. PM's order schedule for the next 6 weeks is as follows:

Week	*Computer Orders*
1	105
2	170
3	230
4	180
5	150
6	250

PM Computers wants to determine a schedule that will indicate how much regular and overtime production it will need each week to meet its orders at the minimum cost. The company wants no inventory left over at the end of the 6-week period.

Decision Variables

This model consists of three different sets of decision variables for computers produced during regular time each week, overtime production each week, and extra computers carried over as inventory each week. This results in a total of 17 decision variables. Because this problem contains a large number of decision variables, we will define them with names that will make them a little easier to keep up with:

$$r_j = \text{regular production of computers per week } j\ (j = 1, 2, 3, 4, 5, 6)$$
$$o_j = \text{overtime production of computers per week } j\ (j = 1, 2, 3, 4, 5, 6)$$
$$i_j = \text{extra computers carried over as inventory in week } j\ (j = 1, 2, 3, 4, 5)$$

This will result in 6 decision variables for regular production (r_1, r_2, etc.) and 6 decision variables for overtime production. There are only 5 decision variables for inventory because the problem stipulates that there is to be no inventory left over at the end of the 6-week period.

Management Science Application

Gasoline Blending at Texaco

The petroleum industry first began using linear programming to solve gasoline blending problems in the 1950s. A single grade of gasoline can be a blend of from 3 to 10 different components. A typical refinery might have as many as 20 different components it blends into four or more grades of gasoline. Each grade of gasoline differs according to octane level, volatility, and area marketing requirements.

At Texaco, for example, the typical gasoline blends are Power and unleaded regular, Plus, and Power Premium. These different grades are blended from a variety of available stocks that are intermediate refinery products, such as distilled gasoline, reformate gasoline, and catalytically cracked gasoline. Additives include, among other things, octane enhancers. As many as 15 stocks can be blended to yield up to eight different blends. The properties or attributes of a blend are determined by a combination of properties that exist in the gasoline stocks and those of any additives. Examples of stock properties (that originally emanated from crude oil) include to some extent vapor pressure, sulfur content, aromatic content, and octane value, among other items. A linear programming model determines the volume of each blend, subject to constraints for stock availability, demand, and the property (or attribute) specifications for each blend. A single blend may have up to 14 different characteristics. In a typical blend analysis involving seven input stocks and four blends, the problem will include 40 variables and 71 constraints.

Texaco, Inc.

Sources: C. E. Bodington and T. E. Baker, "A History of Mathematical Programming in the Petroleum Industry," *Interfaces* 20, no. 4 (July–August 1990): 117–27; and C. W. DeWitt et al., "OMEGA: An Improved Gasoline Blending System for Texaco," *Interfaces* 19, no. 1 (January–February 1989): 85–101.

The Objective Function

The objective is to minimize total production cost, which is the sum of regular and overtime production costs and inventory costs:

$$\text{minimize } Z = \$190(r_1 + r_2 + r_3 + r_4 + r_5 + r_6) + 260(o_1 + o_2 + o_3 + o_4 + o_5 + o_6) + 10(i_1 + i_2 + i_3 + i_4 + i_5)$$

Model Constraints

This model includes three sets of constraints. The first two sets reflect the available capacity for regular and overtime production, and the third set establishes the production schedule per week.

The available regular production capacity of 160 computers for each of the 6 weeks results in six constraints, as follows:

$$r_j \leq 160 \text{ computers in week } j\ (j = 1, 2, 3, 4, 5, 6)$$

The available overtime production capacity of 50 computers per week also results in six constraints:

$$o_j \leq 50 \text{ computers in week } j\ (j = 1, 2, 3, 4, 5, 6)$$

The next set of six constraints shows the regular and overtime production and inventory necessary to meet the order requirement each week:

$$\begin{aligned} &\textit{week } 1\text{: } r_1 + o_1 - i_1 = 105 \\ &\text{week } 2\text{: } r_2 + o_2 + i_1 - i_2 = 170 \\ &\text{week } 3\text{: } r_3 + o_3 + i_2 - i_3 = 230 \\ &\text{week } 4\text{: } r_4 + o_4 + i_3 - i_4 = 180 \\ &\text{week } 5\text{: } r_5 + o_5 + i_4 - i_5 = 150 \\ &\text{week } 6\text{: } r_6 + o_6 + i_5 = 250 \end{aligned}$$

For example, 105 computers have been ordered in week 1. Regular production, r_1, and overtime production, o_1, will meet this order, whereas any extra production that might be needed in a future week to meet an order, i_1, is subtracted because it does not go to meet the order. Subsequently, in week 2 the order of 170 computers is met by regular and overtime production, $r_2 + o_2$, plus inventory carried over from week 1, i_1.

Model Summary

The complete model for this problem is summarized as follows:

$$\text{minimize } Z = \$190(r_1 + r_2 + r_3 + r_4 + r_5 + r_6) + \$260(o_1 + o_2 + o_3 + o_4 + o_5 + o_6) + 10(i_1 + i_2 + i_3 + i_4 + i_5)$$

subject to

$$\begin{aligned} r_j &\le 160\ (j = 1, 2, 3, 4, 5, 6) \\ o_j &\le 50\ (j = 1, 2, 3, 4, 5, 6) \\ r_1 + o_1 - i_1 &= 105 \\ r_2 + o_2 + i_1 - i_2 &= 170 \\ r_3 + o_3 + i_2 - i_3 &= 230 \\ r_4 + o_4 + i_3 - i_4 &= 180 \\ r_5 + o_5 + i_4 - i_5 &= 150 \\ r_6 + o_6 + i_5 &= 250 \\ r_j, o_j, i_j &\ge 0 \end{aligned}$$

Computer Solution with Excel

The Excel spreadsheet for this multiperiod scheduling example is shown in Exhibit 20, and the accompanying Solver window is shown in Exhibit 21. The formula for the objective

Exhibit 20

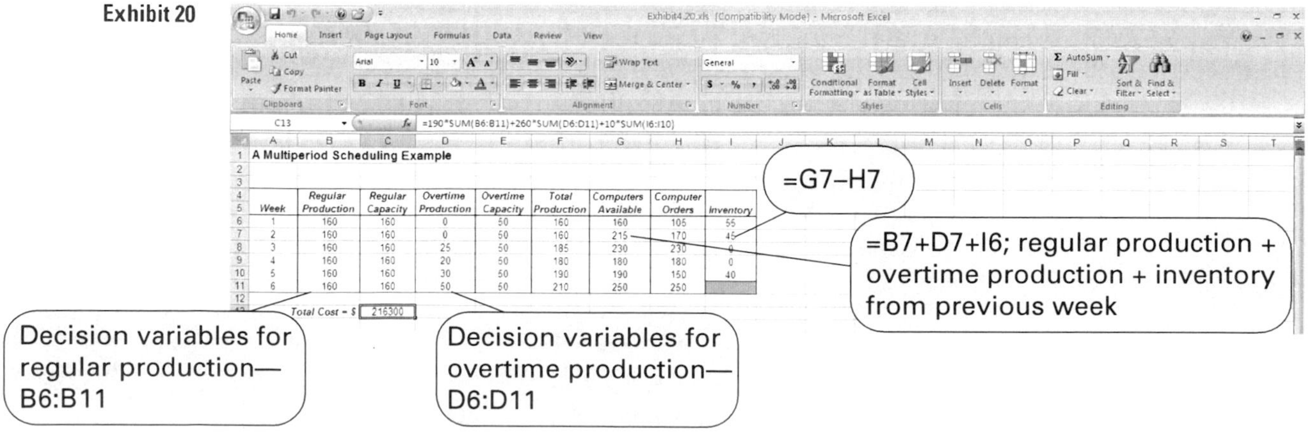

Exhibit 21

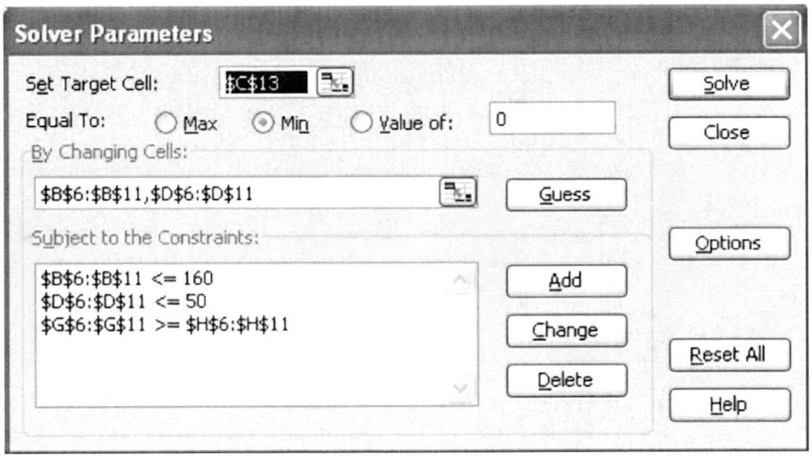

function is embedded in cell C13 and is shown on the formula bar at the top of the screen. The decision variables for regular production are included in cells **B6:B11**, whereas the variables for overtime production are in cells **D6:D11**. The computers available each week in column G includes the regular production plus overtime production plus the inventory from the previous week. For example, cell G7 (computers available in week 2) has the formula =**B7+D7+I6**. Cell I7 (the inventory left over in week 2) includes the formula =**G7–H7** (i.e., computers available minus computers ordered).

The actual constraint for week 2 would be **G7>=H7**. It is also necessary to enter the constraints for available regular and overtime production capacities into Solver. For example, the constraint for regular capacity would be **B6:B11≤ 160**.

Solution Analysis

The solution is

r_1 = 160 computers produced in regular time in week 1
r_2 = 160 computers produced in regular time in week 2
r_3 = 160 computers produced in regular time in week 3
r_4 = 160 computers produced in regular time in week 4
r_5 = 160 computers produced in regular time in week 5
r_6 = 160 computers produced in regular time in week 6
o_3 = 25 computers produced with overtime in week 3
o_4 = 20 computers produced with overtime in week 4
o_5 = 30 computers produced with overtime in week 5
o_6 = 50 computers produced with overtime in week 6
i_1 = 55 computers carried over in inventory in week 1
i_2 = 45 computers carried over in inventory in week 2
i_5 = 40 computers carried over in inventory in week 5

PM Computers must operate with regular production at full capacity during the entire 6-week period. It must also resort to overtime production in weeks 3, 4, 5, and 6 in order to meet heavier order volume in weeks 3 through 6.

As each week passes, PM Computers can use this model to update its production schedule should order sizes change. For example, if PM is in week 2, and the orders for week 5 change from 150 computers to 200, the model can be altered and a new schedule computed.

The model can also be extended further out into the planning horizon to develop future production schedules.

PM may want to consider expanding its regular production capacity because of the heavy overtime requirements in weeks 3 through 6. The dual values (from the sensitivity analysis report from the computer output) for the constraints representing regular production in weeks 3 through 6 show that for each capacity increase for regular production time that will enable the production of one more computer, cost can be reduced by between $70 and $80. (This total reduction would occur if processing time could be reduced without acquiring additional labor, etc. If additional resources were acquired to achieve an increase in capacity, the cost would have to be subtracted from the shadow price.)

A Data Envelopment Analysis Example

Data envelopment analysis (DEA) is a linear programming application that compares a number of service units of the same type—such as banks, hospitals, restaurants, and schools—based on their inputs (resources) and outputs. The model solution result indicates whether a particular unit is less productive, or inefficient, compared with other units. For example, DEA has compared hospitals where inputs include hospital beds and staff size and outputs include patient days for different age groups.

As an example of a DEA linear programming application, consider a town with four elementary schools—Alton, Beeks, Carey, and Delancey. The state has implemented a series of standards of learning (SOL) tests in reading, math, and history that all schools are required to administer to all students in the fifth grade. The average test scores are a measurable output of the school's performance. The school board has identified three key resources, or inputs, that affect a school's SOL scores—the teacher-to-student ratio, supplementary funds per student (i.e., funding generated by the PTA and other private sources over and above the normal budget), and the average educational level of the parents (where 12 = high school graduate, 16 = college graduate, etc.). These inputs and outputs are summarized as follows:

$$\begin{aligned}
\text{input 1} &= \text{teacher-to-student ratio}\\
\text{input 2} &= \text{supplementary funds/student}\\
\text{input 3} &= \text{average educational level of parents}\\
\text{output 1} &= \text{average reading SOL score}\\
\text{output 2} &= \text{average math SOL score}\\
\text{output 3} &= \text{average history SOL score}
\end{aligned}$$

The actual input and output values for each school are

	Inputs			**Outputs**		
School	1	2	3	1	2	3
Alton	.06	$260	11.3	86	75	71
Beeks	.05	320	10.5	82	72	67
Carey	.08	340	12.0	81	79	80
Delancey	.06	460	13.1	81	73	69

For example, at Alton, the teacher-to-student ratio is 0.06 (or approximately one teacher per 16.67 students), there is $260 per student supplemental funds, and the average parent

Management Science Application

Analyzing Bank Branch Efficiency by Using DEA

Data envelopment analysis (DEA) is an application of linear programming that is used to determine the less productive (i.e., inefficient) service units among a group of similar service units. DEA bases this determination on the inputs (resources) and outputs of the service units.

A major northeastern bank, with 33 branches, used DEA to identify ways to improve its productivity. Bank management did not know how to identify the more efficient branches. The bank identified five resource inputs available to all branches—customer service (tellers), sales service, management, expenses, and office space. Five groups of branch outputs were also identified—deposits, withdrawals, and checking; bank and traveler's checks and bonds; night deposits; loans; and new accounts. The DEA model found that only 10 branches were operating efficiently, whereas 23 branches were using excess resources to provide their volume and mix of services and were, thus, inefficient. The DEA model results provided the basis for reviewing and evaluating branch operations, which revealed operating differences between inefficient branches and best-practice branches. The bank was able to improve its branch productivity and profits substantially, reducing its total branch staff by approximately 20% within 1 year of the completion of the DEA analysis and implementing changes in branch operations that resulted in annual savings of over $6 million.

William Taufic/Corbis/Stock Market

Source: H. D. Sherman and G. Ladino, "Managing Bank Productivity Using Data Envelopment Analysis (DEA)," *Interfaces* 25, no. 2 (March–April 1995): 60–73.

educational grade level is 11.3. The average scores on Alton's reading, math, and history tests are 86, 75, and 71, respectively.

The school board wants to identify the school or schools that are less efficient in converting their inputs to outputs relative to the other elementary schools in the town. The DEA linear programming model will compare one particular school with all the others. For a complete analysis, a separate model is necessary for each school. For this example, we will evaluate the Delancey school as compared with the other schools.

Decision Variables

The formulation of a DEA linear programming model is not as readily apparent as the previous example models in this chapter. It is particularly difficult to define the decision variables in a meaningful way.

In a DEA model, the decision variables are defined as a price per unit of each output and each input. These are not the actual prices that inputs or outputs would be valued at. In economic terms, these prices are referred to as *implicit prices*, or *opportunity costs*. These prices are a relative valuation of inputs and outputs among the schools. They do not have much meaning for us, as will become apparent as the model is developed. For now, the decision variables will simply be defined as

$$x_i = \text{a price per unit of each output where } i = 1, 2, 3$$
$$y_i = \text{a price per unit of each input where } i = 1, 2, 3$$

The Objective Function

The objective of our model is to determine whether Delancey is efficient. In a DEA model, when we are attempting to determine whether a unit (i.e., a school) is efficient, it simplifies things to scale the input prices so that the total value of a unit's inputs equals 1. The efficiency of the unit will then equal the value of the unit's outputs. For this example, this means that once we scale Delancey's input prices so that they equal 1 (which we will do by formulating a constraint), the efficiency of Delancey will equal the value of its outputs. The objective, then, is to maximize the value of Delancey's outputs, which also equals efficiency:

$$\text{maximize } Z = 81x_1 + 73x_2 + 69x_3$$

Because the school's inputs will be scaled to 1, the maximum value that Delancey's outputs, as formulated in the objective function, can take on is 1. If the objective function equals 1, the school is efficient; if the objective function is less than 1, the school is inefficient.

Model Constraints

The constraint that will scale the Delancey school's inputs to 1 is formulated as

$$.06y_1 + 460y_2 + 13.1y_3 = 1$$

This sets the value of the inputs to 1 and ultimately forces the value of the outputs to 1 or less. This also has the effect of making the values of the decision variables even less meaningful.

The values of the outputs are forced to be 1 or less by the next set of constraints. In general terms, the efficiency of a school (or any productive unit) can be defined as

$$\text{efficiency} = \frac{\text{value of outputs}}{\text{value of inputs}}$$

It is not possible for a school or any service unit to be more than 100% efficient; thus, the efficiency of the school must be less than or equal to 1 and

$$\frac{\text{value of school's outputs}}{\text{value of school's inputs}} \leq 1$$

Converting this to standard linear form,

$$\text{value of school's outputs} \leq \text{value of school's inputs}$$

Substituting the model's decision variables and parameters for inputs and outputs into this general constraint form results in four constraints, one for each school:

$$86x_1 + 75x_2 + 71x_3 \leq .06y_1 + 260y_2 + 11.3y_3$$
$$82x_1 + 72x_2 + 67x_3 \leq .05y_1 + 320y_2 + 10.5y_3$$
$$81x_1 + 79x_2 + 80x_3 \leq .08y_1 + 340y_2 + 12.0y_3$$
$$81x_1 + 73x_2 + 69x_3 \leq .06y_1 + 460y_2 + 13.1y_3$$

Model Summary

The complete linear programming model for determining the efficiency of the Delancey school is

$$
\begin{aligned}
&\text{maximize } Z = 81x_1 + 73x_2 + 69x_3 \\
&\text{subject to} \\
&.06y_1 + 460y_2 + 13.1y_3 = 1 \\
&\quad 86x_1 + 75x_2 + 71x_3 \le .06y_1 + 260y_2 + 11.3y_3 \\
&\quad 82x_1 + 72x_2 + 67x_3 \le .05y_1 + 320y_2 + 10.5y_3 \\
&\quad 81x_1 + 79x_2 + 80x_3 \le .08y_1 + 340y_2 + 12.0y_3 \\
&\quad 81x_1 + 73x_2 + 69x_3 \le .06y_1 + 460y_2 + 13.1y_3 \\
&\qquad\qquad x_i, y_i \ge 0
\end{aligned}
$$

The objective of this model is to determine whether Delancey is inefficient: If the value of the objective function equals 1, the school is efficient; if it is less than 1, it is inefficient. As mentioned previously, the values of the decision variables, x_i and y_i, have little meaning for us. They are the implicit prices of converting an input into an output, but they have been scaled to 1 to simplify the model. The model solution selects values of x_i and y_i that will maximize the school's efficiency, the maximum of which is 1, but these values have no easily interpretable meaning beyond that.

Computer Solution with Excel

The Excel spreadsheet for this DEA example is shown in Exhibit 22. The Solver window is shown in Exhibit 23. The decision variables are located in cells **B12:B14** and **D12:D14**. The

Exhibit 22

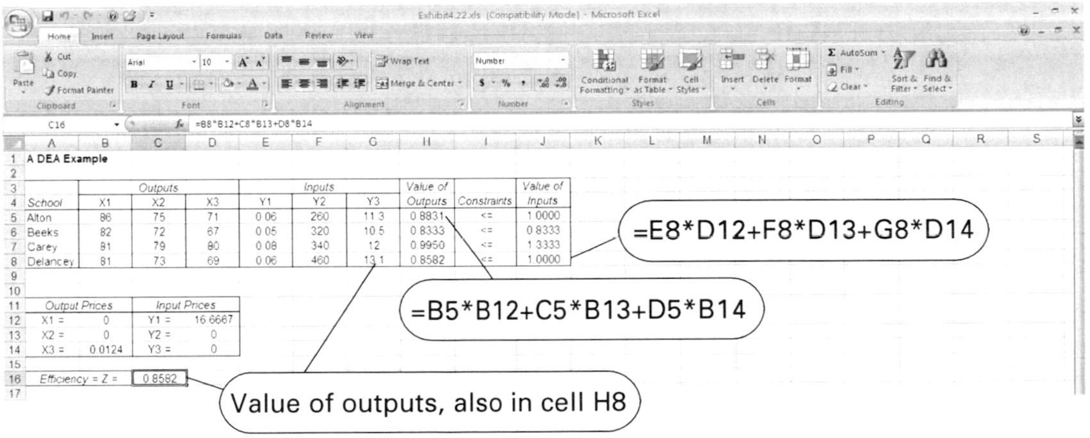

objective function value, Z, which is also the indicator of whether Delancey is inefficient, is shown in cell C16. This value is computed using the formula for the value of the Delancey school's output, =**B8*B12+C8*B13+D8*B14**, which is also shown in cell H8 and is a measure of the school's efficiency.

The output and input values for each school are embedded in cells **H5:H8** and **J5:J8**, respectively. These values are used to develop the model constraints shown in Solver as **H5:H8** $\le$ **J5:J8**. The scaling constraint is shown as **J8=1**, where the formula for the value of the inputs for the Delancey school, =**E8*D12+F8*D13+G8*D14**, is embedded in cell J8.

Exhibit 23

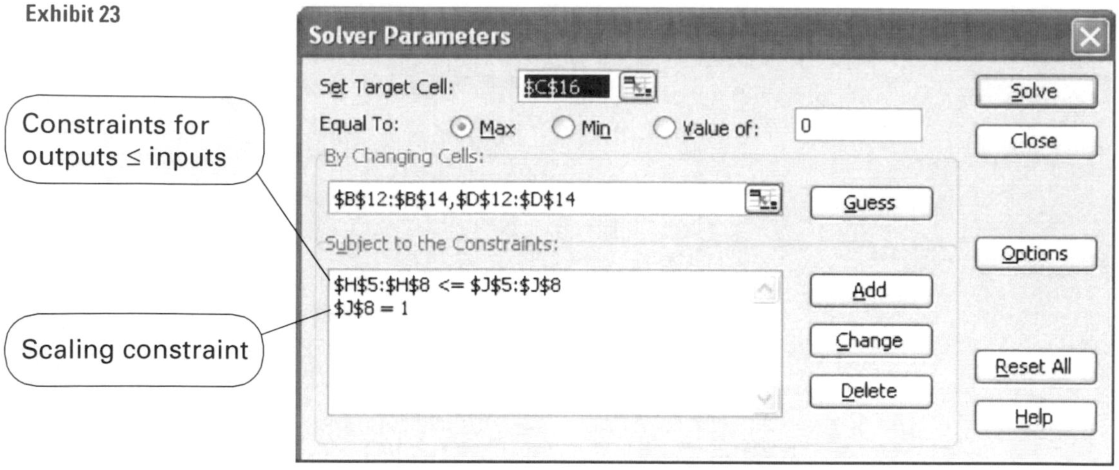

Solution Analysis

The only relevant solution value is the value of the objective function:

$$Z = 0.8582$$

Because this value is less than 1, the Delancey school is inefficient relative to the other schools. It is less efficient at converting its resources into outputs than the other schools. This means that a combination of efficient schools can achieve at least the same level of output as the Delancey school achieved with fewer input resources than required by the Delancey school. In retrospect, we can see that this is a logical result by looking back at the school's inputs and outputs. Although Delancey's input values are among the highest, its output test scores are among the lowest.

It is a simple process to access the efficiency of the other three schools in the town. For example, to ascertain the efficiency of the Alton school, make the value of its output in cell H5 the objective function in Solver, and make the formula for the value of the Alton school's inputs in cell I5 the scaling constraint, **J5=1**, in Solver. The efficiency of the other two schools can be assessed similarly. Doing so indicates an objective function value of 1 for each of the three other schools, indicating that all three are efficient.

Summary

A systematic approach to model formulation is first to define decision variables, construct the objective function, and finally develop each constraint separately; don't try to "see" it all at once.

Generally, it is not feasible to attempt to "see" the whole formulation of the constraints and objective function at once, following the definition of the decision variables. A more prudent approach is to construct the objective function first (without direct concern for the constraints) and then to direct attention to each problem restriction and its corresponding model constraint. This is a systematic approach to model formulation, in which steps are taken one at a time. In other words, it is important not to attempt to swallow the whole problem during the first reading.

Formulating a linear programming model from a written problem statement is often difficult, but formulating a model of a "real" problem that has no written statement is even more difficult. The steps for model formulation described in this section are generally followed; however, the problem must first be defined (i.e., a problem statement or some similar descriptive apparatus must be developed). Developing such a statement can be a formidable task, requiring the assistance of many individuals and units within an organization.

Developing the parameter values that are presented as givens in the written problem statements of this chapter frequently requires extensive data collection efforts. The objective function and model constraints can be very complex, requiring much time and effort to develop. Simply making sure that all the model constraints have been identified and no important problem restrictions have been omitted is difficult. Finally, the problems that one confronts in actual practice are typically much larger than those presented in this chapter. It is not uncommon for linear programming models of real problems to encompass hundreds of functional relationships and decision variables. Unfortunately, it is not possible in a textbook to re-create a realistic problem environment with no written problem statement and a model of large dimensions. What is possible is to provide the fundamentals of linear programming model formulation and solution—prerequisite to solving linear programming problems in actual practice.

References

See the references at the end of this chapter.

Example Problem Solution

As a prelude to the problems, this section presents an example solution of the formulation and computer solution of a linear programming problem.

Problem Statement

Bark's Pet Food Company produces canned cat food called Meow Chow and canned dog food called Bow Chow. The company produces the pet food from horse meat, ground fish, and a cereal additive. Each week the company has 600 pounds of horse meat, 800 pounds of ground fish, and 1,000 pounds of cereal additive available to produce both kinds of pet food. Meow Chow must be at least half fish, and Bow Chow must be at least half horse meat. The company has 2,250 16-ounce cans available each week. A can of Meow Chow earns \$0.80 in profit, and a can of Bow Chow earns \$0.96 in profit. The company wants to know how many cans of Meow Chow and Bow Chow to produce each week in order to maximize profit.

A. Formulate a linear programming model for this problem.
B. Solve the model by using the computer.

Solution

A. Model Formulation

Step 1: Define the Decision Variables

This problem encompasses six decision variables, representing the amount of each ingredient i in pet food j:

x_{ij} = ounces of ingredient i in pet food j per week, where $i = h$ (horse meat), f (fish), and c (cereal), and $j = m$ (Meow Chow) and b (Bow Chow)

To determine the number of cans of each pet food produced per week, the total ounces of Meow Chow produced, $x_{hm} + x_{fm} + x_{cm}$, and the total amount of Bow Chow produced, $x_{hb} + x_{fb} + x_{cb}$, would each be divided by 16 ounces.

Step 2: Formulate the Objective Function

The objective function is to maximize the total profit earned each week, which is determined by multiplying the number of cans of each pet food produced by the profit per can. However, because the decision variables are defined in terms of ounces, they must be converted to equivalent cans by dividing by 16 ounces, as follows:

$$\text{maximize } Z = \frac{0.80}{16}(x_{hm} + x_{fm} + x_{cm}) + \frac{0.96}{16}(x_{hb} + x_{fb} + x_{cb})$$

or

$$\text{maximize } Z = \$0.05(x_{hm} + x_{fm} + x_{cm}) + 0.06(x_{hb} + x_{fb} + x_{cb})$$

Step 3: Formulate the Model Constraints

The first set of constraints represents the amount of each ingredient available each week. The problem provides these in terms of pounds of horse meat, fish, and cereal additives. Thus, because the decision variables are expressed as ounces, the ingredient amounts must be converted to ounces by multiplying each pound by 16 ounces. This results in these three constraints:

$$\begin{aligned} x_{hm} + x_{hb} &\leq 9{,}600 \text{ oz. of horse meat} \\ x_{fm} + x_{fb} &\leq 12{,}800 \text{ oz. of fish} \\ x_{cm} + x_{cb} &\leq 16{,}000 \text{ oz. of cereal additive} \end{aligned}$$

Next, there are two recipe requirements specifying that at least half of Meow Chow be fish and at least half of Bow Chow be horse meat. The requirement for Meow Chow is formulated as

$$\frac{x_{fm}}{x_{hm} + x_{fm} + x_{cm}} \geq \frac{1}{2}$$

or

$$-x_{hm} + x_{fm} - x_{cm} \geq 0$$

The constraint for Bow Chow is developed similarly:

$$\frac{x_{hb}}{x_{hb} + x_{fb} + x_{cb}} \geq \frac{1}{2}$$

or

$$x_{hb} - x_{fb} - x_{cb} \geq 0$$

Finally, the problem indicates that the company has 2,250 16-ounce cans available each week. These cans must also be converted to ounces to conform to our decision variables, which results in the following constraint:

$$x_{hm} + x_{fm} + x_{cm} + x_{hb} + x_{fb} + x_{cb} \leq 36{,}000 \text{ oz.}$$

Step 4: The Model Summary

The complete model is summarized as

$$\text{maximize } Z = \$0.05x_{hm} + 0.05x_{fm} + 0.05x_{cm} + 0.06x_{hb} + 0.06x_{fb} + 0.06x_{cb}$$

subject to

$$\begin{aligned} x_{hm} + x_{hb} &\leq 9{,}600 \\ x_{fm} + x_{fb} &\leq 12{,}800 \end{aligned}$$

$$x_{cm} + x_{cb} \leq 16{,}000$$
$$-x_{hm} + x_{fm} - x_{cm} \geq 0$$
$$x_{hb} - x_{fb} - x_{cb} \geq 0$$
$$x_{hm} + x_{fm} + x_{cm} + x_{hb} + x_{fb} + x_{cb} \leq 36{,}000$$
$$x_{ij} \geq 0$$

B. Computer Solution

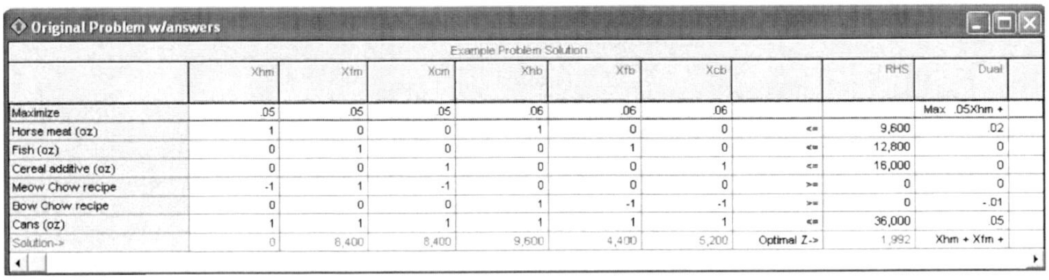

Original Problem w/answers

Example Problem Solution

	Xhm	Xfm	Xcm	Xhb	Xfb	Xcb		RHS	Dual
Maximize	.05	.05	.05	.06	.06	.06			Max .05Xhm +
Horse meat (oz)	1	0	0	1	0	0	<=	9,600	.02
Fish (oz)	0	1	0	0	1	0	<=	12,800	0
Cereal additive (oz)	0	0	1	0	0	1	<=	16,000	0
Meow Chow recipe	-1	1	-1	0	0	0	>=	0	0
Bow Chow recipe	0	0	0	1	-1	-1	>=	0	-.01
Cans (oz)	1	1	1	1	1	1	<=	36,000	.05
Solution->	0	8,400	8,400	9,600	4,400	5,200	Optimal Z->	1,992	Xhm + Xfm +

The computer solution for this model was generated by using the QM for Windows computer software package.

The solution is

$$x_{hm} = 0$$
$$x_{fm} = 8{,}400$$
$$x_{cm} = 8{,}400$$
$$x_{hb} = 9{,}600$$
$$x_{fb} = 4{,}400$$
$$x_{cb} = 5{,}200$$
$$Z = \$1{,}992$$

To determine the number of cans of each pet food, we must sum the ingredient amounts for each pet food and divide by 16 ounces (the size of a can):

$$x_{hm} + x_{fm} + x_{cm} = 0 + 8{,}400 + 8{,}400 = 16{,}800 \text{ oz. of Meow Chow}$$

or

$$16{,}800 \div 16 = 1{,}050 \text{ cans of Meow Chow}$$
$$x_{hb} + x_{fb} + x_{cb} = 9{,}600 + 4{,}400 + 5{,}200 = 19{,}200 \text{ oz. of Bow Chow}$$

or

$$19{,}200 \div 16 = 1{,}200 \text{ cans of Bow Chow}$$

Note that this model has multiple optimal solutions. An alternate optimal solution is $x_{fm} = 10{,}400, x_{cm} = 6{,}400, x_{hb} = 9{,}600$, and $x_{cb} = 9{,}600$. This converts to the same number of cans of each pet food; however, the ingredient mix per can is different.

Problems

1. In the product mix example in this chapter, Quick-Screen is considering adding some extra operators who would reduce processing times for each of the four clothing items by 10%. This would also increase the cost of each item by 10% and thus reduce unit profits by this same amount (because an increase in selling price would not be possible). Can this type of sensitivity analysis be evaluated using only original solution output, or will the model need to be solved again? Should Quick-Screen undertake this alternative?

In this problem, the profit per shirt is computed from the selling price less fixed and variable costs. The computer solution output shows the shadow price for T-shirts to be $4.11. If Quick-Screen decided to acquire extra T-shirts, could the company expect to earn an additional $4.11 for each extra T-shirt it acquires above 500, up to the sensitivity range limit of T-shirts?

If Quick-Screen produced equal numbers of each of the four shirts, how would the company reformulate the linear programming model to reflect this condition? What is the new solution to this reformulated model?

2. In the diet example in this chapter, what would be the effect on the optimal solution of increasing the minimum calorie requirement for the breakfast to 500 calories? to 600 calories?

   Increase the breakfast calorie requirement to 700 calories and reformulate the model to establish upper limits on the servings of each food item to what you think would be realistic and appetizing. Determine the solution for this reformulated model.

3. In the investment example in this chapter, how would the solution be affected if the requirement that the entire $70,000 be invested was relaxed such that it is the maximum amount available for investment?

   If the entire amount available for investment does not have to be invested and the amount available is increased by $10,000 (to $80,000), how much will the total optimal return increase? Will the entire $10,000 increase be invested in one alternative?

4. For the marketing example in this chapter, if the budget is increased by $20,000, how much will audience exposures be increased?

   If Biggs Department Store wanted the same total number of people exposed to each of the three types of advertisements, how should the linear programming model be reformulated? What would be the new solution for this reformulated model?

5. For the transportation example in this chapter, suppose that television sets not shipped were to incur storage costs of $9 at Cincinnati, $6 at Atlanta, and $7 at Pittsburgh. How would these storage costs be reflected in the linear programming model for this example problem, and what would the new solution be, if any?

   The Zephyr Television Company is considering leasing a new warehouse in Memphis. The new warehouse would have a supply of 200 television sets, with shipping costs of $18 to New York, $9 to Dallas, and $12 to Detroit. If the total transportation cost for the company (ignoring the cost of leasing the warehouse) is less than with the current warehouses, the company will lease the new warehouse. Should the warehouse be leased?

   If supply could be increased at any one warehouse, which should it be? What restrictions would there be on the amount of the increase?

6. For the blend example in this chapter, if the requirement that "at least 3,000 barrels of each grade of motor oil" was changed to *exactly* 3,000 barrels of each grade, how would this affect the optimal solution?

   If the company could acquire more of one of the three components, which should it be? What would be the effect on the total profit of acquiring more of this component?

7. On their farm, the Friendly family grows apples that they harvest each fall and make into three products—apple butter, applesauce, and apple jelly. They sell these three items at several local grocery stores, at craft fairs in the region, and at their own Friendly Farm Pumpkin Festival for 2 weeks in October. Their three primary resources are cooking time in their kitchen, their own labor time, and the apples. They have a total of 500 cooking hours available, and it requires 3.5 hours to cook a 10-gallon batch of apple butter, 5.2 hours to cook 10 gallons of applesauce, and 2.8 hours to cook 10 gallons of jelly. A 10-gallon batch of apple butter requires 1.2 hours of labor, a batch of sauce takes 0.8 hour, and a batch of jelly requires 1.5 hours. The Friendly family has 240 hours of labor available during the fall. They produce about 6,500 apples each fall. A batch of apple butter requires

40 apples, a 10-gallon batch of applesauce requires 55 apples, and a batch of jelly requires 20 apples. After the products are canned, a batch of apple butter will generate $190 in sales revenue, a batch of applesauce will generate a sales revenue of $170, and a batch of jelly will generate sales revenue of $155. The Friendlys want to know how many batches of apple butter, applesauce, and apple jelly to produce in order to maximize their revenues.

a. Formulate a linear programming model for this problem.
b. Solve the model by using the computer.

8. a. If the Friendlys in Problem 7 were to use leftover apples to feed livestock, at an estimated cost savings worth $0.08 per apple in revenue, how would this affect the model and solution?
b. Instead of feeding the leftover apples to the livestock, the Friendlys are thinking about producing apple cider. Cider will require 1.5 hours of cooking, 0.5 hour of labor, and 60 apples per batch, and it will sell for $45 per batch. Should the Friendlys use all their apples and produce cider along with their other three products?

9. A hospital dietitian prepares breakfast menus every morning for the hospital patients. Part of the dietitian's responsibility is to make sure that minimum daily requirements for vitamins A and B are met. At the same time, the cost of the menus must be kept as low as possible. The main breakfast staples providing vitamins A and B are eggs, bacon, and cereal. The vitamin requirements and vitamin contributions for each staple follow:

	Vitamin Contributions			
Vitamin	mg/Egg	mg/Bacon Strip	mg/Cereal Cup	**Minimum Daily Requirements**
A	2	4	1	16
B	3	2	1	12

An egg costs $0.04, a bacon strip costs $0.03, and a cup of cereal costs $0.02. The dietitian wants to know how much of each staple to serve per order to meet the minimum daily vitamin requirements while minimizing total cost.

a. Formulate a linear programming model for this problem.
b. Solve the model by using the computer.

10. Lakeside Boatworks is planning to manufacture three types of molded fiberglass recreational boats—a fishing (bass) boat, a ski boat, and a small speedboat. The estimated selling price and variable cost for each type of boat are summarized in the following table:

Boat	Variable Cost	Selling Price
Bass	$12,500	$23,000
Ski	8,500	18,000
Speed	13,700	26,000

The company has incurred fixed costs of $2,800,000 to set up its manufacturing operation and begin production. Lakeside has also entered into agreements with several boat dealers in the region to provide a minimum of 70 bass boats, 50 ski boats, and 50 speedboats. Alternatively, the company is unsure of what actual demand will be, so it has decided to limit production to no more than 120 of any one boat. The company wants to determine the number of boats that it must sell to break even while minimizing its total variable cost.

a. Formulate a linear programming model for this problem.
b. Solve the model by using the computer.

11. The Pyrotec Company produces three electrical products—clocks, radios, and toasters. These products have the following resource requirements:

	Resource Requirements	
	Cost/Unit	Labor Hours/Unit
Clock	$ 7	2
Radio	10	3
Toaster	5	2

The manufacturer has a daily production budget of $2,000 and a maximum of 660 hours of labor. Maximum daily customer demand is for 200 clocks, 300 radios, and 150 toasters. Clocks sell for $15, radios for $20, and toasters for $12. The company wants to know the optimal product mix that will maximize profit.

a. Formulate a linear programming model for this problem.
b. Solve the model by using the computer.

12. Betty Malloy, owner of the Eagle Tavern in Pittsburgh, is preparing for Super Bowl Sunday, and she must determine how much beer to stock. Betty stocks three brands of beer—Yodel, Shotz, and Rainwater. The cost per gallon (to the tavern owner) of each brand is as follows:

Brand	**Cost/Gallon**
Yodel	$1.50
Shotz	0.90
Rainwater	0.50

The tavern has a budget of $2,000 for beer for Super Bowl Sunday. Betty sells Yodel at a rate of $3.00 per gallon, Shotz at $2.50 per gallon, and Rainwater at $1.75 per gallon. Based on past football games, Betty has determined the maximum customer demand to be 400 gallons of Yodel, 500 gallons of Shotz, and 300 gallons of Rainwater. The tavern has the capacity to stock 1,000 gallons of beer; Betty wants to stock up completely. Betty wants to determine the number of gallons of each brand of beer to order so as to maximize profit.

a. Formulate a linear programming model for this problem.
b. Solve the model by using the computer.

13. The Kalo Fertilizer Company produces two brands of lawn fertilizer—Super Two and Green Grow—at plants in Fresno, California, and Dearborn, Michigan. The plant at Fresno has resources available to produce 5,000 pounds of fertilizer daily; the plant at Dearborn has enough resources to produce 6,000 pounds daily. The cost per pound of producing each brand at each plant is as follows:

	Plant	
Product	Fresno	Dearborn
Super Two	$2	$4
Green Grow	2	3

The company has a daily budget of $45,000 for both plants combined. Based on past sales, the company knows the maximum demand (converted to a daily basis) is 6,000 pounds for Super Two and 7,000 pounds for Green Grow. The selling price is $9 per pound for Super Two and $7 per pound for Green Grow. The company wants to know the number of pounds of each brand of fertilizer to produce at each plant in order to maximize profit.

a. Formulate a linear programming model for this problem.
b. Solve the model by using the computer.

14. Grafton Metalworks Company produces metal alloys from six different ores it mines. The company has an order from a customer to produce an alloy that contains four metals according to the following specifications: at least 21% of metal A, no more than 12% of metal B, no more than 7% of metal C, and between 30% and 65% of metal D. The proportion of the four metals in each of the six ores and the level of impurities in each ore are provided in the following table:

	Metal (%)					
Ore	A	B	C	D	**Impurities (%)**	**Cost/Ton**
1	19	15	12	14	40	$27
2	43	10	25	7	15	25
3	17	0	0	53	30	32
4	20	12	0	18	50	22
5	0	24	10	31	35	20
6	12	18	16	25	29	24

When the metals are processed and refined, the impurities are removed.

The company wants to know the amount of each ore to use per ton of the alloy that will minimize the cost per ton of the alloy.

a. Formulate a linear programming model for this problem.
b. Solve the model by using the computer.

15. The Roadnet Transport Company expanded its shipping capacity by purchasing 90 trailer trucks from a bankrupt competitor. The company subsequently located 30 of the purchased trucks at each of its shipping warehouses in Charlotte, Memphis, and Louisville. The company makes shipments from each of these warehouses to terminals in St. Louis, Atlanta, and New York. Each truck is capable of making one shipment per week. The terminal managers have indicated their capacity for extra shipments. The manager at St. Louis can accommodate 40 additional trucks per week, the manager at Atlanta can accommodate 60 additional trucks, and the manager at New York can accommodate 50 additional trucks. The company makes the following profit per truckload shipment from each warehouse to each terminal. The profits differ as a result of differences in products shipped, shipping costs, and transport rates:

	Terminal		
Warehouse	St. Louis	Atlanta	New York
Charlotte	$1,800	$2,100	$1,600
Memphis	1,000	700	900
Louisville	1,400	800	2,200

The company wants to know how many trucks to assign to each route (i.e., warehouse to terminal) to maximize profit.

a. Formulate a linear programming model for this problem.
b. Solve the model by using the computer.

16. The Hickory Cabinet and Furniture Company produces sofas, tables, and chairs at its plant in Greensboro, North Carolina. The plant uses three main resources to make furniture—wood, upholstery, and labor. The resource requirements for each piece of furniture and the total resources available weekly are as follows:

	Resource Requirements		
	Wood (board ft.)	Upholstery (yd.)	Labor (hr.)
Sofa	7	12	6
Table	5	—	9
Chair	4	7	5
Total available resources	2,250	1,000	240

The furniture is produced on a weekly basis and stored in a warehouse until the end of the week, when it is shipped out. The warehouse has a total capacity of 650 pieces of furniture. Each sofa earns \$400 in profit, each table, \$275, and each chair, \$190. The company wants to know how many pieces of each type of furniture to make per week to maximize profit.

a. Formulate a linear programming model for this problem.
b. Solve the model by using the computer.

17. Lawns Unlimited is a lawn care and maintenance company. One of its services is to seed new lawns as well as bare or damaged areas in established lawns. The company uses three basic grass seed mixes it calls Home 1, Home 2, and Commercial 3. It uses three kinds of grass seed—tall fescue, mustang fescue, and bluegrass. The requirements for each grass mix are as follows:

Mix	Mix Requirements
Home 1	No more than 50% tall fescue
	At least 20% mustang fescue
Home 2	At least 30% bluegrass
	At least 30% mustang fescue
	No more than 20% tall fescue
Commercial 3	At least 50% but no more than 70% tall fescue
	At least 10% bluegrass

The company believes it needs to have at least 1,200 pounds of Home 1 mix, 900 pounds of Home 2 mix, and 2,400 pounds of Commercial 3 seed mix on hand. A pound of tall fescue costs the company \$1.70, a pound of mustang fescue costs \$2.80, and a pound of bluegrass costs \$3.25. The company wants to know how many pounds of each type of grass seed to purchase to minimize cost.

a. Formulate a linear programming model for this problem.
b. Solve this model by using the computer.

18. Alexandra Bergson has subdivided her 2,000-acre farm into three plots and has contracted with three local farm families to operate the plots. She has instructed each sharecropper to plant three crops: corn, peas, and soybeans. The size of each plot has been determined by the capabilities of each local farmer. Plot sizes, crop restrictions, and profit per acre are given in the following tables:

Plot	Acreage
1	500
2	800
3	700

	Maximum Acreage	Profit/Acre
Corn	900	$600
Peas	700	450
Soybeans	1,000	300

Any of the three crops may be planted on any of the plots; however, Alexandra has placed several restrictions on the farming operation. At least 60% of each plot must be under cultivation. Further, to ensure that each sharecropper works according to his or her potential and resources (which determined the acreage allocation), she wants the same proportion of each plot to be under cultivation. Her objective is to determine how much of each crop to plant on each plot to maximize profit.

a. Formulate a linear programming model for this problem.
b. Solve the model by using the computer.

19. As a result of a recently passed bill, a congressman's district has been allocated $4 million for programs and projects. It is up to the congressman to decide how to distribute the money. The congressman has decided to allocate the money to four ongoing programs because of their importance to his district—a job training program, a parks project, a sanitation project, and a mobile library. However, the congressman wants to distribute the money in a manner that will please the most voters, or, in other words, gain him the most votes in the upcoming election. His staff's estimates of the number of votes gained per dollar spent for the various programs are as follows:

Program	Votes/Dollar
Job training	0.02
Parks	0.09
Sanitation	0.06
Mobile library	0.04

In order also to satisfy several local influential citizens who financed his election, he is obligated to observe the following guidelines:

- None of the programs can receive more than 40% of the total allocation.
- The amount allocated to parks cannot exceed the total allocated to both the sanitation project and the mobile library.
- The amount allocated to job training must at least equal the amount spent on the sanitation project.

Any money not spent in the district will be returned to the government; therefore, the congressman wants to spend it all. The congressman wants to know the amount to allocate to each program to maximize his votes.

a. Formulate a linear programming model for this problem.
b. Solve the model by using the computer.

20. Anna Broderick is the dietitian for the State University football team, and she is attempting to determine a nutritious lunch menu for the team. She has set the following nutritional guidelines for each lunch serving:

- Between 1,500 and 2,000 calories
- At least 5 mg of iron
- At least 20 but no more than 60 g of fat
- At least 30 g of protein
- At least 40 g of carbohydrates
- No more than 30 mg of cholesterol

She selects the menu from seven basic food items, as follows, with the nutritional contribution per pound and the cost as given:

	Calories (per lb.)	Iron (mg/lb.)	Protein (g/lb.)	Carbohydrates (g/lb.)	Fat (g/lb.)	Cholesterol (mg/lb.)	$/lb.
Chicken	520	4.4	17	0	30	180	0.80
Fish	500	3.3	85	0	5	90	3.70
Ground beef	860	0.3	82	0	75	350	2.30
Dried beans	600	3.4	10	30	3	0	0.90
Lettuce	50	0.5	6	0	0	0	0.75
Potatoes	460	2.2	10	70	0	0	0.40
Milk (2%)	240	0.2	16	22	10	20	0.83

The dietitian wants to select a menu to meet the nutritional guidelines while minimizing the total cost per serving.

a. Formulate a linear programming model for this problem.
b. Solve the model by using the computer.
c. If a serving of each of the food items (other than milk) was limited to no more than a half pound, what effect would this have on the solution?

21. The Midland Tool Shop has four heavy presses it uses to stamp out prefabricated metal covers and housings for electronic consumer products. All four presses operate differently and are of different sizes. Currently the firm has a contract to produce three products. The contract calls for 400 units of product 1; 570 units of product 2; and 320 units of product 3. The time (in minutes) required for each product to be produced on each machine is as follows:

	Machine			
Product	1	2	3	4
1	35	41	34	39
2	40	36	32	43
3	38	37	33	40

Machine 1 is available for 150 hours, machine 2 for 240 hours, machine 3 for 200 hours, and machine 4 for 250 hours. The products also result in different profits, according to the machine they are produced on, because of time, waste, and operating cost. The profit per unit per machine for each product is summarized as follows:

	Machine			
Product	1	2	3	4
1	$7.8	$7.8	$8.2	$7.9
2	6.7	8.9	9.2	6.3
3	8.4	8.1	9.0	5.8

The company wants to know how many units of each product to produce on each machine in order to maximize profit.

a. Formulate this problem as a linear programming model.
b. Solve the model by using the computer.

22. The Cabin Creek Coal (CCC) Company operates three mines in Kentucky and West Virginia, and it supplies coal to four utility power plants along the East Coast. The cost of shipping coal from each mine to each plant, the capacity at each of the three mines, and the demand at each plant are shown in the following table:

	Plant				
Mine	1	2	3	4	**Mine Capacity (tons)**
1	\$7	\$9	\$10	\$12	220
2	9	7	8	12	170
3	11	14	5	7	280
Demand (tons)	110	160	90	180	

The cost of mining and processing coal is \$62 per ton at mine 1, \$67 per ton at mine 2, and \$75 per ton at mine 3. The percentage of ash and sulfur content per ton of coal at each mine is as follows:

Mine	**% Ash**	**% Sulfur**
1	9	6
2	5	4
3	4	3

Each plant has different cleaning equipment. Plant 1 requires that the coal it receives have no more than 6% ash and 5% sulfur; plant 2 coal can have no more than 5% ash and sulfur combined; plant 3 can have no more than 5% ash and 7% sulfur; and plant 4 can have no more than 6% ash and sulfur combined. CCC wants to determine the amount of coal to produce at each mine and ship to its customers that will minimize its total cost.

a. Formulate a linear programming model for this problem.
b. Solve this model by using the computer.

23. Ampco is a manufacturing company that has a contract to supply a customer with parts from April through September. However, Ampco does not have enough storage space to store the parts during this period, so it needs to lease extra warehouse space during the 6-month period. Following are Ampco's space requirements:

Month	**Required Space (ft.^{2})**
April	47,000
May	35,000
June	52,000
July	27,000
August	19,000
September	15,000

The rental agent Ampco is dealing with has provided it with the following cost schedule for warehouse space. This schedule shows that the longer the space is rented, the cheaper it is. For example, if Ampco rents space for all 6 months, it costs $1.00 per square foot per month, whereas if it rents the same space for only 1 month, it costs $1.70 per square foot per month:

Rental Period (months)	$/ft.^{2}/Month
6	$1.00
5	1.05
4	1.10
3	1.20
2	1.40
1	1.70

Ampco can rent any amount of warehouse space on a monthly basis at any time for any number of (whole) months. Ampco wants to determine the least costly rental agreement that will exactly meet its space needs each month and avoid having any unused space.

a. Formulate a linear programming model for this problem.
b. Solve the model by using the computer.
c. Suppose that Ampco relaxed its restriction that it rent exactly the space it needs every month such that it would rent excess space if it was cheaper. How would this affect the optimal solution?

24. Brooks City has three consolidated high schools, each with a capacity of 1,200 students. The school board has partitioned the city into five busing districts—north, south, east, west, and central—each with different high school student populations. The three schools are located in the central, west, and south districts. Some students must be bused outside their districts, and the school board wants to minimize the total bus distance traveled by these students. The average distances from each district to the three schools and the total student population in each district are as follows:

	Distance (miles)			
District	Central School	West School	South School	**Student Population**
North	8	11	14	700
South	12	9	—	300
East	9	16	10	900
West	8	—	9	600
Central	—	8	12	500

The school board wants to determine the number of students to bus from each district to each school to minimize the total busing miles traveled.

a. Formulate a linear programming model for this problem.
b. Solve the model by using the computer.

25. a. In Problem 24 the school board decided that because all students in the north and east districts must be bused, then at least 50% of the students who live in the south, west, and central districts must also be bused to another district. Reformulate the linear programming model to reflect this new set of constraints and solve by using the computer.
b. The school board has further decided that the enrollment at all three high schools should be equal. Formulate this additional restriction in the linear programming model and solve by using the computer.

26. The Southfork Feed Company makes a feed mix from four ingredients—oats, corn, soybeans, and a vitamin supplement. The company has 300 pounds of oats, 400 pounds of corn, 200 pounds of soybeans, and 100 pounds of vitamin supplement available for the mix. The company has the following requirements for the mix:
    - At least 30% of the mix must be soybeans.
    - At least 20% of the mix must be the vitamin supplement.
    - The ratio of corn to oats cannot exceed 2 to 1.
    - The amount of oats cannot exceed the amount of soybeans.
    - The mix must be at least 500 pounds.

    A pound of oats costs \$0.50; a pound of corn, \$1.20; a pound of soybeans, \$0.60; and a pound of vitamin supplement, \$2.00. The feed company wants to know the number of pounds of each ingredient to put in the mix in order to minimize cost.
    a. Formulate a linear programming model for this problem.
    b. Solve the model by using the computer.

27. The United Charities annual fund-raising drive is scheduled to take place next week. Donations are collected during the day and night, by telephone, and through personal contact. The average donation resulting from each type of contact is as follows:

	Phone	Personal
Day	\$2	\$4
Night	3	7

The charity group has enough donated gasoline and cars to make at most 300 personal contacts during one day and night combined. The volunteer minutes required to conduct each type of interview are as follows:

	Phone (min.)	Personal (min.)
Day	6	15
Night	5	12

The charity has 20 volunteer hours available each day and 40 volunteer hours available each night. The chairperson of the fund-raising drive wants to know how many different types of contacts to schedule in a 24-hour period (i.e., 1 day and 1 night) to maximize total donations.
    a. Formulate a linear programming model for this problem.
    b. Solve the model by using the computer.

28. Ronald Thump is interested in expanding his firm. After careful consideration, he has determined three areas in which he might invest additional funds: (1) product research and development, (2) manufacturing operations improvements, and (3) advertising and sales promotion. He has \$500,000 available for investment in the firm. He can invest in its advertising and sales promotion program every year, and each dollar invested in this manner is expected to yield a return of the amount invested plus 20% yearly. He can invest in manufacturing operations improvements every 2 years, with an expected return of the investment plus 30% (at the end of each 2-year period). An investment in product research and development would be for a 3-year period, with an expected return of the investment plus 50% (at the end of the 3-year period). To diversify the total

initial investment, he wishes to include the requirement that at least $30,000 must be invested in the advertising and sales promotion program, at least $40,000 in manufacturing operations improvements, and at least $50,000 in product research and development initially (at the beginning of the first year). Ronald wants to know how much should be invested in each of the three alternatives, during each year of a 4-year period, to maximize the total ending cash value of the initial $500,000 investment.

a. Formulate a linear programming model for this problem.
b. Solve the model by using the computer.

29. Iggy Olweski, a professional football player, is retiring, and he is thinking about going into the insurance business. He plans to sell three types of policies—homeowner's insurance, auto insurance, and life insurance. The average amount of profit returned per year by each type of insurance policy is as follows:

Policy	Yearly Profit/Policy
Homeowner's	$35
Auto	20
Life	58

Each homeowner's policy will cost $14 to sell and maintain; each auto policy, $12; and each life insurance policy, $35. Iggy has projected a budget of $35,000 per year. In addition, the sale of a homeowner's policy will require 6 hours of effort; the sale of an auto policy, 3 hours; and the sale of a life insurance policy, 12 hours. Based on the number of working hours he and several employees could contribute, Iggy has estimated that he would have available 20,000 hours per year. Iggy wants to know how many of each type of insurance policy he would have to sell each year in order to maximize profit.

a. Formulate a linear programming model for this problem.
b. Solve the model by using the computer.

30. A publishing house publishes three weekly magazines—*Daily Life*, *Agriculture Today*, and *Surf's Up*. Publication of one issue of each of the magazines requires the following amounts of production time and paper:

	Production (hr.)	Paper (lb.)
Daily Life	0.01	0.2
Agriculture Today	0.03	0.5
Surf's Up	0.02	0.3

Each week the publisher has available 120 hours of production time and 3,000 pounds of paper. Total circulation for all three magazines must exceed 5,000 issues per week if the company is to keep its advertisers. The selling price per issue is $2.25 for *Daily Life*, $4.00 for *Agriculture Today*, and $1.50 for *Surf's Up*. Based on past sales, the publisher knows that the maximum weekly demand for *Daily Life* is 3,000 issues; for *Agriculture Today*, 2,000 issues; and for *Surf's Up*, 6,000 issues. The production manager wants to know the number of issues of each magazine to produce weekly in order to maximize total sales revenue.

a. Formulate a linear programming model for this problem.
b. Solve the model by using the computer.

31. The manager of a department store in Seattle is attempting to decide on the types and amounts of advertising the store should use. He has invited representatives from the local radio station, television station, and newspaper to make presentations in which they describe their audiences. The television station representative indicates that a TV commercial, which costs $15,000, would reach 25,000 potential customers. The breakdown of the audience is as follows:

	Male	Female
Senior	5,000	5,000
Young	5,000	10,000

The newspaper representative claims to be able to provide an audience of 10,000 potential customers at a cost of $4,000 per ad. The breakdown of the audience is as follows:

	Male	Female
Senior	4,000	3,000
Young	2,000	1,000

The radio station representative says that the audience for one of the station's commercials, which costs $6,000, is 15,000 customers. The breakdown of the audience is as follows:

	Male	Female
Senior	1,500	1,500
Young	4,500	7,500

The store has the following advertising policy:

- Use at least twice as many radio commercials as newspaper ads.
- Reach at least 100,000 customers.
- Reach at least twice as many young people as senior citizens.
- Make sure that at least 30% of the audience is female.

Available space limits the number of newspaper ads to seven. The store wants to know the optimal number of each type of advertising to purchase to minimize total cost.

a. Formulate a linear programming model for this problem.
b. Solve the model by using the computer.
c. Suppose a second radio station approaches the department store and indicates that its commercials, which cost $7,500, reach 18,000 customers with the following demographic breakdown:

	Male	Female
Senior	2,400	3,600
Young	4,000	8,000

If the store considered this station along with the other media alternatives, how would this affect the solution?

32. The Mill Mountain Coffee Shop blends coffee on the premises for its customers. It sells three basic blends in 1-pound bags, Special, Mountain Dark, and Mill Regular. It uses four different types of coffee to produce the blends—Brazilian, mocha, Colombian, and mild. The shop has the following blend recipe requirements:

Blend	Mix Requirements	Selling Price/Pound
Special	At least 40% Columbian, at least 30% mocha	\$6.50
Dark	At least 60% Brazilian, no more than 10% mild	5.25
Regular	No more than 60% mild, at least 30% Brazilian	3.75

The cost of Brazilian coffee is \$2.00 per pound, the cost of mocha is \$2.75 per pound, the cost of Colombian is \$2.90 per pound, and the cost of mild is \$1.70 per pound. The shop has 110 pounds of Brazilian coffee, 70 pounds of mocha, 80 pounds of Colombian, and 150 pounds of mild coffee available per week. The shop wants to know the amount of each blend it should prepare each week to maximize profit.

a. Formulate a linear programming model for this problem.
b. Solve this model by using the computer.

33. Toyz is a large discount toy store in Valley Wood Mall. The store typically has slow sales in the summer months that increase dramatically and rise to a peak at Christmas. During the summer and fall, the store must build up its inventory to have enough stock for the Christmas season. To purchase and build up its stock during the months when its revenues are low, the store borrows money.

Following is the store's projected revenue and liabilities schedule for July through December (where revenues are received and bills are paid at the first of each month):

Month	Revenues	Liabilities
July	\$ 20,000	\$60,000
August	30,000	60,000
September	40,000	80,000
October	50,000	30,000
November	80,000	30,000
December	100,000	20,000

At the beginning of July, the store can take out a 6-month loan that carries an 11% interest rate and must be paid back at the end of December. The store cannot reduce its interest payment by paying back the loan early. The store can also borrow money monthly at a rate of 5% interest per month.

Money borrowed on a monthly basis must be paid back at the beginning of the next month. The store wants to borrow enough money to meet its cash flow needs while minimizing its cost of borrowing.

a. Formulate a linear programming model for this problem.
b. Solve this model by using the computer.
c. What would the effect be on the optimal solution if Toyz could secure a 9% interest rate for a 6-month loan from another bank?

34. The Skimmer Boat Company manufactures the Water Skimmer bass fishing boat. The company purchases the engines it installs in its boats from the Mar-gine Company, which specializes

in marine engines. Skimmer has the following production schedule for April, May, June, and July:

Month	Production
April	60
May	85
June	100
July	120

Mar-gine usually manufactures and ships engines to Skimmer during the month the engines are due. However, from April through July, Mar-gine has a large order with another boat customer, and it can manufacture only 40 engines in April, 60 in May, 90 in June, and 50 in July. Mar-gine has several alternative ways to meet Skimmer's production schedule. It can produce up to 30 engines in January, February, and March and carry them in inventory at a cost of $50 per engine per month until it ships them to Skimmer. For example, Mar-gine could build an engine in January and ship it to Skimmer in April, incurring $150 in inventory charges. Mar-gine can also manufacture up to 20 engines in the month they are due on an overtime basis, with an additional cost of $400 per engine. Mar-gine wants to determine the least costly production schedule that will meet Skimmer's schedule.

a. Formulate a linear programming model for this problem.
b. Solve this model by using the computer.
c. If Mar-gine were able to increase its production capacity in January, February, and March from 30 to 40 engines, what would the effect be on the optimal solution?

35. The Donnor meat processing firm produces wieners from four ingredients: chicken, beef, pork, and a cereal additive. The firm produces three types of wieners: regular, beef, and all-meat. The company has the following amounts of each ingredient available on a daily basis:

	Pounds/Day	Cost/Pound
Chicken	200	$.20
Beef	300	.30
Pork	150	.50
Cereal additive	400	.05

Each type of wiener has certain ingredient specifications, as follows.

	Specifications	Selling Price/Pound
Regular	Not more than 10% beef and pork combined Not less than 20% chicken	$0.90
Beef	Not less than 75% beef	1.25
All-meat	No cereal additive Not more than 50% beef and pork combined	1.75

The firm wants to know how many pounds of wieners of each type to produce to maximize profits.

a. Formulate a linear programming model for this problem.
b. Solve the model by using the computer.

36. Joe Henderson runs a small metal parts shop. The shop contains three machines—a drill press, a lathe, and a grinder. Joe has three operators, each certified to work on all three machines. However, each operator performs better on some machines than on others. The shop has contracted to do a big job that requires all three machines. The times required by the various operators to perform the required operations on each machine are summarized as follows:

Operator	Drill Press (min.)	Lathe (min.)	Grinder (min.)
1	22	18	35
2	41	30	28
3	25	36	18

Joe Henderson wants to assign one operator to each machine so that the total operating time for all three operators is minimized.

a. Formulate a linear programming model for this problem.
b. Solve the model by using the computer.
c. Joe's brother, Fred, has asked him to hire his wife, Kelly, who is a machine operator. Kelly can perform each of the three required machine operations in 20 minutes. Should Joe hire his sister-in-law?

37. Green Valley Mills produces carpet at plants in St. Louis and Richmond. The plants ship the carpet to two outlets in Chicago and Atlanta. The cost per ton of shipping carpet from each of the two plants to the two warehouses is as follows:

	To	
From	Chicago	Atlanta
St. Louis	$40	$65
Richmond	70	30

The plant at St. Louis can supply 250 tons of carpet per week, and the plant at Richmond can supply 400 tons per week. The Chicago outlet has a demand of 300 tons per week; the outlet at Atlanta demands 350 tons per week. Company managers want to determine the number of tons of carpet to ship from each plant to each outlet in order to minimize the total shipping cost.

a. Formulate a linear programming model for this problem.
b. Solve the model by using the computer.

38. Dr. Maureen Becker, the head administrator at Jefferson County Regional Hospital, must determine a schedule for nurses to make sure there are enough of them on duty throughout the day. During the day, the demand for nurses varies. Maureen has broken the day into twelve 2-hour periods. The slowest time of the day encompasses the three periods from 12:00 A.M. to 6:00 A.M., which, beginning at midnight, require a minimum of 30, 20, and 40 nurses, respectively. The demand for nurses steadily increases during the next four daytime periods. Beginning with the 6:00 A.M.–8:00 A.M. period, a minimum of 50, 60, 80, and 80 nurses are required for these four periods, respectively. After 2:00 P.M. the demand for nurses decreases during the afternoon and evening hours. For the five 2-hour periods beginning at 2:00 P.M. and ending at midnight, 70, 70, 60, 50, and 50 nurses are required, respectively. A nurse reports for duty at the beginning of one of the 2-hour periods and works 8 consecutive hours (which is required in the nurses' contract). Dr. Becker wants

to determine a nursing schedule that will meet the hospital's minimum requirements throughout the day while using the minimum number of nurses.

a. Formulate a linear programming model for this problem.
b. Solve this model by using the computer.

39. A manufacturer of bathroom fixtures produces fiberglass bathtubs in an assembly operation that consists of three processes—molding, smoothing, and painting. The number of units that can undergo each process in an hour is as follows:

Process	Output (units/hr.)
Molding	7
Smoothing	12
Painting	10

(*Note:* The three processes are continuous and sequential; thus, no more units can be smoothed or painted than have been molded.) The labor costs per hour are \$8 for molding, \$5 for smoothing, and \$6.50 for painting. The company's labor budget is \$3,000 per week. A total of 120 hours of labor is available for all three processes per week. Each completed bathtub requires 90 pounds of fiberglass, and the company has a total of 10,000 pounds of fiberglass available each week. Each bathtub earns a profit of \$175. The manager of the company wants to know how many hours per week to run each process to maximize profit.

a. Formulate a linear programming model for this problem.
b. Solve the model by using the computer.

40. The admissions office at State University wants to develop a planning model for next year's entering freshman class. The university has 4,500 available openings for freshmen. Tuition is \$8,600 for an in-state student and \$19,200 for an out-of-state student. The university wants to maximize the money it receives from tuition, but by state mandate it can admit no more than 47% out-of-state students. Also, each college in the university must have at least 30% in-state students in its freshman class. In order to be ranked in several national magazines, it wants the freshman class to have an average SAT score of 1150. Following are the average SAT scores for last year's freshman class for in-state and out-of-state students in each college in the university plus the maximum size of the freshman class for each college:

	Average SAT Scores		
College	In-State	Out-of-State	Total Capacity
1. Architecture	1350	1460	470
2. Arts and Sciences	1010	1050	1,300
3. Agriculture	1020	1110	240
4. Business	1090	1180	820
5. Engineering	1360	1420	1,060
6. Human Resources	1000	1400	610

a. Formulate and solve a linear programming model to determine the number of in-state and out-of-state students that should enter each college.
b. If the solution in (a) does not achieve the maximum freshman class size, discuss how you might adjust the model to reach this class size.

41. A manufacturing firm located in Chicago ships its product by railroad to Detroit. Several different routes are available, as shown in the following diagram, referred to as a network:

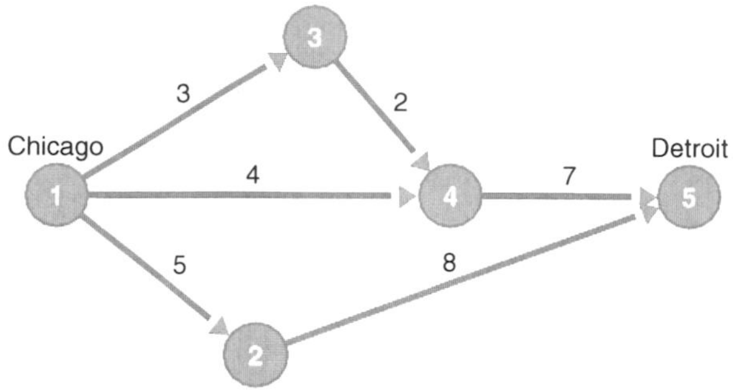

Each circle in the network represents a railroad junction. Each arrow is a railroad branch between two junctions. The number above each arrow is the cost ($1,000s) necessary to ship 1 ton of product from junction to junction. The firm wants to ship 5 tons of its product from Chicago to Detroit at the minimum cost.

a. Formulate a linear programming model for this problem.
b. Solve the model by using the computer.

42. A refinery blends four petroleum components into three grades of gasoline—regular, premium, and diesel. The maximum quantities available of each component and the cost per barrel are as follows:

Component	Maximum Barrels Available/Day	Cost/Barrel
1	5,000	$ 9
2	2,400	7
3	4,000	12
4	1,500	6

To ensure that each gasoline grade retains certain essential characteristics, the refinery has put limits on the percentages of the components in each blend. The limits as well as the selling prices for the various grades are as follows:

Grade	Component Specifications	Selling Price/Barrel
Regular	Not less than 40% of 1	$12
	Not more than 20% of 2	
	Not less than 30% of 3	
Premium	Not less than 40% of 3	18
Diesel	Not more than 50% of 2	10
	Not less than 10% of 1	

The refinery wants to produce at least 3,000 barrels of each grade of gasoline. Management wishes to determine the optimal mix of the four components that will maximize profit.

a. Formulate a linear programming model for this problem.
b. Solve the model by using the computer.

43. The Cash and Carry Building Supply Company has received the following order for boards in three lengths:

Length	Order (quantity)
7 ft.	700
9 ft.	1,200
10 ft.	300

The company has 25-foot standard-length boards in stock. Therefore, the standard-length boards must be cut into the lengths necessary to meet order requirements. Naturally, the company wishes to minimize the number of standard-length boards used. The company must therefore determine how to cut up the 25-foot boards to meet the order requirements and minimize the number of standard-length boards used.

a. Formulate a linear programming model for this problem.
b. Solve the model by using the computer.
c. When a board is cut in a specific pattern, the amount of board left over is referred to as "trim loss." Reformulate the linear programming model for this problem, assuming that the objective is to minimize trim loss rather than to minimize the total number of boards used, and solve this model. How does this affect the solution?

44. An investment firm has $1 million to invest in stocks, bonds, certificates of deposit, and real estate. The firm wishes to determine the mix of investments that will maximize the cash value at the end of 6 years.

Opportunities to invest in stocks and bonds will be available at the beginning of each of the next 6 years. Each dollar invested in stocks will return $1.20 (a profit of $0.20) 2 years later; the return can be immediately reinvested in any alternative. Each dollar invested in bonds will return $1.40 3 years later; the return can be reinvested immediately.

Opportunities to invest in certificates of deposit will be available only once, at the beginning of the second year. Each dollar invested in certificates will return $1.80 four years later. Opportunities to invest in real estate will be available at the beginning of the fifth and sixth years. Each dollar invested will return $1.10 one year later.

To minimize risk, the firm has decided to diversify its investments. The total amount invested in stocks cannot exceed 30% of total investments, and at least 25% of total investments must be in certificates of deposit.

The firm's management wishes to determine the optimal mix of investments in the various alternatives that will maximize the amount of cash at the end of the sixth year.

a. Formulate a linear programming model for this problem.
b. Solve the model by using the computer.

45. The Jones, Jones, Smith, and Rodman commodities trading firm knows the prices at which it will be able to buy and sell a certain commodity during the next 4 months. The buying price (c_i) and selling price (p_i) for each of the given months (i) are as follows:

	Month i			
	1	2	3	4
c_i	$5	$6	$7	$8
p_i	4	8	6	7

The firm's warehouse has a maximum capacity of 10,000 bushels. At the beginning of the first month, 2,000 bushels are in the warehouse. The trading firm wants to know the amounts that should be bought and sold each month in order to maximize profit. Assume that no storage costs are incurred and that sales are made at the beginning of the month, followed by purchases.

a. Formulate a linear programming model for this problem.
b. Solve the model by using the computer.

46. The production manager of Videotechnics Company is attempting to determine the upcoming 5-month production schedule for video recorders. Past production records indicate that 2,000 recorders can be produced per month. An additional 600 recorders can be produced monthly on an overtime basis. Unit cost is $10 for recorders produced during regular working hours and $15 for those produced on an overtime basis. Contracted sales per month are as follows:

Month	Contracted Sales (units)
1	1,200
2	2,100
3	2,400
4	3,000
5	4,000

Inventory carrying costs are $2 per recorder per month. The manager does not want any inventory carried over past the fifth month. The manager wants to know the monthly production that will minimize total production and inventory costs.

a. Formulate a linear programming model for this problem.
b. Solve the model by using the computer.

47. The manager of the Ewing and Barnes Department Store has four employees available to assign to three departments in the store—lamps, sporting goods, and linens. The manager wants each of these departments to have at least one employee, but not more than two. Therefore, two departments will be assigned one employee, and one department will be assigned two. Each employee has different areas of expertise, which are reflected in the daily sales each employee is expected to generate in each department, as follows:

	Department Sales		
Employee	Lamps	Sporting Goods	Linens
1	$130	$150	$ 90
2	275	300	100
3	180	225	140
4	200	120	160

The manager wishes to know which employee(s) to assign to each department in order to maximize expected sales.

a. Formulate a linear programming model for this problem.
b. Solve the model by using the computer.
c. Suppose that the department manager plans to assign only one employee to each department and to lay off the least productive employee. Formulate a new linear programming model that reflects this new condition and solve by using the computer.

48. Tidewater City Bank has four branches with the following inputs and outputs:

input 1 = teller hours (100s)
input 2 = space (100s ft.^{2})
input 3 = expenses ($1,000s)

output 1 = deposits, withdrawals, and checks processed (1,000s)
output 2 = loan applications
output 3 = new accounts (100s)

The monthly output and input values for each bank are as follows:

	Outputs			Inputs		
Bank	1	2	3	1	2	3
A	76	125	12	16	22	12
B	82	105	8	12	19	10
C	69	98	9	17	26	16
D	72	117	14	14	18	14

Using data envelopment analysis (DEA), determine which banks, if any, are inefficient.

49. Carillon Health Systems owns three hospitals, and it wants to determine which, if any, of the hospitals are inefficient. The hospital inputs each month are (1) hospital beds (100s), (2) nonphysician labor (1,000s hrs.), and (3) dollar value of supplies ($1000s). The hospital outputs are patient days (100s) for three age groups—(1) under 15, (2) 15 to 65, and (3) over 65. The output and input values for each hospital are as follows:

	Outputs			Inputs		
Hospital	1	2	3	1	2	3
A	9	5	18	7	12	40
B	6	8	9	5	14	32
C	5	10	12	8	16	47

Using DEA, determine which hospitals are inefficient.

50. Managers at the Transcontinent Shipping and Supply Company want to know the maximum tonnage of goods they can transport from city A to city F. The firm can contract for railroad cars on different rail routes linking these cities via several intermediate stations, shown in the following diagram; all railroad cars are of equal capacity:

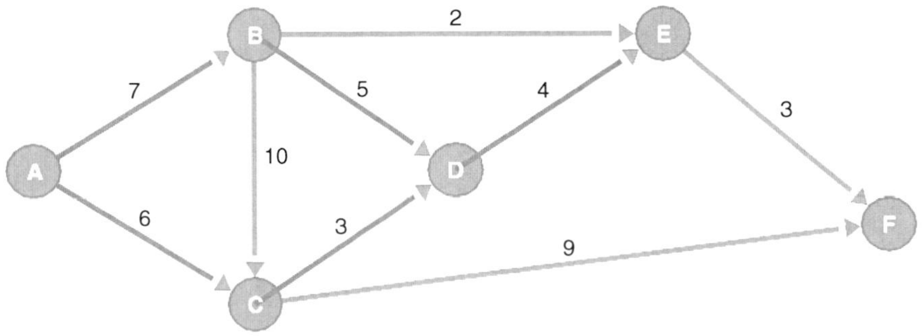

The firm can transport a maximum amount of goods from point to point, based on the maximum number of railroad cars shown on each route segment. Managers want to determine the maximum tonnage that can be shipped from city A to city F.

a. Formulate a linear programming model for this problem.
b. Solve the model by using the computer.

51. The law firm of Smith, Smith, Smith, and Jones is recruiting at law schools for new lawyers for the coming year. The firm has developed the following estimate of the number of hours of casework it will need its new lawyers to handle each month for the following year:

Month	Casework (hr.)	Month	Casework (hr.)
January	650	July	750
February	450	August	900
March	600	September	800
April	500	October	650
May	700	November	700
June	650	December	500

Each new lawyer the firm hires is expected to handle 150 hours per month of casework and to work all year. All casework must be completed by the end of the year. The firm wants to know how many new lawyers it should hire for the year.

a. Formulate a linear programming model for this problem.
b. Solve this model by using the computer.

52. In Problem 51 the optimal solution results in a fractional (i.e., non-integer) number of lawyers being hired. Explain how you would go about logically determining a new solution with a whole (integer) number of lawyers being hired and discuss the difference in results between this new solution and the optimal non-integer solution obtained in Problem 51.

53. The Goliath Tool and Machine Shop produces a single product that consists of three subcomponents that are assembled to form the product. The three components are manufactured in an operation that involves two lathes and three presses. The production time (in minutes per unit) for each machine for the three components is as follows:

	Production Time (min.)		
	Component 1	Component 2	Component 3
Lathe	10	8	6
Press	9	21	15

The shop splits the lathe workload evenly between the two lathes, and it splits the press workload evenly among the three presses. In addition, the firm wishes to produce quantities of components that will balance the daily loading among lathes and presses so that, on the average, no machine is operated more than 1 hour per day longer than any other machine. Each machine operates 8 hours per day.

The firm also wishes to produce a quantity of components that will result in completely assembled products, without any partial assemblies (i.e., in-process inventories). The objective of the firm is to maximize the number of units of assembled product per day.

a. Formulate a linear programming model for this problem.
b. Solve the model by using the computer.

c. The production policies established by the Goliath Tool and Machine Shop are relatively restrictive. If the company were to relax either its machine balancing requirement (that no machine be operated more than an hour longer than any other machine) or its restriction on in-process inventory, which would have the greatest impact on production output? What would be the impact if both requirements were relaxed?

54. A ship has two cargo holds, one fore and one aft. The fore cargo hold has a weight capacity of 70,000 pounds and a volume capacity of 30,000 cubic feet. The aft hold has a weight capacity of 90,000 pounds and a volume capacity of 40,000 cubic feet. The shipowner has contracted to carry loads of packaged beef and grain. The total weight of the available beef is 85,000 pounds; the total weight of the available grain is 100,000 pounds. The volume per mass of the beef is 0.2 cubic foot per pound, and the volume per mass of the grain is 0.4 cubic foot per pound. The profit for shipping beef is $0.35 per pound, and the profit for shipping grain is $0.12 per pound. The shipowner is free to accept all or part of the available cargo; he wants to know how much meat and grain to accept to maximize profit.
    a. Formulate a linear programming model for this problem.
    b. Solve the model by using the computer.

55. Eyewitness News is shown on channel 5 Monday through Friday evenings from 5:00 P.M. to 6:00 P.M. During the hour-long broadcast, 18 minutes are allocated to commercials. The remaining 42 minutes of airtime are allocated to single or multiple time segments for local news and features, national news, sports, and weather. The station has learned through several viewer surveys that viewers do not consistently watch the entire news program; they focus on some segments more closely than others. For example, they tend to pay more attention to the local weather than the national news (because they know they will watch the network news following the local broadcast). As such, the advertising revenues generated for commercials shown during the different broadcast segments are $850 per minute for local news and feature segments, $600 per minute for national news, $750 per minute for sports, and $1,000 per minute for the weather. The production cost for local news is $400 per minute, the cost for national news is $100 per minute, the cost for sports is $175 per minute, and for weather it's $90 per minute. The station budgets $9,000 per show for production costs. The station's policy is that the broadcast time devoted to local news and features must be at least 10 minutes but not more than 25 minutes, whereas national news, sports, and weather must have segments of at least 5 minutes each but not more than 10 minutes. Commercial time must be limited to no more than 6 minutes for each of the four broadcast segment types. The station manager wants to know how many minutes of commercial time and broadcast time to allocate to local news, national news, sports, and weather to maximize advertising revenues.
    a. Formulate a linear programming model for this problem.
    b. Solve by using the computer.

56. The Douglas family raises cattle on their farm in Virginia. They also have a large garden in which they grow ingredients for making two types of relish—chow-chow and tomato. These they sell in 16-ounce jars at local stores and craft fairs in the fall. The profit for a jar of chow-chow is $2.25, and the profit for a jar of tomato relish is $1.95. The main ingredients in each relish are cabbage, tomatoes, and onions. A jar of chow-chow must contain at least 60% cabbage, 5% onions, and 10% tomatoes, and a jar of tomato relish must contain at least 50% tomatoes, 5% onions, and 10% cabbage. Both relishes contain no more than 10% onions. The family has enough time to make no more than 700 jars of relish. In checking sales records for the past 5 years, they know that they will sell at least 30% more chow-chow than tomato relish. They will have 300 pounds of cabbage, 350 pounds of tomatoes, and 30 pounds of onions available. The Douglas family wants to know how many jars of relish to produce to maximize profit.
    a. Formulate a linear programming model for this problem.
    b. Solve by using the computer.

57. The White Horse Apple Products Company purchases apples from local growers and makes applesauce and apple juice. It costs \$0.60 to produce a jar of applesauce and \$0.85 to produce a bottle of apple juice. The company has a policy that at least 30% but not more than 60% of its output must be applesauce.

The company wants to meet but not exceed the demand for each product. The marketing manager estimates that the demand for applesauce is a maximum of 5,000 jars, plus an additional 3 jars for each \$1 spent on advertising. The maximum demand for apple juice is estimated to be 4,000 bottles, plus an additional 5 bottles for every \$1 spent to promote apple juice. The company has \$16,000 to spend on producing and advertising applesauce and apple juice. Applesauce sells for \$1.45 per jar; apple juice sells for \$1.75 per bottle. The company wants to know how many units of each to produce and how much advertising to spend on each to maximize profit.

a. Formulate a linear programming model for this problem.
b. Solve the model by using the computer.

58. Mazy's Department Store has decided to stay open on a 24-hour basis. The store manager has divided the 24-hour day into six 4-hour periods and determined the following minimum personnel requirements for each period:

Time	Personnel Needed
Midnight–4:00 A.M.	90
4:00–8:00 A.M.	215
8:00–Noon	250
Noon–4:00 P.M.	65
4:00–8:00 P.M.	300
8:00–Midnight	125

Personnel must report for work at the beginning of one of these times and work 8 consecutive hours. The store manager wants to know the minimum number of employees to assign for each 4-hour segment to minimize the total number of employees.

a. Formulate a linear programming model for this problem.
b. Solve the model by using the computer.

59. Venture Systems is a consulting firm that develops e-commerce systems and Web sites for its clients. It has six available consultants and eight client projects under contract. The consultants have different technical abilities and experience, and as a result, the company charges different hourly rates for its services. Also, the consultants' skills are more suited for some projects than others, and clients sometimes prefer some consultants over others. The suitability of a consultant for a project is rated according to a 5-point scale, in which 1 is the worst and 5 is the best. The following table shows the rating for each consultant for each project, as well as the hours available for each consultant and the contracted hours and maximum budget for each project.

		Project								
Consultant	Hourly Rate	1	2	3	4	5	6	7	8	Available Hours
A	\$155	3	3	5	5	3	3	3	3	450
B	140	3	3	2	5	5	5	3	3	600
C	165	2	1	3	3	2	1	5	3	500
D	300	1	3	1	1	2	2	5	1	300
E	270	3	1	1	2	2	1	3	3	710
F	150	4	5	3	2	3	5	4	3	860
Project Hours		500	240	400	475	350	460	290	200	
Contract Budget (\$1,000s)		100	80	120	90	65	85	50	55	

The company wants to know how many hours to assign each consultant to each project in order to best utilize the consultants' skills while meeting the clients' needs.

a. Formulate a linear programming model for this problem.
b. Solve the model by using the computer.
c. If the company's objective is to maximize revenue while ignoring client preferences and consultant compatibility, will this change the solution in (b)?

60. Great Northwoods Outfitters is a retail phone-catalog company that specializes in outdoor clothing and equipment. A phone station at the company will be staffed with either full-time operators or temporary operators 8 hours per day. Full-time operators, because of their experience and training, process more orders and make fewer mistakes than temporary operators. However, temporary operators are cheaper because they receive a lower wage rate and are not paid benefits. A full-time operator can process about 360 orders per week, whereas a temporary operator can process about 270 orders per week. A full-time operator averages 1.1 defective orders per week, and a part-time operator incurs about 2.7 defective orders per week. The company wants to limit defective orders to 200 per week. The cost of staffing a station with full-time operators is $610 per week, and the cost of a station with part-time operators is $450 per week. Using historical data and forecasting techniques, the company has developed estimates of phone orders for an 8-week period, as follows:

Week	Orders	Week	Orders
1	19,500	5	33,400
2	21,000	6	29,800
3	25,600	7	27,000
4	27,200	8	31,000

The company does not want to hire or dismiss full-time employees after the first week (i.e., the company wants a constant group of full-time operators over the 8-week period). The company wants to determine how many full-time operators it needs and how many temporary operators to hire each week to meet weekly demand while minimizing labor costs.

a. Formulate a linear programming model for this problem.
b. Solve this model by using the computer.

61. In Problem 60 Great Northwoods Outfitters is going to alter its staffing policy. Instead of hiring a constant group of full-time operators for the entire 8-week planning period, it has decided to hire and add full-time operators as the 8-week period progresses, although once it hires full-time operators, it will not dismiss them. Reformulate the linear programming model to reflect this altered policy and solve to determine the cost savings (if any).

62. Blue Ridge Power and Light Company generates electrical power at four coal-fired power plants along the eastern seaboard in Virginia, North Carolina, Maryland, and Delaware. The company purchases coal from six producers in southwestern Virginia, West Virginia, and Kentucky. Blue Ridge has fixed contracts for coal delivery from the following three coal producers:

Coal Producer	Tons	Cost/Ton	Million BTUs/Ton
ANCO	190,000	$23	26.2
Boone Creek	305,000	28	27.1
Century	310,000	24	25.6

The power-producing capabilities of the coal produced by these suppliers differs according to the quality of the coal. For example, coal produced by ANCO provides 26.2 million BTUs per ton, while coal produced at Boone Creek provides 27.1 million BTUs per ton. Blue Ridge also purchases coal from three backup auxiliary suppliers, as needed (i.e., it does not have fixed contracts with these producers). In general, the coal from these backup suppliers is more costly and lower grade.

Coal Producer	Available Tons	Cost/Ton	Million BTUs/Ton
DACO	125,000	$31	21.4
Eaton	95,000	29	19.2
Franklin	190,000	34	23.6

The demand for electricity at Blue Ridge's four power plants is as follows (note that it requires approximately 10 million BTUs to generate 1 megawatt hour):

Power Plant	Electricity Demand (million BTUs)
1. Afton	4,600,000
2. Surrey	6,100,000
3. Piedmont	5,700,000
4. Chesapeake	7,300,000

For example, the Afton plant must produce at least 4,600,000 million BTUs next year, which translates to approximately 460,000 megawatt hours.

Coal is primarily transported from the producers to the power plants by rail, and the cost of processing coal at each plant is different. Following are the combined transportation and processing costs for coal from each supplier to each plant.

	Power Plant			
Coal Producer	1. Afton	2. Surrey	3. Piedmont	4. Chesapeake
ANCO	$12.20	$14.25	$11.15	$15.00
Boone Creek	10.75	13.70	11.75	14.45
Century	15.10	16.65	12.90	12.00
DACO	14.30	11.90	16.35	11.65
Eaton	12.65	9.35	10.20	9.55
Franklin	16.45	14.75	13.80	14.90

Formulate and solve a linear programming model to determine how much coal should be purchased and shipped from each supplier to each power plant in order to minimize cost.

63. Valley United Soccer Club has 16 boys' and girls' travel soccer teams. The club has access to three town fields, which its teams practice on in the fall during the season. Field 1 is large enough to accommodate two teams at one time, and field 3 can accommodate three teams,

whereas field 2 has enough room for only one team. The teams practice twice per week, either on Monday and Wednesday from 3 P.M. to 5 P.M. or 5 P.M. to 7 P.M., or on Tuesday and Thursday from 3 P.M. to 5 P.M. or 5 P.M. to 7 P.M. Field 3 is in the worst condition of all the fields, so teams generally prefer the other fields; teams also do not like to practice at field 3 because it can get crowded with three teams. In general, the younger teams like to practice right after school, while the older teams like to practice later in the day. In addition, some teams must practice later because their coaches are available only after work. Some teams also prefer specific fields because they're closer to their players' homes. Each team has been asked by the club field coordinator to select three practice locations and times, in priority order, and they have responded as follows:

	Priority		
Team	1	2	3
U11B	2, 3–5M	1, 3–5M	3, 3–5M
U11G	1, 3–5T	2, 3–5T	3, 3–5T
U12B	2, 3–5T	1, 3–5T	3, 3–5T
U12G	1, 3–5M	1, 3–5T	2, 3–5M
U13B	2, 3–5T	2, 3–5M	1, 3–5M
U13G	1, 3–5M	2, 3–5M	1, 3–5T
U14B	1, 5–7M	1, 5–7T	2, 5–7T
U14G	2, 3–5M	1, 3–5M	2, 3–5T
U15B	1, 5–7T	2, 5–7T	1, 5–7M
U15G	2, 5–7M	1, 5–7M	1, 5–7T
U16B	1, 5–7T	2, 5–7T	3, 5–7T
U16G	2, 5–7T	1, 5–7T	3, 5–7T
U17B	2, 5–7M	1, 5–7T	1, 5–7M
U17G	1, 5–7T	2, 5–7T	1, 5–7M
U18B	2, 5–7M	2, 5–7T	1, 5–7M
U18G	1, 5–7M	1, 5–7T	2, 5–7T

For example, the under-11 boys' age group team has selected field 2 from 3 P.M. to 5 P.M. on Monday and Wednesday as its top priority, field 1 from 3 P.M. to 5 P.M. on Monday and Wednesday as its second priority, and so on.

Formulate and solve a linear programming model to optimally assign the teams to fields and times, according to their priorities. Are any of the teams not assigned to one of their top three selections? If not, how might you modify or use the model to assign these teams to the best possible time and location? How could you make sure that the model does not assign teams to unacceptable locations and times—for example, a team whose coach can be at practice only at 5 P.M.?

64. The city of Salem has four police stations, with the following inputs and outputs:

input 1 = number of police officers
input 2 = number of patrol vehicles
input 3 = space (100s ft.^{2})

output 1 = calls responded to (100s)
output 2 = traffic citations (100s)
output 3 = convictions

The monthly output and input data for each station are

	Outputs			Inputs		
Police Station	1	2	3	1	2	3
A	12.7	3.6	35	34	18	54
B	14.2	4.9	42	29	22	62
C	13.8	5.2	56	38	16	50
D	15.1	4.2	39	35	24	57

Help the city council determine which of the police stations are relatively inefficient.

65. USAir South Airlines operates a hub at the Pittsburgh International Airport. During the summer, the airline schedules 7 flights daily from Pittsburgh to Orlando and 10 flights daily from Orlando to Pittsburgh, according to the following schedule:

Flight	Leave Pittsburgh	Arrive Orlando	Flight	Leave Orlando	Arrive Pittsburgh
1	6 A.M.	9 A.M.	A	6 A.M.	9 A.M.
2	8 A.M.	11 A.M.	B	7 A.M.	10 A.M.
3	9 A.M.	Noon	C	8 A.M.	11 A.M.
4	3 P.M.	6 P.M.	D	10 A.M.	1 P.M.
5	5 P.M.	8 P.M.	E	Noon	3 P.M.
6	7 P.M.	10 P.M.	F	2 P.M.	5 P.M.
7	8 P.M.	11 P.M.	G	3 P.M.	6 P.M.
			H	6 P.M.	9 P.M.
			I	7 P.M.	10 P.M.
			J	9 P.M.	Midnight

The flight crews live in Pittsburgh or Orlando, and each day a new crew must fly one flight from Pittsburgh to Orlando and one flight from Orlando to Pittsburgh. A crew must return to its home city at the end of each day. For example, if a crew originates in Orlando and flies a flight to Pittsburgh, it must then be scheduled for a return flight from Pittsburgh back to Orlando. A crew must have at least 1 hour between flights at the city where it arrives. Some scheduling combinations are not possible; for example, a crew on flight 1 from Pittsburgh cannot return on flights A, B, or C from Orlando. It is also possible for a flight to ferry one additional crew to a city in order to fly a return flight, if there are not enough crews in that city.

The airline wants to schedule its crews in order to minimize the total amount of crew ground time (i.e., the time the crew is on the ground between flights). Excessive ground time for a crew lengthens its workday, is bad for crew morale, and is expensive for the airline. Formulate a linear programming model to determine a flight schedule for the airline and solve by using the computer. How many crews need to be based in each city? How much ground time will each crew experience?

66. The National Cereal Company produces a Light-Snak cereal package with a selection of small pouches of four different cereals—Crunchies, Toasties, Snakmix, and Granolies. Each cereal is produced at a different production facility and then shipped to three packaging facilities, where the four different cereal pouches are combined into a single box. The boxes are then sent to one of three distribution centers, where they are combined to fill customer orders and shipped. The following diagram shows the weekly flow of the product through the production, packaging, and distribution facilities (referred to as a "supply chain"):

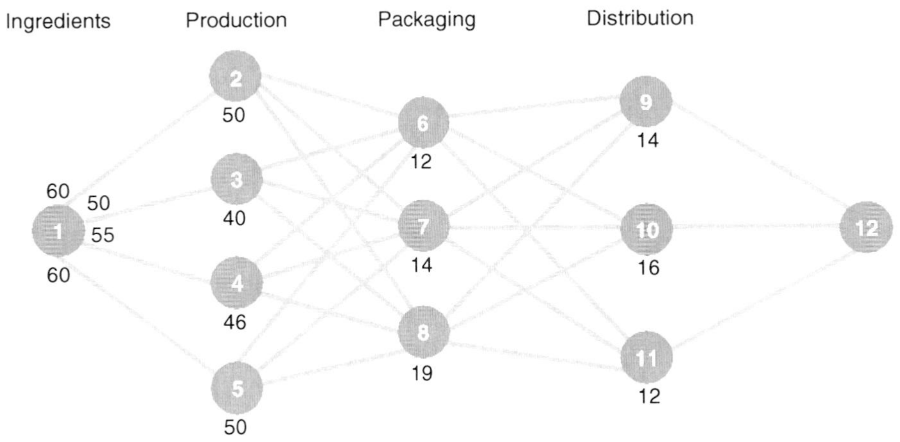

Ingredients capacities (per 1,000 pouches) per week are shown along branches 1–2, 1–3, 1–4, and 1–5. For example, ingredients for 60,000 pouches are available at the production facility, as shown on branch 1–2. The weekly production capacity at each plant (in 1,000s of pouches) is shown at nodes 2, 3, 4, and 5. The packaging facilities at nodes 6, 7, and 8 and the distribution centers at nodes 9, 10, and 11 have capacities for boxes (1,000s) as shown.

The various production, packaging, and distribution costs per unit at each facility are shown in the following table:

Facility	2	3	4	5	6	7	8	9	10	11
Unit cost	$.17	.20	.18	.16	.26	.29	.27	.12	.11	.14

Weekly demand for the Light-Snak product is 37,000 boxes.

Formulate and solve a linear programming model that indicates how much product must be produced at each facility to meet weekly demand at the minimum cost.

67. Valley Fruit Products Company has contracted with apple growers in Ohio, Pennsylvania, and New York to purchase apples that the company then ships to its plants in Indiana and Georgia, where they are processed into apple juice. Each bushel of apples produces 2 gallons of apple juice. The juice is canned and bottled at the plants and shipped by rail and truck to warehouses/distribution centers in Virginia, Kentucky, and Louisiana. The shipping costs per bushel from the farms to the plants and the shipping costs per gallon from the plants to the distribution centers are summarized in the following tables:

	Plant		
Farm	**4. Indiana**	**5. Georgia**	**Supply (bushels)**
1. Ohio	.41	.57	24,000
2. Pennsylvania	.37	.48	18,000
3. New York	.51	.60	32,000
Plant Capacity	48,000	35,000	

Plant	Distribution Centers		
	6. Virginia	7. Kentucky	8. Louisiana
4. Indiana	.22	.10	.20
5. Georgia	.15	.16	.18
Demand (gal.)	9,000	12,000	15,000

Formulate and solve a linear programming model to determine the optimal shipments from the farms to the plants and from the plants to the distribution centers in order to minimize total shipping costs.

68. In the event of a disaster situation at Tech from weather, an accident, or terrorism, victims will be transported by emergency vehicles to three area hospitals: Montgomery Regional, Radford Memorial, and Lewis Galt. Montgomery Regional is (on average) 10 minutes away from Tech, Radford Memorial is 20 minutes away, and Lewis Galt is 35 minutes away. Tech wants to analyze a hypothetical disaster situation in which there are 15 victims with different types of injuries. The emergency facilities at Montgomery Regional can accommodate, at most, 8 victims; Radford Memorial can handle 10 victims; and Lewis Galt can admit 7 victims. A priority has been assigned for each victim according to the hospital that would best treat that victim's type of injury, as shown in the following table (where 1 reflects the best treatment).

Hospital	Patient														
	1	2	3	4	5	6	7	8	9	10	11	12	13	14	15
Montgomery Regional	1	1	2	2	2	1	3	3	3	1	3	3	2	1	3
Radford Memorial	2	2	3	3	1	3	3	1	1	1	3	3	2	2	3
Lewis Galt	3	3	1	1	3	2	1	2	2	2	1	1	1	2	1

For example, for victim 1's type of injury, the best hospital is Montgomery Regional, the next best is Radford Memorial, and Lewis Galt is the third best.

a. Formulate and solve a linear programming model that will send the victims to the hospital best suited to administer to their specific injuries while keeping the average transport time to 22 minutes or less.

b. Formulate and solve a linear programming model that will minimize the average transport time for victims while achieving an average hospital priority of at least 1.50.

Case Problem

SUMMER SPORTS CAMP AT STATE UNIVERSITY

Mary Kelly is a scholarship soccer player at State University. During the summer, she works at a youth all-sports camp that several of the university's coaches operate. The sports camp runs for 8 weeks during July and August. Campers come for a 1-week period, during which time they live in the State dormitories and use the State athletic fields and facilities. At the end of a week, a new group of kids comes in. Mary primarily serves as one of the camp soccer instructors. However, she has also been placed in charge of arranging for sheets for the beds the campers will sleep on in the dormitories. Mary has been instructed to develop a plan for purchasing and cleaning sheets each week of camp at the lowest possible cost.

Clean sheets are needed at the beginning of each week, and the campers use the sheets all week. At the end of the week, the campers strip their beds and place the sheets in large bins. Mary must arrange either to purchase new sheets or to clean old sheets. A set of new sheets costs $10. A local laundry has indicated that it will clean a set of sheets for $4. Also, a couple of Mary's friends have asked her to let them clean some of the sheets. They have told her they will charge only $2 for each set of sheets they clean. However, while the laundry will provide cleaned sheets in a week, Mary's friends can deliver cleaned sheets only in 2 weeks. They are going to summer school and plan to launder the sheets at night at a neighborhood Laundromat.

The accompanying table lists the number of campers who have registered during each of the 8 weeks the camp will operate. Based on discussions with camp administrators from previous summers and on some old camp records and receipts, Mary estimates that each week about 20% of the cleaned sheets that are returned will have to be discarded and replaced. The campers spill food and drinks on the sheets, and sometimes the stains do not come out during cleaning. Also, the campers occasionally tear the sheets, or the sheets get torn at the cleaners. In either case, when the sheets come back from the cleaners and are put on the beds, 20% are taken off and thrown away.

At the beginning of the summer, the camp has no sheets available, so initially sheets must be purchased. Sheets are thrown away at the end of the summer.

Week	Registered Campers
1	115
2	210
3	250
4	230
5	260
6	300
7	250
8	190

Mary's major at State is management science, and she wants to develop a plan for purchasing and cleaning sheets by using linear programming. Help Mary formulate a linear programming model for this problem and solve it by using the computer.

Case Problem

SPRING GARDEN TOOLS

The Spring family has owned and operated a garden tool and implements manufacturing company since 1952. The company sells garden tools to distributors and also directly to hardware stores and home improvement discount chains. The Spring Company's four most popular small garden tools are a trowel, a hoe, a rake, and a shovel. Each of these tools is made from durable steel and has a wooden handle. The Spring family prides itself on its high-quality tools.

The manufacturing process encompasses two stages. The first stage includes two operations—stamping out the metal tool heads and drilling screw holes in them. The completed tool heads then flow to the second stage, which includes an assembly operation where the handles are attached to the tool heads, a finishing step, and packaging. The processing times per tool for each operation are provided in the following table:

	Tool (hr./unit)				
Operation	*Trowel*	*Hoe*	*Rake*	*Shovel*	**Total Hours Available per Month**
Stamping	0.04	0.17	0.06	0.12	500
Drilling	0.05	0.14	—	0.14	400
Assembly	0.06	0.13	0.05	0.10	600
Finishing	0.05	0.21	0.02	0.10	550
Packaging	0.03	0.15	0.04	0.15	500

The steel the company uses is ordered from an iron and steel works in Japan. The company has 10,000 square feet of sheet steel available each month. The metal required for each tool and the monthly contracted production volume per tool are provided in the following table:

	Sheet Metal (ft.^{2})	Monthly Contracted Sales
Trowel	1.2	1,800
Hoe	1.6	1,400
Rake	2.1	1,600
Shovel	2.4	1,800

The primary reasons the company has survived and prospered are its ability always to meet customer demand on time and its high quality. As a result, the Spring Company will produce on an overtime basis in order to meet its sales requirements, and it also has a long-standing arrangement with a local tool and die company to manufacture its tool heads. The Spring Company feels comfortable subcontracting the first-stage operations because it is easier to detect defects prior to assembly and finishing. For the same reason, the company will not subcontract for the entire tool because defects would be particularly hard to detect after the tool was finished and packaged. However, the company does have 100 hours of overtime available each month for each operation in both stages. The regular production and overtime costs per tool for both stages are provided in the following table:

	Stage 1		Stage 2	
	Regular Cost	*Overtime Cost*	*Regular Cost*	*Overtime Cost*
Trowel	$ 6.00	$ 6.20	$3.00	$3.10
Hoe	10.00	10.70	5.00	5.40
Rake	8.00	8.50	4.00	4.30
Shovel	10.00	10.70	5.00	5.40

The cost of subcontracting in stage 1 adds 20% to the regular production cost.

The Spring Company wants to establish a production schedule for regular and overtime production in each stage and for the number of tool heads subcontracted, at the minimum cost. Formulate a linear programming model for this problem and solve the model using the computer. Which resources appear to be most critical in the production process?

Case Problem

SUSAN WONG'S PERSONAL BUDGETING MODEL

After Susan Wong graduated from State University with a degree in management science, she went to work for a computer systems development firm in the Washington, DC, area. As a student at State, Susan paid her normal monthly living expenses for apartment rent, food, and entertainment out of a bank account set up by her parents. Each month they would deposit a specific amount of cash into Susan's account. Her parents also paid her gas, telephone, and bank credit card bills, which were sent directly to them. Susan never had to worry about things like health, car, homeowners', and life insurance; utilities; driver's and car licenses; magazine subscriptions; and so on. Thus, while she was used to spending within a specific monthly budget in college, she was unprepared for the irregular monthly liabilities she encountered once she got a job and was on her own.

In some months Susan's bills would be modest and she would spend accordingly, only to be confronted the next month with a large insurance premium, or a bill for property taxes on her condominium, or a large credit card bill, or a bill for a magazine subscription, and so on the next month. Such unexpected expenditures would result in months when she could not balance her checking account; she would have to pay her bills with her bank credit card and then pay off her accumulated debt in installments while incurring high interest charges. By the end of her first year out of school, she had hoped to have some money saved to begin an investment program, but instead she found herself in debt.

Frustrated by her predicament, Susan decided to get her financial situation in order. First, she sold the condominium that her parents had helped her purchase and moved into a cheaper apartment. This gave her enough cash to clear her outstanding debts, with $3,800 left over to start the new year with. Susan then decided to use some of the management science she had learned in college to help develop a budget. Specifically, she decided to develop a linear programming model to help her decide how much she should put aside each month in short-term investments to meet the demands of irregular monthly liabilities and save some money.

First, Susan went through all her financial records for the year and computed her expected monthly liabilities for the coming year, as shown in the following table:

Month	Bills	Month	Bills
January	$2,750	July	$3,050
February	2,860	August	2,300
March	2,335	September	1,975
April	2,120	October	1,670
May	1,205	November	2,710
June	1,600	December	2,980

Susan's after-taxes-and-benefits salary is $29,400 per year, which she receives in 12 equal monthly paychecks that are deposited directly into her bank account.

Susan has decided that she will invest any money she doesn't use to meet her liabilities each month in either 1-month, 3-month, or 7-month short-term investment vehicles rather than just leaving the money in an interest-bearing checking account. The yield on 1-month investments is 6% per year nominal; on 3-month investments, the yield is 8% per year nominal; and on a 7-month investment, the yield is 12% per year nominal. As part of her investment strategy, any time one of the short-term investments comes due, she uses the principal as part of her budget, but she transfers any interest earned to another long-term investment (which she doesn't consider in her budgeting process). For example, if she has $100 left over in January that she invests for 3 months, in April, when the investment matures, she uses the $100 she originally invested in her budget, but any interest on the $100 is invested elsewhere. (Thus, the interest is not compounded over the course of the year.)

Susan wants to develop a linear programming model to maximize her investment return during the year so she can take that money and reinvest it at the end of the year in a longer-term investment program. However, she doesn't have to confine herself to short-term investments that will all mature by the end of the year; she can continue to put money toward the end of the year in investments that won't mature until the following year. Her budgeting process will continue to the next year, so she can take out any surplus left over after December and reinvest it in a long-term program if she wants to.

A. Help Susan develop a model for the year that will meet her irregular monthly financial obligations while achieving her investment objectives and solve the model.
B. If Susan decides she doesn't want to include all her original $3,800 in her budget at the beginning of the year, but instead she wants to invest some of it directly in alternative longer-term investments, how much does she need to develop a feasible budget?

This case was adapted from T. Lewis, "Personal Operations Research: Practicing OR on Ourselves," *Interfaces* 26, no. 5 (September–October 1996): 34–41.

Case Problem

WALSH'S JUICE COMPANY

Walsh's Juice Company produces three products from unprocessed grape juice—bottled juice, frozen juice concentrate, and jelly. It purchases grape juice from three vineyards near the Great Lakes. The grapes are harvested at the vineyards and immediately converted into juice at plants at the vineyard sites and stored there in refrigerated tanks. The juice is then transported to four different plants in Virginia, Michigan, Tennessee, and Indiana, where it is processed into bottled grape juice, frozen juice concentrate, and jelly. Vineyard output typically differs each month in the harvesting season, and the plants have different processing capacities.

In a particular month the vineyard in New York has 1,400 tons of unprocessed grape juice available, whereas the vineyard in Ohio has 1,700 tons and the vineyard in Pennsylvania has 1,100 tons. The processing capacity per month is 1,200 tons of unprocessed juice at the plant in Virginia, 1,100 tons of juice at the plant in Michigan, 1,400 tons at the plant in Tennessee, and 1,400 tons at the plant in Indiana. The cost per ton of transporting unprocessed juice from the vineyards to the plant is as follows:

	Plant			
Vineyard	*Virginia*	*Michigan*	*Tennessee*	*Indiana*
New York	$850	$720	$910	$750
Pennsylvania	970	790	1,050	880
Ohio	900	830	780	820

The plants are different ages, have different equipment, and have different wage rates; thus, the cost of processing each product at each plant ($/ton) differs, as follows:

	Plant			
Product	*Virginia*	*Michigan*	*Tennessee*	*Indiana*
Juice	$2,100	$2,350	$2,200	$1,900
Concentrate	4,100	4,300	3,950	3,900
Jelly	2,600	2,300	2,500	2,800

This month the company needs to process a total of 1,200 tons of bottled juice, 900 tons of frozen concentrate, and 700 tons of jelly at the four plants combined. However, the production process for frozen concentrate results in some juice dehydration, and the process for jelly includes a cooking stage that evaporates water content. To process 1 ton of frozen concentrate requires 2 tons of unprocessed juice; 1 ton of jelly requires 1.5 tons of unprocessed juice; and 1 ton of bottled juice requires 1 ton of unprocessed juice.

Walsh's management wants to determine how many tons of grape juice to ship from each of the vineyards to each of the plants and the number of tons of each product to process at each plant. Thus, management needs a model that includes both the logistical aspects of this problem and the production processing aspects. It wants a solution that will minimize total costs, including the cost of transporting grape juice from the vineyards to the plants and the product processing costs. Help Walsh's solve this problem by formulating a linear programming model and solve it by using the computer.

Case Problem

THE KING'S LANDING AMUSEMENT PARK

King's Landing is a large amusement theme park located in Virginia. The park hires high school and college students to work during the summer months of May, June, July, August, and September. The student employees operate virtually all the highly mechanized, computerized rides; perform as entertainers; perform most of the custodial work during park hours; make up the workforce for restaurants, food services, retail shops, and stores; drive trams; and park cars. Park management has assessed the park's monthly needs based on previous summers' attendance at the park and the expected available workforce. Park attendance is relatively low in May, until public schools are out, and then it increases through June, July, and August, and decreases dramatically in September, when schools reopen after Labor Day. The park is open 7 days a week through the summer, until September, when it cuts back to weekends only. Management estimates that it will require 22,000 hours of labor in each of the first 2 weeks of May, 25,000 hours during the third week of May, and 30,000 hours during the last week in May. During the first 2 weeks of June, it will require at least 35,000 hours of labor and 40,000 hours during the last 2 weeks in June. In July 45,000 hours will be required each week, and in August 45,000 hours will be needed each week. In September the park will need only 12,000 hours in the first week, 10,000 hours in each of the second and third weeks, and 8,000 hours the last week of the month.

The park hires new employees each week from the first week in May through August. A new employee mostly trains the first week by observing and helping more experienced employees;

however, he or she works approximately 10 hours under the supervision of an experienced employee. An employee is considered experienced after completing 1 week on the job. Experienced employees are considered part-time and are scheduled to work 30 hours per week in order to eliminate overtime and reduce the cost of benefits, and to give more students the opportunity to work. However, no one is ever laid off or will be scheduled for fewer (or more) than 30 hours, even if more employees are available than needed. Management believes this is a necessary condition of employment because many of the student employees move to the area during the summer just to work in the park and live near the beach nearby. If these employees were sporadically laid off and were stuck with lease payments and other expenses, it would be bad public relations and hurt employment efforts in future summers. Although no one is laid off, 15% of all experienced employees quit each week for a variety of reasons, including homesickness, illness, and other personal reasons, plus some are asked to leave because of very poor job performance.

Park management is able to start the first week in May with 700 experienced employees who worked in the park in previous summers and live in the area. These employees are generally able to work a lot of hours on the weekends and then some during the week; however, in May attendance is much heavier on the weekends, so most of the labor hours are needed then. The park expects to have a pool of 1,500 available applicants to hire for the first week in May. After the first week, the pool is diminished by the number of new employees hired the previous week, but each week through June the park gets 200 new job applicants, which decreases to 100 new applicants each week for the rest of the summer. For example, the available applicant pool in the second week in May would be the previous week's pool, which in week 1 is 1,500, minus the number of new employees hired in week 1 plus 200 new applicants. At the end of the last week in August, 75% of all the experienced employees will quit to go back to school, and the park will not hire any new employees in September. The park must operate in September, using experienced employees who live in the area, but the weekly attrition rate for these employees in September drops to 10%.

Formulate and solve a linear programming model to assist the park's management to plan and schedule the number of new employees it hires each week in order to minimize the total number of new employees it must hire during the summer.

References

Baumol, W. J. *Economic Theory and Operations Analysis*, 4th ed. Upper Saddle River, NJ: Prentice Hall, 1977.

Charnes, A., and Cooper, W. W. *Management Models and Industrial Applications of Linear Programming*. New York: John Wiley & Sons, 1961.

Dantzig, G. B. *Linear Programming and Extensions*. Princeton, NJ: Princeton University Press, 1963.

Gass, S. *Linear Programming*, 4th ed. New York: McGraw-Hill, 1975.

Hadley, G. *Linear Programming*. Reading, MA: Addison-Wesley, 1962.

Hillier, F. S., and Lieberman, G. J. *Introduction to Operations Research*, 4th ed. San Francisco: Holden-Day, 1986.

Llewellyn, R. W. *Linear Programming*. New York: Holt, Rinehart and Winston, 1964.

Taha, H. A. *Operations Research, an Introduction*, 4th ed. New York: Macmillan, 1987.

Wagner, H. M. *Principles of Operations Research*, 2nd ed. Upper Saddle River, NJ: Prentice Hall, 1975.

Solutions to Selected Odd-Numbered Problems

1. Model must be resolved; $Z = 43{,}310$, do not implement; no; $x_1 = x_2 = x_3 = x_4 = 112.5$
3. No effect; \$740; $x_1 = 22{,}363.636$, $x_3 = 43{,}636.364$, $x_4 = 14{,}000$
5. Add slack variables for 3 warehouses ≤ constraints; coefficients in objective function—\$9 for s_1, \$6 for s_2, \$7 for s_3, solution does not change
7. (a) max. $Z = 190x_1 + 170x_2 + 155x_3$; s.t. $3.5x_1 + 5.2x_2 + 2.8x_3 \le 500$, $1.2x_1 + 0.8x_2 + 1.5x_3 \le 240$, $40x_1 + 55x_2 + 20x_3 \le 6{,}500$, $x_i \ge 0$; (b) $x_1 = 41.27$, $x_2 = 0$, $x_3 = 126.98$, $Z = 27{,}523.81$
9. (a) min. $Z = 4x_1 + 3x_2 + 2x_3$; s.t. $2x_1 + 4x_2 + x_3 \ge 16$, $3x_1 + 2x_2 + x_3 \ge 12$, $x_i \ge 0$; (b) $x_1 = 2$, $x_2 = 3$, $Z = \$0.17$
11. (a) max. $Z = 8x_1 + 10x_2 + 7x_3$; s.t. $7x_1 + 10x_2 + 5x_3 \le 2{,}000$, $2x_1 + 3x_2 + 2x_3 \le 660$, $x_1 \le 200$, $x_2 \le 300$, $x_3 \le 150$, $x_1 \ge 0$, $x_2 \ge 0$, $x_3 \ge 0$; (b) $x_1 = 178.57$, $x_3 = 150$, $Z = 2{,}478.57$
13. (a) max. $Z = 7x_1 + 5x_2 + 5x_3 + 4x_4$; s.t. $2x_1 + 4x_2 + 2x_3 + 3x_4 \le 45{,}000$, $x_1 + x_2 \le 6{,}000$, $x_3 + x_4 \le 7{,}000$, $x_1 + x_3 \le 5{,}000$, $x_2 + x_4 \le 6{,}000$, $x_1 \ge 0$, $x_2 \ge 0$, $x_3 \ge 0$, $x_4 \ge 0$; (b) $x_1 = 5{,}000$, $x_2 = 1{,}000$, $x_4 = 5{,}000$, $Z = 60{,}000$
15. (a) max. $Z = 1{,}800x_{1a} + 2{,}100x_{1b} + 1{,}600x_{1c} + 1{,}000x_{2a} + 700x_{2b} + 900x_{2c} + 1{,}400x_{3a} + 800x_{3b} + 2{,}200x_{3c}$; s.t. $x_{1a} + x_{1b} + x_{1c} = 30$, $x_{2a} + x_{2b} + x_{2c} = 30$, $x_{3a} + x_{3b} + x_{3c} = 30$, $x_{1a} + x_{2a} + x_{3a} \le 40$, $x_{1b} + x_{2b} + x_{3b} \le 60$, $x_{1c} + x_{2c} + x_{3c} \le 50$, $x_{ij} \ge 0$; (b) $x_{1b} = 30$, $x_{2a} = 30$, $x_{3c} = 30$, $Z = 159{,}000$

17. (a) min. $Z = 1.7(x_{t1} + x_{t2} + x_{t3}) + 2.8(x_{m1} + x_{m2} + x_{m3}) + 3.25(x_{b1} + x_{b2} + x_{b3})$; s.t. $.50x_{t1} - .50x_{m1} - .50x_{b1} \le 0$, $-.20x_{t1} + .80x_{m1} - .20x_{b1} \ge 0$, $-.30x_{t2} - .30x_{m2} + .70x_{b2} \ge 0$, $-.30x_{t2} + .70x_{m2} - .30x_{b2} \ge 0$, $.80x_{t2} - .20x_{m2} - .20x_{b2} \le 0$, $.50x_{t3} - .50x_{m3} - .50x_{b3} \ge 0$, $.30x_{t3} - .70x_{m3} - .70x_{b3} \le 0$, $-.10x_{t3} - .10x_{m3} + .90x_{b3} \ge 0$, $x_{t1} + x_{m1} + x_{b1} \ge 1{,}200$, $x_{t2} + x_{m2} + x_{b2} \ge 900$, $x_{t3} + x_{m3} + x_{b3} \ge 2{,}400$; $x_{ij} \ge 0$; (b) $x_{t1} = 600$, $x_{t2} = 180$, $x_{t3} = 1{,}680$, $x_{m1} = 600$, $x_{m2} = 450$, $x_{m3} = 480$, $x_{b1} = 0$, $x_{b2} = 270$, $x_{b3} = 240$, $Z = 10{,}123.50$

19. (a) max. $Z = .02x_1 + .09x_2 + .06x_3 + .04x_4$; s.t. $x_1 + x_2 + x_3 + x_4 = 4{,}000{,}000$, $x_1 \le 1{,}600{,}000$, $x_2 \le 1{,}600{,}000$, $x_3 \le 1{,}600{,}000$, $x_4 \le 1{,}600{,}000$, $x_2 - x_3 - x_4 \le 0$, $x_1 - x_3 \ge 0$, $x_1 \ge 0$, $x_2 \ge 0$, $x_3 \ge 0$, $x_4 \ge 0$; (b) $x_1 = 800{,}000$, $x_2 = 1{,}600{,}000$, $x_3 = 800{,}000$, $x_4 = 800{,}000$, $Z = 240{,}000$

21. (a) max. $Z = 7.8x_{11} + 7.8x_{12} + 8.2x_{13} + 7.9x_{14} + 6.7x_{21} + 8.9x_{22} + 9.2x_{23} + 6.3x_{24} + 8.4x_{31} + 8.1x_{32} + 9.0x_{33} + 5.8x_{34}$; s.t. $35x_{11} + 40x_{21} + 38x_{31} \le 9{,}000$, $41x_{12} + 36x_{22} + 37x_{32} \le 14{,}400$, $34x_{13} + 32x_{23} + 33x_{33} \le 12{,}000$, $39x_{14} + 43x_{24} + 40x_{34} \le 15{,}000$, $x_{11} + x_{12} + x_{13} + x_{14} = 400$, $x_{21} + x_{22} + x_{23} + x_{24} = 570$, $x_{31} + x_{32} + x_{33} + x_{34} = 320$, $x_{ij} \ge 0$; (b) $x_{11} = 15.385$, $x_{14} = 384.615$, $x_{22} = 400$, $x_{23} = 170$, $x_{31} = 121.212$, $x_{33} = 198.788$, $Z = 11{,}089.73$

23. (a) min. $Z = 1.7x_{11} + 1.4x_{12} + 1.2x_{13} + 1.1x_{14} + 1.05x_{15} + 1.0x_{16} + 1.7x_{21} + 1.4x_{22} + 1.2x_{23} + 1.1x_{24} + 1.05x_{25} + 1.7x_{31} + 1.4x_{32} + 1.2x_{33} + 1.1x_{34} + 1.7x_{41} + 1.4x_{42} + 1.2x_{43} + 1.7x_{51} + 1.4x_{52} + 1.7x_{61}$; s.t. $x_{11} + x_{12} + x_{13} + x_{14} + x_{15} + x_{16} = 47{,}000$, $x_{12} + x_{13} + x_{14} + x_{15} + x_{16} + x_{21} + x_{22} + x_{23} + x_{24} + x_{25} = 35{,}000$, $x_{13} + x_{14} + x_{15} + x_{16} + x_{22} + x_{23} + x_{24} + x_{25} + x_{31} + x_{32} + x_{33} + x_{34} = 52{,}000$, $x_{14} + x_{15} + x_{16} + x_{23} + x_{24} + x_{25} + x_{32} + x_{33} + x_{34} + x_{41} + x_{42} + x_{43} = 27{,}000$, $x_{15} + x_{16} + x_{24} + x_{25} + x_{33} + x_{34} + x_{42} + x_{43} + x_{51} + x_{52} = 19{,}000$, $x_{16} + x_{25} + x_{34} + x_{43} + x_{52} + x_{61} = 15{,}000$, (b) $x_{11} = 12{,}000$, $x_{13} = 25{,}000$, $x_{14} = 8{,}000$, $x_{15} = 2{,}000$, $x_{33} = 2{,}000$, $x_{34} = 15{,}000$, $Z = \$80{,}200$; (c) $x_{16} = 52{,}000$, $Z = \$52{,}000$

25. (a) add $x_{ss} \le 150$, $x_{ww} \le 300$, $x_{cc} \le 250$; $x_{nc} = 700$, $x_{nw} = 0$, $x_{sw} = 150$, $x_{ss} = 150$, $x_{es} = 900$, $x_{wc} = 250$, $x_{ww} = 300$, $x_{cc} = 250$, $x_{cw} = 250$, $x_{ws} = 50$, $Z = 20{,}400$; (b) changes demand constraints from $\le 1{,}200$ to $= 1{,}000$; $x_{nc} = 400$, $x_{nw} = 300$, $x_{sw} = 150$, $x_{ss} = 150$, $x_{ec} = 50$, $x_{es} = 850$, $x_{wc} = 300$, $x_{ww} = 300$, $x_{cc} = 250$, $x_{cw} = 250$, $Z = 21{,}200$

27. (a) max. $Z = 2x_1 + 4x_2 + 3x_3 + 7x_4$; s.t. $x_2 + x_4 \le 300$, $6x_1 + 15x_2 \le 1{,}200$, $5x_3 + 12x_4 \le 2{,}400$, $x_i \ge 0$; (b) $x_1 = 200$, $x_3 = 480$, $Z = 1{,}840$

29. (a) max. $Z = 35x_1 + 20x_2 + 58x_3$; s.t. $14x_1 + 12x_2 + 35x_3 \le 35{,}000$, $6x_1 + 3x_2 + 12x_3 \le 20{,}000$, $x_1 \ge 0$, $x_2 \ge 0$, $x_3 \ge 0$; (b) $x_1 = 2{,}500$, $Z = 87{,}500$

31. (a) min. $Z = 15{,}000x_1 + 4{,}000x_2 + 6{,}000x_3$; s.t. $x_3/x_2 \ge 2/1$, $25{,}000x_1 + 10{,}000x_2 + 15{,}000x_3 \ge 100{,}000$, $(15{,}000x_1 + 3{,}000x_2 + 12{,}000x_3)/(10{,}000x_1 + 7{,}000x_2 + 3{,}000x_3) \ge 2/1$, $(15{,}000x_1 + 4{,}000x_2 + 9{,}000x_3)/(25{,}000x_1 + 10{,}000x_2 + 15{,}000x_3) \ge .30$, $x_2 \le 7$, $x_1 \ge 0$, $x_2 \ge 0$, $x_3 \ge 0$; (b) $x_2 = 2.5$, $x_3 = 5.0$, $Z = 40{,}000$; (c) x_4, no effect

33. (a) min. $Z = .11x_1 + .05 \sum_{6} y_i$; s.t. $x_1 + y_1 + 20{,}000 - c_1 = 60{,}000$, $c_1 + y_2 + 30{,}000 - c_2 = 60{,}000 + y_1$, $c_2 + y_3 + 40{,}000 - c_3 = 80{,}000 + y_2$, $c_3 + y_4 + 50{,}000 - c_4 = 30{,}000 + y_3$, $c_4 + y_5 + 80{,}000 - c_5 = 30{,}000 + y_4$, $c_5 + y_6 + 100{,}000 - c_6 = 20{,}000 + y_5$, $x_1 + y_6 \le c_6$, x_1, y_i, $c_i \ge 0$; (b) $x_1 = 70{,}000$, $y_3 = 40{,}000$, $y_4 = 20{,}000$, $y_1 = y_2 = y_5 = y_6 = 0$, $c_1 = 30{,}000$, $c_5 = 30{,}000$, $c_6 = 110{,}000$, $Z = \$10{,}700$; (c) $x_1 = 90{,}000$, $y_3 = 20{,}000$, $c_1 = 50{,}000$, $c_2 = 20{,}000$, $c_5 = 50{,}000$, $c_6 = 130{,}000$, $Z = \$9{,}100$

35. (a) max. $Z = .7x_{cr} + .6x_{br} + .4x_{pr} + .85x_{ar} + 1.05x_{cb} + .95x_{bb} + .75x_{pb} + 1.20x_{ab} + 1.55x_{cm} + 1.45x_{bm} + 1.25x_{pm} + 1.70x_{am}$; s.t. $x_{cr} + x_{cb} + x_{cm} \le 200$, $x_{br} + x_{bb} + x_{bm} \le 300$, $x_{pr} + x_{pb} + x_{pm} \le 150$, $x_{ar} + x_{ab} + x_{am} \le 400$, $.90x_{br} + .90x_{pr} - .10x_{cr} - .10x_{ar} \le 0$, $.80x_{cr} - .20x_{br} - .20x_{pr} - .20x_{ar} \ge 0$, $.25x_{bb} + .75x_{cb} - .75x_{pb} - .75x_{ab} \ge 0$, $x_{am} = 0$, $.5x_{bm} + .5x_{pm} - .5x_{cm} - .5x_{am} \le 0$, $x_{ij} \ge 0$; (b) $x_{cm} = 125$, $x_{ar} = 300$, $x_{cr} = 75$, $x_{bb} = 300$, $x_{pm} = 125$, $x_{ab} = 100$, $Z = 1{,}602.50$

37. (a) min. $Z = 40x_1 + 65x_2 + 70x_3 + 30x_4$; s.t. $x_1 + x_2 = 250$, $x_3 + x_4 = 400$, $x_1 + x_3 = 300$, $x_2 + x_4 = 350$, $x_1 \ge 0$, $x_2 \ge 0$, $x_3 \ge 0$, $x_4 \ge 0$; (b) $x_1 = 250$, $x_3 = 50$, $x_4 = 350$, $Z = 24{,}000$

39. (a) max. $Z = 175\ (7x_1)$; s.t. $8x_1 + 5x_2 + 6.5x_3 \le 3{,}000$, $x_1 + x_2 + x_3 \le 120$, $90(7x_1) \le 10{,}000$, $7x_1 - 12x_2 = 0$, $12x_2 - 10x_3 = 0$, $7x_1 - 10x_3 = 0$, $x_1 \ge 0$, $x_2 \ge 0$, $x_3 \ge 0$; (b) $x_1 = 15.9$, $x_2 = 9.3$, $x_3 = 11.1$, $Z = 19{,}444.44$

41. (a) min. $Z = 3x_{13} + 4x_{14} + 5x_{12} + 2x_{34} + 7x_{45} + 8x_{25}$; s.t. $x_{13} + x_{14} + x_{12} = 5$, $x_{45} + x_{25} = 5$, $x_{13} = x_{34}$, $x_{14} + x_{34} = x_{45}$, $x_{12} = x_{25}$, $x_{ij} \ge 0$; (b) $x_{14} = 5$, $x_{45} = 5$, $Z = 55{,}000$

43. (a) min. $Z = x_1 + x_2 + x_3 + x_4 + x_5 + x_6$; s.t. $3x_1 + 2x_2 + 2x_3 + x_4 = 700$, $x_3 + 2x_4 + x_5 = 1{,}200$, $x_2 + x_5 + 2x_6 = 300$, $x_i \ge 0$; (b) $x_2 = 50$, $x_4 = 600$, $x_6 = 125$, $Z = 775$; (c) min. $Z = 4x_1 + x_2 + 2x_3 + 0x_4 + 6x_5 + 5x_6$; s.t. $3x_1 + 2x_2 + 2x_3 + x_4 \ge 700$, $x_3 + 2x_4 + x_5 \ge 1{,}200$, $x_2 + x_5 + 2x_6 \ge 300$, $x_i \ge 0$; $x_2 = 300$, $x_4 = 600$, $Z = 300$

45. (a) max. $Z = 4x_1 + 8x_2 + 6x_3 + 7x_4 - 5y_1 - 6y_2 - 7y_3$; s.t. $s_0 = 2{,}000$, $x_1 \le s_0$, $s_1 = s_0 - x_1 + y_1$, $s_1 \le 10{,}000$, $x_2 \le s_1$, $s_2 = s_1 - x_2 + y_2$, $s_2 \le 10{,}000$, $x_3 \le s_2$, $s_3 = s_2 - x_3 + y_3$, $s_3 \le 10{,}000$, $x_4 \le s_3$, $x_i \ge 0$, $y_i \ge 0$, $s_i \ge 0$; (b) $x_1 = 0$, $x_2 = 10{,}000$, $x_4 = 10{,}000$, $y_1 = 8{,}000$, $y_2 = 10{,}000$, $s_0 = 2{,}000$, $s_1 = s_2 = s_3 = 10{,}000$, $Z = 50{,}000$

47. (a) max. $Z = 130x_{1a} + 150x_{1b} + 90x_{1c} + 275x_{2a} + 300x_{2b} + 100x_{2c} + 180x_{3a} + 225x_{3b} + 140x_{3c} + 200x_{4a} + 120x_{4b} + 160x_{4c}$; s.t. $x_{1a} + x_{1b} + x_{1c} = 1$, $x_{2a} + x_{2b} + x_{2c} = 1$, $x_{3a} + x_{3b} + x_{3c} = 1$, $x_{4a} + x_{4b} + x_{4c} = 1$, $1 \le x_{1a} + x_{2a} + x_{3a} + x_{4a} \le 2$, $1 \le x_{1b} + x_{2b} + x_{3b} + x_{4b} \le 2$, $1 \le x_{1c} + x_{2c} + x_{3c} + x_{4c} \le 2$, $x_{ij} \ge 0$; (b) $x_{1a} = 1$, $x_{2b} = 1$, $x_{3b} = 1$, $x_{4c} = 1$, $Z = 815$; (c) max. $Z = 130x_{1a} + 150x_{1b} + 90x_{1c} + 275x_{2a} + 300x_{2b} + 100x_{2c} + 180x_{3a} + 225x_{3b} + 140x_{3c} + 200x_{4a} + 120x_{4b} + 160x_{4c}$; s.t. $x_{1a} + x_{1b} + x_{1c} \le 1$, $x_{2a} + x_{2b} + x_{2c} \le 1$, $x_{3a} + x_{3b} + x_{3c} \le 1$, $x_{4a} + x_{4b} + x_{4c} \le 1$, $x_{1a} + x_{2a} + x_{3a} + x_{4a} = 1$, $x_{1b} + x_{2b} + x_{3b} + x_{4b} = 1$, $x_{1c} + x_{2c} + x_{3c} + x_{4c} = 1$, $x_{ij} \ge 0$; $x_{2a} = 1$, $x_{3b} = 1$, $x_{4c} = 1$, $Z = 660$

49. Z values: A = 1.000, B = 1.000, C = 1.000; all three efficient

51. (a) min. $Z = x$; s.t. $150x = 650 + y_1$, $150x + y_1 = 450 + y_2$, $150x + y_2 = 600 + y_3$, $150x + y_3 = 500 + y_4$, $150x + y_4 = 700 + y_5$, $150x + y_5 = 650 + y_6$, $150x + y_6 = 750 + y_7$, $150x + y_7 = 900 + y_8$, $150x + y_8 = 800 + y_9$, $150x + y_9 = 650 + y_{10}$, $150x + y_{10} = 700 + y_{11}$, $150x + y_{11} \ge 500$; (b) $Z = x = 4.45$, $y_1 = 18.18$, $y_2 = 236.36$, $y_3 = 304.54$, $y_4 = 472.72$, $y_5 = 440.91$, $y_6 = 459.09$, $y_7 = 377.27$, $y_8 = 145.45$, $y_9 = 13.63$, $y_{10} = 31.81$, $y_{11} = 0$

53. (a) max. $Z = y$; s.t. $y - x_1 = 0$, $y - x_2 = 0$, $y - x_3 = 0$, $10x_1 + 8x_2 + 6x_3 \le 960$, $9x_1 + 21x_2 + 15x_3 \le 1{,}440$, $2x_1 - 3x_2 - 2x_3 \le 60$, $-2x_1 + 3x_2 + 2x_3 \le 60$, $x_i \ge 0$, $y \ge 0$; (b) $x_1 = x_2 = x_3 = y = 20$; (c) remove balancing requirement, $x_1 = x_2 = x_3 = y = 32$

55. max. $Z = 850x_1 + 600x_n + 750x_s + 1{,}000x_w$; s.t. $x_1 + x_n + x_s + x_w = 18$, $x_1 + x_n + x_s + x_w + y_1 + y_n + y_s + y_w = 60$, $400y_1 + 100y_n + 175y_s + 90y_w \le 9{,}000$, $10 \le y_1 \le 25$, $5 \le y_n \le 10$, $5 \le y_s \le 10$, $5 \le y_w \le 10$, $x_1 \le 6$, $x_n \le 6$, $x_s \le 6$, $x_w \le 6$, $x_i \ge 0$, $y_i \ge 0$; $x_1 = 6$, $x_n = 0$, $x_s = 6$, $x_w = 6$, $y_1 = 14.44$, $y_n = 10$, $y_s = 7.56$, $y_w = 10$, $Z = 15{,}600$ (multiple optimal)

57. (a) max. $Z = .85x_1 + .90x_2 - y_1 - y_2$; s.t. $x_1 \le 5{,}000 + 3y_1$, $x_2 \le 4{,}000 + 5y_2$, $.60x_1 + .85x_2 + y_1 + y_2 \le 16{,}000$, $x_1 \ge .3(x_1 + x_2)$, $x_1 \le .6(x_1 +$

x_2), $x_1 \geq 0, x_2 \geq 0, y_1 \geq 0, y_2 \geq 0$; (b) $x_1 = 5{,}458.128, x_2 = 12{,}735.63, y_1 = 152.709, y_2 = 1{,}747.126, Z = 14{,}201.64$

59. (a) min. $Z = \Sigma\Sigma$ (ranking)• x_{ij}, s.t. $\Sigma x_{ij} \leq$ hr., Σx_{ij} = project hr., Σ (hourly rate)• $x_{ij} \leq$ budget; (b) $x_{A3} = 400, x_{A4} = 50, x_{B4} = 250, x_{B5} = 350, x_{C4} = 175, x_{C7} = 274.1, x_{C8} = 50.93, x_{D2} = 131.7, x_{D7} = 15.93, x_{E1} = 208.33, x_{E8} = 149.07, x_{F1} = 291.67, x_{F2} = 108.3, x_{F6} = 460, Z = \$12{,}853.33$

61. $x_1 = 0, x_2 = 4, x_3 = 18.4, x_4 = 6.4, x_5 = 24.8, y_1 = 72.22, y_2 = 72.44, y_3 = 64.95, y_4 = 62.34, y_5 = 52.24, y_6 = 38.9, y_7 = 28.53, y_8 = 43.35, Z = \$360{,}196$

63. min. $Z = \Sigma x_{ij}$ (priority ij); s.t. $\sum_{j=1}^{12} x_{ij} = 1, \sum_{i=1}^{16} x_{ij} \leq$ available slots j, U11B: 3-5M, U11G: 3-5T, U12B: 3-5T, U12G: 3-5M, U13B: 3-5T, U13G: 3-5M, U14B: 5-7M, U14G: 3-5M, U15B: 5-7T, U15G: 3-5M, U16B: 5-7T, U16G: 5-7T, U17B: 5-7M, U17G: 5-7T, U18B: 3-5T, U18G: 5-7M, $Z = 27$

65. 1-D (1 hr.), 2-E (1 hr.), 3-F (2 hr.), 3-H (6 hr.), 4-I (1 hr.), 5-J (1 hr.), A-5 (8 hr.), B-4 (5 hr.), C-6 (8 hr.), G-7 (2 hr.), Z = 35 hr.; 6 crews originate in Pittsburgh, 4 in Orlando

67. min. $Z = .41x_{14} + .57x_{15} + .37x_{24} + .48x_{25} + .51x_{34} + .60x_{35} + .22x_{46} + .10x_{47} + .20x_{48} + .15x_{56} + .16x_{57} + .18x_{58}$; s.t. $x_{14} + x_{15} \leq 24{,}000, x_{24} + x_{25} \leq 18{,}000, x_{34} + x_{35} \leq 32{,}000, x_{14} + x_{24} + x_{34} \leq 48{,}000, x_{15} + x_{25} + x_{35} \leq 35{,}000$ $(x_{14} + x_{24} + x_{34})/2 = x_{46} + x_{47} + x_{48}$, $(x_{15} + x_{25} + x_{35})/2 = x_{56} + x_{57} + x_{58}$, $x_{46} + x_{56} = 9{,}000, x_{47} + x_{57} = 12{,}000, x_{47} + x_{58} = 15{,}000, x_{ij} \geq 0$; $x_{14} = 24{,}000, x_{24} = 18{,}000, x_{34} = 6{,}000, x_{35} = 24{,}000, x_{47} = 12{,}000, x_{48} = 12{,}000, x_{56} = 9{,}000, x_{58} = 3{,}000, Z = \$39{,}450$

Project Management

Project Management

One of the most popular uses of networks is for project analysis. Such projects as the construction of a building, the development of a drug, or the installation of a computer system can be represented as networks. These networks illustrate the way in which the parts of the project are organized, and they can be used to determine the time duration of the projects. The network techniques that are used for project analysis are CPM and PERT. CPM stands for *critical path method*, and PERT is an acronym for *project evaluation and review technique*. These two techniques are very similar.

There were originally two primary differences between CPM and PERT. With CPM, a single, or deterministic, estimate for activity time was used, whereas with PERT probabilistic time estimates were employed. The other difference was related to the mechanics of drawing the project network. In PERT, activities were represented as arcs, or arrowed lines, between two nodes, or circles, whereas in CPM, activities were represented as the nodes or circles. However, these were minor differences, and over time CPM and PERT have been effectively merged into a single technique, conventionally referred to as simply CPM/PERT.

CPM and PERT were developed at approximately the same time (although independently) during the late 1950s. The fact that they have already been so frequently and widely applied attests to their value as management science techniques.

The Elements of Project Management

Management is generally perceived to be concerned with the planning, organization, and control of an ongoing process or activity such as the production of a product or delivery of a service. *Project* management is different in that it reflects a commitment of resources and people to a typically important activity for a relatively short time frame, after which the management effort is dissolved. Projects do not have the continuity of supervision that is typical in the management of a production process. As such, the features and characteristics of project management tend to be somewhat unique.

Figure 1 provides an overview of project management, which encompasses three major processes—planning, scheduling, and control. It also includes a number of the more prominent elements of these processes. In the remainder of this section we will discuss some of the features of the project planning process.

Project Planning

Project plans generally include the following basic elements:

- *Objectives*—A detailed statement of what is to be accomplished by the project, how it will achieve the company's goals and meet the strategic plan, and an estimate of when it needs to be completed, the cost, and the return.
- *Project scope*—A discussion of how to approach the project, the technological and resource feasibility, the major tasks involved, and a preliminary schedule; it includes a justification of the project and what constitutes project success.
- *Contract requirements*—A general structure of managerial, reporting, and performance responsibilities, including a detailed list of staff, suppliers, subcontractors, managerial requirements and agreements, reporting requirements, and a projected organizational structure.
- *Schedules*—A list of all major events, tasks, and subschedules, from which a master schedule is developed.
- *Resources*—The overall project budget for all resource requirements and procedures for budgetary control.

Figure 1
The project management process

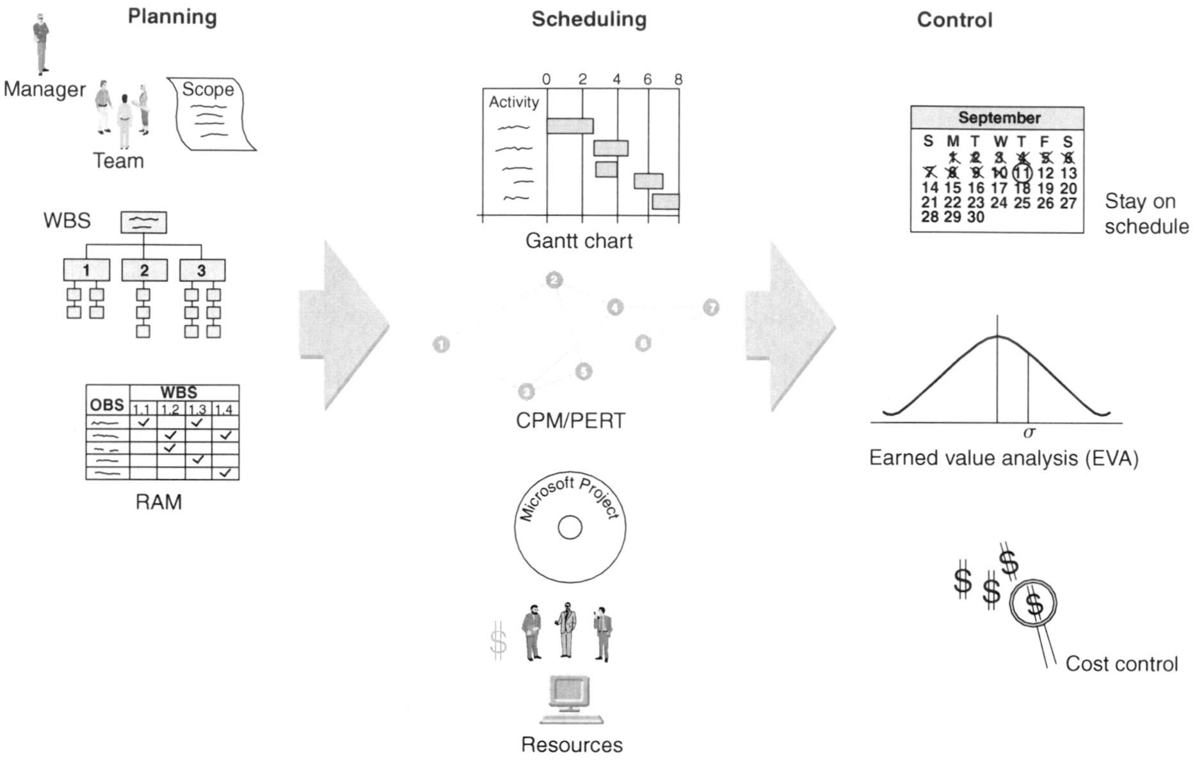

- *Personnel*—Identification and recruitment of personnel required for the project team, including special skills and training.
- *Control*—Procedures for monitoring and evaluating progress and performance, including schedules and cost.
- *Risk and problem analysis*—Anticipation and assessment of uncertainties, problems, and potential difficulties that might increase the risk of project delays and/or failure and threaten project success.

The Project Team

Project teams are made up of individuals from various areas and departments within a company.

A project team typically consists of a group of individuals selected from other areas in the organization, or from consultants outside the organization, because of their special skills, expertise, and experience related to the project activities. Members of the engineering staff, particularly industrial engineering, are often assigned to project work because of their technical skills. The project team may also include various managers and staff personnel from specific areas related to the project. Even workers can be involved on the project team if their jobs are a function of the project activity. For example, a project team for the construction of a new loading dock facility at a plant might logically include truck drivers; forklift operators; dock workers; and staff personnel and managers from purchasing, shipping, receiving, and packaging; as well as engineers to assess vehicle flow, routes, and space considerations.

Assignment to a project team is usually temporary and thus can have both positive and negative repercussions. The temporary loss of workers and staff from their permanent jobs can be disruptive for both the employees and the work area. An employee must sometimes "serve two masters," in a sense, reporting to both the project manager and a regular supervisor. Alternatively, because projects are usually "exciting," they provide an opportunity to do work that is new and innovative, and the employee may be reluctant to report back to a more mundane, regular job after the project is completed.

The project manager is often under great pressure.

The most important member of a project team is the *project manager*. The job of managing a project is subject to a great deal of uncertainty and the distinct possibility of failure. Because each project is unique and usually has not been attempted previously, the outcome is not as certain as the outcome of an ongoing process would be. A degree of security is attained in the supervision of a continuing process that is not present in project management.

Management Science Application

Managing Projects in China

China is the most likely country in the world where U.S. companies will be doing global business in the future. Business between U.S. and Chinese companies includes projects in which diversity and teamwork will be critical factors in determining project success; however, the cultural differences between the United States and China are probably as great as they could possibly be, thus making project teamwork a potential problem that requires special attention. That doesn't mean that the way things are done in the United States (or in China) is better or worse, just different. Following are some examples of these cultural differences that should be addressed to achieve project success.

First, whereas U.S. companies value individualism, China, reflecting 2,000 years of traditional Confucian values, does not. Chinese managers can be good, but their leadership style is typically different from that of U.S. project managers, being more collaborative rather than direct. Relationships are very important in China. The Chinese word *guanxi* (gwan-shee) refers to the strong reliance of business on social connections. A Chinese business partner with strong, well-placed relationships can enhance project success; however, such relationships are developed slowly. The Chinese focus on the long-term rather than the short-term view prevalent in many Western companies. "Face" or *mianzi* (me-ahn-zee) is very important in China. Every conversation, meeting, meal, and social or business engagement is an opportunity for an individual to gain or lose stature. Rudeness and anger have very negative consequences; raising your voice to a Chinese manager will cause him or her shame and embarrassment and brand the offending person as a barbarian. Rank is important in China; people of high rank are afforded an extraordinary degree of deference. Consequently, instructions from team leaders are respected and followed, and advice from junior team members is not generally expected or valued. Humility helps—U.S. food is not better than Chinese food, and the U.S. way of doing business is not better than the Chinese way; they're just different. Gifts are important in China, not so much for their intrinsic value as for their symbolic value (of respect). They should reflect a degree of thoughtfulness and effort, for example, not just a logo T-shirt. Patience is a respected virtue in China, where time is used as a competitive tool. The little things can be important; learn the Chinese way of doing things like smiling, being friendly, and paying attention, which can pay off in successful teamwork.

Getty Images – Digital Vision

Source: Bud Baker, "When in China . . . ," *PM Network* 20, no. 6 (June 2006): 24–25.

The project team members are often from diverse areas of the organization and possess different skills, which must be coordinated into a single, focused effort to successfully complete the project. In addition, the project is invariably subject to time and budgetary constraints that are not the same as normal work schedules and resource consumption in an ongoing process. Overall, there is usually more perceived and real pressure associated with project management than in a normal management position. However, there are potential rewards, including the ability to demonstrate one's management abilities in a difficult situation, the challenge of working on a unique project, and the excitement of doing something new.

Scope Statement

*A **scope statement** includes a project justification and the expected results.*

A **scope statement** is a document that provides a common understanding of a project. It includes a justification for the project that describes what factors have created a need within the company for the project. It also includes an indication of what the expected results of the project will be and what will constitute project success. Further, the scope statement might include a list of the types of planning reports and documents that are part of the project management process.

A similar planning document is the *statement of work (SOW)*. In a large project, the SOW is often prepared for individual team members, groups, departments, subcontractors, and suppliers. This statement describes the work in sufficient detail so that the team member responsible for it knows what is required and whether he or she has sufficient resources to accomplish the work successfully and on time. For suppliers and subcontractors, it is often the basis for determining whether they can perform the work and for bidding on it. Some companies require that an SOW be part of an official contract with a supplier or subcontractor.

Work Breakdown Structure

*A **work breakdown structure** is an organizational chart that break down the project into modules for planning.*

The **work breakdown structure** (WBS) is an organizational chart used for project planning. It organizes the work to be done on a project by breaking down the project into its major components, referred to as *modules*. These components are then subdivided into more detailed subcomponents, which are further broken down into activities, and, finally, into individual tasks. The end result is an organizational structure of the project made up of different levels, with the overall project at the top level and the individual tasks at the bottom. A WBS helps identify activities and determine individual tasks, project workloads, and the resources required. It also helps to identify the relationships between modules and activities and avoid unnecessary duplication of activities. A WBS provides the basis for developing and managing the project schedule, resources, and modifications.

There is no specific model for a WBS, although it is most often in the form of a chart or a table. In general, there are two good ways to develop a WBS. One way is to start at the top and work your way down, asking "What components constitute this level?" until the WBS is developed in sufficient detail. Another way is to brainstorm the entire project, writing down each item on a sticky note and then organizing the sticky notes into a WBS. The upper levels of the WBS tend to contain the summary activities, major components or functional areas involved in the project that indicate what is to be done. The lower levels tend to describe the detailed work activities of the project within the major components or modules. They typically indicate how things are done.

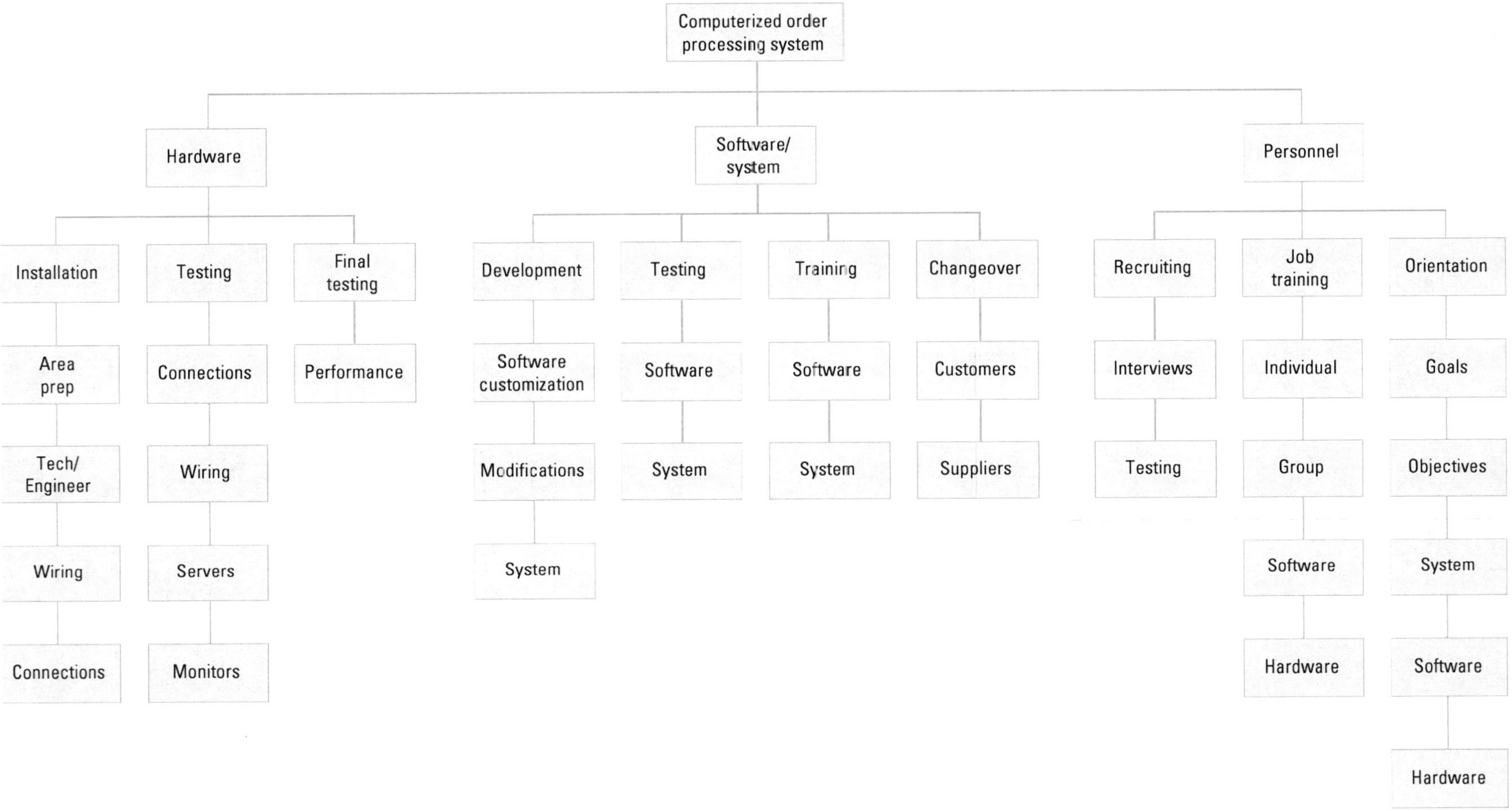

Figure 2
Work breakdown structure for computer order-processing system project

Figure 2 shows a WBS for a project for installing a new computerized order processing system for a manufacturing company that links customers, the manufacturer, and the manufacturer's suppliers. The WBS is organized according to the three major project categories for the development of the system: hardware, software/system, and personnel. Within each of these categories, the major tasks and activities under those tasks are detailed. For example, under hardware, a major task is installation, and activities required in installation include area preparation, technical/engineering layouts and configurations, wiring, and electrical connections.

Responsibility Assignment Matrix

After the WBS is developed, to organize the project work into smaller, manageable elements, the project manager assigns the work elements to organizational units—departments, groups, individuals, or subcontractors—by using an *organizational breakdown structure (OBS)*. An OBS is a table or chart that shows which organizational units are responsible for work items. After the OBS is developed, the project manager can then develop a **responsibility assignment matrix** *(RAM)*. A RAM shows who in the organization is responsible for doing the work in the project. Figure 3 shows a RAM for the "Hardware/Installation" category from the WBS for the computerized order processing project shown in Figure 2. Notice that there are three levels of work assignments in the matrix, reflecting who is responsible for the work, who actually performs the work, and who performs support activities. As with the WBS, there are many different forms both the OBS and RAM can take, depending on the needs and preferences of the company, project team, and project manager.

*A **responsibility assignment matrix** is a table or chart that shows who is responsible for project work.*

Figure 3
A responsibility assignment matrix

	WBS Activities—Hardware/Installation			
OBS Units	1.1.1 Area prep	1.1.2 Tech/Engineer	1.1.3 Wiring	1.1.4 Connections
Hardware engineering	3	1	1	1
Systems engineering		3		3
Software engineering		3		
Technical support	1	2		2
Electrical staff	2		2	2
Hardware vendor	3	3	3	3
Quality manager				3
Customer/supplier liaison				3

Level of responsibility: 1 = Overall responsibility 2 = Performance responsibility 3 = Support

Project Scheduling

A project schedule evolves from the planning documents discussed previously. It is typically the most critical element in the project management process, especially during the implementation phase (i.e., the actual project work), and it is the source of most conflict and problems. One reason is that frequently the single most important criterion for the success of a project is that it be finished on time. If a stadium is supposed to be finished in

TIME OUT *for Henry Gantt*

Both CPM and PERT are based on the network diagram, which is an outgrowth of the bar, or Gantt, chart that was designed to control the time element of a program. Henry Gantt, a pioneer in the field of industrial engineering, first employed the Gantt chart in the artillery ammunition shops at the Frankford Arsenal in 1914, when World War I was declared. The chart graphically depicted actual versus estimated production time.

time for the first game of the season and it's not, there will be a lot of angry ticket holders; if a school building is not completed by the time the school year starts, there will be a lot of angry parents; if a shopping mall is not completed on time, there will be a lot of angry tenants; if a new product is not completed by the scheduled launch date, millions of dollars can be lost; and if a new military weapon is not completed on time, it could affect national security. Also, time is a measure of progress that is very visible. It is an absolute with little flexibility; you can spend less money or use fewer people, but you cannot slow down or stop the passage of time.

Developing a schedule encompasses four basic steps. First, *define the activities* that must be performed to complete the project; second, *sequence the activities* in the order in which they must be completed; third, *estimate the time* required to complete each activity; and fourth, *develop the schedule* based on the sequencing and time estimates of the activities.

Because scheduling involves a quantifiable measure, time, there are several quantitative techniques available that can be used to develop a project schedule, including the Gantt chart and CPM/PERT networks. There are also various computer software packages that can be used to schedule projects, including the popular Microsoft Project. Later in this chapter we will discuss CPM/PERT and Microsoft Project in greater detail. For now, we will describe one of the oldest and most widely used scheduling techniques, the Gantt chart.

The Gantt Chart

*A **Gantt chart** is a graph or bar chart with a bar for each project activity that shows the passage of time.*

Using a **Gantt chart** is a traditional management technique for scheduling and planning small projects that have relatively few activities and precedence relationships. This scheduling technique (also called a *bar chart*) was developed by Henry Gantt, a pioneer in the field of industrial engineering at the artillery ammunition shops of the Frankford Arsenal in 1914. The Gantt chart has been a popular project scheduling tool since its inception and is still widely used today. It is the direct precursor of the CPM/PERT technique, which we will discuss later.

The Gantt chart is a graph with a bar representing time for each activity in the project being analyzed. Figure 4 illustrates a Gantt chart of a simplified project description for building a house. The project contains only seven general activities, such as designing the house, laying the foundation, ordering materials, and so forth. The first activity is "design house and obtain financing," and it requires 3 months to complete, shown by the bar from left to right across the chart. After the first activity is finished, the next two activities, "lay foundation" and "order and receive materials," can start simultaneously. This set of activities demonstrates how a precedence relationship works; the design of the house and the financing must precede the next two activities.

The activity "lay foundation" requires 2 months to complete, so it will be finished, at the earliest, at the end of month 5. "Order and receive materials" requires 1 month to complete, and it could be finished after month 4. However, observe that it is possible to delay the start of this activity 1 month, until month 4. This delay would still enable the activity to be

Figure 4
A Gantt chart

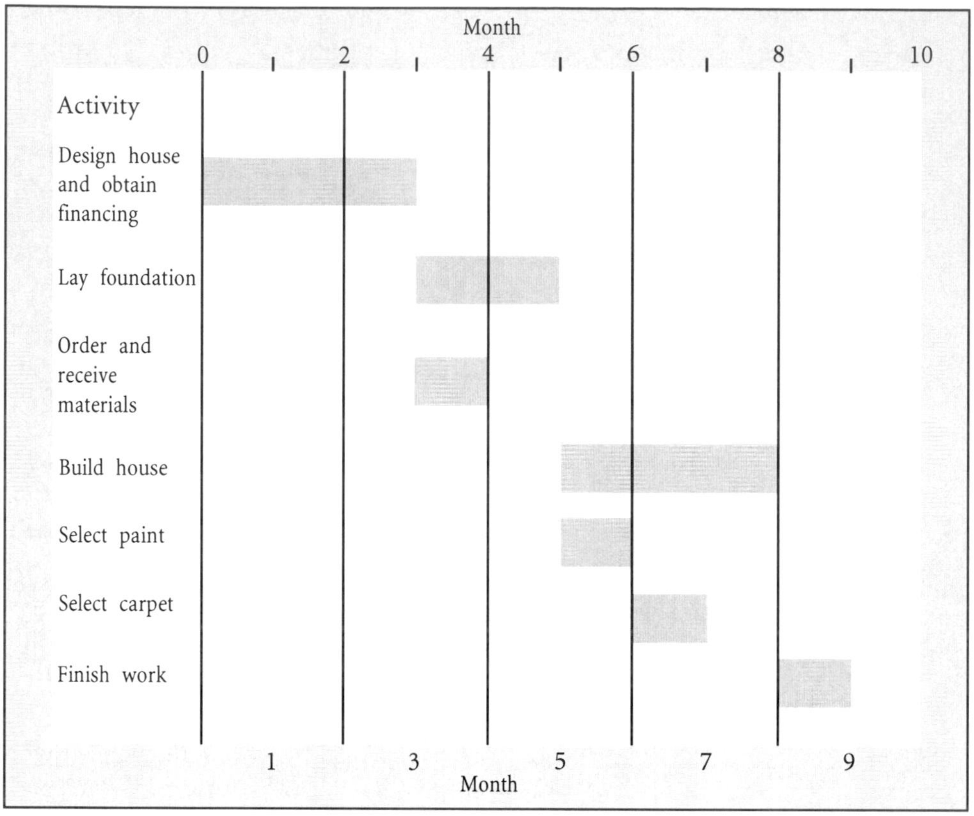

Slack is the amount of time an activity can be delayed without delaying the project.

completed by the end of month 5, when the next activity, "build house," is scheduled to start. This extra time for the activity "order and receive materials" is called **slack.** Slack is the amount of time by which an activity can be delayed without delaying any of the activities that follow it or the project as a whole. The remainder of the Gantt chart is constructed in a similar manner, and the project is scheduled to be completed at the end of month 9.

A Gantt chart provides a visual display of a project schedule, indicating when activities are scheduled to start and to finish and where extra time is available and activities can be delayed. A project manager can use a Gantt chart to monitor the progress of activities and see which ones are ahead of schedule and which ones are behind schedule. A Gantt chart also indicates the precedence relationships between activities; however, these relationships are not always easily discernible. This problem is one of the disadvantages of the Gantt chart method, and it limits the chart's use to smaller projects with relatively few activities. The CPM/PERT network technique, which we will talk about later, does not suffer this disadvantage.

Project Control

Project control is the process of making sure a project progresses toward successful completion. It requires that the project be monitored and progress measured so that any deviations from the project plan, and particularly the project schedule, are minimized. If the project is found to be deviating from the plan (i.e., it is not on schedule, cost overruns are occurring, activity results are not as expected), corrective action must be taken. In the rest of this section we will describe several key elements of project control, including time and cost management and performance monitoring.

Time management is the process of making sure a project schedule does not slip and that a project is on time. This requires monitoring of individual activity schedules and frequent updates. If the schedule is being delayed to an extent that jeopardizes the project success, it may be necessary for the project manager to shift resources to accelerate critical activities. Some activities may have slack time, so resources can be shifted from them to activities that are not on schedule. This is referred to as *time–cost trade-off.* However, this can also push the project cost above the budget. In some cases it may be that the work needs to be corrected or made more efficient. In other cases, it may occur that original activity time estimates upon implementation prove to be unrealistic and the schedule must be changed, and the repercussions of such changes on project success must be evaluated.

Cost management is often closely tied to time management because of the time–cost trade-off occurrences mentioned previously. If the schedule is delayed, costs tend to go up in order to get the project back on schedule. Also, as a project progresses, some cost estimates may prove to be unrealistic or erroneous. Therefore, it may be necessary to revise cost estimates and develop budget updates. If cost overruns are excessive, corrective actions must be taken.

Management Science Application

An Air Flight Safety and Efficiency Project at the FAA

The U.S. Federal Aviation Administration (FAA) operates the nation's air traffic control facilities, which annually handle more than 60 million flights that take off and land at airports across the United States. In 1997 the FAA in conjunction with NASA initiated the Performance Data Analysis and Reporting System (PDARS) project. The purpose of the PDARS project was to create a network of computers in air traffic control facilities around the United States that would continually collect flight plan and radar tracking data; generate data reports; compute quantitative operational performance measures related to safety, delay, flexibility, and predictability that would be used by experts to identify safety and efficiency problems; and maintain performance statistics for research, monitoring and planning. The system could also be used to design and conduct What if? analyses and test air traffic system improvement options. The system was implemented on an incremental basis around the country over an 8-year period and became fully operational in 2005. This incremental approach to the project allowed for the system to be tested and improved as it was being developed. NASA partnered with the FAA because of its interest in improving aviation safety, that is, reducing the probability of an accident despite increasing air traffic. A key aspect of project development was the inclusion of key stakeholders in the project development process, including air traffic controllers, FAA facilities managers, airline facilities personnel, and union representatives. During the 8-year project development period 17 meetings were held for systems users to keep them informed and gather feedback. The fully operational PDARS system provided the FAA with the metrics it needed to meet its performance objectives for safety and efficiency. In 2003 the project team received the Administrators Award from NASA for its significant contribution to NASA's aeronautics objectives.

Chris Rank/Landov Media

Source: Kelley Hunsberger, "Flight Plan," *PM Network* 20, no. 4 (April 2006): 57–61.

Performance management is the process of monitoring a project and developing timed (i.e., daily, weekly, monthly) status reports to make sure that goals are being met and the plan is being followed. It compares planned target dates for events, milestones, and work completion with dates actually achieved to determine whether the project is on schedule or behind schedule. Key measures of performance include deviation from the schedule, resource usage, and cost overruns. The project manager and individuals and organizational units with performance responsibility develop these status reports.

Earned value analysis (EVA) is a specific system for performance management. Activities "earn value" as they are completed. EVA is a recognized standard procedure for numerically measuring a project's progress, forecasting its completion date and final cost, and providing measures of schedule and budget variation as activities are completed. For example, an EVA metric such as *schedule variance* compares the work performed during a time period with the work that was scheduled to be performed; a negative variance means the project is behind schedule. *Cost variance* is the budgeted cost of work performed minus the actual cost of the work; a negative variance means the project is over budget. EVA works best when it is used in conjunction with a WBS that compartmentalizes project work into small packages that are easier to measure. The drawbacks of EVA are that it is sometimes difficult to measure work progress, and the time required for data measurement can be considerable.

CPM/PERT

CPM used a single activity time estimate and in the network activities were nodes.

PERT used multiple activity time estimates and in the network activities were lines between nodes.

Critical path method (CPM) and **project evaluation and review technique** (PERT) were originally developed as separate techniques. (See the TIME OUT box.) Both are derivatives of the Gantt chart and, as a result, are very similar. There were originally two primary differences between CPM and PERT. With CPM, a single estimate for activity time was used that did not allow for variation; activity times were treated as if they were known with certainty. With PERT, multiple time estimates were used for each activity that reflected variation; activity times were treated as probabilistic. The other difference was in the mechanics of drawing a network. In PERT, activities were represented as arcs, or lines with arrows, between circles called *nodes*, whereas in CPM activities were represented by the nodes, and the arrows between them showed precedence relationships (i.e., which activity came before another). However, over time CPM and PERT have effectively merged into a single technique conventionally known as CPM/PERT.

The advantage of CPM/PERT over the Gantt chart is in the use of a network (instead of a graph) to show the precedence relationships between activities. A Gantt chart does not clearly show precedence relationships, especially for larger networks. Put simply, a CPM/PERT network provides a better picture; it is visually easier to use, which makes using CPM/PERT a popular technique for project planners and managers.

AOA Networks

A CPM/PERT network is drawn with branches and nodes, as shown in Figure 5. As previously mentioned, when CPM and PERT were first developed, they employed different conventions for drawing a network. With CPM, the nodes in Figure 5 represent the project activities. The branches with arrows in between the nodes indicate the precedence relationships between activities. For example, in Figure 5, activity 1, represented by node 1, precedes activity 2, and 2 must be finished before 3 can start. This approach to constructing a network is called *activity-on-node (AON)*. Alternatively, with PERT, the branches in between the nodes represent activities, and the nodes reflect events or points in time such as the end of one activity and the start of another. This approach is called *activity-on-arrow (AOA)*, and the activities are identified by the node numbers at the start and end of an activity (for example, activity $1 \longrightarrow 2$, which precedes activity $2 \longrightarrow 3$ in Figure 5). In this chapter we will focus on the AON convention, but we will first provide an overview of the AOA network.

Figure 5
Nodes and branches

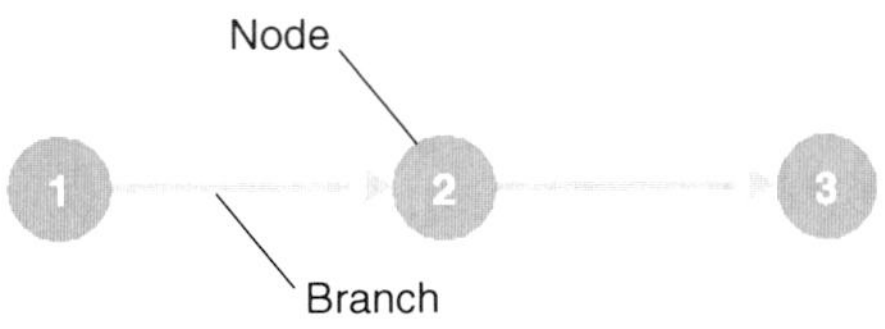

To demonstrate how an AOA network is drawn, we will revisit the example of building a house that we used as a Gantt chart example in Figure 4. The comparable CPM/PERT network for this project is shown in Figure 6. The precedence relationships are reflected in this network by the arrangement of the arrowed (or directed) branches. The first activity in the project is to design the house and obtain financing. This activity must be completed before any subsequent activities can begin. Thus, activity $2 \longrightarrow 3$, laying the foundation, and activity $2 \longrightarrow 4$, ordering and receiving materials, can start only when node 2 is *realized*, indicating that activity $1 \longrightarrow 2$ has been completed. The number 3 above this branch signifies a time estimate of 3 months for the completion of this activity. Activity $2 \longrightarrow 3$ and activity $2 \longrightarrow 4$ can occur concurrently; neither depends on the other, and both depend only on the completion of activity $1 \longrightarrow 2$.

Figure 6
Expanded network for building a house, showing concurrent activities

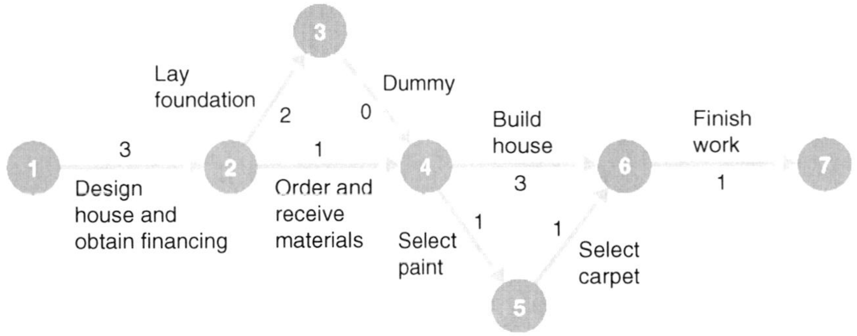

TIME OUT *for Morgan R. Walker, James E. Kelley, Jr., and D. G. Malcolm*

In 1956 a research team at E. I. du Pont de Nemours & Company, Inc., led by a du Pont engineer, Morgan R. Walker, and a Remington-Rand computer specialist, James E. Kelley, Jr., initiated a project to develop a computerized system to improve the planning, scheduling, and reporting of the company's engineering programs (including plant maintenance and construction projects). The resulting network approach is known as the critical path method (CPM). At virtually the same time, the U.S. Navy established a research team composed of members of the Navy Special Projects Office, Lockheed (the prime contractor), and the consulting firm of Booz, Allen, Hamilton, led by D. G. Malcolm, that developed PERT for the design of a management control system for the Polaris Missile Project (a ballistic missile–firing nuclear submarine). The Polaris project eventually included 23 PERT networks encompassing 2,000 events and 3,000 activities.

When the activities of laying the foundation (2 ⟶ 3) and ordering and receiving materials (2 ⟶ 4) are completed, activities 4 ⟶ 5 and 4 ⟶ 6 can begin simultaneously. However, notice activity 3 ⟶ 4, which is referred to as a **dummy activity**. A dummy activity is used in an AOA network to show a precedence relationship, but it does not represent any actual passage of time. These activities have the precedence relationship shown in Figure 7(a). However, in an AOA network, two or more activities are not allowed to share the same start and ending nodes because that would give them the same name designation (i.e., 2 ⟶ 3). Activity 3 ⟶ 4 is inserted to give the two activities separate end nodes and thus separate identities, as shown in Figure 7(b).

*A **dummy activity** shows a precedence relationship but no passage of time.*

Figure 7
A dummy activity

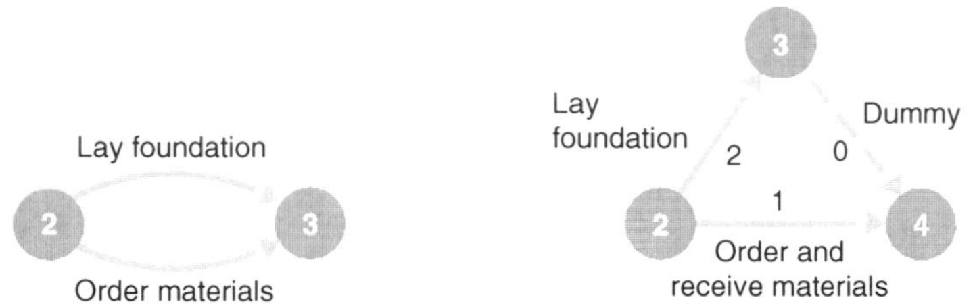

(a) Incorrect precedence relationship

(b) Correct precedence relationship

Returning to the network shown in Figure 6, we see that two activities start at node 4. Activity 4 ⟶ 6 is the actual building of the house, and activity 4 ⟶ 5 is the search for and selection of the paint for the exterior and interior of the house. Activity 4 ⟶ 6 and activity 4 ⟶ 5 can begin simultaneously and take place concurrently. Following the selection of the paint (activity 4 ⟶ 5) and the realization of node 5, the carpet can be selected (activity 5 ⟶ 6) because the carpet color is dependent on the paint color. This activity can also occur concurrently with the building of the house (activity 4 ⟶ 6). When the building is completed and the paint and carpet are selected, the house can be finished (activity 6 ⟶ 7).

AON Networks

Figure 8 shows the comparable AON network to the AOA network in Figure 6 for our house-building project. Notice that the activities and activity times are on the nodes and not on the activities, as with the AOA network. The branches or arrows simply show the precedence relationships between the activities. Also, notice that there is no dummy activity; dummy activities are not required in an AON network because no two activities have the same start and ending nodes, so they will never be confused. This is one of the advantages of the AON convention, although both AOA and AON have minor advantages and disadvantages. In general, the two methods both accomplish the same thing, and the one that is used is usually a matter of individual preference. However, for our purposes, the AON network has one distinct advantage: It is the convention used in the popular Microsoft Project software package. Because we will demonstrate how to use that software later in this chapter, we will use AON.

The Critical Path

A network path is a sequence of connected activities that runs from the start to the end of the network. The network shown in Figure 8 has several paths. In fact, close observation of this network shows four paths, identified in Table 1 as A, B, C, and D.

The project cannot be completed (i.e., the house cannot be built) until the longest path in the network is completed. This is the minimum time in which the project can be

Figure 8
AON network for house-building project

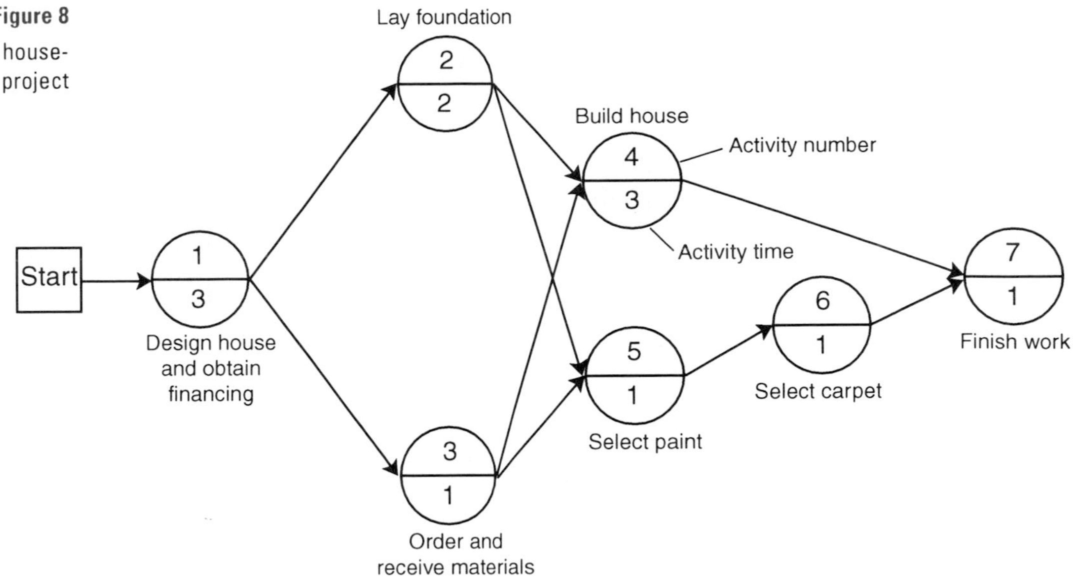

Table 1
Paths through the house-building network

Path	Events
A	1 → 2 → 4 → 7
B	1 → 2 → 5 → 6 → 7
C	1 → 3 → 4 → 7
D	1 → 3 → 5 → 6 → 7

*The **critical path** is the longest path through the network; it is the minimum time in which the network can be completed.*

completed. The longest path is referred to as the **critical path**. To better understand the relationship between the minimum project time and the critical path, we will determine the length of each of the four paths shown in Figure 8.

By summing the activity times (shown in Figure 8) along each of the four paths, we can compute the length of each path, as follows:

path A: 1 → 2 → 4 → 7
$3 + 2 + 3 + 1 = 9$ months
path B: 1 → 2 → 5 → 6 → 7
$3 + 2 + 1 + 1 + 1 = 8$ months
path C: 1 → 3 → 4 → 7
$3 + 1 + 3 + 1 = 8$ months
path D: 1 → 3 → 5 → 6 → 7
$3 + 1 + 1 + 1 + 1 = 7$ months

Because path A is the longest, it is the critical path; thus, the minimum completion time for the project is 9 months. Now let us analyze the critical path more closely. From Figure 9 we can see that activity 3 cannot start until 3 months have passed. It is also easy to see that activity 4 will not start until 5 months have passed (i.e., the sum of activity 1 and 2 times). The start of activity 4 is dependent on the two activities leading into node 4. Activity 2 is completed after 5 months, but activity 3 is completed at the end of 4 months. Thus, we have two possible start times for activity 4: 5 months and 4 months. However, because the activity on node 4 cannot start until all preceding activities have been finished, the soonest node 4 can be started is 5 months.

Figure 9
Activity start time

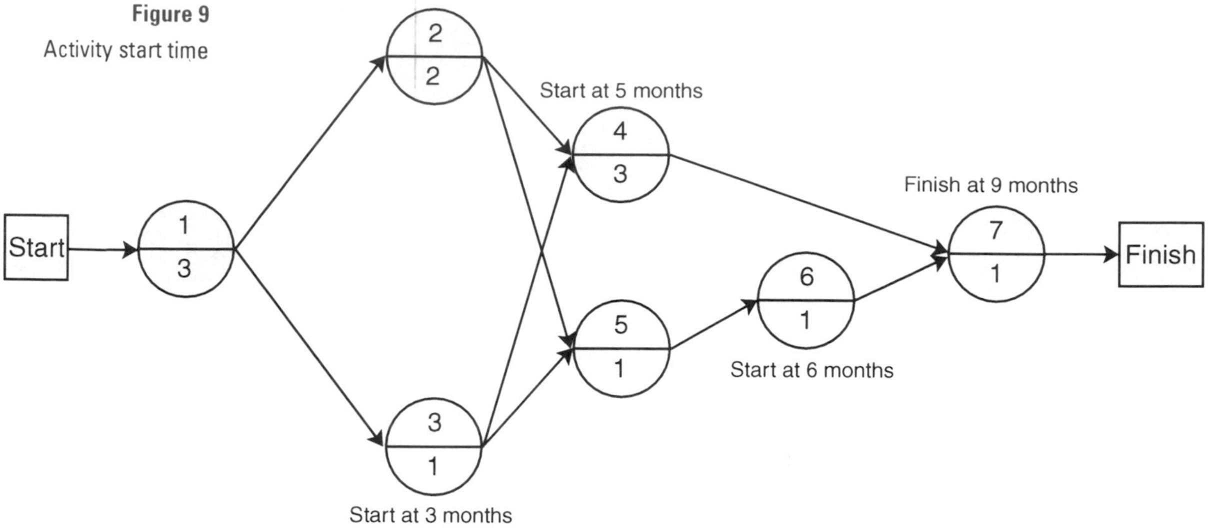

Now let us consider the activity following node 4. Using the same logic as before, we can see that activity 7 cannot start until after 8 months (5 months at node 4 plus the 3 months required by activity 4), or after 7 months. Because all activities preceding node 7 must be completed before activity 7 can start, the soonest this can occur is 8 months. Adding 1 month for activity 7 to the time at node 7 gives a project duration of 9 months. Recall that this is the time of the longest path in the network, or the critical path.

This brief analysis demonstrates the concept of a critical path and the determination of the minimum completion time of a project. However, this is a cumbersome method for determining a critical path. Next, we will discuss a mathematical approach for scheduling the project activities and determining the critical path.

Activity Scheduling

In our analysis of the critical path, we determined the earliest time that each activity could be finished. For example, we found that the earliest time activity 4 could start was at 5 months. This time is referred to as the *earliest start time*, and it is expressed symbolically as *ES*.

ES is the earliest time an activity can start.

In order to show the earliest start time on the network, as well as some other activity times we will develop in the scheduling process, we will alter our node structure a little. Figure 10 shows the structure for node 1, the first activity in our example network for designing a house and obtaining financing.

Figure 10
Activity-on-node configuration

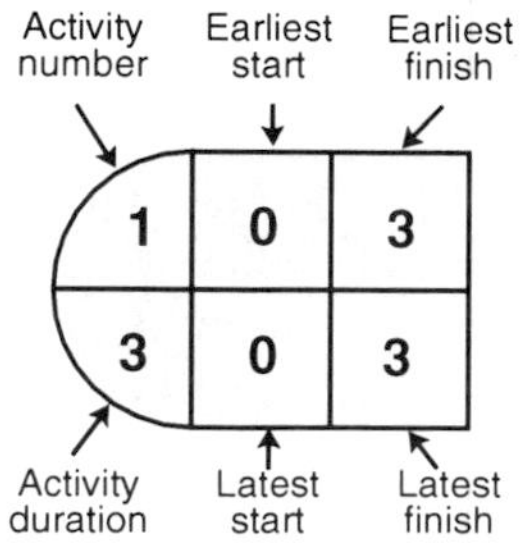

To determine the earliest start time for every activity, we make a *forward pass* through the network. That is, we start at the first node and move forward through the network. The earliest time for an activity is the maximum time for all preceding activities that have been completed—the time when the activity start node is realized.

EF is the earliest start time plus the activity time estimate.

The *earliest finish time, EF,* for an activity is the earliest start time plus the activity time estimate. For example, if the earliest start time for activity 1 is at time 0, then the earliest finish time is 3 months. In general, the earliest start and finish times for an activity are computed according to the following mathematical formulas:

$$ES = \text{Maximum}\ (EF\ \text{immediate predecessors})$$
$$EF = ES + t$$

The earliest start and earliest finish times for all the activities in our project network are shown in Figure 11.

Figure 11

Earliest activity start and finish times

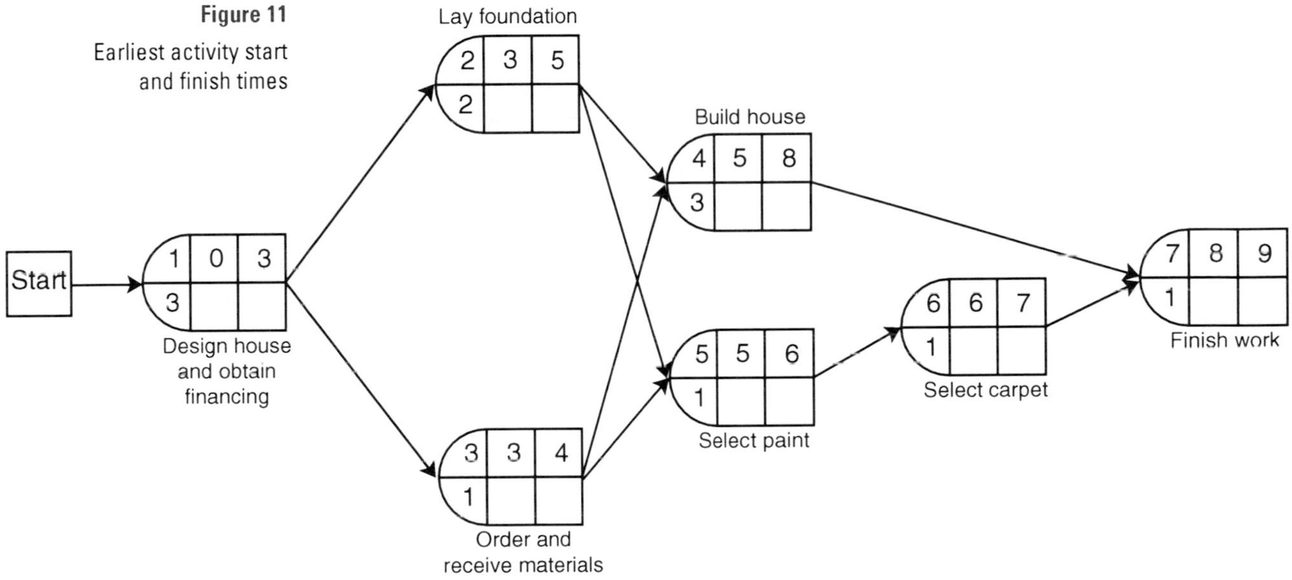

The earliest start time for the first activity in the network (for which there are no pre decessor activities) is always zero, or $ES = 0$. This enables us to compute the earliest finish time for activity 1 as

$$EF = ES + t = 0 + 3 = 3\ \text{months}$$

The earliest start time for activity 2 is

$$ES = \text{Max}\ (EF\ \text{immediate predecessors})$$
$$= 3\ \text{months}$$

The corresponding earliest finish time is

$$EF = ES + t = 3 + 2 = 5\ \text{months}$$

For activity 3 the earliest start time is 3 months, and the earliest finish time is 4 months.

Now consider activity 4, which has two predecessor activities. The earliest start time is computed as

$$ES = \text{Max}\ (EF\ \text{immediate predecessors})$$
$$= \text{Max}\ (5, 4) = 5\ \text{months}$$

and the earliest finish time is

$$EF = ES + t = 5 + 3 = 8 \text{ months}$$

All the remaining earliest start and finish times are computed similarly. Notice in Figure 11 that the earliest finish time for activity 7, the last activity in the network, is 9 months, which is the total project duration, or critical path time.

LS is the latest time an activity can start without delaying the critical path time.

Companions to the earliest start and finish are the *latest start* (*LS*) and *finish* (*LF*) times. The latest start time is the latest time an activity can start without delaying the completion of the project beyond the project critical path time. For our example, the project completion time (and earliest finish time) at node 7 is 9 months. Thus, the objective of determining latest times is to see how long each activity can be delayed without the project exceeding 9 months.

In general, the latest start and finish times for an activity are computed according to the following formulas:

$$LS = LF - t$$
$$LF = \text{Minimum } (LS \text{ immediately following predecessors})$$

*A **forward pass** is used to determine earliest times.*

*A **backward pass** is used to determine latest times.*

Whereas a **forward pass** through the network is made to determine the earliest times, the latest times are computed using a **backward pass**. We start at the end of the network at node 7 and work backward, computing the latest time for each activity. Because we want to determine how long each activity in the network can be delayed without extending the project time, the latest finish time at node 7 cannot exceed the earliest finish time. Therefore, the latest finish time at node 7 is 9 months. This and all other latest times are shown in Figure 12.

Figure 12
Latest activity start and finish times

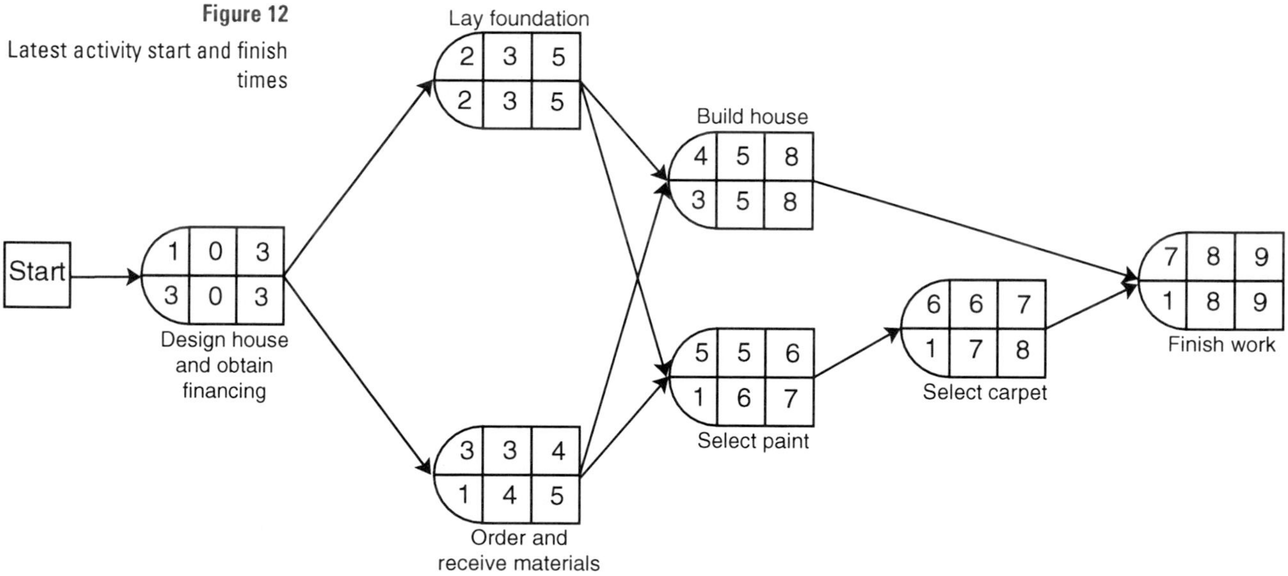

Starting at the end of the network, the critical path time, which is also equal to the earliest finish time of activity 7, is 9 months. This automatically becomes the latest finish time for activity 7, or

$$LF = 9 \text{ months}$$

Using this value, the latest start time for activity 7 can be computed:

$$LS = LF - t = 9 - 1 = 8 \text{ months}$$

The latest finish time for activity 6 is the minimum of the latest start times for the activities following node 6. Because activity 7 follows node 6, the latest start time is computed as follows:

$$\begin{aligned} LF &= \text{Min}\,(LS \text{ following activities}) \\ &= 8 \text{ months} \end{aligned}$$

The latest start time for activity 6 is

$$LS = LF - t = 8 - 1 = 7 \text{ months}$$

For activity 4 the latest finish time is 8 months, and the latest start time is 5 months; for activity 5, the latest finish time is 7 months, and the latest start time is 6 months.

Now consider activity 3, which has two activities following it. The latest finish time is computed as follows:

$$\begin{aligned} LF &= \text{Min}\,(LS \text{ following activities}) \\ &= \text{Min}\,(5, 6) = 5 \text{ months} \end{aligned}$$

The latest start time is

$$LS = LF - t = 5 - 1 = 4 \text{ months}$$

All the remaining latest start and latest finish times are computed similarly. Figure 12 includes the earliest and latest start times and earliest and latest finish times for all activities.

Activity Slack

The project network in Figure 12, with all activity start and finish times, highlights the critical path ($1 \rightarrow 2 \rightarrow 4 \rightarrow 7$) we determined earlier by inspection. Notice that for the activities on the critical path, the earliest start times and latest start times are equal. This means that these activities on the critical path must start exactly on time and cannot be delayed at all. If the start of any activity on the critical path is delayed, then the overall project time will be increased. As a result, we now have an alternative way to determine the critical path besides simply inspecting the network. The activities on the critical path can be determined by seeing for which activities $ES = LS$ or $EF = LF$. In Figure 12, the activities 1, 2, 4, and 7 all have earliest start times and latest start times that are equal (and $EF = LF$); thus, they are on the critical path.

Slack is the amount of time an activity can be delayed without delaying the project.

For those activities not on the critical path, the earliest and latest start times (or earliest and latest finish times) are not equal, and slack time exists. Slack is the amount of time an activity can be delayed without affecting the overall project duration. In effect, it is extra time available for completing an activity.

Slack, S, is computed using either of the following formulas:

$$S = LS - ES$$

or

$$S = LF - EF$$

For example, the slack for activity 3 is computed as follows:

$$S = LS - ES = 4 - 3 = 1 \text{ month}$$

If the start of activity 3 were delayed for 1 month, the activity could still be completed by month 5 without delaying the project completion time. The slack for each activity in our example project network is shown in Table 2 and in Figure 13.

Table 2
Activity slack

Activity	*LS*	*ES*	*LF*	*EF*	Slack, *S*
*1	0	0	3	3	0
*2	3	3	5	5	0
3	4	3	5	4	1
*4	5	5	8	8	0
5	6	5	7	6	1
6	7	6	8	7	1
*7	8	8	9	9	0

*Critical path activities

Figure 13
Activity slack

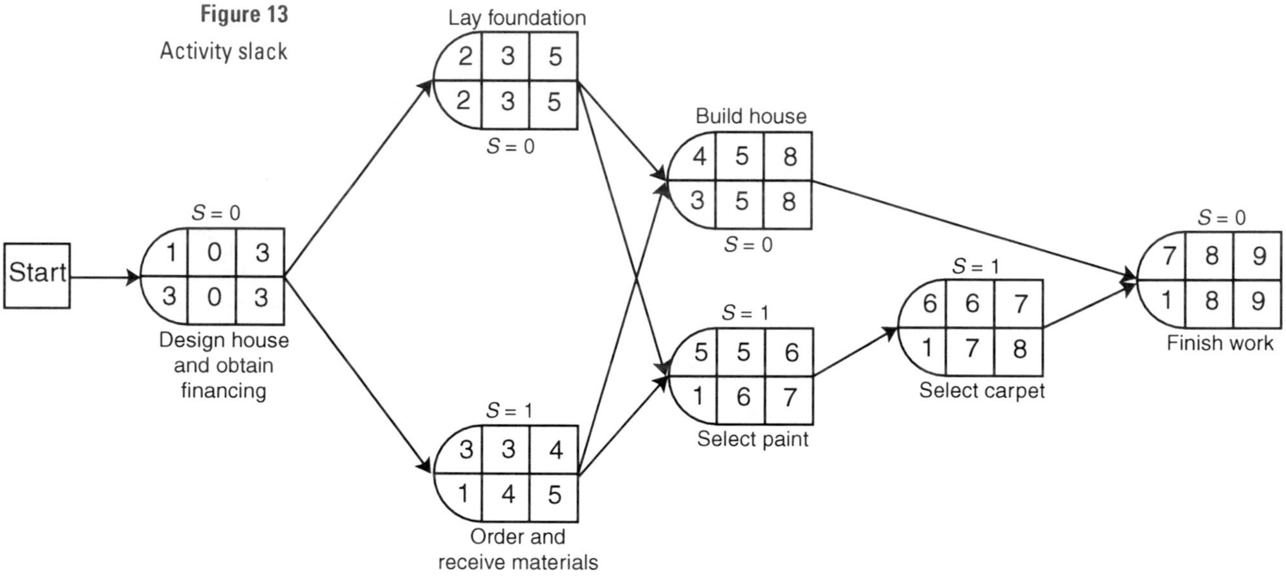

Notice in Figure 13 that activity 3 can be delayed 1 month and activity 5, which follows it, can be delayed 1 more month, but then activity 6 cannot be delayed at all, even though it has 1 month of slack. If activity 3 starts late, at month 4 instead of month 3, then it will be completed at month 5, which will not allow activity 5 to start until month 5. If the start of activity 5 is delayed 1 month, then it will be completed at month 7, and activity 6 cannot be delayed at all without exceeding the critical path time. The slack on these three activities is called **shared slack.** This means that the sequence of activities $3 \rightarrow 5 \rightarrow 6$ can be delayed 2 months jointly without delaying the project, but not 3 months.

Shared slack is total slack available for combination of activities.

Slack is obviously beneficial to a project manager because it enables resources to be temporarily pulled away from activities with slack and used for other activities that might be delayed for various reasons or for which the time estimate has proven to be inaccurate.

The times for the network activities are simply estimates for which there is usually not a lot of historical basis (because projects tend to be unique undertakings). As such, activity time estimates are subject to quite a bit of uncertainty. However, the uncertainty inherent in activity time estimates can be reflected to a certain extent by using probabilistic time estimates instead of the single, deterministic estimates we have used so far.

Probabilistic Activity Times

In the project network for building a house presented in the previous section, all the activity time estimates were single values. By using only a single activity time estimate, we in effect assume that activity times are known with certainty (i.e., they are deterministic). For example, in Figure 8, the time estimate for activity 2 (laying the foundation) is shown to be 2 months. Because only this one value is given, we must assume that the activity time does not vary (or varies very little) from 2 months. In reality, however, it is rare that activity time estimates can be made with certainty. Project activities are likely to be unique, and thus there is little historical evidence that can be used as a basis to predict actual times. However, we earlier indicated that one of the primary differences between CPM and PERT was that PERT used probabilistic activity times. It is this approach to estimating activity times for a project network that we discuss in this section.

Probabilistic Time Estimates

To demonstrate the use of probabilistic activity times, we will employ a new example. (We could use the house-building network from the previous section; however, a network that is a little larger and more complex will provide more experience with different types of projects.) The Southern Textile Company has decided to install a new computerized order processing system that will link the company with customers and suppliers online. In the past, orders for the cloth the company produces were processed manually, which contributed to delays in delivering orders and resulted in lost sales. The company wants to know how long it will take to install the new system.

The network for the installation of the new order processing system is shown in Figure 14. We will briefly describe the activities.

The network begins with three concurrent activities: The new computer equipment is installed (activity 1); the computerized order processing system is developed (activity 2); and people are recruited to operate the system (activity 3). Once people are hired, they are trained for the job (activity 6), and other personnel in the company, such as marketing, accounting, and production personnel, are introduced to the new system (activity 7). Once the system is developed (activity 2), it is tested manually to make sure that it is logical (activity 5). Following activity 1, the new equipment is tested, and any necessary modifications are made (activity 4), and the newly trained personnel begin training on the computerized system (activity 8). Also, node 9 begins the testing of the system on the computer to check for errors (activity 9). The final activities include a trial run and changeover to the system (activity 11) and final debugging of the computer system (activity 10).

At this stage in a project network, we previously assigned a single time estimate to each network activity. In a PERT project network, however, we determine *three time estimates* for each activity, which will enable us to estimate the mean and variance for a **beta distribution** of the activity times. We assume that the activity times can be described by a beta distribution for several reasons. First, the beta distribution mean and variance can be approximated with three estimates. Second, the beta distribution is continuous, but it has no predetermined shape (such as the bell shape of the normal curve). It will take on the shape indicated—that is, be skewed—by the time estimates given. This is beneficial because typically we have no prior knowledge of the shapes of the distributions of activity times in a unique project network. Third, although other types of distributions have been shown to be no more or less accurate than the beta, it has become traditional to use the beta distribution for probabilistic network analysis.

*A **beta distribution** is a probability distribution whose shape is based on 3 time estimates.*

*Three time estimates for each activity—a **most likely**, an **optimistic**, and a **pessimistic**—provide an estimate of the mean and variance of a beta distribution.*

The three time estimates for each activity are the most likely time, the optimistic time, and the pessimistic time. The **most likely time** is the time that would most frequently occur if the activity were repeated many times. The **optimistic time** is the shortest possible time

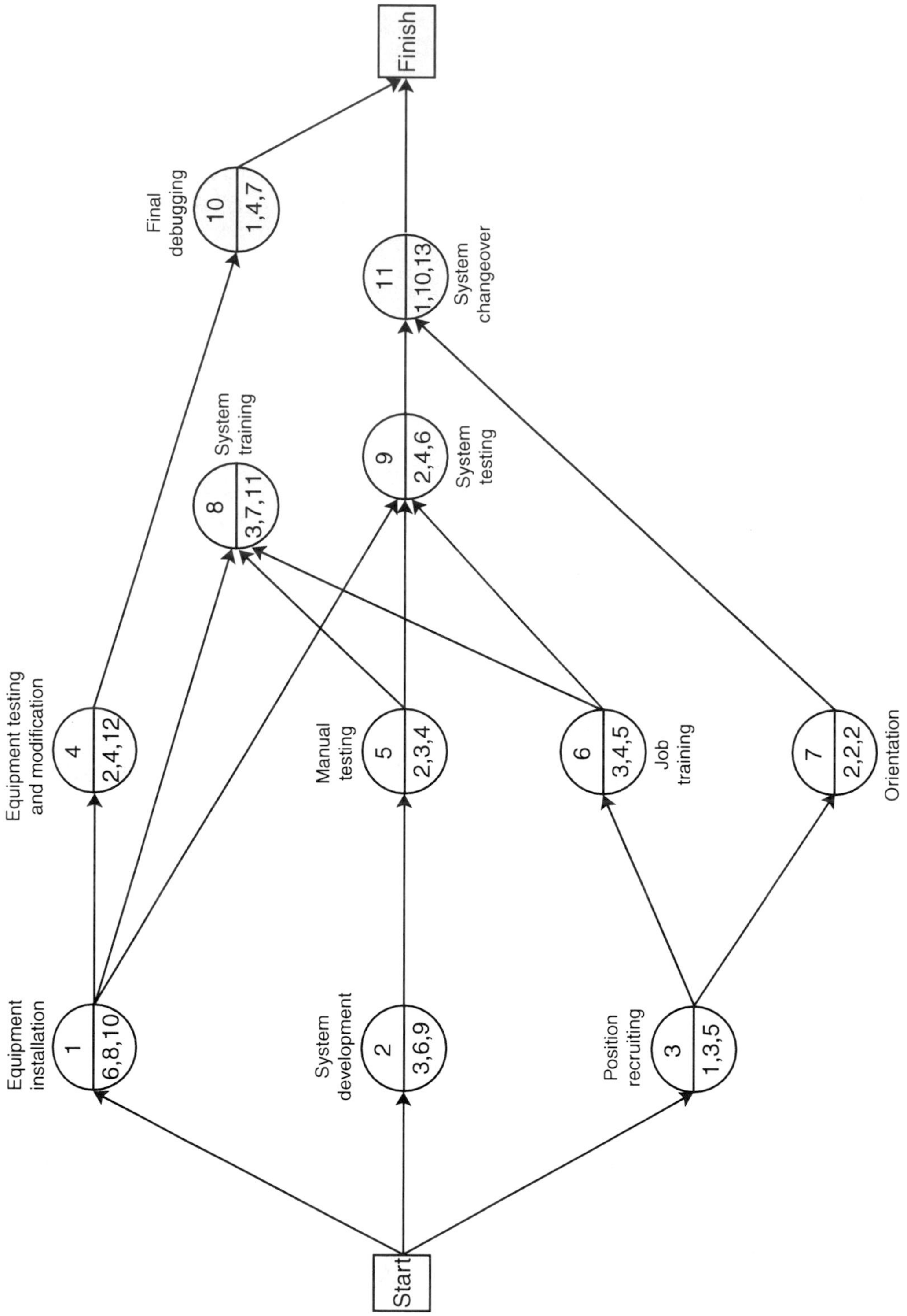

Figure 14
Network for order processing system installation

within which the activity could be completed if everything went right. The **pessimistic time** is the longest possible time the activity would require to be completed, assuming that everything went wrong. In general, the person most familiar with an activity makes these estimates to the best of his or her knowledge and ability. In other words, the estimate is subjective.

These three time estimates can subsequently be used to estimate the mean and variance of a beta distribution. If

$$\begin{aligned} a &= \text{optimistic time estimate} \\ m &= \text{most likely time estimate} \\ b &= \text{pessimistic time estimate} \end{aligned}$$

the mean and variance are computed as follows:

$$\text{mean (expected time)}: t = \frac{a + 4m + b}{6}$$

$$\text{variance}: v = \left(\frac{b - a}{6}\right)^2$$

These formulas provide a reasonable estimate of the mean and variance of the beta distribution, a distribution that is continuous and can take on various shapes—that is, exhibit skewness.

The three time estimates for each activity are shown in Figure 14 and in Table 3. The mean and the variance for all the activities in the network shown in Figure 14 are also given in Table 3.

Table 3
Activity time estimates for Figure 14

	Time Estimates (weeks)			Time	Mean Variance
Activity	a	m	b	t	v
1	6	8	10	8	4/9
2	3	6	9	6	1
3	1	3	5	3	4/9
4	2	4	12	5	25/9
5	2	3	4	3	1/9
6	3	4	5	4	1/9
7	2	2	2	2	0
8	3	7	11	7	16/9
9	2	4	6	4	4/9
10	1	4	7	4	1
11	1	10	13	9	4

As an example of the computation of the individual activity mean times and variances, consider activity 1. The three time estimates ($a = 6, m = 8, b = 10$) are substituted in our beta distribution formulas as follows:

$$t = \frac{a + 4m + b}{6} = \frac{6 + 4(8) + 10}{6} = 8 \text{ weeks}$$

$$v = \left(\frac{b - a}{6}\right)^2 = \left(\frac{10 - 6}{6}\right)^2 = \frac{4}{9} \text{ week}$$

The other values for the mean and variance in Table 3 are computed similarly.

Once the expected activity times have been computed for each activity, we can determine the critical path the same way we did previously, except that we use the expected activity times, *t*. Recall that in the project network, we identified the critical path as the one containing those activities with zero slack. This requires the determination of earliest and latest event times, as shown in Figure 15.

The critical path has no slack.

Observing Figure 15, we can see that the critical path encompasses activities $2 \rightarrow 5 \rightarrow 8 \rightarrow 11$, because these activities have no available slack. We can also see that the *expected* project completion time (t_p) is 25 weeks. However, it is possible to compute the variance for project completion time. To determine the project variance, we *sum the variances for those activities on the critical path.* Using the variances computed in Table 3 and the critical path activities shown in Figure 15, we can compute the variance for project duration (v_p) as follows:

The project variance is the sum of the variance of the critical path activities.

Critical Path Activity	Variance
2	1
5	1/9
8	16/9
11	4
	62/9

$$v_p = 62/9 = 6.9 \text{ weeks}$$

The expected project time is assumed to be normally distributed based on the central limit theorem.

The CPM/PERT method assumes that the activity times are statistically independent, which allows us to sum the individual expected activity times and variances to get an expected *project* time and variance. It is further assumed that the network mean and variance are normally distributed. This assumption is based on the central limit theorem of probability, which for CPM/PERT analysis and our purposes states that if the number of activities is large enough and the activities are statistically independent, then the sum of the means of the activities along the critical path will approach the mean of a normal distribution. For the small examples in this chapter, it is questionable whether there are sufficient activities to guarantee that the mean project completion time and variance are normally distributed. Although it has become conventional in CPM/PERT analysis to employ probability analysis by using the normal distribution, regardless of the network size, the prudent user of CPM/PERT analysis should bear this limitation in mind.

Given these assumptions, we can interpret the expected project time (t_p) and variance (v_p) as the mean (μ) and variance (σ^2) of a normal distribution:

$$\mu = 25 \text{ weeks}$$
$$\sigma^2 = 6.9 \text{ weeks}$$

In turn, we can use these statistical parameters to make probabilistic statements about the project.

Probability Analysis of the Project Network

Using the normal distribution, probabilities can be determined by computing the number of standard deviations (Z) a value is from the mean, as illustrated in Figure 16.

The Z value is computed using the following formula:

$$Z = \frac{x - \mu}{\sigma}$$

This value is then used to find the corresponding probability.

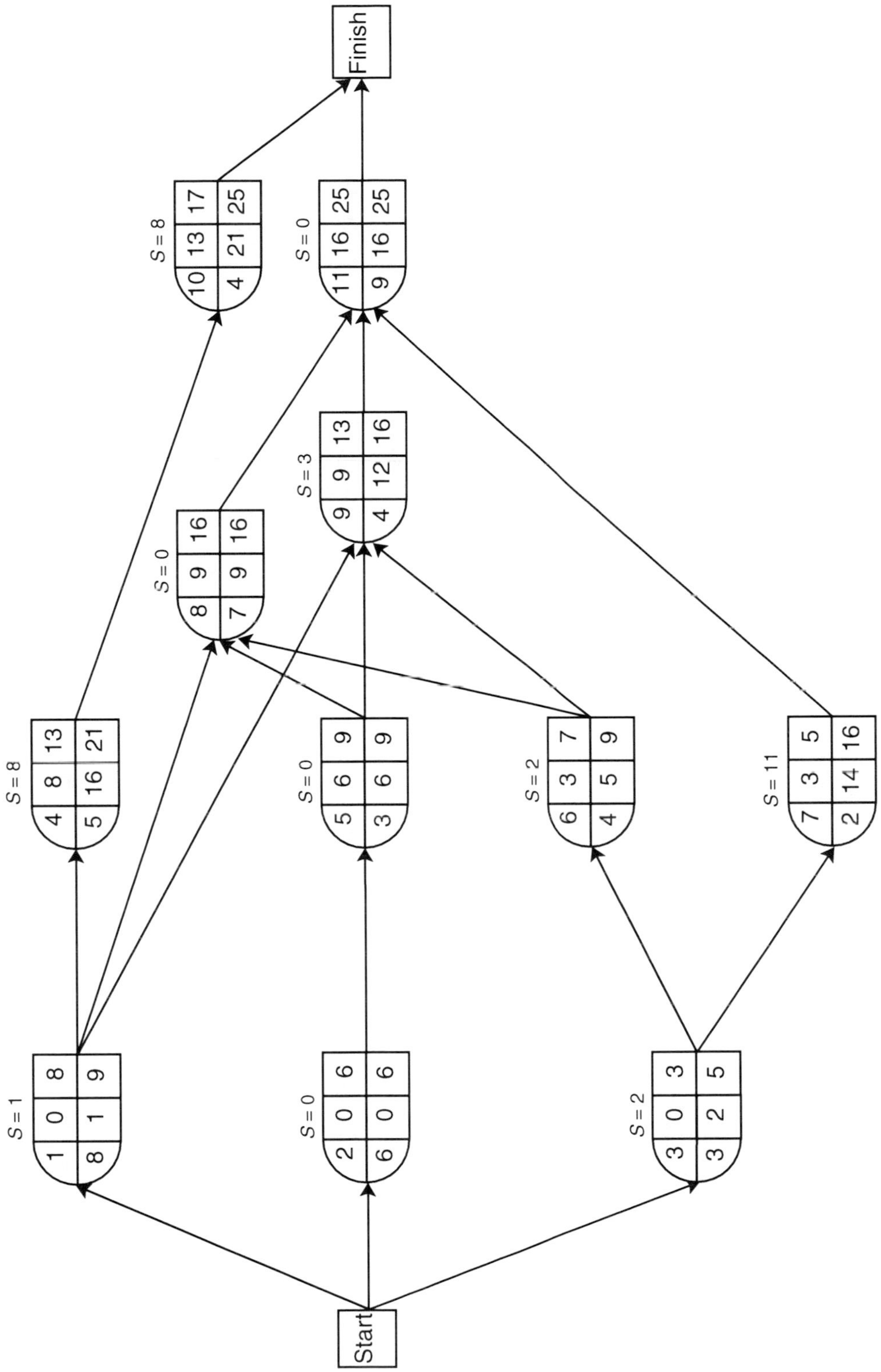

Figure 15
Earliest and latest activity times

Figure 16
Normal distribution of network duration

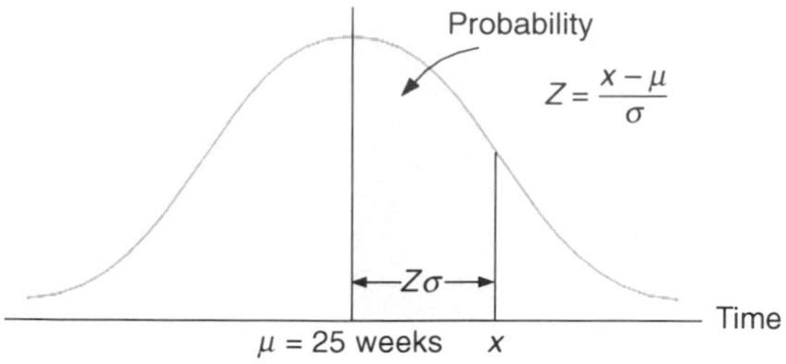

For example, suppose the textile company manager told customers that the new order processing system would be completely installed in 30 weeks. What is the probability that it will, in fact, be ready by that time? This probability is illustrated as the shaded area in Figure 17.

Figure 17
Probability that the network will be completed in 30 weeks or less

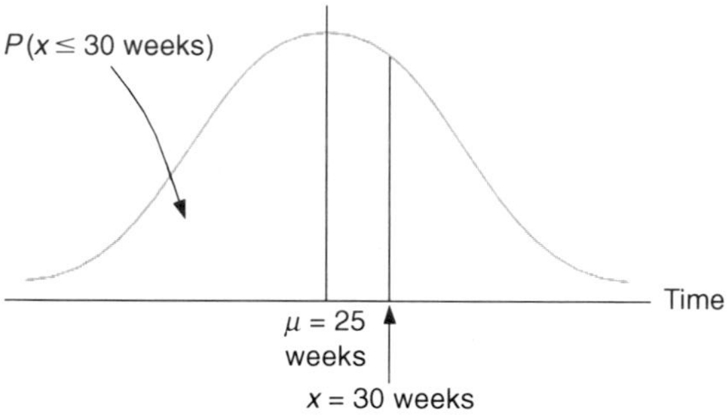

To compute the Z value for a time of 30 weeks, we must first compute the standard deviation (σ) from the variance (σ^2):

$$\sigma^2 = 6.9$$
$$\sigma = \sqrt{6.9} = 2.63$$

Next, we substitute this value for the standard deviation, along with the value for the mean and our proposed project completion time (30 weeks), into the following formula:

$$Z = \frac{x - \mu}{\sigma} = \frac{30 - 25}{2.63} = 1.90$$

A Z value of 1.90 corresponds to a probability of .4713. This means that there is a .9713 (.5000 + .4713) probability of completing the project in 30 weeks or less.

Suppose one customer, frustrated with delayed orders, has told the textile company that if the new ordering system is not working within 22 weeks, she will trade elsewhere. The probability of the project's being completed within 22 weeks is computed as follows:

$$Z = \frac{22 - 25}{2.63} = \frac{-3}{2.63} = -1.14$$

A Z value of 1.14 (the negative is ignored) corresponds to a probability of .3729. Thus, there is only a .1271 probability that the customer will be retained, as illustrated in Figure 18.

Figure 18
Probability that the network will be completed in 22 weeks or less

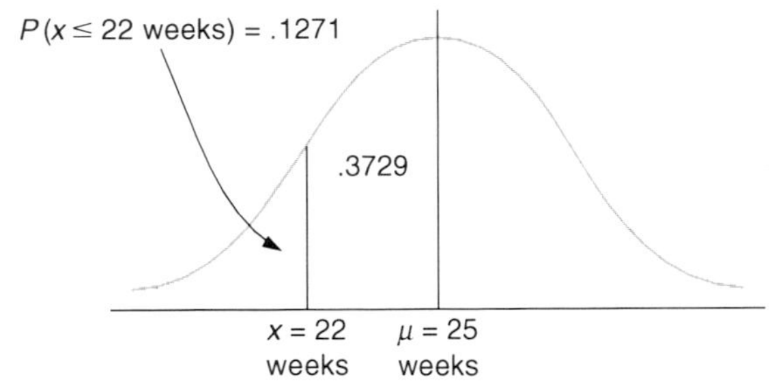

Management Science Application

A Drug Development Project to Combat Malaria

Malaria kills between 1 million and 2 million people worldwide each year. It is an infectious disease caused by a parasite transmitted by female mosquitoes, although it can also be transmitted through blood transfusions, organ transplants, and the shared use of needles. It is typically most often found in the world's warmer regions, including Central and South America, Africa, India, Southeast Asia, and the Middle East—countries that don't have the resources to pay for drugs, or the healthcare facilities to treat the disease. Malaria is one of the biggest infectious disease problems in the world, but because of where it occurs (i.e., in poorer countries), there is virtually no viable market to induce pharmaceutical companies to develop new drugs for malaria. Resistance to older drugs is now so prevalent that countries with malaria epidemics have very limited options for fighting it; less than 1% of global health investments go to malaria treatment research. In response to this scenario a team from the University of California, San Francisco, GlaxoSmithKline (GSK), and the Medicines for Malaria Venture (from Geneva, Switzerland) initiated a project in 1999 to develop drugs that focus on inhibiting *falcipains*, a family of enzymes that fledgling malaria parasites use to build strength, thus hindering the growth of the parasite. The Medicines for Malaria Venture provided a grant of several million dollars to initiate the project. One of the major factors in developing a drug is cost; one of the first compounds developed by the project team had to be abandoned because it was too costly to manufacture. Even a drug treatment costing $1 or $2 is too expensive. Because team members are spread around the world, communication issues are paramount to project success. GSK provides a Web portal for project data that team members around the world can access. Monthly team meetings are held via teleconferencing, and there are two or three physical meetings each year. Although a successful drug has not yet been developed, the project team is in place to eventually achieve the project goals.

Radu Razvan/Shutterstock

Source: Kelley Hunsberger, "Project Rx," *PM Network* 20, no. 5 (May 2006): 54–62.

CPM/PERT Analysis with QM for Windows and Excel QM

The capability to perform CPM/PERT network analysis is a standard feature of most management science software packages for the personal computer. To illustrate the application of QM for Windows and Excel QM we will use our example of installing an order processing system at Southern Textile Company. The QM for Windows solution output is shown in Exhibit 1, and the Excel QM solution is shown in Exhibit 2.

Exhibit 1

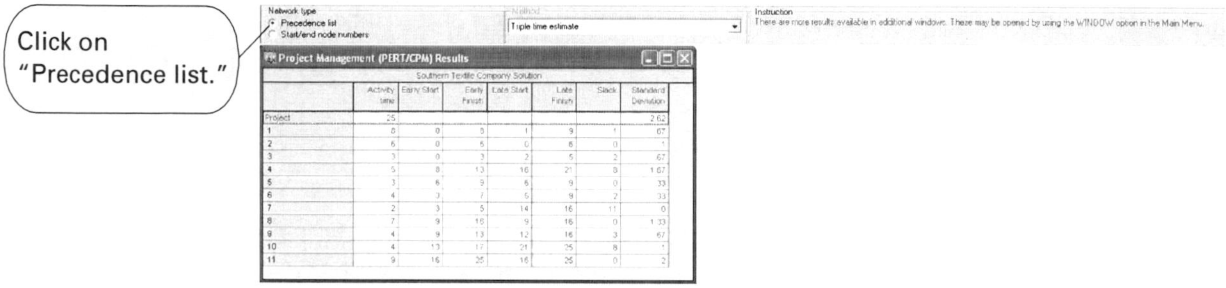

Exhibit 2

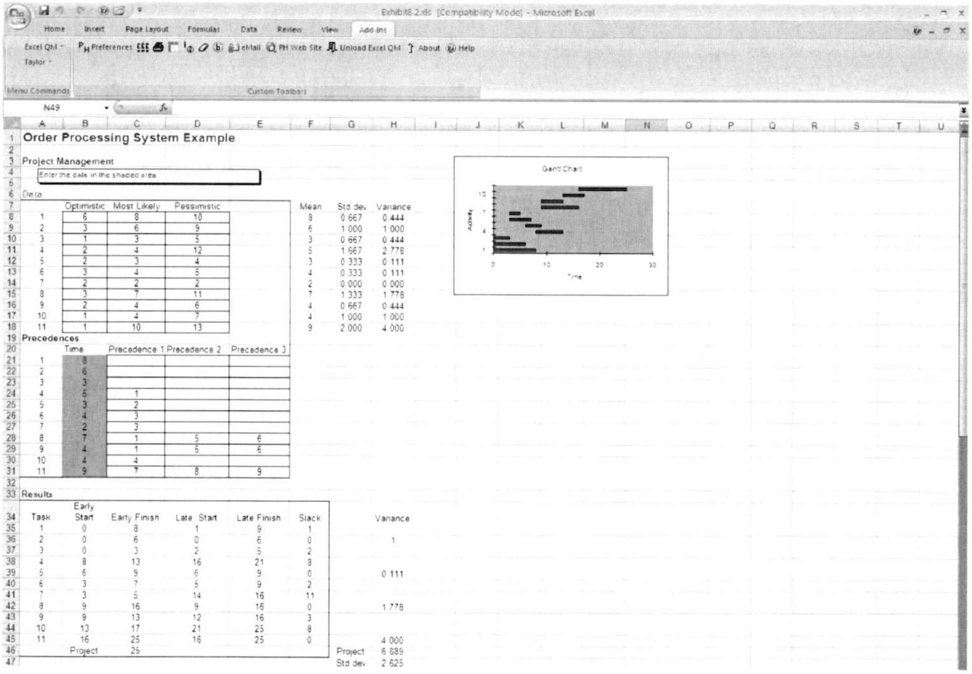

Microsoft Project

Microsoft Project is a very popular and widely used software package for project management and CPM/PERT analysis. It is also relatively easy to use. We will demonstrate how to use Microsoft Project, using the project network for building a house shown in Figure 13. (Note that the Microsoft Project file for this example can be downloaded from the companion Web site.)

Exhibit 3

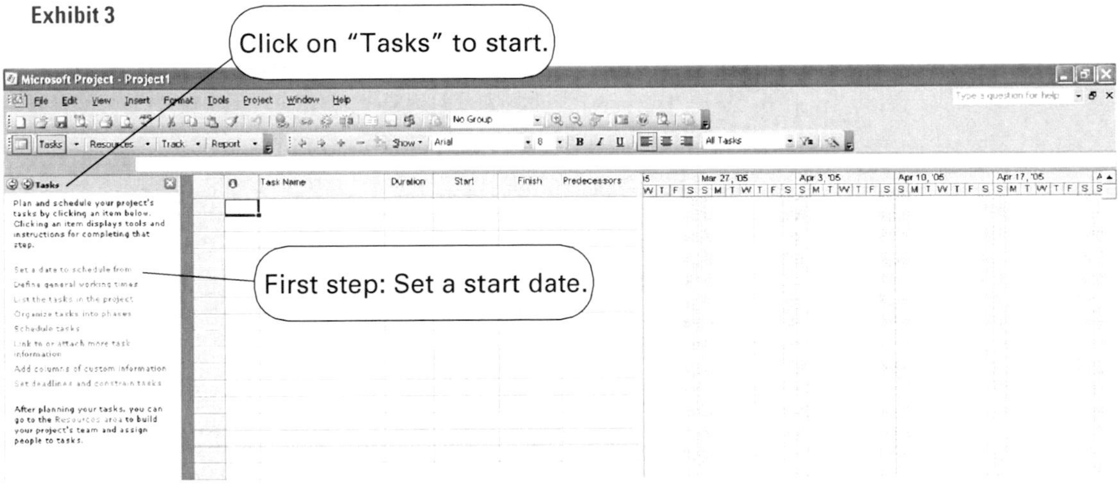

When you open Microsoft Project, a screen comes up for a new project. Click on the "Tasks" button, and the screen like the one shown in Exhibit 3 appears. Notice the set of steps on the left side of the screen, starting with "Set a date to schedule from." If you click on this step, you can set a start date. For our example, we will set the start date for our house-building project as September 1, 2008.

The second step in the "Tasks" menu, "Define general working times," allows the user to specify general work rules and a work calendar, including such things as working hours per day, holidays, and weekend days off. For example, Exhibit 4 shows the screen for selecting the work days and times; in this case, we have selected a "standard" workweek (Monday through Friday) with an 8-hour work day, as shown by the shaded area.

Exhibit 4

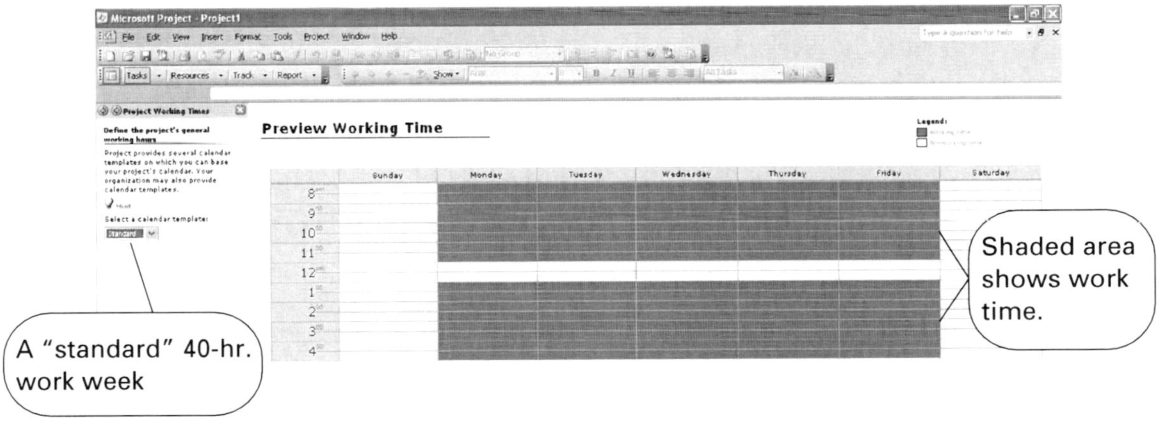

The screen in Exhibit 5 shows how to set holidays and days off. Notice that in this screen for September, we have selected Labor Day as a nonworking time.

The third step in the "Tasks" menu is "List the tasks in the project." The tasks for our house-building project are shown in Exhibit 6. Notice that we have indicated the duration of each task in the "Duration" column. For example, to enter the duration of the first activity, you would type "3 months" in the duration column. Notice that all the tasks show a start date of September 2, 2008, because we haven't set the task sequencing (i.e., precedence relationships) yet. The bars on the far right are for a Gantt chart, but because we haven't established the task sequencing yet, the chart shows nothing but bars across the sheet.

Exhibit 5

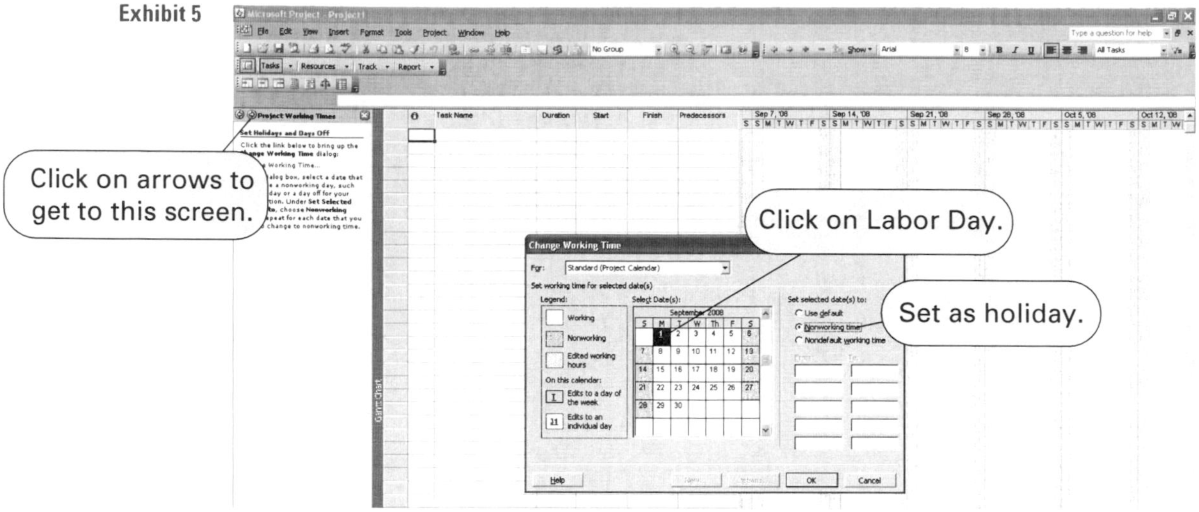

Exhibit 6

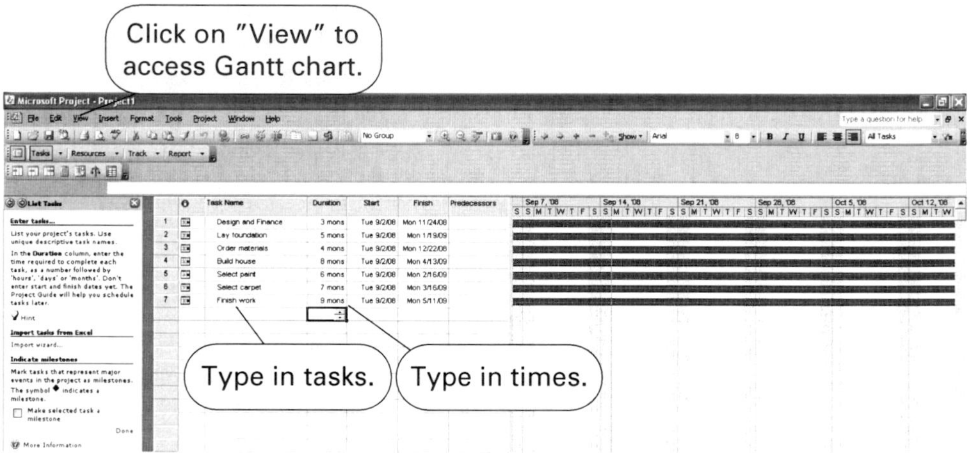

The next step is "Schedule tasks," which we do by specifying the predecessor and successor activities in our network. This is done by using the buttons under "Link dependent tasks" in Exhibit 7. For example, to show that activity 1 precedes activity 2, we put the cursor on activity 1 and then hold down the "Ctrl" key while clicking on activity 2. These two activities should be shaded. Next, we click on the icon on the left side of the spreadsheet to create a finish-to-start link. This makes a finish-to-start link between the two activities, which means that activity 2 cannot start until activity 1 is finished. It creates the precedence relationship between these two activities, as shown under the "Predecessor" column in Exhibit 7.

Exhibit 7 also shows the completed Gantt chart for our network. The Gantt chart is accessed by clicking on the "View" button on the toolbar at the top of the screen and then clicking on "Gantt chart." You may also need to alter the time frame to get all of the Gantt chart on your screen, as shown in Exhibit 7. You can do this by clicking on the "Format" button on the toolbar at the top of the spreadsheet and then clicking on the "Timescale" option. This results in a window from which you can adjust the timescale from days to months, as shown in Exhibit 7. You can show the critical path (which will appear in red)

Exhibit 7

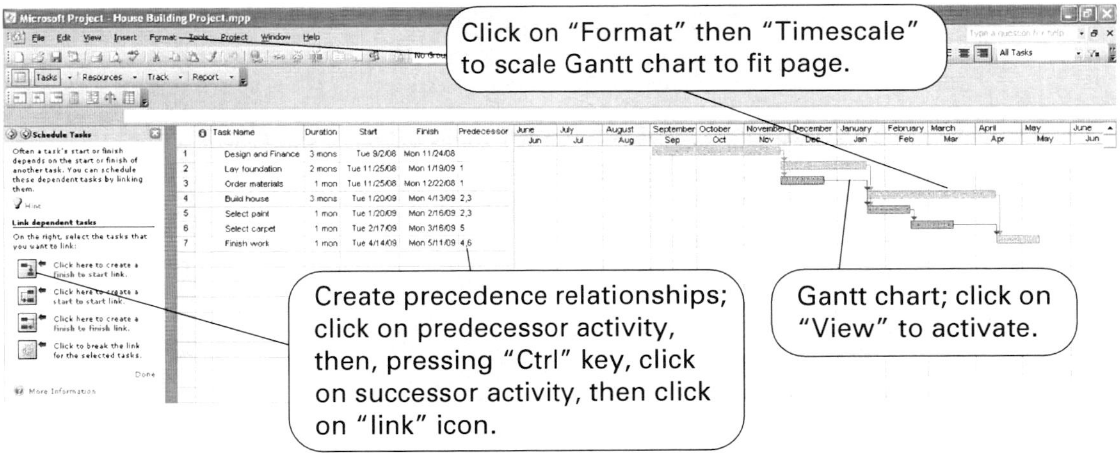

by again clicking on "Format" on the toolbar and then activating "Gantt Chart Wizard," which allows you to highlight the critical path, among other options.

To see the project network, click on the "View" button again on the toolbar and then click on "Network Diagram." Exhibit 8 shows the project network, with the critical path highlighted in red. We used the "Zoom" option under the "View" menu to get the entire network on the screen. (We also removed the "Tasks" menu on the left side of the screen for the moment to show the complete network; it can be restored by clicking on the "Tasks" button again.)

Exhibit 8

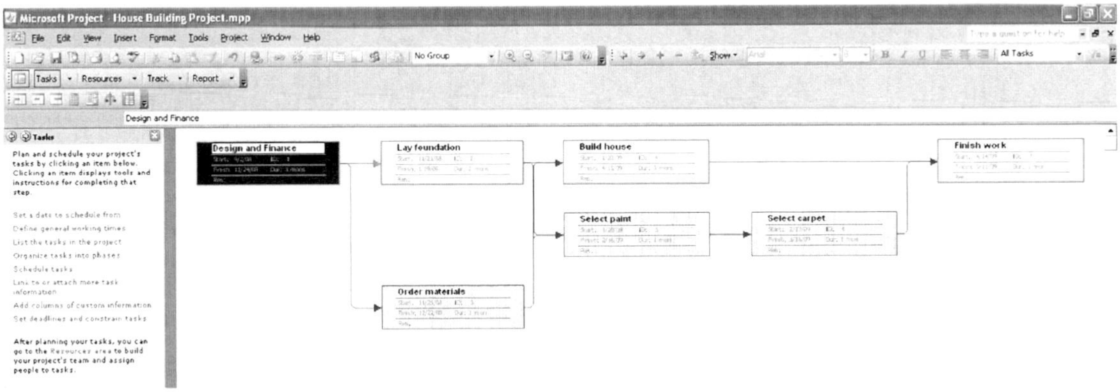

Exhibit 9 shows the project network without using the "Zoom" feature to reduce the network size. This enables you to see the nodes more clearly. Notice that each node includes the start and finish dates and the activity number.

Exhibit 9

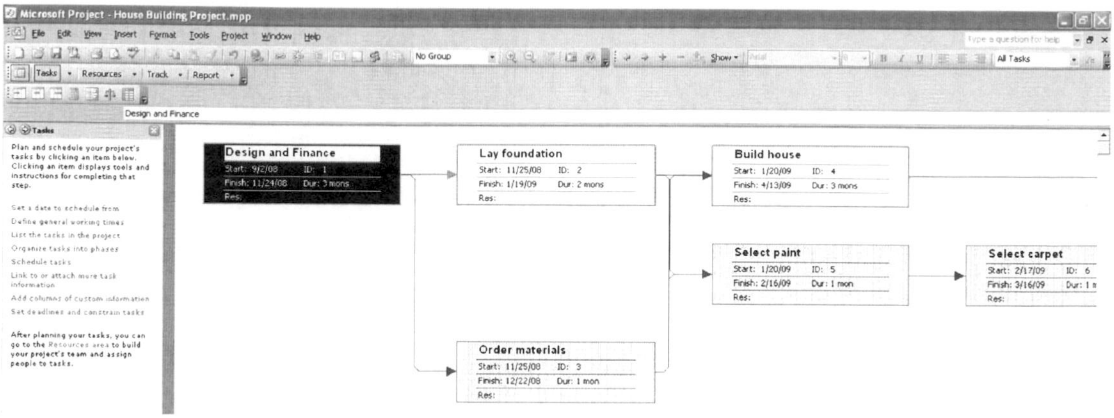

Microsoft Project has many additional tools and features for project updating and resource management. As an example, we will demonstrate one feature that updates the project schedule. First, we double-click on the first task, "Design and Finance," which results in the window labeled Task Information, shown in Exhibit 10. On the "General" tab, we have entered 100% in the "Percent complete" window, meaning this activity has been completed. We have also indicated that activities 2 and 3 have been completed, while activity 4 is 60% complete and activity 5 is 20% complete, by double-clicking on each of these activities and repeating the process. The resulting screen is shown in Exhibit 11. Notice that the dark line through each Gantt chart bar indicates the degree of completion.

Exhibit 10

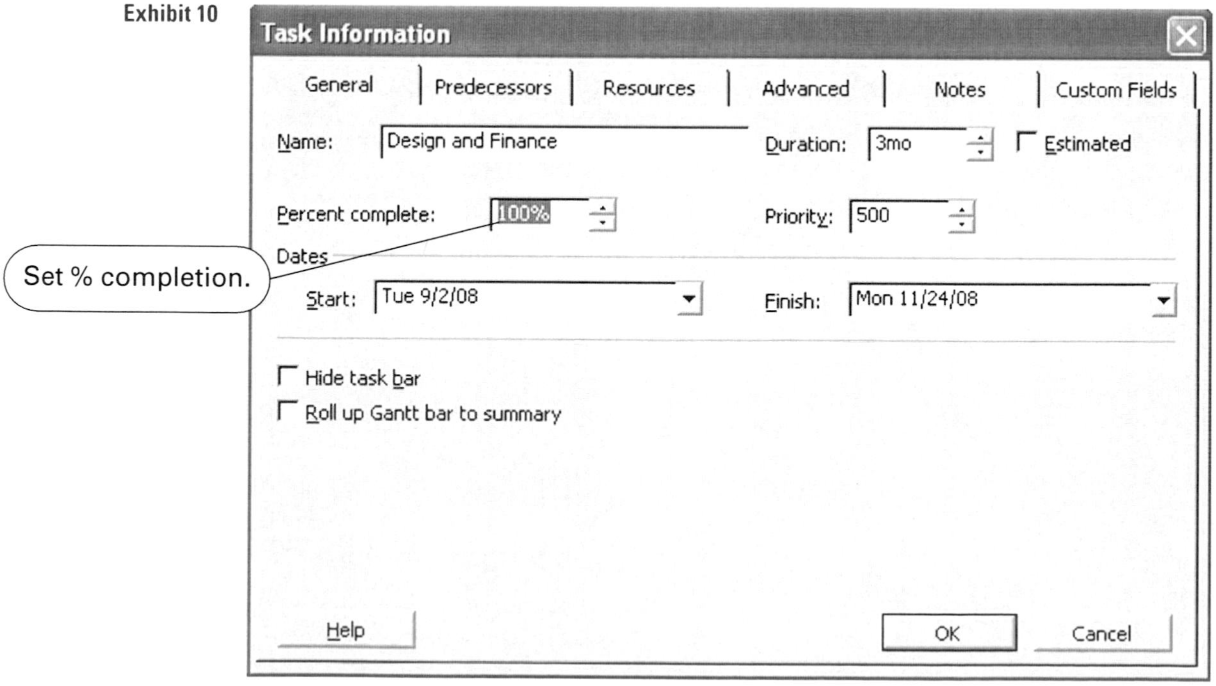

Exhibit 11

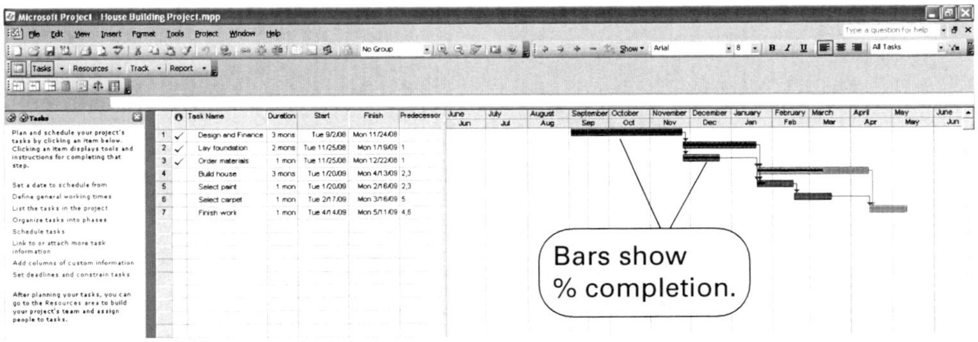

Exhibit 12

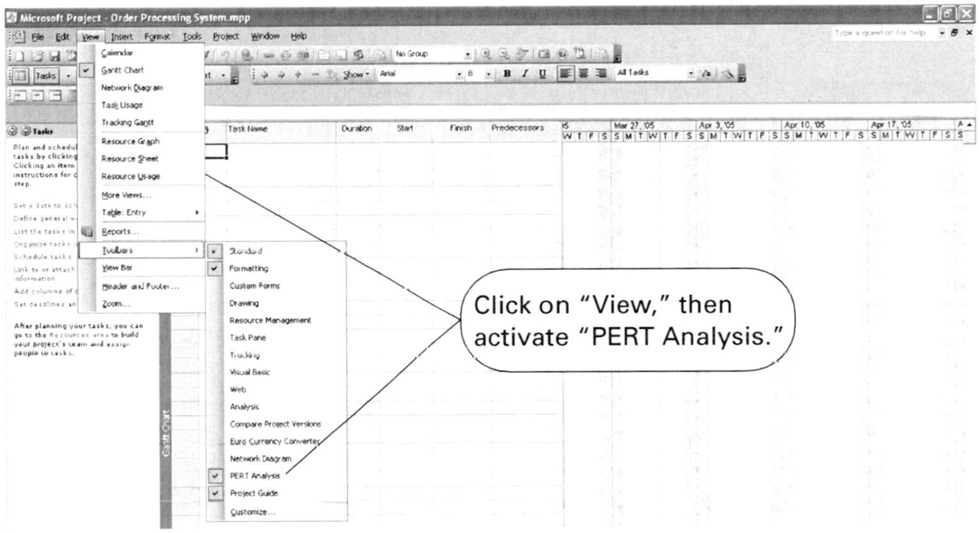

Exhibit 13

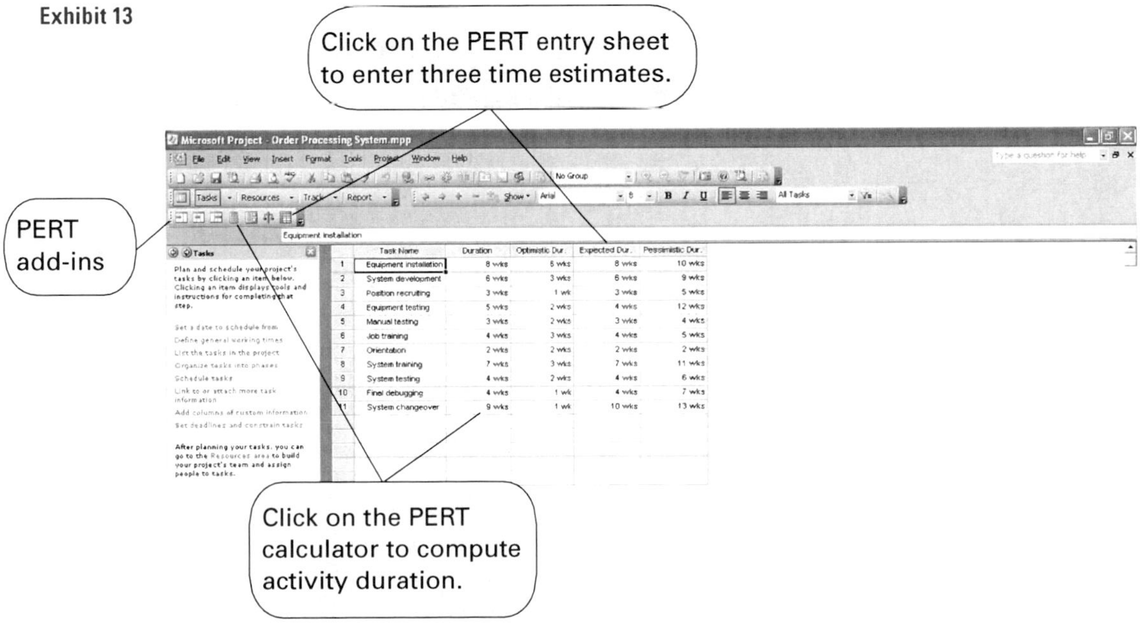

PERT Analysis with Microsoft Project

A PERT network with three time estimates can also be developed by using Microsoft Project. We will demonstrate this capability by using our order processing system project network for the Southern Textile Company, which is shown in Figure 15. After all the project tasks are listed, we enter the three activity time estimates by clicking on the "PERT Entry Sheet" button on the toolbar. If this button is not on your toolbar, you must add it by clicking on "View" and then from the "Toolbars" options selecting "PERT Analysis," as shown in Exhibit 12. (If "PERT Analysis" is still not available to you, you must add it through "COM Add-ins.")

Exhibit 13 shows the PERT time estimate entries for the activities in our order processing system project example, and it shows the activity durations based on the three time estimates for each activity. Exhibit 14 shows the precedence relationships and the project Gantt chart. Exhibit 15 shows the project network.

Exhibit 14

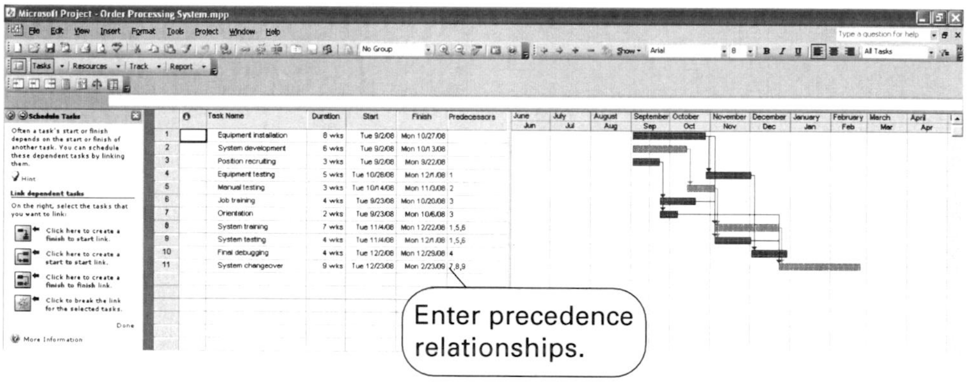

Exhibit 15

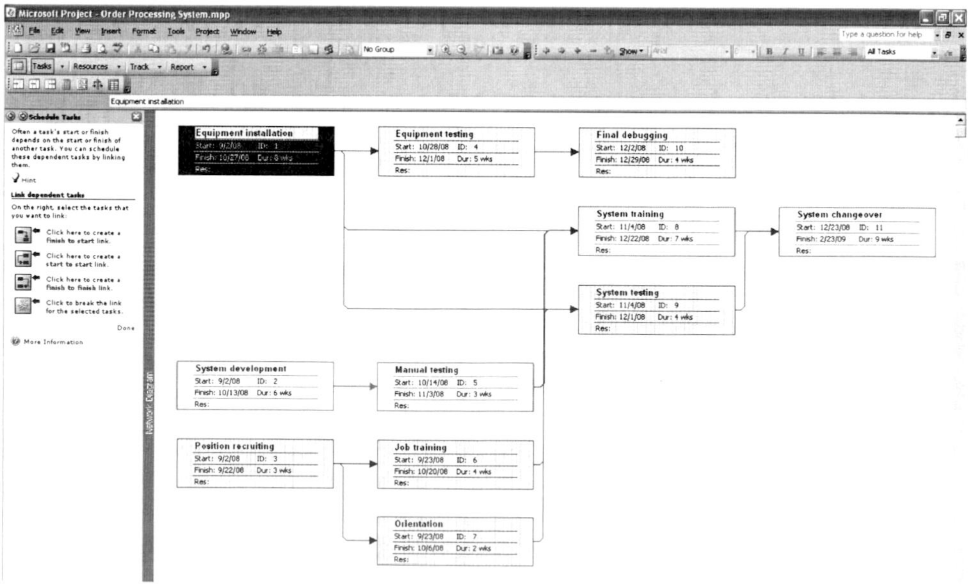

Project Crashing and Time–Cost Trade-Off

To this point we have demonstrated the use of CPM and PERT network analysis for determining project time schedules. This in itself is valuable to a manager planning a project. However, in addition to scheduling projects, a project manager is frequently confronted with the problem of having to reduce the scheduled completion time of a project to meet a deadline. In other words, the manager must finish the project sooner than indicated by the CPM or PERT network analysis.

Project duration can be reduced by assigning more labor to project activities, often in the form of overtime, and by assigning more resources (material, equipment, etc.). However, additional labor and resources cost money and hence increase the overall project cost. Thus, the decision to reduce the project duration must be based on an analysis of the *trade-off* between time and cost.

Project crashing shortens the project time by reducing critical activity times at a cost.

Project crashing is a method for shortening project duration by reducing the time of one or more of the critical project activities to a time that is less than the normal activity time. This reduction in the normal activity times is referred to as *crashing*. Crashing is achieved by devoting more resources, measured in terms of dollars, to the activities to be crashed.

To demonstrate how project crashing works, we will employ the original network for constructing a house shown in Figure 8. This network is repeated in Figure 19, except that the activity times previously shown as months have been converted to weeks. Although this example network encompasses only single-activity time estimates, the project crashing procedure can be applied in the same manner to PERT networks with probabilistic activity time estimates.

Figure 19
The project network for building a house

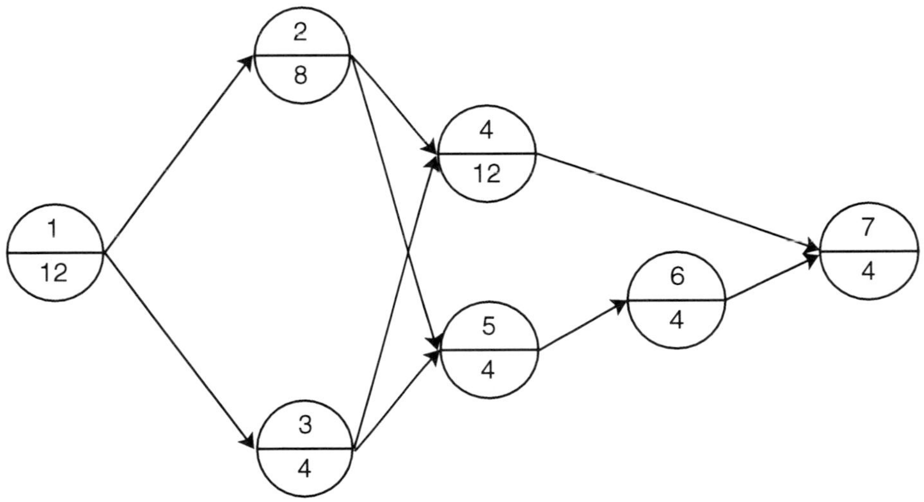

In Figure 19, we will assume that the times (in weeks) shown on the network activities are the *normal activity times*. For example, normally 12 weeks are required to complete activity 1. Furthermore, we will assume that the cost required to complete this activity in the time indicated is \$3,000. This cost is referred to as the *normal activity cost*. Next, we will assume that the building contractor has estimated that activity 1 can be completed in

7 weeks, but it will cost \$5,000 to complete the activity instead of \$3,000. This new estimated activity time is known as the *crash time*, and the revised cost is referred to as the *crash cost*.

Activity 1 can be crashed a total of 5 weeks (normal time − crash time = 12 − 7 = 5 weeks), at a total crash cost of \$2,000 (crash cost − normal cost = \$5,000 − 3,000 = \$2,000). Dividing the total crash cost by the total allowable crash time yields the crash cost per week:

$$\frac{\text{total crash cost}}{\text{total crash time}} = \frac{\$2{,}000}{5} = \$400 \text{ per week}$$

Crash cost and crash time have a linear relationship.

If we assume that the relationship between crash cost and crash time is linear, then activity 1 can be crashed by any amount of time (not exceeding the maximum allowable crash time) at a rate of \$400 per week. For example, if the contractor decided to crash activity 1 by only 2 weeks (for an activity time of 10 weeks), the crash cost would be \$800 (\$400 per week × 2 weeks). The linear relationships between crash cost and crash time and between normal cost and normal time are illustrated in Figure 20.

Figure 20

Time–cost relationship for crashing activity 1.

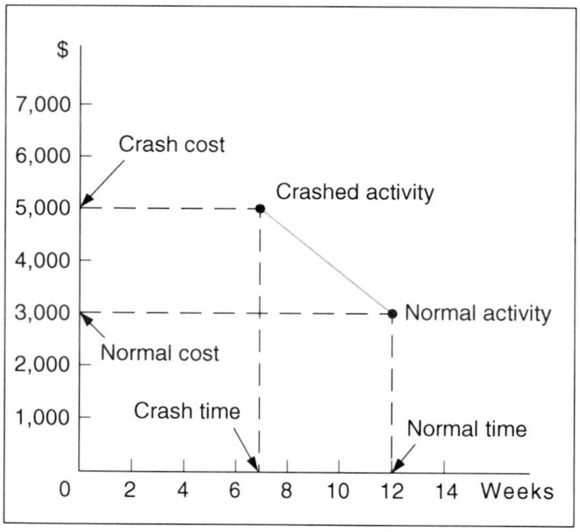

The normal times and costs, the crash times and costs, the total allowable crash times, and the crash cost per week for each activity in the network in Figure 19 are summarized in Table 4.

Recall that the critical path for the house-building network encompassed activities 1 → 2 → 4 → 7, and the project duration was 9 months, or 36 weeks. Suppose that the home builder needed the house in 30 weeks and wanted to know how much extra cost would be incurred to complete the house in this time. To analyze this situation, the contractor would crash the project network to 30 weeks, using the information in Table 4.

As activities are crashed, the critical path may change, and several paths may become critical.

The objective of project crashing is to reduce the project duration while minimizing the cost of crashing. Because the project completion time can be shortened only by crashing

Table 4
Normal activity and crash data for the network in Figure 19

Activity	Normal Time (weeks)	Crash Time (weeks)	Normal Cost	Crash Cost	Total Allowable Crash Time (weeks)	Crash Cost per Week
1	12	7	$ 3,000	$ 5,000	5	$ 400
2	8	5	2,000	3,500	3	500
3	4	3	4,000	7,000	1	3,000
4	12	9	50,000	71,000	3	7,000
5	4	1	500	1,100	3	200
6	4	1	500	1,100	3	200
7	4	3	15,000	22,000	1	7,000
			$75,000	$110,700		

activities on the critical path, it may turn out that not all activities have to be crashed. However, as activities are crashed, the critical path may change, requiring crashing of previously noncritical activities to further reduce the project completion time.

We start the crashing process by looking at the critical path and seeing which activity has the minimum crash cost per week. Observing Table 4 and Figure 21, we see that on the critical path activity 1 has the minimum crash cost of $400. Thus, activity 1 will be reduced as much as possible. Table 4 shows that the maximum allowable reduction for activity 1 is 5 weeks, *but we can reduce activity 1 only to the point where another path becomes critical.* When two paths simultaneously become critical, activities on both must be reduced by the same amount. (If we reduce the activity time beyond the point where another path becomes critical, we may incur an unnecessary cost.) This last stipulation means that we must keep up with all the network paths as we reduce individual activities, a condition that makes manual crashing very cumbersome. Later we will demonstrate an alternative method for project crashing, using linear programming; however, for the moment we will pursue this example in order to demonstrate the logic of project crashing.

It turns out that activity 1 can be crashed by the total amount of 5 weeks without another path's becoming critical because activity 1 is included in all four paths in the network.

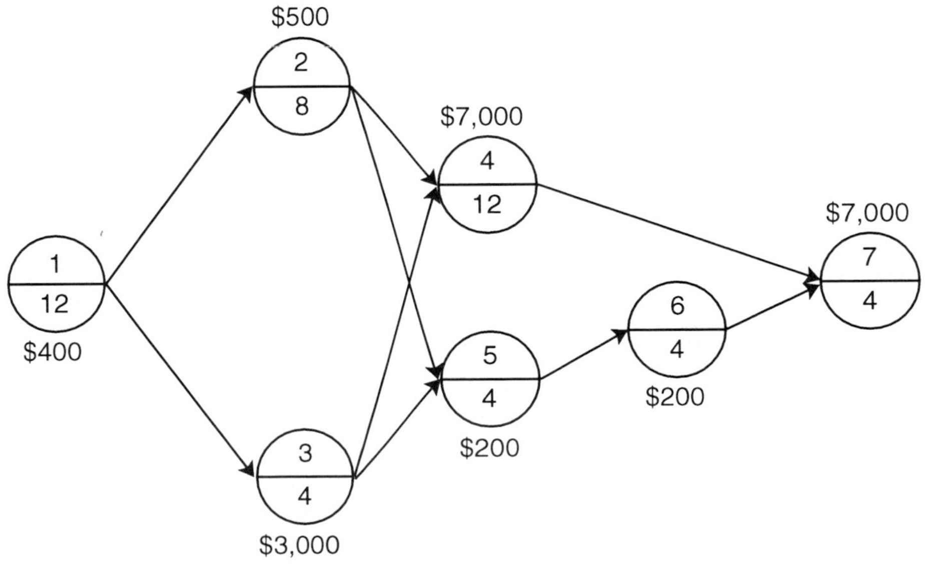

Figure 21
Network with normal activity times and weekly activity crashing costs

Crashing this activity results in a revised project duration of 31 weeks, at a crash cost of $2,000. The revised network is shown in Figure 22.

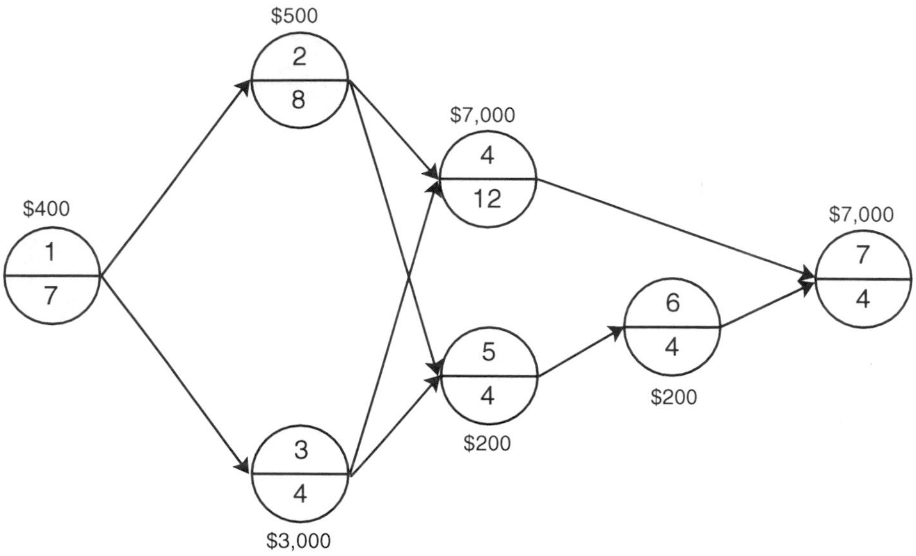

Figure 22
Revised network with activity 1 crashed

This process must now be repeated. The critical path in Figure 22 remains the same, and the new minimum activity crash cost on the critical path is $500 for activity 2. Activity 2 can be crashed a total of 3 weeks, but because the contractor desires to crash the network to only 30 weeks, we need to crash activity 2 by only 1 week. Crashing activity 2 by 1 week does not result in any other path's becoming critical, so we can safely make this reduction. Crashing activity 2 to 7 weeks (i.e., a 1-week reduction) costs $500 and reduces the project duration to 30 weeks.

The extra cost of crashing the project to 30 weeks is $2,500. Thus, the contractor could inform the customer that an additional cost of only $2,500 would be incurred to finish the house in 30 weeks.

As indicated earlier, the manual procedure for crashing a network is very cumbersome and generally unacceptable for project crashing. It is basically a trial-and-error approach that is useful for demonstrating the logic of crashing; however, it quickly becomes unmanageable for larger networks. This approach would have become difficult if we had pursued even the house-building example to a crash time more than 30 weeks.

Project Crashing with QM for Windows

QM for Windows also has the capability to crash a network *completely*. In other words, it crashes the network by the maximum amount possible. In our house-building example in the previous section, we crashed the network to only 30 weeks, and we did not consider by how much the network could have actually been crashed. Alternatively, QM for Windows crashes a network by the maximum amount possible. The QM for Windows solution for our house-building example is shown in Exhibit 16. Notice that the network has been crashed to 24 weeks, at a total crash cost of $31,500.

Exhibit 16

Project Management (PERT/CPM) Results

House Building Example Solution

	Normal time	Crash time	Normal Cost	Crash Cost	Crash cost/pd	Crash by	Crashing cost
Project	36	24					
1	12	7	3000	5000	400	5	2000
2	8	5	2000	3500	500	3	1500
3	4	3	4000	7000	3000	0	0
4	12	9	50000	71000	7000	3	21000
5	4	1	500	1100	200	0	0
6	4	1	500	1100	200	0	0
7	4	3	15000	22000	7000	1	7000
TOTALS			75000				31500

The General Relationship of Time and Cost

In our discussion of project crashing, we demonstrated how the project critical path time could be reduced by increasing expenditures for labor and direct resources. The implicit objective of crashing was to reduce the scheduled completion time for its own sake—that is, to reap the results of the project sooner. However, there may be other important reasons for reducing project time. As projects continue over time, they consume various *indirect*

Management Science Application

Reconstructing the Pentagon After 9/11

On September 11, 2001, at 9:37 A.M., American Airlines flight 77, which had been hijacked by terrorists, was flown into the west face of the Pentagon in Arlington, Virginia. More than 400,000 square feet of office space was destroyed, and an additional 1.6 million square feet was damaged. Almost immediately, the "Phoenix Project" to restore the Pentagon was initiated. A deadline of 1 year was established for project completion, which required the demolition and removal of the destroyed portion of the building, followed by the building restoration, including restoration of the limestone facade. The Pentagon consists of five rings of offices (housing 25,000 employees) that emanate from the center of the building; ring A is the innermost ring, and ring E is the outermost. Ten corridors radiate out from the building's hub, bisecting the ring, and forming the Pentagon's five distinctive wedges. At the time of the attack, the Pentagon was undergoing a 20-year, $1.2 billion renovation program, and the renovation of Wedge 1, which was demolished in the 9/11 attack, was nearing completion. As a result, the Phoenix Project leaders were able to use the Wedge 1 renovation project structure and plans as a basis for their own reconstruction plan and schedule, saving much time in the process. Project leaders were in place and able to assign resources on the very day of the attack. The project included more than 30,000 activities and a 3,000-member project team and required 3 million person-hours of work. Over 56,000 tons of contaminated debris were removed from the site, 2.5 million pounds of limestone were used to reconstruct the facade (using the original drawings from 1941), 21,000 cubic yards of concrete was poured, and 3,800 tons of reinforcing steel were placed. The Phoenix Project was completed almost a month ahead of schedule and nearly $194 million under the original budget estimate of $700 million.

AP Wide World Photos

Source: N. Bauer, "Rising from the Ashes," *PM Network* 18, no. 5 (May 2004): 24–32.

costs, including the cost of facilities, equipment, and machinery; interest on investment; utilities, labor, and personnel costs; and the loss of skills and labor from members of the project team who are not working at their regular jobs. There also may be direct financial penalties for not completing a project on time. For example, many construction contracts and government contracts have penalty clauses for exceeding the project completion date.

Crash costs increase as project time decreases; indirect costs increase as project time increases.

In general, project crash costs and indirect costs have an inverse relationship; crash costs are highest when the project is shortened, whereas indirect costs increase as the project duration increases. This time–cost relationship is illustrated in Figure 23. The best, or optimal, project time is at the minimum point on the total cost curve.

Figure 23
The time–cost trade-off

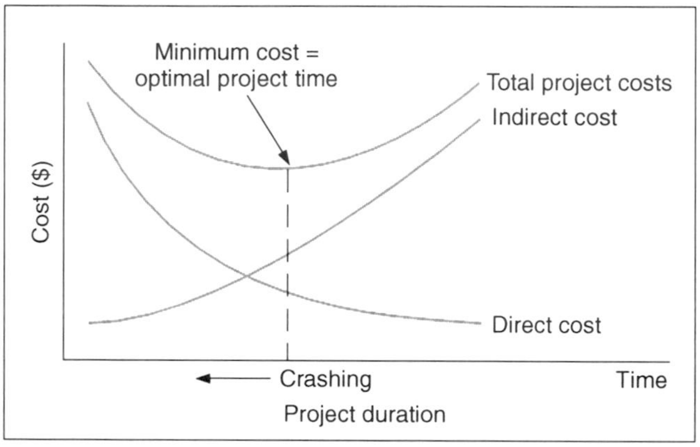

Formulating the CPM/PERT Network as a Linear Programming Model

First we will look at the linear programming formulation of the general CPM/PERT network model and then at the formulation of the project crashing network.

We will formulate the linear programming model of a CPM/PERT network, using the AOA convention. As the first step in formulating the linear programming model, we will define the decision variables. In our discussion of CPM/PERT networks using the AOA convention, we designated an activity by its start and ending node numbers. Thus, an activity starting at node 1 and ending at node 2 was referred to as activity $1 \rightarrow 2$. We will use a similar designation to define the decision variables of our linear programming model.

The objective function for the linear programming model is to minimize project duration.

We will use a different scheduling convention. Instead of determining the earliest activity start time for each activity, we will use the *earliest event time* at each node. This is the earliest time that a node (i or j) can be realized. In other words, it is the earliest time that the event the node represents, either the completion of all the activities leading into it or the start of all activities leaving it, can occur. Thus, for an activity $i \rightarrow j$, the earliest event time of node i will be x_i, and the earliest event time of node j will be x_j.

The objective of the project network is to determine the earliest time the project can be completed (i.e., the critical path time).We have already determined from our discussion of CPM/PERT network analysis that the earliest event time of the last node in the network equals the critical path time. If we let x_i equal the earliest event times of the nodes in the network, then the objective function can be expressed as

$$\text{minimize } Z = \sum_i x_i$$

Because the value of Z is the sum of all the earliest event times, it has no real meaning; however, it will ensure the earliest event time at each node.

Next, we must develop the model constraints. We will define the time for activity $i \longrightarrow j$ as t_{ij} (as we did earlier in this chapter). From our previous discussion of CPM/PERT network analysis, we know that the difference between the earliest event time at node j and the earliest event time at node i must be at least as great as the activity time t_{ij}. A set of constraints that expresses this condition is defined as

$$x_j - x_i \geq t_{ij}$$

The general linear programming model of formulation of a CPM/PERT network can be summarized as

$$\text{minimize } Z = \sum_i x_i$$

subject to

$x_j - x_i \geq t_{ij}$, for all activities $i \longrightarrow j$

$x_i, x_j \geq 0$

where

x_i = earliest event time of node i
x_j = earliest event time of node j
t_{ij} = time of activity $i \longrightarrow j$

The solution of this linear programming model will indicate the earliest event time of each node in the network and the project duration.

As an example of the linear programming model formulation and solution of a project network, we will use the house-building network that we used to demonstrate project crashing. This network, with activity times in weeks and earliest event times, is shown in Figure 24.

Figure 24
CPM/PERT network for the house-building project, with earliest event times

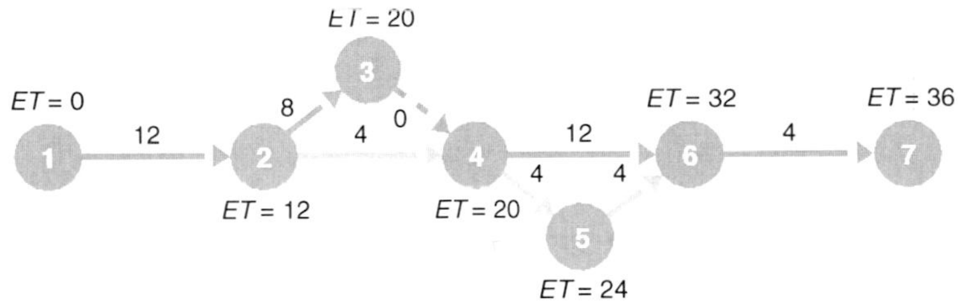

The linear programming model for the network in Figure 24 is

$$\text{minimize } Z = x_1 + x_2 + x_3 + x_4 + x_5 + x_6 + x_7$$

subject to

$$\begin{aligned} x_2 - x_1 &\geq 12 \\ x_3 - x_2 &\geq 8 \\ x_4 - x_2 &\geq 4 \\ x_4 - x_3 &\geq 0 \\ x_5 - x_4 &\geq 4 \\ x_6 - x_4 &\geq 12 \\ x_6 - x_5 &\geq 4 \\ x_7 - x_6 &\geq 4 \\ x_i, x_j &\geq 0 \end{aligned}$$

Notice in this model that there is a constraint for each activity in the network.

Solution of the CPM/PERT Linear Programming Model with Excel

The linear programming model of the CPM/PERT network in the preceding section enables us to use Excel to schedule the project. Exhibit 17 shows an Excel spreadsheet set up to determine the earliest event times for each node—that is, the x_i and x_j values in our linear programming model for our house-building example. The earliest start times are in cells **B6:B12**. Cells **F6:F13** contain the model constraints. For example, cell F6 contains the constraint formula **=B7−B6,** and cell F7 contains the formula **=B8−B7**. These constraint formulas will be set ≥ the activity times in column G when we access Solver. (Also, because activity 3 ⟶ 4 is a dummy, a constraint for **F9=0** must be added to Solver.)

Exhibit 17

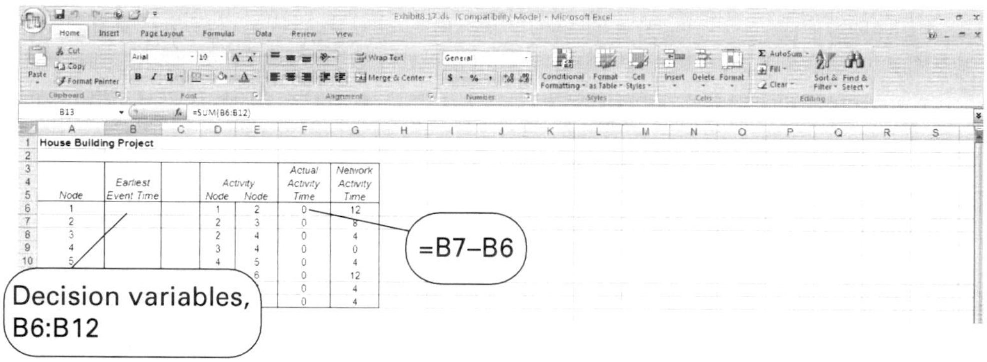

The Solver Parameters window with the model data is shown in Exhibit 18. Notice that the objective is to minimize the project duration in cell B13, which actually contains the earliest event time for node 7.

Exhibit 18

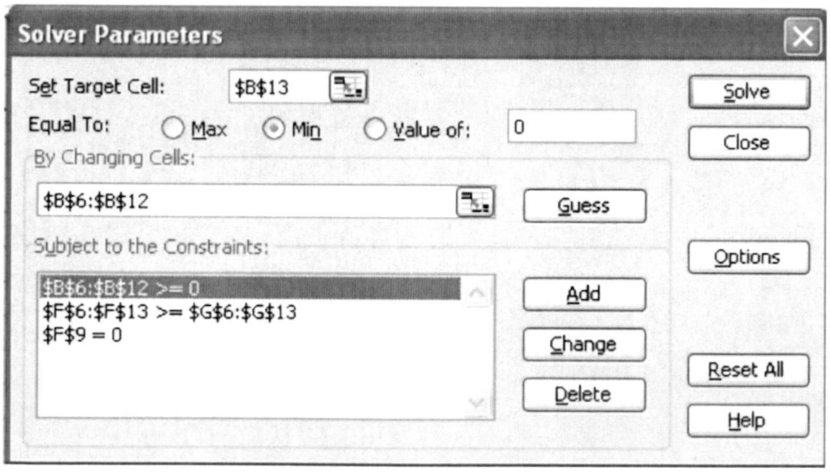

The solution is shown in Exhibit 19. Notice that the earliest time at each node is given in cells **B6:B12**, and the total project duration is 36 weeks. However, this output does not indicate the critical path. The critical path can be determined by accessing the sensitivity report for this problem. Recall that when you click on "Solve" from Solver, a screen comes

Exhibit 19

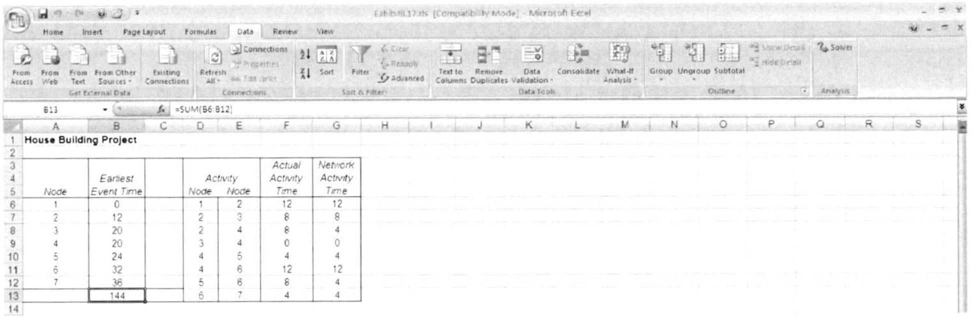

House Building Project

Node	Earliest Event Time	Activity Node	Activity Node	Actual Activity Time	Network Activity Time
1	0	1	2	12	12
2	12	2	3	8	8
3	20	2	4	8	4
4	20	3	4	0	0
5	24	4	5	4	4
6	32	4	6	12	12
7	36	5	6	8	4
	144	6	7	4	4

up, indicating that Solver has reached a solution. This screen also provides the opportunity to generate several different kinds of reports, including an answer report and a sensitivity report. When we click on "Sensitivity" under the report options, the information shown in Exhibit 20 is provided.

Exhibit 20

Constraints

Cell	Name	Final Value	Shadow Price	Constraint R.H. Side	Allowable Increase	Allowable Decrease
F6	Time	12	1	12	1E+30	12
F7	Time	8	1	8	1E+30	4
F8	Time	8	0	4	4	1E+30
F9	Time	0	1	0	1E+30	4
F10	Time	8	0	4	4	1E+30
F11	Time	12	1	12	1E+30	4
F12	Time	4	0	4	4	1E+30
F13	weeks Time	4	1	4	1E+30	36

Indicates critical path

The information in which we are interested is the shadow price for each of the activity constraints. (Remember that to get the shadow prices on the sensitivity report, you must click on "Options" from Solver and then select "Assume Linear Model.") The shadow price for each activity will be either 1 or 0. A positive shadow price of 1 for an activity means that you can reduce the overall project duration by an amount with a corresponding decrease by the same amount in the activity duration. Alternatively, a shadow price of 0 means that the project duration will not change, even if you change the activity duration by some amount. This means that those activities with a shadow price of 1 are on the critical path. Cells F6, F7, F9, F11, and F13 have shadow prices of 1, and referring back to Exhibit 19, we see that these cells correspond to activities $1 \rightarrow 2$, $2 \rightarrow 3$, $3 \rightarrow 4$, $4 \rightarrow 6$, and $6 \rightarrow 7$, which are the activities on the critical path.

Project Crashing with Linear Programming

The linear programming model required to perform project crashing analysis differs from the linear programming model formulated for the general CPM/PERT network in the previous section. The linear programming model for project crashing is somewhat longer and more complex.

The objective of the project crashing model is to minimize the cost of crashing.

The objective for our general linear programming model was to minimize project duration; the objective of project crashing is to minimize the cost of crashing, given the limits on how much individual activities can be crashed. As a result, the general linear programming model formulation must be expanded to include crash times and cost. We will continue to define the earliest event times for activity $i \rightarrow j$ as x_i and x_j. In addition, we will define the amount of time each activity $i \rightarrow j$ is crashed as y_{ij}. Thus, the decision variables are defined as

$$x_i = \text{earliest event time of node } i$$
$$x_j = \text{earliest event time of node } j$$
$$y_{ij} = \text{amount of time by which activity } i \rightarrow j \text{ is crashed (i.e., reduced)}$$

The objective of project crashing is to reduce the project duration at the minimum possible crash cost. For our house-building network, the objective function is written as

$$\text{minimize } Z = \$400y_{12} + 500y_{23} + 3{,}000y_{24} + 200y_{45} + 7{,}000y_{46} + 200y_{56} + 7{,}000y_{67}$$

The objective function coefficients are the activity crash costs per week from Table 4; the variables y_{ij} indicate the number of weeks each activity will be reduced. For example, if activity $1 \rightarrow 2$ is crashed by 2 weeks, then $y_{12} = 2$, and a cost of \$800 is incurred.

The model constraints must specify the limits on the amount of time each activity can be crashed. Using the allowable crash times for each activity from Table 4 enables us to develop the following set of constraints:

$$\begin{aligned} y_{12} &\le 5 \\ y_{23} &\le 3 \\ y_{24} &\le 1 \\ y_{34} &\le 0 \\ y_{45} &\le 3 \\ y_{46} &\le 3 \\ y_{56} &\le 3 \\ y_{67} &\le 1 \end{aligned}$$

For example, the first constraint, $y_{12} \le 5$, specifies that the amount of time by which activity $1 \rightarrow 2$ is reduced cannot exceed 5 weeks.

The next group of constraints must mathematically represent the relationship between earliest event times for each activity in the network, as the constraint $x_j - x_i \ge t_{ij}$ did in our original linear programming model. However, we must now reflect the fact that activity times can be crashed by an amount y_{ij}. Recall the formulation of the activity $1 \rightarrow 2$ constraint for the general linear programming model formulation in the previous section:

$$x_2 - x_1 \ge 12$$

This constraint can also be written as

$$x_1 + 12 \le x_2$$

This latter constraint indicates that the earliest event time at node 1 (x_1), plus the normal activity time (12 weeks) cannot exceed the earliest event time at node 2 (x_2). To reflect the fact that this activity can be crashed, it is necessary only to subtract the amount by which it can be crashed from the left-hand side of the preceding constraint:

$$x_1 + 12 - \underbrace{y_{12}}_{\text{amount activity } 1 \rightarrow 2 \text{ can be crashed}} \le x_2$$

This revised constraint now indicates that the earliest event time at node 2 (x_2) is determined not only by the earliest event time at node 1 plus the activity time but also by the amount the activity is crashed. Each activity in the network must have a similar constraint, as follows:

$$\begin{aligned} x_1 + 12 - y_{12} &\le x_2 \\ x_2 + 8 - y_{23} &\le x_3 \\ x_2 + 4 - y_{24} &\le x_4 \\ x_3 + 0 - y_{34} &\le x_4 \\ x_4 + 4 - y_{45} &\le x_5 \\ x_4 + 12 - y_{46} &\le x_6 \\ x_5 + 4 - y_{56} &\le x_6 \\ x_6 + 4 - y_{67} &\le x_7 \end{aligned}$$

Finally, we must indicate the project duration we are seeking (i.e., the crashed project time). Because the housing contractor wants to crash the project from the 36-week normal critical path time to 30 weeks, our final model constraint specifies that the earliest event time at node 7 should not exceed 30 weeks:

$$x_7 \le 30$$

The complete linear programming model formulation is summarized as follows:

minimize $Z = \$400y_{12} + 500y_{23} + 3{,}000y_{24} + 200y_{45} + 7{,}000y_{46} + 200y_{56} + 7{,}000y_{67}$
subject to

$$\begin{aligned} y_{12} &\le 5 \\ y_{23} &\le 3 \\ y_{24} &\le 1 \\ y_{34} &\le 0 \\ y_{45} &\le 3 \\ y_{46} &\le 3 \\ y_{56} &\le 3 \\ y_{67} &\le 1 \\ y_{12} + x_2 - x_1 &\ge 12 \\ y_{23} + x_3 - x_2 &\ge 8 \\ y_{24} + x_4 - x_2 &\ge 4 \\ y_{34} + x_4 - x_3 &\ge 0 \\ y_{45} + x_5 - x_4 &\ge 4 \\ y_{46} + x_6 - x_4 &\ge 12 \\ y_{56} + x_6 - x_5 &\ge 4 \\ y_{67} + x_7 - x_6 &\ge 4 \\ x_7 &\le 30 \\ x_i, y_{ij} &\ge 0 \end{aligned}$$

Project Crashing with Excel

Because we have been able to develop a linear programming model for project crashing, we can also solve this model by using Excel. Exhibit 21 shows a modified version of the Excel spreadsheet we developed earlier, in Exhibit 16, to determine the earliest event times for our CPM/PERT network for the house-building project. We have added columns H, I, and J for the activity crash costs, the activity crash times, and the actual activity crash times. Cells **J6:J13** correspond to the y_{ij} variables in the linear programming model. The constraint formulas for each activity are included in cells **F6:F13**. For example, cell F6 contains

Exhibit 21

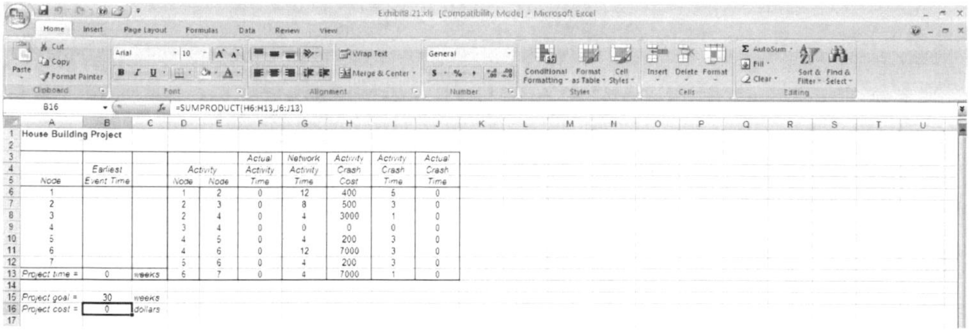

the formula **=J6+B7−B6,** and cell F7 contains the formula **=J7+B8−B7.** These constraints and the others in column F must be set ≥ the activity times in column G. The objective function formula in cell B16 is shown on the formula bar at the top of the spreadsheet. The crashing goal of 30 weeks is included in cell B15.

The problem in Exhibit 21 is solved by using Solver, as shown in Exhibit 22. Notice that there are two sets of variables, in cells **B6:B12** and in cells **J6:J13**. The project crashing solution is shown in Exhibit 23.

Exhibit 22

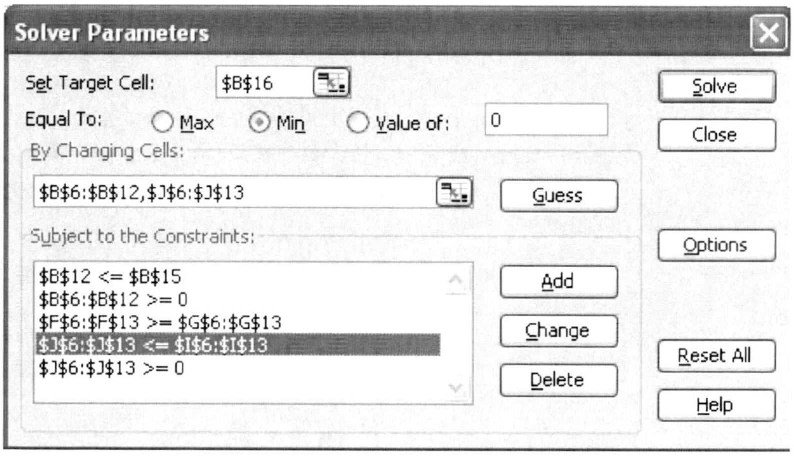

Exhibit 23

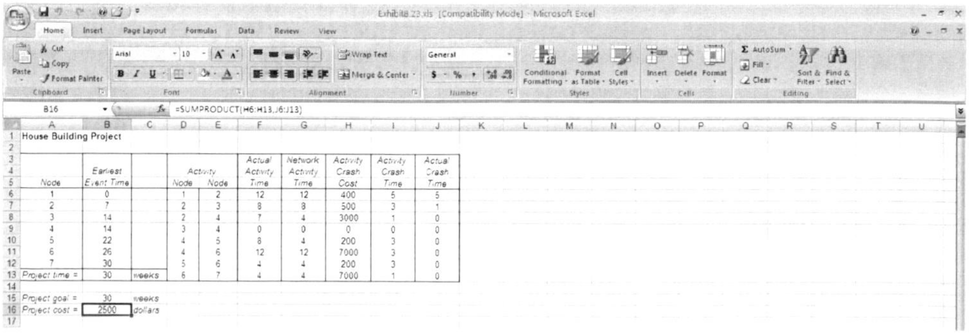

Summary

In this chapter we discussed two of the most popular management science techniques—CPM and PERT networks. Their popularity is due primarily to the fact that a network forms a picture of the system under analysis that is easy for a manager to interpret. Sometimes it is difficult to explain a set of mathematical equations to a manager, but a network often can be easily explained. CPM/PERT has been applied in a variety of government agencies concerned with project control, including various military agencies, the National Aeronautics and Space Administration (NASA), the Federal Aviation Administration (FAA), and the General Services Administration (GSA). These agencies are frequently involved in large-scale projects involving millions of dollars and many subcontractors. Examples of such governmental projects include the development of weapons systems, aircraft, and NASA space exploration projects. It has become a common practice for these agencies to require subcontractors to develop and use a CPM/PERT analysis to maintain management control of the myriad project components and subprojects.

CPM/PERT has also been widely applied in the private sector. Two of the major areas of application of CPM/PERT in the private sector have been research and development (R&D) and construction. CPM/PERT has been applied to various R&D projects, such as developing new drugs, planning and introducing new products, and developing new and more powerful computer systems. CPM/PERT analysis has been particularly applicable to construction projects. Almost every type of construction project—from building a house to constructing a major sports stadium to building a ship to constructing an oil pipeline—has been subjected to network analysis.

Network analysis is also applicable to the planning and scheduling of major events, such as summit conferences, sports festivals, basketball tournaments, football bowl games, parades, political conventions, school registrations, and rock concerts. The availability of powerful, user-friendly project management software packages for the personal computer will serve to increase the use of this technique.

References

Levy, F., Thompson, G., and Wiest, J. "The ABC's of the Critical Path Method." *Harvard Business Review* 41, no. 5 (October 1963).

Moder, J., Phillips, C. R., and Davis, E. W. *Project Management with CPM and PERT and Precedence Diagramming*, 3rd ed. New York: Van Nostrand Reinhold, 1983.

O'Brian, J. *CPM in Construction Management.* New York: McGraw-Hill, 1965.

Wiest, J. D., and Levy, F. K. *A Management Guide to PERT/CPM*, 2nd ed. Upper Saddle River, NJ: Prentice Hall, 1977.

Example Problem Solution

The following example will illustrate CPM/PERT network analysis and probability analysis.

Problem Statement

Given the following AON network and activity time estimates, determine the expected project completion time and variance, as well as the probability that the project will be completed in 28 days or less:

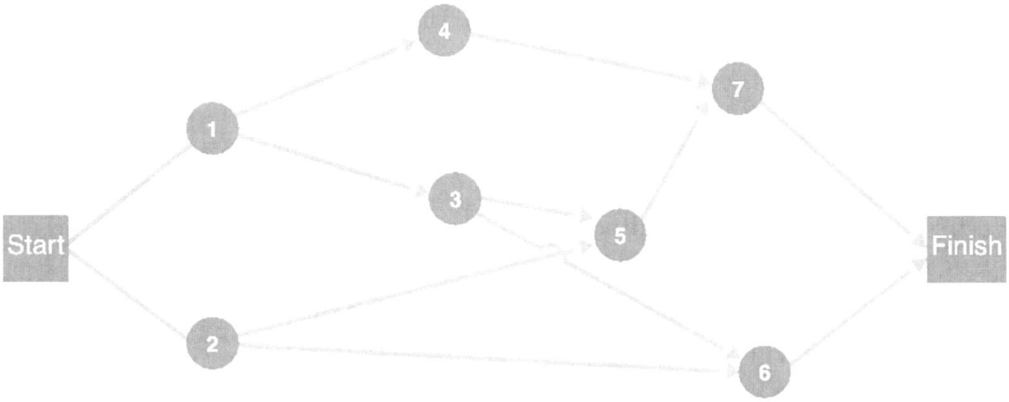

Activity	Time Estimates (weeks)		
	a	m	b
1	5	8	17
2	7	10	13
3	3	5	7
4	1	3	5
5	4	6	8
6	3	3	3
7	3	4	5

Solution

Step 1: Compute the Expected Activity Times and Variances

Using the following formulas, compute the expected time and variance for each activity:

$$t = \frac{a + 4m + b}{6}$$

$$v = \left(\frac{b - a}{6}\right)^2$$

For example, the expected time and variance for activity 1 is

$$t = \frac{5 + 4(8) + 17}{6}$$
$$= 9$$
$$v = \left(\frac{17 - 5}{6}\right)^2$$
$$= 4$$

These values and the remaining expected times and variances for each activity follow:

Activity	t	v
1	9	4
2	10	1
3	5	4/9
4	3	4/9
5	6	4/9
6	3	0
7	4	1/9

Step 2: Determine the Earliest and Latest Times at Each Node

The earliest and latest activity times and the activity slack are shown on the following network:

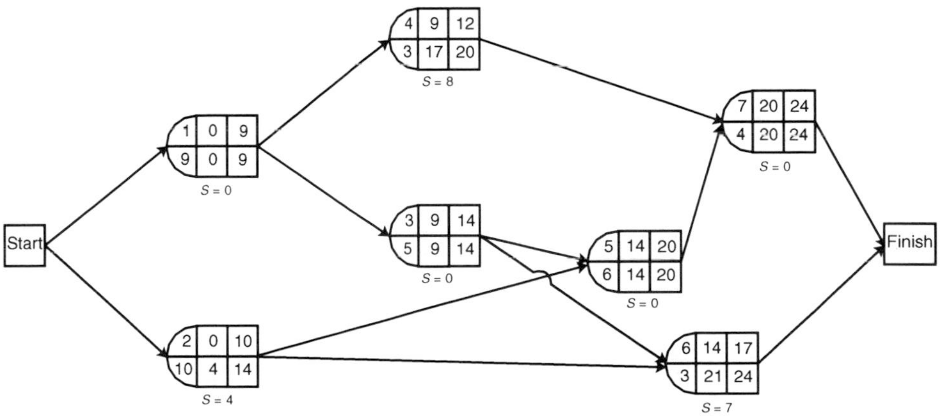

Step 3: Identify the Critical Path and Compute Expected Project Completion Time and Variance

After observing the foregoing network and those activities with no slack (i.e., $S = 0$), we can identify the critical path as $1 \rightarrow 3 \rightarrow 5 \rightarrow 7$. The expected project completion time (t_p) is 24 days. The variance is computed by summing the variances for the activities in the critical path:

$$v_p = 4 + 4/9 + 4/9 + 1/9$$
$$= 5 \text{ days}$$

Step 4: Determine the Probability That the Project Will Be Completed in 28 Days or Less

The following normal probability distribution describes the probability analysis:

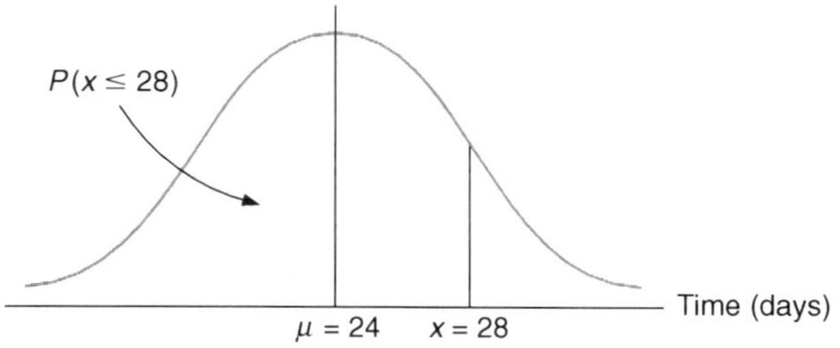

Compute Z by using the following formula:

$$Z = \frac{x - \mu}{\sigma}$$
$$= \frac{28 - 24}{\sqrt{5}}$$
$$= 1.79$$

The corresponding probability is .4633; thus,

$$P(x \leq 28) = .9633$$

Problems

1. Construct a Gantt chart for the following set of activities and indicate the project completion time:

Activity	Activity Predecessor	Time (weeks)
1	—	5
2	—	4
3	1	3
4	2	6

2. Construct a Gantt chart for the following set of activities and indicate the project completion time and slack for each activity:

Activity	Activity Predecessor	Time (weeks)
1	—	3
2	—	7
3	1	2
4	2	5
5	2	6
6	4	1
7	5	4

3. Construct a Gantt chart and project network for the following set of activities, compute the length of each path in the network, and indicate the critical path:

Activity	Activity Predecessor	Time (months)
1	—	4
2	—	7
3	1	8
4	1	3
5	2	9
6	3	5
7	3	2
8	4, 5, 6	6
9	2	5

4. Identify all the paths in the following network, compute the length of each, and indicate the critical path (activity times are in weeks):

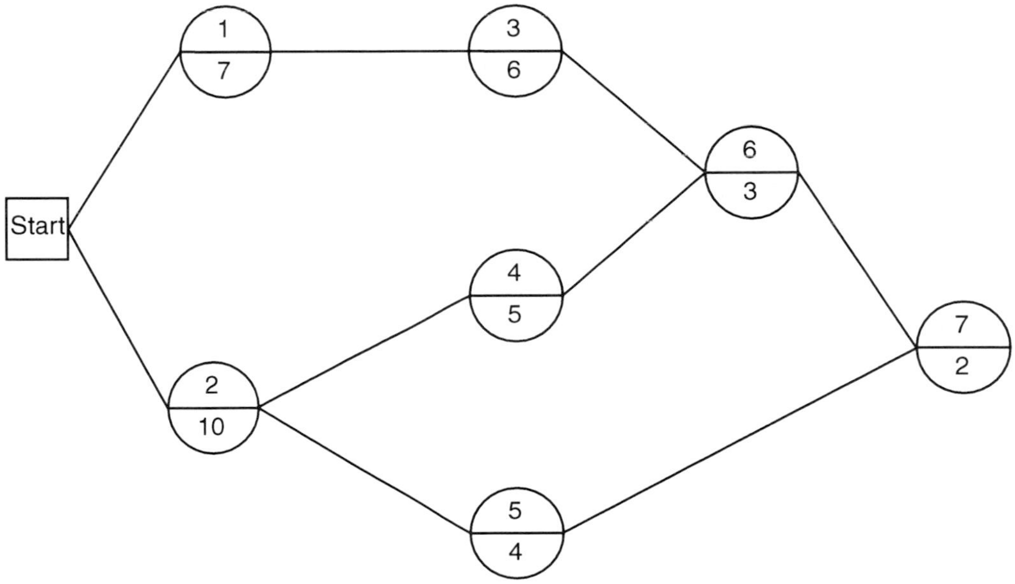

5. For the network in Problem 4, determine the earliest and latest activity times and the slack for each activity. Indicate how the critical path would be determined from this information.

6. Given the following network, with activity times in months, determine the earliest and latest activity times and slack for each activity. Indicate the critical path and the project duration.

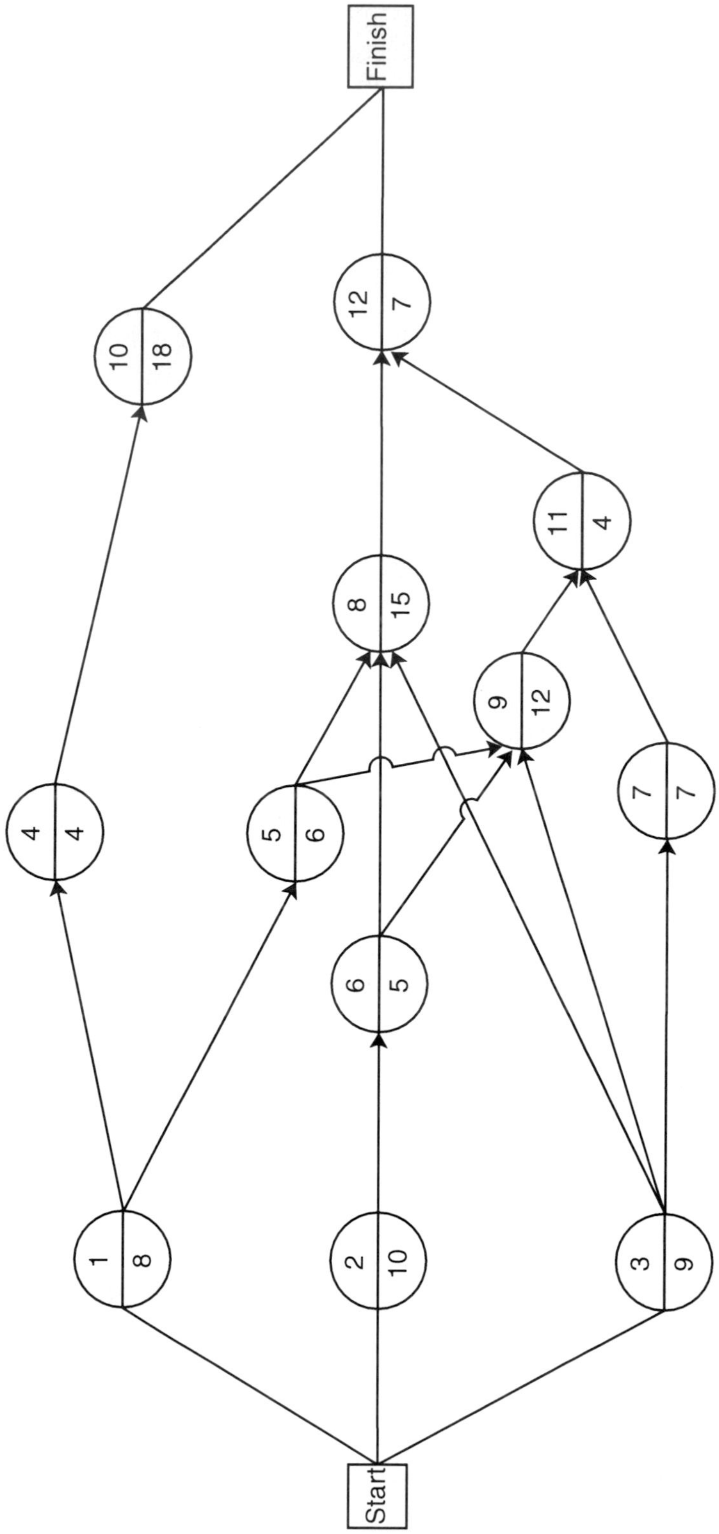
Start
1 8
2 10
3 9
4 4
5 6
6 5
7 7
8 15
9 12
10 18
11 4
12 7
Finish

7. Given the following network, with activity times in weeks, determine the earliest and latest activity times and the slack for each activity. Indicate the critical path and the project duration:

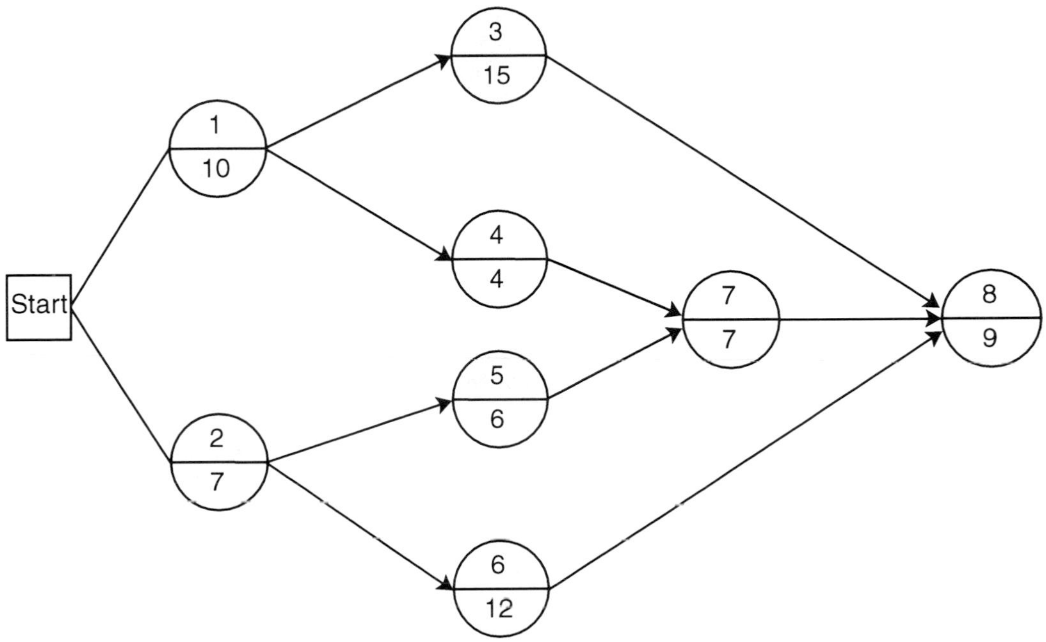

8. In one of the little-known battles of the Civil War, General Tecumseh Beauregard lost the Third Battle of Bull Run because his preparations were not complete when the enemy attacked. If the critical path method had been available, the general could have planned better. Suppose that the following planning network, with activity times in days, had been available:

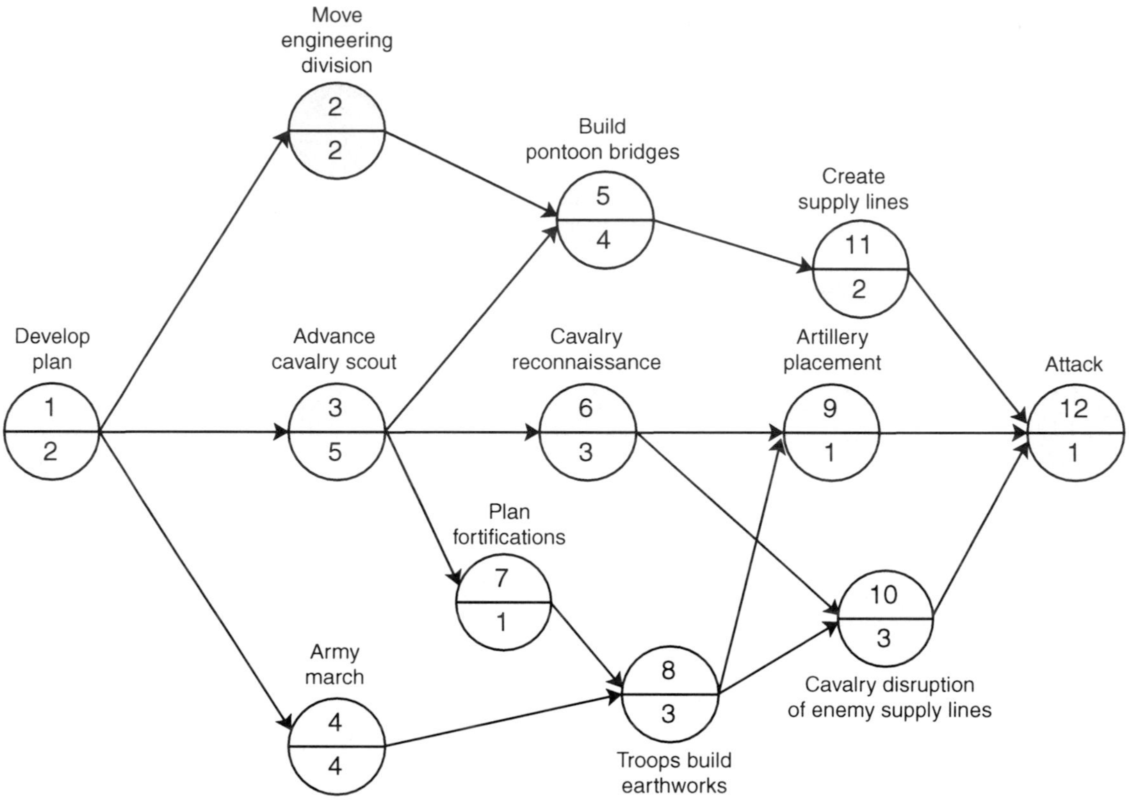

Determine the earliest and latest activity times and the activity slack for the network. Indicate the critical path and the time between the general's receipt of battle orders and the onset of battle.

9. A group of developers is building a new shopping center. A consultant for the developers has constructed the following project network and assigned activity times, in weeks.

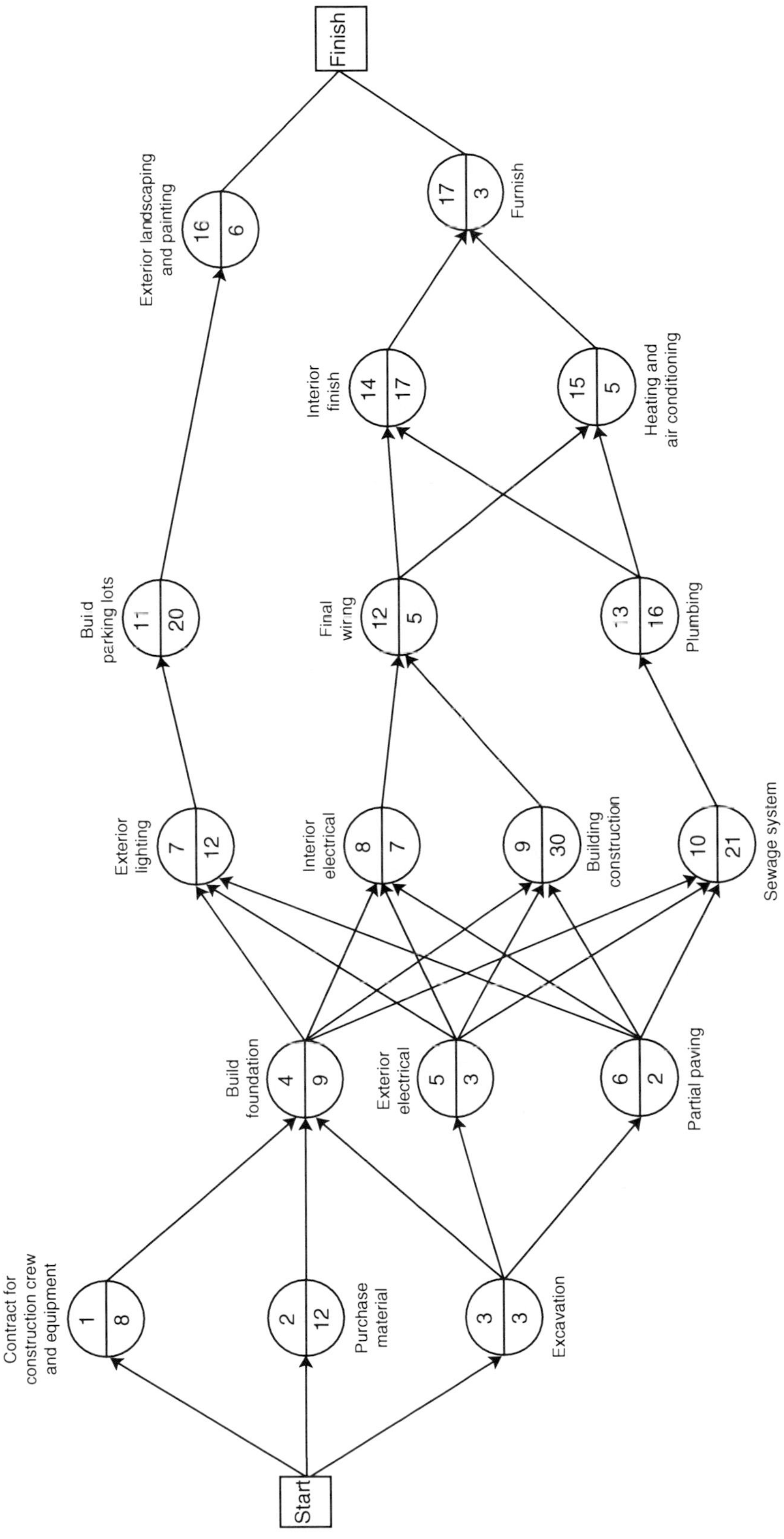

Start
1
8
Contract for construction crew and equipment
2
12
Purchase material
3
3
Excavation
4
9
Build foundation
5
3
Exterior electrical
6
2
Partial paving
7
12
Exterior lighting
8
7
Interior electrical
9
30
Building construction
10
21
Sewage system
11
20
Build parking lots
12
5
Final wiring
13
16
Plumbing
14
17
Interior finish
15
5
Heating and air conditioning
16
6
Exterior landscaping and painting
17
3
Furnish
Finish

Determine the earliest and latest activity times, activity slack, critical path, and duration for the project.

10. A farm owner is going to erect a maintenance building with a connecting electrical generator and water tank. The activities, activity descriptions, and estimated durations are given in the following table:

Activity	Activity Description	Activity Predecessor	Activity Duration (weeks)
a	Excavate	—	2
b	Erect building	a	6
c	Install generator	a	4
d	Install tank	a	2
e	Install maintenance equipment	b	4
f	Connect generator and tank to building	b, c, d	5
g	Paint finish	b	3
h	Check out facility	e, f	2

(Notice that the activities are defined not by node numbers but by activity descriptions. This alternative form of expressing activities and precedence relationships is often used in CPM/PERT.) Construct the network for this project, identify the critical path, and determine the project duration time.

11. Given the following network and activity time estimates, determine the expected time and variance for each activity and indicate the critical path:

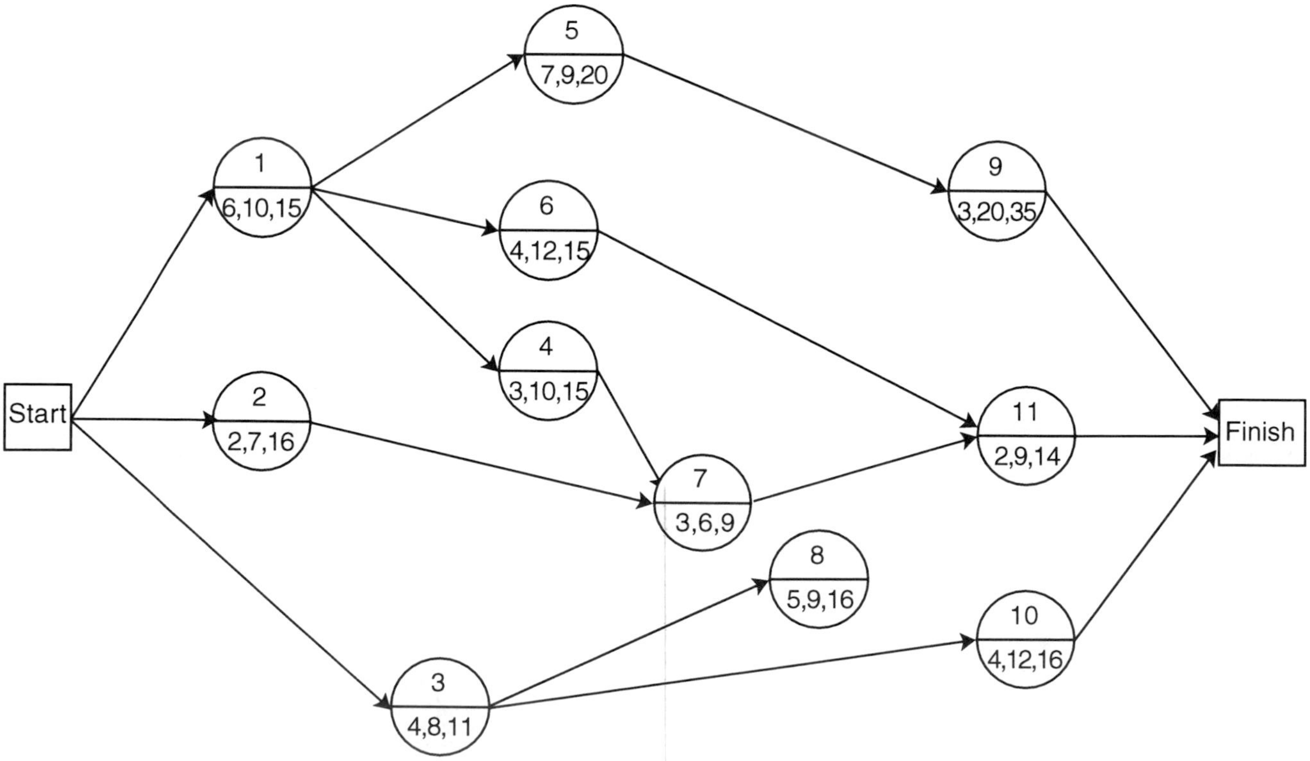

12. The Farmer's American Bank of Leesburg is planning to install a new computerized accounts system. Bank management has determined the activities required to complete the project, the precedence relationships of the activities, and activity time estimates, as shown in the following table:

Activity	Activity Description	Activity Predecessor	Time Estimates (weeks)		
			a	*m*	*b*
a	Position recruiting	—	5	8	17
b	System development	—	3	12	15
c	System training	a	4	7	10
d	Equipment training	a	5	8	23
e	Manual system test	b, c	1	1	1
f	Preliminary system changeover	b, c	1	4	13
g	Computer–personnel interface	d, e	3	6	9
h	Equipment modification	d, e	1	2.5	7
i	Equipment testing	h	1	1	1
j	System debugging and installation	f, g	2	2	2
k	Equipment changeover	g, i	5	8	11

Determine the expected project completion time and variance and determine the probability that the project will be completed in 40 weeks or less.

13. The following activity time estimates are for the network in Problem 6:

Activity	Time Estimates (mo.)		
	a	*m*	*b*
1	4	8	12
2	6	10	15
3	2	10	14
4	1	4	13
5	3	6	9
6	3	6	18
7	2	8	12
8	9	15	22
9	5	12	21
10	7	20	25
11	5	6	12
12	3	8	20

Determine the following:

a. Expected activity times
b. Earliest activity times
c. Latest activity times
d. Activity slack
e. Critical path
f. Expected project duration and variance

14. The following activity time estimates are for the network in Problem 8:

Activity	Time Estimates (days)		
	a	*m*	*b*
1	1	2	6
2	1	3	5
3	3	5	10
4	3	6	14
5	2	4	9
6	2	3	7
7	1	1.5	2
8	1	3	5
9	1	1	5
10	2	4	9
11	1	2	3
12	1	1	1

Determine the following:

a. Expected activity times
b. Earliest activity times
c. Latest activity times
d. Activity slack
e. Critical path
f. Expected project duration and variance

15. For the CPM/PERT network in Problem 13, determine the probability that the network duration will exceed 50 months.

16. The Center for Information Technology at State University has outgrown its office in Bates (B) Hall and is moving to Allen (A) Hall, which has more space. The move will take place during the 3-week break between the end of summer semester and the beginning of fall semester. Movers will be hired from the university's physical plant to move the furniture, boxes of books, and files that the faculty will pack. The center has hired a local retail computer firm to move its office computers so they won't be damaged. Following is a list of activities, their precedence relationships, and probabilistic time estimates for this project:

Activity	Activity Description	Activity Predecessor	Time Estimates (days)		
			a	*m*	*b*
a	Pack A offices	—	1	3	5
b	Network A offices	—	2	3	5
c	Pack B offices	—	2	4	7
d	Movers move A offices	a	1	3	4
e	Paint and clean A offices	d	2	5	8
f	Move computers	b, e	1	2	2
g	Movers move B offices	b, c, e	3	6	8
h	Computer installation	f	2	4	5
i	Faculty move and unpack	g	3	4	6
j	Faculty set up computers and offices	h, i	1	2	4

Determine the earliest and latest start and finish times, the critical path, and the expected project duration. What is the probability that the center will complete its move before the start of the fall semester?

17. Jane and Jim Smith are going to give a dinner party on Friday evening at 7:00 P.M. Their two children, Jerry and Judy, are going to help them get ready. The Smiths will all get home from work and school at 4:00 P.M. Jane and Jim have developed a project network to help them schedule their dinner preparations. Following is a list of the activities, the precedence relationships, and the activity times involved in the project:

Activity	Activity Description	Activity Predecessor	Time Estimates (min.)		
			a	*m*	*b*
a	Prepare salad	—	18	25	31
b	Prepare appetizer	—	15	23	30
c	Dust/clean	—	25	40	56
d	Vacuum	c	20	30	45
e	Prepare dessert	a, b	12	21	30
f	Set table	d	10	17	25
g	Get ice from market	f	5	12	18
h	Prepare/start tenderloin	e	10	20	25
i	Cut and prepare vegetables	e	9	15	22
j	Jim shower and dress	g	8	10	15
k	Jane shower and dress	h, i, j	20	27	40
l	Uncork wine/water carafes	h, i, j	6	10	15
m	Prepare bread	k, l	4	7	10
n	Prepare and set out dishes	k, l	10	14	20
o	Cut meat	k, l	7	15	20
p	Heat vegetable dish	k, l	3	4	6
q	Put out appetizers	m	4	6	7
r	Pour champagne	o	5	8	10

Develop a project network and determine the earliest and latest start and finish times, activity slack, and critical path. Compute the probability that they will be ready by 7:00 P.M.

18. The Stone River Textile Mill was inspected by OSHA and found to be in violation of a number of safety regulations. The OSHA inspectors ordered the mill to alter some existing machinery to make it safer (add safety guards, etc.); purchase some new machinery to replace older, dangerous machinery; and relocate some machinery to make safer passages and unobstructed entrances and exits. OSHA gave the mill only 35 weeks to make the changes; if the changes were not made by then, the mill would be fined $300,000.

The mill determined the activities in a CPM/PERT network that would have to be completed and then estimated the indicated activity times, as shown in the following table:

Activity	Activity Description	Activity Predecessor	Time Estimates (weeks) *a*	*m*	*b*
a	Order new machinery	—	1	2	3
b	Plan new physical layout	—	2	5	8
c	Determine safety changes in existing machinery	—	1	3	5
d	Receive equipment	a	4	10	25
e	Hire new employees	a	3	7	12
f	Make plant alterations	b	10	15	25
g	Make changes in existing machinery	c	5	9	14
h	Train new employees	d, e	2	3	7
i	Install new machinery	d, e, f	1	4	6
j	Relocate old machinery	d, e, f, g	2	5	10
k	Conduct employee safety orientation	h, i, j	2	2	2

Construct the project network for this project and determine the following:

a. Expected activity times
b. Earliest and latest activity times and activity slack
c. Critical path
d. Expected project duration and variance
e. The probability that the mill will be fined $300,000

19. In the Third Battle of Bull Run, for which a CPM/PERT network was developed in Problem 14, General Beauregard would have won if his preparations had been completed in 15 days. What would the probability of General Beauregard's winning the battle have been?

20. On May 21, 1927, Charles Lindbergh landed at Le Bourget Field in Paris, completing his famous transatlantic solo flight. The preparation period prior to his flight was quite hectic, and time was very critical because several other famous pilots of the day were also planning transatlantic flights. Once Ryan Aircraft was contracted to build the *Spirit of St. Louis*, it took only a little over 2.5 months to construct the plane and fly it to New York for the takeoff. If CPM/PERT had been available to Charles Lindbergh, it no doubt would have been useful in helping him plan this project. Use your imagination and assume that a CPM/PERT network with the following estimated activity times was developed for the flight.

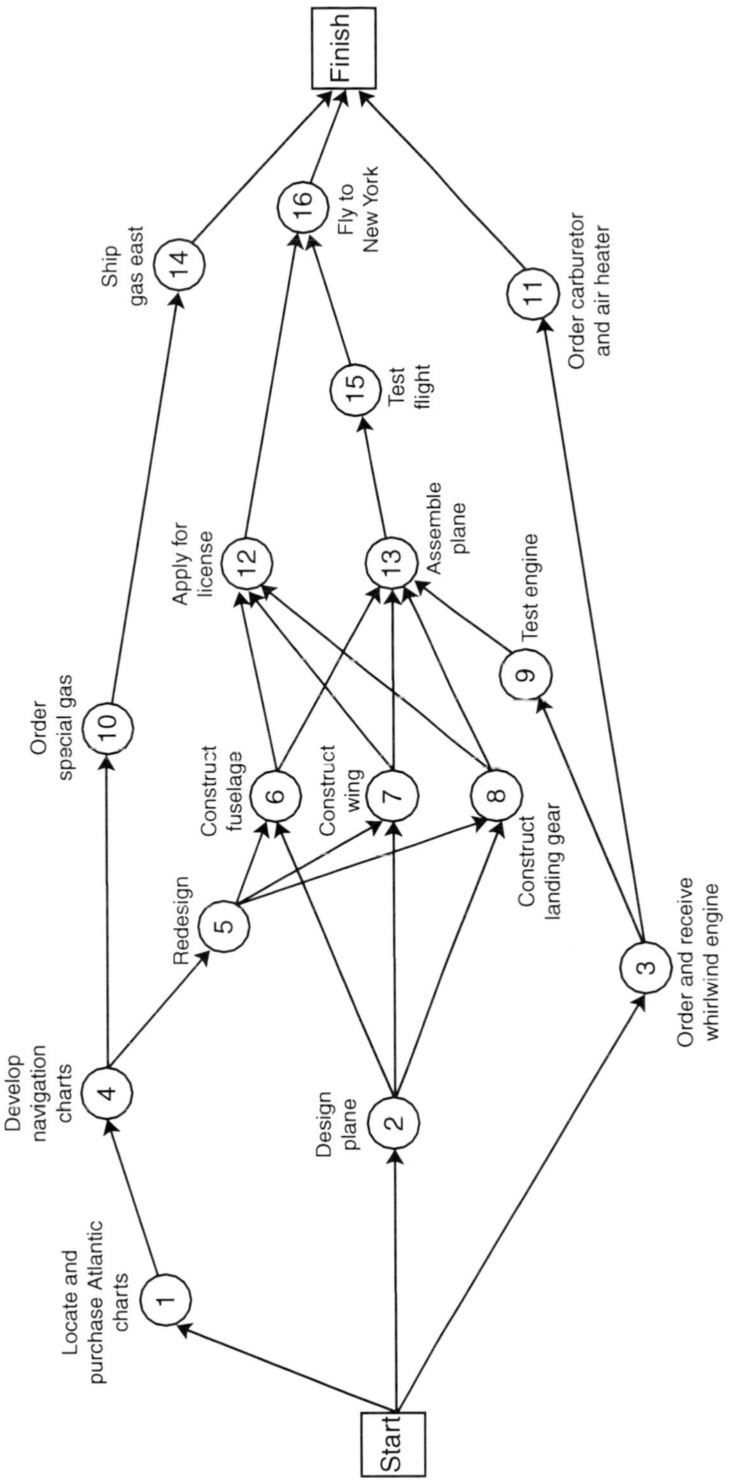

Start
1
Locate and purchase Atlantic charts
2
Design plane
3
Order and receive whirlwind engine
4
Develop navigation charts
5
Redesign
6
Construct fuselage
7
Construct wing
8
Construct landing gear
9
Test engine
10
Order special gas
11
Order carburetor and air heater
12
Apply for license
13
Assemble plane
14
Ship gas east
15
Test flight
16
Fly to New York
Finish

	Time Estimates (days)		
Activity	a	m	b
1	1	3	5
2	4	6	10
3	20	35	50
4	4	7	12
5	2	3	5
6	8	12	25
7	10	16	21
8	5	9	15
9	1	2	2
10	6	8	14
11	5	8	12
12	5	10	15
13	4	7	10
14	5	7	12
15	5	9	20
16	1	3	7

Determine the expected project duration and variance and the probability of completing the project in 67 days.

21. RusTech Tooling is a large job shop operation that builds machine tools and dies to manufacture parts for specialized items. The company primarily bids on government-related contracts to produce parts for such items as military aircraft and weapons systems, as well as the space program. The company is bidding on a contract to produce a component part for the fuselage assembly in a new space shuttle. A major criterion for selecting the winning bid, besides low cost, is the time required to produce the part. However, if the company is awarded the contract, it will be strictly held to the completion date specified in the bid, and any delays will result in severe financial penalties. To determine the project completion time to put in its bid, the company has identified the project activities, precedence relationships, and activity times shown in the following table:

		Time Estimates (weeks)		
Activity	Activity Predecessor	a	m	b
a	—	3	5	9
b	a	2	5	8
c	a	1	4	6
d	a	4	6	10
e	b	2	8	11
f	b	5	9	16
g	c	4	12	20
h	c	6	9	13
i	d	3	7	14
j	d	8	14	22
k	f, g	9	12	20
l	h, i	6	11	15
m	e	4	7	12
n	j	3	8	16
o	n	5	10	18

If RusTech wants to be 90% certain that it can deliver the part without incurring a penalty, what time frame should it specify in the bid?

22. PM Computers is an international manufacturer of computer equipment and software. It is going to introduce a number of new products in the coming year, and it wants to develop marketing programs to accompany the product introductions. The marketing program includes the preparation of printed materials distributed directly by the company and used by the company's marketing personnel, vendors, and representatives; print advertising in regular magazines, trade journals, and newspapers; and television commercials. The program also includes extensive training programs for marketing personnel, vendors, and representatives about the new products. A project management team with members from the marketing department and manufacturing areas has developed the following list of activities for the development of the marketing program:

			Time Estimates (days)		
Activity	Activity Description	Activity Predecessor	*a*	*m*	*b*
a	Preliminary budget and plan approval	—	10	15	20
b	Select marketing personnel for training	—	5	9	12
c	Develop overall media plan	a	15	25	30
d	Prepare separate media plans	c	12	20	25
e	Develop training plan	c	5	8	12
f	Design training course	e	6	14	20
g	Train marketing personnel	b, f	16	20	25
h	Plan TV commercials with agency	d	15	25	35
i	Draft in-house print materials	d	8	15	20
j	Develop print advertising layouts with agency	d	16	23	30
k	Review print advertising layouts	j	4	9	12
l	Review TV commercials	h	3	7	12
m	Review and print in-house materials	i	3	5	7
n	Release advertising to print media	g, i, k	2	4	8
o	Release TV commercials to networks	l	4	7	10
p	Final marketing personnel review	g, i, k	4	5	9
q	Run media advertising, mailings	m, n, o	15	20	30

Construct the network for this project and determine the activity schedule. Identify the critical path and determine the expected project duration time and variance. What is the probability that the program can be completed within 4 months?

23. A marketing firm is planning to conduct a survey of a segment of the potential product audience for one of its customers. The planning process for preparing to conduct the survey consists of six activities, with precedence relationships and activity time estimates as follows:

Activity	Activity Description	Activity Predecessor	Time Estimate (days)
a	Determine survey objectives	—	3
b	Select and hire personnel	a	3
c	Design questionnaire	a	5
d	Train personnel	b, c	4
e	Select target audience	c	3
f	Make personnel assignments	d, e	2

a. Determine all paths through the network from node a to node f and the duration of each. Also indicate the critical path.
b. Determine the earliest and latest activity start and finish times.
c. Determine the slack for each activity.

24. Lakeland-Bering Aircraft Company is preparing a contract proposal to submit to the defense department for a new military aircraft, the X-300J jet fighter. Part of the proposal is a development and productions schedule for completion of the first aircraft. The project consists of three primary categories: engine design and development, development and production of the airframe (e.g., the aircraft body), and design and development of the aircraft avionics (e.g., the electronic systems, equipment, and other devices used to operate and control the aircraft). Following is a list of the project activities, with time estimates (in months):

Activity	Activity Description	Activity Predecessor	Time Estimates (mo.)		
			a	*m*	*b*
1	General design	—	5	10	22
2	Engine design	—	20	33	57
3	Airframe design	1	6	17	33
4	Avionics design	1	2	8	20
5	Develop test engine	2	7	10	12
6	Develop test airframe	3	8	11	18
7	Develop interim avionics	4	7	15	28
8	Develop engine	2	19	24	41
9	Assemble test aircraft	5, 6, 7	4	6	10
10	Test avionics	4	5	10	16
11	Conduct engine/airframe flight trials	9	5	9	12
12	Conduct avionics flight trials	10	5	9	24
13	Produce engine	8	11	14	15
14	Produce airframe	11	12	15	20
15	Produce avionics	11, 12	14	16	25
16	Final assembly/finish	13, 14, 15	2	3	5

Develop the project network and determine the critical path, the expected project duration, and the variance. What is the probability that the project will be completed within 8 years?

25. The Valley United Soccer Club is planning a soccer tournament for the weekend of April 29 and 30. The club's officers know that by March 30 they must send out acceptances to teams that have applied to enter and that by April 15 they must send out the tournament game schedule to teams that have been selected to play. Their tentative plan is to begin the initial activities for tournament preparation, including sending out the application forms to prospective teams, on January 20. Following is a list of tournament activities, their precedence relationships, and estimates of their duration, in days:

Activity	Activity Description	Activity Predecessor	Time Estimates (days)		
			a	m	b
a	Send application forms	—	5	7	10
b	Get volunteer workers	—	10	18	26
c	Line up referees	—	7	10	14
d	Reserve fields	—	14	21	35
e	Receive and process forms	a	30	30	30
f	Determine age divisions	b, c, d, e	4	9	12
g	Assign fields to divisions	f	4	7	10
h	Sell program ads	b	14	21	30
i	Acquire donated items for team gift bags	b	15	20	26
j	Schedule games	g	6	14	18
k	Design ads	h	5	8	10
l	Fill gift bags	i	9	12	17
m	Process team T-shirt orders	e	7	10	14
n	Send acceptance letters	f	4	7	12
o	Design and print programs	j, k, l, n	14	18	24
p	Put together registration boxes (programs, gifts, etc.)	o	5	7	10
q	Send out game schedules	j, k, l, n	5	8	12
r	Assign referees to games	j, k, l, n	4	7	10
s	Get trophies	f	20	28	35
t	Silk-screen T-shirts	m	12	17	25
u	Package team T-shirt orders	t	5	8	12

Develop a project network for the club's tournament preparation process and determine the likelihood that it will meet its schedule milestones and complete the process according to the scheduled tournament date of April 29.

26. During a violent thunderstorm with very high wind gusts in the third week of March, the broadcast tower for the public radio station WVPR, atop Poor Mountain in Roanoke, collapsed. This greatly reduced the strength of the station's signal in the area. The station management immediately began plans to construct a new tower. Following is a list of the required activities for building the new tower with optimistic (a), most likely (m), and pessimistic (b) time estimates (in days); however, the sequence of the activities has not been designated:

Activity	Activity Description	Time Estimates (days)		
		a	m	b
a	Removal of debris	5	8	12
b	Survey new tower site	3	6	8
c	Procure structural steel	15	21	30
d	Procure electrical/broadcasting equipment	18	32	40
e	Grade tower site	4	7	10
f	Pour concrete footings and anchors	10	18	22
g	Deliver and unload steel	3	5	9
h	Deliver and unload electrical/broadcast equipment	1	2	4
i	Erect tower	25	35	50
j	Connect electrical cables between tower and building	4	6	10
k	Construct storm drains and tiles	10	15	21
l	Backfill and grade tower site	4	7	9
m	Clean up	3	6	10
n	Obtain inspection approval	1	4	7

Using your best judgment, develop a CPM/PERT network for this project and determine the expected project completion time. Also determine the probability that the station signal will be back at full strength within 3 months.

27. The following table contains the activities for planning a wedding and the activity time estimates; however, the precedence relationships between activities are not included:

		Time (days)		
Activity	Activity Description	*a*	*m*	*b*
a	Determine date	1	10	15
b	Obtain marriage license	1	5	8
c	Select bridal attendants	3	5	7
d	Order dresses	10	14	21
e	Fit dresses	5	10	12
f	Select groomsmen	1	2	4
g	Order tuxedos	3	5	7
h	Find and rent church	6	14	20
i	Hire florist	3	6	10
j	Develop/print programs	15	22	30
k	Hire photographer	3	10	15
l	Develop guest list	14	25	40
m	Order invitations	7	12	20
n	Address and mail invitations	10	15	25
o	Compile RSVP list	30	45	60
p	Reserve reception hall	3	7	10
q	Hire caterer	2	5	8
r	Determine reception menu	10	12	16
s	Make final order	2	4	7
t	Hire band	10	18	21
u	Decorate reception hall	1	2	3
v	Wedding ceremony	0.5	0.5	0.5
w	Wedding reception	0.5	0.5	0.5

Using your best judgment, determine the project network, critical path, and expected project duration. If it is January 1 and a couple is planning a June 1 wedding, what is the probability that it can be done on time?

28. The following table provides the information necessary to construct a project network and project crash data:

			Activity Time (weeks)		Activity Cost	
Activity	(i, j)	Activity Predecessor	*Normal*	*Crash*	*Normal*	*Crash*
a	(1, 2)	—	20	8	$1,000	$1,480
b	(1, 4)	—	24	20	1,200	1,400
c	(1, 3)	—	14	7	700	1,190
d	(2, 4)	a	10	6	500	820
e	(3, 4)	c	11	5	550	730

a. Construct the project network.

b. Compute the total allowable crash time per activity and the crash cost per week for each activity.

c. Determine the maximum possible crash time for the network and manually crash the network the maximum amount.
d. Compute the normal project cost and the cost of the crashed project.
e. Formulate the general linear programming model for this network and solve it.
f. Formulate the linear programming crashing model that would crash this network by the maximum amount and solve it.

29. The following table provides the information necessary to construct a project network and project crash data:

			Activity Time (weeks)		Activity Cost	
Activity	(i, j)	Activity Predecessor	*Normal*	*Crash*	*Normal*	*Crash*
a	(1, 2)	—	16	8	$2,000	$4,400
b	(1, 3)	—	14	9	1,000	1,800
c	(2, 4)	a	8	6	500	700
d	(2, 5)	a	5	4	600	1,300
e	(3, 5)	b	4	2	1,500	3,000
f	(3, 6)	b	6	4	800	1,600
g	(4, 6)	c	10	7	3,000	4,500
h	(5, 6)	d, e	15	10	5,000	8,000

a. Construct the project network.
b. Manually crash the network to 28 weeks.
c. Formulate the general linear programming model for this network.
d. Formulate the linear programming crashing model that would crash this model by the maximum amount.

30. Formulate the general linear programming model for Problem 4, and solve it.

31. Formulate the general linear programming model for the project network for installing an order processing system shown in Figure 14 and solve it.

32. Reconstruct the example problem at the end of this chapter as an AOA network. Assume that the most likely times (m) are the normal activity times and that the optimistic times (a) are the activity crash times. Further assume that the activities have the following normal and crash costs:

Activity	(i, j)	Costs (normal cost, crash cost)
1	(1, 2)	($100, $400)
2	(1, 3)	($250, $400)
3	(2, 3)	($400, $800)
4	(2, 4)	($200, $400)
5	(3, 4)	($150, $300)
6	(3, 5)	($100, $100)
7	(4, 5)	($300, $500)

a. Formulate the general linear programming model for this project network, using most likely activity times (m).

b. Formulate the linear programming crashing model that would crash this network by the maximum amount.
c. Solve this model by using the computer.

33. The following table provides the crash data for the network project described in Problem 12:

	Activity Time (weeks)		Activity Cost	
Activity	*Normal*	*Crash*	*Normal*	*Crash*
a	9	7	$4,800	$ 6,300
b	11	9	9,100	15,500
c	7	5	3,000	4,000
d	10	8	3,600	5,000
e	1	1	0	0
f	5	3	1,500	2,000
g	6	5	1,800	2,000
h	3	3	0	0
i	1	1	0	0
j	2	2	0	0
k	8	6	5,000	7,000

The normal activity times are considered to be deterministic and not probabilistic. Using the computer, crash the network to 26 weeks. Indicate how much it would cost the bank and then indicate the critical path.

34. The following table provides the crash data for the network project described in Problem 6:

	Activity Time (months)		Activity Cost ($1,000s)	
Activity	*Normal*	*Crash*	*Normal*	*Crash*
1	8	5	$ 700	$1,200
2	10	9	1,600	2,000
3	9	7	900	1,500
4	4	2	500	700
5	6	3	500	900
6	5	4	500	800
7	7	5	700	1,000
8	15	12	1,400	2,000
9	12	10	1,800	2,300
10	18	14	1,400	3,200
11	4	3	500	800
12	7	6	800	1,400

Using the computer, crash the network to 32 months. Indicate the first critical path activities and then the cost of crashing the network.

Case Problem

THE BLOODLESS COUP CONCERT

John Aaron called the meeting of the Programs and Arts Committee of the Student Government Association to order.

"Okay, okay, everybody, quiet down. I have an important announcement to make," he shouted above the noise. The room got quiet, and John started again, "Well, you guys, we can have the Coup."

His audience looked puzzled, and Randy Jones asked, "What coup have we scored this time, John?"

"The Coup, the Coup! You know, the rock group, the Bloodless Coup!"

Everyone in the room cheered and started talking excitedly. John stood up and waved his arms and shouted, "Hey, calm down, everybody, and listen up." The room quieted again, and everyone focused on John. "The good news is that they can come." He paused a moment. "The bad news is that they will be here in 18 days."

The students groaned and seemed to share Jim Hastings' feelings: "No way, man. It can't be done. Why can't we put it off for a couple of weeks?"

John answered, "They're just starting their new tour and are looking for some warm-up concerts. They'll be traveling near here for their first concert date in DC and saw they had a letter from us, so they said they could come now. But that's it—now or never." He looked around the room at the solemn faces. "Look, you guys, we can handle this. Let's think of what we have to do. Come on, perk up. Let's make a list of everything we have to do to get ready and figure out how long it will take. So somebody tell me what we have to do first!"

Anna Mendoza shouted from the back of the room, "We have to find a place; you know, get an auditorium somewhere. I've done that before, and it should take anywhere from 2 days up to 7 days, most likely about 4 days."

"Okay, that's great," John said, as he wrote down the activity "Secure auditorium" on the blackboard, with the times out to the side. "What's next?"

"We need to print tickets—and quick," Tracey Shea called. "It could only take 1 day if the printer isn't busy, but it could take up to 4 days if he is. It should probably take about 2 days."

"But we can't print tickets until we know where the concert will be because of the security arrangement," Andy Taylor noted.

"Right," said John. "Get the auditorium first; then print the tickets. What else?"

"We need to make hotel and transportation arrangements for the Coup and their entourage while they're here," Jim Hastings proposed. "But we better not do that until we get the auditorium. If we can't find a place for the concert, everything falls through."

"How long do you think it will take to make the arrangements?" John asked.

"Oh, between 3 and 10 days, probably about 5, most likely," Jim answered.

"We also have to negotiate with the local union for concert employees, stagehands, and whoever else we need to hire," Reggie Wilkes interjected. "That could take 1 day or up to 8 days, but 3 days would be my best guess."

"We should probably also hold off on talking to the union until we get the auditorium," John added. "That will probably be a factor in the negotiations."

"After we work things out with the union, we can hire some stagehands," Reggie continued. "That could take as few as 2 days but as long as 7. I imagine it'll take about 4 days. We should also be able to get some student ushers at the same time, once we get union approval. That could take only 1 day, but it has taken 5 days in the past; 3 days is probably the most likely."

"We need to arrange a press conference," said Art Cohen, who was leaning against a wall. "This is a heavy group, big time."

"But doesn't a press conference usually take place at the hotel?" John asked.

"Yeah, that's right," Art answered. "We can't make arrangements for the press conference until we work things out with the hotel. When we do that, it should take about 3 days to set up a press conference—2 days if we're lucky, and 4 at the most."

The room got quiet as everyone thought.

"What else?" John asked.

"Hey, I know," Annie Roark spoke up. "Once we hire the stagehands, they have to set up the stage. I think that could be done in a couple of days, but it could take up to 6 days, with 3 most likely." She paused for a moment before adding, "And we can also assign the ushers to their jobs once we hire them. That shouldn't take long, maybe only 1 day—3 days worst, probably 2 days would be a good time to put down."

"We also have to do some advertising and promotion if we want people to show up for this thing," mentioned Art nonchalantly. "I guess we need to wait until we print the tickets, so we'll have something to sell. That depends on the media, the paper, and radio stations. I've worked with this before. It could get done really quick, like 2 days, if we can make the right contacts. But it could take a lot longer, like 12 days, if we hit any snags. We probably ought to count on 6 days as our best estimate."

"Hey, if we're going to promote this, shouldn't we also have a preliminary act, some other group?" Annie asked.

"Wow, I forgot all about that!" John exclaimed. "Hiring another act will take me between 4 and 8 days; I can probably do it in 5. I can start on that right away, at the same time you guys are arranging for an auditorium." He thought for a moment. "But we really can't begin to work on the promotion until I get the lead-in group. So what's left?"

"Sell the tickets," shouted several people at once.

"Right," said John. "We have to wait until they're printed; but I don't think we have to wait for the advertising and promotion to start, do we?"

"No," Jim replied. "But we should hire the preliminary act first so people will know what they're buying a ticket for."

"Agreed," said John. "The tickets could go quick; I suppose in the first day."

"Or," interrupted Mike Eggleston, "it could take longer. I remember 2 years ago, it took 12 days to sell out for the Cosmic Modem."

"Okay, so it's between 1 and 12 days to sell the tickets," said John, "but I think about 5 days is more likely. Everybody agree?"

The group nodded in unison, and they all turned at once to the list of activities and times John had written on the blackboard.

Use PERT analysis to determine the probability that the concert preparations will be completed in time.

Case Problem

MOORE HOUSING CONTRACTORS

Moore Housing Contractors is negotiating a deal with Countryside Realtors to build six houses in a new development. Countryside wants Moore Contractors to start in late winter or early spring, when the weather begins to moderate, and build on through the summer and into the fall. The summer months are an especially busy time for the realty company, and it believes it can sell the houses almost as soon as they are ready, and maybe even before. The houses all have similar floor plans and are of approximately equal size; only the exteriors are noticeably different. The completion time is so critical for Countryside Realtors that it is insisting that a project management network accompany the contractor's bid for the job, with an estimate of the completion time for a house. The realtor also needs to be able to plan its offerings and marketing for the summer. It wants each house to be completed within 45 days after it is started. If a house is not completed within this time frame, it wants to be able to charge the contractor a penalty. Mary and Sandy Moore, the president and vice president, respectively, of Moore Contractors, are concerned about the prospect of a penalty charge. They want to be very confident that they can meet the deadline for a house before they enter into any kind of agreement with a penalty involved. (If there is a reasonable likelihood that they cannot finish a house within 45 days, they want to increase their bid to cover potential penalty charges.)

The Moores are experienced home builders, so it was not difficult for them to list the activities involved in building a house or to estimate activity times. However, they made their estimates conservatively and tended to increase their pessimistic estimates to compensate for the possibility of bad weather and variations in their workforce. Following is a list of the activities involved in building a house and the activity time estimates:

Activity	Activity Description	Predecessors	Time (days) a	m	b
a	Excavation, pour footers	—	3	4	6
b	Lay foundation	a	2	3	5
c	Frame and roof	b	2	4	5
d	Lay drain tiles	b	1	2	4
e	Sewer (floor) drains	b	1	2	3
f	Install insulation	c	2	4	5
g	Pour basement floor	e	2	3	5
h	Rough plumbing, pipes	e	2	4	7
i	Install windows	f	1	3	4
j	Rough electrical wiring	f	1	2	4
k	Install furnace, air conditioner	c, g	3	5	8
l	Exterior brickwork	i	5	6	10
m	Install plasterboard, mud, plaster	j, h, k	6	8	12
n	Roof shingles, flashing	l	2	3	6
o	Attach gutter, downspouts	n	1	2	5
p	Grading	d, o	2	3	7
q	Lay subflooring	m	3	4	6
r	Lay driveway, walks, landscape	p	4	6	10
s	Finish carpentry	q	3	5	12
t	Kitchen cabinetry, sink, and appliances	q	2	4	8
u	Bathroom cabinetry, fixtures	q	2	3	6
v	Painting (interior and exterior)	t, u	4	6	10
w	Finish wood floors, lay carpet	v, s	2	5	8
x	Final electrical, light fixtures	v	1	3	4

a. Develop a CPM/PERT network for Moore Housing Contractors and determine the probability that the company can complete a house within 45 days. Does it appear that the Moores might need to increase their bid to compensate for potential penalties?

b. Indicate which project activities Moore Housing Contractors should be particularly diligent to keep on schedule by making sure workers and materials are always available. Also indicate which activities the company might shift workers from as the need arises.

Solutions to Selected Odd-Numbered Problems

1. 1–3–4 = 10
3. 1–3–6–8 = 23
5. 1: $ES = 0, EF = 7, LS = 2, LF = 9, S = 2$; 2: $ES = 0, EF = 10, LS = 0, LF = 10, S = 0$; 3: $ES = 7, EF = 13, LS = 9, LF = 15, S = 2$; 4: $ES = 10, EF = 15, LS = 10, LF = 15, S = 0$; 5: $ES = 10, EF = 14, LS = 14, LF = 18, S = 4$; 6: $ES = 15, EF = 18, LS = 15, LF = 18, S = 0$; 7: $ES = 18, EF = 20, LS = 18, LF = 20, S = 0$; 2–4–6–7 = 20
7. 1: $ES = 0, EF = 10, LS = 0, LF = 10, S = 0$; 2: $ES = 0, EF = 7, LS = 5, LF = 12, S = 5$; 4: $ES = 10, EF = 14, LS = 14, LF = 18, S = 4$; 3: $ES = 10, EF = 25, LS = 10, LF = 25, S = 0$; 5: $ES = 7, EF = 13, LS = 12, LF = 18, S = 5$; 6: $ES = 7, EF = 19, LS = 13, LF = 25, S = 6$; 7: $ES = 14, EF = 21, LS = 18, LF = 25, S = 4$; 8: $ES = 25, EF = 34, LS = 25, LF = 34, S = 0$; 1–3–8 = 34
9. 2–4–10–13–14–17 = 78 wk.
11. 1–5–9 = 40.33, $\sigma = 5.95$
13. (e) 2–6–9–11–12; (f) $\mu = 46$ mo., $\sigma = 5$ mo.
15. $P(x \geq 50) = .2119$
17. c–d–f–g–j–k–o–r = 160.83 min.; $P(x \leq 180) = .9875$
19. $P(x \leq 15) = .0643$
21. a–d–j–n–o, $\mu = 42.3$ wk., $\sigma = 4.10$ wk., 47.59 wk.
23. a–c–d–f = 14 days
25. a–e–f–g–j–o–p = 91.67 days, $\sigma = 3.308$, $P(x \leq 101) = .9976$
27. a–h–l–m–n–o–s–w = 126.67 days; $P(x \leq 150) = .9979$
29. (c) min. $Z = x_6$; s.t. $x_2 - x_1 \geq 16, x_3 - x_1 \geq 14, x_4 - x_2 \geq 8, x_5 - x_2 \geq 5, x_5 - x_3 \geq 4, x_6 - x_3 \geq 6, x_6 - x_4 \geq 10, x_6 - x_5 \geq 15, x_i, x_j \geq 0$
31. min. $Z = x_9$; s.t. $x_2 - x_1 \geq 8, x_3 - x_1 \geq 6, x_4 - x_1 \geq 3, x_5 - x_2 \geq 0, x_6 - x_2 \geq 5, x_5 - x_3 \geq 3, x_5 - x_4 \geq 4, x_7 - x_5 \geq 7, x_7 - x_8 \geq 0, x_8 - x_5 \geq 4, x_8 - x_4 \geq 2, x_9 - x_6 \geq 4, x_9 - x_7 \geq 9, x_i, x_j \geq 0; x_1 = 0, x_2 = 9, x_3 = 6, x_4 = 3, x_5 = 9, x_6 = 14, x_7 = 16, x_8 = 16, x_9 = 25$
33. a–d–g–k; crash cost = \$5,100; total network cost = \$33,900

Decision Analysis

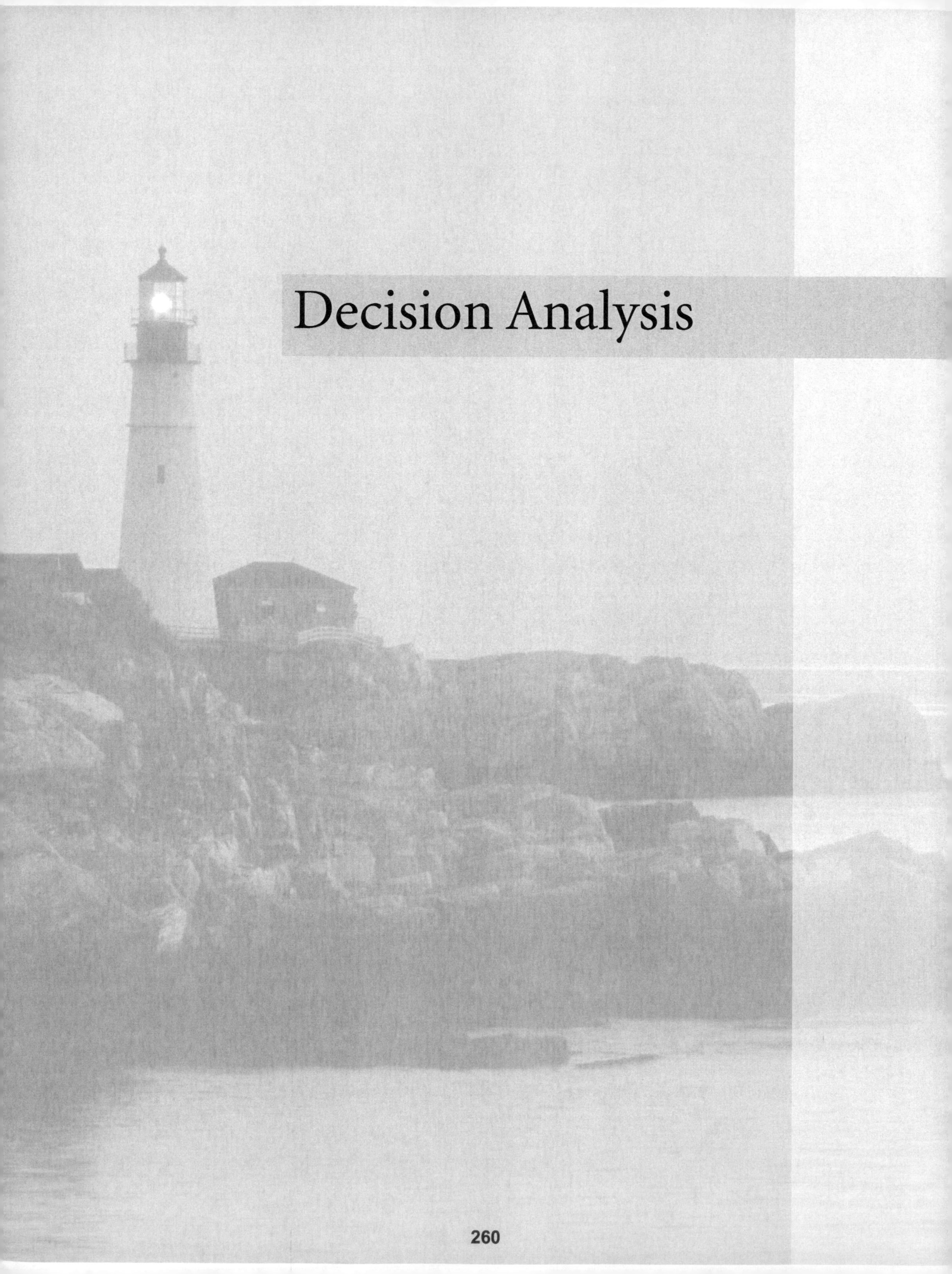

Decision Analysis

In actual practice, many decision-making situations occur under conditions of *uncertainty*. For example, the demand for a product may be not 100 units next week, but 50 or 200 units, depending on the state of the market (which is uncertain). Several decision-making techniques are available to aid the decision maker in dealing with this type of decision situation in which there is uncertainty.

The two categories of decision situations are probabilities that can *be assigned to future occurrences and probabilities that* cannot *be assigned.*

Decision situations can be categorized into two classes: situations in which probabilities *cannot* be assigned to future occurrences and situations in which probabilities *can* be assigned. In this chapter we will discuss each of these classes of decision situations separately and demonstrate the decision-making criterion most commonly associated with each. Decision situations in which there are two or more decision makers who are in competition with each other are the subject of *game theory*, a topic included on the companion CD.

Components of Decision Making

A decision-making situation includes several components—the decisions themselves *and* the actual events that may occur in the future, known as **states of nature**. At the time a decision is made, the decision maker is uncertain which states of nature will occur in the future and has no control over them.

*A **state of nature** is an actual event that may occur in the future.*

Suppose a distribution company is considering purchasing a computer to increase the number of orders it can process and thus increase its business. If economic conditions remain good, the company will realize a large increase in profit; however, if the economy takes a downturn, the company will lose money. In this decision situation, the possible decisions are to purchase the computer and to not purchase the computer. The states of nature are *good* economic conditions and *bad* economic conditions. The state of nature that occurs will determine the outcome of the decision, and it is obvious that the decision maker has no control over which state will occur.

As another example, consider a concessions vendor who must decide whether to stock coffee for the concession stands at a football game in November. If the weather is cold, most of the coffee will be sold, but if the weather is warm, very little coffee will be sold. The decision is to order or not to order coffee, and the states of nature are warm and cold weather.

*Using a **payoff table** is a means of organizing a decision situation, including the payoffs from different decisions, given the various states of nature.*

To facilitate the analysis of these types of decision situations so that the best decisions result, they are organized into **payoff tables**. In general, a payoff table is a means of organizing and illustrating the payoffs from the different decisions, given the various states of nature in a decision problem. A payoff table is constructed as shown in Table 1.

Each decision, 1 or 2, in Table 1 will result in an outcome, or *payoff*, for the particular state of nature that will occur in the future. Payoffs are typically expressed in terms of profit rev-

Table 1
Payoff table

	State of Nature	
Decision	*a*	*b*
1	Payoff 1*a*	Payoff 1*b*
2	Payoff 2*a*	Payoff 2*b*

enues, or cost (although they can be expressed in terms of a variety of values). For example, if decision 1 is to purchase a computer and state of nature *a* is good economic conditions, payoff 1*a* could be $100,000 in profit.

It is often possible to assign probabilities to the states of nature to aid the decision maker in selecting the decision that has the best outcome. However, in some cases the decision maker is not able to assign probabilities, and it is this type of decision-making situation that we will address first.

Decision Making without Probabilities

The following example will illustrate the development of a payoff table without probabilities. An investor is to purchase one of three types of real estate, as illustrated in Figure 1. The investor must decide among an apartment building, an office building, and a warehouse. The

Figure 1

Decision situation with real estate investment alternatives

future states of nature that will determine how much profit the investor will make are good economic conditions and poor economic conditions. The profits that will result from each decision in the event of each state of nature are shown in Table 2.

Table 2
Payoff table for the real estate investments

Decision (Purchase)	State of Nature: Good Economic Conditions	State of Nature: Poor Economic Conditions
Apartment building	$ 50,000	$ 30,000
Office building	100,000	−40,000
Warehouse	30,000	10,000

Decision-Making Criteria

Once the decision situation has been organized into a payoff table, several criteria are available for making the actual decision. These decision criteria, which will be presented in this section, include maximax, maximin, minimax regret, Hurwicz, and equal likelihood. On occasion these criteria will result in the same decision; however, often they will yield different decisions. The decision maker must select the criterion or combination of criteria that best suits his or her needs.

The Maximax Criterion

*The **maximax criterion** results in the maximum of the maximum payoffs.*

With the **maximax criterion**, the decision maker selects the decision that will result in the maximum of the maximum payoffs. (In fact, this is how this criterion derives its name—a maximum of a maximum.) The maximax criterion is very optimistic. The decision maker assumes that the most favorable state of nature for each decision alternative will occur. Thus, for example, using this criterion, the investor would optimistically assume that good economic conditions will prevail in the future.

The maximax criterion is applied in Table 3. The decision maker first selects the maximum payoff for each decision. Notice that all three maximum payoffs occur under good economic conditions. Of the three maximum payoffs—$50,000, $100,000, and $30,000—the maximum is $100,000; thus, the corresponding decision is to purchase the office building.

Table 3
Payoff table illustrating a maximax decision

Decision (Purchase)	State of Nature: Good Economic Conditions	State of Nature: Poor Economic Conditions
Apartment building	$ 50,000	$ 30,000
Office building	100,000	−40,000
Warehouse	30,000	10,000

Maximum payoff (→ 100,000)

Although the decision to purchase an office building will result in the largest payoff ($100,000), such a decision completely ignores the possibility of a potential loss of $40,000. The decision maker who uses the maximax criterion assumes a very optimistic future with respect to the state of nature.

Management Science Application

Decision Analysis at DuPont

DuPont has used decision analysis extensively since the mid-1960s to create, evaluate, and implement strategic alternatives within 10 of its businesses, each worldwide in scope. As an example, one of these DuPont businesses was experiencing declining financial performance due to eroding prices and loss of market share to European and Japanese competitors. The business identified three possible strategies to evaluate from a number of alternatives. These strategies were (1) to continue with the current strategy, (2) to reestablish product leadership by strengthening new product development efforts and product differentiation, and (3) to establish a low-cost market position by closing a plant and streamlining the product line to improve production efficiency. Uncertainties in the evaluation process derived from competitor strategies and from market size, share, and prices. The decision criterion was net present value for each of the three strategies, calculated using a Super Tree spreadsheet model. The ultimate decision was to strengthen product development and product differentiation. The selected strategy resulted in an approximate increase in value of $175 million.

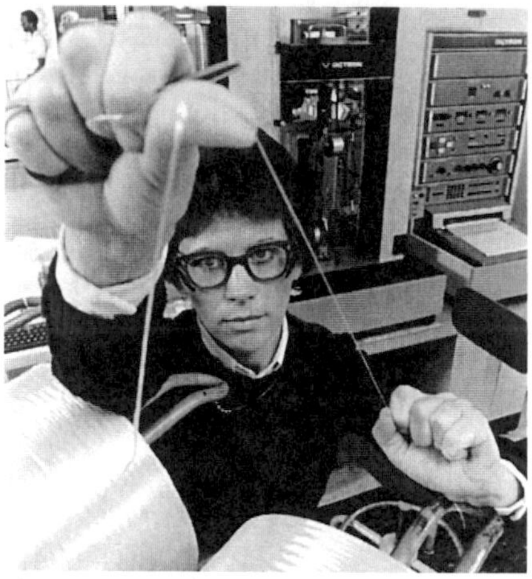

Photo courtesy of DuPont Kevlar®

Source: F. Krumm and C. Rolle, "Management and Application of Decision and Risk Analysis in DuPont," *Interfaces* 22, no. 6 (November–December 1992): 84–93.

Before the next criterion is presented, it should be pointed out that the maximax decision rule as presented here deals with *profit*. However, if the payoff table consisted of costs, the opposite selection would be indicated: the minimum of the minimum costs, or a *minimin* criterion. For the subsequent decision criteria we encounter, the same logic in the case of costs can be used.

The Maximin Criterion

*The **maximin criterion** results in the maximum of the minimum payoff.*

In contrast with the maximax criterion, which is very optimistic, the **maximin criterion** is pessimistic. With the maximin criterion, the decision maker selects the decision that will reflect the *maximum* of the *minimum* payoffs. For each decision alternative, the decision maker assumes that the minimum payoff will occur. Of these minimum payoffs, the maximum is selected. The maximin criterion for our investment example is demonstrated in Table 4.

Table 4
Payoff table illustrating a maximin decision

Decision (Purchase)	State of Nature: Good Economic Conditions	State of Nature: Poor Economic Conditions	
Apartment building	$ 50,000	$ 30,000	← Maximum payoff
Office building	100,000	−40,000	
Warehouse	30,000	10,000	

The minimum payoffs for our example are \$30,000, −\$40,000, and \$10,000. The maximum of these three payoffs is \$30,000; thus, the decision arrived at by using the maximin criterion would be to purchase the apartment building. This decision is relatively conservative because the alternatives considered include only the worst outcomes that could occur. The decision to purchase the office building as determined by the maximax criterion includes the possibility of a large loss (−\$40,000). The worst that can occur from the decision to purchase the apartment building, however, is *a gain of \$30,000*. On the other hand, the largest possible gain from purchasing the apartment building is much less than that of purchasing the office building (i.e., \$50,000 vs. \$100,000).

If Table 4 contained costs instead of profits as the payoffs, the conservative approach would be to select the maximum cost for each decision. Then the decision that resulted in the minimum of these costs would be selected.

The Minimax Regret Criterion

Regret is the difference between the payoff from the best decision and all other decision payoffs.

*The **minimax regret criterion** minimizes the maximum regret.*

In our example, suppose the investor decided to purchase the warehouse, only to discover that economic conditions in the future were better than expected. Naturally, the investor would be disappointed that she had not purchased the office building because it would have resulted in the largest payoff (\$100,000) under good economic conditions. In fact, the investor would *regret* the decision to purchase the warehouse, and the *degree of* **regret** *would be \$70,000*, the difference between the payoff for the investor's choice and the best choice.

This brief example demonstrates the principle underlying the decision criterion known as **minimax regret criterion.** With this decision criterion, the decision maker attempts to avoid regret by selecting the decision alternative that minimizes the maximum regret.

To use the minimax regret criterion, a decision maker first selects the maximum payoff under each state of nature. For our example, the maximum payoff under good economic conditions is \$100,000, and the maximum payoff under poor economic conditions is \$30,000. All other payoffs under the respective states of nature are subtracted from these amounts, as follows:

Good Economic Conditions	*Poor Economic Conditions*
\$100,000 − 50,000 = \$50,000	\$30,000 − 30,000 = \$0
\$100,000 − 100,000 = \$0	\$30,000 − (−40,000) = \$70,000
\$100,000 − 30,000 = \$70,000	\$30,000 − 10,000 = \$20,000

These values represent the regret that the decision maker would experience if a decision were made that resulted in less than the maximum payoff. The values are summarized in a modified version of the payoff table known as a *regret table*, shown in Table 5. (Such a table is sometimes referred to as an *opportunity loss table*, in which case the term *opportunity loss* is synonymous with *regret*.)

Table 5 Regret table

	State of Nature	
Decision (Purchase)	Good Economic Conditions	Poor Economic Conditions
Apartment building	\$50,000	\$ 0
Office building	0	70,000
Warehouse	70,000	20,000

To make the decision according to the minimax regret criterion, the maximum regret for *each decision* must be determined. The decision corresponding to the minimum of these regret values is then selected. This process is illustrated in Table 6.

Table 6
Regret table illustrating the minimax regret decision

Decision (Purchase)	State of Nature: Good Economic Conditions	State of Nature: Poor Economic Conditions
Apartment building	$50,000	$ 0
Office building	0	70,000
Warehouse	70,000	20,000

The minimum regret value (→ $50,000)

According to the minimax regret criterion, the decision should be to purchase the apartment building rather than the office building or the warehouse. This particular decision is based on the philosophy that the investor will experience the least amount of regret by purchasing the apartment building. In other words, if the investor purchased either the office building or the warehouse, $70,000 worth of regret could result; however, the purchase of the apartment building will result in, at most, $50,000 in regret.

The Hurwicz Criterion

*The **Hurwicz criterion** is a compromise between the maximax and maximin criteria.*

*The **coefficient of optimism**, α, is a measure of the decision maker's optimism.*

*The **Hurwicz criterion** multiplies the best payoff by α, the coefficient of optimism, and the worst payoff by $1 - \alpha$, for each decision, and the best result is selected.*

The **Hurwicz criterion** strikes a compromise between the maximax and maximin criteria. The principle underlying this decision criterion is that the decision maker is neither totally optimistic (as the maximax criterion assumes) nor totally pessimistic (as the maximin criterion assumes). With the Hurwicz criterion, the decision payoffs are weighted by a **coefficient of optimism**, a measure of the decision maker's optimism. The coefficient of optimism, which we will define as α, is between zero and one (i.e., $0 \leq \alpha \leq 1.0$). If $\alpha = 1.0$, then the decision maker is said to be completely optimistic; if $\alpha = 0$, then the decision maker is completely pessimistic. (Given this definition, if α is the coefficient of optimism, $1 - \alpha$ is the *coefficient of pessimism.*)

The Hurwicz criterion requires that for each decision alternative, the maximum payoff be multiplied by α and the minimum payoff be multiplied by $1 - \alpha$. For our investment example, if α equals .4 (i.e., the investor is slightly pessimistic), $1 - \alpha = .6$, and the following values will result:

Decision	***Values***
Apartment building	$ 50,000(.4) + 30,000(.6) = $38,000
Office building	$100,000(.4) − 40,000(.6) = $16,000
Warehouse	$ 30,000(.4) + 10,000(.6) = $18,000

The Hurwicz criterion specifies selection of the decision alternative corresponding to the maximum weighted value, which is $38,000 for this example. Thus, the decision would be to purchase the apartment building.

It should be pointed out that when $\alpha = 0$, the Hurwicz criterion is actually the maximin criterion; when $\alpha = 1.0$, it is the maximax criterion. A limitation of the Hurwicz criterion is the fact that α must be determined by the decision maker. It can be quite difficult for a decision maker to accurately determine his or her degree of optimism. Regardless of how the decision maker determines α, it is still a completely *subjective* measure of the decision maker's degree of optimism. Therefore, the Hurwicz criterion is a completely subjective decision-making criterion.

The Equal Likelihood Criterion

When the maximax criterion is applied to a decision situation, the decision maker implicitly assumes that the most favorable state of nature for each decision will occur. Alternatively, when the maximin criterion is applied, the least favorable states of nature are assumed. The **equal likelihood**, or **LaPlace, criterion** weights each state of nature equally, thus assuming that the states of nature are equally likely to occur.

*The **equal likelihood criterion** multiplies the decision payoff for each state of nature by an equal weight.*

Because there are two states of nature in our example, we assign a weight of .50 to each one. Next, we multiply these weights by each payoff for each decision:

Decision	***Values***
Apartment building	\$ 50,000(.50) + 30,000(.50) = \$40,000
Office building	\$100,000(.50) − 40,000(.50) = \$30,000
Warehouse	\$ 30,000(.50) + 10,000(.50) = \$20,000

As with the Hurwicz criterion, we select the decision that has the maximum of these weighted values. Because \$40,000 is the highest weighted value, the investor's decision would be to purchase the apartment building.

In applying the equal likelihood criterion, we are assuming a 50% chance, or .50 probability, that either state of nature will occur. Using this same basic logic, it is possible to weight the states of nature differently (i.e., unequally) in many decision problems. In other words, different probabilities can be assigned to each state of nature, indicating that one state is more likely to occur than another. The application of different probabilities to the states of nature is the principle behind the decision criteria to be presented in the section on expected value.

Summary of Criteria Results

The decisions indicated by the decision criteria examined so far can be summarized as follows:

Criterion	***Decision (Purchase)***
Maximax	Office building
Maximin	Apartment building
Minimax regret	Apartment building
Hurwicz	Apartment building
Equal likelihood	Apartment building

The decision to purchase the apartment building was designated most often by the various decision criteria. Notice that the decision to purchase the warehouse was never indicated by any criterion. This is because the payoffs for an apartment building, under either set of future economic conditions, are always better than the payoffs for a warehouse. Thus, given any situation with these two alternatives (and any other choice, such as purchasing the office building), the decision to purchase an apartment building will always be made over the decision to purchase a warehouse. In fact, the warehouse decision alternative could have been eliminated from consideration under each of our criteria. The alternative of purchasing a warehouse is said to be *dominated* by the alternative of purchasing an apartment building. In general, dominated decision alternatives can be removed from the payoff table and not considered when the various decision-making criteria are applied. This reduces the complexity of the decision analysis somewhat. However, in our discussions throughout this chapter of the application of decision criteria, we will leave the dominated alternative in the payoff table for demonstration purposes.

*A **dominant** decision is one that has a better payoff than another decision under each state of nature.*

The appropriate criterion is dependent on the risk personality and philosophy of the decision maker.

The use of several decision criteria often results in a mix of decisions, with no one decision being selected more than the others. The criterion or collection of criteria used and the resulting decision depend on the characteristics and philosophy of the decision maker. For example, the extremely optimistic decision maker might eschew the majority of the foregoing results and make the decision to purchase the office building because the maximax criterion most closely reflects his or her personal decision-making philosophy.

Solution of Decision-Making Problems Without Probabilities with QM for Windows

QM for Windows includes a module to solve decision analysis problems. QM for Windows will be used to illustrate the use of the maximax, maximin, minimax regret, equal likelihood, and Hurwicz criteria for the real estate problem considered in this section. The problem data are input very easily. A summary of the input and solution output for the maximax, maximin, and Hurwicz criteria is shown in Exhibit 1. The decision with the equal likelihood criterion can be determined by using an alpha value for the Hurwicz criterion equal to the equal likelihood weight, which is .5 for our real estate investment example. The solution output with alpha equal to .5 is shown in Exhibit 2. The decision with the minimax regret criterion is shown in Exhibit 3.

Exhibit 1

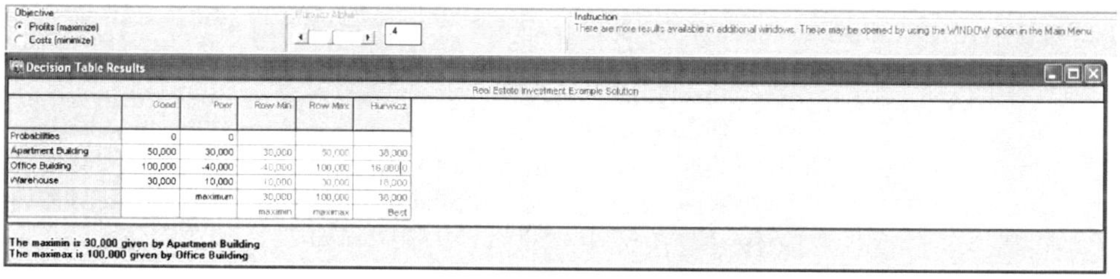

	Good	Poor	Row Min	Row Max	Hurwicz
Probabilities	0	0			
Apartment Building	50,000	30,000	30,000	50,000	38,000
Office Building	100,000	-40,000	-40,000	100,000	16,000
Warehouse	30,000	10,000	10,000	30,000	18,000
		maximum	30,000	100,000	38,000
			maximin	maximax	Best

Exhibit 2

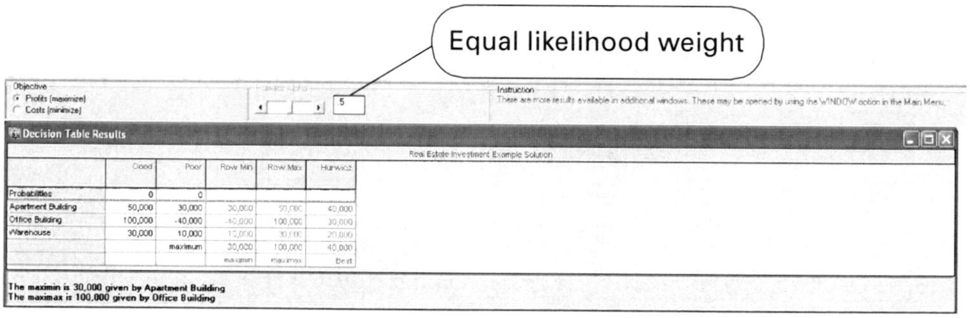

	Good	Poor	Row Min	Row Max	Hurwicz
Probabilities	0	0			
Apartment Building	50,000	30,000	30,000	50,000	40,000
Office Building	100,000	-40,000	-40,000	100,000	30,000
Warehouse	30,000	10,000	10,000	30,000	20,000
		maximum	30,000	100,000	40,000
			maximin	maximax	Best

Exhibit 3

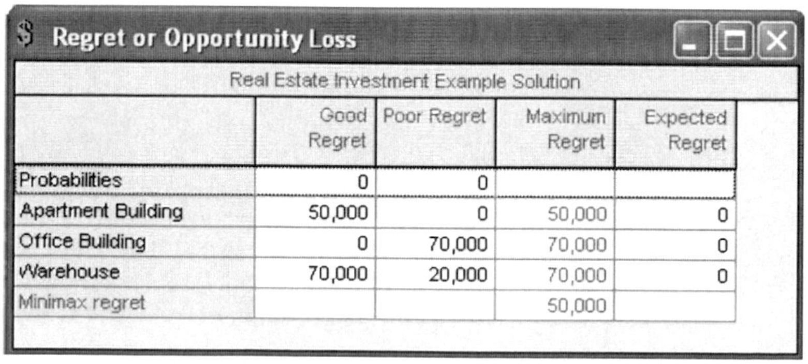

	Good Regret	Poor Regret	Maximum Regret	Expected Regret
Probabilities	0	0		
Apartment Building	50,000	0	50,000	0
Office Building	0	70,000	70,000	0
Warehouse	70,000	20,000	70,000	0
Minimax regret			50,000	

Solution of Decision-Making Problems Without Probabilities with Excel

Excel can also be used to solve decision analysis problems using the decision-making criteria presented in this section. Exhibit 4 illustrates the application of the maximax, minimax, minimax regret, Hurwicz, and equal likelihood criteria for our real estate investment example.

Exhibit 4

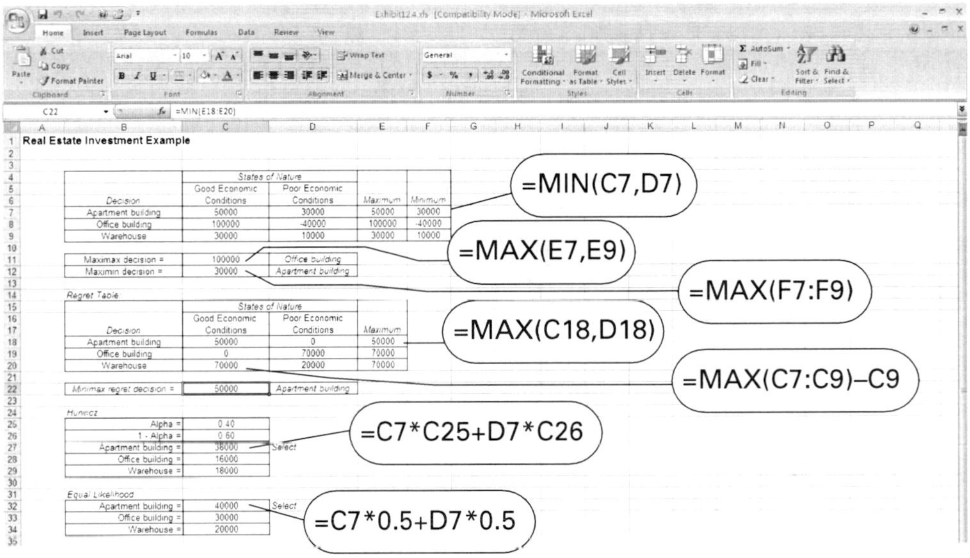

In cell E7 the formula **=MAX(C7,D7)** selects the maximum payoff outcome for the decision to purchase the apartment building. Next, in cell C11 the maximum of the maximum payoffs is determined with the formula **=MAX(E7:E9)**. The maximin decision is determined similarly.

In the regret table in Exhibit 4, in cell C18 the formula **=MAX(C7:C9) – C7** computes the regret for the apartment building decision under good economic conditions, and then the maximum regret for the apartment building is determined in cell E18, using the formula **=MAX(C18,D18)**. The minimax regret value is determined in cell C22 with the formula **=MIN(E18:E20)**.

The Hurwicz and equal likelihood decisions are determined using their respective formulas in cells **C27:C29** and **C32:C34**.

Decision Making with Probabilities

The decision-making criteria just presented were based on the assumption that no information regarding the likelihood of the states of nature was available. Thus, no *probabilities of occurrence* were assigned to the states of nature, except in the case of the equal likelihood criterion. In that case, by assuming that each state of nature was equally likely and assigning a weight of .50 to each state of nature in our example, we were implicitly assigning a probability of .50 to the occurrence of each state of nature.

It is often possible for the decision maker to know enough about the future states of nature to assign probabilities to their occurrence. Given that probabilities can be assigned, several decision criteria are available to aid the decision maker. We will consider two of these criteria: *expected value* and *expected opportunity loss* (although several others, including the *maximum likelihood criterion*, are available).

Expected Value

Expected value is computed by multiplying each decision outcome under each state of nature by the probability of its occurrence.

To apply the concept of **expected value** as a decision-making criterion, the decision maker must first estimate the probability of occurrence of each state of nature. Once these estimates have been made, the expected value for each decision alternative can be computed. The expected value is computed by multiplying each outcome (of a decision) by the probability of its occurrence and then summing these products. The expected value of a random variable x, written symbolically as $EV(x)$, is computed as follows:

$$EV(x) = \sum_{i=1}^{n} x_i P(x_i)$$

where

n = number of values of the random variable x

Using our real estate investment example, let us suppose that, based on several economic forecasts, the investor is able to estimate a .60 probability that good economic conditions will prevail and a .40 probability that poor economic conditions will prevail. This new information is shown in Table 7.

Table 7
Payoff table with probabilities for states of nature

	State of Nature	
Decision (Purchase)	Good Economic Conditions .60	Poor Economic Conditions .40
Apartment building	$ 50,000	$ 30,000
Office building	100,000	−40,000
Warehouse	30,000	10,000

The expected value (EV) for each decision is computed as follows:

$$EV(\text{apartment}) = \$50{,}000(.60) + 30{,}000(.40) = \$42{,}000$$
$$EV(\text{office}) = \$100{,}000(.60) - 40{,}000(.40) = \$44{,}000$$
$$EV(\text{warehouse}) = \$30{,}000(.60) + 10{,}000(.40) = \$22{,}000$$

The best decision is the one with the greatest expected value. Because the greatest expected value is $44,000, the best decision is to purchase the office building. This does not mean that $44,000 will result if the investor purchases the office building; rather, it is assumed that one of the payoff values will result (either $100,000 or −$40,000). The expected value means that if this decision situation occurred a large number of times, an *average* payoff of $44,000 would result. Alternatively, if the payoffs were in terms of costs, the best decision would be the one with the lowest expected value.

Expected Opportunity Loss

Expected opportunity loss is the expected value of the regret for each decision.

A decision criterion closely related to expected value is **expected opportunity loss**. To use this criterion, we multiply the probabilities by the regret (i.e., opportunity loss) for each decision outcome rather than multiplying the decision outcomes by the probabilities of their occurrence, as we did for expected monetary value.

The concept of regret was introduced in our discussion of the minimax regret criterion. The regret values for each decision outcome in our example were shown in Table 6. These values are repeated in Table 8, with the addition of the probabilities of occurrence for each state of nature.

Table 8
Regret (opportunity loss) table with probabilities for states of nature

	State of Nature	
Decision (Purchase)	GOOD ECONOMIC CONDITIONS .60	POOR ECONOMIC CONDITIONS .40
Apartment building	$50,000	$ 0
Office building	0	70,000
Warehouse	70,000	20,000

The expected opportunity loss (*EOL*) for each decision is computed as follows:

$$
\begin{aligned}
EOL(\text{apartment}) &= \$50{,}000(.60) + 0(.40) = \$30{,}000 \\
EOL(\text{office}) &= \$0(.60) + 70{,}000(.40) = \$28{,}000 \\
EOL(\text{warehouse}) &= \$70{,}000(.60) + 20{,}000(.40) = \$50{,}000
\end{aligned}
$$

As with the minimax regret criterion, the best decision results from minimizing the regret, or, in this case, minimizing the *expected* regret or opportunity loss. Because $28,000 is the minimum expected regret, the decision is to purchase the office building.

The expected value and expected opportunity loss criteria result in the same decision.

Notice that the decisions recommended by the expected value and expected opportunity loss criteria were the same—to purchase the office building. This is not a coincidence because these two methods always result in the same decision. Thus, it is repetitious to apply both methods to a decision situation when one of the two will suffice.

In addition, note that the decisions from the expected value and expected opportunity loss criteria are totally dependent on the probability estimates determined by the decision maker. Thus, if inaccurate probabilities are used, erroneous decisions will result. It is therefore important that the decision maker be as accurate as possible in determining the probability of each state of nature.

Solution of Expected Value Problems with QM for Windows

QM for Windows not only solves decision analysis problems without probabilities but also has the capability to solve problems using the expected value criterion. A summary of the input data and the solution output for our real estate example is shown in Exhibit 5. Notice that the expected value results are included in the third column of this solution screen.

Exhibit 5

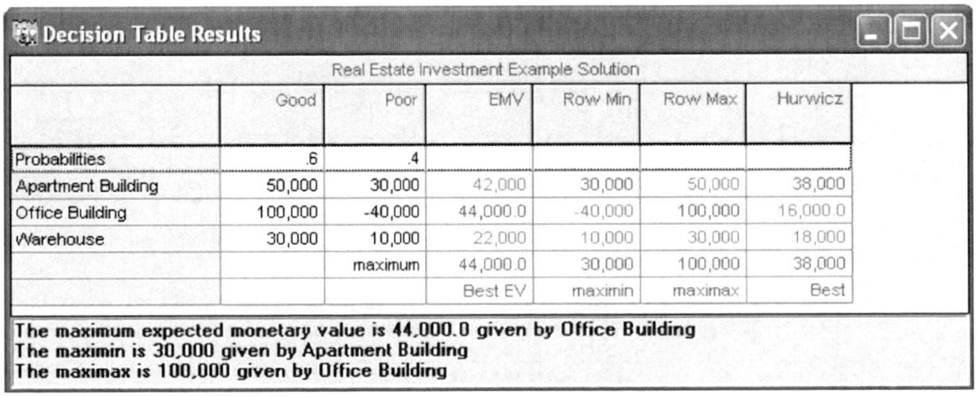
Decision Table Results

Real Estate Investment Example Solution

	Good	Poor	EMV	Row Min	Row Max	Hurwicz
Probabilities	.6	.4				
Apartment Building	50,000	30,000	42,000	30,000	50,000	38,000
Office Building	100,000	-40,000	44,000.0	-40,000	100,000	16,000.0
Warehouse	30,000	10,000	22,000	10,000	30,000	18,000
		maximum	44,000.0	30,000	100,000	38,000
			Best EV	maximin	maximax	Best

The maximum expected monetary value is 44,000.0 given by Office Building
The maximin is 30,000 given by Apartment Building
The maximax is 100,000 given by Office Building

Solution of Expected Value Problems with Excel and Excel QM

This type of expected value problem can also be solved by using an Excel spreadsheet. Exhibit 6 shows our real estate investment example set up in a spreadsheet format. Cells E7, E8, and E9 include the expected value formulas for this example. The expected value formula for the first decision, purchasing the apartment building, is embedded in cell E7 and is shown on the formula bar at the top of the spreadsheet.

Exhibit 6

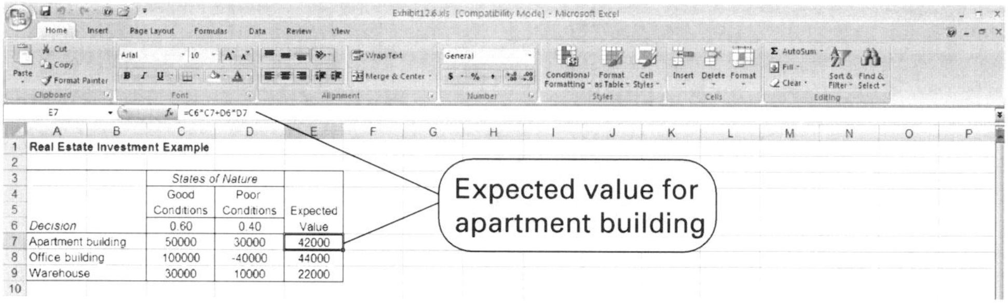

Excel QM is a set of spreadsheet macros that is included on the companion Web site that accompanies this text, and it has a macro to solve decision analysis problems. Once activated, clicking on "Decision Analysis" will result in a Spreadsheet Initialization window. After entering several problem parameters, including the number of decisions and states of nature, and then clicking on "OK," the spreadsheet shown in Exhibit 7 will result. Initially, this spreadsheet contains example values in cells **B8:C11**. Exhibit 7 shows the spreadsheet with our problem data already typed in. The results are computed automatically as the data are entered, using the cell formulas already embedded in the macro.

Exhibit 7

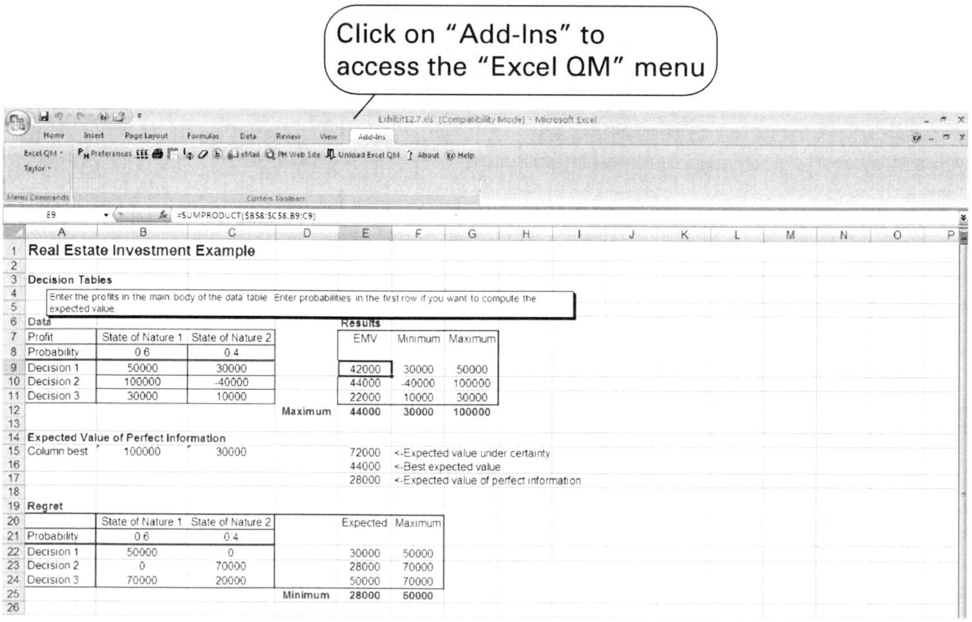

Expected Value of Perfect Information

It is often possible to purchase additional information regarding future events and thus make a better decision. For example, a real estate investor could hire an economic forecaster to perform an analysis of the economy to more accurately determine which economic condition will occur in the future. However, the investor (or any decision maker) would be foolish to pay more for this information than he or she stands to gain in extra profit from having the information. That is, the information has some maximum value that represents the limit of what the decision maker would be willing to spend. This value of information can be computed as an expected value—hence its name, the **expected value of perfect information** (also referred to as **EVPI**).

The ***expected value of perfect information*** *is the maximum amount a decision maker would pay for additional information.*

To compute the expected value of perfect information, we first look at the decisions under each state of nature. If we could obtain information that assured us which state of nature was going to occur (i.e., perfect information), we could select the best decision for that state of nature. For example, in our real estate investment example, if we know for sure that good economic conditions will prevail, then we will decide to purchase the office building. Similarly, if we know for sure that poor economic conditions will occur, then we will decide to purchase the apartment building. These hypothetical "perfect" decisions are summarized in Table 9.

Table 9
Payoff table with decisions, given perfect information

	State of Nature	
Decision (Purchase)	GOOD ECONOMIC CONDITIONS .60	POOR ECONOMIC CONDITIONS .40
Apartment building	$ 50,000	**$ 30,000**
Office building	**100,000**	−40,000
Warehouse	30,000	10,000

The probabilities of each state of nature (i.e., .60 and .40) tell us that good economic conditions will prevail 60% of the time and poor economic conditions will prevail 40% of the time (if this decision situation is repeated many times). In other words, even though perfect information enables the investor to make the right decision, each state of nature will occur only a certain portion of the time. Thus, each of the decision outcomes obtained using perfect information must be weighted by its respective probability:

$$\$100{,}000(.60) + 30{,}000(.40) = \$72{,}000$$

The amount $72,000 is the expected value of the decision, *given* perfect information, not the expected value *of* perfect information. The expected value of perfect information is the maximum amount that would be paid to gain information that would result in a decision better than the one made without perfect information. Recall that the expected value decision without perfect information was to purchase an office building, and the expected value was computed as

$$EV(\text{office}) = \$100{,}000(.60) - 40{,}000(.40) = \$44{,}000$$

EVPI equals the expected value, given perfect information, minus the expected value without perfect information.

The expected value of perfect information is computed by subtracting the expected value without perfect information ($44,000) from the expected value given perfect information ($72,000):

$$EVPI = \$72{,}000 - 44{,}000 = \$28{,}000$$

The expected value of perfect information, $28,000, is the maximum amount that the investor would pay to purchase perfect information from some other source, such as an economic forecaster. Of course, perfect information is rare and usually unobtainable. Typically, the decision maker would be willing to pay some amount less than $28,000, depending on how accurate (i.e., close to perfection) the decision maker believed the information was.

The expected value of perfect information equals the expected opportunity loss for the best decision.

It is interesting to note that the expected value of perfect information, $28,000 for our example, is the same as the *expected opportunity loss (EOL)* for the decision selected, using this later criterion:

$$EOL(\text{office}) = \$0(.60) + 70{,}000(.40) = \$28{,}000$$

This will always be the case, and logically so, because regret reflects the *difference between the best decision under a state of nature and the decision actually made.* This is actually the same thing determined by the expected value of perfect information.

Excel QM for decision analysis computes the expected value of perfect information, as shown in cell E17 at the bottom of the spreadsheet in Exhibit 7. The expected value of perfect information can also be determined by using Excel. Exhibit 8 shows the *EVPI* for our real estate investment example.

Exhibit 8

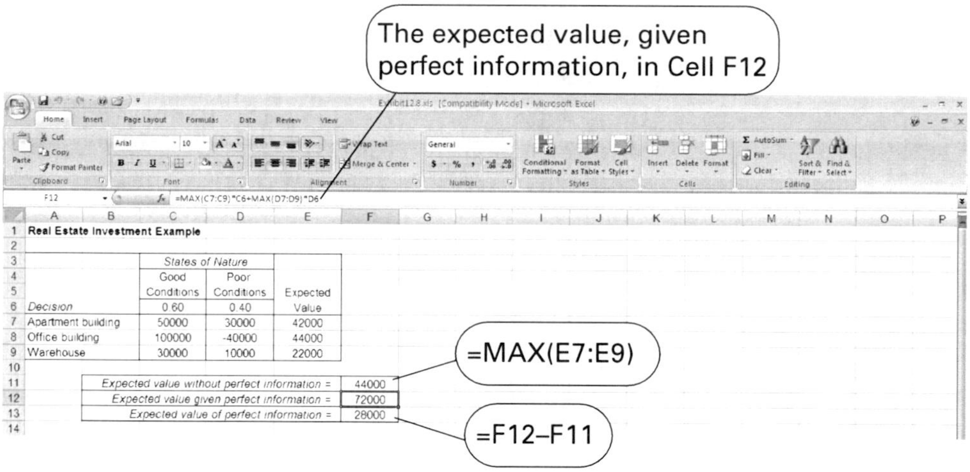

Real Estate Investment Example

	States of Nature		
	Good Conditions	Poor Conditions	Expected Value
Decision	0.60	0.40	
Apartment building	50000	30000	42000
Office building	100000	-40000	44000
Warehouse	30000	10000	22000

Expected value without perfect information =	44000
Expected value given perfect information =	72000
Expected value of perfect information =	28000

Decision Trees

*A **decision tree** is a diagram consisting of square decision nodes, circle probability nodes, and branches representing decision alternatives.*

Another useful technique for analyzing a decision situation is using a **decision tree.** A decision tree is a graphical diagram consisting of nodes and branches. In a decision tree the user computes the expected value of each outcome and makes a decision based on these expected values. The primary benefit of a decision tree is that it provides an illustration (or picture) of the decision-making process. This makes it easier to correctly compute the necessary expected values and to understand the process of making the decision.

We will use our example of the real estate investor to demonstrate the fundamentals of decision tree analysis. The various decisions, probabilities, and outcomes of this example, initially presented in Table 7, are repeated in Table 10. The decision tree for this example is shown in Figure 2.

Table 10
Payoff table for real estate investment example

Decision (Purchase)	State of Nature: Good Economic Conditions .60	Poor Economic Conditions .40
Apartment building	$ 50,000	$ 30,000
Office building	100,000	−40,000
Warehouse	30,000	10,000

Figure 2
Decision tree for real estate investment example

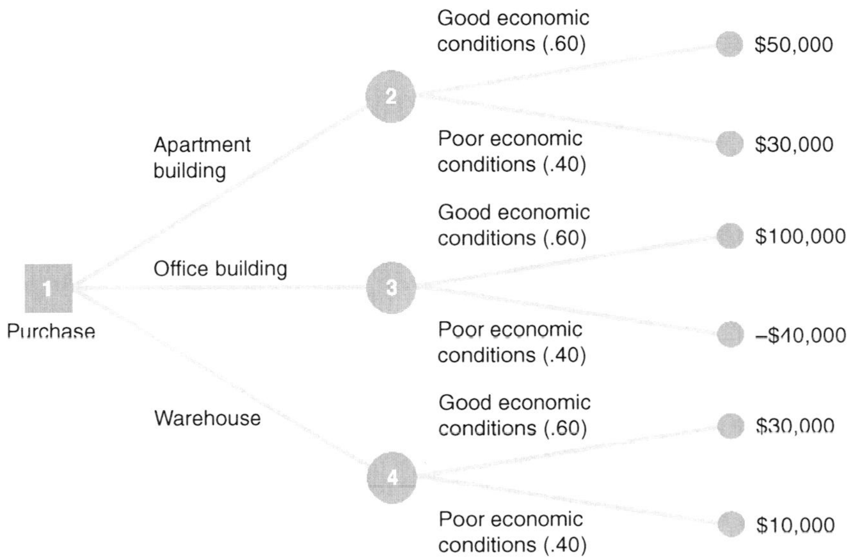

The circles (●) and the square (■) in Figure 2 are referred to as *nodes*. The square is a decision node, and the *branches* emanating from a decision node reflect the alternative decisions possible at that point. For example, in Figure 2, node 1 signifies a decision to purchase an apartment building, an office building, or a warehouse. The circles are probability, or event, nodes, and the branches emanating from them indicate the states of nature that can occur: good economic conditions or poor economic conditions.

The expected value is computed at each probability node.

The decision tree represents the sequence of events in a decision situation. First, one of the three decision choices is selected at node 1. Depending on the branch selected, the decision maker arrives at probability node 2, 3, or 4, where one of the states of nature will prevail, resulting in one of six possible payoffs.

Determining the best decision by using a decision tree involves computing the expected value at each probability node. This is accomplished by starting with the final outcomes (payoffs) and working backward through the decision tree toward node 1. First, the expected value of the payoffs is computed at each probability node:

$$EV(\text{node } 2) = .60(\$50{,}000) + .40(\$30{,}000) = \$42{,}000$$
$$EV(\text{node } 3) = .60(\$100{,}000) + .40(-\$40{,}000) = \$44{,}000$$
$$EV(\text{node } 4) = .60(\$30{,}000) + .40(\$10{,}000) = \$22{,}000$$

Branches with the greatest expected value are selected.

These values are now shown as the *expected* payoffs from each of the three branches emanating from node 1 in Figure 3. Each of these three expected values at nodes 2, 3, and 4 is the outcome of a possible decision that can occur at node 1. Moving toward node 1, we

Figure 3
Decision tree with expected value at probability nodes

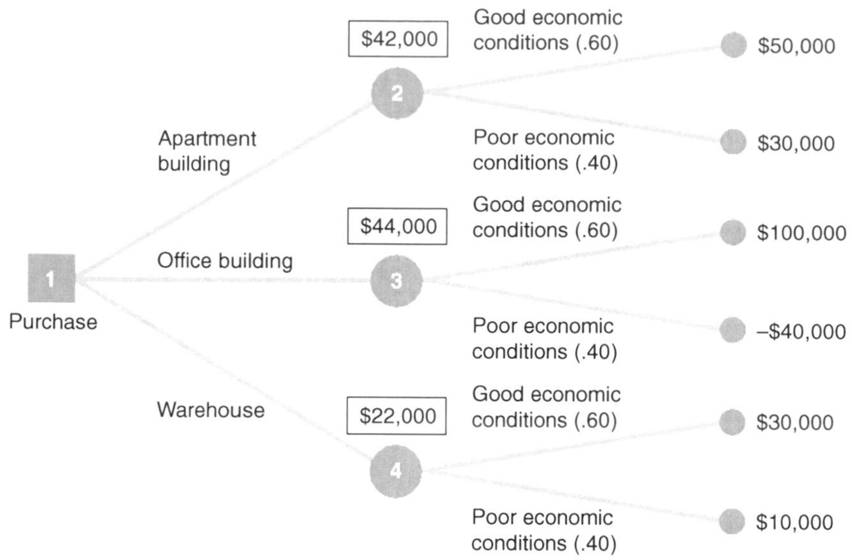

select the branch that comes from the probability node with the highest expected payoff. In Figure 3, the branch corresponding to the highest payoff, $44,000, is from node 1 to node 3. This branch represents the decision to purchase the office building. The decision to purchase the office building, with an expected payoff of $44,000, is the same result we achieved earlier by using the expected value criterion. In fact, when only one decision is to be made (i.e., there is not a series of decisions), the decision tree will always yield the same decision and expected payoff as the expected value criterion. As a result, in these decision situations a decision tree is not very useful. However, when a sequence or series of decisions is required, a decision tree can be very useful.

Decision Trees with QM for Windows

In QM for Windows, when the "Decision Analysis" module is accessed and you click on "New" to input a new problem, a menu appears that allows you to select either "Decision Tables" or "Decision Trees." Exhibit 9 shows the Decision Tree Results solution screen for our real estate investment example. Notice that QM for Windows requires that all nodes

Exhibit 9

Decision Tree Results

Real Estate Investment Example Solution

	Start Node	End Node	Branch Probability	Profit	Branch Use	End node	Node Type	Node Value
Start	0	1	0	0		1	Decision	44,000.0
Purchase apartment	1	2	0	0		2	Chance	42,000.0
Purchase office	1	3	0	0	Always	3	Chance	44,000.0
Purchase warehouse	1	4	0	0		4	Chance	22,000
Good conditions	2	5	.6	50,000		5	Final	50,000
Poor conditions	2	6	.4	30,000		6	Final	30,000
Good conditions	3	7	.6	100,000		7	Final	100,000
Poor conditions	3	8	.4	-40,000		8	Final	-40,000
Good conditions	4	9	.6	30,000		9	Final	30,000
Poor conditions	4	10	.4	10,000		10	Final	10,000

For the branch used columns the meanings are as follows:
Always - these are branches that should always be included
Possibly - these are branches that should be included if you get there and you MIGHT get there.
Backwards - these are branches that should be used if you get there BUT you should NOT get there.
(They are used for the backwards pass from right to left).

be numbered, including the end, or terminal, nodes, which are shown as solid dots in Figure 3. For QM for Windows, we have numbered these end nodes 5 through 10.

Decision Trees with Excel and TreePlan

TreePlan is an Excel add-in program developed by Michael Middleton to construct and solve decision trees in an Excel spreadsheet format. Although Excel has the graphical and computational capability to develop decision trees, it is a difficult and slow process. TreePlan is basically a decision tree template that greatly simplifies the process of setting up a decision tree in Excel.

The first step in using TreePlan is to gain access to it. The best way to go about this is to copy the TreePlan add-in file, TreePlan.xla, from the companion Web site onto your hard drive and then add it to the "Data/Add-Ins" menu that you access at the top of your spreadsheet screen. Once you have added TreePlan to the "Add-Ins" menu, you can invoke it by clicking on the "Decision Trees" menu item.

We will demonstrate how to use TreePlan with our real estate investment example shown in Figure 3. The first step in using TreePlan is to generate a new tree on which to begin work. Exhibit 10 shows a new tree that we generated by positioning the cursor on cell B1 and then invoking the "Add-ins" menu and clicking on "Decision Trees." This results in a menu from which we click on "New Tree," which creates the decision tree shown in Exhibit 10.

Exhibit 10

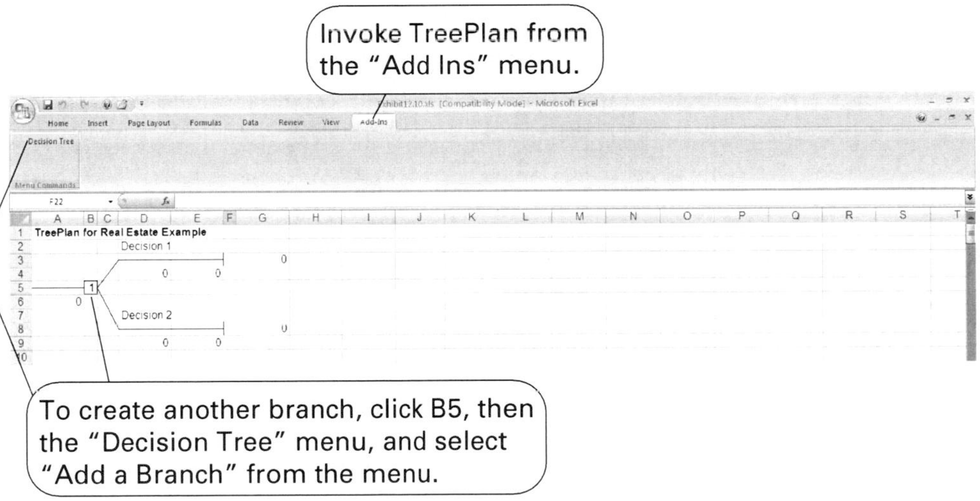

The decision tree in Exhibit 10 uses the normal nodal convention we used in creating the decision trees in Figures 2 and 3—squares for decision nodes and circles for probability nodes (which TreePlan calls *event nodes*). However, this decision tree is only a starting point or template that we need to expand to replicate our example decision tree in Figure 3.

In Figure 3, three branches emanate from the first decision node, reflecting the three investment decisions in our example. To create a third branch using TreePlan, click on the decision node in cell B5 in Exhibit 10 and then invoke TreePlan from the "Add-Ins" menu. A window will appear, with several menu items, including "Add a Branch." Select this menu item and click on "OK." This will create a third branch on our decision tree, as shown in Exhibit 11.

Exhibit 11

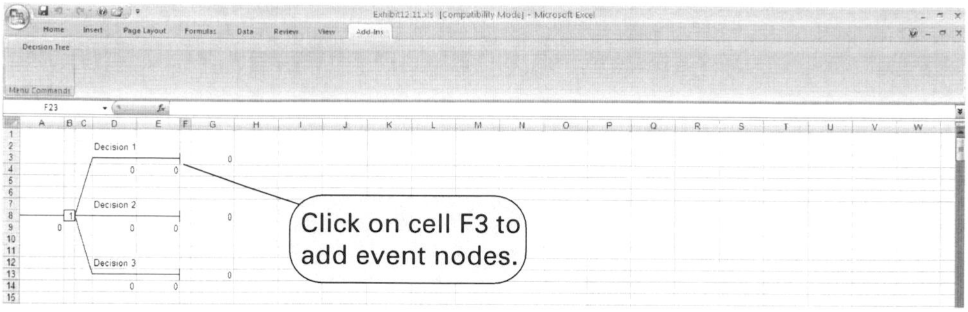

Next we need to expand our decision tree in Exhibit 11 by adding probability nodes (2, 3, and 4 in Figure 3) and branches from these nodes for our example. To add a new node, click on the end node in cell F3 in Exhibit 11 and then invoke TreePlan from the "Add-Ins" menu. From the menu window that appears, select "Change to Event Node" and then select "Two Branches" from the same menu and click on "OK." This process must be repeated two more times for the other two end nodes (in cells F8 and F13) to create our three probability nodes. The resulting decision tree is shown in Exhibit 12, with the new probability nodes at cells F5, F15, and F25 and with accompanying branches.

Exhibit 12

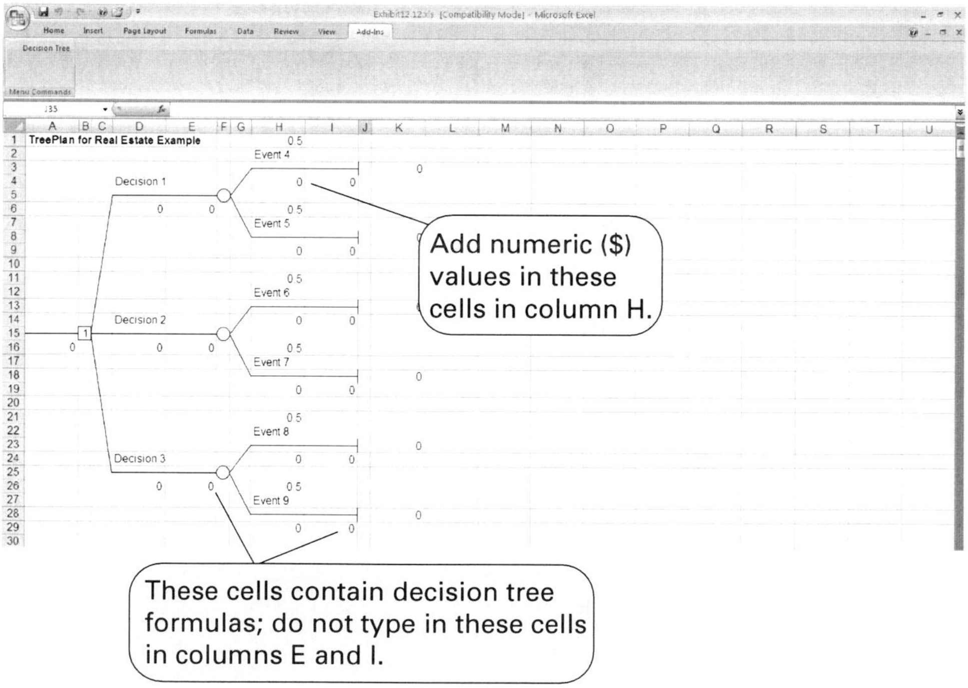

The next step is to edit the decision tree labels and add the numeric data from our example. Generic descriptive labels are shown above each branch in Exhibit 12—for example, "Decision 1" in cell D4 and "Event 4" in cell H2. We edit the labels the same way we would edit any spreadsheet. For example, if we click on cell D4, we can type in "Apartment Building" in place of "Decision 1," reflecting the decision corresponding to this branch in our example, as shown in Figure 3. We can change the other labels on the other branches the same way. The decision tree with the edited labels corresponding to our example is shown in Exhibit 13.

Exhibit 13

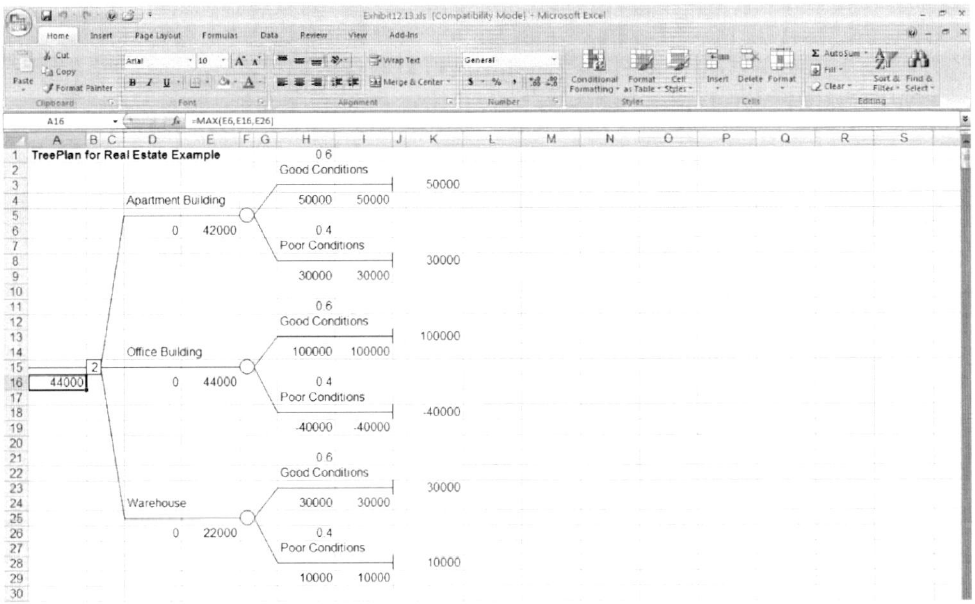

Looking back to Exhibit 12 for a moment, focus on the two 0 values below each branch—for example, in cells D6 and E6 and in cells H9 and I4. The first 0 cell is where we type in the numeric value (i.e., \$ amount) for that branch. For our example, we would type in 50,000 in cell H4, 30,000 in H9, 100,000 in H14, and so on. These values are shown on the decision tree in Exhibit 13. Likewise, we would type in the probabilities for the branches in the cells just above the branch—H1, H6, H11, and so on. For example, we would type in 0.60 in cell H1 and 0.40 in cell H6. These probabilities are also shown in Exhibit 13. However, we need to be very careful not to type anything into the second 0 branch cell—for example, E6, I4, I9, E16, I14, I19, and so on. These cells automatically contain the decision tree formulas that compute the expected values at each node and select the best decision branches, so we do not want to type anything in these cells that would eliminate these formulas. For example, in Exhibit 12 the formula in cell E6 is shown on the formula bar at the top of the screen. This is the expected value for that probability node.

The expected value for this decision tree and our example, \$44,000, is shown in cell A16 in Exhibit 13.

Sequential Decision Trees

A sequential decision tree illustrates a situation requiring a series of decisions.

As noted earlier, when a decision situation requires only a single decision, an expected value payoff table will yield the same result as a decision tree. However, a payoff table is usually limited to a single decision situation, as in our real estate investment example. If a decision situation requires a series of decisions, then a payoff table cannot be created, and a decision tree becomes the best method for decision analysis.

To demonstrate the use of a decision tree for a sequence of decisions, we will alter our real estate investment example to encompass a 10-year period during which several decisions must be made. In this new example, the *first decision* facing the investor is whether to purchase an apartment building or land. If the investor purchases the apartment building, two

Management Science Application

Evaluating Electric Generator Maintenance Schedules Using Decision Tree Analysis

Electric utility companies plan annual outage periods for preventive maintenance on generators. The outages are typically part of 5- to-20-year master schedules. However, at Entergy Electric Systems these scheduled outages were traditionally based on averages that did not reflect short-term fluctuations in demand due to breakdowns and bad weather conditions. The master schedule had to be reviewed each week by outage planners who relied on their experience to determine whether the schedule needed to be changed. A user-friendly software system was developed to assist planners at Entergy Electric Systems in making changes in their schedule. The system is based on decision tree analysis.

Each week in the master schedule is represented by a decision tree that is based on changes in customer demand, unexpected generator breakdowns, and delays in returning generators from planned outages. The numeric outcome of the decision tree is the average reserve margin of megawatts (MW) for a specific week. This value enables planners to determine whether customer demand will be met and whether the maintenance schedule planned for the week is acceptable. The planner's objective is to avoid negative power reserves by making changes in the generators' maintenance schedule. The branches of the decision tree, their probabilities of occurrence, and the branch MW values are based on historical data. The system has enabled Entergy Electric Systems to isolate high-risk weeks and to develop timely maintenance schedules on short notice. The new computerized system has reduced the maintenance schedules review time for as many as 260 weeks from several days to less than an hour.

Lester Lefkowitz/Corbis/Stock Market

Source: H. A. Taha and H. M. Wolf, "Evaluation of Generator Maintenance Schedules at Entergy Electric Systems," *Interfaces* 26, no. 4 (July–August 1996): 56–65.

states of nature are possible: Either the population of the town will grow (with a probability of .60) or the population will not grow (with a probability of .40). Either state of nature will result in a payoff. On the other hand, if the investor chooses to purchase land, 3 years in the future another decision will have to be made regarding the development of the land. The decision tree for this example, shown in Figure 4, contains all the pertinent data, including decisions, states of nature, probabilities, and payoffs.

At decision node 1 in Figure 4, the decision choices are to purchase an apartment building or to purchase land. Notice that the cost of each venture ($800,000 and $200,000, respectively) is shown in parentheses. If the apartment building is purchased, two states of nature are possible at probability node 2: The town may exhibit population growth, with a probability of .60, or there may be no population growth or a decline, with a probability of .40. If the population grows, the investor will achieve a payoff of $2,000,000 over a 10-year period. (Note that this whole decision situation encompasses a 10-year time span.) However, if no population growth occurs, a payoff of only $225,000 will result.

If the decision is to purchase land, two states of nature are possible at probability node 3. These two states of nature and their probabilities are identical to those at node 2; however, the payoffs are different. If population growth occurs *for a 3-year period*, no payoff will occur, but the investor will make another decision at node 4 regarding development of the land. At that point, either apartments will be built, at a cost of $800,000, or the land will be sold, with a payoff of $450,000. Notice that the decision situation at node 4 can occur only if population

Figure 4
Sequential decision tree

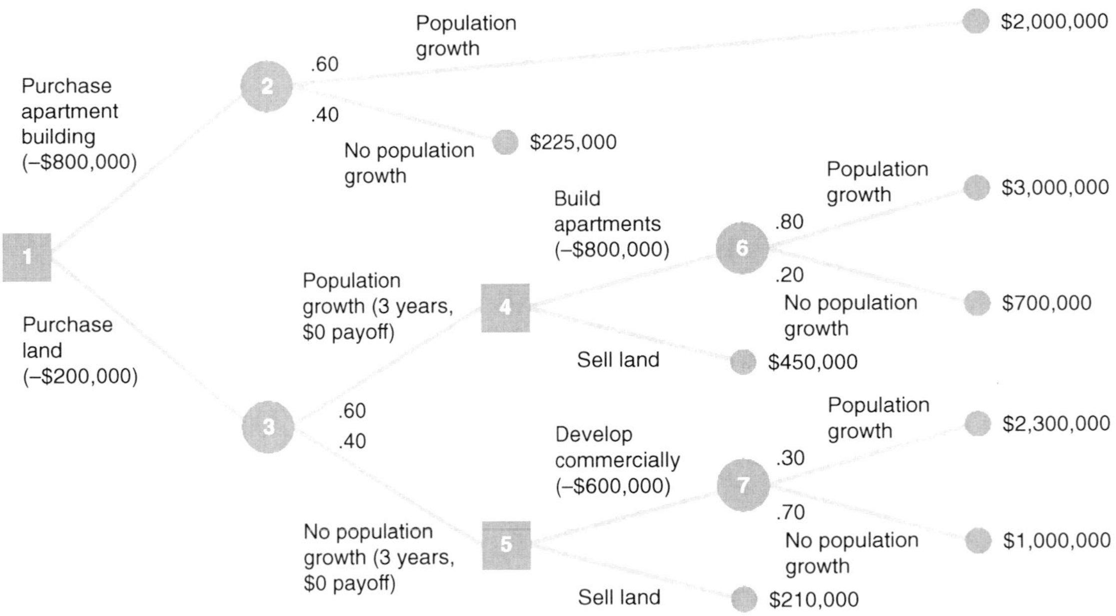

growth occurs first. If no population growth occurs at node 3, there is no payoff, and another decision situation becomes necessary at node 5: The land can be developed commercially at a cost of \$600,000, or the land can be sold for \$210,000. (Notice that the sale of the land results in less profit if there is no population growth than if there is population growth.)

If the decision at decision node 4 is to build apartments, two states of nature are possible: The population may grow, with a conditional probability of .80, or there may be no population growth, with a conditional probability of .20. The probability of population growth is higher (and the probability of no growth is lower) than before because there has already been population growth for the first 3 years, as shown by the branch from node 3 to node 4. The payoffs for these two states of nature at the end of the 10-year period are \$3,000,000 and \$700,000, respectively, as shown in Figure 4.

If the investor decides to develop the land commercially at node 5, then two states of nature can occur: Population growth can occur, with a probability of .30 and an eventual payoff of \$2,300,000, or no population growth can occur, with a probability of .70 and a payoff of \$1,000,000. The probability of population growth is low (i.e., .30) because there has already been no population growth, as shown by the branch from node 3 to node 5.

This decision situation encompasses several sequential decisions that can be analyzed by using the decision tree approach outlined in our earlier (simpler) example. As before, we start at the end of the decision tree and work backward toward a decision at node 1.

First, we must compute the expected values at nodes 6 and 7:

$$EV(\text{node } 6) = .80(\$3{,}000{,}000) + .20(\$700{,}000) = \$2{,}540{,}000$$
$$EV(\text{node } 7) = .30(\$2{,}300{,}000) + .70(\$1{,}000{,}000) = \$1{,}390{,}000$$

These expected values (and all other nodal values) are shown in boxes in Figure 5.

At decision nodes 4 and 5, we must make a decision. As with a normal payoff table, we make the decision that results in the greatest expected value. At node 4 we have a choice between two values: \$1,740,000, the value derived by subtracting the cost of building an apartment building (\$800,000) from the expected payoff of \$2,540,000, *or* \$450,000, the

Figure 5 Sequential decision tree with nodal expected values

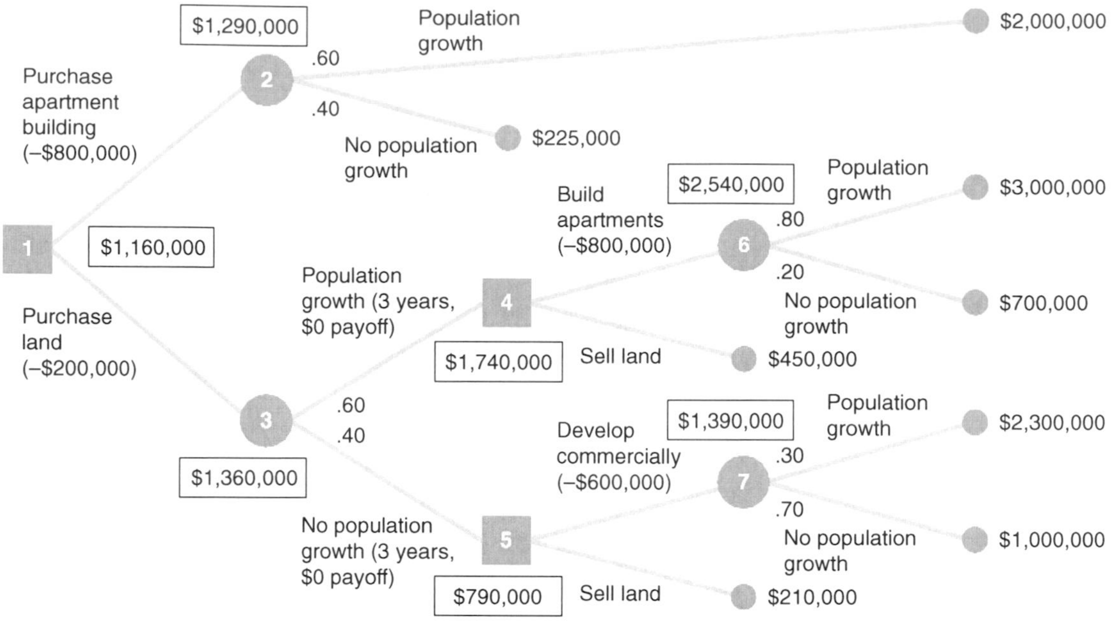

expected value of selling the land computed with a probability of 1.0. The decision is to build the apartment building, and the value at node 4 is $1,740,000.

This same process is repeated at node 5. The decisions at node 5 result in payoffs of $790,000 (i.e., $1,390,000 − 600,000 = $790,000) and $210,000. Because the value $790,000 is higher, the decision is to develop the land commercially.

Next, we must compute the expected values at nodes 2 and 3:

$$EV(\text{node } 2) = .60(\$2{,}000{,}000) + .40(\$225{,}000) = \$1{,}290{,}000$$
$$EV(\text{node } 3) = .60(\$1{,}740{,}000) + .40(\$790{,}000) = \$1{,}360{,}000$$

(Note that the expected value for node 3 is computed from the decision values previously determined at nodes 4 and 5.)

Now we must make the final decision for node 1. As before, we select the decision with the greatest expected value *after the cost of each decision is subtracted out*:

$$\text{apartment building: } \$1{,}290{,}000 - 800{,}000 = \$490{,}000$$
$$\text{land: } \$1{,}360{,}000 - 200{,}000 = \$1{,}160{,}000$$

Because the highest *net* expected value is $1,160,000, the decision is to purchase land, and the payoff of the decision is $1,160,000.

This example demonstrates the usefulness of decision trees for decision analysis. A decision tree allows the decision maker to see the logic of decision making because it provides a picture of the decision process. Decision trees can be used for decision problems more complex than the preceding example without too much difficulty.

Sequential Decision Tree Analysis with QM for Windows

We have already demonstrated the capability of QM for Windows to perform decision tree analysis. For the sequential decision tree example described in the preceding section and

Exhibit 14

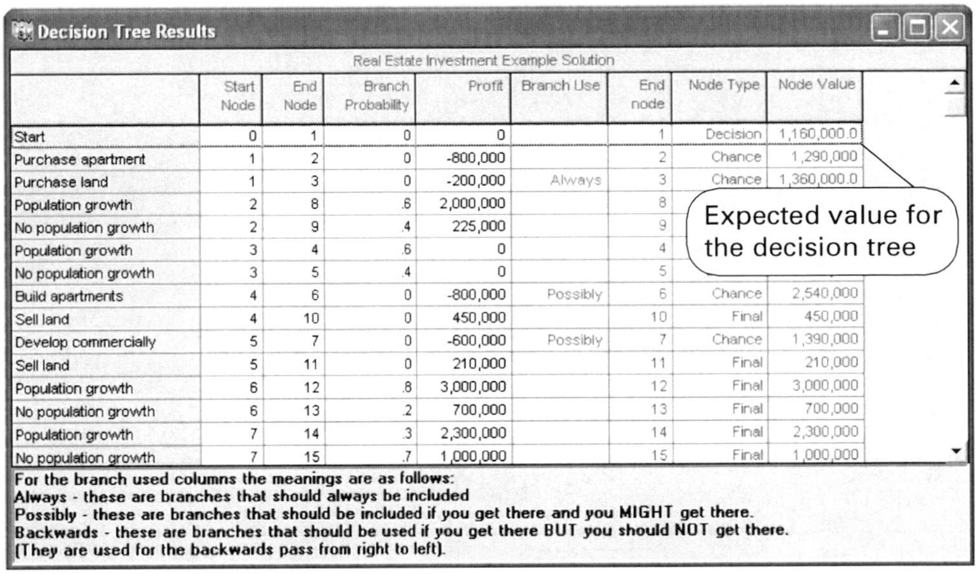

Real Estate Investment Example Solution

	Start Node	End Node	Branch Probability	Profit	Branch Use	End node	Node Type	Node Value
Start	0	1	0	0		1	Decision	1,160,000.0
Purchase apartment	1	2	0	-800,000		2	Chance	1,290,000
Purchase land	1	3	0	-200,000	Always	3	Chance	1,360,000.0
Population growth	2	8	.6	2,000,000		8		
No population growth	2	9	.4	225,000		9		
Population growth	3	4	.6	0		4		
No population growth	3	5	.4	0		5		
Build apartments	4	6	0	-800,000	Possibly	6	Chance	2,540,000
Sell land	4	10	0	450,000		10	Final	450,000
Develop commercially	5	7	0	-600,000	Possibly	7	Chance	1,390,000
Sell land	5	11	0	210,000		11	Final	210,000
Population growth	6	12	.8	3,000,000		12	Final	3,000,000
No population growth	6	13	.2	700,000		13	Final	700,000
Population growth	7	14	.3	2,300,000		14	Final	2,300,000
No population growth	7	15	.7	1,000,000		15	Final	1,000,000

For the branch used columns the meanings are as follows:
Always - these are branches that should always be included
Possibly - these are branches that should be included if you get there and you MIGHT get there.
Backwards - these are branches that should be used if you get there BUT you should NOT get there.
(They are used for the backwards pass from right to left).

illustrated in Figures 4 and 5, the program input and solution screen for QM for Windows is shown in Exhibit 14.

Notice that the expected value for the decision tree, $1,160,000, is given in the first row of the last column on the solution screen in Exhibit 14.

Sequential Decision Tree Analysis with Excel and TreePlan

The sequential decision tree example shown in Figure 5, developed and solved by using TreePlan, is shown in Exhibit 15. Although this TreePlan decision tree is larger than the one we previously developed in Exhibit 13, it was accomplished in exactly the same way.

Exhibit 15

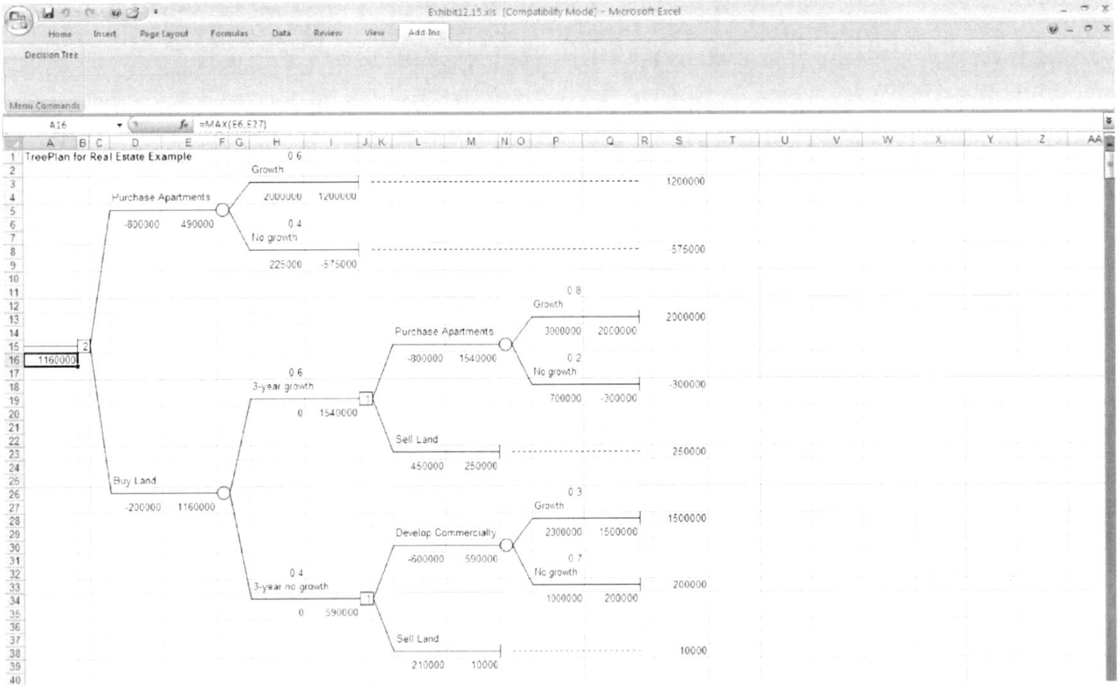

Decision Analysis with Additional Information

Earlier in this chapter we discussed the concept of the *expected value of perfect information.* We noted that if perfect information could be obtained regarding which state of nature would occur in the future, the decision maker could obviously make better decisions. Although perfect information about the future is rare, it is often possible to gain some amount of additional (imperfect) information that will improve decisions.

*In **Bayesian analysis** additional information is used to alter the marginal probability of the occurrence of an event.*

In this section we will present a process for using additional information in the decision-making process by applying **Bayesian analysis.** We will demonstrate this process using the real estate investment example employed throughout this chapter. Let's review this example briefly: A real estate investor is considering three alternative investments, which will occur under one of the two possible economic conditions (states of nature) shown in Table 11.

Table 11
Payoff table for the real estate investment example

	State of Nature	
	GOOD ECONOMIC CONDITIONS	POOR ECONOMIC CONDITIONS
Decision (Purchase)	.60	.40
Apartment building	$ 50,000	$ 30,000
Office building	100,000	−40,000
Warehouse	30,000	10,000

Recall that, using the expected value criterion, we found the best decision to be the purchase of the office building, with an expected value of $44,000. We also computed the expected value of perfect information to be $28,000. Therefore, the investor would be willing to pay up to $28,000 for information about the states of nature, depending on how close to perfect the information was.

Now suppose that the investor has decided to hire a professional economic analyst who will provide additional information about future economic conditions. The analyst is constantly researching the economy, and the results of this research are what the investor will be purchasing.

*A **conditional probability** is the probability that an event will occur, given that another event has already occurred.*

The economic analyst will provide the investor with a report predicting one of two outcomes. The report will be either positive, indicating that good economic conditions are most likely to prevail in the future, or negative, indicating that poor economic conditions will probably occur. Based on the analyst's past record in forecasting future economic conditions, the investor has determined **conditional probabilities** of the different report outcomes, given the occurrence of each state of nature in the future. We will use the following notations to express these conditional probabilities:

g = good economic conditions
p = poor economic conditions
P = positive economic report
N = negative economic report

Management Science Application

Decision Analysis in the Electric Power Industry

Oglethorpe Power Corporation (OPC), a wholesale power generation and transmission cooperative, provides power to 34 consumer-owned distribution cooperatives in Georgia, representing 20% of the power in the state. Georgia Power Company meets the remaining power demand in Georgia. In general, Georgia has the ability to produce surplus power, whereas Florida, because of its rapidly growing population, must buy power from outside the state to meet its demand. In 1990, OPC learned that Florida Power Corporation wanted to add a transmission line to Georgia capable of transmitting an additional 1,000 megawatts (MW). OPC had to decide whether to add this additional capacity at a cost of around $100 million, with annual savings of around $20 million or more. OPC used decision analysis and, specifically, decision trees to help make its ultimate decision. Decision analysis has become a very popular form of quantitative analysis in the electric power industry in the United States. OPC's decision tree analysis included a series of decisions combined with uncertainties. The initial decision alternatives in the tree were whether to build a new transmission line alone, build it in a joint venture with Georgia Power, or not build a new line at all. Subsequent decisions included whether to upgrade existing facilities to meet Florida's needs plus control of the new facilities. Uncertainties included construction costs, Florida's demand for power, competition from other power sellers to Florida, and the share of Florida power for which OPC would be able to contract. The full decision tree for this decision problem, including all combinations of decision nodes and probability nodes, includes almost 8,000 possible decision paths. The decision tree helped OPC understand its decision process better and enabled it to approach the problem so that it would understand its competitive situation with Florida Power Corporation to a greater extent before making a final decision.

Courtesy of Oglethorpe Power Corporation

Source: A. Borison, "Oglethorpe Power Corporation Decides about Investing in a Major Transmission System," *Interfaces* 25, no. 2 (March–April 1995): 25–36.

The conditional probability of each report outcome, given the occurrence of each state of nature, follows:

$$P(\text{P}|\text{g}) = .80$$
$$P(\text{N}|\text{g}) = .20$$
$$P(\text{P}|\text{p}) = .10$$
$$P(\text{N}|\text{p}) = .90$$

For example, if the future economic conditions are, in fact, good (g), the probability that a positive report (P) will have been given by the analyst, $P(\text{P}|\text{g})$, is .80. The other three conditional probabilities can be interpreted similarly. Notice that these probabilities indicate that the analyst is a relatively accurate forecaster of future economic conditions.

The investor now has quite a bit of probabilistic information available—not only the conditional probabilities of the report but also the *prior probabilities* that each state of nature will occur. These prior probabilities that good or poor economic conditions will occur in the future are

$$P(\text{g}) = .60$$
$$P(\text{p}) = .40$$

*A **posterior probability** is the altered marginal probability of an event, based on additional information.*

Given the conditional probabilities, the prior probabilities can be revised to form **posterior probabilities** by means of Bayes's rule. If we know the conditional probability that a positive report was presented, given that good economic conditions prevail, $P(\text{P}|\text{g})$, the posterior probability of good economic conditions, given a positive report, $P(g\,|\,\text{P})$, can be determined using Bayes's rule, as follows:

$$\begin{aligned} P(\text{g}|\text{P}) &= \frac{P(\text{P}|\text{g})P(\text{g})}{P(\text{P}|\text{g})P(\text{g}) + P(\text{P}|\text{p})P(\text{p})} \\ &= \frac{(.80)(.60)}{(.80)(.60) + (.10)(.40)} \\ &= .923 \end{aligned}$$

The prior probability that good economic conditions will occur in the future is .60. However, by obtaining the additional information of a positive report from the analyst, the investor can revise the prior probability of good conditions to a .923 probability that good economic conditions will occur. The remaining posterior (revised) probabilities are

$$\begin{aligned} P(\text{g}|\text{N}) &= .250 \\ P(\text{p}|\text{P}) &= .077 \\ P(\text{p}|\text{N}) &= .750 \end{aligned}$$

Decision Trees with Posterior Probabilities

The original decision tree analysis of the real estate investment example is shown in Figures 2 and 3. Using these decision trees, we determined that the appropriate decision was the purchase of an office building, with an expected value of $44,000. However, if the investor hires an economic analyst, the decision regarding which piece of real estate to invest in will not be made until after the analyst presents the report. This creates an additional stage in the decision-making process, which is shown in the decision tree in Figure 6. This decision tree differs in two respects from the decision trees in Figures 2 and 3. The first difference is that there are two new branches at the beginning of the decision tree that represent the two report outcomes. Notice, however, that given either report outcome, the decision alternatives, the possible states of nature, and the payoffs are the same as those in Figures 2 and 3.

The second difference is that the probabilities of each state of nature are no longer the prior probabilities given in Figure 2; instead, they are the revised posterior probabilities computed in the previous section, using Bayes's rule. If the economic analyst issues a positive report, then the upper branch in Figure 6 (from node 1 to node 2) will be taken. If an apartment building is purchased (the branch from node 2 to node 4), the probability of good economic conditions is .923, whereas the probability of poor conditions is .077. These are the revised posterior probabilities of the economic conditions, given a positive report. However, before we can perform an expected value analysis using this decision tree, one more piece of probabilistic information must be determined—the initial branch probabilities of positive and negative economic reports.

The probability of a positive report, $P(\text{P})$, and of a negative report, $P(\text{N})$, can be determined according to the following logic. The probability that two dependent events, A and B, will both occur is

$$P(\text{AB}) = P(\text{A}|\text{B})P(\text{B})$$

If event A is a positive report and event B is good economic conditions, then according to the preceding formula,

$$P(\text{Pg}) = P(\text{P}|\text{g})P(\text{g})$$

Figure 6
Decision tree with posterior probabilities

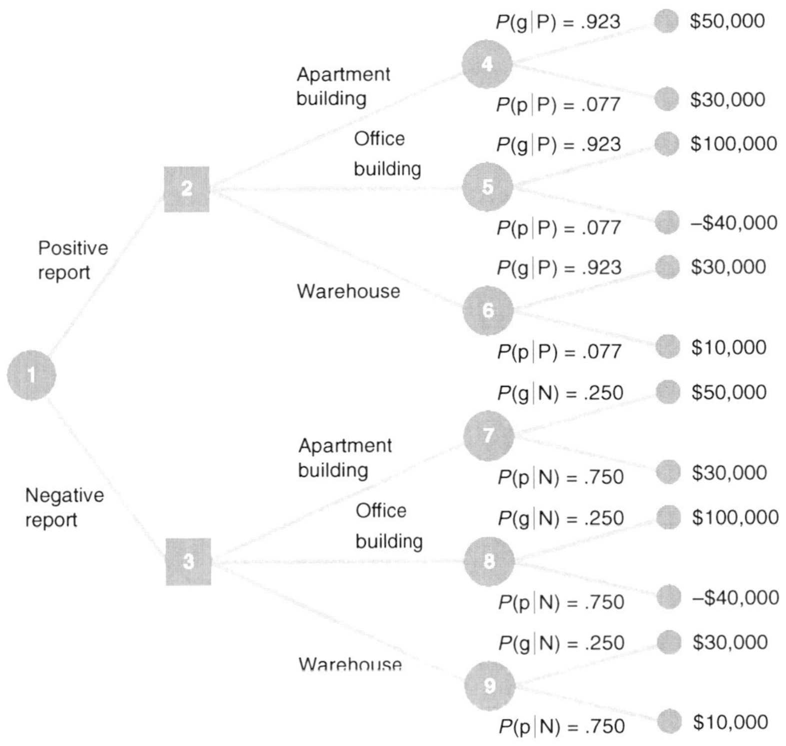

Management Science Application

Discount Fare Allocation at American Airlines

The management of its reservation system, referred to as *yield management*, is a significant factor in American Airlines's profitability. At American Airlines, yield management consists of three functions: overbooking, discount fare allocation, and traffic management. Overbooking is the practice of selling more reservations for a flight than there are available seats, to compensate for no-shows and cancellations. Discount allocation is the process of determining the number of discount fares to make available on a flight. Too few discount fares will leave a flight with empty seats, while too many will limit the number of flights to schedule to maximize revenues.

The process of determining the allocation of discount fares for a flight is essentially a decision analysis model with a decision tree. The initial decision is to accept or reject a discount fare request. If the initial decision is to reject the request, there is a probability, p, that the seat will eventually be sold at full fare and a probability, $1 - p$, that the seat will not be sold at all. The estimate of p is updated several times before flight departure, depending on the forecast for seat demand and the number of available seats remaining. If the expected value of the decision to reject—that is, *EV* (reject discount fare) = (p) ($full fare)—is greater than the discount fare, then the request is rejected.

American Airlines

Source: B. Smith, J. Leimkuhler, and R. Darrow, "Yield Management at American Airlines," *Interfaces* 22, no. 1 (January–February 1992): 8–31.

We can also determine the probability of a positive report and poor economic conditions the same way:

$$P(\text{Pp}) = P(\text{P}|\text{p})P(\text{p})$$

Next, we consider the two probabilities $P(\text{Pg})$ and $P(\text{Pp})$, also called *joint probabilities.* These are, respectively, the probability of a positive report and good economic conditions and the probability of a positive report and poor economic conditions. These two sets of occurrences are **mutually exclusive** because both good and poor economic conditions cannot occur simultaneously in the immediate future. Conditions will be either good or poor, but not both. To determine the probability of a positive report, we add the mutually exclusive probabilities of a positive report with good economic conditions and a positive report with poor economic conditions, as follows:

*Events are **mutually exclusive** if only one can occur at a time.*

$$P(\text{P}) = P(\text{Pg}) + P(\text{Pp})$$

Now, if we substitute into this formula the relationships for $P(\text{Pg})$ and $P(\text{Pp})$ determined earlier, we have

$$P(\text{P}) = P(\text{P}|\text{g})P(\text{g}) + P(\text{P}|\text{p})P(\text{p})$$

You might notice that the right-hand side of this equation is the denominator of the Bayesian formula we used to compute $P(\text{g}|\text{P})$ in the previous section. Using the conditional and prior probabilities that have already been established, we can determine that the probability of a positive report is

$$P(\text{P}) = P(\text{P}|\text{g})P(\text{g}) + P(\text{P}|\text{p})P(\text{p}) = (.80)(.60) + (.10)(.40) = .52$$

Similarly, the probability of a negative report is

$$P(\text{N}) = P(\text{N}|\text{g})P(\text{g}) + P(\text{N}|\text{p})P(\text{p}) = (.20)(.60) + (.90)(.40) = .48$$

$P(\text{P})$ and $P(\text{N})$ are also referred to as *marginal probabilities.*

Now we have all the information needed to perform a decision tree analysis. The decision tree analysis for our example is shown in Figure 7. To see how the decision tree analysis is conducted, consider the result at node 4 first. The value \$48,460 is the expected value of the purchase of an apartment building, given both states of nature. This expected value is computed as follows:

$$EV(\text{apartment building}) = \$50{,}000(.923) + 30{,}000(.077) = \$48{,}460$$

The expected values at nodes 5, 6, 7, 8, and 9 are computed similarly.

The investor will actually make the decision about the investment at nodes 2 and 3. It is assumed that the investor will make the best decision in each case. Thus, the decision at node 2 will be to purchase an office building, with an expected value of \$89,220; the decision at node 3 will be to purchase an apartment building, with an expected value of \$35,000. These two results at nodes 2 and 3 are referred to as *decision strategies.* They represent a plan of decisions to be made, given either a positive or a negative report from the economic analyst.

The final step in the decision tree analysis is to compute the expected value of the decision strategy, given that an economic analysis is performed. This expected value, shown as \$63,194 at node 1 in Figure 7, is computed as follows:

$$\begin{aligned} EV(\text{strategy}) &= \$89{,}220(.52) + 35{,}000(.48) \\ &= \$63{,}194 \end{aligned}$$

This amount, \$63,194, is the expected value of the investor's decision strategy, given that a report forecasting future economic condition is generated by the economic analyst.

Figure 7
Decision tree analysis for real estate investment example

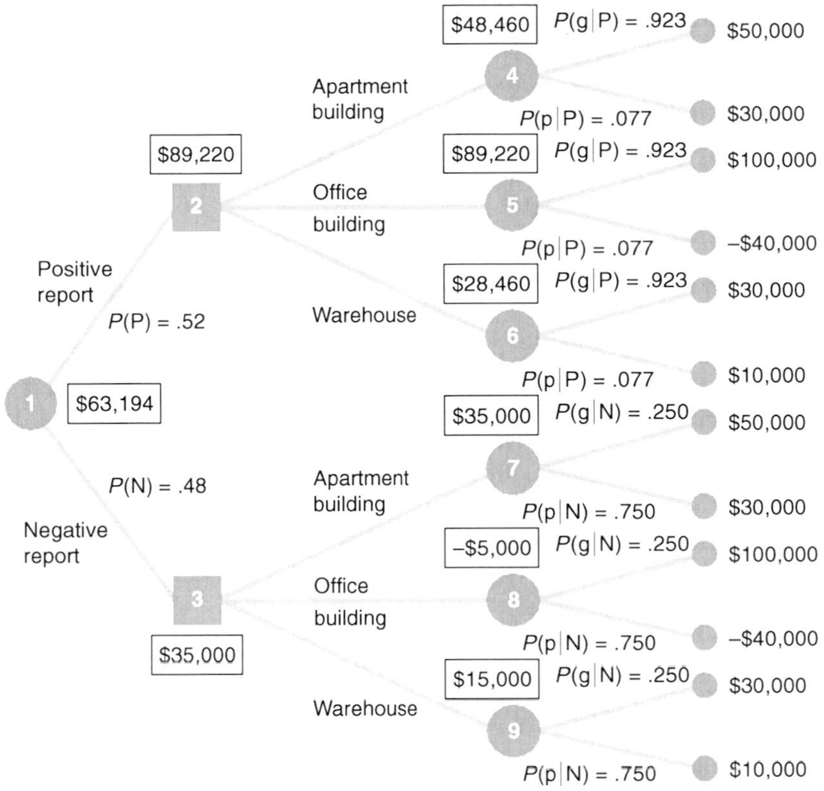

Computing Posterior Probabilities with Tables

One of the difficulties that can occur with decision analysis with additional information is that as the size of the problem increases (i.e., as we add more decision alternatives and states of nature), the application of Bayes's rule to compute the posterior probabilities becomes more complex. In such cases, the posterior probabilities can be computed by using tables. This tabular approach will be demonstrated with our real estate investment example. The table for computing posterior probabilities for a positive report and $P(P)$ is initially set up as shown in Table 12.

Table 12
Computation of posterior probabilities

(1) State of Nature	(2) Prior Probability	(3) Conditional Probability	(4) Prior Probability × Conditional Probability: (2) × (3)	(5) Posterior Probability: (4) ÷ Σ(4)
Good conditions	$P(g) = .60$	$P(P\|g) = .80$	$P(Pg) = .48$	$P(g\|P) = \frac{.48}{.52} = .923$
Poor conditions	$P(p) = .40$	$P(P\|p) = .10$	$P(Pp) = .04$ $\sum = P(P) = .52$	$P(p\|P) = \frac{.04}{.52} = .077$

The posterior probabilities for either state of nature (good or poor economic conditions), given a negative report, are computed similarly.

No matter how large the decision analysis, the steps of this tabular approach can be followed the same way as in this relatively small problem. This approach is more systematic than the direct application of Bayes's "rule," making it easier to compute the posterior probabilities for larger problems.

Computing Posterior Probabilities with Excel

The posterior probabilities computed in Table 12 can also be computed by using Excel. Exhibit 16 shows Table 12 set up in an Excel spreadsheet format, as well as the table for computing $P(\text{N})$.

Exhibit 16

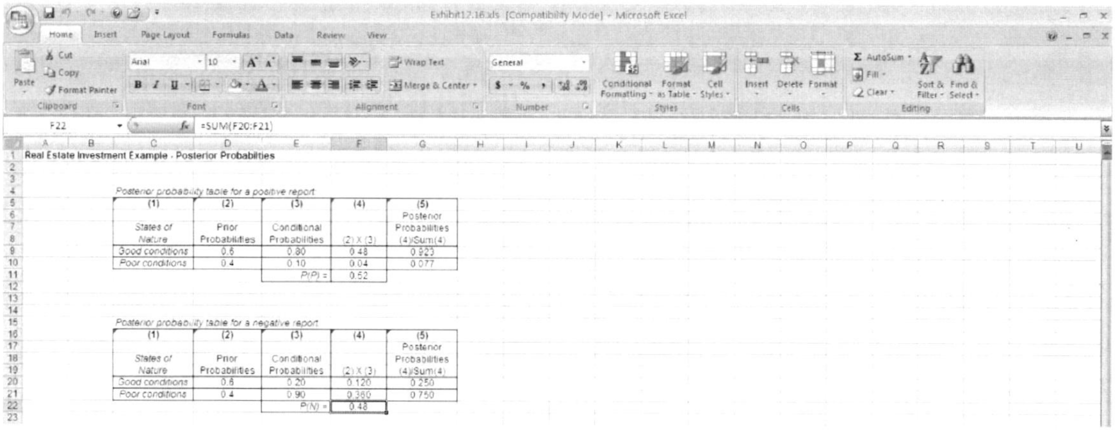

Real Estate Investment Example - Posterior Probabilties

Posterior probability table for a positive report

(1) States of Nature	(2) Prior Probabilities	(3) Conditional Probabilities	(4) (2) X (3)	(5) Posterior Probabilities (4)/Sum(4)
Good conditions	0.6	0.80	0.48	0.923
Poor conditions	0.4	0.10	0.04	0.077
		P(P) =	0.52	

Posterior probability table for a negative report

(1) States of Nature	(2) Prior Probabilities	(3) Conditional Probabilities	(4) (2) X (3)	(5) Posterior Probabilities (4)/Sum(4)
Good conditions	0.6	0.20	0.120	0.250
Poor conditions	0.4	0.90	0.360	0.750
		P(N) =	0.48	

The Expected Value of Sample Information

Recall that we computed the expected value of our real estate investment example to be \$44,000 when we did not have any additional information. After obtaining the additional information provided by the economic analyst, we computed an expected value of \$63,194, using the decision tree in Figure 7. The difference between these two expected values is called the **expected value of sample information** (EVSI), and it is computed as follows:

*The **expected value of sample information** is the difference between the expected value with and without additional information.*

$$EVSI = EV_{\text{with information}} - EV_{\text{without information}}$$

For our example, the expected value of sample information is

$$EVSI = \$63{,}194 - 44{,}000 = \$19{,}194$$

This means that the real estate investor would be willing to pay the economic analyst up to \$19,194 for an economic report that forecasted future economic conditions.

After we computed the expected value of the investment without additional information, we computed the *expected value of perfect information*, which equaled \$28,000. However, the expected value of the sample information was only \$19,194. This is a logical result because it is rare that absolutely perfect information can be determined. Because the additional information that is obtained is less than perfect, it will be worth less to the decision maker. We can determine how close to perfect our sample information is by computing the **efficiency of sample information** as follows:

*The **efficiency of sample information** is the ratio of the expected value of sample information to the expected value of perfect information.*

$$\text{efficiency} = EVSI \div EVPI = \$19{,}194 \,/\, 28{,}000 = .69$$

Thus, the analyst's economic report is viewed by the investor to be 69% as efficient as perfect information. In general, a high efficiency rating indicates that the information is very good, or close to being perfect information, and a low rating indicates that the additional

Management Science Application

Scheduling Refueling at the Indian Point 3 Nuclear Power Plant

The New York Power Authority (NYPA) owns and operates 12 power projects that provide roughly one-fourth of all the electricity used in New York State. Approximately 20% of NYPA's electrical power (supplying Westchester County and New York City) is generated by the Indian Point 3 (IP3) nuclear power plant, located on the Hudson River. IP3 withdraws 840,000 gallons of water per minute from the river for cooling steam and then returns it to the river. When water is withdrawn from the river, fish, especially small fish and eggs, do not always survive as they pass through the cooling system. The NYPA can reduce the negative effects by scheduling plant shutdowns to refuel IP3 when fish eggs and small fish are most abundant in the Hudson River. In the past, NYPA developed a refueling schedule according to a 10-year planning horizon, although unforeseen events often altered this schedule. There is uncertainty in the future about possible deregulation of the electric utility industry and its effect on the price of replacement power during refueling outages. The NYPA must consider these uncertainties in its attempt to provide low-cost power and minimize the environmental effects of refueling outages. The NYPA developed a decision analysis model to compare alternative strategies for refueling that balanced fish protection, the cost of buying fuel, and the uncertainties of deregulation.

The key decisions of the model were the times of year that refueling outages should occur, which affects the level of fish protection, and the amount of fuel that should be ordered for the nuclear reactor core that allows for operation for a target number of days, which affects the cost of the operation. The cost consideration comprises three objectives: minimizing the cost of replacement electricity when IP3 is shut down, minimizing the amount of unused fuel at the end of an operating cycle, and minimizing the time that IP3 would operate at less than full power before refueling. The objective of fish protection was to minimize the sum of the average percentage reduction in the mortality rate caused by water removal at IP3 for five types of fish over the 10-year planning horizon. The three major uncertainties in the model were the cost of refueling, how long it takes IP3 to refuel and how well it operates, and when New York State is likely to deregulate the electric utility industry. The decision analysis model considered five strategies based on different schedules that reflected different time windows when fish were most vulnerable. The model showed that no strategy simultaneously minimized refueling cost while minimizing fish mortality rates. The strategy that was selected restricted the starting date for refueling to the third week in May, when fish protection would meet accepted standards, at a cost savings of $10 million over the previous refueling schedule. The NYPA used the decision analysis model to develop its refueling schedule for the 10-year period from 1999 to 2008.

AP Wide World Photos

Source: D. J. Dunning, S. Lockfort, Q. E. Ross, P. C. Beccue, and J. S. Stonebraker, "New York Power Authority Uses Decision Analysis to Schedule Refueling of Its Indian Point 3 Nuclear Power Plant," *Interfaces* 31, no. 5 (September–October 2001): 121–35.

information is not very good. For our example, the efficiency of .69 is relatively high; thus, it is doubtful that the investor would seek additional information from an alternative source. (However, this is usually dependent on how much money the decision maker has available to purchase information.) If the efficiency had been lower, however, the investor might seek additional information elsewhere.

Utility

All the decision-making criteria presented so far in this chapter have been based on monetary value. In other words, decisions have been based on the potential dollar payoffs of the alternatives. However, there are certain decision situations in which individuals do not make decisions based on the expected dollar gain or loss.

For example, consider an individual who purchases automobile insurance. The decisions are to purchase and to not purchase, and the states of nature are *an accident* and *no accident*. The payoff table for this decision situation, including probabilities, is shown in Table 13.

Table 13
Payoff table for auto insurance example

	State of Nature	
Decision	No Accident .992	Accident .008
Purchase insurance	$500	$ 500
Do not purchase insurance	0	10,000

The dollar outcomes in Table 13 are the *costs* associated with each outcome. The insurance costs $500 whether there is an accident or no accident. If the insurance is not purchased and there is no accident, then there is no cost at all. However, if an accident does occur, the individual will incur a cost of $10,000.

The expected cost (*EC*) for each decision is

$$EC(\text{insurance}) = .992(\$500) + .008(\$500) = \$500$$
$$EC(\text{no insurance}) = .992(\$0) + .008(\$10{,}000) = \$80$$

Because the *lower* expected cost is $80, the decision *should be* not to purchase insurance. However, people almost always purchase insurance (even when they are not legally required to do so). This is true of all types of insurance, such as accident, life, or fire.

Why do people shun the greater *expected* dollar outcome in this type of situation? The answer is that people want to avoid a ruinous or painful situation. When faced with a relatively small dollar cost versus a disaster, people typically pay the small cost to avert the disaster. People who display this characteristic are referred to as **risk averters** because they avoid risky situations.

*People who forgo a high expected value to avoid a disaster with a low probability are **risk averters**.*

Alternatively, people who go to the track to wager on horse races, travel to Atlantic City to play roulette, or speculate in the commodities market decide to take risks even though the greatest *expected value* would occur if they simply held on to the money. These people shun the greater expected value accruing from a sure thing (keeping their money) in order to take a chance on receiving a "bonanza." Such people are referred to as **risk takers**.

*People who take a chance on a bonanza with a very low probability of occurrence in lieu of a sure thing are **risk takers**.*

For both risk averters and risk takers (as well as those who are indifferent to risk), the decision criterion is something other than the expected dollar outcome. This alternative criterion is known as **utility**. Utility is a measure of the satisfaction derived from money. In our examples of risk averters and risk takers presented earlier, the utility derived from their decisions *exceeded* the expected dollar value. For example, the utility to the average decision maker of having insurance is much greater than the utility of not having insurance.

***Utility** is a measure of personal satisfaction derived from money.*

As another example, consider two people, each of whom is offered $100,000 to perform some particularly difficult and strenuous task. One individual has an annual income of $10,000; the other individual is a multimillionaire. It is reasonable to assume that the average person with an annual income of only $10,000 would leap at the opportunity to earn $100,000, whereas the multimillionaire would reject the offer. Obviously, $100,000 has more *utility* (i.e., value) for one individual than for the other.

In general, the same incremental amount of money does not have the same intrinsic value to every person. For individuals with a great deal of wealth, more money does not usually have as much intrinsic value as it does for individuals who have little money. In other words, although the dollar value is the same, the value as measured by utility is different, depending on how much wealth a person has. Thus, utility in this case is a measure of the pleasure or satisfaction an individual would receive from an incremental increase in wealth.

Utiles are units of subjective measures of utility.

In some decision situations, decision makers attempt to assign a subjective value to utility. This value is typically measured in terms of units called **utiles**. For example, the $100,000 offered to the two individuals may have a utility value of 100 utiles to the person with a low income and 0 utiles to the multimillionaire.

In our automobile insurance example, the *expected utility* of purchasing insurance could be 1,000 utiles, and the expected utility of not purchasing insurance only 1 utile. These utility values are completely reversed from the *expected monetary values* computed from Table 13, which explains the decision to purchase insurance.

As might be expected, it is usually very difficult to measure utility and the number of utiles derived from a decision outcome. The process is a very subjective one in which the decision maker's psychological preferences must be determined. Thus, although the concept of utility is realistic and often portrays actual decision-making criteria more accurately than does expected monetary value, its application is difficult and, as such, somewhat limited.

Summary

The purpose of this chapter was to demonstrate the concepts and fundamentals of decision making when uncertainty exists. Within this context, several decision-making criteria were presented. The maximax, maximin, minimax regret, equal likelihood, and Hurwicz decision criteria were demonstrated for cases in which probabilities could not be attached to the occurrence of outcomes. The expected value criterion and decision trees were discussed for cases in which probabilities could be assigned to the states of nature of a decision situation.

All the decision criteria presented in this chapter were demonstrated via rather simplified examples; actual decision-making situations are usually more complex. Nevertheless, the process of analyzing decisions presented in this chapter is the logical method that most decision makers follow to make a decision.

References

Baumol, W. J. *Economic Theory and Operations Analysis*, 4th ed. Upper Saddle River, NJ: Prentice Hall, 1977.

Bell, D. "Bidding for the S.S. *Kuniang*." *Interfaces* 14, no. 2 (March–April 1984): 17–23.

Dorfman, R., Samuelson, P. A., and Solow, R. M. *Linear Programming and Economic Analysis*. New York: McGraw-Hill, 1958.

Holloway, C. A. *Decision Making Under Uncertainty*. Upper Saddle River, NJ: Prentice Hall, 1979.

Howard, R. A. "An Assessment of Decision Analysis." *Operations Research* 28, no. 1 (January–February 1980): 4–27.

Keeney, R. L. "Decision Analysis: An Overview." *Operations Research* 30, no. 5 (September–October 1982): 803–38.

Luce, R. D., and Raiffa, H. *Games and Decisions*. New York: John Wiley & Sons, 1957.

Von Neumann, J., and Morgenstern, O. *Theory of Games and Economic Behavior*, 3rd ed. Princeton, NJ: Princeton University Press, 1953.

Williams, J. D. *The Compleat Strategyst*, rev. ed. New York: McGraw-Hill, 1966.

Example Problem Solution

The following example will illustrate the solution procedure for a decision analysis problem.

Problem Statement

T. Bone Puckett, a corporate raider, has acquired a textile company and is contemplating the future of one of its major plants, located in South Carolina. Three alternative decisions are being considered: (1) expand the plant and produce lightweight, durable materials for possible sales to the military, a market with little foreign competition; (2) maintain the status quo at the plant, continuing production of textile goods that are subject to heavy foreign competition; or (3) sell the plant now. If one of the first two alternatives is chosen, the plant will still be sold at the end of a year. The amount of profit that could be earned by selling the plant in a year depends on foreign market conditions, including the status of a trade embargo bill in Congress. The following payoff table describes this decision situation:

	State of Nature	
Decision	*Good Foreign Competitive Conditions*	*Poor Foreign Competitive Conditions*
Expand	\$ 800,000	\$ 500,000
Maintain status quo	1,300,000	−150,000
Sell now	320,000	320,000

A. Determine the best decision by using the following decision criteria:
   1. Maximax
   2. Maximin
   3. Minimax regret
   4. Hurwicz ($\alpha = .3$)
   5. Equal likelihood

B. Assume that it is now possible to estimate a probability of .70 that good foreign competitive conditions will exist and a probability of .30 that poor conditions will exist. Determine the best decision by using expected value and expected opportunity loss.

C. Compute the expected value of perfect information.

D. Develop a decision tree, with expected values at the probability nodes.

E. T. Bone Puckett has hired a consulting firm to provide a report on future political and market situations. The report will be positive (P) or negative (N), indicating either a good (g) or poor (p) future foreign competitive situation. The conditional probability of each report outcome, given each state of nature, is

$$P(\text{P} \mid \text{g}) = .70$$
$$P(\text{N} \mid \text{g}) = .30$$
$$P(\text{P} \mid \text{p}) = .20$$
$$P(\text{N} \mid \text{p}) = .80$$

   Determine the posterior probabilities by using Bayes's rule.

F. Perform a decision tree analysis by using the posterior probability obtained in (E).

Solution

Step 1 (part A): Determine Decisions Without Probabilities

Maximax:

Expand	\$ 800,000	
Status quo	1,300,000	← Maximum
Sell	320,000	

Decision: Maintain status quo.

Maximin:

Expand	\$ 500,000	←	Maximum
Status quo	−150,000		
Sell	320,000		

Decision: Expand.

Minimax regret:

Expand	\$500,000	←	Minimum
Status quo	650,000		
Sell	980,000		

Decision: Expand.

Hurwicz ($\alpha = .3$):

Expand	\$800,000(.3) + 500,000(.7) = \$590,000
Status quo	\$1,300,000(.3) − 150,000(.7) = \$285,000
Sell	\$320,000(.3) + 320,000(.7) = \$320,000

Decision: Expand.

Equal likelihood:

Expand	\$800,000(.50) + 500,000(.50) = \$650,000
Status quo	\$1,300,000(.50) − 150,000(.50) − \$575,000
Sell	\$320,000(.50) + 320,000(.50) = \$320,000

Decision: Expand.

Step 2 (part B): Determine Decisions with *EV* and *EOL*

Expected value:

Expand	\$800,000(.70) + 500,000(.30) = \$710,000
Status quo	\$1,300,000(.70) − 150,000(.30) = \$865,000
Sell	\$320,000(.70) + 320,000(.30) = \$320,000

Decision: Maintain status quo.

Expected opportunity loss:

Expand	\$500,000(.70) + 0(.30) = \$350,000
Status quo	\$0(.70) + 650,000(.30) = \$195,000
Sell	\$980,000(.70) + 180,000(.30) = \$740,000

Decision: Maintain status quo.

Step 3 (part C): Compute *EVPI*

$$\text{expected value given perfect information} = 1{,}300{,}000(.70) + 500{,}000(.30) = \$1{,}060{,}000$$

$$\text{expected value without perfect information} = \$1{,}300{,}000(.70) - 150{,}000(.30)$$
$$= \$865{,}000$$
$$EVPI = \$1{,}060{,}000 - 865{,}000 = \$195{,}000$$

Step 4 (part D): Develop a Decision Tree

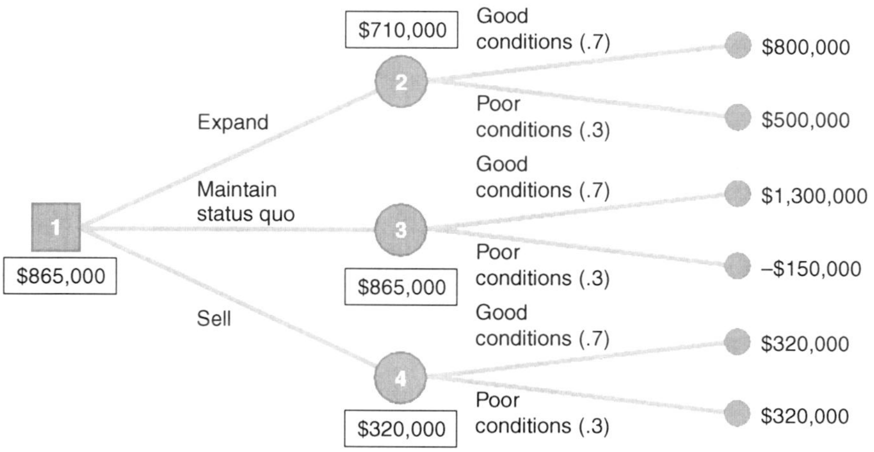

Step 5 (part E): Determine Posterior Probabilities

$$P(\mathrm{g}|\mathrm{P}) = \frac{P(\mathrm{P}|\mathrm{g})P(\mathrm{g})}{P(\mathrm{P}|\mathrm{g})P(\mathrm{g}) + P(\mathrm{P}|\mathrm{p})P(\mathrm{p})}$$
$$= \frac{(.70)(.70)}{(.70)(.70) + (.20)(.30)}$$
$$= .891$$
$$P(\mathrm{p}|\mathrm{P}) = .109$$
$$P(\mathrm{g}|\mathrm{N}) = \frac{P(\mathrm{N}|\mathrm{g})P(\mathrm{g})}{P(\mathrm{N}|\mathrm{g})P(\mathrm{g}) + P(\mathrm{N}|\mathrm{p})P(\mathrm{p})}$$
$$= \frac{(.30)(.70)}{(.30)(.70) + (.80)(.30)}$$
$$= .467$$
$$P(\mathrm{p}|\mathrm{N}) = .533$$

Step 6 (part F): Perform Decision Tree Analysis with Posterior Probabilities

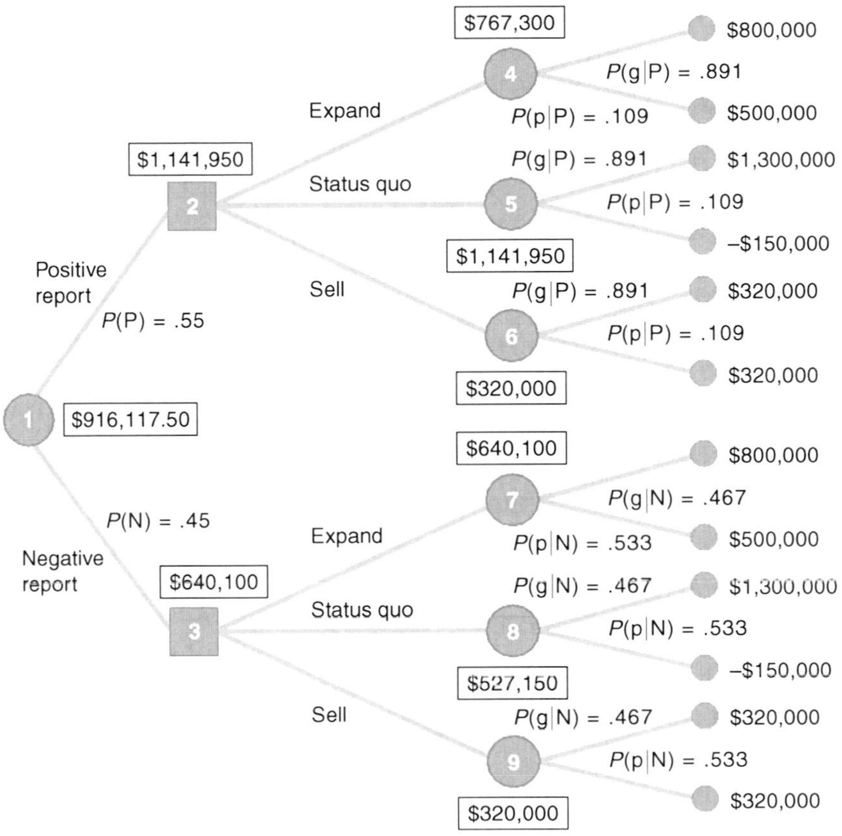

Problems

1. A farmer in Iowa is considering either leasing some extra land or investing in savings certificates at the local bank. If weather conditions are good next year, the extra land will give the farmer an excellent harvest. However, if weather conditions are bad, the farmer will lose money. The savings certificates will result in the same return, regardless of the weather conditions. The return for each investment, given each type of weather condition, is shown in the following payoff table:

	Weather	
Decision	Good	Bad
Lease land	$90,000	$-40,000
Buy savings certificate	10,000	10,000

Select the best decision, using the following decision criteria:

a. Maximax
b. Maximin

2. The owner of the Burger Doodle Restaurant is considering two ways to expand operations: open a drive-up window or serve breakfast. The increase in profits resulting from these proposed expansions depends on whether a competitor opens a franchise down the street. The possible profits from each expansion in operations, given both future competitive situations, are shown in the following payoff table:

	Competitor	
Decision	Open	Not Open
Drive-up window	$−6,000	$20,000
Breakfast	4,000	8,000

Select the best decision, using the following decision criteria.
a. Maximax
b. Maximin

3. Stevie Stone, a bellhop at the Royal Sundown Hotel in Atlanta, has been offered a management position. Although accepting the offer would assure him a job if there was a recession, if good economic conditions prevailed, he would actually make less money as a manager than as a bellhop (because of the large tips he gets as a bellhop). His salary during the next 5 years for each job, given each future economic condition, is shown in the following payoff table:

	Economic Conditions	
Decision	Good	Recession
Bellhop	$120,000	$60,000
Manager	85,000	85,000

Select the best decision, using the following decision criteria.
a. Minimax regret
b. Hurwicz ($\alpha = .4$)
c. Equal likelihood

4. Brooke Bentley, a student in business administration, is trying to decide which management science course to take next quarter—I, II, or III. "Steamboat" Fulton, "Death" Ray, and "Sadistic" Scott are the three management science professors who teach the courses. Brooke does not know who will teach what course. Brooke can expect a different grade in each of the courses, depending on who teaches it next quarter, as shown in the following payoff table:

	Professor		
Course	Fulton	Ray	Scott
I	B	D	D
II	C	B	F
III	F	A	C

Determine the best course to take next quarter, using the following criteria.
a. Maximax
b. Maximin

5. A farmer in Georgia must decide which crop to plant next year on his land: corn, peanuts, or soybeans. The return from each crop will be determined by whether a new trade bill with Russia passes the Senate. The profit the farmer will realize from each crop, given the two possible results on the trade bill, is shown in the following payoff table:

	Trade Bill	
Crop	Pass	Fail
Corn	$35,000	$ 8,000
Peanuts	18,000	12,000
Soybeans	22,000	20,000

Determine the best crop to plant, using the following decision criteria.

a. Maximax
b. Maximin
c. Minimax regret
d. Hurwicz ($\alpha = .3$)
e. Equal likelihood

6. A company must decide now which of three products to make next year to plan and order proper materials. The cost per unit of producing each product will be determined by whether a new union labor contract passes or fails. The cost per unit for each product, given each contract result, is shown in the following payoff table:

	Contract Outcome	
Product	Pass	Fail
1	$7.50	$6.00
2	4.00	7.00
3	6.50	3.00

Determine which product should be produced, using the following decision criteria.

a. Minimin
b. Minimax

7. The owner of the Columbia Construction Company must decide between building a housing development, constructing a shopping center, and leasing all the company's equipment to another company. The profit that will result from each alternative will be determined by whether material costs remain stable or increase. The profit from each alternative, given the two possibilities for material costs, is shown in the following payoff table:

	Material Costs	
Decision	Stable	Increase
Houses	$ 70,000	$30,000
Shopping center	105,000	20,000
Leasing	40,000	40,000

Determine the best decision, using the following decision criteria.

a. Maximax
b. Maximin

c. Minimax regret
d. Hurwicz ($\alpha = .2$)
e. Equal likelihood

8. A local real estate investor in Orlando is considering three alternative investments: a motel, a restaurant, or a theater. Profits from the motel or restaurant will be affected by the availability of gasoline and the number of tourists; profits from the theater will be relatively stable under any conditions. The following payoff table shows the profit or loss that could result from each investment:

	Gasoline Availability		
Investment	Shortage	Stable Supply	Surplus
Motel	\$−8,000	\$15,000	\$20,000
Restaurant	2,000	8,000	6,000
Theater	6,000	6,000	5,000

Determine the best investment, using the following decision criteria.
a. Maximax
b. Maximin
c. Minimax regret
d. Hurwicz ($\alpha = .4$)
e. Equal likelihood

9. A television network is attempting to decide during the summer which of the following three football games to televise on the Saturday following Thanksgiving Day: Alabama versus Auburn, Georgia versus Georgia Tech, or Army versus Navy. The estimated viewer ratings (millions of homes) for the games depend on the win–loss records of the six teams, as shown in the following payoff table:

	Number of Viewers (1,000,000s)		
Game	Both Teams Have Winning Records	One Team Has Winning Record; One Team Has Losing Record	Both Teams Have Losing Records
Alabama vs. Auburn	10.2	7.3	5.4
Georgia vs. Georgia Tech	9.6	8.1	4.8
Army vs. Navy	12.5	6.5	3.2

Determine the best game to televise, using the following decision criteria.
a. Maximax
b. Maximin
c. Equal likelihood

10. Ann Tyler has come into an inheritance from her grandparents. She is attempting to decide among several investment alternatives. The return after 1 year is primarily dependent on the interest rate during the next year. The rate is currently 7%, and Ann anticipates that it will stay the same or go

up or down by at most two points. The various investment alternatives plus their returns ($10,000s), given the interest rate changes, are shown in the following table:

	Interest Rate				
Investments	5%	6%	7%	8%	9%
Money market fund	2	3.1	4	4.3	5
Stock growth fund	−3	−2	2.5	4	6
Bond fund	6	5	3	3	2
Government fund	4	3.6	3.2	3	2.8
Risk fund	−9	−4.5	1.2	8.3	14.7
Savings bonds	3	3	3.2	3.4	3.5

Determine the best investment, using the following decision criteria.

a. Maximax
b. Maximin
c. Equal likelihood

11. The Tech football coaching staff has six basic offensive plays it runs every game. Tech has an upcoming game against State on Saturday, and the Tech coaches know that State employs five different defenses. The coaches have estimated the number of yards Tech will gain with each play against each defense, as shown in the following payoff table:

	Defense				
Play	54	63	Wide Tackle	Nickel	Blitz
Off tackle	3	−2	9	7	−1
Option	−1	8	−2	9	12
Toss sweep	6	16	−5	3	14
Draw	−2	4	3	10	−3
Pass	8	20	12	−7	−8
Screen	−5	−2	8	3	16

a. If the coaches employ an offensive game plan, they will use the maximax criterion. What will be their best play?
b. If the coaches employ a defensive plan, they will use the maximin criterion. What will be their best play?
c. What will be their best offensive play if State is equally likely to use any of its five defenses?

12. Microcomp is a U.S.-based manufacturer of personal computers. It is planning to build a new manufacturing and distribution facility in either South Korea, China, Taiwan, the Philippines, or Mexico. It will take approximately 5 years to build the necessary infrastructure (roads, etc.), construct the new facility, and put it into operation. The eventual cost of the facility will differ between countries and will even vary within countries depending on the financial, labor, and political climate, including monetary exchange rates. The company has estimated the facility cost (in $1,000,000s) in each country under three different future economic and political climates, as follows:

Country	Economic/Political Climate		
	Decline	Same	Improve
South Korea	21.7	19.1	15.2
China	19.0	18.5	17.6
Taiwan	19.2	17.1	14.9
Philippines	22.5	16.8	13.8
Mexico	25.0	21.2	12.5

Determine the best decision, using the following decision criteria.

a. Minimin
b. Minimax
c. Hurwicz ($\alpha = .4$)
d. Equal likelihood

13. Place-Plus, a real estate development firm, is considering several alternative development projects. These include building and leasing an office park, purchasing a parcel of land and building an office building to rent, buying and leasing a warehouse, building a strip mall, and building and selling condominiums. The financial success of these projects depends on interest rate movement in the next 5 years. The various development projects and their 5-year financial return (in $1,000,000s) given that interest rates will decline, remain stable, or increase, are shown in the following payoff table:

Project	**Interest Rate**		
	Decline	Stable	Increase
Office park	$0.5	$1.7	$4.5
Office building	1.5	1.9	2.5
Warehouse	1.7	1.4	1.0
Mall	0.7	2.4	3.6
Condominiums	3.2	1.5	0.6

Determine the best investment, using the following decision criteria.

a. Maximax
b. Maximin
c. Equal likelihood
d. Hurwicz ($\alpha = .3$)

14. The Oakland Bombers professional basketball team just missed making the playoffs last season and believes it needs to sign only one very good free agent to make the playoffs next season. The team is considering four players: Barry Byrd, Rayneal O'Neil, Marvin Johnson, and Michael Gordan. Each player differs according to position, ability, and attractiveness to fans. The payoffs (in $1,000,000s) to the team for each player, based on the contract, profits from attendance, and team product sales for several different season outcomes, are provided in the following table:

Player	**Season Outcome**		
	Loser	Competitive	Makes Playoffs
Byrd	$−3.2	$ 1.3	4.4
O'Neil	−5.1	1.8	6.3
Johnson	−2.7	0.7	5.8
Gordan	−6.3	−1.6	9.6

Determine the best decision, using the following decision criteria.

a. Maximax
b. Maximin
c. Hurwicz (α = .60)
d. Equal likelihood

15. A machine shop owner is attempting to decide whether to purchase a new drill press, a lathe, or a grinder. The return from each will be determined by whether the company succeeds in getting a government military contract. The profit or loss from each purchase and the probabilities associated with each contract outcome are shown in the following payoff table:

Purchase	Contract .40	No Contract .60
Drill press	$40,000	$−8,000
Lathe	20,000	4,000
Grinder	12,000	10,000

Compute the expected value for each purchase and select the best one.

16. A concessions manager at the Tech versus A&M football game must decide whether to have the vendors sell sun visors or umbrellas. There is a 30% chance of rain, a 15% chance of overcast skies, and a 55% chance of sunshine, according to the weather forecast in College Junction, where the game is to be held. The manager estimates that the following profits will result from each decision, given each set of weather conditions:

	Weather Conditions		
Decision	Rain .30	Overcast .15	Sunshine .55
Sun visors	$−500	$−200	$1,500
Umbrellas	2,000	0	−900

a. Compute the expected value for each decision and select the best one.
b. Develop the opportunity loss table and compute the expected opportunity loss for each decision.

17. Allen Abbott has a wide-curving, uphill driveway leading to his garage. When there is a heavy snow, Allen hires a local carpenter, who shovels snow on the side in the winter, to shovel his driveway. The snow shoveler charges $30 to shovel the driveway. Following is a probability distribution of the number of heavy snows each winter:

Heavy Snows	Probability
1	.13
2	.18
3	.26
4	.23
5	.10
6	.07
7	.03
	1.00

Allen is considering purchasing a new self-propelled snowblower for $625 that would allow him, his wife, or his children to clear the driveway after a snow. Discuss what you think Allen's decision should be and why.

18. The Miramar Company is going to introduce one of three new products: a widget, a hummer, or a nimnot. The market conditions (favorable, stable, or unfavorable) will determine the profit or loss the company realizes, as shown in the following payoff table:

	Market Conditions		
	Favorable	Stable	Unfavorable
Product	.2	.7	.1
Widget	$120,000	$70,000	$−30,000
Hummer	60,000	40,000	20,000
Nimnot	35,000	30,000	30,000

a. Compute the expected value for each decision and select the best one.
b. Develop the opportunity loss table and compute the expected opportunity loss for each product.
c. Determine how much the firm would be willing to pay to a market research firm to gain better information about future market conditions.

19. The financial success of the Downhill Ski Resort in the Blue Ridge Mountains is dependent on the amount of snowfall during the winter months. If the snowfall averages more than 40 inches, the resort will be successful; if the snowfall is between 20 and 40 inches, the resort will receive a moderate financial return; and if snowfall averages less than 20 inches, the resort will suffer a financial loss. The financial return and probability, given each level of snowfall, follow:

Snowfall Level (in.)	Financial Return
>40, .4	$ 120,000
20–40, .2	40,000
<20, .4	−40,000

A large hotel chain has offered to lease the resort for the winter for $40,000. Compute the expected value to determine whether the resort should operate or lease. Explain your answer.

20. An investor must decide between two alternative investments—stocks and bonds. The return for each investment, given two future economic conditions, is shown in the following payoff table:

	Economic Conditions	
Investment	Good	Bad
Stocks	$10,000	$−4,000
Bonds	7,000	2,000

What probability for each economic condition would make the investor indifferent to the choice between stocks and bonds?

21. In Problem 10, Ann Tyler, with the help of a financial newsletter and some library research, has been able to assign probabilities to each of the possible interest rates during the next year, as follows:

Interest Rate (%)	Probability
5	.2
6	.3
7	.3
8	.1
9	.1

Using expected value, determine her best investment decision.

22. In Problem 11 the Tech coaches have reviewed game films and have determined the following probabilities that State will use each of its defenses:

Defense	Probability
54	.40
63	.10
Wide tackle	.20
Nickel	.20
Blitz	.10

a. Using expected value, rank Tech's plays from best to worst.
b. During the actual game, a situation arises in which Tech has a third down and 10 yards to go, and the coaches are 60% certain State will blitz, with a 10% chance of any of the other four defenses. What play should Tech run? Is it likely the team will make the first down?

23. A global economist hired by Microcomp, the U.S.-based computer manufacturer in Problem 12, estimates that the probability that the economic and political climate overseas and in Mexico will decline during the next 5 years is .40, the probability that it will remain approximately the same is .50, and the probability that it will improve is .10. Determine the best country to construct the new facility in and the expected value of perfect information.

24. In Problem 13 the Place-Plus real estate development firm has hired an economist to assign a probability to each direction interest rates may take over the next 5 years. The economist has determined that there is a .50 probability that interest rates will decline, a .40 probability that rates will remain stable, and a .10 probability that rates will increase.
   a. Using expected value, determine the best project.
   b. Determine the expected value of perfect information.

25. Fenton and Farrah Friendly, husband-and-wife car dealers, are soon going to open a new dealership. They have three offers: from a foreign compact car company, from a U.S.-producer of full-sized cars, and from a truck company. The success of each type of dealership will depend on how

much gasoline is going to be available during the next few years. The profit from each type of dealership, given the availability of gas, is shown in the following payoff table:

Dealership	Gasoline Availability	
	Shortage .6	Surplus .4
Compact cars	$ 300,000	$150,000
Full-sized cars	−100,000	600,000
Trucks	120,000	170,000

Determine which type of dealership the couple should purchase.

26. The Steak and Chop Butcher Shop purchases steak from a local meatpacking house. The meat is purchased on Monday at $2.00 per pound, and the shop sells the steak for $3.00 per pound. Any steak left over at the end of the week is sold to a local zoo for $.50 per pound. The possible demands for steak and the probability of each are shown in the following table:

Demand (lb.)	Probability
20	.10
21	.20
22	.30
23	.30
24	.10
	1.00

The shop must decide how much steak to order in a week. Construct a payoff table for this decision situation and determine the amount of steak that should be ordered, using expected value.

27. The Loebuck Grocery must decide how many cases of milk to stock each week to meet demand. The probability distribution of demand during a week is shown in the following table:

Demand (cases)	Probability
15	.20
16	.25
17	.40
18	.15
	1.00

Each case costs the grocer $10 and sells for $12. Unsold cases are sold to a local farmer (who mixes the milk with feed for livestock) for $2 per case. If there is a shortage, the grocer considers the cost of customer ill will and lost profit to be $4 per case. The grocer must decide how many cases of milk to order each week.

a. Construct the payoff table for this decision situation.
b. Compute the expected value of each alternative amount of milk that could be stocked and select the best decision.
c. Construct the opportunity loss table and determine the best decision.
d. Compute the expected value of perfect information.

28. The manager of the greeting card section of Mazey's department store is considering her order for a particular line of Christmas cards. The cost of each box of cards is \$3; each box will be sold for \$5 during the Christmas season. After Christmas, the cards will be sold for \$2 a box. The card section manager believes that all leftover cards can be sold at that price. The estimated demand during the Christmas season for the line of Christmas cards, with associated probabilities, is as follows:

Demand (boxes)	Probability
25	.10
26	.15
27	.30
28	.20
29	.15
30	.10

a. Develop the payoff table for this decision situation.
b. Compute the expected value for each alternative and identify the best decision.
c. Compute the expected value of perfect information.

29. The Palm Garden Greenhouse specializes in raising carnations that are sold to florists. Carnations are sold for \$3.00 per dozen; the cost of growing the carnations and distributing them to the florists is \$2.00 per dozen. Any carnations left at the end of the day are sold to local restaurants and hotels for \$0.75 per dozen. The estimated cost of customer ill will if demand is not met is \$1.00 per dozen. The expected daily demand (in dozens) for the carnations is as follows:

Daily Demand	Probability
20	.05
22	.10
24	.25
26	.30
28	.20
30	.10
	1.00

a. Develop the payoff table for this decision situation.
b. Compute the expected value of each alternative number of (dozens of) carnations that could be stocked and select the best decision.
c. Construct the opportunity loss table and determine the best decision.
d. Compute the expected value of perfect information.

30. Assume that the probabilities of demand in Problem 28 are no longer valid; the decision situation is now one without probabilities. Determine the best number of cards to stock, using the following decision criteria.
   a. Maximin
   b. Maximax
   c. Hurwicz ($\alpha = .4$)
   d. Minimax regret

31. In Problem 14, the Bombers' management has determined the following probabilities of the occurrence of each future season outcome for each player:

	Probability		
Player	Loser	Competitive	Makes Playoffs
Byrd	.15	.55	.30
O'Neil	.18	.26	.56
Johnson	.21	.32	.47
Gordan	.30	.25	.45

Compute the expected value for each player and indicate which player the team should try to sign.

32. The director of career advising at Orange Community College wants to use decision analysis to provide information to help students decide which 2-year degree program they should pursue. The director has set up the following payoff table for six of the most popular and successful degree programs at OCC that shows the estimated 5-year gross income ($) from each degree for four future economic conditions:

	Economic Conditions			
Degree Program	Recession	Average	Good	Robust
Graphic design	145,000	175,000	220,000	260,000
Nursing	150,000	180,000	205,000	215,000
Real estate	115,000	165,000	220,000	320,000
Medical technology130,000	180,000	210,000	280,000	
Culinary technology	115,000	145,000	235,000	305,000
Computer information technology	125,000	150,000	190,000	250,000

Determine the best degree program in terms of projected income, using the following decision criteria:

a. Maximax
b. Maximin
c. Equal likelihood
d. Hurwicz ($\alpha = .50$)

33. In Problem 32 the director of career advising at Orange Community College has paid a small fee to a local investment firm to indicate a probability for each future economic condition over the next 5 years. The firm estimates that there is a .20 probability of a recession, a .40 probability that the economy will be average, a .30 probability that the economy will be good, and a .10 probability that it will be robust. Using expected value determine the best degree program in terms of projected income. If you were the director of career advising, which degree program would you recommend?

34. The Blue Sox American League baseball team is going to enter the free-agent market over the winter to sign a new starting pitcher. They are considering five prospects who will enter the free-agent market. All five pitchers are in their mid-20s, have been in the major leagues for approximately 5 years, and have been relatively successful. The team's general manager has compiled a lot of information about the pitchers from scouting reports and their playing histories since high school. He has developed a chart projecting how many wins each pitcher will likely have during the next

10 years given three possible future states of nature: the pitchers will be relatively injury free, they will have a normal career with injuries, or they will have excessive injuries, as shown in the following payoff table:

	Physical Condition		
Pitcher	No injuries	Normal	Excessive injuries
Jose Diaz	153	122	76
Jerry Damon	173	135	46
Frank Thompson	133	115	88
Derek Rodriguez	105	101	95
Ken Griffin	127	98	75

Determine the best pitcher to sign, using the following decision criteria:

a. Maximax
b. Maximin
c. Equal likelihood
d. Hurwicz ($\alpha = .35$)

35. In Problem 34 the Blue Sox general manager has asked a superscout to assign a probability to each of the three states of nature for the pitchers during the next 10 years. The scout estimates there is a .10 probability that these pitchers at this stage of their careers will have no injuries, a .60 probability that they will have a career with the normal number of injuries, and a .30 probability that they will have excessive injuries.
   a. Using expected value, determine the best pitcher to sign.
   b. Given the following 10-year contract price for each pitcher (in $millions), which would you recommend signing?

Jose Diaz	$ 97.3
Jerry Damon	$121.5
Frank Thompson	$ 73.5
Derek Rodriguez	$103.4
Ken Griffin	$ 85.7

   c. Suppose that the general manager asked the superscout to determine the probabilities of each state of nature for each individual pitcher, and the results were as follows:

	Physical Condition		
Pitcher	No injuries	Normal	Excessive injuries
Jose Diaz	0.30	0.45	0.25
Jerry Damon	0.13	0.47	0.40
Frank Thompson	0.45	0.35	0.20
Derek Rodriguez	0.50	0.40	0.10
Ken Griffin	0.15	0.60	0.25

Determine the expected number of wins for each pitcher, and combined with the contract price in part b, indicate which pitcher you would recommend signing.

36. Construct a decision tree for the decision situation described in Problem 25 and indicate the best decision.

37. Given the following sequential decision tree, determine which is the optimal investment, A or B:

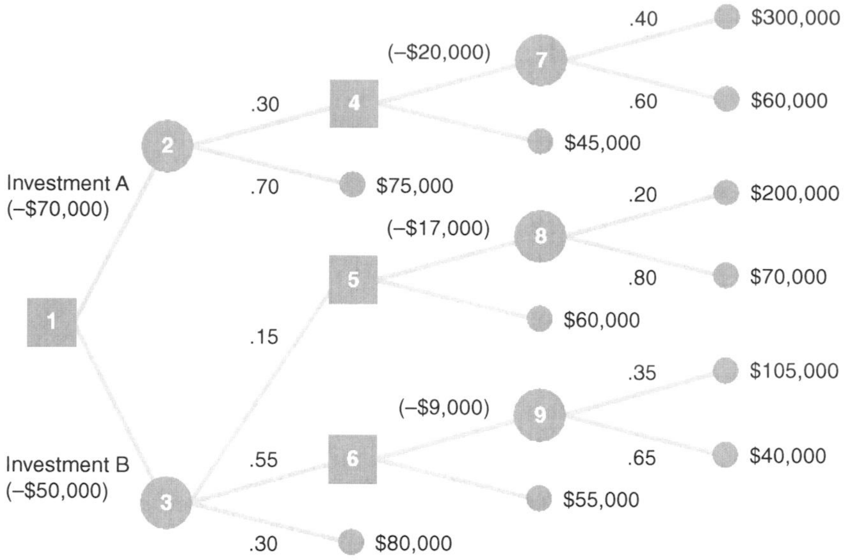

38. The management of First American Bank was concerned about the potential loss that might occur in the event of a physical catastrophe such as a power failure or a fire. The bank estimated that the loss from one of these incidents could be as much as $100 million, including losses due to interrupted service and customer relations. One project the bank is considering is the installation of an emergency power generator at its operations headquarters. The cost of the emergency generator is $800,000, and if it is installed, no losses from this type of incident will be incurred. However, if the generator is not installed, there is a 10% chance that a power outage will occur during the next year. If there is an outage, there is a .05 probability that the resulting losses will be very large, or approximately $80 million in lost earnings. Alternatively, it is estimated that there is a .95 probability of only slight losses of around $1 million. Using decision tree analysis, determine whether the bank should install the new power generator.

39. The Americo Oil Company is considering making a bid for a shale oil development contract to be awarded by the federal government. The company has decided to bid $112 million. The company estimates that it has a 60% chance of winning the contract with this bid. If the firm wins the contract, it can choose one of three methods for getting the oil from the shale. It can develop a new method for oil extraction, use an existing (inefficient) process, or subcontract the processing to a number of smaller companies once the shale has been excavated. The results from these alternatives are as follows:

Develop new process:

Outcomes	*Probability*	*Profit ($1,000,000s)*
Great success	.30	$ 600
Moderate success	.60	300
Failure	.10	−100

Use present process:

Outcomes	*Probability*	*Profit ($1,000,000s)*
Great success	.50	$ 300
Moderate success	.30	200
Failure	.20	−40

Subcontract:

Outcome	*Probability*	*Profit ($1,000,000s)*
Moderate success	1.00	250

The cost of preparing the contract proposal is $2 million. If the company does not make a bid, it will invest in an alternative venture with a guaranteed profit of $30 million. Construct a sequential decision tree for this decision situation and determine whether the company should make a bid.

40. The machine shop owner in Problem 15 is considering hiring a military consultant to ascertain whether the shop will get the government contract. The consultant is a former military officer who uses various personal contacts to find out such information. By talking to other shop owners who have hired the consultant, the owner has estimated a .70 probability that the consultant would present a favorable report, given that the contract is awarded to the shop, and a .80 probability that the consultant would present an unfavorable report, given that the contract is not awarded. Using decision tree analysis, determine the decision strategy the owner should follow, the expected value of this strategy, and the maximum fee the owner should pay the consultant.

41. The Miramar Company in Problem 18 is considering contracting with a market research firm to do a survey to determine future market conditions. The results of the survey will indicate either positive or negative market conditions. There is a .60 probability of a positive report, given favorable conditions; a .30 probability of a positive report, given stable conditions; and a .10 probability of a positive report, given unfavorable conditions. There is a .90 probability of a negative report, given unfavorable conditions; a .70 probability, given stable conditions; and a .40 probability, given favorable conditions. Using decision tree analysis *and* posterior probability tables, determine the decision strategy the company should follow, the expected value of the strategy, and the maximum amount the company should pay the market research firm for the survey results.

42. The Friendlys in Problem 25 are considering hiring a petroleum analyst to determine the future availability of gasoline. The analyst will report that either a shortage or a surplus will occur. The probability that the analyst will indicate a shortage, given that a shortage actually occurs is .90; the probability that the analyst will indicate a surplus, given that a surplus actually occurs is .70.
    a. Determine the decision strategy the Friendlys should follow, the expected value of this strategy, and the maximum amount the Friendlys should pay for the analyst's services.
    b. Compute the efficiency of the sample information for the Friendly car dealership.

43. Jeffrey Mogul is a Hollywood film producer, and he is currently evaluating a script by a new screenwriter and director, Betty Jo Thurston. Jeffrey knows that the probability of a film by a new director being a success is about .10 and that the probability it will flop is .90. The studio accounting department estimates that if this film is a hit, it will make $25 million in profit, whereas if it is a box office failure, it will lose $8 million. Jeffrey would like to hire noted film critic Dick Roper to read the script and assess its chances of success. Roper is generally able to correctly predict a successful film 70% of the time and correctly predict an unsuccessful film 80% of the time. Roper wants a fee of $1 million. Determine whether Roper should be hired, the strategy Mogul should follow if Roper is hired, and the expected value.

44. Tech is playing State in the last conference game of the season. Tech is trailing State 21 to 14, with 7 seconds left in the game, when Tech scores a touchdown. Still trailing 21 to 20, Tech can either go for 2 points and win or go for 1 point to send the game into overtime. The conference championship will be determined by the outcome of this game. If Tech wins, it will go to the Sugar Bowl, with a payoff of $7.2 million; if it loses, it will go to the Gator Bowl, with a payoff of $1.7 million. If Tech goes for 2 points, there is a 33% chance it will be successful and win (and a 67% chance it will fail and lose). If it goes for 1 point, there is a 0.98 probability of success and a tie and a 0.02

probability of failure. If the teams tie, they will play overtime, during which Tech believes it has only a 20% chance of winning because of fatigue.

a. Use decision tree analysis to determine whether Tech should go for 1 or 2 points.
b. What would Tech's probability of winning the game in overtime have to be to make Tech indifferent to going for either 1 or 2 points?

45. Jay Seago is suing the manufacturer of his car for $3.5 million because of a defect that he believes caused him to have an accident. The accident kept him out of work for a year. The company has offered him a settlement of $700,000, of which Jay would receive $600,000 after attorneys' fees. His attorney has advised him that he has a 50% chance of winning his case. If he loses, he will incur attorneys' fees and court costs of $75,000. If he wins, he is not guaranteed his full requested settlement. His attorney believes that there is a 50% chance he could receive the full settlement, in which case Jay would realize $2 million after his attorney takes her cut, and a 50% chance that the jury will award him a lesser amount of $1 million, of which Jay would get $500,000.

Using decision tree analysis, decide whether Jay should proceed with his lawsuit against the manufacturer.

46. Tech has three health care plans for its faculty and staff to choose from, as follows:

Plan 1—monthly cost of $32, with a $500 deductible; the participants pay the first $500 of medical costs for the year; the insurer pays 90% of all remaining expenses.

Plan 2—monthly cost of $5 but a deductible of $1,200, with the insurer paying 90% of medical expenses after the insurer pays the first $1,200 in a year.

Plan 3—monthly cost of $24, with no deductible; the participants pay 30% of all expenses, with the remainder paid by the insurer.

Tracy McCoy, an administrative assistant in the management science department, estimates that her annual medical expenses are defined by the following probability distribution:

Annual Medical Expenses	Probability
$ 100	.15
500	.30
1,500	.35
3,000	.10
5,000	.05
10,000	.05

Determine which medical plan Tracy should select.

47. The Valley Wine Company purchases grapes from one of two nearby growers each season to produce a particular red wine. It purchases enough grapes to produce 3,000 bottles of the wine. Each grower supplies a certain portion of poor-quality grapes, resulting in a percentage of bottles being used as fillers for cheaper table wines, according to the following probability distribution:

	Probability of Percentage Defective	
Defective (%)	Grower A	Grower B
2	.15	.30
4	.20	.30
6	.25	.20
8	.30	.10
10	.10	.10

The two growers charge different prices for their grapes and, because of differences in taste, the company charges different prices for its wine, depending on which grapes it uses. Following is the annual profit from the wine produced from each grower's grapes for each percentage defective:

	Profit	
Defective (%)	Grower A	Grower B
2	$44,200	$42,600
4	40,200	40,300
6	36,200	38,000
8	32,200	35,700
10	28,200	33,400

Use decision tree analysis to determine from which grower the company should purchase grapes.

48. Kroft Food Products is attempting to decide whether it should introduce a new line of salad dressings called Special Choices. The company can test market the salad dressings in selected geographic areas or bypass the test market and introduce the product nationally. The cost of the test market is $150,000. If the company conducts the test market, it must wait to see the results before deciding whether to introduce the salad dressings nationally. The probability of a positive test market result is estimated to be 0.6. Alternatively, the company can decide not to conduct the test market and go ahead and make the decision to introduce the dressings or not. If the salad dressings are introduced nationally and are a success, the company estimates that it will realize an annual profit of $1.6 million, whereas if the dressings fail, it will incur a loss of $700,000. The company believes the probability of success for the salad dressings is 0.50 if they are introduced without the test market. If the company does conduct the test market and it is positive, then the probability of successfully introducing the salad dressings increases to 0.8. If the test market is negative and the company introduces the salad dressings anyway, the probability of success drops to 0.30.

    Using decision tree analysis, determine whether the company should conduct the test market.

49. In Problem 48, determine the expected value of sample information (*EVSI*) (i.e., the test market value) and the expected value of perfect information (*EVPI*).

50. Ellie Daniels has $200,000 and is considering three mutual funds for investment—a global fund, an index fund, and an Internet stock fund. During the first year of investment, Ellie estimates that there is a .70 probability that the market will go up and a .30 probability that the market will go down. Following are the returns on her $200,000 investment at the end of the year under each market condition:

	Market Conditions	
Fund	Up	Down
Global	$25,000	$ −8,000
Index	35,000	5,000
Internet	60,000	−35,000

At the end of the first year, Ellie will either reinvest the entire amount plus the return or sell and take the profit or loss. If she reinvests, she estimates that there is a .60 probability the market will go up and a .40 probability the market will go down. If Ellie reinvests in the global fund after it has gone up, her return on her initial $200,000 investment plus her $25,000 return after 1 year will be

$45,000. If the market goes down, her loss will be $15,000. If she reinvests after the market has gone down, her return will be $34,000, and her loss will be $17,000. If Ellie reinvests in the index fund after the market has gone up, after 2 years her return will be $65,000 if the market continues upward, but only $5,000 if the market goes down. Her return will be $55,000 if she reinvests and the market reverses itself and goes up after initially going down, and it will be $5,000 if the market continues to go down. If Ellie invests in the Internet fund, she will make $60,000 if the market goes up, but she will lose $35,000 if it goes down. If she reinvests as the market continues upward, she will make an additional $100,000; but if the market reverses and goes down, she will lose $70,000. If she reinvests after the market has initially gone down, she will make $65,000, but if the market continues to go down, she will lose an additional $75,000.

Using decision tree analysis, determine which fund Ellie should invest in and its expected value.

51. Blue Ridge Power and Light is an electric utility company with a large fleet of vehicles, including automobiles, light trucks, and construction equipment. The company is evaluating four alternative strategies for maintaining its vehicles at the lowest cost: (1) do no preventive maintenance at all and repair vehicle components when they fail; (2) take oil samples at regular intervals and perform whatever preventive maintenance is indicated by the oil analysis; (3) change the vehicle oil on a regular basis and perform repairs when needed; (4) change the oil at regular intervals, take oil samples regularly, and perform maintenance repairs as indicated by the sample analysis.

For autos and light trucks, strategy 1 (no preventive maintenance) costs nothing to implement and results in two possible outcomes: There is a .10 probability that a defective component will occur, requiring emergency maintenance at a cost of $1,200, or there is a .90 probability that no defects will occur and no maintenance will be necessary.

Strategy 2 (take oil samples) costs $20 to implement (i.e., take a sample), and there is a .10 probability that there will be a defective part and .90 probability that there will not be a defect. If there is actually a defective part, there is a .70 probability that the sample will correctly identify it, resulting in preventive maintenance at a cost of $500. However, there is a .30 probability that the sample will not identify the defect and indicate that everything is okay, resulting in emergency maintenance later at a cost of $1,200. On the other hand, if there are actually no defects, there is a .20 probability that the sample will erroneously indicate that there is a defect, resulting in unnecessary maintenance at a cost of $250. There is an .80 probability that the sample will correctly indicate that there are no defects, resulting in no maintenance and no costs.

Strategy 3 (changing the oil regularly) costs $14.80 to implement and has two outcomes: a .04 probability of a defective component, which will require emergency maintenance at a cost of $1,200, and a .96 probability that no defects will occur, resulting in no maintenance and no cost.

Strategy 4 (changing the oil and sampling) costs $34.80 to implement and results in the same probabilities of defects and no defects as strategy 3. If there is a defective component, there is a .70 probability that the sample will detect it and $500 in preventive maintenance costs will be incurred. Alternatively, there is a .30 probability that the sample will not detect the defect, resulting in emergency maintenance at a cost of $1,200. If there is no defect, there is a .20 probability that the sample will indicate that there is a defect, resulting in an unnecessary maintenance cost of $250, and there is an .80 probability that the sample will correctly indicate no defects, resulting in no cost.

Develop a decision strategy for Blue Ridge Power and Light and indicate the expected value of this strategy.[1]

52. In Problem 51, the decision analysis is for automobiles and light trucks. Blue Ridge Power and Light would like to reformulate the problem for its heavy construction equipment. Emergency maintenance is much more expensive for heavy equipment, costing $15,000. Required preventive

[1]This problem is based on J. Mellichamp, D. Miller, and O.-J. Kwon, "The Southern Company Uses a Probability Model for Cost Justification of Oil Sample Analysis," *Interfaces* 23, no. 3 (May–June 1993): 118–24.

maintenance costs $2,000, and unnecessary maintenance costs $1,200. The cost of an oil change is $100, and the cost of taking an oil sample and analyzing it is $30. All the probabilities remain the same. Determine the strategy Blue Ridge Power and Light should use for its heavy equipment.

53. In Problem 14, the management of the Oakland Bombers is considering hiring superscout Jerry McGuire to evaluate the team's chances for the coming season. McGuire will evaluate the team, assuming that it will sign one of the four free agents. The team's management has determined the probability that the team will have a losing record with any of the free agents to be .21 by averaging the probabilities of losing for the four free agents in Problem 31. The probability that the team will have a competitive season but not make the playoffs is developed similarly, and it is .35. The probability that the team will make the playoffs is .44. The probability that McGuire will correctly predict that the team will have a losing season is .75, whereas the probability that he will predict a competitive season, given that it has a losing season, is .15, and the probability that he will incorrectly predict a playoff season, given that the team has a losing season, is .10. The probability that he will successfully predict a competitive season is .80, whereas the probability that he will incorrectly predict a losing season, given that the team is competitive, is .10, and the probability that he will incorrectly predict a playoff season, given the team has a competitive season, is .10. The probability that he will correctly predict a playoff season is .85, whereas the probability that he will incorrectly predict a losing season, given that the team makes the playoffs, is .05, and the probability that he will predict a competitive season, given the team makes the playoffs, is .10. Using decision tree analysis and posterior probabilities, determine the decision strategy the team should follow, the expected value of the strategy, and the maximum amount the team should pay for Jerry McGuire's predictions.

54. The Place-Plus real estate development firm in Problem 24 is dissatisfied with the economist's estimate of the probabilities of future interest rate movement, so it is considering having a financial consulting firm provide a report on future interest rates. The consulting firm is able to cite a track record which shows that 80% of the time when interest rates declined, it had predicted they would, whereas 10% of the time when interest rates declined, the firm had predicted they would remain stable and 10% of the time it had predicted they would increase. The firm has been correct 70% of the time when rates have remained stable, whereas 10% of the time it has incorrectly predicted that rates would decrease, and 20% of the time it has incorrectly predicted that rates would increase. The firm has correctly predicted that interest rates would increase 90% of the time and incorrectly predicted rates would decrease 2% and remain stable 8% of the time. Assuming that the consulting firm could supply an accurate report, determine how much Place-Plus should be willing to pay the consulting firm and how efficient the information will be.

55. A young couple has $5,000 to invest in either savings bonds or a real estate deal. The expected return on each investment, given good and bad economic conditions, is shown in the following payoff table:

	Economic Conditions	
Investment	Good .6	Bad .4
Savings bonds	$ 1,000	$ 1,000
Real estate	10,000	−2,000

The expected value of investing in savings bonds is $1,000, and the expected value of the real estate investment is $5,200. However, the couple decides to invest in savings bonds. Explain the couple's decision in terms of the utility they might associate with each investment.

56. Annie Hays recently sold a condominium she had bought and lived in while she was a college student over 15 years ago. She received $200,000 for the condominium and is considering two investment alternatives. Annie can invest the entire amount in a bank money market for 1 year at 8% interest and thus receive $162,000 at the end of a year, or she can invest in a speculative oil exploration project with a 50–50 chance of doubling her investment at the end of the year or losing everything.
    a. Determine which alternative Annie should invest in, according to the expected value criterion, and indicate whether that is the alternative you would also select.
    b. Suppose Annie determined that the probability of success for the oil exploration investment would have to be .80 before she would be indifferent between the two alternatives. In other words, if the probability of success for the oil exploration investment was less than .80, Annie would invest in the money market, but if the probability of success was greater than .80, she would invest in the oil exploration. In this case, .80 is the utility value of the $162,000 safe return. Determine the preferred alternative, according to the expected utility value.

Case Problem

STEELEY ASSOCIATES VERSUS CONCORD FALLS

Steeley Associates, Inc., a property development firm, purchased an old house near the town square in Concord Falls, where State University is located. The old house was built in the mid-1800s, and Steeley Associates restored it. For almost a decade, Steeley has leased it to the university for academic office space. The house is located on a wide lawn and has become a town landmark.

However, in 2008, the lease with the university expired, and Steeley Associates decided to build high-density student apartments on the site, using all the open space. The community was outraged and objected to the town council. The legal counsel for the town spoke with a representative from Steeley and hinted that if Steeley requested a permit, the town would probably reject it. Steeley had reviewed the town building code and felt confident that its plan was within the guidelines, but that did not necessarily mean that it could win a lawsuit against the town to force the town to grant a permit.

The principals at Steeley Associates held a series of meetings to review their alternatives. They decided that they had three options: They could request the permit, they could sell the property, or they could request a permit for a low-density office building, which the town had indicated it would not fight. Regarding the last two options, if Steeley sells the house and property, it thinks it can get $900,000. If it builds a new office building, its return will depend on town business growth in the future. It feels that there is a 70% chance of future growth, in which case Steeley will see a return of $1.3 million (over a 10-year planning horizon); if no growth (or erosion) occurs, it will make only $200,000.

If Steeley requests a permit for the apartments, a host of good and bad outcomes are possible. The immediate good outcome is approval of its permit, which it estimates will result in a return of $3 million. However, Steeley gives that result only a 10% chance that it will occur. Alternatively, Steeley thinks there is a 90% chance that the town will reject its application, which will result in another set of decisions.

Steeley can sell the property at that point. However, the rejection of the permit will undoubtedly decrease the value to potential buyers, and Steeley estimates that it will get only $700,000. Alternatively, it can construct the office building and face the same potential outcomes it did earlier, namely, a 30% chance of no town growth and a $200,000 return or a 70% chance of growth with a return of $1.3 million. A third option is to sue the town. On the surface, Steeley's case looks good, but the town building code is vague, and a sympathetic judge could throw out its suit. Whether or not it wins, Steeley estimates its possible legal fees to be $300,000, and it feels it has only a 40% chance of winning. However, if Steeley does win, it estimates that the award will be approximately $1 million, and it will also get its $3 million return for building the apartments. Steeley also estimates that there is a 10% chance that the suit could linger on in the courts for such a long time that any future return would be negated during its planning horizon, and it would incur an additional $200,000 in legal fees.

If Steeley loses the suit, it will then be faced with the same options of selling the property or constructing an office building. However, if the suit is carried this far into the future, it feels that the selling price it can ask will be somewhat dependent on the town's growth prospects at that time, which it feels it can estimate at only 50–50. If the town is in a growth mode that far in the future, Steeley thinks that $900,000 is a conservative estimate of the potential sale price, whereas if the town is not growing, it thinks $500,000 is a more likely estimate. Finally, if Steeley constructs the office building, it feels that the chance of town growth is 50%, in which case the return will be only $1.2 million. If no growth occurs, it conservatively estimates only a $100,000 return.

A. Perform a decision tree analysis of Steeley Associates's decision situation, using expected value, and indicate the appropriate decision with these criteria.
B. Indicate the decision you would make and explain your reasons.

Case Problem

TRANSFORMER REPLACEMENT AT MOUNTAIN STATES ELECTRIC SERVICE

Mountain States Electric Service is an electrical utility company serving several states in the Rocky Mountains region. It is considering replacing some of its equipment at a generating substation and is attempting to decide whether it should replace an older, existing PCB transformer. (PCB is a toxic chemical known formally as polychlorinated biphenyl.) Even though the PCB generator meets all current regulations, if an incident occurred, such as a fire, and PCB contamination caused harm either to neighboring businesses or farms or to the environment, the company would be liable for damages. Recent court cases have shown that simply meeting utility regulations does not relieve a utility of liability if an incident causes harm to others. Also, courts have been awarding large damages to individuals and businesses harmed by hazardous incidents.

If the utility replaces the PCB transformer, no PCB incidents will occur, and the only cost will be the cost of the transformer, $85,000. Alternatively, if the company decides to keep the existing PCB transformer, then management estimates that there is a 50–50 chance of there being a high likelihood of an incident or a low likelihood of an incident. For the case in which there is a high likelihood that an incident will occur, there is a .004 probability that a fire will occur sometime during the remaining life of the transformer and a .996 probability that no fire will occur. If a fire occurs, there is a .20 probability that it will be bad and the utility will incur a very high cost of approximately $90 million for the cleanup, whereas there is an .80 probability that the fire will be minor and cleanup can be accomplished at a low cost of approximately $8 million. If no fire occurs, no cleanup costs will occur. For the case in which there is a low likelihood that an incident will occur, there is a .001 probability that a fire will occur during the life of the existing transformer and a .999 probability that a fire will not occur. If a fire does occur, the same probabilities exist for the incidence of high and low cleanup costs, as well as the same cleanup costs, as indicated for the previous case. Similarly, if no fire occurs, there is no cleanup cost.

Perform a decision tree analysis of this problem for Mountain States Electric Service and indicate the recommended solution. Is this the decision you believe the company should make? Explain your reasons.

This case was adapted from W. Balson, J. Welsh, and D. Wilson, "Using Decision Analysis and Risk Analysis to Manage Utility Environmental Risk," *Interfaces* 22, no. 6 (November–December 1992): 126–39.

Case Problem

THE CAROLINA COUGARS

The Carolina Cougars is a major league baseball expansion team beginning its third year of operation. The team had losing records in each of its first 2 years and finished near the bottom of its division. However, the team was young and generally competitive. The team's general manager, Frank Lane, and manager, Biff Diamond, believe that with a few additional good players, the Cougars can become a contender for the division title and perhaps even for the pennant. They have prepared several proposals for free-agent acquisitions to present to the team's owner, Bruce Wayne.

Under one proposal the team would sign several good available free agents, including two pitchers, a good fielding shortstop, and two power-hitting outfielders for $52 million in bonuses and annual salary. The second proposal is less ambitious, costing $20 million to sign a relief pitcher, a solid, good-hitting infielder, and one power-hitting outfielder. The final proposal would be to stand pat with the current team and continue to develop.

General Manager Lane wants to lay out a possible season scenario for the owner so he can assess the long-run ramifications of each decision strategy. Because the only thing the owner understands is money, Frank wants this analysis to be quantitative, indicating the money to be made or lost from each strategy. To help develop this analysis, Frank has hired his kids, Penny and Nathan, both management science graduates from Tech.

Penny and Nathan analyzed league data for the previous five seasons for attendance trends, logo sales (i.e., clothing, souvenirs, hats, etc.), player sales and trades, and revenues. In addition, they interviewed several other owners, general managers, and league officials. They also analyzed the free agents that the team was considering signing.

Based on their analysis, Penny and Nathan feel that if the Cougars do not invest in any free agents, the team will have a 25% chance of contending for the division title and a 75% chance of being out of contention most of the season. If the team is a contender, there is a .70 probability that attendance will increase as the season progresses and the team will have high attendance levels (between 1.5 million and 2.0 million) with profits of $170 million from ticket sales, concessions, advertising sales, TV and radio sales, and logo sales. They estimate a .25 probability that the team's attendance will be mediocre (between 1.0 million and 1.5 million) with profits of $115 million and a .05 probability that the team will suffer low attendance (less than 1.0 million) with profit of $90 million. If the team is not a contender, Penny and Nathan estimate that there is .05 probability of high attendance with profits of $95 million, a .20 probability of medium attendance with profits of $55 million, and a .75 probability of low attendance with profits of $30 million.

If the team marginally invests in free agents at a cost of $20 million, there is a 50–50 chance it will be a contender. If it is a contender, then later in the season it can either stand pat with its existing roster or buy or trade for players that could improve the team's chances of winning the division. If the team stands pat, there is a .75 probability that attendance will be high and profits will be $195 million. There is a .20 probability that attendance will be mediocre with profits of $160 million and a .05 probability of low attendance and profits of $120 million. Alternatively, if the team decides to buy or trade for players, it will cost $8 million, and the probability of high attendance with profits of $200 million will be .80. The probability of mediocre attendance with $170 million in profits will be .15, and there will be a .05 probability of low attendance, with profits of $125 million.

If the team is not in contention, then it will either stand pat or sell some of its players, earning approximately $8 million in profit. If the team stands pat, there is a .12 probability of high attendance, with profits of $110 million; a .28 probability of mediocre attendance, with profits of $65 million; and a .60 probability of low attendance, with profits of $40 million. If the team sells players, the fans will likely lose interest at an even faster rate, and the probability of high attendance with profits of $100 million will drop to .08, the probability of mediocre attendance with profits of $60 million will be .22, and the probability of low attendance with profits of $35 million will be .70.

The most ambitious free-agent strategy will increase the team's chances of being a contender to 65%. This strategy will also excite the fans most during the off-season and boost ticket sales and advertising and logo sales early in the year. If the team does contend for the division title, then later in the season it will have to decide whether to invest in more players. If the Cougars stand pat, the probability of high attendance with profits of $210 million will be .80, the probability of mediocre attendance with profits of $170 million will be .15, and the probability of low attendance with profits of $125 million will be .05. If the team buys players at a cost of $10 million, then the probability of having high attendance with profits of $220 million will increase to .83, the probability of mediocre attendance with profits of $175 million will be .12, and the probability of low attendance with profits of $130 million will be .05.

If the team is not in contention, it will either sell some players' contracts later in the season for profits of around $12 million or stand pat. If it stays with its roster, the probability of high attendance with profits of $110 million will be .15, the probability of mediocre attendance with profits of $70 million will be .30, and the probability of low attendance with profits of $50 million will be .55. If the team sells players late in the season, there will be a .10 probability of high attendance with profits of $105 million, a .30 probability of mediocre attendance with profits of $65 million, and a .60 probability of low attendance with profits of $45 million.

Assist Penny and Nathan in determining the best strategy to follow and its expected value.

Case Problem

EVALUATING R&D PROJECTS AT WESTCOM SYSTEMS PRODUCTS COMPANY

WestCom Systems Products Company develops computer systems and software products for commercial sale. Each year it considers and evaluates a number of different R&D projects to undertake. It develops a road map for each project, in the form of a standardized decision tree that identifies the different decision points in the R&D process from the initial decision to invest in a project's development through the actual commercialization of the final product.

The first decision point in the R&D process is whether to fund a proposed project for 1 year. If the decision is no, then there is no resulting cost; if the decision is yes, then the project proceeds at an incremental cost to the company. The company establishes specific short-term, early technical milestones for its projects after 1 year. If the early milestones are achieved, the project proceeds to the next phase of project development; if the milestones are not achieved, the project is abandoned. In its planning process the company develops probability estimates of achieving and not achieving the early milestones. If the early milestones are achieved, the project is funded for further development during an extended time frame specific to a project. At the end of this time frame, a project is evaluated according to a second set of (later) technical milestones. Again, the company attaches probability estimates for achieving and not achieving these later milestones. If the later milestones are not achieved, the project is abandoned.

If the later milestones are achieved, technical uncertainties and problems have been overcome, and the company next assesses the project's ability to meet its strategic business objectives. At this stage, the company wants to know if the eventual product coincides with the company's competencies and whether there appears to be an eventual, clear market for the product. It invests in a product "prelaunch" to ascertain the answers to these questions. The outcomes of the prelaunch are that either there is a strategic fit or there is not, and the company assigns probability estimates to each of these two possible outcomes. If there is not a strategic fit at this point, the project is abandoned and the company loses its investment in the prelaunch process. If it is determined that there is a strategic fit, then three possible decisions result: (1) The company can invest in the product's launch, and a successful or unsuccessful outcome will result, each with an estimated probability of occurrence; (2) the company can delay the product's launch and at a later date decide whether to launch or abandon; and (3) if it launches later, the outcomes are success or failure, each with an estimated probability of occurrence. Also, if the product launch is delayed, there is always a likelihood that the technology will become obsolete or dated in the near future, which tends to reduce the expected return.

The following table provides the various costs, event probabilities, and investment outcomes for five projects the company is considering:

	Project				
Decision Outcomes/Event	*1*	*2*	*3*	*4*	*5*
Fund—1 year	\$ 200,000	\$ 350,000	\$ 170,000	\$ 230,000	\$ 400,000
P(Early milestones—yes)	.70	.67	.82	.60	.75
P(Early milestones—no)	.30	.33	.18	.40	.25
Long-term funding	\$ 650,000	780,000	450,000	300,000	450,000
P(Late milestones—yes)	.60	.56	.65	.70	.72
P(Late milestones—no)	.40	.44	.35	.30	.28
Prelaunch funding	\$ 300,000	450,000	400,000	500,000	270,000
P(Strategic fit—yes)	.80	.75	.83	.67	.65
P(Strategic fit—no)	.20	.25	.17	.33	.35
P(Invest—success)	.60	.65	.70	.75	.80
P(Invest—failure)	.40	.35	.30	.25	.20
P(Delay—success)	.80	.70	.65	.80	.85
P(Delay—failure)	.20	.30	.35	.20	.15
Invest—success	\$ 7,300,000	8,000,000	4,500,000	5,200,000	3,800,000
Invest—failure	−2,000,000	3,500,000	−1,500,000	−2,100,000	−900,000
Delay—success	4,500,000	6,000,000	3,300,000	2,500,000	2,700,000
Delay—failure	−1,300,000	−4,000,000	−800,000	−1,100,000	−900,000

Determine the expected value for each project and then rank the projects accordingly for the company to consider.

This case was adapted from R. K. Perdue, W. J. McAllister, P. V. King, and B. G. Berkey, "Valuation of R and D Projects Using Options Pricing and Decision Analysis Models," *Interfaces* 29, no. 6 (November–December 1999): 57–74.

Solutions to Selected Odd-Numbered Problems

1. (a) lease land; (b) savings certificate
3. (a) bellhop; (b) management; (c) bellhop
5. (a) corn; (b) soybeans; (c) corn; (d) soybeans; (e) corn
7. (a) build shopping center; (b) lease equipment; (c) build shopping center; (d) lease equipment; (e) build shopping center
9. (a) Army vs. Navy; (b)Alabama vs. Auburn; (c) Alabama vs. Auburn
11. (a) pass; (b) off tackle or option; (c) toss sweep
13. (a) office park; (b) office building; (c) office park or shopping center; (d) office building
15. press
17. *EV* (shoveler) = \$99.6
19. *EV* (operate) same as leasing; conservative decision is to lease
21. bond fund
23. Taiwan, *EVPI* = \$0.47 million
25. compact car dealership
27. (b) Stock 16 cases; (c) stock 16 cases; (d) \$5.80
29. (b) Stock 26 dozen; (c) stock 26 dozen; (d) \$3.10
31. O'Neil
33. *EV* (graphic design) = 191,000
35. (a) *EV* (Damon) = 121.5, (c) *EV*(Diaz) = 119.8
37. *A*, *EV*(A) = \$23,300
39. make bid, *EV* = \$142
41. produce widget, *EV* = \$69,966
43. hire Roper, *EVSI* = \$5.01M
45. Jay should settle; *EV* = 600,000
47. grower B, *EV* = 39,380
49. *EVSI* = \$234,000, *EVPI* = \$350,000
51. oil change, *EV* = \$62.80
53. *EV* = \$3.75 million, *EVSI* = \$670,000
55. risk averters

Forecasting

A **forecast** is a prediction of what will occur in the future. Meteorologists forecast the weather, sportscasters predict the winners of football games, and managers of business firms attempt to predict how much of their product will be demanded in the future. In fact, managers are constantly trying to predict the future, making decisions in the present that will ensure the continued success of their firms. Often a manager will use judgment, opinion, or past experiences to forecast what will occur in the future. However, a number of mathematical methods are also available to aid managers in making decisions. In this chapter, we present two of the traditional forecasting methods: time series analysis and regression. Although no technique will result in a totally accurate forecast (i.e., it is impossible to predict the future exactly), these forecasting methods can provide reliable guidelines for decision making.

Forecasting Components

A variety of forecasting methods exist, and their applicability is dependent on the *time frame* of the forecast (i.e., how far in the future we are forecasting), the *existence of patterns* in the forecast (i.e., seasonal trends, peak periods), and the *number of variables* to which the forecast is related. We will discuss each of these factors separately.

Short-range forecasts are daily operations.

Medium-range forecasts are usually from a month up to a year.

Long-range forecasts are more strategic and for over a year.

In general, forecasts can be classified according to three time frames: short range, medium range, and long range. **Short-range forecasts** typically encompass the immediate future and are concerned with the daily operations of a business firm, such as daily demand or resource requirements. A short-range forecast rarely goes beyond a couple months into the future. A **medium-range forecast** typically encompasses anywhere from 1 or 2 months to 1 year. A forecast of this length is generally more closely related to a yearly production plan and will reflect such items as peaks and valleys in demand and the necessity to secure additional resources for the upcoming year. A **long-range forecast** typically encompasses a period longer than 1 or 2 years. Long-range forecasts are related to management's attempt to plan new products for changing markets, build new facilities, or secure long-term financing. In general, the farther into the future one seeks to predict, the more difficult forecasting becomes.

These classifications should be viewed as generalizations. The line of demarcation between medium- and long-range forecasts is often quite arbitrary and not always distinct. For some firms a medium-range forecast could be several years, and for other firms a long-range forecast could be in terms of months.

*A **trend** is a gradual, long-term, up-or-down movement of demand.*

__Random variations__ are unpredictable movements in demand that follow no pattern.

Forecasts often exhibit patterns, or trends. A **trend** is a long-term movement of the item being forecast. For example, the demand for personal computers has shown an upward trend during the past decade, without any long downward movement in the market. Trends are the easiest patterns of demand behavior to detect and are often the starting point for developing a forecast. Figure 1(a) illustrates a demand trend in which there is a general upward movement or increase. Notice that Figure 1(a) also includes several random movements up and down. **Random variations** are movements that are not predictable and follow no pattern (and thus are virtually unpredictable).

*A **cycle** is an up-and-down repetitive movement in demand.*

A **cycle** is an undulating movement in demand, up and down, that repeats itself over a lengthy time span (i.e., more than 1 year). For example, new housing starts and thus construction-related products tend to follow cycles in the economy. Automobile sales tend to follow cycles in the same fashion. The demand for winter sports equipment increases every 4 years, before and after the Winter Olympics. Figure 1(b) shows the general behavior of a demand cycle.

*A **seasonal pattern** is an up-and-down, repetitive movement within a trend occurring periodically.*

A **seasonal pattern** is an oscillating movement in demand that occurs periodically (in the short run) and is repetitive. Seasonality is often weather related. For example, every winter the

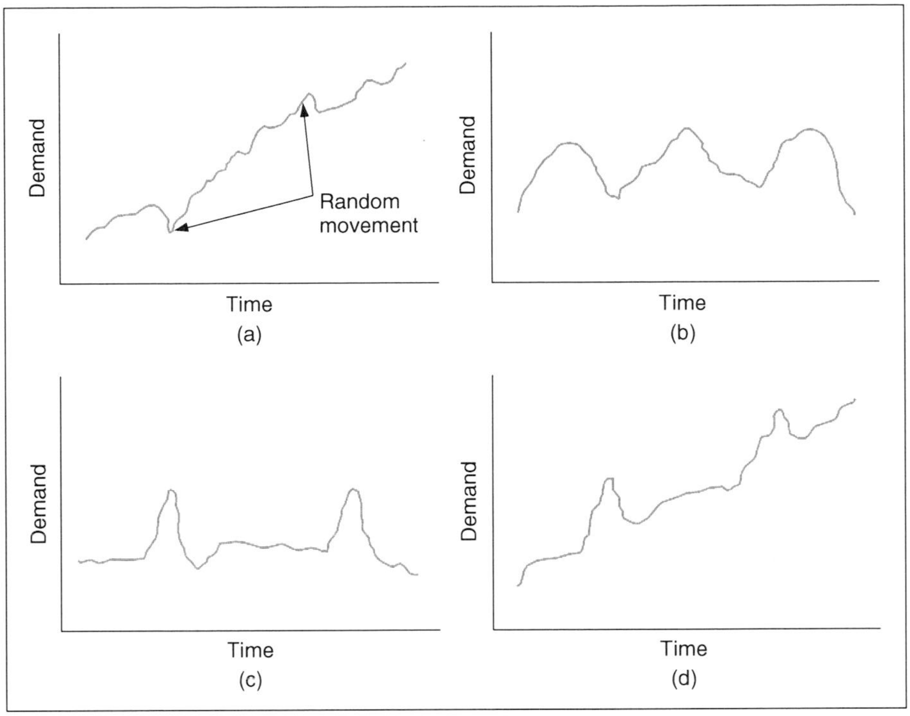

Figure 1

Forms of forecast movement: (a) trend, (b) cycle, (c) seasonal pattern, and (d) trend with seasonal pattern

demand for snowblowers and skis increases dramatically, and retail sales in general increase during the Christmas season. However, a seasonal pattern can occur on a daily or weekly basis. For example, some restaurants are busier at lunch than at dinner, and shopping mall stores and theaters tend to have higher demand on weekends. Figure 1(c) illustrates a seasonal pattern in which the same demand behavior is repeated each period at the same time.

Of course, demand behavior will frequently display several of these characteristics simultaneously. Although housing starts display cyclical behavior, there has been an upward trend in new house construction over the years. As we noted, demand for skis is seasonal; however, there has been a general upward trend in the demand for winter sports equipment during the past 2 decades. Figure 1(d) displays the combination of two demand patterns, a trend with a seasonal pattern.

There are instances in which demand behavior exhibits no pattern. These are referred to as *irregular movements*, or variations. For example, a local flood might cause a momentary increase in carpet demand, or negative publicity resulting from a lawsuit might cause product demand to drop for a period of time. Although this behavior is causal, and thus not totally random, it still does not follow a pattern that can be reflected in a forecast.

Types of forecasting methods are time series, regression, and qualitative.

Forecasting Methods

Time series forecasts are statistical techniques that use historical data.

Regression develops a mathematical relationship between the forecasted item and factors that cause it to behave the way it does.

The factors discussed previously determine to a certain extent the type of forecasting method that can or should be used. In this chapter we discuss the basic types of forecasting: *time series*, *regression methods*, and *qualitative methods*. **Time series** is a category of statistical techniques that uses historical data to predict future behavior. **Regression** (or causal) methods attempt to develop a mathematical relationship (in the form of a regression model) between the item being forecast and factors that cause it to behave the way it does. Most of the remainder of this chapter is about time series and regression forecasting methods. In this section we focus our discussion on qualitative forecasting.

Qualitative methods use judgement, expertise and opinion to make forecasts.

Qualitative methods use management judgment, expertise, and opinion to make forecasts. Often called "the jury of executive opinion," they are the most common type of forecasting method for the long-term strategic planning process. There are normally individuals or groups within an organization whose judgments and opinions regarding the future are as valid or more valid than those of outside experts or other structured approaches. Top managers are the key group involved in the development of forecasts for strategic plans. They are generally most familiar with their firms' own capabilities and resources and the markets for their products.

The sales force is a direct point of contact with the consumer. This contact provides an awareness of consumer expectations in the future that others may not possess. Engineering personnel have an innate understanding of the technological aspects of the type of products that might be feasible and likely in the future.

Management Science Application

Forecasting Advertising Demand at NBC

NBC Universal, a subsidiary of General Electric Company, owns and operates the most profitable television network in the United States, with revenues of over $14 billion. More than 60% of these revenues are generated by on-air advertising time on its television networks and stations. The major television networks announce their new programming schedules for the upcoming season (which starts in late September) in mid-May. NBC begins selling advertising time very soon after the new schedule is announced in May, and 60% to 80% of its air-time inventory is sold in the following 2- to 3-week period (to approximately 400 advertisers), known as the *upfront market*. Immediately following the announcement of its new season schedule in May, NBC forecasts ratings and estimates market demand for its shows. The ratings forecasts are estimates of the number of people in several demographic groups who are expected to watch each airing of the shows in the schedule for the entire year, which are, in turn, based on such factors as a show's strength, historical time-slot ratings, and the ratings performance of adjacent shows. Total market demand depends primarily on the strength of the economy and the expected performance of the network's schedule. Based on this ratings forecast and market demand, NBC develops pricing strategies and sets the prices for commercials on its shows. Forecasting the upfront market has always been a challenging process for NBC. The network used to use historical patterns, expert knowledge, and intuition to forecast demand, then later it switched to time series forecasting models based on historical demand. However, these models were unsatisfactory because of the unique nature of NBC's demand population of advertisers. NBC ultimately developed a unique approach to forecasting its upfront market for demand that includes a combination of the Delphi technique and a "grassroots" forecasting approach. The Delphi technique seeks to develop a consensus (or at least a compromise) forecast from among a group of experts, whereas a grassroots approach to forecasting asks the individuals closest to the final customer, such as salespeople, about the customers' purchasing plans. In their forecasting approach NBC used its (more than 100) account executives, who interact closely with the network's (more than 400) advertisers, to build a knowledge base in order to estimate individual advertiser demand, aggregate this demand into a total demand forecast, and then continuously and iteratively update demand estimates based on the account executives' expertise. Previous forecasting methods had resulted in forecast errors of 5% to 12%, whereas this new forecasting process resulted in a forecast error of only 2.8%, the most accurate forecast NBC had ever achieved for its upfront market.

Source: S. Bollapragada, S. Gupta, B. Hurwitz, P. Miles, and R. Tyagi, "NBC-Universal Uses a Novel Qualitative Forecasting Technique to Predict Advertising Demand," *Interfaces* 38, no. 2 (March–April 2008): 103–11.

Consumer, or market, research is an organized approach that uses surveys and other research techniques to determine what products and services customers want and will purchase, and to identify new markets and sources of customers. Consumer and market research is normally conducted by the marketing department within an organization, by industry organizations and groups, and by private marketing or consulting firms. Although market research can provide accurate and useful forecasts of product demand, it must be skillfully and correctly conducted, and it can be expensive.

*The **Delphi method** forecasts future using informed judgement and opinions from knowledgeable individuals.*

The **Delphi method** is a procedure for acquiring informed judgments and opinions from knowledgeable individuals, using a series of questionnaires to develop a consensus forecast about what will occur in the future. It was developed at the RAND Corporation shortly after World War II to forecast the impact of a hypothetical nuclear atack on the United States. Although the Delphi method has been used for a variety of applications, forecasting has been one of its primary uses. It has been especially useful for forecasting technological change and advances.

Technological forecasting has become increasingly crucial for successful competition in today's global business environment. New enhanced computer technology, new production methods, and advanced machinery and equipment are constantly being made available to companies. These advances enable them to introduce more new products into the marketplace faster than ever before. The companies that succeed do so by getting a technological jump on their competitors through accurate prediction of future technology and its capabilities. What new products and services will be technologically feasible, when they can be introduced, and what their demand will be are questions about the future for which answers cannot be predicted from historical data. Instead, the informed opinion and judgment of experts are necessary to make these types of single, long-term forecasts.

Time Series Methods

Time series methods are statistical techniques that make use of historical data accumulated over a period of time. Time series methods assume that what has occurred in the past will continue to occur in the future. As the name *time series* suggests, these methods relate the forecast to only one factor—*time*. Time series methods tend to be most useful for short-range forecasting, although they can be used for longer-range forecasting. We will discuss two types of time series methods: the *moving average* and *exponential smoothing*.

Moving Average

A time series forecast can be as simple as using demand in the current period to predict demand in the next period. For example, if demand is 100 units this week, the forecast for next week's demand would be 100 units; if demand turned out to be 90 units instead, then the following week's demand would be 90 units, and so forth. This is sometimes referred to as *naïve* forecasting. However, this type of forecasting method does not take into account any type of historical demand behavior; it relies only on demand in the current period. As such, it reacts directly to the normal, random up-and-down movements in demand.

*The **moving average** method is good for stable demand with no pronounced behavioral patterns.*

Alternatively, the **moving average** method uses several values during the recent past to develop a forecast. This tends to *dampen*, or *smooth out*, the random increases and decreases of a forecast that uses only one period. As such, the simple moving average is particularly useful for forecasting items that are relatively stable and do not display any pronounced behavior, such as a trend or seasonal pattern.

Moving averages are computed for specific periods, such as 3 months or 5 months, depending on how much the forecaster desires to smooth the data. The longer the moving average period, the smoother the data will be. The formula for computing the simple moving average is as follows:

$$MA_n = \frac{\sum_{i=1}^{n} D_i}{n}$$

where

n = number of periods in the moving average
D_i = data in period i

To demonstrate the *moving average* forecasting method, we will use an example. The Instant Paper Clip Supply Company sells and delivers office supplies to various companies, schools, and agencies within a 30-mile radius of its warehouse. The office supply business is extremely competitive, and the ability to deliver orders promptly is an important factor in gettting new customers and keeping old ones. (Offices typically order not when their inventory of supplies is getting low but when they completely run out. As a result, they need their orders immediately.) The manager of the company wants to be certain that enough drivers and delivery vehicles are available so that orders can be delivered promptly. Therefore, the manager wants to be able to forecast the number of orders that will occur during the next month (i.e., to forecast the demand for deliveries).

From records of delivery orders, the manager has accumulated data for the past 10 months. These data are shown in Table 1.

Table 1
Orders for 10-month period

Month	Orders Delivered per Month
January	120
February	90
March	100
April	75
May	110
June	50
July	75
August	130
September	110
October	90

The moving average forecast is computed by dividing the sum of the values of the forecast variable, orders per month for a sequence of months, by the number of months in the sequence. Frequently, a moving average is calculated for three or five time periods. The forecast resulting from either the 3- or the 5-month moving average is typically for the next month in the sequence, which in this case is November. The moving average is computed from the demand for orders for the last 3 months in the sequence, according to the following formula:

$$MA_3 = \frac{\sum_{i=1}^{3} D_i}{3} = \frac{90 + 110 + 130}{3} = 110 \text{ orders}$$

The 5-month moving average is computed from the last 5 months of demand data, as follows:

$$MA_5 = \frac{\sum_{i=1}^{5} D_i}{5} = \frac{90 + 110 + 130 + 75 + 50}{5} = 91 \text{ orders}$$

The 3- and 5-month moving averages for all the months of demand data are shown in Table 2. Notice that we have computed forecasts for all the months. Actually, only the forecast for November, based on the most recent monthly demand, would be used by the manager. However, the earlier forecasts for prior months allow us to compare the forecast with actual demand to see how accurate the forecasting method is (i.e., how well it does).

Table 2
Three- and 5-month averages

Month	Orders per Month	3-Month Moving Average	5-Month Moving Average
January	120	—	—
February	90	—	—
March	100	—	—
April	75	103.3	—
May	110	88.3	—
June	50	95.0	99.0
July	75	78.3	85.0
August	130	78.3	82.0
September	110	85.0	88.0
October	90	105.0	95.0
November	—	110.0	91.0

Both moving average forecasts in Table 2 tend to smooth out the variability occurring in the actual data. This smoothing effect can be observed in Figure 2, in which the 3-month and 5-month averages have been superimposed on a graph of the original data. The extremes in the actual orders per month have been reduced. This is beneficial if these extremes simply reflect random fluctuations in orders per month because our moving average forecast will not be strongly influenced by them.

Figure 2
Three- and 5-month moving averages

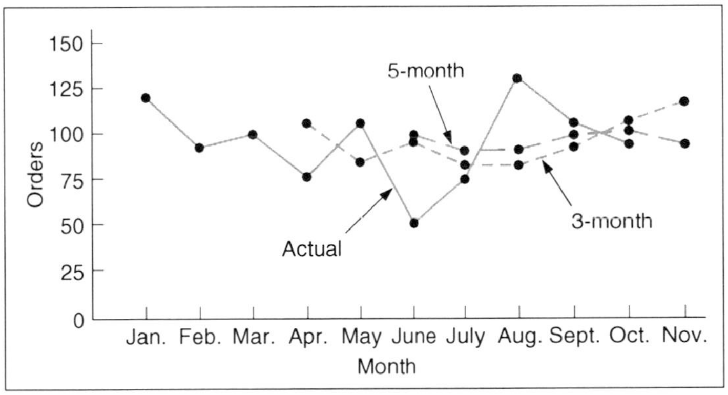

Longer-period moving averages react more slowly to recent demand changes than do shorter-period moving averages.

Notice that the 5-month moving average in Figure 2 smooths out fluctuations to a greater extent than the 3-month moving average. However, the 3-month average more closely reflects the most recent data available to the office supply manager. (The 5-month average forecast considers data all the way back to June; the 3-month average does so only to August.) In general, forecasts computed using the longer-period moving average are slower to react to recent changes in demand than those made using shorter-period moving averages. The extra periods of data dampen the speed with which the forecast responds. Establishing the appropriate number of periods to use in a moving average forecast often requires some amount of trial-and-error experimentation.

One additional point to mention relates to the period of the forecast. Sometimes a forecaster will need to forecast for a short planning horizon rather than just a single period. For both the 3- and 5-month moving average forecasts computed in Table 2, the final forecast is for one period only in the future. Because the moving average includes multiple periods of data for each forecast, and it is most often used to forecast in a stable demand environment, it would be appropriate to use the forecast for multiple periods in the future. It could then be updated as actual demand data became available.

The major disadvantage of the moving average method is that it does not react well to variations that occur for a reason, such as trends and seasonal effects (although this method does reflect trends to a moderate extent). Those factors that cause changes are generally ignored. It is basically a "mechanical" method that reflects historical data in a consistent fashion. However, the moving average method does have the advantage of being easy to use, quick, and relatively inexpensive, although moving averages for a substantial number of periods for many different items can result in the accumulation and storage of a large amount of data. In general, this method can provide a good forecast for the short run, but an attempt should not be made to push the forecast too far into the distant future.

Weighted Moving Average

*In a **weighted moving average**, weights are assigned to the most recent data.*

The moving average method can be adjusted to reflect more closely more recent fluctuations in the data and seasonal effects. This adjusted method is referred to as a **weighted moving average** method. In this method, weights are assigned to the most recent data according to the following formula:

$$WMA_n = \sum_{i=1}^{n} W_i D_i$$

where

W_i = the weight for period i, between 0% and 100% (i.e., between 0 and 1.0)

ΣW_i = 1.00

For example, if the Instant Paper Clip Supply Company wants to compute a 3-month weighted moving average with a weight of 50% for the October data, a weight of 33% for the September data, and a weight of 17% for August, it is computed as

$$WMA_3 = \sum_{i=1}^{3} W_i D_i = (.50)(90) + (.33)(110) + (.17)(130) = 103.4 \text{ orders}$$

Notice that the forecast includes a fractional part, .4. Because .4 order would be impossible, this appears to be unrealistic. In general, the fractional parts need to be included in the computation to achieve mathematical accuracy, but when the final forecast is achieved, it must be rounded up or down.

Also notice that this forecast is slightly lower than our previously computed 3-month average forecast of 110 orders, reflecting the lower number of orders in October (the most recent month in the sequence).

Determining the precise weights to use for each period of data frequently requires some trial-and-error experimentation, as does determining the exact number of periods to include in the moving average. If the most recent months are weighted too heavily, the forecast might overreact to a random fluctuation in orders; if they are weighted too lightly, the forecast might underreact to an actual change in the pattern of orders.

Exponential Smoothing

***Exponential smoothing** is an averaging method that reacts more strongly to recent changes in demand than to more distant past data.*

The **exponential smoothing** forecast method is an averaging method that weights the most recent past data more strongly than more distant past data. Thus, the forecast will react more strongly to immediate changes in the data. This is very useful if the recent changes in

Management Science Application

Forecasting at Goodyear Tire and Rubber Company

Goodyear, with net sales of almost $20 billion, is one of the world's leading tire manufacturing companies and the number one tire maker in North America. Forecasting customer demand has always been recognized as an important part of its production and distribution planning processes, and it has historically used such forecasting techniques as time series analysis and exponential smoothing. For example, in the early 1990s in the United States Goodyear was experiencing large errors in its 60-day advance planning forecasts, so it replaced its linear regression models with a single exponential smoothing model, which increased forecast accuracy by 20%. In the mid-1990s the company developed a forecast system that analyzed the performance of more than 20 mathematical forecasting models for different products using historical demand data. It then picked the forecasting model that resulted in the lowest mean absolute percent error (MAPE). In the late 1990s Goodyear upgraded its planning systems and simultaneously consolidated all its forecasting systems in North America (i.e., the United States and Canada) into a single integrated system. However, as the complexity of its business increased, so did its forecasting errors. To resolve this problem Goodyear created forecasts based on products, customers, and location to enhance its customer-specific forecasting capabilities. This required a collaborative relationship between Goodyear and its customers that included shared demand data and forecasts. For example, Goodyear used EDI technology to receive a customer's forecast and incorporate it into its own production planning process. By the mid-2000s Goodyear had experienced a 10% improvement in the accuracy of its 60-day forecast.

Landov Media

Source: S. D. Miller and K. M. Liem, "Collaborative Forecasting: Goodyear Tire and Rubber Company's Journey," *Journal of Business Forecasting* 22, no. 1 (Fall 2004): 23–27.

the data are the results of an *actual* change (e.g., a seasonal pattern) instead of just random fluctuations (for which a simple moving average forecast would suffice).

We will consider two forms of exponential smoothing: *simple exponential smoothing* and *adjusted exponential smoothing* (adjusted for trends, seasonal patterns, etc.). We will discuss the simple exponential smoothing case first, followed by the adjusted form.

To demonstrate simple exponential smoothing, we will return to the Instant Paper Clip Supply Company example. The simple exponential smoothing forecast is computed by using the formula

$$F_{t+1} = \alpha D_t + (1 - \alpha)F_t$$

where

F_{t+1} = the forecast for the next period
D_t = actual demand in the present period
F_t = the previously determined forecast for the present period
α = a weighting factor referred to as the *smoothing constant*

The smoothing constant, α, is between zero and one. It reflects the weight given to the most recent demand data. For example, if $\alpha = .20$,

$$F_{t+1} = .20D_t + .80F_t$$

Management Science Application

Forecasting Customer Demand at Taco Bell

Taco Bell is an international fast-food business with 6,500 locations worldwide, with annual sales of approximately $4.6 billion.

Labor costs at Taco Bell are approximately 30% of every sales dollar, and these costs are very difficult to manage because labor is so closely linked to sales demand. It is not possible for Taco Bell to produce its food products in advance and store them in inventory like a manufacturing company; instead, it must prepare its food products on demand—that is, when they are ordered. Demand is highly variable during both the day and the week, with 52% of sales occurring during the 3-hour lunch period from 11:00 A.M. to 2:00 P.M. Determining how many employees to schedule at given times during the day is very difficult. This problem is exacerbated by the fact that quality service is determined by the speed of service.

To develop an effective labor-management system, Taco Bell needed an accurate forecasting model to predict customer demand—that is, arrivals and sales. Taco Bell determined that the best forecasting method was a 6-week moving average for each 15-minute interval of every day of the week. For example, customer demand at a particular restaurant for all Thursdays from 11:00 A.M. to 11:15 A.M. for a 6-week period constitutes the time series database to forecast customer transactions for the next Thursday in the future. On a weekly basis, the forecasts are compared to statistical forecasting control limits that are continuously updated, and the length of the moving average is adjusted when the forecasts move out of control. Taco Bell achieved labor savings of over $40 million from 1993 to 1996 by using the new labor-management system, of which this forecasting model is an integral part.

Source: J. Hueter and W. Swart, "An Integrated Labor-Management System for Taco Bell," *Interfaces* 28, no. 1 (January–February 1998): 75–91.

which means that our forecast for the next period is based on 20% of recent demand (D_t) and 80% of past demand (in the form of the forecast F_t because F_t is derived from previous demands and forecasts). If we go to one extreme and let $\alpha = 0.0$, then

$$\begin{aligned} F_{t+1} &= 0D_t + 1F_t \\ &= F_t \end{aligned}$$

The closer α is to one, the greater the reaction to the most recent demand.

and the forecast for the next period is the same as for this period. In other words, *the forecast does not reflect the most recent demand at all.*

On the other hand, if $\alpha = 1.0$, then

$$\begin{aligned} F_{t+1} &= 1D_t + 0F_t \\ &= D_t \end{aligned}$$

and we have considered only the most recent occurrence in our data (demand in the present period) and nothing else. Thus, we can conclude that the higher α is, the more sensitive the forecast will be to changes in recent demand. Alternatively, the closer α is to zero, the greater will be the dampening or smoothing effect. As α approaches zero, the forecast will react and adjust more slowly to differences between the actual demand and the forecasted demand. The most commonly used values of α are in the range from .01 to .50. However, the determination of α is usually judgmental and subjective and will often be based on trial-and-error experimentation. An inaccurate estimate of α can limit the usefulness of this forecasting technique.

To demonstrate the computation of an exponentially smoothed forecast, we will use an example. PM Computer Services assembles customized personal computers from generic parts. The company was formed and is operated by two part-time State University students, Paulette Tyler and Maureen Becker, and has had steady growth since it started. The company assembles computers mostly at night, using other part-time students as labor. Paulette and Maureen purchase generic computer parts in volume at a discount from a variety of sources whenever they see a good deal. It is therefore important that they develop a good forecast of demand for their computers so that they will know how many computer component parts to purchase and stock.

The company has accumulated the demand data in Table 3 for its computers for the past 12 months, from which it wants to compute exponential smoothing forecasts, using smoothing constants (α) equal to .30 and .50.

Table 3
Demand for personal computers

Period	Month	Demand
1	January	37
2	February	40
3	March	41
4	April	37
5	May	45
6	June	50
7	July	43
8	August	47
9	September	56
10	October	52
11	November	55
12	December	54

To develop the series of forecasts for the data in Table 3, we will start with period 1 (January) and compute the forecast for period 2 (February) by using $\alpha = .30$. The formula for exponential smoothing also requires a forecast for period 1, which we do not have, so we will use the demand for period 1 as both demand and *the forecast for period 1.* Other ways to determine a starting forecast include averaging the first three or four periods and making a subjective estimate. Thus, the forecast for February is

$$F_2 = \alpha D_1 + (1 - \alpha)F_1 = (.30)(37) + (.70)(37) = 37 \text{ units}$$

The forecast for period 3 is computed similarly:

$$F_3 = \alpha D_2 + (1 - \alpha)F_2 = (.30)(40) + (.70)(37) = 37.9 \text{ units}$$

The remaining monthly forecasts are shown in Table 4. The final forecast is for period 13, January, and is the forecast of interest to PM Computer Services:

$$F_{13} = \alpha D_{12} + (1 - \alpha)F_{12} = (.30)(54) + (.70)(50.84) = 51.79 \text{ units}$$

Table 4 also includes the forecast values by using $\alpha = .50$. Both exponential smoothing forecasts are shown in Figure 3, together with the actual data.

In Figure 3, the forecast using the higher smoothing constant, $\alpha = .50$, reacts more strongly to changes in demand than does the forecast with $\alpha = .30$, although both smooth out the random fluctuations in the forecast. Notice that both forecasts lag the actual demand. For example, a pronounced downward change in demand in July is not reflected

Table 4
Exponential smoothing forecasts, α = .30 and α = .50

Period	Month	Demand	Forecast, F_{t+1} $\alpha = .30$	Forecast, F_{t+1} $\alpha = .50$
1	January	37	—	—
2	February	40	37.00	37.00
3	March	41	37.90	38.50
4	April	37	38.83	39.75
5	May	45	38.28	38.37
6	June	50	40.29	41.68
7	July	43	43.20	45.84
8	August	47	43.14	44.42
9	September	56	44.30	45.71
10	October	52	47.81	50.85
11	November	55	49.06	51.42
12	December	54	50.84	53.21
13	January	—	51.79	53.61

Figure 3
Exponential smoothing forecasts

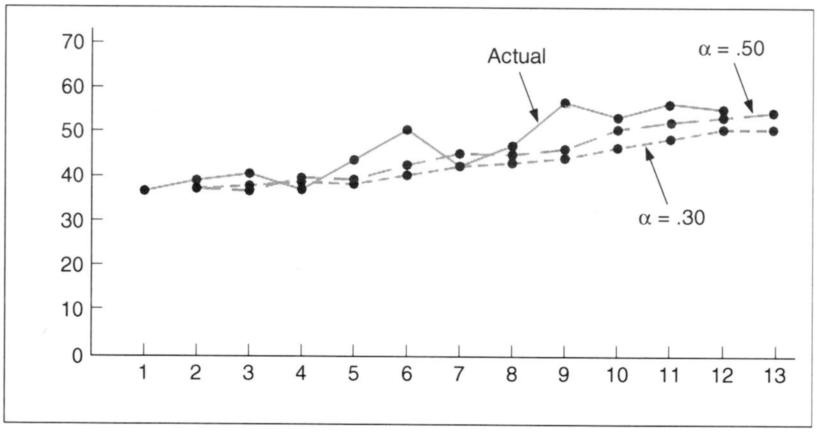

in the forecast until August. If these changes mark a change in trend (i.e., a long-term upward or downward movement) rather than just a random fluctuation, then the forecast will always lag this trend. We can see a general upward trend in delivered orders throughout the year. Both forecasts tend to be consistently lower than the actual demand; that is, the forecasts lag behind the trend.

Based on simple observation of the two forecasts in Figure 3, $\alpha = .50$ seems to be the more accurate of the two, in the sense that it seems to follow the actual data more closely. (Later in this chapter we will discuss several quantitative methods for determining forecast accuracy.) In general, when demand is relatively stable, without any trend, using a small value for α is more appropriate to simply smooth out the forecast. Alternatively, when actual demand displays an increasing (or decreasing) trend, as is the case in Figure 3, a larger value of α is generally better. It will react more quickly to the more recent upward or downward movements in the actual data. In some approaches to exponential smoothing, the accuracy of the forecast is monitored in terms of the difference between the actual values and the forecasted values. If these differences become larger, then α is changed (higher or lower) in an attempt to adapt the forecast to the actual data. However, the exponential smoothing forecast can also be adjusted for the effects of a trend.

As we noted with the moving average forecast, the forecaster sometimes needs a forecast for more than one period into the future. In our PM Computer Services example, the final forecast computed was for 1 month, January. A forecast for 2 or 3 months could have been computed by grouping the demand data into the required number of periods and then using these values in the exponential smoothing computations. For example, if a 3-month forecast was needed, demand for January, February, and March could be summed and used to compute the forecast for the next 3-month period, and so on, until a final 3-month forecast resulted. Alternatively, if a trend was present, the final period forecast could be used for an extended forecast by adjusting it by a trend factor.

Adjusted Exponential Smoothing

Adjusted exponential smoothing is the exponential smoothing forecast with an adjustment for a trend added to it.

The **adjusted exponential smoothing** forecast consists of the exponential smoothing forecast with a trend adjustment factor added to it. The formula for the adjusted forecast is

$$AF_{t+1} = F_{t+1} + T_{t+1}$$

where
T = an exponentially smoothed trend factor

The trend factor is computed much the same as the exponentially smoothed forecast. It is, in effect, a forecast model for trend:

$$T_{t+1} = \beta(F_{t+1} - F_t) + (1 - \beta)T_t$$

where
T_t = the last period trend factor
β = a smoothing constant for trend

The closer β is to one, the stronger a trend is reflected.

Like α, β is a value between zero and one. It reflects the weight given to the most recent trend data. Also like α, β is often determined subjectively, based on the judgment of the forecaster. A high β reflects trend changes more than a low β. It is not uncommon for β to equal α in this method.

Notice that this formula for the trend factor reflects a weighted measure of the increase (or decrease) between the current forecast, F_{t+1}, and the previous forecast, F_t.

As an example, PM Computer Services now wants to develop an adjusted exponentially smoothed forecast, using the same 12 months of demand shown in Table 3. It will use the exponentially smoothed forecast with $\alpha = .50$ computed in Table 4 with a smoothing constant for trend, β, of .30.

The formula for the adjusted exponential smoothing forecast requires an initial value for T_t to start the computational process. This initial trend factor is most often an estimate determined subjectively or based on past data by the forecaster. In this case, because we have a relatively long sequence of demand data (i.e., 12 months), we will start with the trend, T_t, equal to zero. By the time the forecast value of interest, F_{13}, is computed, we should have a relatively good value for the trend factor.

The adjusted forecast for February, AF_2, is the same as the exponentially smoothed forecast because the trend computing factor will be zero (i.e., F_1 and F_2 are the same and $T_2 = 0$). Thus, we will compute the adjusted forecast for March, AF_3, as follows, starting with the determination of the trend factor, T_3:

$$T_3 = \beta(F_3 - F_2) + (1 - \beta)T_2 = (.30)(38.5 - 37.0) + (.70)(0) = 0.45$$

and

$$AF_3 = F_3 + T_3 = 38.5 + 0.45 = 38.95$$

This adjusted forecast value for period 3 is shown in Table 5, with all other adjusted forecast values for the 12-month period plus the forecast for period 13, computed as follows:

$$T_{13} = \beta(F_{13} - F_{12}) + (1 - \beta)T_{12} = (.30)(53.61 - 53.21) + (.70)(1.77) = 1.36$$

Table 5
Adjusted exponentially smoothed forecast values

Period	Month	Demand	Forecast (F_{t+1})	Trend (T_{t+1})	Adjusted Forecast (AF_{t+1})
1	January	37	37.00	—	—
2	February	40	37.00	0.00	37.00
3	March	41	38.50	0.45	38.95
4	April	37	39.75	0.69	40.44
5	May	45	38.37	0.07	38.44
6	June	50	41.68	1.04	42.73
7	July	43	45.84	1.97	47.82
8	August	47	44.42	0.95	45.37
9	September	56	45.71	1.05	46.76
10	October	52	50.85	2.28	53.13
11	November	55	51.42	1.76	53.19
12	December	54	53.21	1.77	54.98
13	January	—	53.61	1.36	54.96

and

$$AF_{13} = F_{13} + T_{13} = 53.61 + 1.36 = 54.96 \text{ units}$$

The adjusted exponentially smoothed forecast values shown in Table 5 are compared with the exponentially smoothed forecast values and the actual data in Figure 4.

Figure 4
Adjusted, exponentially smoothed forecast

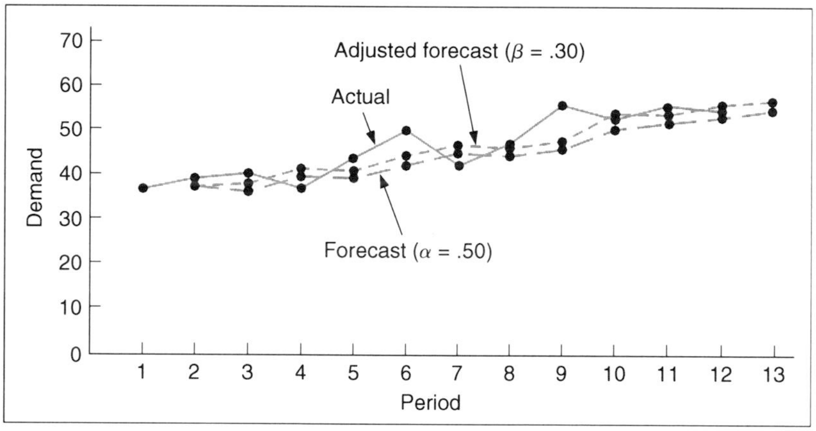

Notice that the adjusted forecast is consistently higher than the exponentially smoothed forecast and is thus more reflective of the generally increasing trend of the actual data. However, in general, the pattern, or degree of smoothing, is very similar for both forecasts.

Linear Trend Line

Linear regression is most often thought of as a causal method of forecasting in which a mathematical relationship is developed between demand and some other factor that causes demand behavior. However, when demand displays an obvious trend over time, a least squares regression line, or **linear trend line**, can be used to forecast demand.

A ***linear trend line*** *is a linear regression model that relates demand to time.*

A linear trend line relates a dependent variable, which for our purposes is demand, to one independent variable, time, in the form of a linear equation, as follows:

$$y = a + bx$$

Management Science Application

Seasonal Forecasting at Dell

Dell is the largest computer company in the world. Its founder, Michael Dell, formed the company based on the idea of selling personal computers directly to customers and bypassing retailers; Dell Inc. sells computer systems directly to customers via phone and Internet orders. Once an order is received and processed, it is sent to an assembly plant in Austin, Texas, where Dell builds, tests, and packages a product within 8 hours.

Dell's direct sales model is dependent upon its arrangements with its suppliers, many of which are located in Southeast Asia, with shipping times to Austin of 7 to 30 days. To compensate for these long lead times, Dell requires its suppliers to keep specified (i.e., target) inventory levels—typically 10 days of inventory—on hand at small warehouses, called "revolvers" (short for *revolving inventory*). In this type of vendor-managed inventory (VMI) arrangement, Dell's suppliers determine how much inventory to order and when to order to meet Dell's target inventory levels at the revolvers.

To help its suppliers make good ordering decisions, Dell shares its demand forecast with them on a monthly basis. Dell uses a 6-month rolling forecast developed by its marketing department that is updated weekly. Buyers receive weekly forecasts from commodity teams that break down the forecasts for specific parts and components. These forecasts reflect product-specific trends and seasonality. For home computer systems, Christmas is the major sales period of the year. Other high-demand periods include the back-to-school season and the end of the year, when the government makes big purchases.

AP Wide World Photos

Source: R. Kapuscinski, R. Zhang, P. Carbonneau, R. Moore, and B. Reeves, "Inventory Decisions in Dell's Supply Chain," *Interfaces* 34, no. 3 (May–June 2004): 191–205.

where

a = intercept (at period 0)
b = slope of the line
x = the time period
y = forecast for demand for period x

These parameters of the linear trend line can be calculated by using the least squares formulas for linear regression:

$$b = \frac{\Sigma xy - n\bar{x}\bar{y}}{\Sigma x^2 - n\bar{x}^2}$$
$$a = \bar{y} - b\bar{x}$$

where

n = number of periods

$$\bar{x} = \frac{\Sigma x}{n}$$

$$\bar{y} = \frac{\Sigma y}{n}$$

As an example, consider the demand data for PM Computer Services shown in Table 3. They appear to follow an increasing linear trend. As such, the company wants to compute a linear trend line as an alternative to the exponential smoothing and adjusted exponential smoothing forecasts shown in Tables 4 and 5. The values that are required for the least squares calculations are shown in Table 6.

Table 6
Least squares calculations

x (period)	y (demand)	xy	x^2
1	37	37	1
2	40	80	4
3	41	123	9
4	37	148	16
5	45	225	25
6	50	300	36
7	43	301	49
8	47	376	64
9	56	504	81
10	52	520	100
11	55	605	121
12	54	648	144
78	557	3,867	650

Using these values for $\bar{x}$ and $\bar{y}$ and the values from Table 6, the parameters for the linear trend line are computed as follows:

$$\bar{x} = \frac{78}{12} = 6.5$$
$$\bar{y} = \frac{557}{12} = 46.42$$
$$b = \frac{\Sigma xy - n\bar{x}\bar{y}}{\Sigma x^2 - n\bar{x}^2} = \frac{3{,}867 - (12)(6.5)(46.42)}{650 - 12(6.5)^2} = 1.72$$
$$a = \bar{y} - b\bar{x} = 46.42 - (1.72)(6.5) = 35.2$$

Therefore, the linear trend line is

$$y = 35.2 + 1.72x$$

To calculate a forecast for period 13, $x = 13$ would be substituted in the linear trend line:

$$y = 35.2 + 1.72(13) = 57.56$$

A linear trend line will not adjust to a change in trend as will exponential smoothing.

Figure 5 shows the linear trend line in comparison to the actual data. The trend line visibly appears to closely reflect the actual data (i.e., to be a "good fit") and would thus be a

Figure 5
Linear trend line

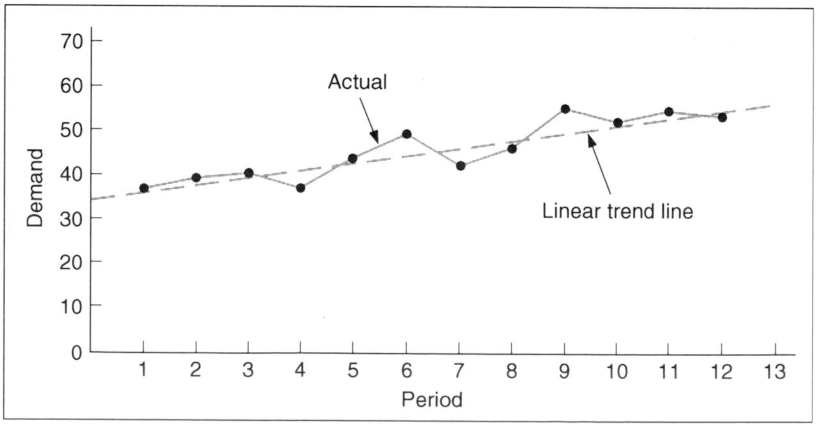

good forecast model for this problem. However, a disadvantage of the linear trend line is that it will not adjust to a change in the trend as the exponential smoothing forecast methods will (i.e., it is assumed that all future forecasts will follow a straight line). This limits the use of this method to a shorter time frame in which the forecaster is relatively certain that the trend will not change.

Seasonal Adjustments

As we mentioned at the beginning of this chapter, a seasonal pattern is a repetitive up-and-down movement in demand. Many demand items exhibit seasonal behavior. Clothing sales follow annual seasonal patterns, with demand for warm clothes increasing in the fall and winter and declining in the spring and summer, as the demand for cooler clothing increases. Demand for many retail items—including toys, sports equipment, clothing, electronic appliances, hams, turkeys, wine, and fruit—increases during the Christmas season. Greeting card demand increases in conjunction with various special days, such as Valentine's Day and Mother's Day. Seasonal patterns can also occur on a monthly, weekly, or even daily basis. Some restaurants have higher demand in the evening than at lunch, or on weekends as opposed to weekdays. Traffic and sales picks up at shopping malls on Friday and Saturday.

*It is possible to adjust for seasonality by multiplying the normal forecast by a **seasonal factor**.*

There are several methods available for reflecting seasonal patterns in a time series forecast. We will describe one of the simpler methods—using a **seasonal factor**, which is a numerical value that is multiplied by the normal forecast to get a seasonally adjusted forecast.

One method for developing a demand for seasonal factors is dividing the actual demand for each seasonal period by the total annual demand, according to the following formula:

$$S_i = \frac{D_i}{\Sigma D}$$

The resulting seasonal factors between zero and one are, in effect, the portion of total annual demand assigned to each season. These seasonal factors are thus multiplied by the annual forecasted demand to yield seasonally adjusted forecasts for each period.

As an example, Wishbone Farms is a company that raises turkeys, which it sells to a meat-processing company throughout the year. However, the peak season obviously occurs during the fourth quarter of the year, October to December. Wishbone Farms has experienced a demand for turkeys for the past 3 years as shown in Table 7.

Table 7
Demand for turkeys at Wishbone Farms

	Demand (1,000s)				
Year	QUARTER 1	QUARTER 2	QUARTER 3	QUARTER 4	TOTAL
1	12.6	8.6	6.3	17.5	45.0
2	14.1	10.3	7.5	18.2	50.1
3	15.3	10.6	8.1	19.6	53.6
Total	42.0	29.5	21.9	55.3	148.7

Because we have 3 years of demand data, we can compute the seasonal factors by dividing total quarterly demand for the 3 years by total demand across all 3 years:

$$S_1 = \frac{D_1}{\Sigma D} = \frac{42.0}{148.7} = 0.28$$

$$S_2 = \frac{D_2}{\Sigma D} = \frac{29.5}{148.7} = 0.20$$

$$S_3 = \frac{D_3}{\Sigma D} = \frac{21.9}{148.7} = 0.15$$

$$S_4 = \frac{D_4}{\Sigma D} = \frac{55.3}{148.7} = 0.37$$

Next, we want to multiply the forecasted demand for year 4 by each of the seasonal factors to get the forecasted demand for each quarter. However, to accomplish this, we need a demand forecast for year 4. In this case, because the demand data in Table 7 seem to exhibit a generally increasing trend, we compute a linear trend line for the 3 years of data in Table 7 to use as a rough forecast estimate:

$$y = 40.97 + 4.30x = 40.97 + 4.30(4) = 58.17$$

Thus, the forecast for year 4 is 58.17, or 58,170 turkeys.

Using this annual forecast of demand, the seasonally adjusted forecasts, SF_i, for 2004 are as follows:

$$SF_1 = (S_1)(F_5) = (.28)(58.17) = 16.28$$
$$SF_2 = (S_2)(F_5) = (.20)(58.17) = 11.63$$

Management Science Application

Developing Joint Forecasts at Boeing and Alcoa

Boeing is the world's largest manufacturer of commercial jetliners, with total revenues of approximately \$55 billion, and more than 154,000 employees in 48 U.S. states and 67 countries. One of the key stages in its large and complex supply chain is its Skin and Spar business unit, which supplies large wing products for most of Boeing's commercial jets. One of the Skin and Spar unit's major raw material suppliers is Alcoa, which is the world's leading producer of fabricated aluminum, with 130,000 employees and more than \$26 billion in total revenues. The two companies experienced difficulties with their supply chain relationship that resulted in unreliable deliveries, and shortages of some parts and excessive inventories of others. They identified two primary difficulties: the transportation system (i.e., railcars) and forecast reliability. Boeing and Alcoa used a team approach to find a solution, which included a new forecasting process that included an integrated information system and the real-time exchange of forecast data. Specifically, Boeing developed an electronic forecasting system to send weekly electronic forecasts directly to Alcoa. The forecast is generated automatically from Boeing's planning system each week. Boeing increased its forecast accuracy by making production plans visible to everyone in the supply chain at Alcoa and Boeing so Alcoa would know when changes were made in the production plan that were not reflected in the planning forecast—for example, when parts were pulled out of buffer stocks. In addition, Boeing developed a spreadsheet approach to monitor aggregate demand on a monthly basis and adjust its forecast accordingly for any unexpected changes.

Alamy Images

Source: V. A. Micheau, "How Boeing and Alcoa Implemented a Successful Vendor Managed Inventory Program," *Journal of Business Forecasting* 24, no. 1 (Spring 2005): 17–19.

$$SF_3 = (S_3)(F_5) = (.15)(58.17) = 8.73$$
$$SF_4 = (S_4)(F_5) = (.37)(58.17) = 21.53$$

Comparing these quarterly forecasts with the actual demand values in Table 7 shows them to be relatively good forecast estimates, reflecting both the seasonal variations in the data and the general upward trend.

Forecast Accuracy

*The **forecast error** is the difference between the forecast and actual demand.*

It is not probable that a forecast will be completely accurate; forecasts will always deviate from the actual demand. This difference between the forecast and the actual demand is referred to as the **forecast error**. Although some amount of forecast error is inevitable, the objective of forecasting is for the error to be as slight as possible. Of course, if the degree of error is not small, this may indicate either that the forecasting technique being used is the wrong one or that the technique needs to be adjusted by changing its parameters (for example, α in the exponential smoothing forecast).

There are a variety of different measures of forecast error, and in this section we discuss several of the most popular ones: mean absolute deviation (*MAD*), mean absolute percent deviation (*MAPD*), cumulative error (*E*), average error or bias ($\overline{E}$), and mean squared error (*MSE*).

Mean Absolute Deviation

MAD is the average, absolute difference between the forecast and the demand.

The **mean absolute deviation (MAD)** is one of the most popular and simplest-to-use measures of forecast error. *MAD* is an average of the difference between the forecast and actual demand, as computed by the following formula:

$$MAD = \frac{\Sigma|D_t - F_t|}{n}$$

where

t = the period number
D_t = demand in period t
F_t = the forecast for period t
n = the total number of periods
$||$ = the absolute value

In our examples for PM Computer Services, forecasts were developed using exponential smoothing (with $\alpha = .30$ and with $\alpha = .50$), adjusted exponential smoothing ($\alpha = .50$, $\beta = .30$), and a linear trend line for the demand data. The company wants to compare the accuracy of these different forecasts by using *MAD*.

We will compute *MAD* for all four forecasts; however, we will only present the computational detail for the exponential smoothing forecast with $\alpha = .30$. Table 8 shows the values necessary to compute *MAD* for the exponential smoothing forecast.

Using the data in Table 8, we compute *MAD* as

$$MAD = \frac{\Sigma|D_t - F_t|}{n} = \frac{53.41}{11} = 4.85$$

The lower the value of MAD relative to the magnitude of the data, the more accurate the forecast.

In general, the smaller the value of *MAD*, the more accurate the forecast, although, viewed alone, *MAD* is difficult to assess. In this example, the data values were relatively small, and the *MAD* value of 4.85 should be judged accordingly. Overall, it would seem to be a "low" value (i.e., the forecast appears to be relatively accurate). However, if the magnitude of the data values were in the thousands or millions, then a *MAD* value of a similar

Table 8
Computational values for *MAD* and error

Period	Demand, D_t	Forecast, F_t ($\alpha = .30$)	Error ($D_t - F_t$)	$\lvert D_t - F_t \rvert$	Error^2 ($D_t - F_t)^2$
1	37	37.00	—	—	—
2	40	37.00	3.00	3.00	9.00
3	41	37.90	3.10	3.10	9.61
4	37	38.83	−1.83	1.83	3.35
5	45	38.28	6.72	6.72	45.15
6	50	40.29	9.71	9.71	94.28
7	43	43.20	−0.20	0.20	0.04
8	47	43.14	3.86	3.86	14.90
9	56	44.30	11.70	11.70	136.89
10	52	47.81	4.19	4.19	17.56
11	55	49.06	5.94	5.94	35.28
12	54	50.84	3.16	3.16	9.98
	520*		49.31	53.41	376.04

*Because the computation of *MAD* will be based on the 11 periods 2 through 12, $\Sigma D_t = 520$, excluding the demand value of 37.

magnitude might not be bad either. The point is that you cannot compare a *MAD* value of 4.85 with a *MAD* value of 485 and say the former is good and the latter is bad; they depend to a certain extent on the relative magnitude of the data.

One benefit of *MAD* is being able to compare the accuracy of several different forecasting techniques, as we are doing in this example. The *MAD* values for the remaining forecasts are

- Exponential smoothing ($\alpha = .50$): $MAD = 4.04$
- Adjusted exponential smoothing ($\alpha = .50, \beta = .30$): $MAD = 3.81$
- Linear trend line: $MAD = 2.29$

When we compare all four forecasts, the linear trend line has the lowest *MAD* value, of 2.29. It would seem to be the most accurate, although it does not appear to be significantly better than the adjusted exponential smoothing forecast. Furthermore, we can deduce from these *MAD* values that increasing α from .30 to .50 enhanced the accuracy of the exponentially smoothed forecast. The adjusted forecast is even more accurate.

MAPD is absolute error as a percentage of demand.

A variation of *MAD* is the **mean absolute percent deviation (MAPD)**. It measures the absolute error as a percentage of demand rather than per period. As a result, it eliminates the problem of interpreting the measure of accuracy relative to the magnitude of the demand and forecast values, as *MAD* does. *MAPD* is computed according to the following formula:

$$MAPD = \frac{\Sigma \lvert D_t - F_t \rvert}{\Sigma D_t}$$

Using the data from Table 8 for the exponential smoothing forecast ($\alpha = .30$) for PM Computer Services, *MAPD* is computed as

$$MAPD = \frac{53.41}{520} = .103, \text{ or } 10.3\%$$

A lower *MAPD* implies a more accurate forecast. The *MAPD* values for our other three forecasts are

- Exponential smoothing ($\alpha = .50$): $MAPD = 8.5\%$
- Adjusted exponential smoothing ($\alpha = .50, \beta = .30$): $MAPD = 8.1\%$
- Linear trend line: $MAPD = 4.9\%$

Cumulative Error

Cumulative error is the sum of the forecast errors.

Cumulative error is computed simply by summing the forecast errors, as shown in the following formula:

$$E = \Sigma e_t$$

A relatively large positive value indicates that the forecast is probably consistently lower than the actual demand or is biased low. A large negative value implies that the forecast is consistently higher than actual demand or is biased high. Also, when the errors for each period are scrutinized and there appears to be a preponderance of positive values, this shows that the forecast is consistently less than actual, and vice versa.

The cumulative error for the exponential smoothing forecast ($\alpha = .30$) for PM Computer Services can be read directly from Table 8; it is simply the sum of the values in the "Error" column:

$$E = \Sigma e_t = 49.31$$

This relatively large-value positive error for cumulative error and the fact that the individual errors for each period in Table 8 are positive indicate that this forecast is frequently below the actual demand. A quick glance back at the plot of the exponential smoothing ($\alpha = .30$) forecast in Figure 3 visually verifies this result.

The cumulative errors for the other forecasts are

- Exponential smoothing ($\alpha = .50$): $E = 33.21$
- Adjusted exponential smoothing ($\alpha = .50, \beta = .30$): $E = 21.14$

We did not show the cumulative error for the linear trend line. E will always be near zero for the linear trend line; thus, it is not a good measure on which to base comparisons with other forecast methods.

Average error is the per-period average of cumulative error.

A measure closely related to cumulative error is the **average error**. It is computed by averaging the cumulative error over the number of time periods:

$$\bar{E} = \frac{\Sigma e_t}{n}$$

For example, the average error for the exponential smoothing forecast ($\alpha = .30$) is computed as follows (notice that the value of 11 was used for n because we used actual demand for the first-period forecast, resulting in no error, i.e., $D_1 = F_1 = 37$):

$$\bar{E} = \frac{49.31}{11} = 4.48$$

Large $+\bar{E}$ indicates that a forecast is biased low; large $-\bar{E}$ indicates that a forecast is biased high.

The average error is interpreted similarly to the cumulative error. A positive value indicates low bias, and a negative value indicates high bias. A value close to zero implies a lack of bias.

Mean squared error individual error values are squared and then summed and averaged.

Another measure of forecast accuracy related to error is **mean squared error** (MSE). With *MSE*, each individual error value is squared, and then these values are summed and averaged. The last column in Table 8 shows the sum of the squared forecast errors (i.e., 376.04) for the PM Computer example forecast ($\alpha = 0.30$). The *MSE* is computed as

$$MSE = \frac{376.04}{11} = 34.18$$

As with other measures of forecast accuracy, the smaller the *MSE*, the better.

Table 9 summarizes the measures of forecast accuracy we have discussed in this section for the four example forecasts we developed in the previous section for PM Computer Services. The results are consistent for all four forecasts, indicating that for the PM Computer

Management Science Application

Forecasting at Bayer Consumer Care

Since its development of aspirin in 1899, The Bayer Group has grown into a company with a global workforce of 110,000, more than 5,000 products, and annual sales exceeding 27,380 million Euros. Bayer HealthCare, one of the three operational subgroups of Bayer AG, researches, develops, manufactures, and markets products for the prevention, diagnosis, and treatment of diseases. The Consumer Care Division of Bayer HealthCare markets over-the-counter medications such as aspirin, Aleve, Midol, Alka-Seltzer, milk of magnesia, and One-A-Day and Flintstones vitamins. Forecasting is an important function at Bayer Consumer Care because of the competitiveness in the over-the-counter pharmaceutical market and the seasonality of its products. The supply chain planning process at Bayer's Consumer Care division in the EU is based on each country customer's forecasts of its future sales for 18 months into the future, which they share (along with inventory information) with Bayer. Bayer uses this information to develop its production plans, generate customer orders, and establish shipment schedules. This forecasting approach is necessary because the pharmaceutical industry has long lead times for raw materials and ingredients, plus uncertainty created by irregular product trends, seasonality, and promotions. To remain competitive Bayer guarantees its customers close to a 100% service level, and thus it seeks an inventory level that will meet this goal, which decreases as its forecast accuracy increases. Initially the company discovered that forecast errors resulted from the number of different forecasts that were being used by different supply chain members in each country. To resolve this problem, monthly round-table meetings were established to develop a consensus forecast in each EU country. To determine forecast accuracy three performance measures were used: absolute percent forecast error (for a 3-month horizon), percent forecast error, and standard deviation of percent forecast error. Forecast accuracy in most countries is around 80% and forecasting bias approaches zero.

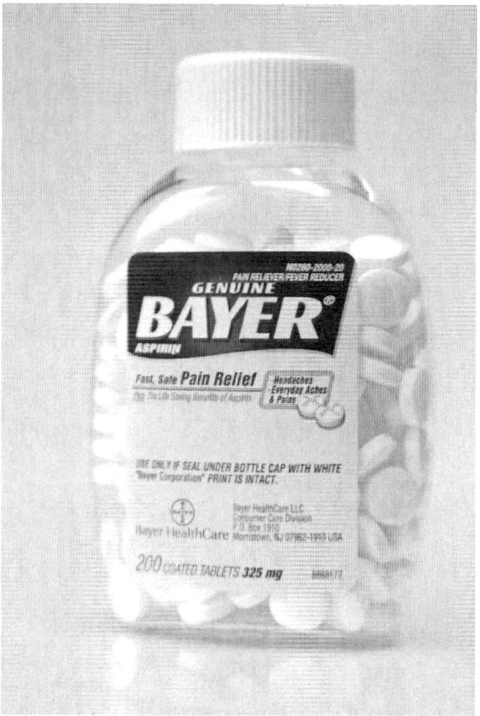

Joe Kohen/Landov Media

Source: H. Petersen, "Integrating the Forecasting Process with the Supply Chain: Bayer HealthCare's Journey," *Journal of Business Forecasting* 22, no. 4 (Winter 2003–4): 11–15.

Table 9
Comparison of forecasts for PM Computer Services

Forecast	*MAD*	*MAPD* (%)	*E*	$\bar{E}$	*MSE*
Exponential smoothing ($\alpha = .30$)	4.85	10.3	49.31	4.48	34.18
Exponential smoothing ($\alpha = .50$)	4.04	8.5	33.21	3.02	24.64
Adjusted exponential smoothing ($\alpha = .50, \beta = .30$)	3.81	8.1	21.14	1.92	21.58
Linear trend line	2.29	4.9	—	—	8.67

Services example data, a larger value of α is preferable for the exponential smoothing forecast. The adjusted forecast is more accurate than the exponential smoothing forecasts, and the linear trend is more accurate than all the others. Although these results are example specific, they do indicate how the different forecast measures for accuracy can be used to adjust a forecasting method or select the best method.

Time Series Forecasting Using Excel

All the time series forecasts we have presented can also be developed with Excel spreadsheets. Exhibit 1 shows an Excel spreadsheet set up to compute the exponentially smoothed forecast and adjusted exponentially smoothed forecast for the PM Computer Services example summarized in Table 5. Notice that the formula for computing the trend factor in cell D10 is shown on the formula bar on the top of the spreadsheet. The adjusted forecast in column E is computed by typing the formula =**C9**+**D9** in cell E9 and copying it to cells **E10:E20** (using the "Copy" and "Paste" options that appear after clicking the right mouse button).

Exhibit 1

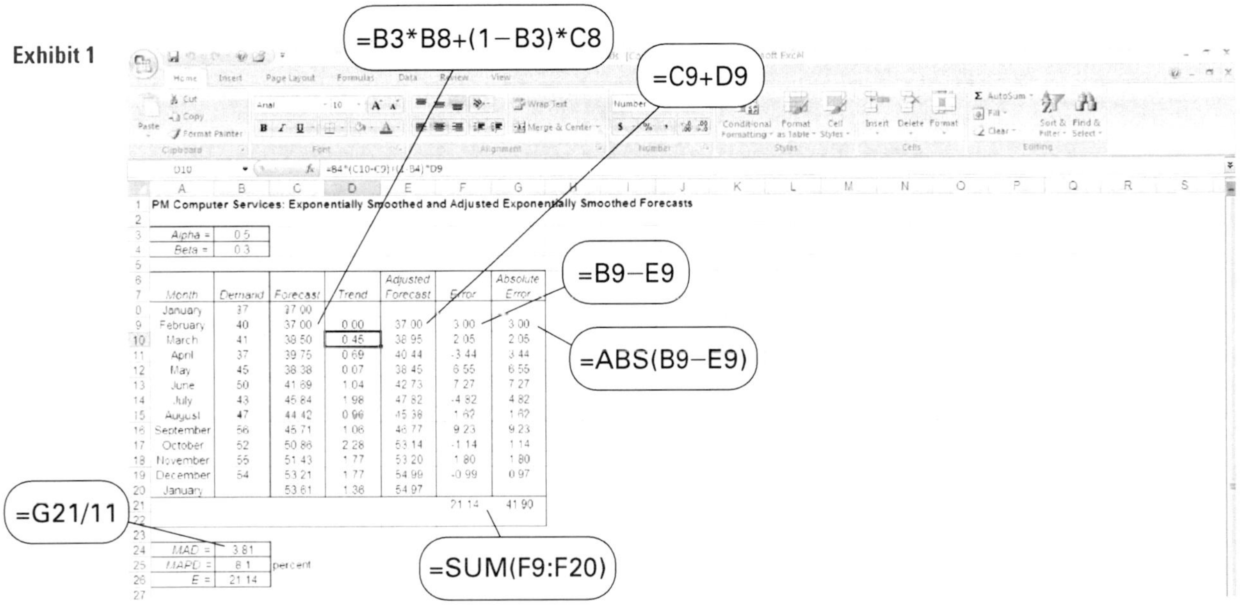

The exponential smoothing forecast can also be developed directly from Excel without "customizing" a spreadsheet and entering our own formulas, as we did in Exhibit 1. From the "Data" menu at the top of the spreadsheet, select the "Data Analysis" option. (If your "Data" menu does not include this menu item, you should add it by accessing the "Add-Ins" option from the "Data" menu or by loading from the original Excel or Office software.) Exhibit 2 shows the Data Analysis window and the "Exponential Smoothing" menu item you should select and then click on "OK." The resulting Exponential Smoothing window is

Exhibit 2

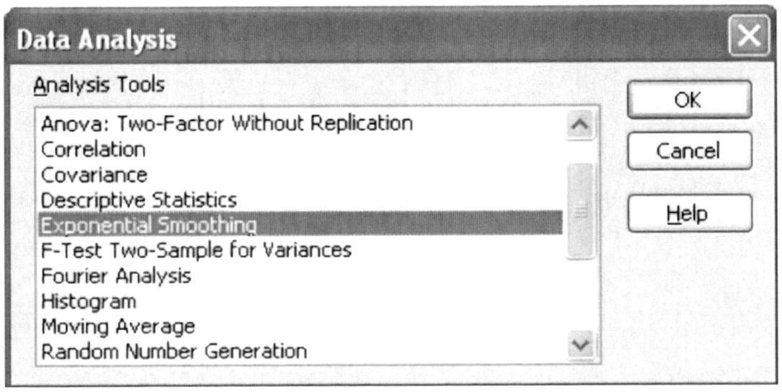

shown in Exhibit 3. The input range includes the demand values in column B in Exhibit 1, the damping factor is alpha (α), which in this case is 0.5, and the output should be placed in column C in Exhibit 1. Clicking on "OK" will result in the same forecast values in column C of Exhibit 1 that we computed using our own exponential smoothing formula. Note that the "Data Analysis" group of analysis tools does not have an adjusted exponential smoothing selection; that is the reason we developed our own customized spreadsheet in Exhibit 1. The "Data Analysis" tools also have a "Moving Average" menu item from which a moving average forecast can be computed.

Exhibit 3

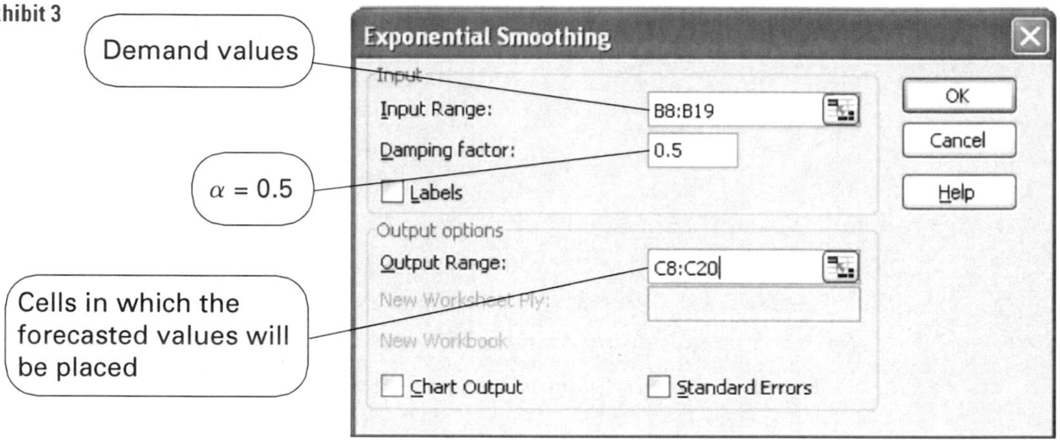

Excel can also be used to develop seasonally adjusted forecasts. Exhibit 4 shows an Excel spreadsheet set up to develop the seasonally adjusted forecast for the demand for turkeys at Wishbone Farms. You will notice that the seasonally adjusted forecasts for each quarter are slightly different from the forecasts computed manually (e.g., SF_1 with Excel equals 16.43, whereas SF_1 computed manually equals 16.28). This is due to the rounding done in the manual computations.

Exhibit 4

B12 =(B8/F8)*E10

Wishbone Farms : Seasonally Adjusted Forecast

	Demand (1,000s) per Quarter				
Year	1	2	3	4	Total
2003	12.6	8.6	6.3	17.5	45
2004	14.1	10.3	7.5	18.2	50.1
2005	15.3	10.6	8.1	19.6	53.6
Total	42.0	29.5	21.9	55.3	148.7

Linear trend line forecast for 2006 =	58.17

SF1 =	16.43
SF2 =	11.54
SF3 =	8.57
SF4 =	21.63

Computing the Exponential Smoothing Forecast with Excel QM

Excel QM includes a spreadsheet macro for exponential smoothing. After it is activated, the Excel QM menu is accessed by clicking on "Add-Ins" on the menu bar at the top of the spreadsheet. Clicking on "Forecasting" from this menu results in a Spreadsheet Initialization window, in which you enter the problem title and the number of periods of past demand. Clicking on "OK" will result in the spreadsheet shown in Exhibit 5. Initially, this spreadsheet will have

Exhibit 5

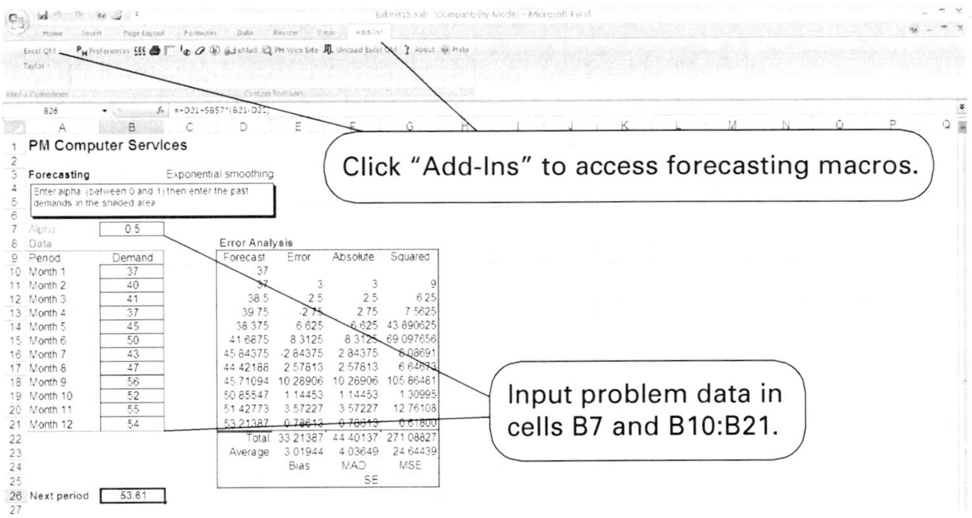

example values in the (shaded) data cells, **B7** and **B10:B21**. Thus, the first step in using this macro is to type in the data for our PM Computer Services problem: alpha (α) = 0.50 in cell B7 and our demand values in cells **B10:B21**. The forecast results are computed automatically from formulas already embedded in the spreadsheet. The resulting next-period forecast for January is shown in cell B26, and the monthly forecasts are shown in cells **D10:D21**. (Do not confuse this exponentially smoothed forecast and the values for *MAD* and the like with the *adjusted* exponentially smoothed forecast and *MAD* value in Exhibit 1.)

Time Series Forecasting Using QM for Windows

QM for Windows has the capability to perform forecasting for all the time series methods we have described so far. QM for Windows has modules for moving averages, exponential smoothing and adjusted exponential smoothing, and linear regression.

To demonstrate the forecasting capability of QM for Windows, we will generate the exponential smoothing (α = .30) forecast computed manually for PM Computer Services (Table 4). The solution output is shown in Exhibit 6.

Exhibit 6

Details and Error Analysis

PM Computer Services Example Solution

	Demand(y)	Forecast	Error	|Error|	Error^2	|Pct Error|
1	37					
2	40	37	3	3	9	.075
3	41	37.9	3.1	3.1	9.61	.0756
4	37	38.83	-1.83	1.83	3.3489	.0495
5	45	38.281	6.719	6.719	45.1449	.1493
6	50	40.2967	9.7033	9.7033	94.154	.1941
7	43	43.2077	-.2077	.2077	.0431	.0048
8	47	43.1454	3.8546	3.8546	14.8581	.082
9	56	44.3018	11.6982	11.6982	136.8486	.2089
10	52	47.8112	4.1888	4.1888	17.5457	.0806
11	55	49.0679	5.9321	5.9321	35.1902	.1079
12	54	50.8475	3.1525	3.1525	9.9382	.0584
TOTALS	557		49.3108	53.3862	375.6818	1.086
AVERAGE	46.4167		4.4828	4.8533	34.1529	.0987
Next period forecast		51.7933	(Bias)	(MAD)	(MSE)	(MAPE)
				Std err	6.4608	

Notice that the solution summary includes the forecast per period and the forecast for the next period (13), as well as three measures of forecast accuracy: average error (bias), mean absolute deviation (*MAD*), and mean squared error (*MSE*).

The least squares module or the simple linear regression module in QM for Windows can be used to develop a linear trend line forecast. Using the least squares module, the solution summary for the linear trend line forecast we developed for PM Computer Services is shown in Exhibit 7.

Exhibit 7

Forecasting Results

PM Computer Services Example Summary

Measure	Value	Future Period	Forecast
Error Measures		13	57.6212
Bias (Mean Error)	0	14	59.345
MAD (Mean Absolute Deviation)	2.2892	15	61.0688
MSE (Mean Squared Error)	8.6672	16	62.7925
Standard Error (denom=n-2=10)	3.225	17	64.5163
MAPE (Mean Absolute Percent Error)	.0499	18	66.2401
Regression line		19	67.9639
Demand(y) = 35.21213		20	69.6876
+ 1.7238 * Time(x)		21	71.4114
Statistics		22	73.1352
Correlation coefficient	.8963	23	74.859
Coefficient of determination (r^2)	.8034	24	76.5827
		25	78.3065
		26	80.0303

Regression Methods

The time series techniques of exponential smoothing and moving average relate a single variable being forecast (such as demand) to *time*. In contrast, *regression* is a forecasting technique that measures the relationship of one variable to one or more other variables. For example, if we know that something has caused product demand to behave in a certain way in the past, we might like to identify that relationship. If the same thing happens again in the future, we can then predict what demand will be. For example, there is a well-known relationship between increased demand in new housing and lower interest rates. Correspondingly, a myriad of building products and services display increased demand if new housing starts increase. Similarly, an increase in sales of DVD players results in an increase in demand for DVDs.

The simplest form of regression is linear regression, which you will recall we used previously to develop a linear trend line for forecasting. In the following section we will show how to develop a regression model for variables related to items other than time.

Linear Regression

Linear regression relates demand (dependent variable) to an independent variable.

Simple **linear regression** relates one dependent variable to one independent variable in the form of a linear equation:

$$y = a + bx$$

dependent variable (y), intercept (a), slope (b), independent variable (x)

To develop the linear equation, the slope, b, and the intercept, a, must first be computed by using the following least squares formulas:

$$a = \bar{y} - b\bar{x}$$

$$b = \frac{\Sigma xy - n\bar{x}\bar{y}}{\Sigma x^2 - n\bar{x}^2}$$

where

$$\bar{x} = \frac{\Sigma x}{n} = \text{mean of the } x \text{ data}$$

$$\bar{y} = \frac{\Sigma y}{n} = \text{mean of the } y \text{ data}$$

We will consider regression within the context of an example. The State University athletic department wants to develop its budget for the coming year, using a forecast for football attendance. Football attendance accounts for the largest portion of its revenues, and the athletic director believes attendance is directly related to the number of wins by the team. The business manager has accumulated total annual attendance figures for the past 8 years:

Wins	Attendance
4	36,300
6	40,100
6	41,200
8	53,000
6	44,000
7	45,600
5	39,000
7	47,500

Given the number of returning starters and the strength of the schedule, the athletic director believes the team will win at least seven games next year. He wants to develop a simple regression equation for these data to forecast attendance for this level of success.

The computations necessary to compute a and b, using the least squares formulas, are summarized in Table 10. (Note that the magnitude of y has been reduced to make manual computation easier.)

Table 10
Least squares computations

x (wins)	y (attendance, 1,000s)	xy	x^2
4	36.3	145.2	16
6	40.1	240.6	36
6	41.2	247.2	36
8	53.0	424.0	64
6	44.0	264.0	36
7	45.6	319.2	49
5	39.0	195.0	25
7	47.5	332.5	49
49	346.7	2,167.7	311

$$\bar{x} = \frac{49}{8} = 6.125$$

$$\bar{y} = \frac{346.9}{8} = 43.34$$

$$b = \frac{\Sigma xy - n\bar{x}\bar{y}}{\Sigma x^2 - n\bar{x}^2}$$

$$= \frac{(2{,}167.7) - (8)(6.125)(43.34)}{(311) - (8)(6.125)^2} = 4.06$$

$$a = \bar{y} - b\bar{x} = 43.34 - (4.06)(6.125) = 18.46$$

Substituting these values for a and b into the linear equation line, we have

$$y = 18.46 + 4.06x$$

Thus, for $x = 7$ (wins), the forecast for attendance is

$$y = 18.46 + 4.06(7) = 46.88 \text{ or } 46{,}880$$

The data points with the regression line are shown in Figure 6. Observing the regression line relative to the data points, it would appear that the data follow a distinct upward linear trend, which would indicate that the forecast should be relatively accurate. In fact, the *MAD* value for this forecasting model is 1.41, which suggests an accurate forecast.

Correlation

Correlation is a measure of the strength of the relationship between independent and dependent variables.

Correlation in a linear regression equation is a measure of the strength of the relationship between the independent and dependent variables. The formula for the correlation coefficient is

$$r = \frac{n\Sigma xy - \Sigma x \Sigma y}{\sqrt{[n\Sigma x^2 - (\Sigma x)^2][n\Sigma y^2 - (\Sigma y)^2]}}$$

Figure 6
Linear regression line

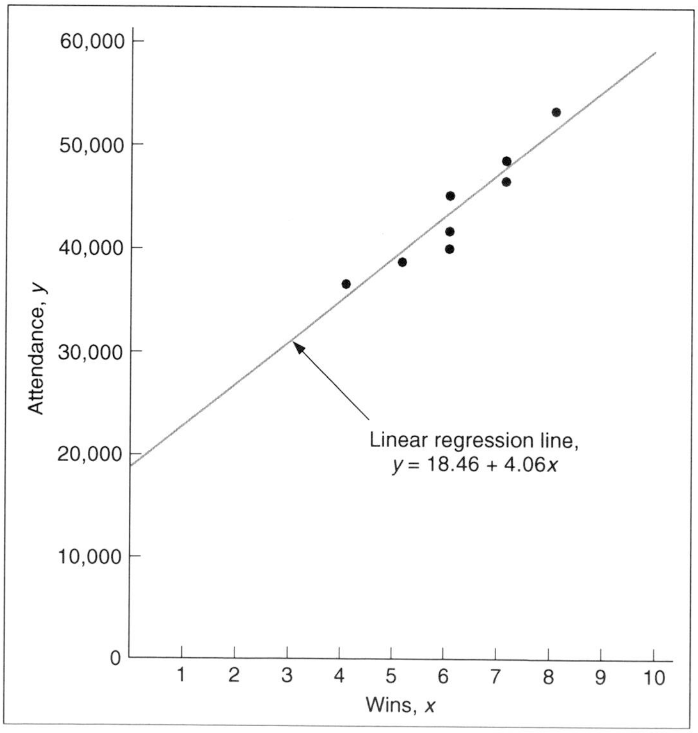

The value of r varies between -1.00 and $+1.00$, with a value of ± 1.00 indicating a strong linear relationship between the variables. If $r = 1.00$, then an increase in the independent variable will result in a corresponding linear increase in the dependent variable. If $r = -1.00$, an increase in the dependent variable will result in a linear decrease in the dependent variable. A value of r near zero implies that there is little or no linear relationship between variables.

We can determine the correlation coefficient for the linear regression equation determined in our State University example by substituting most of the terms calculated for the least squares formula (except for Σy^2) into the formula for r:

$$r = \frac{(8)(2{,}167.7) - (49)(346.7)}{\sqrt{[(8)(311) - (49)^2][(8)(15{,}224.7) - (346.7)^2]}}$$
$$= .948$$

This value for the correlation coefficient is very close to one, indicating a strong linear relationship between the number of wins and home attendance.

Management Science Application

An Airline Passenger Forecasting Model

Following the terrorist attacks of September 11, 2001, Congress created the Transportation Security Administration (TSA), which became part of the Department of Homeland Security in March 2003. The TSA has responsibility for national transportation security and, specifically, U.S. commercial aviation system security. The TSA put into effect a number of procedures, processes, and regulations to safeguard against terrorism, the unintended consequences of which were long lines and waiting times at security checkpoints in airports. To address the problems created by the new security measures, the TSA joined with the commercial airlines to form the U.S. Commercial Aviation Partnership (USCAP). The goal of this partnership was to maintain the health of U.S. commercial aviation while ensuring that security requirements were implemented efficiently and effectively. To achieve this goal, USCAP used its technical professionals to develop mathematical models to analyze, define, and predict the operational and economic effects of air travel security measures. The key component of this modeling effort was a model to forecast air travel passenger demand. Previously most air travel forecasting models focused on long-term trends with time horizons of 5 to 20 years, which weren't effective for making near-term tactical decisions and reflecting the immediate impact of security policies. The model developed by USCAP used multiple regression to forecast passenger demand based on six causal factors including the economy (reflected by U.S. gross domestic product); ticket prices (represented by the average fare for a 1,000-mile trip); travel time (from door to door); fear (represented by the reduction in plane boardings owing to an event causing fear); a hassle factor (created by the reduction in plane boardings owing to an event causing hassle); and an operations factor (resulting from a reduction in plane boardings owing to a reduction in operations caused by an event). A detailed regression analysis Solver tool with special capabilities was developed for this model. The forecasting model was subsequently used as the basis for other analytical models to explore numerous questions concerning airport security procedures, such as staffing for security screening, the number of screening lanes at airports, security processing times, security credentials for employees, and what-if? analyses of proposed security measures such as passenger security fees. The immediate financial savings of the models developed by USCAP, in addition to improved security procedures, were in the tens of billions of dollars with an estimated 20-year impact of more than $100 billion.

Bill Aron/PhotoEdit Inc.

Source: R. Peterson, R. Bittel, C. Forgie, W. Lee, and J. Nestor, "Using USCAP's Analytical Models, the Transportation Security Administration Balances the Impacts of Aviation Security Policies on Passengers and Airlines," *Interfaces* 37, no. 1 (January–February 2007): 52–67.

*The **coefficient of determination** is the percentage of the variation in the dependent variable that results from the independent variable.*

Another measure of the strength of the relationship between the variables in a linear regression equation is the **coefficient of determination.** It is computed by simply squaring the value of r. It indicates the percentage of the variation in the dependent variable that is a result of the behavior of the independent variable. For our example, $r = .948$; thus, the coefficient of determination is

$$\begin{aligned} r^2 &= (.948)^2 \\ &= .899 \end{aligned}$$

This value for the coefficient of determination means that 89.9% of the amount of variation in attendance can be attributed to the number of wins by the team (with the remaining 10.1% due to other unexplained factors, such as weather, a good or poor start, publicity, etc.). A value of one (or 100%) would indicate that attendance totally depends on wins. However, because 10.1% of the variation is a result of other factors, some amount of forecast error can be expected.

Regression Analysis with Excel

Exhibit 8 shows a spreadsheet set up to develop the linear regression forecast for our State University athletic department example. Notice that Excel computes the slope directly with the formula =**SLOPE(B5:B12,A5:A12)** entered in cell E7 and shown on the formula bar at the top of the spreadsheet. The formula for the intercept in cell E6 is =**INTERCEPT(B5:B12,A5:A12)**. The values for the slope and intercept are subsequently entered in cells E9 and G9 to form the linear regression equation. The correlation coefficient in cell E13 is computed by using the formula =**CORREL(B5:B12,A5:A12)**. Although it is not shown on the spreadsheet, the coefficient of determination (r^2) could be computed by using the formula =**RSQ(B5:B12,A5:A12)**.

Exhibit 8

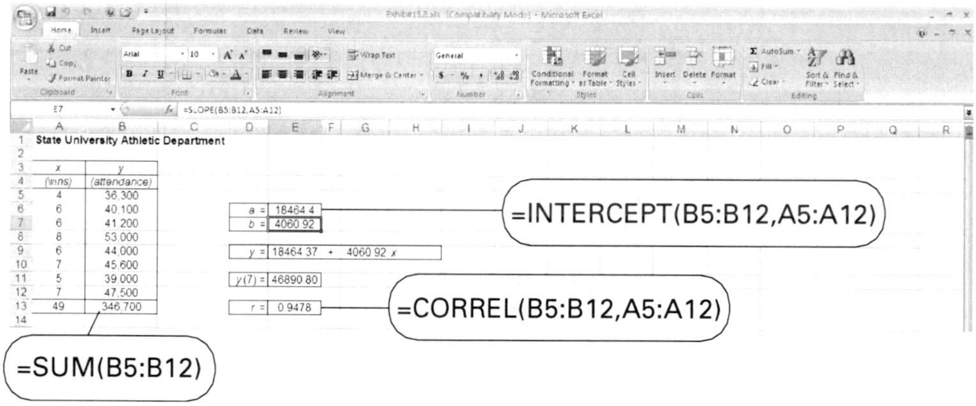

The same linear regression equation could be computed in Excel if we had developed and entered the mathematical formulas for computing the slope and intercept we developed in the previous section, although that would have been more time-consuming and tedious.

It is also possible to develop a scatter diagram of our example data similar to the chart shown in Figure 6 by using Excel. First, cover the example data in cells **A5:B12** on the spreadsheet in Exhibit 8. Next click on the "Insert" tab on the toolbar at the top of the spreadsheet. This will result in the toolbar menu shown in Exhibit 9.

On the "Charts" segment from this menu select the "Scatter" chart as shown in Exhibit 9. Exhibit 9 shows the spreadsheet with the scatter diagram chart for our example data.

A linear regression forecast can also be developed directly with Excel by using the "Data Analysis" Add-In option from the "Data" toolbar we accessed previously to develop an exponentially smoothed forecast. Exhibit 10 shows the "Regression" selection from the

Exhibit 9

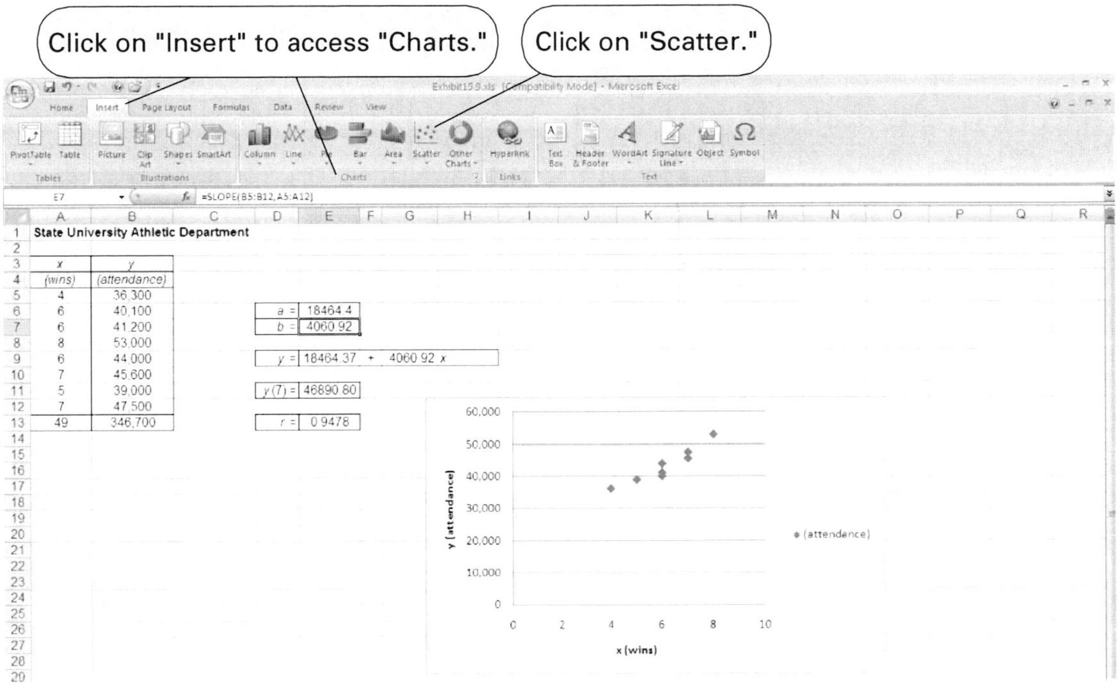

Exhibit 10

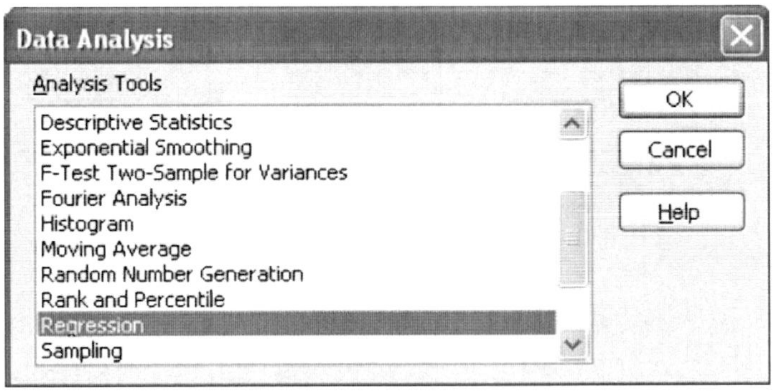

Data Analysis window and Exhibit 11 shows the Regression window. We first enter the cells from Exhibit 8 that include the *y* values (for attendance), **B5:B12**. Next, we enter the *x* value cells, **A5:A12**. The output range is the location on the spreadsheet where we want to put the output results. This range needs to be large (18 cells by 9 cells) and must not overlap with anything else on the spreadsheet. Clicking on "OK" will result in the spreadsheet shown in Exhibit 12. (Note that the "Summary Output" section has been slightly edited—i.e., moved around—so that all the results could be included on the screen in Exhibit 12.)

The "Summary Output" section in Exhibit 12 provides a large amount of statistical information, the explanation and use of which are beyond the scope of this text. The essential items that interest us are the intercept and slope (labeled "X Variable 1") in the "Coefficients" column at the bottom of the spreadsheet and the "Multiple R" (or correlation coefficient) value shown under "Regression Statistics."

Note that Excel QM also has a spreadsheet macro for regression analysis that can be accessed in much the same way as was the exponentially smoothed forecast in Exhibit 5.

Exhibit 11

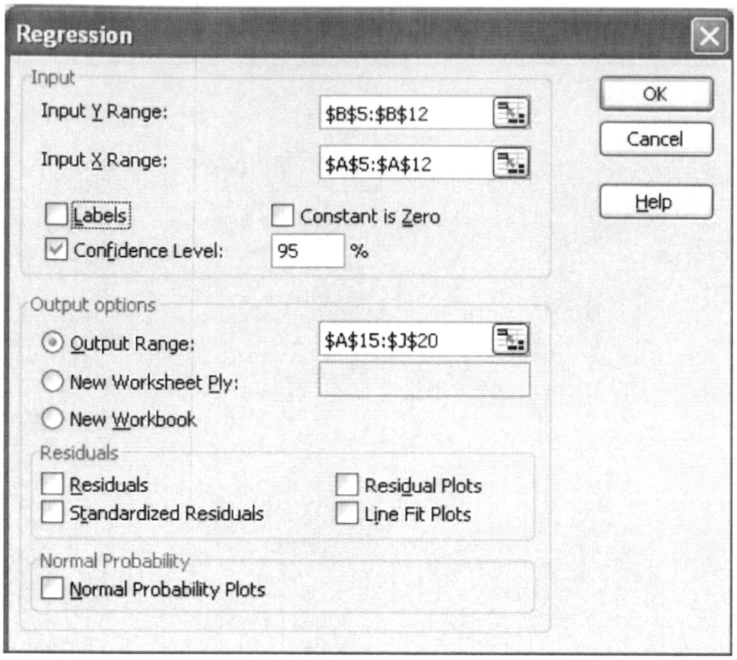

Exhibit 12

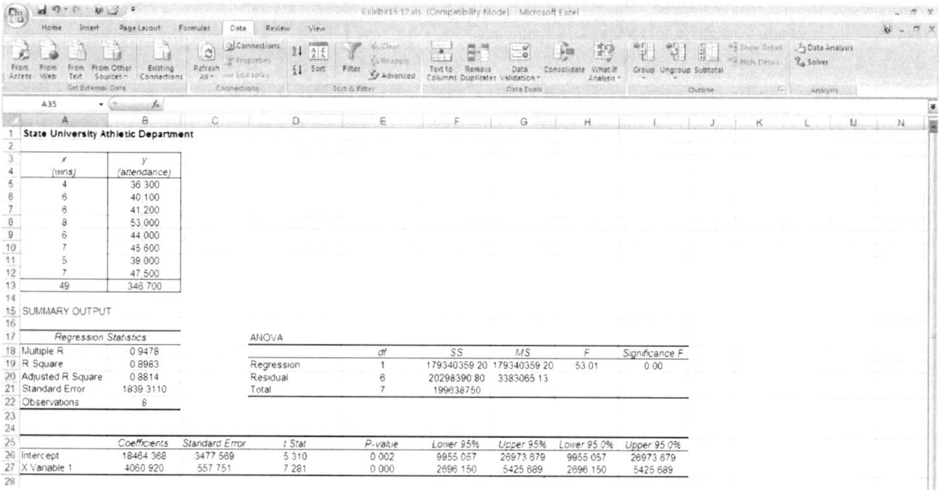

Regression Analysis with QM for Windows

QM for Windows has the capability to perform linear regression, as demonstrated earlier. To demonstrate this program module, we will use our State University athletic department example. The program output, including the linear equation and correlation coefficient, is shown in Exhibit 13.

Multiple Regression with Excel

Multiple regression relates demand to two or more independent variables.

Another causal method of forecasting is **multiple regression**, a more powerful extension of linear regression. Linear regression relates a dependent variable such as demand to one other independent variable, whereas multiple regression reflects the relationship between a dependent variable and *two or more* independent variables. A multiple regression model has the following general form:

$$y = \beta_0 + \beta_1 x_1 + \beta_2 x_2 + \cdots + \beta_k x_k$$

Exhibit 13

Forecasting Results

State University Athletic Department Summary

Measure	Value
Error Measures	
Bias (Mean Error)	.001
MAD (Mean Absolute Deviation)	1,412.644
MSE (Mean Squared Error)	2,537,298.0
Standard Error (denom=n-2-0=6)	1,839.311
MAPE (Mean Absolute Percent Error)	.033
Regression line	
Dpndnt var, Y = 18,464.37	
+ 4,060.919 * X1	
Statistics	
Correlation coefficient	.9478
Coefficient of determination (r^2)	.8983

where

β_0 = the intercept
$\beta_1 \ldots \beta_k$ = parameters representing the contribution of the independent variables
$x_1 \ldots x_k$ = independent variables

For example, the demand for new housing (y) in a region or an urban area might be a function of several independent variables, including interest rates, population, housing prices, and personal income. Development and computation of the multiple regression equation, including the compilation of data, are quite a bit more complex than linear regression. Therefore, the only viable means for forecasting using multiple regression problems is by using a computer.

To demonstrate the capability to solve multiple regression problems with Excel spreadsheets, we will expand our State University athletic department example for forecasting attendance at football games that we used to demonstrate linear regression. Instead of attempting to predict attendance based on only one variable (wins), we will include a second variable for advertising and promotional expenditures, as follows:

Wins	Promotion	Attendance
4	$29,500	36,300
6	55,700	40,100
6	71,300	41,200
8	87,000	53,000
6	75,000	44,000
7	72,000	45,600
5	55,300	39,000
7	81,600	47,500

We will use the "Data Analysis" option (Add-In) from the "Data" menu at the top of the spreadsheet that we used in the previous section to develop our linear regression equation, and then we will use the "Regression" option from the "Data Analysis" menu. The resulting spreadsheet, with the multiple regression statistics, is shown in Exhibit 14.

Note that the data need to be set up on the spreadsheet so that the x variables are in adjacent columns (in this case, columns A and B). Then we enter the "Input X Range" as **A4:B12**, as

Exhibit 14

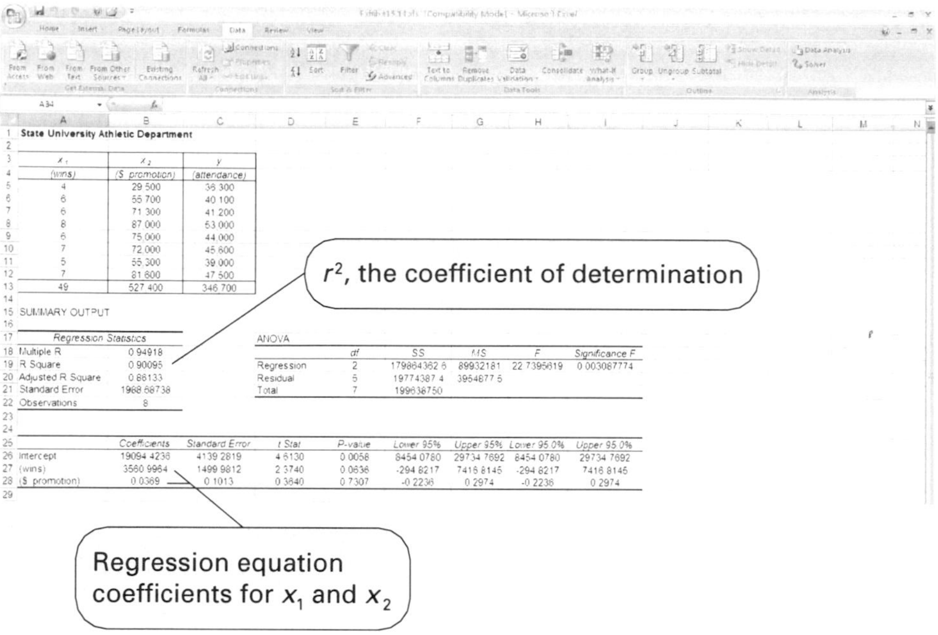

shown in Exhibit 15. Notice that we have also included cells A4, B4, and C4, which include our variable headings (i.e., "wins," "$ promotion," and "attendance"), in the input ranges. By clicking on "Labels," headings can be placed on our spreadsheet in cells A27 and A28.

The regression coefficients for our x variables, wins and promotion, are shown in cells B27 and B28 in Exhibit 14. Thus, the multiple regression equation is formulated as

$$y = 19{,}094.42 + 3{,}560.99x_1 + .0368x_2$$

This equation can now be used to forecast attendance based on both projected football wins and promotional expenditure. For example, if the athletic department expects the

Exhibit 15

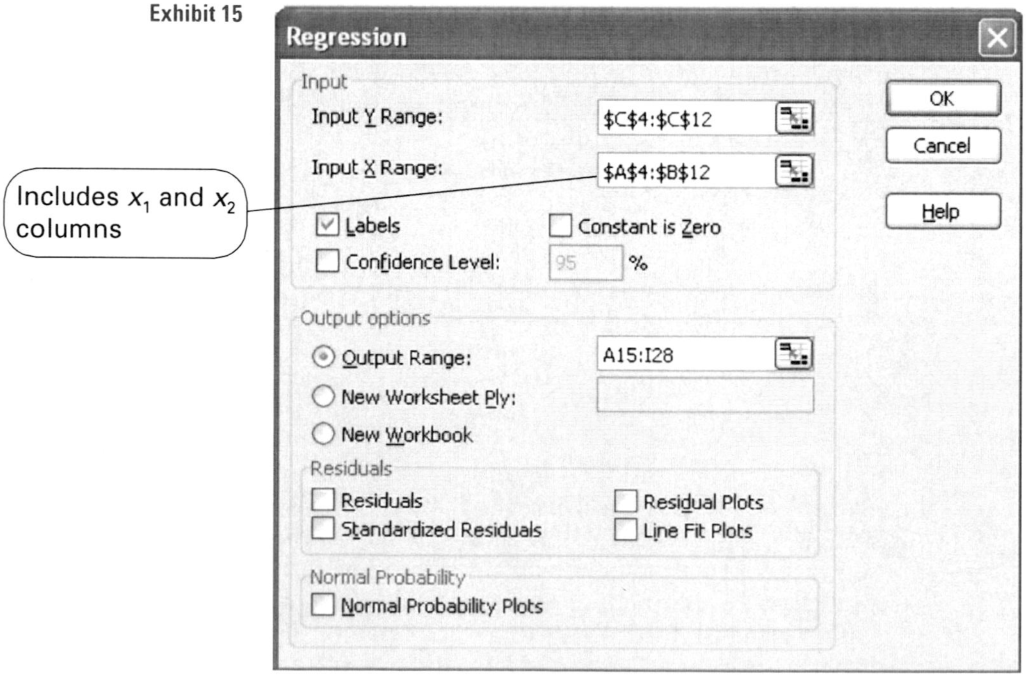

team to win seven games and plans to spend \$60,000 on promotion and advertising, the forecasted attendance is

$$\begin{aligned} y &= 19{,}094.42 + 3{,}560.99(7) + .0368(60{,}000) \\ &= 46{,}229.35 \end{aligned}$$

If the promotional expenditure is held constant, every win will increase attendance by 3,560.99, whereas if the wins are held constant, every \$1,000 of advertising money spent will increase attendance by 36.8 fans. This would seem to suggest that number of wins has a more significant impact on attendance than promotional expenditures.

The coefficient of determination, r^2, shown in cell B19 in Exhibit 14, is .90, which suggests that 90% of the amount of variation in attendance can be attributed to the number of wins and the promotional expenditures. However, as we have already noted, the number of wins probably accounts for a larger part of the variation in attendance.

A problem often encountered in multiple regression is *multicollinearity*, or the amount of "overlapping" information about the dependent variable that is provided by several independent variables. This problem usually occurs when the independent variables are highly correlated, as in this example, in which wins and promotional expenditures are both positively correlated; that is, more wins coincide with higher promotional expenditures and vice versa. (Possibly the athletic department increased promotional expenditures when it thought it would have a better team that would achieve more wins.) Multicollinearity and how to cope with it are beyond the scope of this text and this brief section on multiple regression; however, most statistics texts discuss this topic in detail.

Summary

We have presented several methods of forecasting that are useful for different time frames. Time series and regression methods can be used to develop forecasts encompassing horizons of any length time, although they tend to be used most frequently for short- and medium-range forecasts. These quantitative forecasting techniques are generally easy to understand, simple to use, and not especially costly, unless the data requirements are substantial. They also have exhibited a good track record of performance for many companies that have used them. For these reasons, regression methods, and especially times series, are widely popular.

When managers and students are first introduced to forecasting methods, they are sometimes surprised and disappointed at the lack of exactness of the forecasts. However, they soon learn that forecasting is not easy and exactness is not possible. Forecasting is a lot like playing horseshoes: It's great to get a "ringer," but you can win by just getting close, although those who have the skill and experience to get ringers will beat those who just get close. Often forecasts are used as inputs to other decision models—for example, in inventory models, the subject of the next chapter. The primary factor in determining the amount of inventory a firm should order (i.e., prepare to have on hand) is the demand that will occur in the future—forecasted demand.

References

Box, G. E. P., and Jenkins, G. M. *Time Series Analysis: Forecasting and Control*, 2nd ed. Oakland, CA: Holden-Day, 1976.

Brown, R. G. *Statistical Forecasting for Inventory Control*. New York: McGraw-Hill, 1959.

Gardner, E. S., and Dannenbring, D. G. "Forecasting with Exponential Smoothing: Some Guidelines for Model Selection." *Decision Sciences* 11, no. 2 (1980): 370–83.

Makridakis, S., Wheelwright, S. C., and McGee, V. E. *Forecasting: Methods and Applications*, 2nd ed. New York: John Wiley & Sons, 1983.

Example Problem Solutions

The following problem provides an example of the computation of exponentially smoothed and adjusted exponentially smoothed forecasts.

Problem Statement

A computer software firm has experienced the following demand for its Personal Finance software package:

Period	Units
1	56
2	61
3	55
4	70
5	66
6	65
7	72
8	75

Develop an exponential smoothing forecast, using $\alpha = .40$, and an adjusted exponential smoothing forecast, using $\alpha = .40$ and $\beta = .20$. Compare the accuracy of the two forecasts, using *MAD* and cumulative error.

Solution

Step 1: Compute the Exponential Smoothing Forecast

$$F_{t+1} = \alpha D_t + (1 - \alpha)F_t$$

For period 2 the forecast (assuming that $F_1 = 56$) is

$$F_2 = \alpha D_1 + (1 - \alpha)F_1 = (.40)(56) + (.60)(56) = 56$$

For period 3 the forecast is

$$F_3 = (.40)(61) + (.60)(56) = 58$$

The remaining forecasts are computed similarly and are shown in the table.

Step 2: Compute the Adjusted Exponential Smoothing Forecast

$$AF_{t+1} = F_{t+1} + T_{t+1}$$
$$T_{t+1} = \beta(F_{t+1} - F_t) + (1 - \beta)T_t$$

Starting with the forecast for period 3 (because $F_1 = F_2$ and we will assume that $T_2 = 0$),

$$T_3 = \beta(F_3 - F_2) + (1 - \beta)T_2 = (.20)(58 - 56) + (.80)(0) = .40$$
$$AF_3 = F_3 + T_3 = 58 + .40 = 58.40$$

The remaining adjusted forecasts are computed similarly and are shown in the following table:

Period	D_t	F_t	AF_t	$D_t - F_t$	$D_t - AF_t$
1	56	—	—	—	—
2	61	56.00	56.00	5.00	5.00
3	55	58.00	58.40	−3.00	−3.40
4	70	56.80	56.88	13.20	13.12
5	66	62.08	63.20	3.92	2.80
6	65	63.65	64.86	1.35	0.14
7	72	64.18	65.26	7.81	6.73
8	75	67.31	68.80	7.68	6.20
9	—	70.39	72.19	—	—
				35.97	30.60

Step 3: Compute the *MAD* Values

$$MAD(F_t) = \frac{\Sigma|D_t - F_t|}{n} = \frac{41.97}{7} = 5.99$$

$$MAD(AF_t) = \frac{\Sigma|D_t - AF_t|}{n} = \frac{37.39}{7} = 5.34$$

Step 4: Compute the Cumulative Error

$$E(F_t) = 35.97$$
$$E(AF_t) = 30.60$$

Because both *MAD* and the cumulative error are less for the adjusted forecast, it would appear to be the most accurate.

The following problem provides an example of the computation of a linear regression forecast.

Problem Statement

A local building products store has accumulated sales data for two-by-four lumber (in board feet) and the number of building permits in its area for the past 10 quarters:

Quarter	Building Permits, x	Lumber Sales (1,000s of bd. ft.), y
1	8	12.6
2	12	16.3
3	7	9.3
4	9	11.5
5	15	18.1
6	6	7.6
7	5	6.2
8	8	14.2
9	10	15.0
10	12	17.8

Develop a linear regression model for these data and determine the strength of the linear relationship by using correlation. If the model appears to be relatively strong, determine the forecast for lumber, given 10 building permits in the next quarter.

Solution

Step 1: Compute the Components of the Linear Regression Equation

$$\bar{x} = \frac{92}{10} = 9.2$$

$$\bar{y} = \frac{128.6}{10} = 12.86$$

$$b = \frac{\Sigma xy - n\bar{x}\bar{y}}{\Sigma x^2 - n\bar{x}^2} = \frac{(1{,}290.3) - (10)(9.2)(12.86)}{(932) - (10)(9.2)^2}$$

$$b = 1.25$$

$$a = \bar{y} - b\bar{x} = 12.86 - (1.25)(9.2)$$

$$a = 1.36$$

Step 2: Develop the Linear Regression Equation

$$y = a + bx$$

$$y = 1.36 + 1.25x$$

Step 3: Compute the Correlation Coefficient

$$r = \frac{n\Sigma xy - \Sigma x \Sigma y}{\sqrt{[n\Sigma x^2 - (\Sigma x)^2][n\Sigma y^2 - (\Sigma y)^2]}}$$

$$= \frac{(10)(1{,}290.3) - (92)(128.6)}{\sqrt{[(10)(932) - (92)^2][(10)(1{,}810.48) - (128.6)^2]}}$$

$$= .925$$

Thus, there appears to be a strong linear relationship.

Step 4: Calculate the Forecast for $x = 10$ Permits

$$y = a + bx$$

$$= 1.36 + 1.25(10)$$

$$= 13.86 \text{ or } 1{,}386 \text{ bd. ft.}$$

Problems

1. The Saki motorcycle dealer in the Minneapolis–St. Paul area wants to make an accurate forecast of demand for the Saki Super TXII motorcycle during the next month. Because the manufacturer is in Japan, it is difficult to send motorcycles back or reorder if the proper number is not ordered a month ahead. From sales records, the dealer has accumulated the following data for the past year:

Month	Motorcycle Sales
January	9
February	7
March	10
April	8
May	7
June	12
July	10
August	11
September	12
October	10
November	14
December	16

a. Compute a 3-month moving average forecast of demand for April through January (of the next year).
b. Compute a 5-month moving average forecast for June through January.
c. Compare the two forecasts computed in (a) and (b), using *MAD*. Which one should the dealer use for January of the next year?

2. The manager of the Carpet City outlet needs to make an accurate forecast of the demand for Soft Shag carpet (its biggest seller). If the manager does not order enough carpet from the carpet mill, customers will buy their carpet from one of Carpet City's many competitors. The manager has collected the following demand data for the past 8 months:

Month	Demand for Soft Shag Carpet (1,000 yd.)
1	8
2	12
3	7
4	9
5	15
6	11
7	10
8	12

a. Compute a 3-month moving average forecast for months 4 through 9.
b. Compute a weighted 3-month moving average forecast for months 4 through 9. Assign weights of .55, .33, and .12 to the months in sequence, starting with the most recent month.
c. Compare the two forecasts by using *MAD*. Which forecast appears to be more accurate?

3. The Fastgro Fertilizer Company distributes fertilizer to various lawn and garden shops. The company must base its quarterly production schedule on a forecast of how many tons of fertilizer will be demanded from it. The company has gathered the following data for the past 3 years from its sales records:

Year	Quarter	Demand for Fertilizer (tons)
1	1	105
	2	150
	3	93
	4	121
2	5	140
	6	170
	7	105
	8	150
3	9	150
	10	170
	11	110
	12	130

a. Compute a three-quarter moving average forecast for quarters 4 through 13 and compute the forecast error for each quarter.
b. Compute a five-quarter moving average forecast for quarters 6 through 13 and compute the forecast error for each quarter.
c. Compute a weighted three-quarter moving average forecast, using weights of .50, .33, and .17 for the most recent, next most recent, and most distant data, respectively, and compute the forecast error for each quarter.
d. Compare the forecasts developed in (a), (b), and (c), using cumulative error. Which forecast appears to be most accurate? Do any of them exhibit any bias?

4. Graph the demand data in Problem 3. Can you identify any trends, cycles, or seasonal patterns?

5. The chairperson of the department of management at State University wants to forecast the number of students who will enroll in production and operations management (POM) next semester, in order to determine how many sections to schedule. The chair has accumulated the following enrollment data for the past eight semesters:

Semester	Students Enrolled in POM
1	400
2	450
3	350
4	420
5	500
6	575
7	490
8	650

   a. Compute a three-semester moving average forecast for semesters 4 through 9.
   b. Compute the exponentially smoothed forecast ($\alpha = .20$) for the enrollment data.
   c. Compare the two forecasts by using *MAD* and indicate the more accurate of the two.

6. The manager of the Petroco Service Station wants to forecast the demand for unleaded gasoline next month so that the proper number of gallons can be ordered from the distributor. The owner has accumulated the following data on demand for unleaded gasoline from sales during the past 10 months:

Month	Gasoline Demanded (gal.)
October	800
November	725
December	630
January	500
February	645
March	690
April	730
May	810
June	1,200
July	980

   a. Compute an exponentially smoothed forecast, using an α value of .30.
   b. Compute an adjusted exponentially smoothed forecast (with $\alpha = .30$ and $\beta = .20$).
   c. Compare the two forecasts by using *MAPD* and indicate which seems to be more accurate.

7. The Victory Plus Mutual Fund of growth stocks has had the following average monthly price for the past 10 months:

Month	Fund Price
1	62.7
2	63.9
3	68.0
4	66.4
5	67.2
6	65.8
7	68.2
8	69.3
9	67.2
10	70.1

Compute the exponentially smoothed forecast with $\alpha = .40$ the adjusted exponential smoothing forecast with $\alpha = .40$ and $\beta = .30$, and the linear trend line forecast. Compare the accuracy of the three forecasts, using cumulative error and *MAD*, and indicate which forecast appears to be most accurate.

8. The Bayside Fountain Hotel is adjacent to County Coliseum, a 24,000-seat arena that is home to the city's professional basketball and ice hockey teams and that hosts a variety of concerts, trade shows, and conventions throughout the year. The hotel has experienced the following occupancy rates for the past 9 years, since the coliseum opened:

Year	Occupancy Rate (%)
1	83
2	78
3	75
4	81
5	86
6	85
7	89
8	90
9	86

Compute an exponential smoothing forecast with $\alpha = .20$, an adjusted exponential smoothing forecast with $\alpha = .20$ and $\beta = .20$, and a linear trend line forecast. Compare the three forecasts, using *MAD* and average error ($\overline{E}$), and indicate which seems to be most accurate.

9. Emily Andrews has invested in a science and technology mutual fund. Now she is considering liquidating and investing in another fund. She would like to forecast the price of the science and technology fund for the next month before making a decision. She has collected the following data on the average price of the fund during the past 20 months:

Month	Fund Price
1	\$63 1/4
2	60 1/8
3	61 3/4
4	64 1/4
5	59 3/8
6	57 7/8
7	62 1/4
8	65 1/8
9	68 1/4
10	65 1/2
11	68 1/8
12	63 1/4
13	64 3/8
14	68 5/8
15	70 1/8
16	72 3/4
17	74 1/8
18	71 3/4
19	75 1/2
20	76 3/4

a. Using a 3-month average, forecast the fund price for month 21.
b. Using a 3-month weighted average with the most recent month weighted 0.60, the next most recent month weighted 0.30, and the third month weighted 0.10, forecast the fund price for month 21.
c. Compute an exponentially smoothed forecast, using $\alpha = .40$, and forecast the fund price for month 21.
d. Compare the forecasts in (a), (b), and (c), using *MAD*, and indicate the most accurate.

10. Eurotronics manufactures components for use in small electronic products such as computers, CD players, and radios at plants in Belgium, Germany, and France. The parts are transported by truck to Hamburg, where they are shipped overseas to customers in Mexico, South America, the United States, and the Pacific Rim. The company has to reserve space on ships months and sometimes years in advance. This requires an accurate forecasting model. Following are the number of cubic feet of container space the company has used in each of the past 18 months:

Month	Space (1,000s ft.^{3})
1	10.6
2	12.7
3	9.8
4	11.3
5	13.6
6	14.4
7	12.2
8	16.7
9	18.1
10	19.2
11	16.3
12	14.7
13	18.2
14	19.6
15	21.4
16	22.8
17	20.6
18	18.7

Develop a forecasting model that you believe would provide the company with relatively accurate forecasts for the next year and indicate the forecasted shipping space required for the next 3 months.

11. The Whistle Stop Cafe in Weems, Georgia, is well known for its popular homemade ice cream, made in a small plant in back of the cafe. People drive all the way from Atlanta and Macon to buy the ice cream. The two women who own the cafe want to develop a forecasting model so they can plan their ice cream production operation and determine the number of employees they need to sell ice cream in the cafe. They have accumulated the following sales records for their ice cream for the past 12 quarters:

Year	Quarter	Ice Cream Sales (gal.)
1	1	350
	2	510
	3	750
	4	420
2	5	370
	6	480
	7	860
	8	500
3	9	450
	10	550
	11	820
	12	570

Develop an adjusted exponential smoothing model with $\alpha = .50$ and $\beta = .50$ to forecast demand and assess its accuracy using cumulative error (E) and average error ($\overline{E}$). Does there appear to be any bias in the forecast?

12. For the demand data in Problem 11, develop a seasonally adjusted forecast for year 4. (Use a linear trend line model to develop a forecast estimate for year 4.) Which forecast model do you perceive to be more accurate: the exponential smoothing model from Problem 11 or the seasonally adjusted forecast?

13. Develop a seasonally adjusted forecast for the demand data for fertilizer found in Problem 3. Then use a linear trend line model to compute a forecast estimate for demand in year 4.

14. Monaghan's Pizza delivery service has randomly selected 8 weekdays during the past month and recorded orders for pizza at four different time periods per day:

	Day							
Time Period	1	2	3	4	5	6	7	8
10:00 A.M.–3:00 P.M.	62	49	53	35	43	48	56	43
3:00 P.M.–7:00 P.M.	73	55	81	77	60	66	85	70
7:00 P.M.–11:00 P.M.	42	38	45	50	29	37	35	44
11:00 P.M.–12:00 A.M.	35	40	36	39	26	25	36	31

Develop a seasonally adjusted forecasting model for daily pizza demand and forecast demand for each of the time periods for a single upcoming day.

15. The Cat Creek Mining Company mines and ships coal. It has experienced the following demand for coal during the past 8 years:

Year	Coal Sales (tons)
1	4,260
2	4,510
3	4,050
4	3,720
5	3,900
6	3,470
7	2,890
8	3,100

Develop an adjusted exponential smoothing model ($\alpha = .30$, $\beta = .20$) and a linear trend line model and compare the forecast accuracy of the two by using *MAD*. Indicate which forecast seems to be more accurate.

16. The Northwoods Outdoor Company is a catalog sales operation that specializes in outdoor recreational clothing. Demand for its items is very seasonal, peaking during the Christmas season and during the spring. It has accumulated the following data for orders per season (quarter) during the past 5 years:

	Orders (1,000s)/Year				
Quarter	1	2	3	4	5
January–March	18.6	18.1	22.4	23.2	24.5
April–June	23.5	24.7	28.8	27.6	31.0
July–September	20.4	19.5	21.0	24.4	23.7
October–December	41.9	46.3	45.5	47.1	52.8

a. Develop a seasonally adjusted forecast model for these order data. Forecast demand for each quarter for year 6 (using a linear trend line forecast estimate for orders in year 6).
b. Develop a separate linear trend line forecast for each of the four seasons and forecast each season for year 6.
c. Which of the two approaches used in (a) and (b) appears to be the more accurate? Use *MAD* to verify your selection.

17. Metro Food Vending operates vending machines in office buildings, the airport, bus stations, colleges, and other businesses and agencies around town, and it operates vending trucks for building and construction sites. The company believes its sandwich sales follow a seasonal pattern. It has accumulated the following data for sandwich sales per season during the past 4 years:

	Sandwich Sales (1,000s)/Year			
Season	1	2	3	4
Fall	42.7	44.3	45.7	40.6
Winter	36.9	42.7	34.8	41.5
Spring	51.3	55.6	49.3	47.3
Summer	62.9	64.8	71.2	74.5

Develop a seasonally adjusted forecast model for these sandwich sales data. Forecast demand for each season for year 5 by using a linear trend line estimate for sales in year 5. Do the data appear to have a seasonal pattern?

18. The Hillsboro Aquatic Center has an indoor pool with lanes for lap swimming and an open area for recreational swimming and various exercise and water aerobics programs. From June to mid-August it operates on a summer schedule, and from mid-August to the end of May it operates according to normal weekday and weekend schedules. The center's policy for the pool is to have a lifeguard-to-patron ratio of 1:40. The center director wants to develop a forecast of pool attendance for the weekday schedule in order to determine the number of lifeguards to hire. The director believes pool attendance follows a seasonal pattern during the day and has accumulated the following data for average daily attendance for each hour of the day that the pool is open to the public (i.e., there are no swim team practices):

	Year					
Time	1	2	3	4	5	6
7:00 A.M.	56	64	66	60	72	65
8:00	31	41	37	44	52	46
9:00	15	22	24	30	19	26
10:00	34	35	38	31	28	33
11:00	45	52	55	49	57	50
Noon	63	71	57	65	75	70
1:00 P.M.	35	30	41	42	33	45
2:00	24	28	32	30	35	33
3:00	27	19	24	23	25	27
6:00	31	47	36	45	40	46
7:00	25	35	41	43	39	45
8:00	14	20	18	17	23	27
9:00	10	8	16	14	15	18

Develop a seasonally adjusted forecast model for these data for hourly pool attendance. Forecast attendance for each hour for year 7 by using a linear trend line estimate for pool attendance in year 7. Do the data appear to have a seasonal pattern?

19. Develop an adjusted exponential smoothing forecast ($\alpha = .30, \beta = .20$) for the annual pool attendance data in Problem 18. Does this forecast appear to be more or less accurate than the linear trend line model for forecasting annual pool attendance developed in Problem 18?

20. The emergency room at the new Community Hospital selected every other week during the past 5 months to observe the number of patients during two parts of each week—the weekend (Friday through Sunday) and weekdays (Monday through Thursday). They typically experience greater patient traffic on weekends than during the week:

	Number of Patients	
Week	Weekend	Weekdays
1	116	83
2	126	92
3	125	97
4	132	91
5	128	103
6	139	88
7	145	96
8	137	106
9	151	95
10	148	102

Develop a seasonally adjusted forecasting model for the number of patients during each part of the week for week 11.

21. Aztec Industries has developed a forecasting model that was used to forecast during a 10-month period. The forecasts and actual demand were as follows:

Month	Actual Demand	Forecast Demand
1	160	170
2	150	165
3	175	157
4	200	166
5	190	183
6	220	186
7	205	203
8	210	204
9	200	207
10	220	203

Measure the accuracy of the forecast by using *MAD*, *MAPD*, and cumulative error. Does the forecast method appear to be accurate?

22. RAP Computers assembles personal computers from generic parts it purchases at a discount, and it sells the units via phone orders it receives from customers responding to the company's ads in trade journals. The business has developed an exponential smoothing forecast model to forecast future computer demand. Actual demand for the company's computers for the past 8 months as well as a forecast are shown in the following table:

Month	Demand	Forecast
March	120	—
April	110	120.0
May	150	116.0
June	130	129.6
July	160	129.7
August	165	141.8
September	140	151.1
October	155	146.7
November	—	150.0

   a. Using a measure of forecast accuracy of your choice, ascertain whether the forecast appears to be accurate.
   b. Determine whether a 3-month moving average would provide a better forecast.

23. Develop an exponential smoothing forecast with $\alpha = .20$ for the demand data in Problem 1. Compare this forecast with the 3-month moving average computed in part (a) of Problem 1, using *MAD*, and indicate which forecast seems to be more accurate.

24. The Jersey Dairy Products Company produces cheese, which it sells to supermarkets and food-processing companies. Because of concerns about cholesterol and fat in cheese, the company has seen demand for its products decline during the past decade. It is now considering introducing some alternative low-fat dairy products and wants to determine how much available plant capacity it will have next year. The company has developed an exponential smoothing forecast with $\alpha = .40$ to forecast cheese demand. The actual demand and the forecasts from the model are as follows:

Year	Demand (1,000 lb.)	Forecast
1	16.8	—
2	14.1	16.8
3	15.3	15.7
4	12.7	15.5
5	11.9	14.4
6	12.3	13.4
7	11.5	12.9
8	10.8	12.4

Assess the accuracy of the forecast model by using *MAD* and cumulative error. If the exponential smoothing forecast model does not appear to be accurate, determine whether a linear trend model would provide a more accurate forecast.

25. The manager of the Ramona Inn Hotel near Cloverleaf Stadium believes that how well the local Blue Sox professional baseball team is playing has an impact on the occupancy rate at the hotel during the summer months. Following are the number of victories for the Blue Sox (in a 162-game schedule) for the past 8 years and the hotel occupancy rates:

Year	Blue Sox Wins	Occupancy Rate (%)
1	75	83
2	70	78
3	85	86
4	91	85
5	87	89
6	90	93
7	87	92
8	67	91

Develop a linear regression model for these data and forecast the occupancy rate for next year if the Blue Sox win 88 games.

26. Carpet City wants to develop a means to forecast its carpet sales. The store manager believes that the store's sales are directly related to the number of new housing starts in town. The manager has gathered data from county records on monthly house construction permits and from store records on monthly sales. These data are as follows:

Monthly Carpet Sales (1,000 yd.)	Monthly Construction Permits
5	21
10	35
4	10
3	12
8	16
2	9
12	41
11	15
9	18
14	26

a. Develop a linear regression model for these data and forecast carpet sales if 30 construction permits for new homes are filed.
b. Determine the strength of the causal relationship between monthly sales and new home construction by using correlation.

27. The manager of Gilley's Ice Cream Parlor needs an accurate forecast of the demand for ice cream. The store orders ice cream from a distributor a week ahead; if the store orders too little, it loses business, and if it orders too much, the extra must be thrown away. The manager believes that a major determinant of ice cream sales is temperature (i.e., the hotter the weather, the more ice cream people buy). Using an almanac, the manager has determined the average daytime temperature for 10 weeks, selected at random, and from store records he has determined the ice cream consumption for the same 10 weeks. These data are summarized as follows:

Week	Average Temperature (degrees)	Ice Cream Sold (gal.)
1	73	110
2	65	95
3	81	135
4	90	160
5	75	97
6	77	105
7	82	120
8	93	175
9	86	140
10	79	121

a. Develop a linear regression model for these data and forecast the ice cream consumption if the average weekly daytime temperature is expected to be 85 degrees.
b. Determine the strength of the linear relationship between temperature and ice cream consumption by using correlation.

28. Compute the coefficient of determination for the data in Problem 27 and explain its meaning.

29. Administrators at State University believe that decreases in the number of freshman applications that they have experienced are directly related to tuition increases. They have collected the following enrollment and tuition data for the past decade:

Year	Freshman Applications	Annual Tuition
1	6,050	\$3,600
2	4,060	3,600
3	5,200	4,000
4	4,410	4,400
5	4,380	4,500
6	4,160	5,700
7	3,560	6,000
8	2,970	6,000
9	3,280	7,500
10	3,430	8,000

a. Develop a linear regression model for these data and forecast the number of applications for State University if tuition increases to $9,000 per year and if tuition is lowered to $7,000 per year.
b. Determine the strength of the linear relationship between freshman applications and tuition by using correlation.
c. Describe the various planning decisions for State University that would be affected by the forecast for freshman applications.

30. Develop a linear trend line model for the freshman applications data at State University in Problem 29.
    a. Does this forecast appear to be more or less accurate than the linear regression forecast developed in Problem 29? Justify your answer.
    b. Compute the correlation coefficient for the linear trend line forecast and explain its meaning.

31. Explain the numerical value of the slope of the linear regression equation in Problem 27.

32. Some members of management of the Fairface Cosmetics Firm believe that demand for its products is related to the promotional activities of local department stores where the cosmetics are sold. However, others in management believe that other factors, such as local demographics, are stronger determinants of demand behavior. The following data for local annual promotional expenditures for Fairface products and local annual unit sales for Fairface lip gloss have been collected from 20 stores selected at random from different localities:

Store	Annual Unit Sales (1,000s)	Annual Promotional Expenditures ($1,000s)
1	3.5	$12.6
2	7.2	15.5
3	3.1	10.8
4	1.6	8.7
5	8.9	20.3
6	5.7	21.9
7	6.3	25.6
8	9.1	14.3
9	10.2	15.1
10	7.3	18.7
11	2.5	9.6
12	4.6	12.7
13	8.1	16.3
14	2.5	8.1
15	3.0	7.5
16	4.8	12.4
17	10.2	17.3
18	5.1	11.2
19	11.3	18.5
20	10.4	16.7

Based on these data, does it appear that the strength of the relationship between sales and promotional expenditures is sufficient to warrant using a linear regression forecasting model? Explain your response.

33. Employees at Precision Engine Parts Company produce parts according to exact design specifications. The employees are paid according to a piece-rate system, wherein the faster they work and

the more parts they produce, the greater their chances for monthly bonuses. Management suspects that this method of pay may contribute to an increased number of defective parts. A specific part requires a normal, standard time of 23 minutes to produce. The quality control manager has checked the actual average times to produce this part for 10 different employees during 20 days selected at random during the past month and determined the corresponding percentage of defective parts, as follows:

Average Time (min.)	Defective (%)	Average Time (min.)	Defective (%)
21.6	3.1	20.8	2.7
22.5	4.6	18.9	4.5
23.1	2.7	21.4	2.8
24.6	1.8	23.7	1.9
22.8	3.5	23.8	1.1
23.7	3.2	24.9	1.2
20.9	3.7	19.8	2.3
19.7	4.5	19.7	5.1
24.5	0.8	21.2	3.6
26.7	1.2	20.8	4.2

Develop a linear regression model relating average production time to percentage defects to determine whether a relationship exists and the percentage of defective items that would be expected with a normal production time of 23 minutes.

34. Apperson and Fitz is a chain of clothing stores that caters to high school and college students. It publishes a quarterly catalog and operates a Web site that features provocatively attired males and females. The Web site is very expensive to maintain, and company executives are not sure whether the number of hits at the site relate to sales (i.e., people may be looking at the site's pictures only). The Web master has accumulated the following data for hits per month and orders placed at the Web site for the past 20 months:

Month	Hits (1,000s)	Orders (1,000s)
1	34.2	7.6
2	28.5	6.3
3	36.7	8.9
4	42.3	5.7
5	25.8	5.9
6	52.3	6.3
7	35.2	7.2
8	27.9	4.1
9	31.4	3.7
10	29.4	5.9
11	46.7	10.8
12	43.5	8.7
13	52.6	9.3
14	61.8	6.5
15	37.3	4.8
16	28.9	3.1
17	26.4	6.2
18	39.4	5.9
19	44.7	7.2
20	46.3	5.5

Develop a linear regression model for these data and indicate whether there appears to be a strong relationship between Web site hits and orders. What would be the forecast for orders with 50,000 hits per month?

35. The Gametime Hat Company manufactures baseball caps that have various team logos in an assortment of designs and colors. The company has had monthly sales for the past 24 months as follows:

Month	Demand (1,000s)
1	8.2
2	7.5
3	8.1
4	9.3
5	9.1
6	9.5
7	10.4
8	9.7
9	10.2
10	10.6
11	8.2
12	9.9
13	10.3
14	10.5
15	11.7
16	9.8
17	10.8
18	11.3
19	12.6
20	11.5
21	10.8
22	11.7
23	12.5
24	12.8

Develop a forecast model using the method you believe best and justify your selection by using a measure (or measures) of forecast accuracy.

36. Infoworks is a large computer discount store that sells computers and ancillary equipment and software in the town where State University is located. Infoworks has collected historical data on computer sales and printer sales for the past 10 years, as follows:

Year	Personal Computers Sold	Printers Sold
1	1,045	326
2	1,610	510
3	860	296
4	1,211	478
5	975	305
6	1,117	506
7	1,066	612
8	1,310	560
9	1,517	590
10	1,246	676

a. Develop a linear trend line forecast to forecast printer demand in year 11.
b. Develop a linear regression model relating printer sales to computer sales in order to forecast printer demand in year 11 if 1,300 computers are sold.
c. Compare the forecasts developed in (a) and (b) and indicate which one appears to be more accurate.

37. Develop an exponential smoothing model with $\alpha = .30$ for the data in Problem 36 to forecast printer demand in year 11 and compare its accuracy to the linear trend line forecast developed in (a).

38. Arrow Air is a regional East Coast airline that has collected data for the percentage available seats occupied on its flights for four quarters—(1) January–March, (2) April–June, (3) July–September, and (4) October–December—for the past 5 years. Arrow Air also has collected data for the average percentage fare discount for each of these quarters, as follows:

Year	Quarter	Average Fare Discount (%)	Seat Occupancy (%)
1	1	63	21
	2	75	34
	3	76	18
	4	58	26
2	1	59	18
	2	62	40
	3	81	25
	4	76	30
3	1	65	23
	2	70	28
	3	78	30
	4	69	35
4	1	59	20
	2	61	35
	3	83	26
	4	71	30
5	1	60	25
	2	66	37
	3	86	25
	4	74	30

a. Develop a seasonally adjusted forecast model for seat occupancy. Forecast seat occupancy for year 6 by using a linear trend line forecast estimate for seat occupancy in year 6.
b. Develop linear regression models relating seat occupancy to discount fares in order to forecast seat occupancy for each quarter in year 6. Assume a fare discount of 20% for quarter 1, 36% for quarter 2, 25% for quarter 3, and 30% for quarter 4.
c. Compare the forecasts developed in (a) and (b) and indicate which one appears to be the best.

39. Develop an adjusted exponential smoothing forecast model ($\alpha = .40$ and $\beta = .40$) for the data in Problem 38 to forecast seat occupancy, and compare its accuracy with the seasonally adjusted model developed in (a).

40. The consumer loan department at Central Union Bank and Trust wants to develop a forecasting model to help determine its potential loan application volume for the coming year. Because

adjustable-rate home mortgages are based on government long-term treasury note rates, the department collected the following data for 3- to 5-year treasury note interest rates for the past 24 years:

Year	Rate	Year	Rate	Year	Rate
1	5.77	9	9.71	17	7.68
2	5.85	10	11.55	18	8.26
3	6.92	11	14.44	19	8.55
4	7.82	12	12.92	20	8.26
5	7.49	13	10.45	21	6.80
6	6.67	14	11.89	22	6.12
7	6.69	15	9.64	23	5.48
8	8.29	16	7.06	24	6.09

Develop an appropriate forecast model for the bank to use to forecast treasury note rates in the future and indicate how accurate it appears to be compared to historical data.

41. The busiest time of the day at the Taco Town fast-food restaurant is between 11:00 A.M. and 2:00 P.M. Taco Town's service is very labor dependent, and a critical factor for providing quick service is the number of employees on hand during this 3-hour period. To determine the number of employees it needs during each hour of the 3-hour lunch period, Taco Town requires an accurate forecasting model. Following are the number of customers served at Taco Town during each hour of the lunch period for the past 20 weekdays:

	Hour		
Day	11–12	12–1	1–2
1	90	125	87
2	76	131	93
3	87	112	99
4	83	149	78
5	71	156	83
6	94	178	89
7	56	101	124
8	63	91	66
9	73	146	119
10	101	104	96
11	57	114	106
12	68	125	95
13	75	206	102
14	94	117	118
15	103	145	122
16	67	121	93
17	94	113	76
18	83	166	94
19	79	124	87
20	81	118	115

Develop a forecast model that you believe will best forecast Taco Town's customer demand for the next day and explain why you selected this model.

42. The Wellton Fund is a balanced mutual fund that includes a mix of stocks and bonds. Following are the year-end share prices of the fund and Dow Jones Industrial Average (DJIA) for a 20-year period:

Year	Share Price	DJIA
1	$14.75	1,046
2	15.06	1,258
3	14.98	1,211
4	15.73	1,546
5	16.11	1,895
6	16.07	1,938
7	16.78	2,168
8	17.69	2,753
9	16.90	2,633
10	17.81	3,168
11	19.08	3,301
12	20.40	3,754
13	19.39	3,834
14	24.43	5,117
15	26.46	6,448
16	29.45	7,908
17	29.35	9,181
18	27.96	11,497
19	28.21	10,786
20	27.26	10,150

Develop a linear regression model for these data and forecast the fund share price for a DJIA of 12,000. Does there appear to be a strong relationship between the fund's share price and the DJIA?

43. The Valley United Soccer Club has boys' and girls' travel soccer teams at all age levels up to 18 years. The club has been successful and grown in popularity over the years; however, an obstacle to its continued growth is a shortage of practice and game soccer fields in the area. The club has tried to make a case to the town council and the parks and recreation committee that it needs more soccer fields to accommodate the increasing number of kids who want to play on club teams. The number of kids who have played soccer on club teams and the town's population for the past 15 years are as follows:

Year	Club Soccer Players	Town Population
1	146	18,060
2	135	18,021
3	159	18,110
4	161	18,125
5	176	18,240
6	190	18,231
7	227	18,306
8	218	18,477
9	235	18,506
10	231	18,583
11	239	18,609
12	251	18,745
13	266	19,003
14	301	19,062
15	327	19,114

The soccer club wants to develop a forecasting model to demonstrate to the town council its expected growth in the future.

a. Develop a linear trend line forecast to predict the number of soccer players the club can expect next year.
b. The town planning department has told the soccer club that the town expects to grow to a population of 19,300 by next year and to 20,000 in 5 years. Develop a linear regression model, using the town's population as a predictor of the number of club soccer players, and compare this forecasting model to the one developed in part (a). Which forecasting model should the club use to support its request for new fields?

44. The Port of Savannah is considering an expansion of its container terminal. The port has experienced the following container throughput during the past 12 years, expressed as TEUs (i.e., 20-foot equivalent units, a standard unit of measure for containers):

Year	TEUs (1,000s)
1	526.1
2	549.4
3	606.0
4	627.0
5	695.7
6	734.9
7	761.1
8	845.4
9	1,021.1
10	1,137.1
11	1,173.6
12	1,233.4

a. Develop a linear trend line forecast for these data and forecast the number of TEUs for year 13.
b. How strong is the linear relationship for these data?

45. The admission data for freshmen at Tech during the past 10 years are as follows:

Year	Applicants	Offers	% Offers	Acceptances	% Acceptances
1	13,876	11,200	80.7	4,112	36.7
2	14,993	11,622	77.8	4,354	37.3
3	14,842	11,579	78.0	4,755	41.1
4	16,285	13,207	81.1	5,068	38.0
5	16,922	11,382	73.2	4,532	39.8
6	16,109	11,937	74.1	4,655	39.0
7	15,883	11,616	73.1	4,659	40.1
8	18,407	11,539	62.7	4,620	40.0
9	18,838	13,138	69.7	5,054	38.5
10	17,756	11,952	67.3	4,822	40.3

Tech's admission objective is a class of 5,000 entering freshmen, and Tech wants to forecast the percentage of offers it will likely have to make in order to achieve this objective.

a. Develop a linear trend line to forecast next year's applicants and percentage of acceptances and use these results to estimate the percentage of offers that Tech should expect to make.

b. Develop a linear trend line to forecast the percentage of offers that Tech should expect to make and compare this result with the result in (a). Which forecast do you think is more accurate?
c. Assume that Tech receives 18,300 applicants in year 11. How many offers do you think it should make to get 5,000 acceptances?

46. The State of Virginia has instituted a series of standards of learning (SOL) tests in math, history, English, and science that all high school students must pass with a grade of 70 before they are allowed to graduate and receive their diplomas. The school superintendent of Montgomery County believes the tests are unfair because the test scores are closely related to teacher salary and tenure (i.e., the years a teacher has been at a school). The superintendent has sampled 12 other county school systems in the state and accumulated the following data for average teacher salary and average teacher tenure:

School	Average SOL Score	Average Teacher Salary	Average Teacher Tenure (yr.)
1	81	$34,300	9.3
2	78	28,700	10.1
3	76	26,500	7.6
4	77	36,200	8.2
5	84	35,900	8.8
6	86	32,500	12.7
7	79	31,800	8.4
8	91	38,200	11.5
9	68	27,100	8.3
10	73	31,500	7.3
11	90	37,600	12.3
12	85	40,400	14.2

a. Using Excel or QM for Windows, develop the multiple regression equation for these data.
b. What is the coefficient of determination for this regression equation? Do you think the superintendent is correct in his beliefs?
c. Montgomery County has an average SOL score of 74, with an average teacher salary of $27,500 and an average teacher tenure of 7.8 years. The superintendent has proposed to the school board a salary increase that would raise the average salary to $30,000 as well as a benefits program, with the goal of increasing the average tenure to 9 years. He has suggested that if the board passes his proposals, then the average SOL score will increase to 80. Is he correct, according to the forecasting model?

47. Tech administrators believe their freshman applications are influenced by two variables: tuition and the size of the applicant pool of eligible high school seniors in the state. The following data for an 8-year period show the tuition rates (per semester) and the sizes of the applicant pool for each year:

Tuition	Applicant Pool	Applicants
$ 900	76,200	11,060
1,250	78,050	10,900
1,375	67,420	8,670
1,400	70,390	9,050
1,550	62,550	7,400
1,625	59,230	7,100
1,750	57,900	6,300
1,930	60,080	6,100

a. Using Excel, develop the multiple regression equation for these data.
b. What is the coefficient of determination for this regression equation?
c. Determine the forecast for freshman applicants for a tuition rate of $1,500 per semester, with a pool of applicants of 60,000.

48. In Problem 36, Infoworks believes its printer sales are also related to the average price of its printers. It has collected historical data on average printer prices for the past 10 years, as follows:

Year	Average Printer Price
1	$475
2	490
3	520
4	420
5	410
6	370
7	350
8	300
9	280
10	250

a. Using Excel, develop the multiple regression equation for these data.
b. What is the coefficient of determination for this regression equation?
c. Determine the forecast for printer sales, based on personal computer sales of 1,500 units and an average printer price of $300.

49. The manager of the Bayville police department motor pool wants to develop a forecast model for annual maintenance on police cars, based on mileage in the past year and age of the cars. The following data have been collected for eight different cars:

Miles Driven	Car Age (yr.)	Maintenance Cost
16,320	7	$1,200
15,100	8	1,400
18,500	8	1,820
10,200	3	900
9,175	3	650
12,770	7	1,150
8,600	2	875
7,900	3	900

a. Using Excel, develop a multiple regression equation for these data.
b. What is the coefficient of determination for this regression equation?
c. Forecast the annual maintenance cost for a police car that is 5 years old and will be driven 10,000 miles in 1 year.

50. The dean of the college of business at Tech has initiated a fund-raising campaign. One of the selling points he plans to use with potential donors is that increasing the college's private endowment

will improve its ranking among all business schools, as published each year by the magazine *The Global News and Business Report*. He would like to demonstrate that there is a relationship between funding and the rankings. He has collected the following data, showing the private endowments ($1,000,000s) and annual budgets ($1,000,000s) from state and private sources for eight of Tech's peer institutions plus Tech, and the ranking of each school:

Private Endowment ($1,000,000s)	Annual Budget ($1,000,000s)	Ranking
$ 2.5	$ 8.1	87
52.0	26.0	20
12.7	7.5	122
63.0	33.0	32
46.0	12.0	54
27.1	16.1	76
23.3	17.0	103
46.4	14.9	40
48.9	21.8	98

a. Using Excel, develop a linear regression model for the amount of the private endowment and the ranking and forecast a ranking for a private endowment of $70 million. Does there appear to be a strong relationship between the endowment and the ranking?
b. Using Excel, develop a multiple regression equation for all these data, including private endowment and annual budget, and forecast a ranking for a private endowment of $70 million and an annual budget of $40 million. How does this forecast compare with the forecast in part (a)?

Case Problem

Forecasting at State University

During the past few years, the legislature has severely reduced funding for State University. In reaction, the administration at State has significantly raised tuition each year for the past 5 years. Perceived as a bargain 5 years ago, State is now considered one of the more expensive state-supported universities. This has led some parents and students to question the value of a State education, and applications for admission have declined. Because a portion of state educational funding is based on a formula tied to enrollments, State has maintained its enrollment levels by going deeper into its applicant pool and accepting less-qualified students.

On top of these problems, a substantial increase in the college-age population is expected in the next decade. Key members of the state legislature have told the university administration that State will be expected to absorb additional students during the next decade. However, because of the economic outlook and the budget situation, the university should not expect any funding increases for additional facilities, classrooms, dormitory rooms, or faculty. The university already has a classroom deficit in excess of 25%, and class sizes are above the averages of the peer institutions.

The president of the university, Alva McMahon, established several task forces consisting of faculty and administrators to address these problems. These groups made several wide-ranging general recommendations, including the implementation of appropriate management practices and more in-depth, focused planning.

Discuss in general terms how forecasting might be used for university planning to address these specific problem areas. Include in your discussion the types of forecasting methods that might be used.

Case Problem

THE UNIVERSITY BOOKSTORE STUDENT COMPUTER PURCHASE PROGRAM

The University Bookstore is owned and operated by State University through an independent corporation with its own board of directors. The bookstore has three locations on or near the State University campus. It stocks a range of items, including textbooks, trade books, logo apparel, drawing and educational supplies, and computers and related products, including printers, modems, and software. The bookstore has a program to sell personal computers to incoming freshmen and other students at a substantial educational discount, partly passed on from computer manufacturers. This means that the bookstore just covers computer costs, with a very small profit margin remaining.

Each summer all incoming freshmen and their parents come to the State campus for a 3-day orientation program. The students come in groups of 100 throughout the summer. During their visit the students and their parents are given details about the bookstore's computer purchase program. Some students place their computer orders for the fall semester at this time, whereas others wait until later in the summer. The bookstore also receives orders from returning students throughout the summer. This program presents a challenging management problem for the bookstore.

Orders come in throughout the summer, many only a few weeks before school starts in the fall, and the computer suppliers require at least 6 weeks for delivery. Thus, the bookstore must forecast computer demand to build up inventory to meet student demand in the fall. The student computer program and the forecast of computer demand have repercussions all along the bookstore supply chain. The bookstore has a warehouse near campus where it must store all computers because it has no storage space at its retail locations. Ordering too many computers not only ties up the bookstore's cash reserves, it also takes up limited storage space and limits inventories for other bookstore products during the bookstore's busiest sales period. Because the bookstore has such a low profit margin on computers, its bottom line depends on these other products. Because competition for good students has increased, the university has become very quality conscious and insists that all university facilities provide exemplary student service, which for the bookstore means meeting all student demands for computers when fall semester starts. The number of computers ordered also affects the number of temporary warehouse and bookstore workers who must be hired for handling and assisting with PC installations. The number of truck trips from the warehouse to the bookstore each day of fall registration is also affected by computer sales.

The bookstore student computer purchase program has been in place for 14 years. Although the student population has remained stable during this period, computer sales have been somewhat volatile. Following are the historical sales data for computers during the first month of fall registration:

Year	*Computers Sold*	*Year*	*Computers Sold*
1	518	8	792
2	651	9	877
3	708	10	693
4	921	11	841
5	775	12	1,009
6	810	13	902
7	856	14	1,103

Develop an appropriate forecast model for bookstore management to use to forecast computer demand for next fall semester and indicate how accurate it appears to be. What other forecasts might be useful to the bookstore?

Case Problem

VALLEY SWIM CLUB

The Valley Swim Club has 300 stockholders, each holding one share of stock in the club. A share of club stock allows the shareholder's family to use the club's heated outdoor pool during the summer, upon payment of annual membership dues of $175. The club has not issued any stock in years, and only a few of the existing shares come up for sale each year. The board of directors administers the sale of all stock. When a shareholder wants to sell, he or she turns the stock in to the board, which sells it to the person at the top of the waiting list. For the past few years, the length of the waiting list has remained relatively steady, at approximately 20 names.

However, during the past winter two events occurred that have suddenly increased the demand for shares in the club. The winter was especially severe, and subzero weather and heavy ice storms caused both the town and the county pools to buckle and crack. The problems were not discovered until maintenance crews began to prepare the pools for the summer, and repairs cannot be completed until the fall. Also during the winter, the manager of the local country club had an argument with her board of directors and one night burned down the clubhouse. Although the pool itself was not damaged, the dressing room facilities, showers, and snack bar were destroyed. As a result of these two events, the Valley Swim Club was inundated with applications to purchase shares. The waiting list suddenly grew to 250 people as the summer approached.

The board of directors of the swim club had refrained from issuing new shares in the past because there never was a very great demand, and the demand that did exist was usually absorbed within a year by stock turnover. In addition, the board has a real concern about overcrowding. It seemed like the present membership was about right, and there were very few complaints about overcrowding, except on holidays such as Memorial Day and the Fourth of July. However, at a recent board meeting, a number of new applicants had attended and asked the board to issue new shares. In addition, a number of current shareholders suggested that this might be an opportunity for the club to raise some capital for needed repairs and to improve some of the existing facilities. This was tempting to the board. Although it had set the share price at $500 in the past, the board could set it at a much higher level now. In addition, an increase in attendance could create a need for more lifeguards.

Before the board of directors could make a decision on whether to sell more shares and, if so, how many, the board members felt they needed more information. Specifically, they would like a forecast of the average number of people (family members, guests, etc.) who might attend the pool each day during the summer, with the current number of shares.

The board of directors has the following daily attendance records for June through August from the previous summer; it thinks the figures would provide accurate estimates for the upcoming summer:

M-139	W-380	F-193	Su-399	T-177	Th-238
T-273	Th-367	Sa-378	M-197	W-161	F-224
W-172	F-359	Su-461	T-273	Th-308	Sa-368
Th-275	Sa-463	M-242	W-213	F-256	Su-541
F-337	Su-578	T-177	Th-303	Sa-391	M-235
Sa-402	M-287	W-245	F-262	Su-400	T-218
Su-487	T-247	Th-390	Sa-447	M-224	W-271
M-198	W-356	F-284	Su-399	T-239	Th-259
T-310	Th-322	Sa-417	M-275	W-274	F-232
W-347	F-419	Su-474	T-241	Th-205	Sa-317
Th-393	Sa-516	M-194	W-190	F-361	Su-369
F-421	Su-478	T-207	Th-243	Sa-411	M-361
Sa-595	M-303	W-215	F-277	Su-419	
Su-497	T-223	Th-304	Sa-241	M-258	
M-341	W-315	F-331	Su-384	T-130	
T-291	Th-258	Sa-407	M-246	W-195	

Develop a forecasting model to forecast daily demand during the summer.

Case Problem

Forecasting Airport Passenger Arrivals

Since the terrorist attacks of 9/11 and because of the ensuing measures to increase airline security, airports have faced the problem of long waiting lines and waiting times at security gates. Waiting lines can be as long as hundreds of yards, and waiting times can sometimes be hours. In their efforts to reduce waiting lines and times, or at least to not have them become longer as airline demand increases, airports have analyzed their existing security systems and sought quantitative solutions. One of the key components of any effort to operationally improve airport security procedures is forecasting passenger arrivals at security checkpoints in order to determine how many security checkpoints and staff are needed. At Berry International Airport (BEI), security analysts would like to forecast passenger arrivals for next July, the airport's busiest travel month of the year, for the purpose of determining how many security checkpoints they should staff during the month so that waiting lines and times will not be excessively long. Demand for airline travel has generally been increasing during the past 3 years. There are two main concourses at BEI, North and South, each serving different airlines. The following table shows passenger arrivals at the South concourse for 10 days (selected randomly) in 2-hour segments from 4:00 A.M. to 10:00 P.M. for the month of July for the past 3 years.

	Day	4–6 A.M.	6–8 A.M.	8–10 A.M.	10–Noon	Noon–2 P.M.	2–4 P.M.	4–6 P.M.	6–8 P.M.	8–10 P.M.
Year One	1	2400	2700	3200	1400	1700	1800	1600	800	200
	2	1900	2500	3100	1600	1800	2000	1800	900	300
	3	2300	3100	2500	1500	1500	1800	1900	1100	200
	4	2200	3200	3100	2200	1900	2400	2100	1200	400
	5	2400	3300	3400	1700	2200	2100	2000	1000	600
	6	2600	2800	3500	1500	1700	1900	1500	1100	300
	7	1900	2800	3100	1200	1500	2000	1400	900	400
	8	2000	2700	2500	1500	2000	2300	1900	1000	200
	9	2400	3200	3600	1600	2100	2500	1800	1400	200
	10	2600	3300	3100	200	2500	2600	2400	1100	400
Year Two	11	3100	3900	4100	2200	2600	2300	2500	1100	300
	12	2800	3400	3900	1900	2100	2500	2000	1200	300
	13	2700	3800	4300	2100	2400	2400	2400	1200	400
	14	2400	3500	4100	2400	3000	3200	2600	1200	700
	15	3300	3700	4000	2600	2600	2700	2900	1000	300
	16	3500	4000	3800	2300	2700	3100	3000	900	200
	17	2900	4100	3900	2400	3000	3200	2500	1100	500
	18	3400	3800	4200	2000	2500	3000	2200	1000	300
	19	3600	3600	4000	2300	2600	2800	2600	1200	200
	20	3700	3700	4000	2200	2600	2700	2400	1200	200
Year Three	21	4400	4400	4500	2600	3300	3400	3000	1200	400
	22	4200	4500	4300	2500	3400	3600	3100	1400	300
	23	4500	4500	4700	2700	3400	3500	2900	1200	300
	24	4600	4600	4600	2500	3200	3500	2800	1300	300
	25	4500	4300	4400	2900	3300	3300	3300	1500	400
	26	4200	4300	4500	3000	4000	3400	3000	1500	600
	27	4500	4500	5100	3300	4000	3700	3100	1200	300
	28	4300	4200	4300	2800	3500	4000	3300	1100	400
	29	4900	4100	4200	3100	3600	3900	3400	1400	500
	30	4700	4500	4100	3000	4000	3700	3400	1200	500

Develop a forecast for daily passenger arrivals at the South concourse at BEI for each time period for July of year 4. Discuss the various forecast model variations that might be used to develop this forecast.

Solutions to Selected Odd-Numbered Problems

1. (a) Apr = 8.67, May = 8.33, Jun = 8.33, Jul = 9.00, Aug = 9.67, Sep = 11.00, Oct = 11.00, Nov = 11.00, Dec = 12.00, Jan = 13.33; (b) Jun = 8.20, Jul = 8.80, Aug = 9.40, Sep = 9.60, Oct = 10.40, Nov = 11.00, Dec = 11.40, Jan = 12.60; (c) $MAD(3) = 1.89$, $MAD(5) = 2.43$

3. (a) $F_4 = 116.00$, $F_5 = 121.33$, $F_6 = 118.00$, $F_7 = 143.67$, $F_8 = 138.33$, $F_9 = 141.67$, $F_{10} = 135.00$, $F_{11} = 156.67$, $F_{12} = 143.33$, $F_{13} = 136.67$; (b) $F_6 = 121.80$, $F_7 = 134.80$, $F_8 = 125.80$, $F_9 = 137.20$, $F_{10} = 143.00$, $F_{11} = 149.00$, $F_{12} = 137.00$, $F_{13} = 142.00$; (c) $F_4 = 113.85$, $F_5 = 116.69$, $F_6 = 125.74$, $F_7 = 151.77$, $F_8 = 132.4$, $F_9 = 138.55$, $F_{10} = 142.35$, $F_{11} = 160.0$, $F_{12} = 136.69$, $F_{13} = 130.20$; (d) 3–qtr *MA*: $E = 32.0$, 5–qtr *MA*: $E = 36.4$, weighted *MA*: $E = 28.09$

5. (a) $F_4 = 400.000$, $F_5 = 406.67$, $F_6 = 423.33$, $F_7 = 498.33$, $F_8 = 521.67$, $F_9 = 571.67$; (b) $F_2 = 400.00$, $F_3 = 410.00$, $F_4 = 398.00$, $F_5 = 402.40$, $F_6 = 421.92$, $F_7 = 452.53$, $F_8 = 460.00$, $F_9 = 498.02$; (c) 3-sem. $MAD = 80.33$, exp. smooth. $MAD = 87.16$

7. F_{11} (exp. smooth) = 68.6, F_{11} (adjusted) = 69.17, F_{11} (linear trend) = 70.22; exp. smooth: $E = 14.75$, $MAD = 1.89$; adjusted: $E = 10.73$, $MAD = 1.72$; linear trend: $MAD = 1.09$

9. (a) $F_{21} = 74.67$, $MAD = 3.12$; (b) $F_{21} = 75.875$, $MAD = 2.98$; (c) $F_{21} = 74.60$, $MAD = 2.87$; (d) 3-mo. moving average and exponentially smoothed

11. $F_{13} = 631.22$, $\bar{E} = 26.30$, $E = 289.33$, biased low

13. $F_1 = 155.6$, $F_2 = 192.9$, $F_3 = 118.2$, $F_4 = 155.6$

15. F_{04} (adjusted) = 3,313.19, F_{04} (linear trend) = 2,785.00; adjusted: MAD = 431.71; linear trend: MAD = 166.25
17. fall = 44.61, winter = 40.08, spring = 52.29, summer = 70.34; yes
19. F_9 (exp. smooth) = 492.31, F_9 (adjusted) = 503.27
21. E = 86.00, $\bar{E}$ = 8.60, MAD = 15.00, $MAPD$ = 0.08
23. MAD: MA = 1.89, exp. smooth = 2.16; 3-mo. moving average
25. $y = 0.67 + .223x$, 88.58%
27. (a) $y = -113.4 + 2.986x$, 140.43 gal.; (b) .929
29. (a) $y = 6{,}541.66 - .448x$; $y(\$9{,}000) = 2{,}503.2$, $y(\$7{,}000) = 3{,}400.6$; (b) −.754
31. b = 2.98, the number of gallons sold per each degree increase
33. $y = 13.476 - 0.4741x$, $r = -0.76$, $r^2 = 0.58$; yes, relationship; y = 2.57% defects
35. linear trend line, 3-mo. MA and adj. exp. smooth all are relatively accurate
37. exponential smoothing appears to be less accurate than linear trend line
39. F_6 (adj.) = 74.19 seat occupancy, $\bar{E}$ = 1.08, MAD = 8.6
41. student choice of model
43. (a) $y = 119.27 + 12.28x$, y (lb.) = 315.67; (b) $y = -2504.18 + .147x$, $r^2 = .966$
45. (a) $y = 13{,}803.07 + 470.55x$, 65.15%; (b) $y = 83 - 1.68x$; 64.5%
47. (a) $y = 745.91 - 2.226x_1 + .163x_2$; (b) $r^2 = .992$; (c) $y = 7{,}186.91$
49. (a) $y = 117.128 + .072x_1 + 19.148x_2$; (b) $r^2 = .822$; (c) $y = \$940.60$

Inventory Management

Inventory Management

Inventory analysis is one of the most popular topics in management science. One reason is that almost all types of business organizations have inventory. Although we tend to think of inventory only in terms of stock on a store shelf, it can take on a variety of forms, such as partially finished products at different stages of a manufacturing process, raw materials, resources, labor, or cash. In addition, the purpose of inventory is not always simply to meet customer demand. For example, companies frequently stock large inventories of raw materials as a hedge against strikes. Whatever form inventory takes or whatever its purpose, it often represents a significant cost to a business firm. It is estimated that the average annual cost of manufactured goods inventory in the United States is approximately 30% of the total value of the inventory. Thus, if a company has \$10.0 million worth of products in inventory, the cost of holding the inventory (including insurance, obsolescence, depreciation, interest, opportunity costs, storage costs, etc.) would be approximately \$3.0 million. If the amount of inventory could be reduced by half to \$5.0 million, then \$1.5 million would be saved in inventory costs, a significant cost reduction.

In this chapter we describe the classic economic order quantity models, which represent the most basic and fundamental form of inventory analysis. These models provide a means for determining how much to order (the order quantity) and when to place an order so that inventory-related costs are minimized. The underlying assumption of these models is that demand is known with certainty and is constant. In addition, we will describe models for determining the order size and reorder points (when to place an order) when demand is uncertain.

Elements of Inventory Management

Inventory is a stock of items kept on hand to meet demand.

Inventory is defined as a stock of items kept on hand by an organization to use to meet customer demand. Virtually every type of organization maintains some form of inventory. A department store carries inventories of all the retail items it sells; a nursery has inventories of different plants, trees, and flowers; a rental car agency has inventories of cars; and a major league baseball team maintains an inventory of players on its minor league teams. Even a family household will maintain inventories of food, clothing, medical supplies, personal hygiene products, and so on.

The Role of Inventory

A company or an organization keeps stocks of inventory for a variety of important reasons. The most prominent is holding finished goods inventories to meet customer demand for a product, especially in a retail operation. However, customer demand can also be in the form of a secretary going to a storage closet to get a printer cartridge or paper, or a carpenter getting a board or nail from a storage shed. A level of inventory is normally maintained that will meet anticipated or expected customer demand. However, because demand is usually not known with certainty, additional amounts of inventory, called **safety**, or ***buffer*, stocks**, are often kept on hand to meet unexpected variations in excess of expected demand.

Safety stocks are additional inventory to compensate for demand uncertainty.

Additional stocks of inventories are sometimes built up to meet seasonal or cyclical demand. Companies will produce items when demand is low to meet high seasonal demand for which their production capacity is insufficient. For example, toy manufacturers produce large inventories during the summer and fall to meet anticipated demand during the Christmas season. Doing so enables them to maintain a relatively smooth production flow throughout the year. They would not normally have the production capacity or logistical support to produce enough to meet all of the Christmas demand during that season. Correspondingly, retailers might find it necessary to keep large stocks of inventory on their shelves to meet peak seasonal demand, such as at Christmas, or for display purposes to attract buyers.

A company will often purchase large amounts of inventory to take advantage of price discounts, as a hedge against anticipated future price increases, or because it can get a lower price by purchasing in volume. For example, Wal-Mart has long been known to purchase an entire manufacturer's stock of soap powder or other retail items because it can get a very low price, which it subsequently passes on to its customers. Companies will often purchase large stocks of items when a supplier liquidates to get a low price. In some cases, large orders will be made simply because the cost of an order may be very high, and it is more cost-effective to have higher inventories than to make a lot of orders.

Many companies find it necessary to maintain in-process inventories at different stages in a manufacturing process to provide independence between operations and to avoid work stoppages or delays. Inventories of raw materials and purchased parts are kept on hand so that the production process will not be delayed as a result of missed or late deliveries or shortages from a supplier. Work-in-process inventories are kept between stages in the manufacturing process so that production can continue smoothly if there are temporary machine breakdowns or other work stoppages. Similarly, a stock of finished parts or products allows customer demand to be met in the event of a work stoppage or problem with the production process.

Demand

A crucial component and the basic starting point for the management of inventory is customer demand. Inventory exists for the purpose of meeting the demand of customers. Customers can be inside the organization, such as a machine operator waiting for a part or a partially completed product to work on, or outside the organization, such as an individual purchasing groceries or a new stereo. As such, an essential determinant of effective inventory management is an accurate forecast of demand. For this reason the topics of forecasting and inventory management are directly interrelated.

__Dependent demand__ items are used internally to produce a final product.

In general, the demand for items in inventory is classified as dependent or independent. **Dependent demand** items are typically component parts, or materials, used in the process of producing a final product. For example, if an automobile company plans to produce 1,000 new cars, it will need 5,000 wheels and tires (including spares). In this case the demand for wheels is dependent on the production of cars; that is, the demand for one item is a function of demand for another item.

__Independent demand__ items are final products demanded by an external customer.

Alternatively, cars are an example of an **independent demand** item. In general, independent demand items are final or finished products that are not a function of, or dependent upon, internal production activity. Independent demand is usually external, and, thus, beyond the direct control of the organization. In this chapter we will focus on the management of inventory for independent demand items.

Inventory Costs

Inventory costs include __carrying__, not __ordering__, and __shortage costs__.

__Carrying costs__ are the costs of holding inventory in storage.

There are three basic costs associated with inventory: carrying (or holding) costs, ordering costs, and shortage costs. **Carrying costs** are the costs of holding items in storage. These vary with the level of inventory and occasionally with the length of time an item is held; that is, the greater the level of inventory over time, the higher the carrying cost(s). Carrying costs can include the cost of losing the use of funds tied up in inventory; direct storage costs, such as rent, heating, cooling, lighting, security, refrigeration, record keeping, and logistics; interest on loans used to purchase inventory; depreciation; obsolescence as markets for products in inventory diminish; product deterioration and spoilage; breakage; taxes; and pilferage.

Carrying costs are normally specified in one of two ways. The most general form is to assign total carrying costs, determined by summing all the individual costs mentioned previously, on a per-unit basis per time period, such as a month or a year. In this form, carrying

Management Science Application

Evaluating Inventory Costs at Hewlett-Packard

Rick Maiman/Landov Media

Hewlett-Packard, with annual revenues exceeding $90 billion and 150,000 employees worldwide, is the *Fortune 500* 11th-ranked company. Although demand for PCs increased by fivefold in the 1990s, becoming a veritable household product, many PC companies struggled to remain profitable. By the end of the 1990s HP was struggling to make a profit in the increasingly competitive global PC market because of price cuts throughout the decade. Because prices were not really controllable, inventory costs became especially critical in the PC profit equation. Rapid technological advancements render new PC products obsolete in a few months, and, in general, it's believed that the value of a PC decreases at the rate of 1% per week. Consequently, holding any excess inventory is very costly.

In the late 1990s, to return its PC business to more sustainable profitability, HP undertook an extensive evaluation of its inventory costs. It discovered that inventory-related costs were the main determinants of overall PC cost, and, in fact, in 1 year alone inventory-related costs equaled the PC business's total operating margin. Further, HP determined that the traditional inventory carrying (or holding) costs (which encompass capital costs plus storage, taxes, insurance, breakage, etc.) accounted for less than 10% of the total inventory-related costs. HP identified four additional inventory costs in their PC business that were a major factor in overall supply chain costs. The single biggest inventory cost was determined to be the "component devaluation cost." This is the penalty cost HP incurred when the price dropped for excess components and parts (for example, CPUs, memory, and chips) being held in inventory. HP held inventories of parts and components in factories, in distribution centers, and in transit and incurred a devaluation cost at all these points in its supply chain whenever a price reduction occurred. Another inventory cost is the "price protection cost," which occurs when the retail price of a product drops after it has already been shipped to the sales outlet. HP had to reimburse its sales partners for the difference in price for any unsold units so its partners wouldn't incur a loss. Given how fast PC products lose their value, excess inventory can result in large protection costs. A third inventory-related cost in the PC business is the "product return cost." This is the cost of a full refund HP paid its distributors when unsold products were returned; essentially it is a 100% price protection cost. In some cases sales partners and distributors returned excess unsold inventory valued at more than 10% of a product's revenue. The fourth inventory cost is "obsolescence cost," which is the cost of writing-off unsold products in inventory after the life of the product ends. Because PC products' life cycles are so short, there is the potential for large costs if excessive inventories are held. Related costs include price discounts for products that are about to be discontinued and the marketing costs to quickly reduce inventory. The Mobile Computing Division (which manufactures notebooks) was the first HP PC business unit to focus on all these inventory-related costs in redesigning its supply chain. The original supply chain consisted of a central manufacturing facility with local product configuration occurring at regional sites. (In this configuration about 40% of the total supply chain cost was related to inventory.) In the redesigned supply chain there is a central manufacturing facility, and products are air freighted directly to customers around the world. Positive results were immediate; in a 2-year period inventory-related costs dropped from almost 19% of total revenue to less than 4%, and the notebook division became profitable. As a result, all other HP PC operations began using these inventory costs to evaluate and redesign their supply chains.

Source: Reprinted by permission of *Harvard Business Review.* From "*Inventory Driven Costs,*" by G. Callioni, X. de Montgros, R. Slagmulder, L. N. Van Wassenove, and L. Wright. March 2005.

costs would commonly be expressed as a per-unit dollar amount on an annual basis (for example, $10 per year). Alternatively, carrying costs are sometimes expressed as a percentage of the value of an item or as a percentage of average inventory value. It is generally estimated that carrying costs range from 10% to 40% of the value of a manufactured item.

Ordering costs are the cost of replenishing inventory.

Ordering costs are the costs associated with replenishing the stock of inventory being held. These are normally expressed as a dollar amount per order and are independent of the order size. Thus, ordering costs vary with the number of orders made (i.e., as the number of orders increases, the ordering cost increases). Costs incurred each time an order is made can include requisition costs, purchase orders, transportation and shipping, receiving, inspection, handling and placing in storage, and accounting and auditing.

Ordering costs generally react inversely to carrying costs. As the size of orders increases, fewer orders are required, thus reducing annual ordering costs. However, ordering larger amounts results in higher inventory levels and higher carrying costs. In general, as the order size increases, annual ordering costs decrease and annual carrying costs increase.

Shortage costs are incurred when customer demand cannot be met.

Shortage costs, also referred to as *stockout costs*, occur when customer demand cannot be met because of insufficient inventory on hand. If these shortages result in a permanent loss of sales for items demanded but not provided, shortage costs include the loss of profits. Shortages can also cause customer dissatisfaction and a loss of goodwill that can result in a permanent loss of customers and future sales. In some instances the inability to meet customer demand or lateness in meeting demand results in specified penalties in the form of price discounts or rebates. When demand is internal, a shortage can cause work stoppages in the production process and create delays, resulting in downtime costs and the cost of lost production (including indirect and direct production costs).

Costs resulting from immediate or future lost sales because demand could not be met are more difficult to determine than carrying or ordering costs. As a result, shortage costs are frequently subjective estimates and many times no more than educated guesses.

Shortages occur because it is costly to carry inventory in stock. As a result, shortage costs have an inverse relationship to carrying costs; as the amount of inventory on hand increases, the carrying cost increases, while shortage costs decrease.

*The purpose of **inventory management** is to determine how much and when to order.*

The objective of **inventory management** is to employ an inventory control system that will indicate how much should be ordered and when orders should take place to minimize the sum of the three inventory costs described here.

Inventory Control Systems

An inventory system is a structure for controlling the level of inventory by determining how much to order (the level of replenishment) and when to order. There are two basic types of inventory systems: a *continuous* (or *fixed–order quantity*) *system* and a *periodic* (or *fixed–time period*) *system*. The primary difference between the two systems is that in a continuous system, an order is placed for the same constant amount whenever the inventory on hand decreases to a certain level, whereas in a periodic system, an order is placed for a variable amount after an established passage of time.

Continuous Inventory Systems

In a continuous inventory system, a constant amount is ordered when inventory declines to a predetermined level.

In a *continuous inventory system*, alternatively referred to as a *perpetual system* or a *fixed–order quantity system*, a continual record of the inventory level for every item is maintained. Whenever the inventory on hand decreases to a predetermined level, referred to as the *reorder point*, a new order is placed to replenish the stock of inventory. The order that is placed is for a "fixed" amount that minimizes the total inventory carrying, ordering, and shortage costs. This fixed order quantity is called the *economic order quantity*; its determination will be discussed in greater detail in a later section.

A positive feature of a continuous system is that the inventory level is closely and continuously monitored so that management always knows the inventory status. This is especially advantageous for critical inventory items such as replacement parts or raw materials and supplies. However, the cost of maintaining a continual record of the amount of inventory on hand can also be a disadvantage of this type of system.

A simple example of a continuous inventory system is a ledger-style checkbook that many of us use on a daily basis. Our checkbook comes with 300 checks; after the 200th check has been used (and there are 100 left), there is an order form for a new batch of checks that has been inserted by the printer. This form, when turned in at the bank, initiates an order for a new batch of 300 checks from the printer. Many office inventory systems use "reorder" cards that are placed within stacks of stationery or at the bottom of a case of pens or paper clips to signal when a new order should be placed. If you look behind the items on a hanging rack in a Kmart store, you will see a card indicating that it is time to place an order for this item, for an amount indicated on the card.

A more sophisticated example of a continuous inventory system is a computerized checkout system with a laser scanner, used by many supermarkets and retail stores. In this system a laser scanner reads the Universal Product Code (UPC), or bar code, off the product package, and the transaction is instantly recorded and the inventory level updated. Such a system is not only quick and accurate, but it also provides management with continuously updated information on the status of inventory levels. Although not as publicly visible as supermarket systems, many manufacturing companies, suppliers, and distributors also use bar code systems and handheld laser scanners to inventory materials, supplies, equipment, in-process parts, and finished goods.

Because continuous inventory systems are much more common than periodic systems, models that determine fixed order quantities and the time to order will receive most of our attention in this chapter.

Periodic Inventory Systems

In a periodic inventory system, an order is placed for a variable amount after a fixed passage of time.

In a **periodic inventory system**, also referred to as a *fixed–time period system* or *periodic review system*, the inventory on hand is counted at specific time intervals—for example, every week or at the end of each month. After the amount of inventory in stock is determined, an order is placed for an amount that will bring inventory back up to a desired level. In this system the inventory level is not monitored at all during the time interval between orders, so it has the advantage of requiring little or no record keeping. However, it has the disadvantage of less direct control. This typically results in larger inventory levels for a periodic inventory system than in a continuous system, to guard against unexpected stockouts early in the fixed period. Such a system also requires that a new order quantity be determined each time a periodic order is made.

Periodic inventory systems are often found at a college or university bookstore. Textbooks are normally ordered according to a periodic system, wherein a count of textbooks in stock (for every course) is made after the first few weeks or month during the semester or quarter. An order for new textbooks for the next semester is then made according to estimated course enrollments for the next term (i.e., demand) and the number remaining in stock. Smaller retail stores, drugstores, grocery stores, and offices often use periodic systems; the stock level is checked every week or month, often by a vendor, to see how much (if anything) should be ordered.

Time Out *for Ford Harris*

The earliest published derivation of the classic economic lot size model is credited to Ford Harris of Westinghouse Corporation in 1915. His equation determined a minimum sum of inventory costs and setup costs, given demand that was known and constant and a rate of production that was assumed to be higher than demand.

Economic Order Quantity Models

EOQ is a continuous inventory system.

You will recall that in a continuous or fixed–order quantity system, when inventory reaches a specific level, referred to as the *reorder point*, a fixed amount is ordered. The most widely used and traditional means for determining how much to order in a continuous system is the **economic order quantity (EOQ)** model, also referred to as the economic lot size model.

The function of the EOQ model is to determine the optimal order size that minimizes total inventory costs. There are several variations of the EOQ model, depending on the assumptions made about the inventory system. In this and following sections we will describe three model versions: the basic EOQ model, the EOQ model with noninstantaneous receipt, and the EOQ model with shortages.

The Basic EOQ Model

EOQ is the optimal order quantity that will minimize total inventory costs.

The simplest form of the economic order quantity model on which all other model versions are based is called the basic EOQ model. It is essentially a single formula for determining the optimal order size that minimizes the sum of carrying costs and ordering costs. The model formula is derived under a set of simplifying and restrictive assumptions, as follows:

Assumptions of the EOQ model include constant demand, no shortages, constant lead time, and instantaneous order receipt.

- Demand is known with certainty and is relatively constant over time.
- No shortages are allowed.
- Lead time for the receipt of orders is constant.
- The order quantity is received all at once.

The graph in Figure 1 reflects these basic model assumptions.

Figure 1
The inventory order cycle

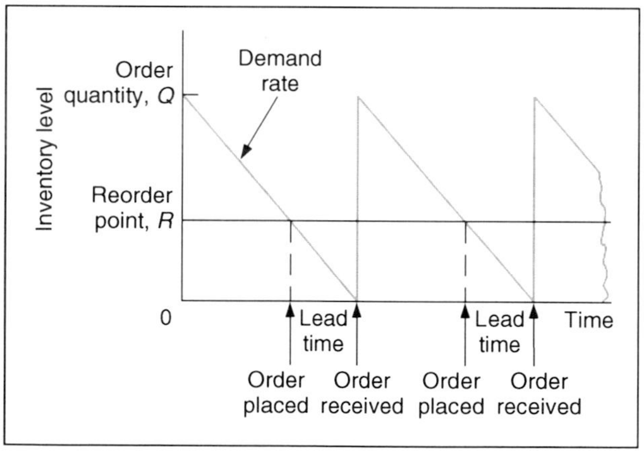

Figure 1 describes the continuous inventory order cycle system inherent in the EOQ model. An order quantity, Q, is received and is used up over time at a constant rate. When the inventory level decreases to the reorder point, R, a new order is placed, and a period of time, referred to as the *lead time*, is required for delivery. The order is received all at once, just at the moment when demand depletes the entire stock of inventory (and the inventory level reaches zero), thus allowing no shortages. This cycle is continuously repeated for the same order quantity, reorder point, and lead time.

As we mentioned earlier, Q is the order size that minimizes the sum of carrying costs and holding costs. These two costs react inversely to each other in response to an increase in the order size. As the order size increases, fewer orders are required, causing the ordering cost to decline, whereas the average amount of inventory on hand increases, resulting in an increase in carrying costs. Thus, in effect, the optimal order quantity represents a compromise between these two conflicting costs.

Carrying Cost

Carrying cost is usually expressed on a per-unit basis for some period of time (although it is sometimes given as a percentage of average inventory). Traditionally, the carrying cost is referred to on an annual basis (i.e., per year).

The total carrying cost is determined by the amount of inventory on hand during the year. The amount of inventory available during the year is illustrated in Figure 2.

Figure 2
Inventory usage

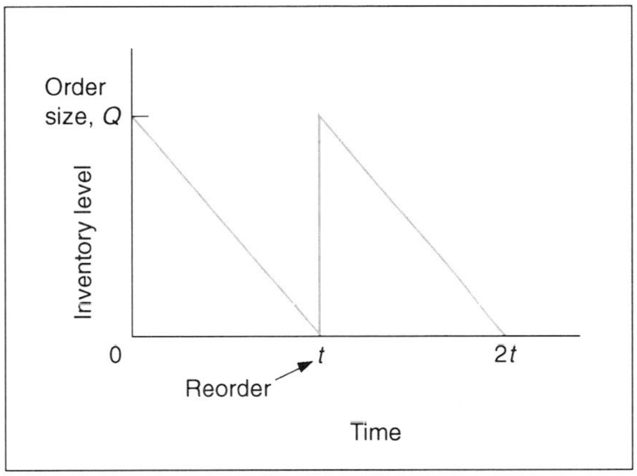

In Figure 2, Q represents the size of the order needed to replenish inventory, which is what a manager wants to determine. The line connecting Q to time, t, in our graph represents the rate at which inventory is depleted, or *demand*, during the time period, t. Demand is assumed to be *known with certainty* and is thus constant, which explains why the line representing demand is straight. Also, notice that inventory never goes below zero; shortages do not exist. In addition, when the inventory level does reach zero, it is assumed that an order arrives immediately after an infinitely small passage of time, a condition referred to as **instantaneous receipt**. This is a simplifying assumption that we will maintain for the moment.

Instantaneous receipt means inventory is received almost immediately after it is ordered.

Referring to Figure 2, we can see that the amount of inventory is Q, the size of the order, for an infinitely small period of time because Q is always being depleted by demand. Similarly, the amount of inventory is zero for an infinitely small period of time because the only time there is no inventory is at the specific time t. Thus, the amount of inventory available is somewhere between these two extremes. A logical deduction is that the amount of inventory available is the *average inventory* level, defined as

$$\text{average inventory} = \frac{Q}{2}$$

To verify this relationship, we can specify any number of points—values of Q—over the entire time period, t, and divide by the number of points. For example, if $Q = 5{,}000$, the six points designated from 5,000 to 0, as shown in Figure 3, are summed and divided by 6:

$$\begin{aligned}\text{average inventory} &= \frac{5{,}000 + 4{,}000 + 3{,}000 + 2{,}000 + 1{,}000 + 0}{6} \\ &= 2{,}500\end{aligned}$$

Figure 3
Levels of *Q*

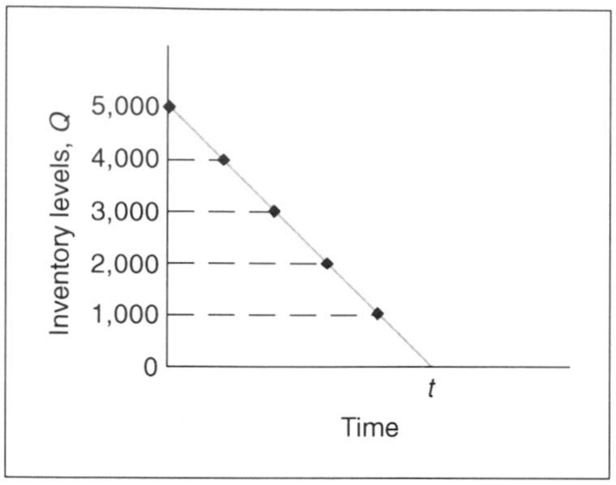

Alternatively, we can sum just the two extreme points (which also encompass the range of time, t) and divide by 2. This also equals 2,500. This computation is the same, in principle, as adding Q and 0 and dividing by 2, which equals $Q/2$. This relationship for average inventory is maintained, regardless of the size of the order, Q, or the frequency of orders (i.e., the time period, t). Thus, the average inventory on an *annual basis* is also $Q/2$, as shown in Figure 4.

Figure 4
Annual average inventory

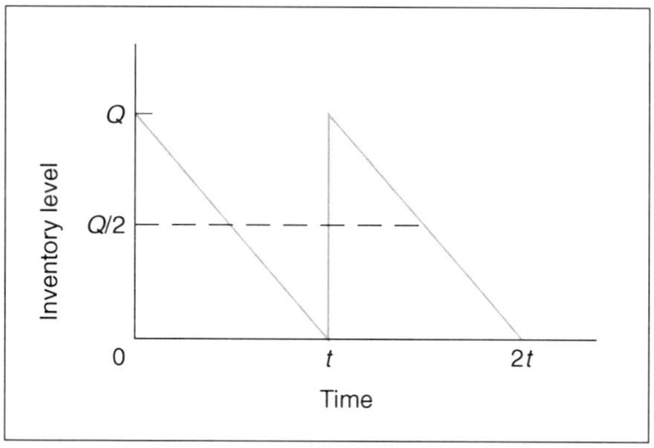

Now that we know that the amount of inventory available *on an annual basis* is the average inventory, $Q/2$, we can determine the total annual carrying cost by multiplying the average number of units in inventory by the carrying cost per unit per year, C_c:

$$\text{annual carrying cost} = C_c \frac{Q}{2}$$

Ordering Cost

The total annual ordering cost is computed by multiplying the cost per order, designated as C_o, by the number of orders per year. Because annual demand is assumed to be known and constant, the number of orders will be D/Q, where Q is the order size:

$$\text{annual ordering cost} = C_o \frac{D}{Q}$$

The only variable in this equation is Q; both C_o and D are constant parameters. In other words, demand is known with certainty. Thus, the relative magnitude of the ordering cost is dependent upon the order size.

Total Inventory Cost

The total annual inventory cost is simply the sum of the ordering and carrying costs:

$$TC = C_o \frac{D}{Q} + C_c \frac{Q}{2}$$

These cost functions are shown in Figure 5. Notice the inverse relationship between ordering cost and carrying cost, resulting in a convex total cost curve.

Figure 5
The EOQ cost model

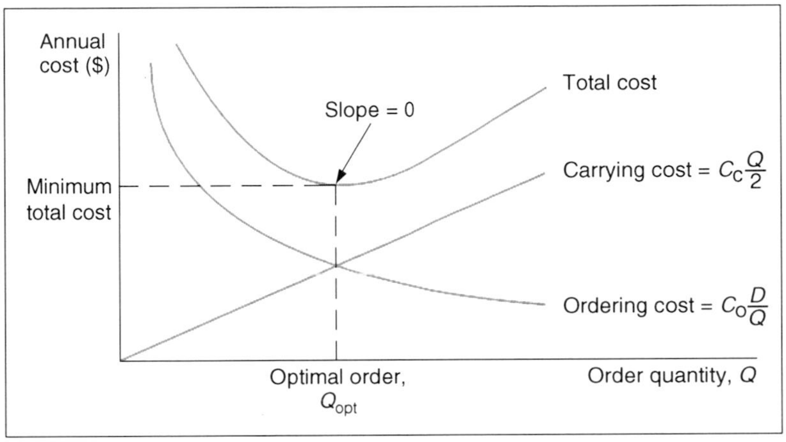

Observe the general upward trend of the total carrying cost curve. As the order size Q (shown on the horizontal axis) increases, the total carrying cost (shown on the vertical axis) increases. This is logical because larger orders will result in more units carried in inventory. Next, observe the ordering cost curve in Figure 5. As the order size, Q, increases, the ordering cost *decreases* (just the opposite of what occurred with the carrying cost). This is logical, because an increase in the size of the orders will result in fewer orders being placed each year. Because one cost increases as the other decreases, the result of summing the two costs is a convex total cost curve.

The optimal value of Q corresponds to the lowest point on the total cost curve.

The optimal order quantity occurs at the point in Figure 5 where the total cost curve is at a minimum, which also coincides exactly with the point where the ordering cost curve intersects with the carrying cost curve. This enables us to determine the optimal value of Q by equating the two cost functions and solving for Q, as follows:

$$C_o \frac{D}{Q} = C_c \frac{Q}{2}$$

$$Q^2 = \frac{2C_oD}{C_c}$$

$$Q_{opt} = \sqrt{\frac{2C_oD}{C_c}}$$

Alternatively, the optimal value of Q can be determined by differentiating the total cost curve with respect to Q, setting the resulting function equal to zero (the slope at the minimum point on the total cost curve), and solving for Q, as follows:

$$TC = C_o \frac{D}{Q} + C_c \frac{Q}{2}$$

$$\frac{\delta TC}{\delta Q} = -\frac{C_oD}{Q^2} + \frac{C_c}{2}$$

$$0 = -\frac{C_o D}{Q^2} + \frac{C_c}{2}$$

$$Q_{opt} = \sqrt{\frac{2C_o D}{C_c}}$$

The total minimum cost is determined by substituting the value for the optimal order size, Q_{opt}, into the total cost equation:

$$TC_{min} = \frac{C_o D}{Q_{opt}} + C_o \frac{Q_{opt}}{2}$$

We will use the following example to demonstrate how the optimal value of Q is computed. The I-75 Carpet Discount Store in north Georgia stocks carpet in its warehouse and sells it through an adjoining showroom. The store keeps several brands and styles of carpet in stock; however, its biggest seller is Super Shag carpet. The store wants to determine the optimal order size and total inventory cost for this brand of carpet, given an estimated annual demand of 10,000 yards of carpet, an annual carrying cost of \$0.75 per yard, and an ordering cost of \$150. The store would also like to know the number of orders that will be made annually and the time between orders (i.e., the order cycle), given that the store is open every day except Sunday, Thanksgiving Day, and Christmas Day (that is not on a Sunday).

We can summarize the model parameters as follows:

$$\begin{aligned} C_c &= \$0.75 \\ C_o &= \$150 \\ D &= 10{,}000 \text{ yd.} \end{aligned}$$

The optimal order size is computed as follows:

$$\begin{aligned} Q_{opt} &= \sqrt{\frac{2C_o D}{C_c}} \\ &= \sqrt{\frac{2(150)(10{,}000)}{(0.75)}} \\ Q_{opt} &= 2{,}000 \text{ yd.} \end{aligned}$$

The total annual inventory cost is determined by substituting Q_{opt} into the total cost formula, as follows:

$$\begin{aligned} TC_{min} &= C_o \frac{D}{Q_{opt}} + C_c \frac{Q_{opt}}{2} \\ &= (150)\frac{10{,}000}{2{,}000} + (0.75)\frac{(2{,}000)}{2} \\ &= \$750 + 750 \\ TC_{min} &= \$1{,}500 \end{aligned}$$

The number of orders per year is computed as follows:

$$\text{number of orders per year} = \frac{D}{Q_{opt}} = \frac{10{,}000}{2{,}000} = 5$$

Given that the store is open 311 days annually (365 days minus 52 Sundays, plus Thanksgiving and Christmas), the order cycle is determined as follows:

$$\text{order cycle time} = \frac{311 \text{ days}}{D/Q_{opt}} = \frac{311}{5} = 62.2 \text{ store days}$$

The EOQ model is robust; because Q is a square root, errors in the estimation of D, C_c, and C_o are dampened.

It should be noted that the optimal order quantity determined in this example, and in general, is an approximate value because it is based on estimates of carrying and ordering costs as well as uncertain demand (although all these parameters are treated as known, certain values in the EOQ model). Thus, in practice it is acceptable to round off the Q values to the nearest whole number. The precision of a decimal place generally is neither necessary nor appropriate. In addition, because the optimal order quantity is computed from a square root, errors or variations in the cost parameters and demand tend to be dampened. For instance, if the order cost had actually been a third higher, or \$200, the resulting optimal order size would have varied by about 15% (i.e., 2,390 yards instead of 2,000 yards). In addition, variations in both inventory costs will tend to offset each other because they have an inverse relationship. As a result, the EOQ model is relatively robust, or resilient to errors in the cost estimates and demand, which has tended to enhance its popularity.

EOQ Analysis Over Time

One aspect of inventory analysis that can be confusing is the time frame encompassed by the analysis. Therefore, we will digress for just a moment to discuss this aspect of EOQ analysis.

Recall that previously we developed the EOQ model "regardless of order size, Q, and time, *t*." Now we will verify this condition. We will do so by developing our EOQ model on a *monthly basis*. First, demand is equal to 833.3 yards per month (which we determined by dividing the annual demand of 10,000 yards by 12 months). Next, by dividing the annual carrying cost, C_c, of \$0.75 by 12, we get the monthly (per-unit) carrying cost: $C_c = \$0.0625$. (The ordering cost of \$150 is not related to time.) We thus have the values

$$\begin{aligned} D &= 833.3 \text{ yd. per month} \\ C_c &= \$0.0625 \text{ per yd. per month} \\ C_o &= \$150 \text{ per order} \end{aligned}$$

which we can substitute into our EOQ formula:

$$\begin{aligned} Q_{opt} &= \sqrt{\frac{2C_oD}{C_c}} \\ &= \sqrt{\frac{2(150)(833.3)}{(0.0625)}} = 2{,}000 \text{ yd.} \end{aligned}$$

This is the same optimal order size that we determined on an annual basis. Now we will compute total monthly inventory cost:

$$\begin{aligned} \text{total monthly inventory cost} &= C_c\frac{Q_{opt}}{2} + C_o\frac{D}{Q_{opt}} \\ &= (\$0.0625)\frac{(2{,}000)}{2} + (\$150)\frac{(833.3)}{(2{,}000)} \\ &= \$125 \text{ per month} \end{aligned}$$

To convert this monthly total cost to an annual cost, we multiply it by 12 (months):

$$\text{total annual inventory cost} = (\$125)(12) = \$1{,}500$$

This brief example demonstrates that regardless of the time period encompassed by EOQ analysis, the economic order quantity (Q_{opt}) is the same.

The EOQ Model with Noninstantaneous Receipt

*The **noninstantaneous receipt model** relaxes the assumption that Q is received all at once.*

A variation of the basic EOQ model is achieved when the assumption that orders are received all at once is relaxed. This version of the EOQ model is known as the **noninstantaneous receipt model,** also referred to as the *gradual usage*, or **production lot size, model.** In this EOQ variation, the order quantity is received gradually over time and the inventory level is depleted at the same time it is being replenished. This is a situation most commonly found when the inventory user is also the producer, as, for example, in a manufacturing operation where a part is produced to use in a larger assembly. This situation can also occur when orders are delivered gradually over time or the retailer and producer of a product are one and the same. The noninstantaneous receipt model is illustrated graphically in Figure 6, which highlights the difference between this variation and the basic EOQ model.

Figure 6

The EOQ model with noninstantaneous order receipt

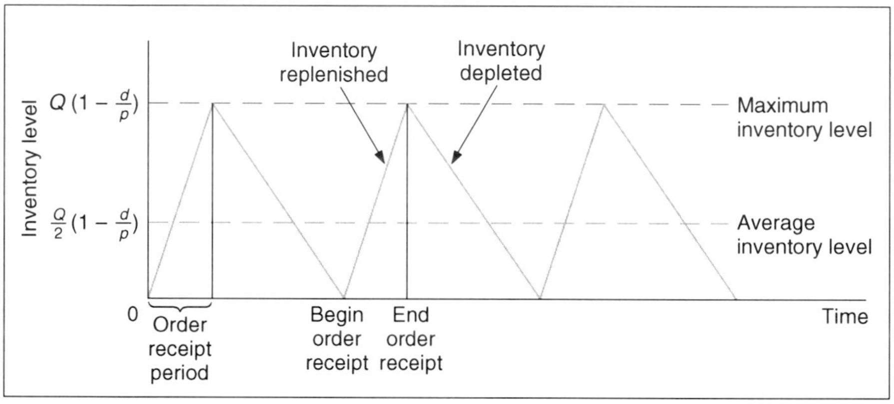

The ordering cost component of the basic EOQ model does not change as a result of the gradual replenishment of the inventory level because it is dependent only on the number of annual orders. However, the carrying cost component is not the same for this model variation because average inventory is different. In the basic EOQ model, average inventory was half the maximum inventory level, or $Q/2$, but in this variation, the maximum inventory level is not simply Q; it is an amount somewhat lower than Q, adjusted for the fact that the order quantity is depleted during the order receipt period.

To determine the average inventory level, we define the following parameters that are unique to this model:

p = daily rate at which the order is received over time, also known as the *production rate*
d = the daily rate at which inventory is demanded

The demand rate cannot exceed the production rate because we are still assuming that no shortages are possible, and if $d = p$, then there is no order size because items are used as fast as they are produced. Thus, for this model, the production rate must exceed the demand rate, or $p > d$.

Figure 6 shows that the time required to receive an order is the order quantity divided by the rate at which the order is received, or Q/p. For example, if the order size is 100 units and the production rate, p, is 20 units per day, the order will be received in 5 days. The amount of inventory that will be depleted or used up during this time period is determined by multiplying by the demand rate, or $(Q/p)d$. For example, if it takes 5 days to receive the order and during this time inventory is depleted at the rate of 2 units per day, then a total of 10 units is used. As a result, the maximum amount of inventory that is on hand is the order size minus the amount depleted during the receipt period, computed as follows and shown earlier in Figure 6:

$$\begin{aligned}\text{maximum inventory level} &= Q - \frac{Q}{p}d \\ &= Q\left(1 - \frac{d}{p}\right)\end{aligned}$$

Because this is the maximum inventory level, the average inventory level is determined by dividing this amount by 2, as follows:

$$\begin{aligned}\text{average inventory level} &= \frac{1}{2}\left[Q\left(1 - \frac{d}{p}\right)\right] \\ &= \frac{Q}{2}\left(1 - \frac{d}{p}\right)\end{aligned}$$

The total carrying cost, using this function for average inventory, is

$$\text{total carrying cost} = C_c\frac{Q}{2}\left(1 - \frac{d}{p}\right)$$

Thus, the total annual inventory cost is determined according to the following formula:

$$TC = C_o\frac{D}{Q} + C_c\frac{Q}{2}\left(1 - \frac{d}{p}\right)$$

The total inventory cost is a function of two other costs, just as in our previous EOQ model. Thus, the minimum inventory cost occurs when the total cost curve is lowest and where the carrying cost curve and ordering cost curve intersect (see Figure 5). Therefore, to find optimal Q_{opt}, we equate total carrying cost with total ordering cost:

$$\begin{aligned}C_c\frac{Q}{2}\left(1 - \frac{d}{p}\right) &= C_o\frac{D}{Q} \\ C_c\frac{Q^2}{2}\left(1 - \frac{d}{p}\right) &= C_oD \\ Q_{opt} &= \sqrt{\frac{2C_oD}{C_c(1 - d/p)}}\end{aligned}$$

For our previous example we will now assume that the I-75 Carpet Discount Store has its own manufacturing facility, in which it produces Super Shag carpet. We will further assume that the ordering cost, C_o, is the cost of setting up the production process to make Super Shag carpet. Recall that C_c = \$0.75 per yard and D = 10,000 yards per year. The manufacturing facility operates the same days the store is open (i.e., 311 days) and produces 150 yards of the carpet per day. The optimal order size, the total inventory cost, the length of time to receive an order, the number of orders per year, and the maximum inventory level are computed as follows:

$$\begin{aligned}C_o &= \$150 \\ C_c &= \$0.75 \text{ per unit} \\ D &= 10{,}000 \text{ yd.} \\ d &= \frac{10{,}000}{311} = 32.2 \text{ yd. per day} \\ p &= 150 \text{ yd. per day}\end{aligned}$$

The optimal order size is determined as follows:

$$Q_{opt} = \sqrt{\frac{2C_oD}{C_c\left(1 - \frac{d}{p}\right)}}$$

$$= \sqrt{\frac{2(150)(10{,}000)}{0.75\left(1 - \frac{32.2}{150}\right)}}$$

$$Q_{opt} = 2{,}256.8 \text{ yd.}$$

This value is substituted into the following formula to determine total minimum annual inventory cost:

$$TC_{min} = C_o\frac{D}{Q} + C_c\frac{Q}{2}\left(1 - \frac{d}{p}\right)$$

$$= (150)\frac{(10{,}000)}{(2{,}256.8)} + (0.75)\frac{(2{,}256.8)}{2}\left(1 - \frac{32.2}{150}\right)$$

$$= \$1{,}329$$

The length of time to receive an order for this type of manufacturing operation is commonly called the length of the *production run*. It is computed as follows:

$$\text{production run length} = \frac{Q}{p} = \frac{2{,}256.8}{150} = 15.05 \text{ days}$$

The number of orders per year is actually the number of production runs that will be made, computed as follows:

$$\text{number of production runs} = \frac{D}{Q}$$

$$= \frac{10{,}000}{2{,}256.8}$$

$$= 4.43 \text{ runs}$$

Finally, the maximum inventory level is computed as follows:

$$\text{maximum inventory level} = Q\left(1 - \frac{d}{p}\right)$$

$$= 2{,}256.8\left(1 - \frac{32.2}{150}\right)$$

$$= 1{,}755 \text{ yd.}$$

The EOQ Model with Shortages

The EOQ model with shortages relaxes the assumption that shortages cannot exist.

One of the assumptions of our basic EOQ model is that shortages and back ordering are not allowed. The third model variation that we will describe, the EOQ model with shortages, relaxes this assumption. However, it will be assumed that all demand not met because of inventory shortage can be back-ordered and delivered to the customer later. Thus, all demand is eventually met. The EOQ model with shortages is illustrated in Figure 7.

Figure 7
The EOQ model with shortages

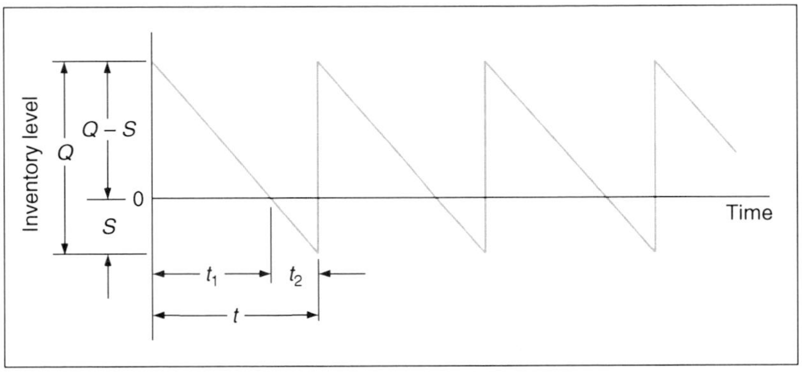

Because back-ordered demand, or shortages, S, are filled when inventory is replenished, the maximum inventory level does not reach Q, but instead a level equal to $Q - S$. It can be seen from Figure 7 that the amount of inventory on hand $(Q - S)$ decreases as the amount of the shortage increases, and vice versa. Therefore, the cost associated with shortages, which we described earlier in this chapter as primarily the cost of lost sales and lost customer goodwill, has an inverse relationship to carrying costs. As the order size, Q, increases, the carrying cost increases and the shortage cost declines. This relationship between carrying and shortage cost as well as ordering cost is shown in Figure 8.

Figure 8
Cost model with shortages

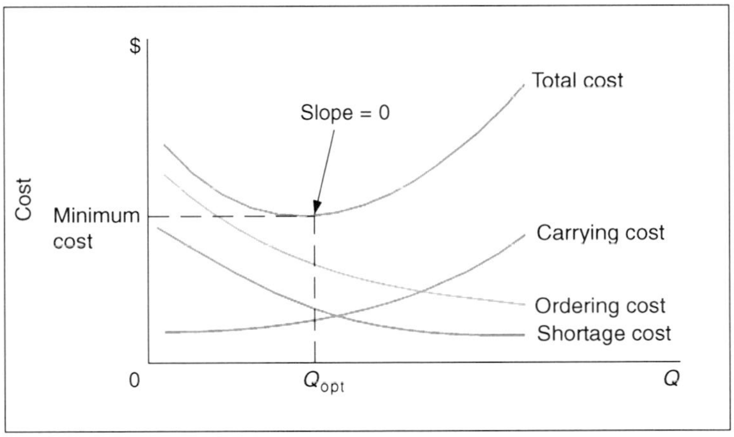

We will forgo the lengthy derivation of the individual cost components of the EOQ model with shortages, which requires the application of plane geometry to the graph in Figure 8. The individual cost functions are provided as follows, where S equals the shortage level and C_s equals the annual per-unit cost of shortages:

$$\text{total shortage cost} = C_s \frac{S^2}{2Q}$$

$$\text{total carrying cost} = C_c \frac{(Q - S)^2}{2Q}$$

$$\text{total ordering cost} = C_o \frac{D}{Q}$$

Combining these individual cost components results in the total inventory cost formula:

$$TC = C_s \frac{S^2}{2Q} + C_c \frac{(Q - S)^2}{2Q} + C_o \frac{D}{Q}$$

You will notice in Figure 8 that the three cost component curves do not intersect at a common point, as was the case in the basic EOQ model. As a result, the only way to determine the optimal order size *and the optimal shortage level, S,* is to differentiate the total cost function with respect to Q and S, set the two resulting equations equal to zero, and solve them simultaneously. Doing so results in the following formulas for the optimal order quantity and shortage level:

$$Q_{opt} = \sqrt{\frac{2C_oD}{C_c}\left(\frac{C_s + C_c}{C_s}\right)}$$

$$S_{opt} = Q_{opt}\left(\frac{C_c}{C_c + C_s}\right)$$

For example, we will now assume that the I-75 Carpet Discount Store allows shortages and the shortage cost, C_s, is \$2 per yard per year. All other costs and demand remain the same ($C_c = \$0.75$, $C_o = \$150$, and $D = 10{,}000$ yd.). The optimal order size and shortage level and total minimum annual inventory cost are computed as follows:

$$\begin{aligned}
C_o &= \$150 \\
C_c &= \$0.75 \text{ per yd.} \\
C_s &= \$2 \text{ per yd.} \\
D &= 10{,}000 \text{ yd.} \\
Q_{opt} &= \sqrt{\frac{2C_oD}{C_c}\left(\frac{C_s + C_c}{C_s}\right)} \\
&= \sqrt{\frac{2(150)(10{,}000)}{0.75}\left(\frac{2 + 0.75}{2}\right)} \\
&= 2{,}345.2 \text{ yd} \\
S_{opt} &= Q_{opt}\left(\frac{C_c}{C_c + C_s}\right) \\
&= 2{,}345.2\left(\frac{0.75}{2 + 0.75}\right) \\
&= 639.6 \text{ yd} \\
TC_{min} &= \frac{C_sS^2}{2Q} + \frac{C_c(Q - S)^2}{2Q} + C_o\frac{D}{Q} \\
&= \frac{(2)(639.6)^2}{2(2{,}345.2)} + \frac{(0.75)(1{,}705.6)^2}{2(2{,}345.2)} + \frac{(150)(10{,}000)}{2{,}345.2} \\
&= \$174.44 + 465.16 + 639.60 \\
&= \$1{,}279.20
\end{aligned}$$

Several additional parameters of the EOQ model with shortages can be computed for this example, as follows:

$$\text{number of orders} = \frac{D}{Q} = \frac{10{,}000}{2{,}345.2} = 4.26 \text{ orders per year}$$

$$\text{maximum inventory level} = Q - S = 2{,}345.2 - 639.6 = 1{,}705.6 \text{ yd.}$$

The time between orders, identified as t in Figure 7, is computed as follows:

$$t = \frac{\text{days per year}}{\text{number of orders}} = \frac{311}{4.26} = 73.0 \text{ days between orders}$$

The time during which inventory is on hand, t_1 in Figure 7, and the time during which there is a shortage, t_2 in Figure 7, during each order cycle can be computed using the following formulas:

$$\begin{aligned} t_1 &= \frac{Q - S}{D} \\ &= \frac{2{,}345.2 - 639.6}{10{,}000} \\ &= 0.171 \text{ year, or } 53.2 \text{ days} \\ t_2 &= \frac{S}{D} \\ &= \frac{639.6}{10{,}000} \\ &= 0.064 \text{ year, or } 19.9 \text{ days} \end{aligned}$$

Management Science Application

Determining Inventory Ordering Policy at Dell

Dell Inc., the world's largest computer-systems company, bypasses retailers and sells directly to customers via phone or the Internet. After an order is processed, it is sent to one of its assembly plants in Austin, Texas, where the product is built, tested, and packaged within 8 hours.

Dell carries very little components inventory itself. Technology changes occur so fast that holding inventory can be a huge liability; some components lose 0.5% to 2.0% of their value per week. In addition, many of Dell's suppliers are located in Southeast Asia, and their shipping times to Austin range from 7 days for air transport to 30 days for water and ground transport. To compensate for these factors, Dell's suppliers keep inventory in small warehouses called "revolvers" (for revolving inventory), which are a few miles from Dell's assembly plants. Dell keeps very little inventory at its own plants, so it withdraws inventory from the revolvers every few hours, and most of Dell's suppliers deliver to their revolvers three times per week.

The cost of carrying inventory by Dell's suppliers is ultimately reflected in the final price of a computer. Thus, in order to maintain a competitive price advantage in the market, Dell strives to help its suppliers reduce inventory costs. Dell has a vendor-managed inventory (VMI) arrangement with its suppliers, who decide how much to order and when to send their orders to the revolvers. Dell's suppliers order in batches (to offset ordering costs), using a continuous ordering system with a batch order size, Q, and a reorder point, R, where R is the sum of the inventory on order and a safety stock. The order size estimate, based on long-term data and forecasts, is held constant. Dell sets target inventory levels for its suppliers—typically 10 days of inventory—and keeps track of how much suppliers deviate from these targets and reports this information back to suppliers so that they can make adjustments accordingly.

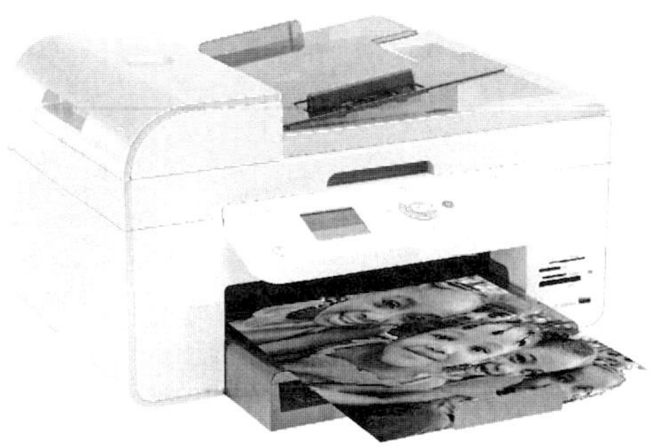

Source: R. Kapuscinski, R. Zhang, P. Carbonneau, R. Moore, and B. Reeves, "Inventory Decisions in Dell's Supply Chain," *Interfaces* 34, no. 3 (May–June 2004): 191–205.

EOQ Analysis with QM for Windows

QM for Windows has modules for all the EOQ models we have presented, including the basic model, the noninstantaneous receipt model, and the model with shortages. To demonstrate the capabilities of this program, we will use our basic EOQ example, for which the solution output summary is shown in Exhibit 1.

Exhibit 1

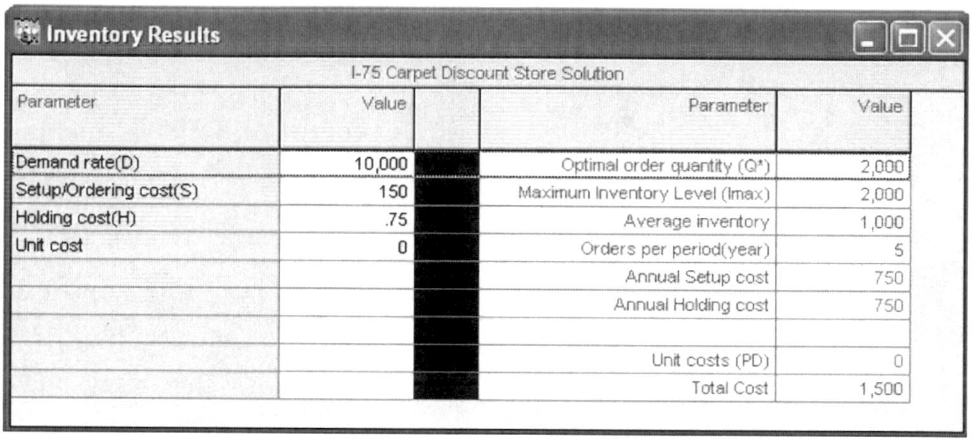

Inventory Results

I-75 Carpet Discount Store Solution

Parameter	Value		Parameter	Value
Demand rate(D)	10,000		Optimal order quantity (Q*)	2,000
Setup/Ordering cost(S)	150		Maximum Inventory Level (Imax)	2,000
Holding cost(H)	.75		Average inventory	1,000
Unit cost	0		Orders per period(year)	5
			Annual Setup cost	750
			Annual Holding cost	750
			Unit costs (PD)	0
			Total Cost	1,500

EOQ Analysis with Excel and Excel QM

Exhibit 2 shows an Excel spreadsheet set up to perform EOQ analysis for our noninstantaneous receipt model example. The parameters of the model have been input in cells **D3:D8**, and all the formulas for optimal Q, total cost, and so on have been embedded in cells **D10:D14**. Notice that the formula for computing optimal Q in cell D10 is shown on the formula bar at the top of the screen.

Exhibit 2

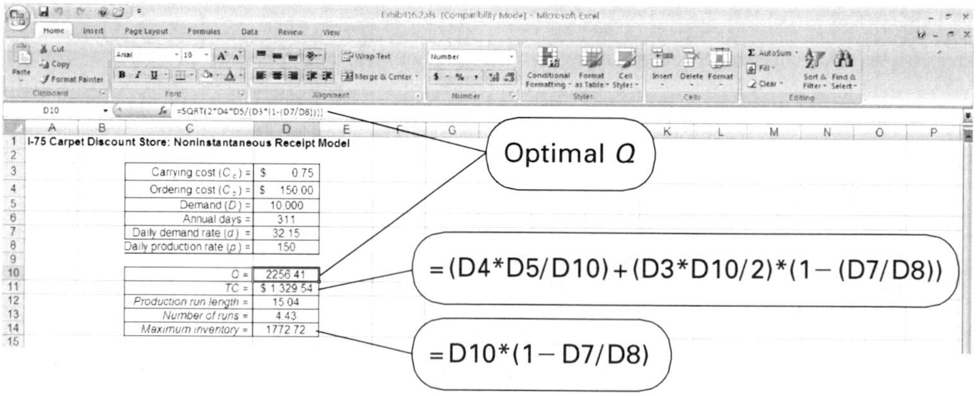

Excel QM includes a set of spreadsheet macros for "Inventory" that includes EOQ analysis. After Excel QM is activated, the "Excel QM" menu is accessed by clicking on

"Add-Ins" on the menu bar at the top of the spreadsheet. Clicking on "Inventory" from this menu results in a Spreadsheet Initialization window, in which you enter the problem title and the form of holding (or carrying) cost. Clicking on "OK" will result in the spreadsheet shown in Exhibit 3. Initially, this spreadsheet will have example values in the data cells **B8:B13**. Thus, the first step in using this macro is to type in cells **B8:B13** the data for the noninstantaneous receipt model for our I-75 Carpet Discount Store problem. The model results are computed automatically in cells **B16:B26** from formulas already embedded in the spreadsheet.

Exhibit 3

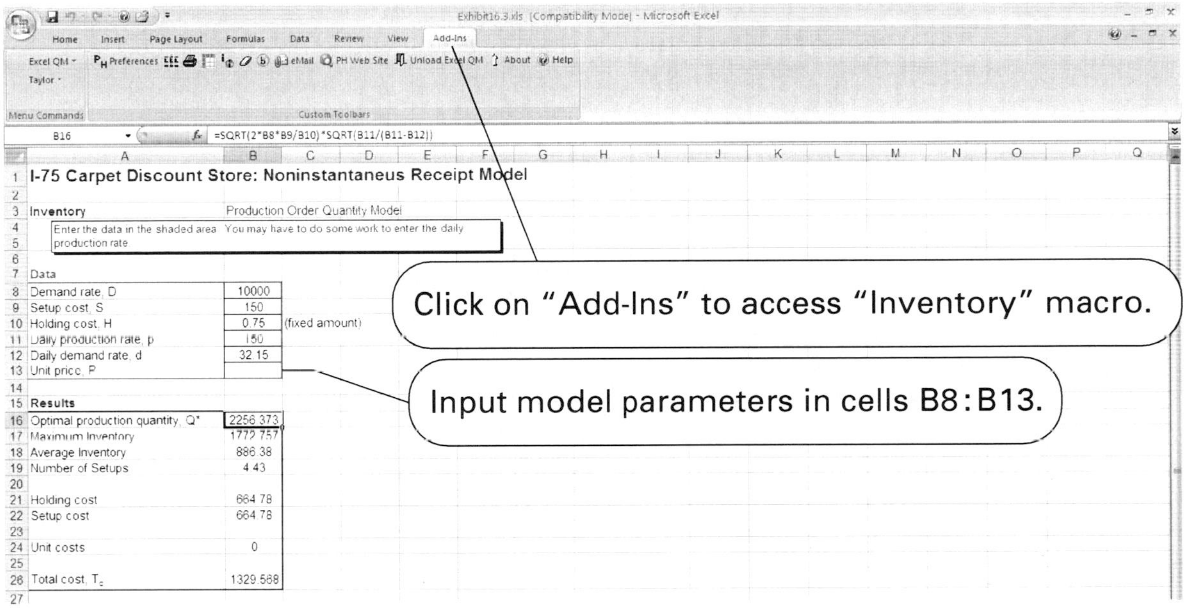

Quantity Discounts

It is often possible for a customer to receive a price discount on an item if a predetermined number of units are ordered. For example, occasionally in the back of a magazine you might see an advertisement for a firm that will produce a coffee mug (or hat) with a company or organizational logo on it, and the price will be $5 per mug if you purchase 100, $4 per mug if you purchase 200, or $3 per mug if you purchase 500 or more. Many manufacturing companies receive price discounts for ordering materials and supplies in high volume, and retail stores receive price discounts for ordering merchandise in large quantities.

Determining whether an order size with a discount is more cost-effective than optimal Q.

The basic EOQ model can be used to determine the optimal order size with quantity discounts; however, the application of the model is slightly altered. The total inventory cost function must now include the purchase price for the order, as follows:

$$TC = C_o \frac{D}{Q} + C_c \frac{Q}{2} + PD$$

where

$P =$ per unit price of the item
$D =$ annual demand

Purchase price was not considered as part of our basic EOQ formulation earlier because it had no real impact on the optimal order size. *PD* in the foregoing formula is a constant value that would not alter the basic shape of the total cost curve (i.e., the minimum point on the cost curve would still be at the same location, corresponding to the same value of *Q*). Thus, the optimal order size will be the same, no matter what the purchase price. However, when a discount price is available, it is associated with a specific order size that may be different from the optimal order size, and the customer must evaluate the trade-off between possibly higher carrying costs with the discount quantity versus EOQ cost. As a result, the purchase price does influence the order size decision when a discount is available.

Quantity discounts are evaluated with constant C_c and as a percentage of price.

Quantity discounts can be evaluated using the basic EOQ model under two different scenarios—with constant carrying costs and with carrying costs as a percentage of the purchase price. It is not uncommon for carrying costs to be determined as a percentage of purchase price, although it was not considered as such in our previous basic EOQ model. Carrying cost very well could have been a percentage of purchase price, but it was reflected as a constant value, C_c, in the basic EOQ model because the purchase price was not part of the EOQ formula. However, in the case of a quantity discount, carrying cost will vary with the change in price if it is computed as a percentage of purchase price.

Quantity Discounts with Constant Carrying Costs

In the EOQ cost model with constant carrying costs, the optimal order size, Q_{opt}, is the same, regardless of the discount price. Although total cost decreases with each discount in price because ordering and carrying cost are constant, the optimal order size, Q_{opt}, does not change. The total cost with Q_{opt} must be compared with any lower total cost with a discount price to see which is the minimum.

The following example will illustrate the evaluation of an EOQ model with a quantity discount when the carrying cost is a constant value. Comptek Computers wants to reduce a large stock of personal computers it is discontinuing. It has offered the University Bookstore at Tech a quantity discount pricing schedule if the store will purchase the personal computers in volume, as follows:

Quantity	***Price***
1–49	\$1,400
50–89	1,100
90+	900

The annual carrying cost for the bookstore for a computer is \$190, the ordering cost is \$2,500, and annual demand for this particular model is estimated to be 200 units. The bookstore wants to determine whether it should take advantage of this discount or order the basic EOQ order size.

First, determine both the optimal order size and the total cost by using the basic EOQ model:

$$\begin{aligned} C_o &= \$2{,}500 \\ C_c &= \$190 \text{ per unit} \\ D &= 200 \\ Q_{opt} &= \sqrt{\frac{2C_oD}{C_c}} \\ &= \sqrt{\frac{2(2{,}500)(200)}{190}} \\ Q_{opt} &= 72.5 \end{aligned}$$

This order size is eligible for the first discount of \$1,100; therefore, this price is used to compute total cost, as follows:

$$TC = \frac{C_oD}{Q_{opt}} + C_c\frac{Q_{opt}}{2} + PD$$
$$= \frac{(2{,}500)(200)}{(72.5)} + (190)\frac{(72.5)}{2} + (1{,}100)(200)$$
$$TC_{min} = \$233{,}784$$

Because there is a discount for an order size larger than 72.5, this total cost of \$233,784 must be compared with total cost with an order size of 90 and a price of \$900, as follows:

$$TC = \frac{C_oD}{Q} + C_c\frac{Q}{2} + PD$$
$$= \frac{(2{,}500)(200)}{(90)} + \frac{(190)(90)}{2} + (900)(200)$$
$$= \$194{,}105$$

Because this total cost is lower (\$194,105 < \$233,784), the maximum discount price should be taken and 90 units ordered.

Quantity Discounts with Constant Carrying Costs as a Percentage of Price

The difference between the model in the previous section and the quantity discount model with carrying cost as a percentage of price is that there is a different optimal order size, Q_{opt}, for each price discount. This requires that the optimal order size with a discount be determined a little differently from the case for a constant carrying cost.

The optimal order size and total cost are determined by using the basic EOQ model for the case with no quantity discount. This total cost value is then compared with the various discount quantity order sizes to determine the minimum cost order size. However, once this minimum cost order size is determined, it must be compared with the EOQ-determined order size for the specific discount price because the EOQ order size, Q_{opt}, will change for every discount level.

Reconsider our previous example, except now assume that the annual carrying cost for a computer at the University Bookstore is 15% of the purchase price. Using the same discount pricing schedule, determine the optimal order size.

The annual carrying cost is determined as follows:

Quantity	*Price*	*Carrying Cost*
0–49	\$1,400	1,400(.15) = \$210
50–89	1,100	1,100(.15) = 165
90+	900	900(.15) = 135

$$C_o = \$2{,}500$$
$$D = 200 \text{ computers per year}$$

First, compute the optimal order size for the purchase price without a discount and with $C_c = \$210$, as follows:

$$Q_{opt} = \sqrt{\frac{2C_oD}{C_c}}$$
$$= \sqrt{\frac{2(2{,}500)(200)}{210}}$$
$$Q_{opt} = 69$$

Because this order size exceeds 49 units, it is not feasible for this price, and a lower total cost will automatically be achieved with the first price discount of \$1,100. However, the optimal order size will be different for this price discount because carrying cost is no longer constant. Thus, the new order size is computed as follows:

$$Q_{\text{opt}} = \sqrt{\frac{2(2{,}500)(200)}{165}} = 77.8$$

This order size is the true optimum for this price discount instead of the 50 units required to receive the discount price; thus, it will result in the minimum total cost, computed as follows:

$$\begin{aligned} TC &= \frac{C_o D}{Q} + C_c\frac{Q}{2} + PD \\ &= \frac{(2{,}500)(200)}{77.8} + 165\frac{(77.8)}{2} + (1{,}100)(200) \\ &= \$232{,}845 \end{aligned}$$

Management Science Application

Quantity Discount Orders at Mars

Mars is one of the world's largest privately owned companies, with over \$14 billion in annual sales. It has grown from making and selling buttercream candies door-to-door to a global business spanning 100 countries that includes food, pet care, beverage vending, and electronic payment systems. It produces such well-known products as Mars candies, M&M's, Snickers, and Uncle Ben's rice.

Mars relies on a small number of suppliers for each of the huge number of materials it uses in its products. One way that Mars purchases materials from its suppliers is through online electronic auctions, in which Mars buyers negotiate bids for orders from suppliers. The most important purchases are those of high value and large volume, for which the suppliers provide quantity discounts. The suppliers provide a pricing schedule that includes quantity ranges associated with each price level. Such quantity-discount auctions are tailored (by online brokers) for industries in which volume discounts are common, such as bulk chemicals and agricultural commodities.

A Mars buyer selects the bids that minimize total purchasing costs, subject to several rules: There must be a minimum and maximum number of suppliers so that Mars is not dependent on too few suppliers nor loses quality control by having too many; there must be a maximum amount purchased from each supplier to limit the influence of any one supplier; and a minimum amount must be ordered to avoid economically inefficient orders (i.e., less than a full truckload).

Source: G. Hohner, J. Rich, E. Ng, A. Davenport, J. Kalagnanam, H. Lee, and C. An, "Combinatorial and Quantity-Discount Procurement Auctions Benefit Mars, Incorporated and Its Suppliers," *Interfaces* 33, no. 1 (January–February 2003): 23–35.

Will Burgess/Reuters Landov Media

This cost must still be compared with the total cost for lowest discount price ($900) and order quantity (90 units), computed as follows:

$$TC = \frac{(2{,}500)(200)}{90} + \frac{(135)(90)}{2} + (900)(200)$$
$$= \$191{,}630$$

Because this total cost is lower ($\$191{,}630 < \$232{,}845$), the maximum discount price should be taken and 90 units ordered. However, as before, we still must check to see whether there is a new optimal order size for this discount that will result in an even lower cost. The optimal order size with $C_c = \$135$ is computed as follows:

$$Q_{opt} = \sqrt{\frac{2(2{,}500)(200)}{135}} = 86.1$$

Because this order size is less than the 90 units required to receive the discount, it is not feasible; thus, the optimal order size is 90 units.

Quantity Discount Model Solution with QM for Windows

QM for Windows has the capability to perform EOQ analysis with quantity discounts when carrying costs are constant. Exhibit 4 shows the solution summary for our University Bookstore example.

Exhibit 4

Inventory Results

University Bookstore Example Solution

Parameter	Value				Parameter	Value
Demand rate(D)	200	XXXXXXX	XXXXXXX		Optimal order quantity (Q*)	90
Setup/Ordering cost(S)	2,500	XXXXXXX	XXXXXXX		Maximum Inventory Level	90
Holding cost(H)	190	XXXXXXX	XXXXXXX		Average inventory	45
					Orders per period(year)	2.2222
	From	To	Price		Annual Setup cost	5,555.556
1	1	49	1,400		Annual Holding cost	8,550
2	50	89	1,100			
3	90	999,999	900		Unit costs (PD)	180,000
					Total Cost	194,105.6

Quantity Discount Model Solution with Excel

It is also possible to use Excel to solve the quantity discount model with constant carrying costs. Exhibit 5 shows the Excel solution screen for the University Bookstore example. Notice that the selection of the appropriate order size, Q, that results in the minimum total cost for each discount range is determined by the formulas embedded in cells E8, E9, and E10. For example, the formula for the first quantity discount range, 1–49, is embedded in cell E8 and shown on the formula bar at the top of the screen, **=IF(D8>=B8,D8,B8)**. This means that if the discount order size in cell D8 (i.e., $Q = 72.55$) is greater than or equal to the quantity in cell B8 (i.e., 1), the quantity in cell D8 (72.55) is selected; otherwise, the amount in cell B8 is selected. The formulas in cells E9 and E10 are constructed similarly. The result is that the order quantity for the final discount range, $Q = 90$, is selected.

Exhibit 5

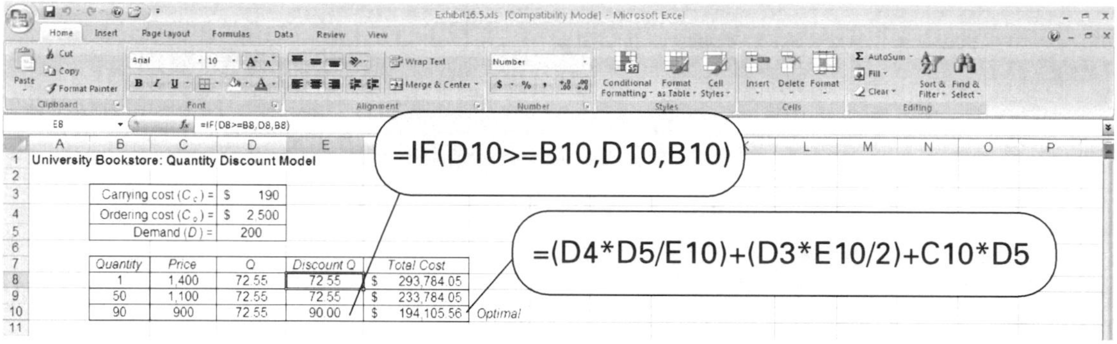

Carrying cost (C_c) =	$ 190
Ordering cost (C_o) =	$ 2,500
Demand (D) =	200

Quantity	Price	Q	Discount Q	Total Cost
1	1,400	72.55	72.55	$ 293,784.05
50	1,100	72.55	72.55	$ 233,784.05
90	900	72.55	90.00	$ 194,105.56

Reorder Point

In our presentation of the basic EOQ model in the previous section, we addressed one of the two primary questions related to inventory management: *How much should be ordered?* In this section we will discuss the other aspect of inventory management: *When to order?* The determinant of when to order in a continuous inventory system is the **reorder point**, the inventory level at which a new order is placed.

The concept of lead time is illustrated graphically in Figure 9. Notice that the order must be made prior to the time when the level of inventory falls to zero. Because demand is consuming the inventory while the order is being shipped, the order must be made while there is enough inventory in stock to meet demand during the lead-time period. This level of inventory is referred to as the *reorder point* and is so designated in Figure 9.

Figure 9
Reorder point and lead time

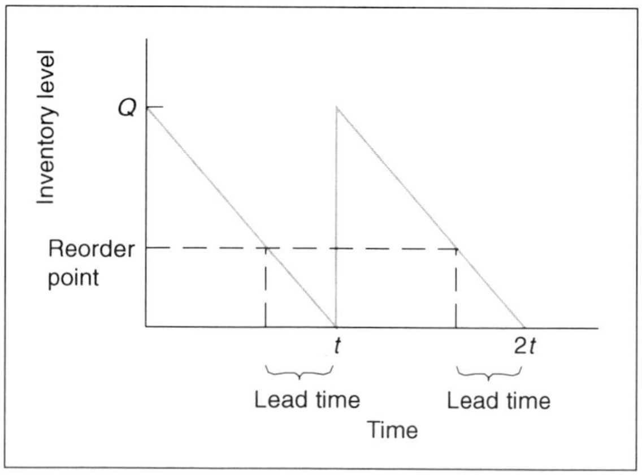

The reorder point for our basic EOQ model with constant demand and a constant lead time to receive an order is relatively straightforward. It is simply equal to the amount demanded during the lead-time period, computed using the following formula:

$$R = dL$$

where

$d =$ demand rate per time period (e.g., daily)
$L =$ lead time

Consider the I-75 Carpet Discount Store example described previously. The store is open 311 days per year. If annual demand is 10,000 yards of Super Shag carpet and the lead time to receive an order is 10 days, the reorder point for carpet is determined as follows:

$$\begin{aligned} R &= dL \\ &= \left(\frac{10{,}000}{311}\right)(10) \\ &= 321.54 \text{ yd.} \end{aligned}$$

Thus, when the inventory level falls to approximately 321 yards of carpet, a new order is placed. Notice that the reorder point is not related to the optimal order quantity or any of the inventory costs.

Safety Stocks

In our previous example for determining the reorder point, an order is made when the inventory level reaches the reorder point. During the lead time, the remaining inventory in stock is depleted as a constant demand rate, such that the new order quantity arrives at exactly the same moment as the inventory level reaches zero in Figure 9. Realistically, however, demand—and to a lesser extent lead time—is uncertain. The inventory level might be depleted at a slower or faster rate during lead time. This is depicted in Figure 10 for uncertain demand and a constant lead time.

Figure 10
Inventory model with uncertain demand

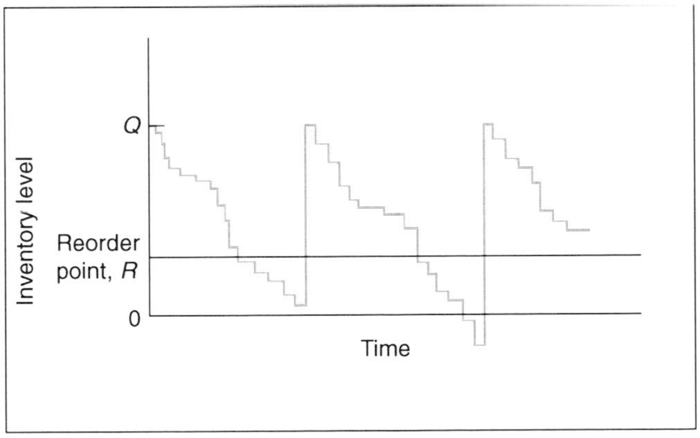

Notice in the second order cycle that a stockout occurs when demand exceeds the available inventory in stock. As a hedge against stockouts when demand is uncertain, a safety (or buffer) stock of inventory is frequently added to the demand during lead time. The addition of a safety stock is shown in Figure 11.

Figure 11
Inventory model with safety stock

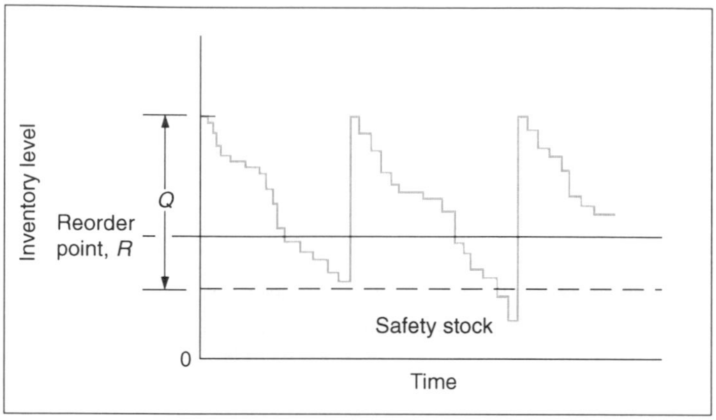

Determining Safety Stock by Using Service Levels

The service level is the probability that the inventory available during the lead time will meet demand.

There are several approaches to determining the amount of the safety stock needed. One of the most popular methods is to establish a safety stock that will meet a specified **service level**. The service level is the probability that the amount of inventory on hand during the lead time is sufficient to meet expected demand (i.e., the probability that a stockout will not occur). The word *service* is used because the higher the probability that inventory will be on hand, the more likely that customer demand will be met (i.e., the customer can be served). For example, a service level of 90% means that there is a .90 probability that demand will be met during the lead time period and a .10 probability that a stockout will occur. The specification of the service level is typically a policy decision based on a number of factors, including costs for the "extra" safety stock and present and future lost sales if customer demand cannot be met.

Reorder Point with Variable Demand

To compute the reorder point with a safety stock that will meet a specific service level, we will assume that the individual demands during each day of lead time are uncertain and independent and can be described by a normal probability distribution. The average demand for the lead-time period is the sum of the average daily demands for the days of the lead time, which is also the product of the average daily demand multiplied by the lead time. Likewise, the variance of the distribution is the sum of the daily variances for the number of days in the lead-time period. Using these parameters, the reorder point to meet a specific service level can be computed as follows:

$$R = \bar{d}L + Z\sigma_d\sqrt{L}$$

where

$\bar{d}$ = average daily demand
L = lead time
σ_d = the standard deviation of daily demand
Z = number of standard deviations corresponding to the service level probability
$Z\sigma_d\sqrt{L}$ = safety stock

The term $\sigma_d\sqrt{L}$ in this formula for reorder point is the square root of the sum of the daily variances during lead time:

$$\text{variance} = (\text{daily variances}) \times (\text{number of days of lead time}) = \sigma_d^2 L$$
$$\text{standard deviation} = \sqrt{\sigma_d^2 L} = \sigma_d\sqrt{L}$$

The reorder point relative to the service level is shown in Figure 12. The service level is the shaded area, or probability, to the left of the reorder point, R.

Figure 12

Reorder point for a service level

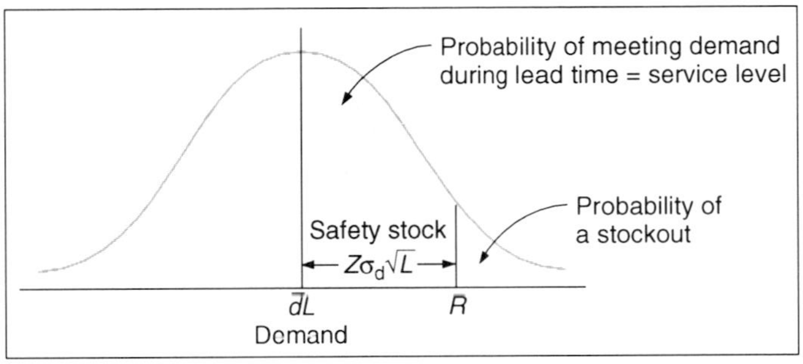

The I-75 Carpet Discount Store sells Super Shag carpet. The average daily customer demand for the carpet stocked by the store is normally distributed, with a mean daily demand of 30 yards and a standard deviation of 5 yards of carpet per day. The lead time for receiving a new order of carpet is 10 days. The store wants a reorder point and safety stock for a service level of 95%, with the probability of a stockout equal to 5%:

$$\bar{d} = 30 \text{ yd. per day}, L = 10 \text{ days}, \sigma_d = 5 \text{ yd. per day}$$

For a 95% service level, the value of Z (from Table A.1 in Appendix A) is 1.65. The reorder point is computed as follows:

$$R = \bar{d}L + Z\sigma_d\sqrt{L} = 30(10) + (1.65)(5)(\sqrt{10}) = 300 + 26.1 = 326.1 \text{ yd.}$$

The safety stock is the second term in the reorder point formula:

$$\text{safety stock} = Z\sigma_d\sqrt{L} = (1.65)(5)(\sqrt{10}) = 26.1 \text{ yd.}$$

Determining the Reorder Point Using Excel

Excel can be used to determine the reorder point with variable demand. Exhibit 6 shows an Excel spreadsheet set up to compute the reorder point for our I-75 Carpet Discount Store example. Notice that the formula for computing the reorder point in cell E7 is shown on the formula bar at the top of the spreadsheet.

Exhibit 6

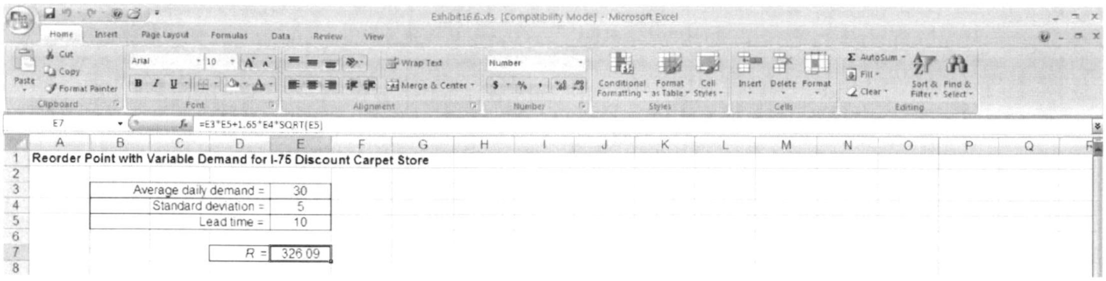

Reorder Point with Variable Lead Time

In the model in the previous section for determining the reorder point, we assumed a variable demand rate and a constant lead time. In the case where demand is constant and the lead time varies, we can use a similar formula, as follows:

$$R = d\bar{L} + Zd\sigma_L$$

where

d = constant daily demand
$\bar{L}$ = average lead time
σ_L = standard deviation of lead time
$d\sigma_L$ = standard deviation of demand during lead time
$Zd\sigma_L$ = safety stock

For our previous example of the I-75 Carpet Discount Store, we will now assume that daily demand for Super Shag carpet is a constant 30 yards. Lead time is normally distributed, with a mean of 10 days and a standard deviation of 3 days. The reorder point and safety stock corresponding to a 95% service level are computed as follows:

$$\begin{aligned} d &= 30 \text{ yd. per day} \\ \bar{L} &= 10 \text{ days} \\ \sigma_L &= 3 \text{ days} \\ Z &= 1.65 \text{ for a } 95\% \text{ service level} \\ R &= d\bar{L} + Zd\sigma_L = (30)(10)+(1.65)(30)(3) = 300+148.5 = 448.5 \text{ yd.} \end{aligned}$$

Reorder Point with Variable Demand and Lead Time

The final reorder point case we will consider is the case in which both demand and lead time are variables. The reorder point formula for this model is as follows:

$$R = \bar{d}\bar{L} + Z\sqrt{\sigma_d^2\bar{L} + \sigma_L^2\bar{d}^2}$$

where

$\bar{d}$ = average daily demand
$\bar{L}$ = average lead time
$\sqrt{\sigma_d^2\bar{L} + \sigma_L^2\bar{d}^2}$ = standard deviation of demand during lead time
$Z\sqrt{\sigma_d^2\bar{L} + \sigma_L^2\bar{d}^2}$ = safety stock

Management Science Application

Establishing Inventory Safety Stocks at Kellogg's

Richard Levine/Frances Roberts/Levine Roberts Photography

Kellogg's is the world's largest cereal producer and a leading maker of convenience foods. The company started with a single product, Kellogg's Corn Flakes, in 1906, and over the years has developed a product line of other cereals, including Rice Krispies and Corn Pops, as well as convenience foods, such as Pop-Tarts and Nutri-Grain cereal bars. Kellogg's operates five plants in the United States and Canada and seven distribution centers, and it contracts with 15 co-packers to produce or pack some Kellogg's products. Kellogg's must coordinate the production, packaging, inventory, and distribution of roughly 80 cereal products alone at these various facilities.

Kellogg's uses a model called the Kellogg Planning System (KPS) to plan its weekly production, inventory, and distribution decisions. The data used in the model are subject to much uncertainty, and the greatest uncertainty is in product demand. Demand in the first few weeks of a planning horizon is based on customer orders and is fairly accurate; however, demand in the third and fourth weeks may be significantly different from marketing forecasts. However, Kellogg's primary goal is to meet customer demand, and in order to achieve this goal, Kellogg's employs safety stocks as a buffer against uncertain demand. The safety stock for a product at a specific production facility in week t is the sum of demands for weeks t and $t + 1$. However, for a product that is being promoted in an advertising campaign, the safety stock is the sum of forecasted demand for a 4-week horizon or longer. KPS has saved Kellogg's many millions of dollars since the mid-1990s. The tactical version of KPS recently helped the company consolidate production capacity, with estimated projected savings of almost $40 million.

Source: G. Brown, J. Keegan, B. Vigus, and K. Wood, "The Kellogg Company Optimizes Production, Inventory, and Distribution," *Interfaces* 31, no. 6 (November–December 2001): 1–15.

Again we will consider the I-75 Carpet Discount Store example, used previously. In this case, daily demand is normally distributed, with a mean of 30 yards and a standard deviation of 5 yards. Lead time is also assumed to be normally distributed, with a mean of 10 days and a standard deviation of 3 days. The reorder point and safety stock for a 95% service level are computed as follows:

$$\begin{aligned}
\bar{d} &= 30 \text{ yd./day} \\
\sigma_d &= 5 \text{ yd./day} \\
\bar{L} &= 10 \text{ days} \\
\sigma_L &= 3 \text{ days} \\
Z &= 1.65 \text{ for a } 95\% \text{ service level} \\
R &= \bar{d}\,\bar{L} + Z\sqrt{\sigma_d^2\bar{L} + \sigma_L^2\bar{d}^2} \\
&= (30)(10) + (1.65)\sqrt{(5)^2(10) + (3)^2(30)^2} \\
&= 300 + 150.8 \\
R &= 450.8 \text{ yd.}
\end{aligned}$$

Thus, the reorder point is 450.8 yards, with a safety stock of 150.8 yards. Notice that this reorder point encompasses the largest safety stock of our three reorder point examples, which would be anticipated, given the increased variability resulting from variable demand and lead time.

Order Quantity for a Periodic Inventory System

*A **periodic inventory** system uses variable order sizes at fixed time intervals.*

Previously we defined a continuous, or fixed–order quantity, inventory system as one in which the order quantity was constant and the time between orders varied. So far, this type of inventory system has been the primary focus of our discussion. The less common **periodic**, or *fixed–time period*, **inventory system** is one in which the time between orders is constant and the order size varies. A drugstore is one example of a business that sometimes uses a fixed-period inventory system. Drugstores stock a number of personal hygiene and health-related products, such as shampoo, toothpaste, soap, bandages, cough medicine, and aspirin. Normally, the vendors that provide these items to the store will make periodic visits—for example, every few weeks or every month—and count the stock of inventory on hand for their products. If the inventory is exhausted or at some predetermined reorder point, a new order will be placed for an amount that will bring the inventory level back up to the desired level. The drugstore managers will generally not monitor the inventory level between vendor visits but instead rely on the vendor to take inventory at the time of the scheduled visit.

A periodic inventory system normally requires a larger safety stock.

A limitation of this type of inventory system is that inventory can be exhausted early in the time period between visits, resulting in a stockout that will not be remedied until the next scheduled order. Alternatively, in a fixed–order quantity system, when inventory reaches a reorder point, an order is made that minimizes the time during which a stockout might exist. As a result of this drawback, a larger safety stock is normally required for the fixed-interval system.

Order Quantity with Variable Demand

If the demand rate and lead time are constant, then the fixed-period model will have a fixed order quantity that will be made at specified time intervals, which is the same as the fixed quantity (EOQ) model under similar conditions. However, as we have already explained, the fixed-period model reacts significantly differently from the fixed–order quantity model when demand is a variable.

The order size for a fixed-period model, given variable daily demand that is normally distributed, is determined by the following formula:

$$Q = \bar{d}(t_b + L) + Z\sigma_d\sqrt{t_b + L} - I$$

where

$\bar{d}$ = average demand rate
t_b = the fixed time between orders
L = lead time
σ_d = standard deviation of demand
$Z\sigma_d\sqrt{t_b + L}$ = safety stock
I = inventory in stock

The first term in the preceding formula, $d(t_b + L)$, is the average demand during the order cycle time plus the lead time. It reflects the amount of inventory that will be needed to protect against shortages during the entire time from this order to the next and the lead time, until the order is received. The second term, $Z\sigma_d\sqrt{t_b + L}$, is the safety stock for a specific service level, determined in much the same way as previously described for a reorder point. The final term, I, is the amount of inventory on hand when the inventory level is checked and an order is made. We will demonstrate the computation of Q with an example.

The Corner Drug Store stocks a popular brand of sunscreen. The average demand for the sunscreen is 6 bottles per day, with a standard deviation of 1.2 bottles. A vendor for the sunscreen producer checks the drugstore stock every 60 days, and during a particular visit the drugstore had 8 bottles in stock. The lead time to receive an order is 5 days. The order size for this order period that will enable the drugstore to maintain a 95% service level is computed as follows:

$$
\begin{aligned}
\bar{d} &= 6 \text{ bottles per day} \\
\sigma_d &= 1.2 \text{ bottles} \\
t_b &= 60 \text{ days} \\
L &= 5 \text{ days} \\
I &= 8 \text{ bottles} \\
Z &= 1.65 \text{ for } 95\% \text{ service level} \\
Q &= \bar{d}(t_b + L) + Z\sigma_d\sqrt{t_b + L} - I \\
&= (6)(60 + 5) + (1.65)(1.2)\sqrt{60 + 5} - 8 \\
&= 398 \text{ bottles}
\end{aligned}
$$

Determining the Order Quantity for the Fixed-Period Model with Excel

Exhibit 7 shows an Excel spreadsheet set up to compute the order quantity for the fixed-period model with variable demand for our Corner Drug Store example. Notice that the formula for the order quantity in cell D10 is shown on the formula bar at the top of the spreadsheet.

Exhibit 7

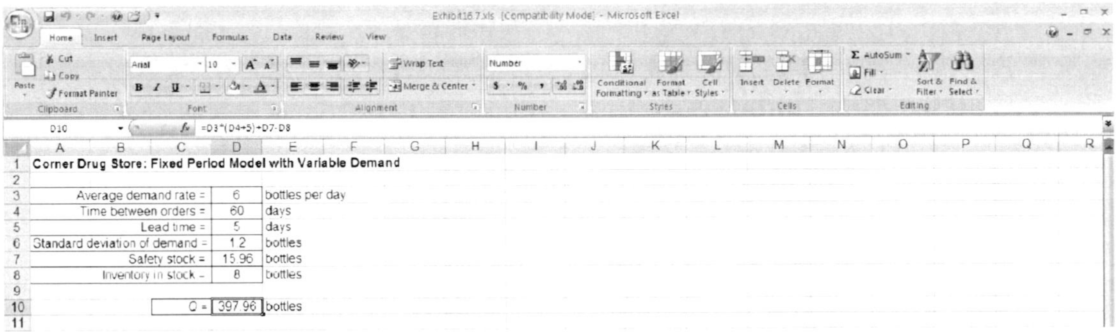

Summary

In this chapter the classical economic order quantity model was presented. The basic form of the EOQ model we discussed included simplifying assumptions regarding order receipt, no shortages, and constant demand known with certainty. By relaxing some of these assumptions, we were able to create increasingly complex but realistic models. These EOQ variations included the reorder point model, the noninstantaneous receipt model, the model with shortages, and models with safety stocks. The techniques for inventory analysis presented in this chapter are not widely used to analyze other types of problems. The wide use of management science techniques for inventory analysis attests to the importance of inventory to all types of organizations.

References

Buchan, J., and Koenigsberg, E. *Scientific Inventory Management.* Upper Saddle River, NJ: Prentice Hall, 1963.

Buffa, E. S., and Miller, J. G. *Production-Inventory Systems: Planning and Control,* 3rd ed. Homewood, IL: Irwin, 1979.

Churchman, C. W., Ackoff, R. L., and Arnoff, E. L. *Introduction to Operations Research.* New York: John Wiley & Sons, 1957.

Hadley, G., and Whitin, T. M. *Analysis of Inventory Systems.* Upper Saddle River, NJ: Prentice Hall, 1963.

Johnson, L. A., and Montgomery, D. C. *Operations Research in Production Planning, Scheduling and Inventory Control.* New York: John Wiley & Sons, 1974.

Magee, J. F., and Boodman, D. M. *Production Planning and Inventory Control,* 2nd ed. New York: McGraw-Hill, 1967.

Starr, M. K., and Miller, D. W. *Inventory Control: Theory and Practice.* Upper Saddle River, NJ: Prentice Hall, 1962.

Wagner, H. M. *Statistical Management of Inventory Systems.* New York: John Wiley & Sons, 1962.

Whitin, T. M. *The Theory of Inventory Management.* Princeton, NJ: Princeton University Press, 1957.

Example Problem Solutions

The following example will demonstrate EOQ analysis for the classical model and the model with shortages and back ordering.

Problem Statement

Electronic Village stocks and sells a particular brand of personal computer. It costs the store $450 each time it places an order with the manufacturer for the personal computers. The annual cost of carrying the PCs in inventory is $170. The store manager estimates the annual demand for the PCs will be 1,200 units.

a. Determine the optimal order quantity and the total minimum inventory cost.
b. Assume that shortages are allowed and that the shortage cost is $600 per unit per year. Compute the optimal order quantity and the total minimum inventory cost.

Solution

Step 1: (part a): Determine the Optimal Order Quantity

$$\begin{aligned} D &= 1{,}200 \text{ personal computers} \\ C_c &= \$170 \\ C_o &= \$450 \\ Q &= \sqrt{\frac{2C_oD}{C_c}} \\ &= \sqrt{\frac{2(450)(1{,}200)}{170}} \\ &= 79.7 \text{ personal computers} \\ \text{total cost} &= C_c\frac{Q}{2} + C_o\frac{D}{Q} \\ &= 170\left(\frac{79.7}{2}\right) + 450\left(\frac{1{,}200}{79.7}\right) \\ &= \$13{,}549.91 \end{aligned}$$

Step 2: (part b): Compute the EOQ with Shortages

$$\begin{aligned} C_s &= \$600 \\ Q &= \sqrt{\frac{2C_oD}{C_c}\left(\frac{C_s + C_c}{C_s}\right)} \end{aligned}$$

$$= \sqrt{\frac{2(450)(1{,}200)}{170}\left(\frac{600 + 170}{600}\right)}$$
$$= 90.3 \text{ personal computers}$$
$$S = Q\left(\frac{C_c}{C_c + C_s}\right)$$
$$= 90.3\left(\frac{170}{170 + 600}\right)$$
$$= 19.9 \text{ personal computers}$$
$$\text{total cost} = \frac{C_s S^2}{2Q} + C_c\frac{(Q - S)^2}{2Q} + \frac{C_o D}{Q}$$
$$= \frac{(600)(19.9)^2}{2(90.3)} + 170\frac{(90.3 - 19.9)^2}{2(90.3)} + 450\left(\frac{1{,}200}{90.3}\right)$$
$$= \$1{,}315.65 + 4{,}665.27 + 5{,}980.07$$
$$= \$11{,}960.98$$

Problem Statement

A computer products store stocks color graphics monitors, and the daily demand is normally distributed, with a mean of 1.6 monitors and a standard deviation of 0.4 monitor. The lead time to receive an order from the manufacturer is 15 days. Determine the reorder point that will achieve a 98% service level.

Solution

Step 1: Identify Parameters

$$\bar{d} = 1.6 \text{ monitors per day}$$
$$L = 15 \text{ days}$$
$$\sigma_d = 0.4 \text{ monitor per day}$$
$$Z = 2.05 \text{ (for a 98\% service level)}$$

Step 2: Solve for R

$$R = \bar{d}L + Z\sigma_d\sqrt{L} = (1.6)(15) + (2.05)(0.4)\sqrt{15} = 24 + 3.18 = 27.18 \text{ monitors}$$

Problems

1. Hayes Electronics stocks and sells a particular brand of personal computer. It costs the firm $450 each time it places an order with the manufacturer for the personal computers. The cost of carrying one PC in inventory for a year is $170. The store manager estimates that total annual demand for the computers will be 1,200 units, with a constant demand rate throughout the year. Orders are received within minutes after placement from a local warehouse maintained by the manufacturer. The store policy is never to have stockouts of the PCs. The store is open for business every day of the year except Christmas Day. Determine the following:
   a. The optimal order quantity per order
   b. The minimum total annual inventory costs
   c. The optimal number of orders per year
   d. The optimal time between orders (in working days)

2. Hayes Electronics in Problem 1 assumed with certainty that the ordering cost is $450 per order and the inventory carrying cost is $170 per unit per year. However, the inventory model parameters are frequently only estimates that are subject to some degree of uncertainty. Consider four cases of variation in the model parameters: (a) Both ordering cost and carrying cost are 10% less than originally estimated, (b) both ordering cost and carrying cost are 10% higher than originally estimated, (c) ordering cost is 10% higher and carrying cost is 10% lower than originally estimated, and (d) ordering cost is 10% lower and carrying cost is 10% higher than originally estimated. Determine the optimal order quantity and total inventory cost for each of the four cases. Prepare a table with values from all four cases and compare the sensitivity of the model solution to changes in parameter values.

3. A firm is faced with the attractive situation in which it can obtain immediate delivery of an item it stocks for retail sale. The firm has therefore not bothered to order the item in any systematic way. Recently, however, profits have been squeezed due to increasing competitive pressures, and the firm has retained a management consultant to study its inventory management. The consultant has determined that the various costs associated with making an order for the item stocked are approximately $30 per order. She has also determined that the costs of carrying the item in inventory amount to approximately $20 per unit per year (primarily direct storage costs and foregone profit on investment in inventory). Demand for the item is reasonably constant over time, and the forecast is for 19,200 units per year. When an order is placed for the item, the entire order is immediately delivered to the firm by the supplier. The firm operates 6 days a week plus a few Sundays, or approximately 320 days per year. Determine the following:
   a. The optimal order quantity per order
   b. The total annual inventory costs
   c. The optimal number of orders to place per year
   d. The number of operating days between orders, based on the optimal number of orders

4. The Western Jeans Company purchases denim from Cumberland Textile Mills. The Western Jeans Company uses 35,000 yards of denim per year to make jeans. The cost of ordering denim from the textile company is $500 per order. It costs Western $0.35 per yard annually to hold a yard of denim in inventory. Determine the optimal number of yards of denim the Western Jeans Company should order, the minimum total annual inventory cost, the optimal number of orders per year, and the optimal time between orders.

5. The Metropolitan Book Company purchases paper from the Atlantic Paper Company. Metropolitan produces magazines and paperbacks that require 1,215,000 pounds of paper per year. The cost per order for the company is $1,200; the cost of holding 1 pound of paper in inventory is $0.08 per year. Determine the following:
   a. The economic order quantity
   b. The minimum total annual cost
   c. The optimal number of orders per year
   d. The optimal time between orders

6. The Simple Simon Bakery produces fruit pies for freezing and subsequent sale. The bakery, which operates 5 days per week, 52 weeks per year, can produce pies at the rate of 64 pies per day. The bakery sets up the pie production operation and produces until a predetermined number (Q) of pies has been produced. When not producing pies, the bakery uses its personnel and facilities for producing other bakery items. The setup cost for a production run of fruit pies is $500. The cost of holding frozen pies in storage is $5 per pie per year. The annual demand for frozen fruit pies, which is constant over time, is 5,000 pies. Determine the following:
   a. The optimal production run quantity (Q)

b. The total annual inventory costs
c. The optimal number of production runs per year
d. The optimal cycle time (time between run starts)
e. The run length, in working days

7. The Pedal Pusher Bicycle Shop operates 7 days per week, closing only on Christmas Day. The shop pays $300 for a particular bicycle purchased from the manufacturer. The annual holding cost per bicycle is estimated to be 25% of the dollar value of inventory. The shop sells an average of 25 bikes per week. Frequently, the dealer does not have a bike in stock when a customer purchases it, and the bike is back-ordered. The dealer estimates his shortage cost per unit back-ordered, on an annual basis, to be $250 due to lost future sales (and profits). The ordering cost for each order is $100. Determine the optimal order quantity and shortage level and the total minimum cost.

8. The Petroco Company uses a highly toxic chemical in one of its manufacturing processes. It must have the product delivered by special cargo trucks designed for safe shipment of chemicals. As such, ordering (and delivery) costs are relatively high, at $2,600 per order. The chemical product is packaged in 1-gallon plastic containers. The cost of holding the chemical in storage is $50 per gallon per year. The annual demand for the chemical, which is constant over time, is 2,000 gallons per year. The lead time from time of order placement until receipt is 10 days. The company operates 310 working days per year. Compute the optimal order quantity, the total minimum inventory cost, and the reorder point.

9. The Big Buy Supermarket stocks Munchies Cereal. Demand for Munchies is 4,000 boxes per year (365 days). It costs the store $60 per order of Munchies, and it costs $0.80 per box per year to keep the cereal in stock. Once an order for Munchies is placed, it takes 4 days to receive the order from a food distributor. Determine the following:
   a. The optimal order size
   b. The minimum total annual inventory cost
   c. The reorder point

10. The Wood Valley Dairy makes cheese to supply to stores in its area. The dairy can make 250 pounds of cheese per day (365 days per year), and the demand at area stores is 180 pounds per day. Each time the dairy makes cheese, it costs $125 to set up the production process. The annual cost of carrying a pound of cheese in a refrigerated storage area is $12. Determine the optimal order size and the minimum total annual inventory cost.

11. The Rainwater Brewery produces Rainwater Light Beer, which it stores in barrels in its warehouse and supplies to its distributors on demand. The demand for Rainwater is 1,500 barrels of beer per day (365 days per year). The brewery can produce 2,000 barrels of Rainwater per day. It costs $6,500 to set up a production run for Rainwater. Once it is brewed, the beer is stored in a refrigerated warehouse at an annual cost of $50 per barrel. Determine the economic order quantity and the minimum total annual inventory cost.

12. The purchasing manager for the Atlantic Steel Company must determine a policy for ordering coal to operate 12 converters. Each converter requires exactly 5 tons of coal per day to operate, and the firm operates 360 days per year. The purchasing manager has determined that the ordering cost is $80 per order and the cost of holding coal is 20% of the average dollar value of inventory held. The purchasing manager has negotiated a contract to obtain the coal for $12 per ton for the coming year.
    a. Determine the optimal quantity of coal to receive in each order.
    b. Determine the total inventory-related costs associated with the optimal ordering policy (do not include the cost of the coal).
    c. If 5 days of lead time are required to receive an order of coal, how much coal should be on hand when an order is placed?

13. The Pacific Lumber Company and Mill processes 10,000 logs annually, operating 250 days per year. Immediately upon receiving an order, the logging company's supplier begins delivery to the lumber mill, at a rate of 60 logs per day. The lumber mill has determined that the ordering cost is $1,600 per order and the cost of carrying logs in inventory before they are processed is $15 per log on an annual basis. Determine the following:
    a. The optimal order size
    b. The total inventory cost associated with the optimal order quantity
    c. The number of operating days between orders
    d. The number of operating days required to receive an order

14. The Roadking Tire Store sells a brand of tires called the Roadrunner. The annual demand from the store's customers for Roadrunner tires is 3,700. The cost to order tires from the tire manufacturer is $420 per order. The annual carrying cost is $1.75 per tire. The store allows shortages, and the annual shortage cost per tire is $4. Determine the optimal order size, maximum shortage level, and minimum total annual inventory cost.

15. The Laurel Creek Lawn Shop sells Fastgro Fertilizer. The annual demand for the fertilizer is 270,000 pounds. The cost to order the fertilizer from the Fastgro Company is $105 per order. The annual carrying cost is $0.25 per pound. The store operates with shortages, and the annual shortage cost is $0.70 per pound. Compute the optimal order size, minimum total annual inventory cost, and maximum shortage level.

16. Videoworld is a discount store that sells color televisions. The annual demand for color television sets is 400. The cost per order from the manufacturer is $650. The carrying cost is $45 per set each year. The store has an inventory policy that allows shortages. The shortage cost per set is estimated at $60. Determine the following:
    a. The optimal order size
    b. The maximum shortage level
    c. The minimum total annual inventory cost

17. The University Bookstore at Tech stocks the required textbook for Management Science 2405. The demand for this text is 1,200 copies per year. The cost of placing an order is $350, and the annual carrying cost is $2.75 per book. If a student requests the book and it is not in stock, the student will likely go to the privately owned Tech Bookstore. It is likely that the student will not buy books at the University Bookstore in the future; thus the shortage cost to the University Bookstore is estimated to be $45 per book. Determine the optimal order size, the maximum shortage level, and the total inventory cost.

18. The A-to-Z Office Supply Company is open from 8:00 A.M. to 6:00 P.M., and it receives 200 calls per day for delivery orders. It costs A-to-Z $20 to send out its trucks to make deliveries. The company estimates that each minute a customer spends waiting for an order costs A-to-Z $0.20 in lost sales.
    a. How frequently should A-to-Z send out its delivery trucks each day? Indicate the total daily cost of deliveries.
    b. If a truck could carry only six orders, how often would deliveries be made, and what would be the cost?

19. The Union Street Microbrewery makes 1220 Union beer, which it bottles and sells in its adjoining restaurant and by the case. It costs $1,700 to set up, brew, and bottle a batch of the beer. The annual cost to store the beer in inventory is $1.25 per bottle. The annual demand for the beer is 18,000 bottles, and the brewery has the capacity to produce 30,000 bottles annually.
    a. Determine the optimal order quantity, the total annual inventory cost, the number of production runs per year, and the maximum inventory level.

b. If the microbrewery has only enough storage space to hold a maximum of 2,500 bottles of beer in inventory, how will that affect total inventory costs?

20. Eurotronics is a European manufacturer of electronic components. During the course of a year, it requires container cargo space on ships leaving Hamburg bound for the United States, Mexico, South America, and Canada. Annually, the company needs 160,000 cubic feet of cargo space. The cost of reserving cargo space is $7,000, and the cost of holding cargo space is $0.80 per cubic foot. Determine how much storage space Eurotronics should optimally order, the total cost, and how many times per year it should place orders to reserve space.

21. The Summer Outdoor Furniture Company produces wooden lawn chairs. The annual demand from its store customers is 17,400 chairs per year. The transport and handling costs are $2,600 each time a shipment of chairs is delivered to stores from its warehouse. The annual carrying cost is $3.75 per chair.
    a. Determine the optimal order quantity and minimum total annual cost.
    b. The company is thinking about relocating its warehouse closer to its customers, which would reduce transport and handling costs to $1,900 per order but increase carrying costs to $4.50 per chair per year. Should the company relocate based on inventory costs?

22. The Spruce Creek Vegetable Farm produces organically grown greenhouse tomatoes that are sold to area grocery stores. The annual demand for Spruce Creek's tomatoes is 270,000 pounds. The farm is able to produce 305,000 pounds annually. The cost to transport the tomatoes from the farm to the stores is $620 per load. The annual carrying cost is $0.12 per pound.
    a. Compute the optimal order size, the maximum inventory level, and the total minimum cost.
    b. If Spruce Creek can increase production capacity to 360,000 tomatoes per year, will it reduce total inventory cost?

23. The Uptown Kiln is an importer of ceramics from overseas. It has arranged to purchase a particular type of ceramic pottery from a Korean artisan. The artisan makes the pottery in 120-unit batches and will ship only that exact number of units. The transportation and handling cost of a shipment is $7,600 (not including the unit cost). The Uptown Kiln estimates its annual demand to be 900 units. What storage and handling cost per unit does it need to achieve in order to minimize its inventory cost?

24. The I-75 Carpet Discount Store has an annual demand of 10,000 yards of Super Shag carpet. The annual carrying cost for a yard of this carpet is $0.75, and the ordering cost is $150. The carpet manufacturer normally charges the store $8 per yard for the carpet; however, the manufacturer has offered a discount price of $6.50 per yard if the store will order 5,000 yards. How much should the store order, and what will be the total annual inventory cost for that order quantity?

25. The Fifth Quarter Bar buys Old World draft beer by the barrel from a local distributor. The bar has an annual demand of 900 barrels, which it purchases at a price of $205 per barrel. The annual carrying cost is 12% of the price, and the cost per order is $160. The distributor has offered the bar a reduced price of $190 per barrel if it will order a minimum of 300 barrels. Should the bar take the discount?

26. The bookstore at State University purchases from a vendor sweatshirts emblazoned with the school name and logo. The vendor sells the sweatshirts to the store for $38 apiece. The cost to the bookstore for placing an order is $120, and the carrying cost is 25% of the average annual inventory value. The bookstore manager estimates that 1,700 sweatshirts will be sold during the year. The vendor has offered the bookstore the following volume discount schedule:

Order Size	Discount %
1–299	0
300–499	2
500–799	4
800+	5

The bookstore manager wants to determine the bookstore's optimal order quantity, given the foregoing quantity discount information.

27. Determine the optimal order quantity of sweatshirts and total annual cost in Problem 26 if the carrying cost is a constant $8 per sweatshirt per year.

28. The office manager for the Gotham Life Insurance Company orders letterhead stationery from an office products firm in boxes of 500 sheets. The company uses 6,500 boxes per year. Annual carrying costs are $3 per box, and ordering costs are $28. The following discount price schedule is provided by the office supply company:

Order Quantity (boxes)	Price per Box
200–999	$16
1,000–2,999	14
3,000–5,999	13
6,000+	12

Determine the optimal order quantity and the total annual inventory cost.

29. Determine the optimal order quantity and total annual inventory cost for boxes of stationery in Problem 28 if the carrying cost is 20% of the price of a box of stationery.

30. The 23,000-seat City Coliseum houses the local professional ice hockey, basketball, indoor soccer, and arena football teams, as well as various trade shows, wrestling and boxing matches, tractor pulls, and circuses. Coliseum vending annually sells large quantities of soft drinks and beer in plastic cups, with the name of the coliseum and the various team logos on them. The local container cup manufacturer that supplies the cups in boxes of 100 has offered coliseum management the following discount price schedule for cups:

Order Quantity (boxes)	Price per Box
2,000–6,999	$47
7,000–11,999	43
12,000–19,999	41
20,000+	38

The annual demand for cups is 2.3 million, the annual carrying cost per box of cups is $1.90, and the ordering cost is $320. Determine the optimal order quantity and total annual inventory cost.

31. Community Hospital orders latex sanitary gloves from a hospital supply firm. The hospital expects to use 40,000 pairs of gloves per year. The cost to order and to have the gloves delivered is $180. The annual carrying cost is $0.18 per pair of gloves. The hospital supply firm offers the following quantity discount pricing schedule:

Quantity	Price
0–9,999	$0.34
10,000–19,999	0.32
20,000–29,999	0.30
30,000–39,999	0.28
40,000–49,999	0.26
50,000+	0.24

Determine the order size for the hospital.

32. Tracy McCoy is the office administrator for the department of management science at Tech. The faculty uses a lot of printer paper, and although Tracy is constantly reordering, paper frequently runs out. She orders the paper from the university central stores. Several faculty members have determined that the lead time to receive an order is normally distributed, with a mean of 2 days and a standard deviation of 0.5 day. The faculty has also determined that daily demand for the paper is normally distributed, with a mean of 2 packages and a standard deviation of 0.8 package. What reorder point should Tracy use in order not to run out 99% of the time?

33. Determine the optimal order quantity and total annual inventory cost for cups in Problem 30 if the carrying cost is 5% of the price of a box of cups.

34. The amount of denim used daily by the Western Jeans Company in its manufacturing process to make jeans is normally distributed, with an average of 3,000 yards of denim and a standard deviation of 600 yards. The lead time required to receive an order of denim from the textile mill is a constant 6 days. Determine the safety stock and reorder point if the Western Jeans Company wants to limit the probability of a stockout and work stoppage to 5%.

35. In Problem 34, what level of service would a safety stock of 2,000 yards provide?

36. The Atlantic Paper Company produces paper from wood pulp ordered from a lumber products firm. The paper company's daily demand for wood pulp is a constant 8,000 pounds. Lead time is normally distributed, with an average of 7 days and a standard deviation of 1.6 days. Determine the reorder point if the paper company wants to limit the probability of a stockout and work stoppage to 2%.

37. The Uptown Bar and Grill serves Rainwater draft beer to its customers. The daily demand for beer is normally distributed, with an average of 18 gallons and a standard deviation of 4 gallons. The lead time required to receive an order of beer from the local distributor is normally distributed, with a mean of 3 days and a standard deviation of 0.8 day. Determine the safety stock and reorder point if the restaurant wants to maintain a 90% service level. What would be the increase in the safety stock if a 95% service level were desired?

38. In Problem 37, the manager of the Uptown Bar and Grill has negotiated with the beer distributor for the lead time to receive orders to be a constant 3 days. What effect does this have on the reorder point developed in Problem 37 for a 90% service level?

39. The daily demand for Sunlight paint at the Rainbow Paint Store in East Ridge is normally distributed, with a mean of 26 gallons and a standard deviation of 10 gallons. The lead time for receiving an order of paint from the Sunlight distributor is 9 days. Because this is the only paint store in East Ridge, the manager is interested in maintaining only a 75% service level. What reorder point should be used to meet this service level? The manager subsequently has learned that a new paint store will open soon in East Ridge, which has prompted her to increase the service level to 95%. What reorder point will maintain this service level?

40. PM Computers assembles personal computers from generic components. It purchases its color monitors from a manufacturer in Taiwan; thus, there is a long and uncertain lead time for receiving orders. Lead time is normally distributed, with a mean of 25 days and a standard deviation of 10 days. Daily demand is also normally distributed, with a mean of 2.5 monitors and a standard

deviation of 1.2 monitors. Determine the safety stock and reorder point corresponding to a 90% service level.

41. PM Computers in Problem 40 is considering purchasing monitors from an American manufacturer that would guarantee a lead time of 8 days, instead of the Taiwanese company. Determine the new reorder point, given this lead time, and identify the factors that would enter into the decision to change manufacturers.

42. The Corner Drug Store fills prescriptions for a popular children's antibiotic, amoxicillin. The daily demand for amoxicillin is normally distributed, with a mean of 200 ounces and a standard deviation of 80 ounces. The vendor for the pharmaceutical firm that supplies the drug calls the drugstore pharmacist every 30 days to check the inventory of amoxicillin. During a call, the druggist indicated that the store had 60 ounces of the antibiotic in stock. The lead time to receive an order is 4 days. Determine the order size that will enable the drugstore to maintain a 95% service level.

43. The Fast Service Food Mart stocks frozen pizzas in a refrigerated display case. The average daily demand for the pizzas is normally distributed, with a mean of 8 pizzas and a standard deviation of 2.5 pizzas. A vendor for a packaged food distributor checks the market's inventory of frozen foods every 10 days, and during a particular visit, there were no pizzas in stock. The lead time to receive an order is 3 days. Determine the order size for this order period that will result in a 99% service level. During the vendor's following visit, there were 5 frozen pizzas in stock. What is the order size for the next order period?

44. The Impanema Restaurant stocks a red Brazilian table wine it purchases from a wine merchant in a nearby city. The daily demand for the wine at the restaurant is normally distributed, with a mean of 18 bottles and a standard deviation of 4 bottles. The wine merchant sends a representative to check the restaurant's wine cellar every 30 days, and during a recent visit, there were 25 bottles in stock. The lead time to receive an order is 2 days. The restaurant manager has requested an order size that will enable him to limit the probability of a stockout to 2%. Determine the order size.

45. The concession stand at the Blacksburg High School stadium sells slices of pizza during soccer games. Concession stand sales are a primary source of revenue for high school athletic programs, so the athletic director wants to sell as much food as possible. However, any pizza not sold is given away to the players, coaches, and referees, or it is thrown away. The athletic director wants to determine a reorder point that will meet, not exceed, the demand for pizza. Pizza sales are normally distributed, with a mean of 6 pizzas per hour and a standard deviation of 2.5 pizzas. The pizzas are ordered from Pizza Town restaurant, and the mean delivery time is 30 minutes, with a standard deviation of 8 minutes.
    a. Currently, the concession stand places an order when it has 1 pizza left. What level of service does this result in?
    b. What should the reorder point be to have a 98% service level?

Case Problem

THE NORTHWOODS GENERAL STORE

The Northwoods General Store in Vermont sells a variety of outdoor clothing items and equipment and several food products at its modern but rustic-looking retail store. Its food products include salmon and maple syrup. The store also runs a lucrative catalog operation. One of its most popular products is maple syrup, which is sold in metal half-gallon cans with a picture of the store on the front.

Maple syrup was one of the first products the store produced and sold, and it continues to do so. Setting up the syrup-making equipment to produce a batch of syrup costs $450. Storing the syrup for sales throughout the year is a tricky process because the syrup must be kept in a temperature-controlled facility. The annual cost of carrying a gallon of the syrup is $15. Based on past sales data, the store has forecasted a demand of 7,500 gallons of maple syrup for the coming year. The store can produce approximately 100 gallons of syrup per day during the maple syrup season, which runs from February through May.

Because of the short season when the store can actually get sap out of trees, it obviously must produce enough during this 4-month season to meet demand for the whole year. Specifically, store management would like a production and inventory schedule that minimizes costs and indicates when during the year they need to start operating the syrup-making facility full time on a daily basis to meet demand for the remaining 8 months.

Develop a syrup production and inventory schedule for the Northwoods General Store.

Case Problem

THE TEXANS STADIUM STORE

The Fort Worth Texans have won three Super Bowls in the past 5 years, including two in a row the past 2 years. As a result, sportswear such as hats, sweatshirts, sweatpants, and jackets with the Texans logo are particularly popular in Texas. The Texans operate a stadium store outside the football stadium where they play. It is near a busy highway, so the store has heavy customer traffic throughout the year, not just on game days. In addition, the stadium holds high school or college football and soccer games almost every week in the fall, and it holds baseball games in the spring and summer. The most popular single item the stadium store sells is a blue and silver baseball cap with the Texans logo embroidered on it in a special and very attractive manner. The cap has an elastic headband inside it, which automatically conforms to different head sizes. However, the store has had a difficult time keeping the cap in stock, especially during the time between the placement and receipt of an order. Often customers come to the store just for the hat; when it is not in stock, customers are visibly upset, and the store management believes they tend to go to competing stores to purchase their Texans clothing. To rectify this problem, the store manager, Jenny Jones, would like to develop an inventory control policy that would ensure that customers would be able to purchase the cap 99% of the time they asked for it. Jenny has accumulated the following demand data for the cap for a 30-week period:

Week	*Demand*	*Week*	*Demand*	*Week*	*Demand*
1	38	11	28	21	52
2	51	12	41	22	38
3	25	13	37	23	49
4	60	14	44	24	46
5	35	15	45	25	47
6	42	16	56	26	41
7	29	17	62	27	39
8	46	18	53	28	50
9	55	19	46	29	28
10	19	20	41	30	34

(Demand includes actual sales plus a record of the times a cap has been requested but not available and an estimate of the number of times a customer wanted a cap when it was not available but did not ask for it.)

The store purchases the hats from a small manufacturing company in Jamaica. The shipments from Jamaica are somewhat erratic, with a lead time anywhere between 10 days and 1 month. The following lead time data (in days) were accumulated during approximately a 1-year period:

Order	*Lead Time*	*Order*	*Lead Time*
1	12	11	14
2	16	12	16
3	25	13	23
4	18	14	18
5	10	15	21
6	30	16	19
7	24	17	17
8	19	18	16
9	17	19	22
10	15	20	18

In the past, Jenny placed an order whenever the stock got down to 150 caps. To what level of service does this reorder point correspond? What would the reorder point and safety stock need to be to attain the desired service level? Discuss how Jenny might determine the order size for caps and what additional, if any, information would be needed to determine the order size.

Case Problem

THE A-TO-Z OFFICE SUPPLY COMPANY

Christine Yamaguchi is the manager of the A-to-Z Office Supply Company in Charlotte. The company attempts to gain an advantage over its competitors by providing quality customer service, which includes prompt delivery of orders by truck or van and always being able to meet customer demand from its stock. In order to achieve this degree of customer service, A-to-Z must stock a large volume of items on a daily basis at a central warehouse and at three retail stores in the city and suburbs. Christine maintains these inventory levels by borrowing cash on a daily basis from the First Piedmont Bank. She estimates that for the coming fiscal year, the company's demand for cash to pay for inventory will be $17,000 per day for 305 working days. Any money she borrows during the year must be repaid with interest by the end of the year. The annual interest rate currently charged by the bank is 9%. Any time Christine takes out a loan to purchase inventory, the bank charges the company a loan origination fee of $1,200 plus 2¼ points (2.25% of the amount borrowed).

Christine often uses EOQ analysis to determine optimal amounts of inventory to order for different office supplies. Now she is wondering if she can use the same type of analysis to determine an optimal borrowing policy. Determine the amount of the loan Christine should secure from the bank, the total annual cost of the company's borrowing policy, and the number of loans the company should obtain during the year. Also determine the level of cash on hand at which the company should apply for a new loan, given that it takes 15 days for a loan to be processed by the bank.

Suppose the bank offers Christine a discount, as follows: On any loan amount equal to or greater than $500,000, the bank will lower the number of points charged on the loan origination fee from 2.25% to 2.00%. What would the company's optimal loan amount be?

Case Problem

DIAMANT FOODS COMPANY

Diamant Foods Company produces a variety of food products, including a line of candies. One of its most popular candy items is Divine Diamonds, a bag of a dozen individually wrapped diamond-shaped candies made primarily from a blend of dark and milk chocolates, macadamia nuts, and a blend of heavy cream fillings. The item is relatively expensive, so Diamant Foods produces it only for its eastern market, encompassing urban areas such as New York, Atlanta, Philadelphia, and Boston. The item is not sold in grocery or discount stores but mainly in specialty shops and specialty groceries, candy stores, and department stores. Diamant Foods supplies the candy to a single food distributor, which has several warehouses on the East Coast. The candy is shipped in cases of 60 bags of the candy per case. Diamonds sell well, despite the fact that they are expensive, at $9.85 per bag (wholesale). Diamant uses high-quality, fresh ingredients and does not store large stocks of the candy in inventory for very long periods of time.

Diamant's distributor believes that demand for the candy follows a seasonal pattern. It has collected demand data (i.e., cases sold) for Diamonds from its warehouses and the stores it supplies for the past 3 years, as follows:

	Demand (cases)		
Month	*Year 1*	*Year 2*	*Year 3*
January	192	212	228
February	210	223	231
March	205	216	226
April	260	252	293
May	228	235	246
June	172	220	229
July	160	209	217
August	147	231	226
September	256	263	302
October	342	370	411
November	251	260	279
December	273	277	293

The distributor must hold the candy inventory in climate-controlled warehouses and be careful in handling it. The annual carrying cost is $116 per case. Diamonds must be shipped a long distance from the manufacturer to the distributor, and in order to keep the candy as fresh as possible, trucks must be air-conditioned, shipments must be direct, and shipments are often less than a truckload. As a result, the ordering cost is $4,700.

Diamant Foods makes Diamonds from three primary ingredients it orders from different suppliers: dark and milk chocolate, macadamia nuts, and a special heavy cream filling. Except for its unique shape, a Diamond is almost like a chocolate truffle. Each Diamond weighs 1.2 ounces and requires 0.70 ounce of blended chocolates, 0.50 ounce of macadamia nuts, and 0.40 ounce of filling to produce (including spillage and waste). Diamant Foods orders chocolate, nuts, and filling from its suppliers by the pound. The annual ordering cost is $5,700 for chocolate, and the annual carrying cost is $0.45 per pound. The ordering cost for macadamia nuts is $6,300, and the annual carrying cost is $0.63 per pound. The ordering cost for filling is $4,500, and the annual carrying cost is $0.55 per pound.

Each of the suppliers offers the candy manufacturer a quantity discount price schedule for the ingredients, as follows:

Chocolate		Macadamia Nuts		Filling	
Price	*Quantity (lb.)*	*Price*	*Quantity (lb.)*	*Price*	*Quantity (lb.)*
$3.05	0–50,000	$6.50	0–30,000	$1.50	0–40,000
2.90	50,001–100,000	6.25	30,001–70,000	1.35	40,001–80,000
2.75	100,001–150,000	5.95	70,001+	1.25	80,001+
2.60	150,001+				

Determine the inventory order quantity for Diamant's distributor. Compare the optimal order quantity with a seasonally adjusted forecast for demand. Does the order quantity seem adequate to meet the seasonal demand pattern for Diamonds (i.e., is it likely that shortages or excessive inventories will occur)? Can you identify the causes of the seasonal demand pattern for Diamonds? Determine the inventory order quantity for each of the three primary ingredients that Diamant Foods orders from its suppliers.

Solutions to Selected Odd-Numbered Problems

1. (a) $Q = 79.7$; (b) \$13,550; (c) 15.05 orders; (d) 24.18 days
3. (a) $Q = 240$; (b) \$4,800; (c) 80 orders; (d) 4 days
5. (a) $Q = 190{,}918.8$ yd.; (b) \$15,273.51; (c) 6.36 orders; (d) 57.4 days
7. $Q = 67.13$, $S = 15.49$, $TC = \$3{,}872.98$
9. (a) $Q = 774.6$ boxes, $TC = \$619.68$, $R = 43.84$ boxes
11. $Q = 23{,}862$, $TC = \$298{,}276$
13. (a) $Q = 2{,}529.8$ logs; (b) $TC = \$12{,}649.11$; (c) $T_b = 63.3$ days; (d) 42.16 days
15. $Q = 17{,}544.2$; $S = 4{,}616.84$; $TC = \$3{,}231.84$
17. $Q = 569.32$, $S = 32.79$, $TC = \$1{,}475.45$
19. (a) $Q = 11{,}062.62$, $TC = \$5{,}532.14$, runs = 1.63, max. level = 4,425.7; (b) $Q = 6{,}250$, $TC = \$6{,}458.50$
21. (a) $Q = 4{,}912.03$, $TC = \$18{,}420.11$; (b) $Q = 3{,}833.19$, $TC = \$17{,}249.36$; select new location
23. $C_c = \$950$
25. take discount, $Q = 300$
27. $Q = 500$, $TC = \$64{,}424$
29. $Q = 6{,}000$, $TC = \$85{,}230.33$
31. $Q = 30{,}000$, $TC = \$14{,}140$
33. $Q = 20{,}000$, $TC = \$893{,}368$
35. 91%
37. $R(90\%) = 74.61$ gal; increase safety stock to 26.37 gal.
39. 254.4 gal.
41. $R = 24.38$
43. 120 pizzas
45. (a) 15.15%; (b) $R = 6.977$ pizzas

Material Requirements Planning (MRP) and ERP

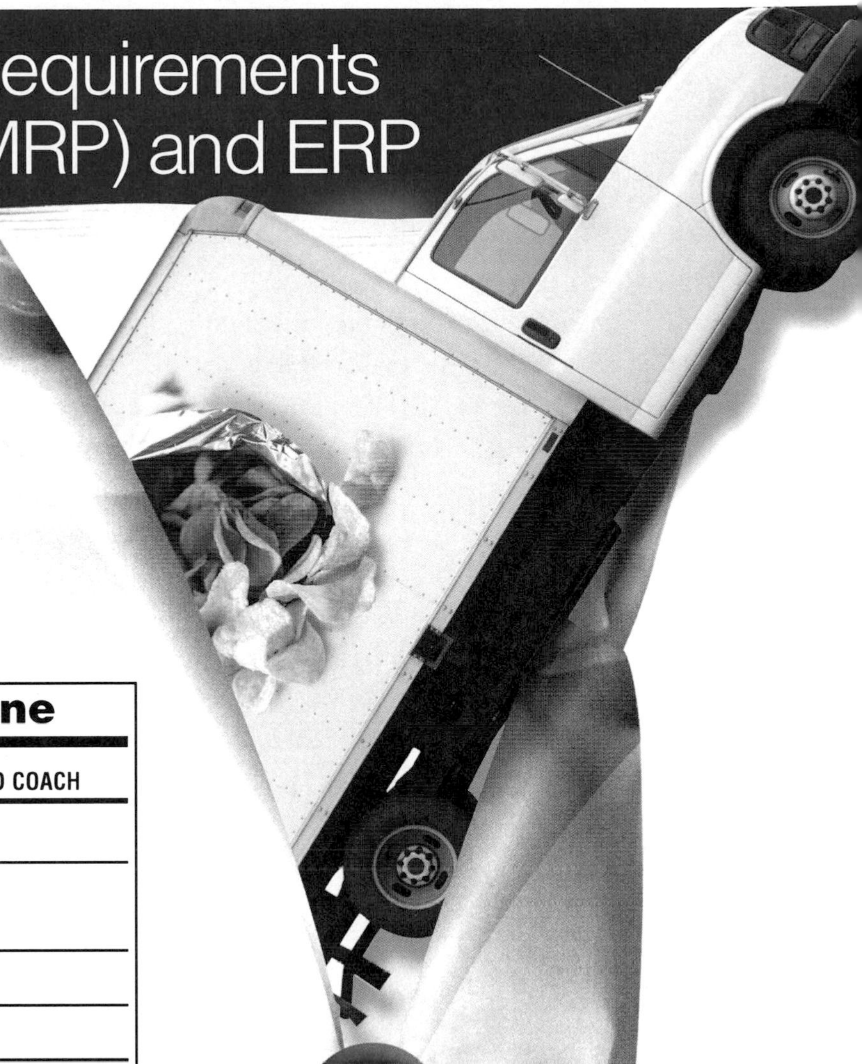

Chapter Outline

10

OM Strategy Decisions

- ► Design of Goods and Services
- ► Managing Quality
- ► Process Strategy
- ► Location Strategies
- ► Layout Strategies
- ► Human Resources
- ► Supply-Chain Management
- ► Inventory Management
  - Independent Demand
  - Dependent Demand
  - JIT and Lean Operations
- ► Scheduling
- ► Maintenance

MRP PROVIDES A COMPETITIVE ADVANTAGE FOR WHEELED COACH

Wheeled Coach, headquartered in Winter Park, Florida, is the largest manufacturer of ambulances in the world. The $200 million firm is an international competitor that sells more than 25% of its vehicles to markets outside the U.S. Twelve major ambulance designs are produced on assembly lines (i.e., a repetitive process) at the Florida plant, using 18,000 different inventory items, of which 6,000 are manufactured and 12,000 purchased. Most of the product line is custom designed and assembled to meet the specific and often unique requirements

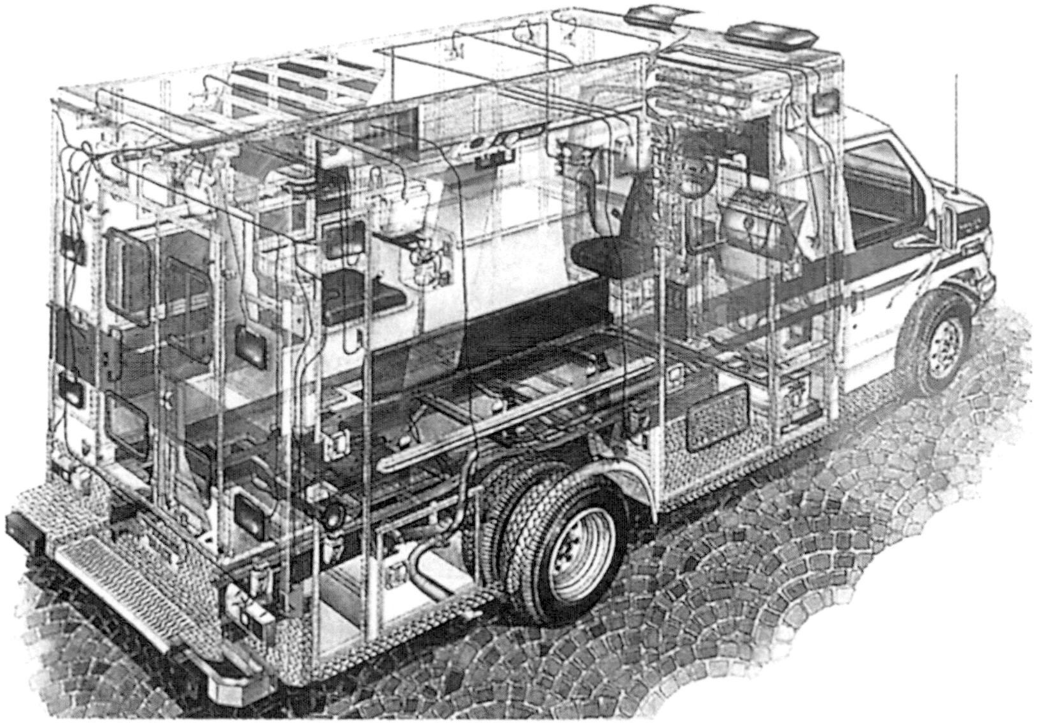

This cutaway of one ambulance interior indicates the complexity of the product, which for some rural locations may be the equivalent of a hospital emergency room in miniature. To complicate production, virtually every ambulance is custom ordered. This customization necessitates precise orders, excellent bills of materials, exceptional inventory control from supplier to assembly, and an MRP system that works.

Collins Industries, Inc.

Wheeled Coach Industries Incorporated

Wheeled Coach uses work cells to feed the assembly line. It maintains a complete carpentry shop (to provide interior cabinetry), a paint shop (to prepare, paint, and detail each vehicle), an electrical shop (to provide for the complex electronics in a modern ambulance), an upholstery shop (to make interior seats and benches), and as shown here, a metal fabrication shop (to construct the shell of the ambulance).

demanded by the ambulance's application and customer preferences.

This variety of products and the nature of the process demand good material requirements planning. Effective use of an MRP system requires accurate bills of material and inventory records. The Wheeled Coach system, which uses MAPICS DB software, provides daily updates and has reduced inventory by more than 30% in just 2 years.

Wheeled Coach insists that four key tasks be performed properly. First, the material plan must meet both the requirements of the master schedule and the capabilities of the production facility. Second, the plan must be executed as designed. Third, inventory investment must be minimized through effective "time-phased" material deliveries, consignment inventories, and a constant review of purchase methods. Finally, excellent record integrity must be maintained. Record accuracy is recognized as a fundamental ingredient of Wheeled Coach's successful MRP program. Its cycle counters are charged with material audits that not only correct errors but also investigate and correct problems.

Wheeled Coach Industries uses MRP as the catalyst for low inventory, high quality, tight schedules, and accurate records. Wheeled Coach has found competitive advantage via MRP.

On six parallel lines, ambulances move forward each day to the next workstation. The MRP system makes certain that just the materials needed at each station arrive overnight for assembly the next day.

Wheeled Coach Industries Incorporated

VIDEO 14.1
MRP at Wheeled Coach Ambulances

Here an employee is installing the wiring for an ambulance. There are an average of 15 miles of wire in a Wheeled Coach vehicle. This compares to 17 miles of wire in a sophisticated F-16 fighter jet.

Collins Industries, Inc.

Learning Objectives

LO1: Develop a product structure

LO2: Build a gross requirements plan

LO3: Build a net requirements plan

LO4: Determine lot sizes for lot-for-lot, EOQ, and PPB

LO5: Describe MRP II

LO6: Describe closed-loop MRP

LO7: Describe ERP

AUTHOR COMMENT
"Dependent demand" means the demand for one item is related to the demand for another item.

DEPENDENT DEMAND

Wheeled Coach, the subject of the *Global Company Profile*, and many other firms have found important benefits in MRP. These benefits include (1) better response to customer orders as the result of improved adherence to schedules, (2) faster response to market changes, (3) improved utilization of facilities and labor, and (4) reduced inventory levels. Better response to customer orders and to the market wins orders and market share. Better utilization of facilities and labor yields higher productivity and return on investment. Less inventory frees up capital and floor space for other uses. These benefits are the result of a strategic decision to use a *dependent* inventory scheduling system. Demand for every component of an ambulance is dependent.

Demand for items is dependent when the relationship between the items can be determined. Therefore, once management receives an order or makes a forecast for the final product, quantities for all components can be computed. All components are dependent items. The Boeing Aircraft operations manager who schedules production of one plane per week, for example, knows the requirements down to the last rivet. For any product, all components of that product are dependent demand items. *More generally, for any product for which a schedule can be established, dependent techniques should be used.*

Material requirements planning (MRP)
A dependent demand technique that uses a bill-of-material, inventory, expected receipts, and a master production schedule to determine material requirements.

When the requirements of MRP are met, dependent models are preferable to some EOQ models.[1] Dependent models are better not only for manufacturers and distributors but also for a wide variety of firms from restaurants to hospitals. The dependent technique used in a production environment is called **material requirements planning (MRP)**.

Because MRP provides such a clean structure for dependent demand, it has evolved as the basis for Enterprise Resource Planning (ERP). ERP is an information system for identifying and planning the enterprise-wide resources needed to take, make, ship, and account for customer orders. We will discuss ERP in the latter part of this chapter.

DEPENDENT INVENTORY MODEL REQUIREMENTS

Effective use of dependent inventory models requires that the operations manager know the following:

1. Master production schedule (what is to be made and when)
2. Specifications or bill of material (materials and parts required to make the product)
3. Inventory availability (what is in stock)
4. Purchase orders outstanding (what is on order, also called expected receipts)
5. Lead times (how long it takes to get various components)

We now discuss each of these requirements in the context of material requirements planning.

Master Production Schedule

Master production schedule (MPS)
A timetable that specifies what is to be made and when.

A **master production schedule (MPS)** specifies what is to be made (i.e., the number of finished products or items) and when. The schedule must be in accordance with a production plan. The production plan sets the overall level of output in broad terms (e.g., product families, standard

[1]These inventory models (EOQ) assume that the demand for one item was independent of the demand for another item. For example, EOQ assumes the demand for refrigerator parts is *independent* of the demand for refrigerators and that demand for parts is constant.

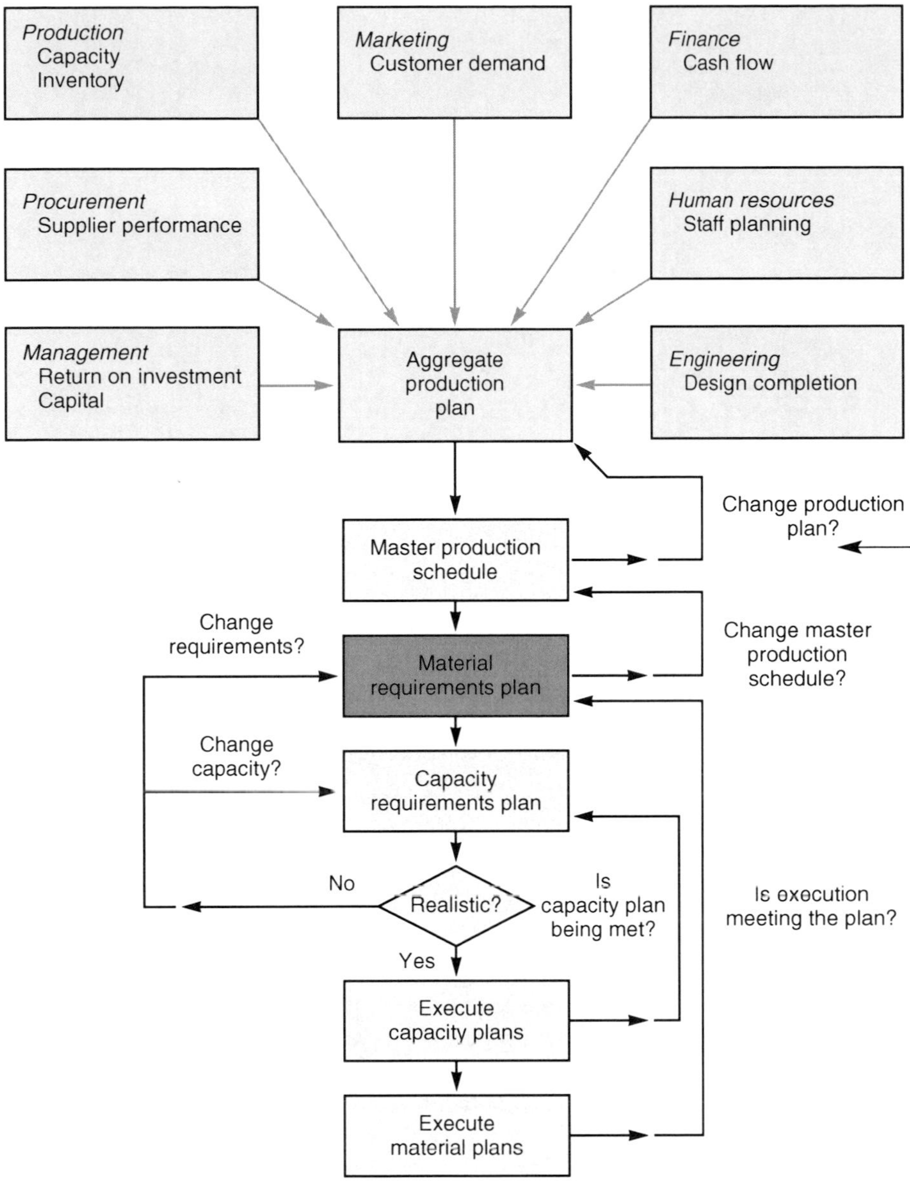

◀ **FIGURE 1**
The Planning Process

AUTHOR COMMENT
The master production schedule is derived from the aggregate schedule.

hours, or dollar volume). The plan also includes a variety of inputs, including financial plans, customer demand, engineering capabilities, labor availability, inventory fluctuations, supplier performance, and other considerations. Each of these inputs contributes in its own way to the production plan, as shown in Figure 1.

As the planning process moves from the production plan to execution, each of the lower-level plans must be feasible. When one is not, feedback to the next higher level is used to make the necessary adjustment. One of the major strengths of MRP is its ability to determine precisely the feasibility of a schedule within aggregate capacity constraints. This planning process can yield excellent results. The production plan sets the upper and lower bounds on the master production schedule. The result of this production planning process is the master production schedule.

The master production schedule tells us what is required to satisfy demand and meet the production plan. This schedule establishes what items to make and when: It *disaggregates* the aggregate production plan. While the *aggregate production plan* is established in gross terms such as families of products or tons of steel, the *master production schedule* is established in terms of specific products. Figure 2 shows the master production schedules for three stereo models that flow from the aggregate production plan for a family of stereo amplifiers.

Managers must adhere to the schedule for a reasonable length of time (usually a major portion of the production cycle—the time it takes to produce a product). Many organizations establish a master production schedule and establish a policy of not changing ("fixing") the near-term portion of the plan. This near-term portion of the plan is then referred to as the "fixed," "firm," or "frozen"

▶ **FIGURE 2**
The Aggregate Production Plan Is the Basis for Development of the Detailed Master Production Schedule

Months	January				February			
Aggregate Production Plan (Shows the total quantity of amplifiers)	1,500				1,200			
Weeks	1	2	3	4	5	6	7	8
Master Production Schedule (Shows the specific type and quantity of amplifier to be produced)								
240-watt amplifier	100		100		100		100	
150-watt amplifier		500		500		450		450
75-watt amplifier			300				100	

schedule. Wheeled Coach, the subject of the *Global Company Profile* for this chapter, fixes the last 14 days of its schedule. Only changes farther out, beyond the fixed schedule, are permitted. The master production schedule is a "rolling" production schedule. For example, a fixed 7-week plan has an additional week added to it as each week is completed, so a 7-week fixed schedule is maintained. Note that the master production schedule is a statement of *what is to be produced*, not a forecast of demand. The master schedule can be expressed in any of the following terms:

1. A *customer order in a job shop* (make-to-order) company
2. *Modules in a repetitive* (assemble-to-order or forecast) company
3. An *end item in a continuous* (stock-to-forecast) company

This relationship of the master production schedule to the processes is shown in Figure 3.

A master production schedule for two of Nancy's Specialty Foods' products, crabmeat quiche and spinach quiche, might look like Table 1.

Bills of Material

Bill of material (BOM)
A listing of the components, their description, and the quantity of each required to make one unit of a product.

Defining what goes into a product may seem simple, but it can be difficult in practice. To aid this process, manufactured items are defined via a bill of material. A **bill of material (BOM)** is a list of quantities of components, ingredients, and materials required to make a product. Individual drawings describe not only physical dimensions but also any special processing as well as the raw material from which each part is made. Nancy's Specialty Foods has a recipe

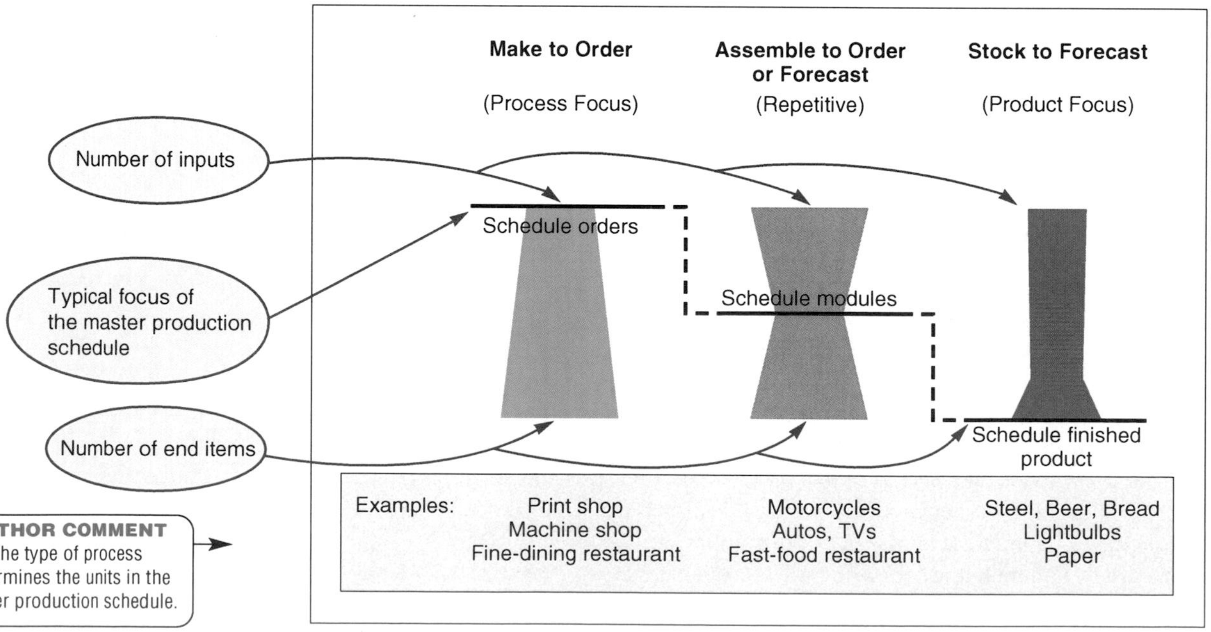

AUTHOR COMMENT
The type of process determines the units in the master production schedule.

▲ **FIGURE 3** **Typical Focus of the Master Production Schedule in Three Process Strategies**

Gross Requirements for Crabmeat Quiche										
Day	6	7	8	9	10	11	12	13	14	and so on
Amount	50		100	47	60		110	75		

Gross Requirements for Spinach Quiche											
Day	7	8	9	10	11	12	13	14	15	16	and so on
Amount	100	200	150			60	75		100		

◀ **TABLE 1**
Master Production Schedule for Crabmeat Quiche and Spinach Quiche at Nancy's Specialty Foods

for quiche, specifying ingredients and quantities, just as Wheeled Coach has a full set of drawings for an ambulance. Both are bills of material (although we call one a recipe, and they do vary somewhat in scope).

Because there is often a rush to get a new product to market, however, drawings and bills of material may be incomplete or even nonexistent. Moreover, complete drawings and BOMs (as well as other forms of specifications) often contain errors in dimensions, quantities, or countless other areas. When errors are identified, engineering change notices (ECNs) are created, further complicating the process. An *engineering change notice* is a change or correction to an engineering drawing or bill of material.

One way a bill of material defines a product is by providing a product structure. Example 1 shows how to develop the product structure and "explode" it to reveal the requirements for each component. A bill of material for item A in Example 1 consists of items B and C. Items above any level are called *parents*; items below any level are called *components* or *children*. By convention, the top level in a BOM is the 0 level.

◀ **EXAMPLE 1**

Developing a product structure and gross requirements

Speaker Kits, Inc., packages high-fidelity components for mail order. Components for the top-of-the-line speaker kit, "Awesome" (A), include 2 standard 12-inch speaker kits (Bs) and 3 speaker kits with amp-boosters (Cs).

Each B consists of 2 speakers (Ds) and 2 shipping boxes each with an installation kit (E). Each of the three 300-watt speaker kits (Cs) has 2 speaker boosters (Fs) and 2 installation kits (Es). Each speaker booster (F) includes 2 speakers (Ds) and 1 amp-booster (G). The total for each Awesome is 4 standard 12-inch speakers and twelve 12-inch speakers with the amp-booster. (Most purchasers require hearing aids within 3 years, and at least one court case is pending because of structural damage to a men's dormitory.) As we can see, the demand for B, C, D, E, F, and G is completely dependent on the master production schedule for A—the Awesome speaker kits.

APPROACH ▶ Given the above information, we construct a product structure and "explode" the requirements.

LO1: Develop a product structure.

SOLUTION ▶ This structure has four levels: 0, 1, 2, and 3. There are four parents: A, B, C, and F. Each parent item has at least one level below it. Items B, C, D, E, F, and G are components because each item has at least one level above it. In this structure, B, C, and F are both parents and components. The number in parentheses indicates how many units of that particular item are needed to make the item immediately above it. Thus, $B_{(2)}$ means that it takes two units of B for every unit of A, and $F_{(2)}$ means that it takes two units of F for every unit of C.

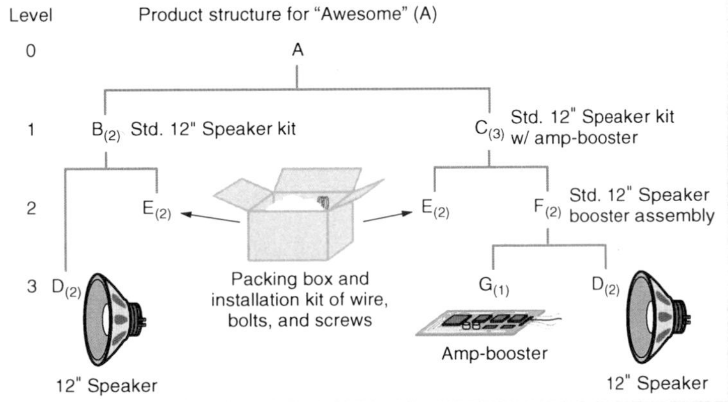

Once we have developed the product structure, we can determine the number of units of each item required to satisfy demand for a new order of 50 Awesome speaker kits. We "explode" the requirements as shown:

Part B:	2 × number of As =	(2)(50) =	100
Part C:	3 × number of As =	(3)(50) =	150
Part D:	2 × number of Bs + 2 × number of Fs =	(2)(100) + (2)(300) =	800
Part E:	2 × number of Bs + 2 × number of Cs =	(2)(100) + (2)(150) =	500
Part F:	2 × number of Cs =	(2)(150) =	300
Part G:	1 × number of Fs =	(1)(300) =	300

INSIGHT ▶ We now have a visual picture of the Awesome speaker kit requirements and knowledge of the quantities required. Thus, for 50 units of A, we will need 100 units of B, 150 units of C, 800 units of D, 500 units of E, 300 units of F, and 300 units of G.

LEARNING EXERCISE ▶ If there are 100 Fs in stock, how many Ds do you need? [Answer: 600.]

RELATED PROBLEMS ▶ 14.1, 14.3a, 14.13a, 14.25a

EXCEL OM Data File **Ch14Ex1.xls** can be found at **www.pearsonhighered.com/heizer.**

Bills of material not only specify requirements but also are useful for costing, and they can serve as a list of items to be issued to production or assembly personnel. When bills of material are used in this way, they are usually called *pick lists*.

Modular bills
Bills of material organized by major subassemblies or by product options.

Modular Bills Bills of material may be organized around product modules. *Modules* are not final products to be sold but are components that can be produced and assembled into units. They are often major components of the final product or product options. Bills of material for modules are called **modular bills**. Bills of material are sometimes organized as modules (rather than as part of a final product) because production scheduling and production are often facilitated by organizing around relatively few modules rather than a multitude of final assemblies. For instance, a firm may make 138,000 different final products but may have only 40 modules that are mixed and matched to produce those 138,000 final products. The firm builds an aggregate production plan and prepares its master production schedule for the 40 modules, not the 138,000 configurations of the final product. This approach allows the MPS to be prepared for a reasonable number of items (the narrow portion of the middle graphic in Figure 3) and to postpone assembly. The 40 modules can then be configured for specific orders at final assembly.

Planning bills (or **kits**)
A material grouping created in order to assign an artificial parent to a bill of material; also called "pseudo" bills.

Phantom bills of material
Bills of material for components, usually assemblies, that exist only temporarily; they are never inventoried.

Planning Bills and Phantom Bills Two other special kinds of bills of material are planning bills and phantom bills. **Planning bills** (sometimes called "pseudo" bills or super bills) are created in order to assign an artificial parent to the bill of material. Such bills are used (1) when we want to group subassemblies so the number of items to be scheduled is reduced and (2) when we want to issue "kits" to the production department. For instance, it may not be efficient to issue inexpensive items such as washers and cotter pins with each of numerous subassemblies, so we call this a *kit* and generate a planning bill. The planning bill specifies the *kit* to be issued. Consequently, a planning bill may also be known as **kitted material**, or **kit**. **Phantom bills of material** are bills of material for components, usually subassemblies, that exist only temporarily. These components go directly into another assembly and are never inventoried. Therefore, components of phantom bills of material are coded to receive special treatment; lead times are zero, and they are handled as an integral part of their parent item. An example is a transmission shaft with gears and bearings assembly that is placed directly into a transmission.

Low-level coding
A number that identifies items at the lowest level at which they occur.

Low-Level Coding Low-level coding of an item in a BOM is necessary when identical items exist at various levels in the BOM. **Low-level coding** means that the item is coded at the lowest level at which it occurs. For example, item D in Example 1 is coded at the lowest level at which it is used. Item D could be coded as part of B and occur at level 2. However, because D is also part of F, and F is level 2, item D becomes a level-3 item. Low-level coding is a convention to allow easy computing of the requirements of an item. When the BOM has thousands of items or when requirements are frequently recomputed, the ease and speed of computation become a major concern.

Accurate Inventory Records

Knowledge of what is in stock is the result of good inventory management. Good inventory management is an absolute necessity for an MRP system to work. If the firm does not exceed 99% record accuracy, then material requirements planning will not work.[2]

Purchase Orders Outstanding

Knowledge of outstanding orders exists as a by-product of well-managed purchasing and inventory-control departments. When purchase orders are executed, records of those orders and their scheduled delivery dates must be available to production personnel. Only with good purchasing data can managers prepare meaningful production plans and effectively execute an MRP system.

Lead time
In purchasing systems, the time between recognition of the need for an order and receiving it; in production systems, it is the order, wait, move, queue, setup, and run times for each component.

Lead Times for Components

Once managers determine when products are needed, they determine when to acquire them. The time required to acquire (that is, purchase, produce, or assemble) an item is known as **lead time**. Lead time for a manufactured item consists of *move*, *setup*, and *assembly* or *run times* for each component. For a purchased item, the lead time includes the time between recognition of need for an order and when it is available for production.

When the bill of material for Awesome speaker kits (As), in Example 1, is turned on its side and modified by adding lead times for each component (see Table 2), we then have a *time-phased product structure*. Time in this structure is shown on the horizontal axis of Figure 4 with item A due for completion in week 8. Each component is then offset to accommodate lead times.

▼ **TABLE 2**
Lead Times for Awesome Speaker Kits (As)

Component	Lead Time
A	1 week
B	2 weeks
C	1 week
D	1 week
E	2 weeks
F	3 weeks
G	2 weeks

MRP STRUCTURE

Although most MRP systems are computerized, the MRP procedure is straightforward and we can illustrate a small one by hand. A master production schedule, a bill of material, inventory and purchase records, and lead times for each item are the ingredients of a material requirements planning system (see Figure 5).

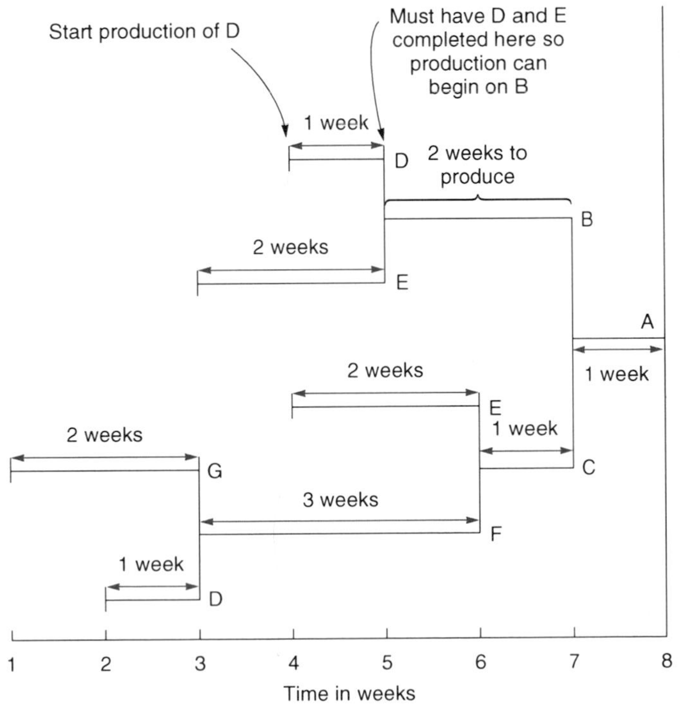

◄ **FIGURE 4**
Time-Phased Product Structure

AUTHOR COMMENT
This is a product structure on its side, with lead times.

[2]Record accuracy of 99% may sound good, but note that even when each component has an availability of 99% and a product has only seven components, the likelihood of a product being completed is only .932 (because $.99^7 = .932$).

▶ FIGURE 5
Structure of the MRP System

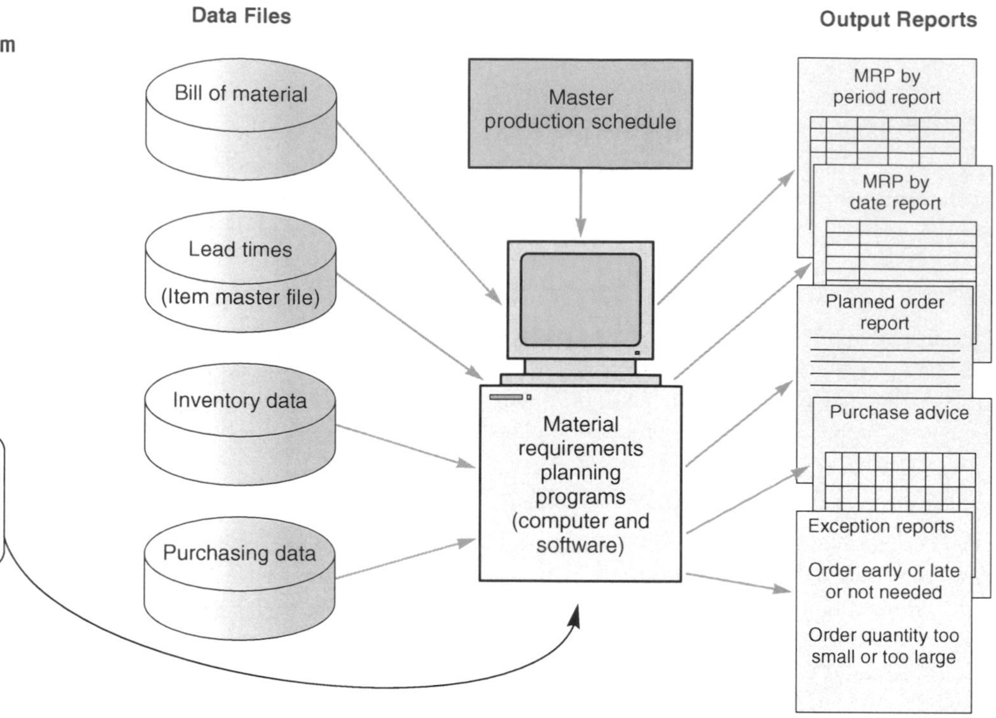

AUTHOR COMMENT
MRP software programs are popular because manual approaches are slow and error prone.

Gross material requirements plan
A schedule that shows the total demand for an item (prior to subtraction of on-hand inventory and scheduled receipts) and (1) when it must be ordered from suppliers, or (2) when production must be started to meet its demand by a particular date.

Once these ingredients are available and accurate, the next step is to construct a gross material requirements plan. The **gross material requirements plan** is a schedule, as shown in Example 2. It combines a master production schedule (that requires one unit of A in week 8) and the time-phased schedule (Figure 4). It shows when an item must be ordered from suppliers if there is no inventory on hand or when the production of an item must be started to satisfy demand for the finished product by a particular date.

EXAMPLE 2 ▶ Building a gross requirements plan

Each Awesome speaker kit (item A of Example 1) requires all the items in the product structure for A. Lead times are shown in Table 2.

APPROACH ▶ Using the information in Example 1 and Table 2, we construct the gross material requirements plan with a production schedule that will satisfy the demand of 50 units of A by week 8.

SOLUTION ▶ We prepare a schedule as shown in Table 3.

▶ TABLE 3
Gross Material Requirements Plan for 50 Awesome Speaker Kits (As)

	Week								
	1	2	3	4	5	6	7	8	Lead Time
A. Required date								50	
Order release date							50		1 week
B. Required date							100		
Order release date					100				2 weeks
C. Required date							150		
Order release date						150			1 week
E. Required date					200	300			
Order release date			200	300					2 weeks
F. Required date						300			
Order release date			300						3 weeks
D. Required date			600		200				
Order release date		600		200					1 week
G. Required date			300						
Order release date	300								2 weeks

LO2: Build a gross requirements plan

You can interpret the gross material requirements shown in Table 3 as follows: If you want 50 units of A at week 8, you must start assembling A in week 7. Thus, in week 7, you will need 100 units of B and 150 units of C. These two items take 2 weeks and 1 week, respectively, to produce. Production of B, therefore, should start in week 5, and production of C should start in week 6 (lead time subtracted from the required date for these items). Working backward, we can perform the same computations for all of the other items. Because D and E are used in two different places in Awesome speaker kits, there are two entries in each data record.

INSIGHT ▶ The gross material requirements plan shows when production of each item should begin and end in order to have 50 units of A at week 8. Management now has an initial plan.

LEARNING EXERCISE ▶ If the lead time for G decreases from 2 weeks to 1 week, what is the new order release date for G? [Answer: 300 in week 2.]

RELATED PROBLEMS ▶ 14.2, 14.4, 14.6, 14.8b, 14.9, 14.10a, 14.11a, 14.13b, 14.25b

So far, we have considered *gross material requirements*, which assumes that there is no inventory on hand. When there is inventory on hand, we prepare a **net requirements plan**. When considering on-hand inventory, we must realize that many items in inventory contain subassemblies or parts. If the gross requirement for Awesome speaker kits (As) is 100 and there are 20 of those speakers on hand, the net requirement for Awesome speaker kits (As) is 80 (that is, 100 – 20). However, each Awesome speaker kit on hand contains 2 Bs. As a result, the requirement for Bs drops by 40 Bs (20 A kits on hand × 2 Bs per A). Therefore, if inventory is on hand for a parent item, the requirements for the parent item and all its components decrease because each Awesome kit contains the components for lower-level items. Example 3 shows how to create a net requirements plan.

Net material requirements
The result of adjusting gross requirements for inventory on hand and scheduled receipts.

◄ EXAMPLE 3

Determining net requirements

Speaker Kits, Inc., developed a product structure from a bill of material in Example 1. Example 2 developed a gross requirements plan. Given the following on-hand inventory, Speaker Kits, Inc., now wants to construct a net requirements plan.

Item	On Hand	Item	On Hand
A	10	E	10
B	15	F	5
C	20	G	0
D	10		

APPROACH ▶ A net material requirements plan includes gross requirements, on-hand inventory, net requirements, planned order receipt, and planned order release for each item. We begin with A and work backward through the components.

SOLUTION ▶ Shown in the chart on the next page is the net material requirements plan for product A.

Constructing a net requirements plan is similar to constructing a gross requirements plan. Starting with item A, we work backward to determine net requirements for all items. To do these computations, we refer to the product structure, on-hand inventory, and lead times. The gross requirement for A is 50 units in week 8. Ten items are on hand; therefore, the net requirements and the scheduled **planned order receipt** are both 40 items in week 8. Because of the 1-week lead time, the **planned order release** is 40 items in week 7 (see the arrow connecting the order receipt and order release). Referring to week 7 and the product structure in Example 1, we can see that 80 (2 × 40) items of B and 120 (3 × 40) items of C are required in week 7 to have a total for 50 items of A in week 8. The letter superscripted A to the right of the gross figure for items B and C was generated as a result of the demand for the parent, A. Performing the same type of analysis for B and C yields the net requirements for D, E, F, and G. Note the on-hand inventory in row E in week 6 is zero. It is zero because the on-hand inventory (10 units) was used to make B in week 5. By the same token, the inventory for D was used to make F in week 3.

Planned order receipt
The quantity planned to be received at a future date.

Planned order release
The scheduled date for an order to be released.

INSIGHT ▶ Once a net requirement plan is completed, management knows the quantities needed, an ordering schedule, and a production schedule for each component.

▼ Net Material Requirements Plan for Product A *(the superscript is the source of the demand)*

Lot Size	Lead Time (weeks)	On Hand	Safety Stock	Allo- cated	Low- Level Code	Item Identi- fication			Week							
									1	2	3	4	5	6	7	8
Lot-for-Lot	1	10	—	—	0	A	Gross Requirements									50
							Scheduled Receipts									
							Projected On Hand	10	10	10	10	10	10	10	10	10
							Net Requirements									40
							Planned Order Receipts									40
							Planned Order Releases								40	
Lot-for-Lot	2	15	—	—	1	B	Gross Requirements								80^A	
							Scheduled Receipts									
							Projected On Hand	15	15	15	15	15	15	15	15	
							Net Requirements								65	
							Planned Order Receipts								65	
							Planned Order Releases						65			
Lot-for-Lot	1	20	—	—	1	C	Gross Requirements								120^A	
							Scheduled Receipts									
							Projected On Hand	20	20	20	20	20	20	20	20	
							Net Requirements								100	
							Planned Order Receipts								100	
							Planned Order Releases							100		
Lot-for-Lot	2	10	—	—	2	E	Gross Requirements						130^B	200^C		
							Scheduled Receipts									
							Projected On Hand	10	10	10	10	10	10			
							Net Requirements						120	200		
							Planned Order Receipts						120	200		
							Planned Order Releases				120	200				
Lot-for-Lot	3	5	—	—	2	F	Gross Requirements							200^C		
							Scheduled Receipts									
							Projected On Hand	5	5	5	5	5	5	5		
							Net Requirements							195		
							Planned Order Receipts							195		
							Planned Order Releases				195					
Lot-for-Lot	1	10	—	—	3	D	Gross Requirements				390^F		130^B			
							Scheduled Receipts									
							Projected On Hand	10	10	10	10					
							Net Requirements				380		130			
							Planned Order Receipts				380		130			
							Planned Order Releases			380		130				
Lot-for-Lot	2	0	—	—	3	G	Gross Requirements				195^F					
							Scheduled Receipts									
							Projected On Hand				0					
							Net Requirements				195					
							Planned Order Receipts				195					
							Planned Order Releases		195							

LEARNING EXERCISE ▶ If the on-hand inventory quantity of component F is 95 rather than 5, how many units of G will need to be ordered in week 1? [Answer: 105 units.]

RELATED PROBLEMS ▶ 14.5, 14.7, 14.8c, 14.10b, 14.11b, 14.12, 14.13c, 14.14b, 14.15a,b,c, 14.16a, 14.25c, 14.27

ACTIVE MODEL 14.1 This example is further illustrated in Active Model 1 at **www.pearsonhighered.com/heizer**.

Examples 2 and 3 considered only product A, the Awesome speaker kit, and its completion only in week 8. Fifty units of A were required in week 8. Normally, however, there is a demand for many products over time. For each product, management must prepare a master production schedule (as we saw earlier in Table 1). Scheduled production of each product is added to the

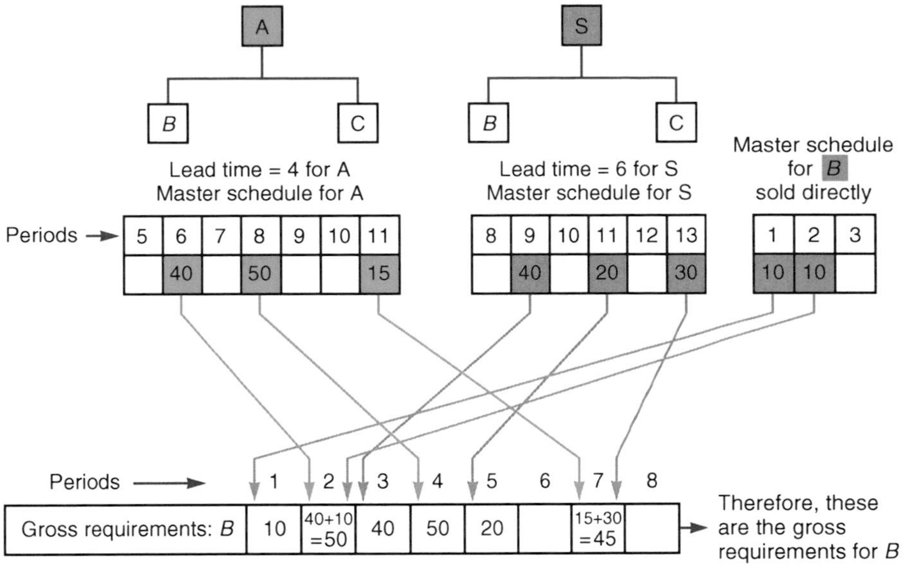

◀ **FIGURE 6**
Several Schedules Contributing to a Gross Requirements Schedule for B
One B is in each A, and one B is in each S; in addition, 10 Bs sold directly are scheduled in week 1, and 10 more that are sold directly are scheduled in week 2.

AUTHOR COMMENT
MRP gross requirements can combine multiple products, spare parts, and items sold directly.

master schedule and ultimately to the net material requirements plan. Figure 6 shows how several product schedules, including requirements for components sold directly, can contribute to one gross material requirements plan.

Most inventory systems also note the number of units in inventory that have been assigned to specific future production but not yet used or issued from the stockroom. Such items are often referred to as *allocated* items. Allocated items increase requirements and may then be included in an MRP planning sheet, as shown in Figure 7.

The allocated quantity has the effect of increasing the requirements (or, alternatively, reducing the quantity on hand). The logic, then, of a net requirements MRP is:

$$\underbrace{[(\text{Gross requirements}) + (\text{Allocations})]}_{\text{Total requirements}} - \underbrace{[(\text{On hand}) + (\text{Scheduled receipts})]}_{\text{Available inventory}} = \text{Net requirements}$$

LO3: Build a net requirements plan

Safety Stock The continuing task of operations managers is to remove variability. This is the case in MRP systems as in other operations systems. Realistically, however, managers need to realize that bills of material and inventory records, like purchase and production quantities, as well as lead times, may not be perfect. This means that some consideration of safety stock may be prudent. Because of the significant domino effect of any change in requirements, safety stock should be minimized, with a goal of ultimate elimination. When safety stock is deemed absolutely necessary, the usual policy is to build it into the projected on-hand inventory of the MRP logic. Distortion can be minimized when safety stock is held at the finished goods level and at the purchased component or raw material level.

▼ **FIGURE 7 Sample MRP Planning Sheet for Item Z**

Lot Size	Lead Time	On Hand	Safety Stock	Allocated	Low-Level Code	Item ID		Period 1	2	3	4	5	6	7	8
Lot For Lot	1	0	0	10	0	Z	Gross Requirements								~~80~~ 90
							Scheduled Receipts								0
							Projected On Hand 0	0	0	0	0	0	0	0	0
							Net Requirements								90
							Planned Order Receipts								90
							Planned Order Releases							90	

AUTHOR COMMENT
Using MRP to the utmost is serious work.

MRP MANAGEMENT

The material requirements plan is not static. And since MRP systems increasingly are integrated with just-in-time (JIT) techniques, we now discuss these two issues.

MRP Dynamics

Bills of material and material requirements plans are altered as changes in design, schedules, and production processes occur. In addition, changes occur in material requirements whenever the master production schedule is modified. Regardless of the cause of any changes, the MRP model can be manipulated to reflect them. In this manner, an up-to-date requirements schedule is possible.

The inputs to MRP (the master schedule, BOM, lead times, purchasing, and inventory) frequently change. Conveniently, a central strength of MRP systems is timely and accurate replanning. This occurs in one of two ways: by recomputing (also known as "regenerating") the requirement and schedule periodically, often weekly, or via a "net change" calculation. Net change in an MRP system means the MRP system creates new requirements in response to transactions. However, many firms find they do not want to respond to minor scheduling or quantity changes even if they are aware of them. These frequent changes generate what is called **system nervousness** and can create havoc in purchasing and production departments if implemented. Consequently, OM personnel reduce such nervousness by evaluating the need and impact of changes prior to disseminating requests to other departments. Two tools are particularly helpful when trying to reduce MRP system nervousness.

System nervousness
Frequent changes in an MRP system.

The first is time fences. **Time fences** allow a segment of the master schedule to be designated as "not to be rescheduled." This segment of the master schedule is therefore not changed during the periodic regeneration of schedules. The second tool is pegging. **Pegging** means tracing upward in the BOM from the component to the parent item. By pegging upward, the production planner can determine the cause for the requirement and make a judgment about the necessity for a change in the schedule.

Time fences
A means for allowing a segment of the master schedule to be designated as "not to be rescheduled."

Pegging
In material requirements planning systems, tracing upward in the bill of material from the component to the parent item.

With MRP, the operations manager *can* react to the dynamics of the real world. How frequently the manager wishes to impose those changes on the firm requires professional judgment. Moreover, if the nervousness is caused by legitimate changes, then the proper response may be to investigate the production environment—not adjust via MRP.

MRP and JIT

MRP does not do detailed scheduling—it plans. MRP will tell you that a job needs to be completed on a certain week or day but does not tell you that Job X needs to run on Machine A at 10:30 A.M. and be completed by 11:30 A.M. so that Job X can then run on machine B. MRP is also a planning technique with *fixed* lead times. Fixed lead times can be a limitation. For instance, the lead time to produce 50 units may vary substantially from the lead time to produce 5 units. These limitations complicate the marriage of MRP and just-in-time (JIT). What is needed is a way to make MRP more responsive to moving material rapidly in small batches. An MRP system combined with JIT can provide the best of both worlds. MRP provides the plan and an accurate picture of requirements; then JIT rapidly moves material in small batches, reducing work-in-process inventory. Let's look at four approaches for integrating MRP and JIT: finite capacity scheduling, small buckets, balanced flow, and supermarkets.

Finite Capacity Scheduling (FCS) Most MRP software loads work into infinite size "buckets." The **buckets** are time units, usually one week. Traditionally, when work is to be done in a given week, MRP puts the work there without regard to capacity. Consequently, MRP is considered an *infinite* scheduling technique. Frequently, as you might suspect, this is not realistic. Finite capacity scheduling (FCS) considers department and machine capacity, which is *finite*, hence the name. FCS provides the precise scheduling needed for rapid material movement. We are now witnessing a convergence of FCS and MRP. Sophisticated FCS systems modify the output from MRP systems to provide a finite schedule.

Buckets
Time units in a material requirements planning system.

Small Bucket Approach MRP is an excellent tool for resource and scheduling management in process-focused facilities, that is, in job shops. Such facilities include machine shops, hospitals, and restaurants, where lead times are relatively stable and poor balance between work centers is expected. Schedules are often driven by work orders, and lot sizes are the exploded bill-of-material size. In these enterprises, MRP can be integrated with JIT through the following steps.

STEP 1: Reduce MRP "buckets" from weekly to daily to perhaps hourly. Buckets are time units in an MRP system. Although the examples in this chapter have used weekly *time buckets*, many firms now use daily or even fraction-of-a-day time buckets. Some systems use a **bucketless system** in which all time-phased data have dates attached rather than defined time periods or buckets.

STEP 2: The planned receipts that are part of a firm's planned orders in an MRP system are communicated to the work areas for production purposes and used to sequence production.

STEP 3: Inventory is moved through the plant on a JIT basis.

STEP 4: As products are completed, they are moved into inventory (typically finished-goods inventory) in the normal way. Receipt of these products into inventory reduces the quantities required for subsequent planned orders in the MRP system.

STEP 5: A system known as *back flush* is used to reduce inventory balances. **Back flushing** uses the bill of material to deduct component quantities from inventory as each unit is completed.

Bucketless system
Time-phased data are referenced using dated records rather than defined time periods, or buckets.

Back flush
A system to reduce inventory balances by deducting everything in the bill of material on completion of the unit.

The focus in these facilities becomes one of maintaining schedules. Nissan achieves success with this approach by computer communication links to suppliers. These schedules are confirmed, updated, or changed every 15 to 20 minutes. Suppliers provide deliveries 4 to 16 times per day. Master schedule performance is 99% on time, as measured every hour. On-time delivery from suppliers is 99.9% and for manufactured piece parts, 99.5%.

Balanced Flow Approach MRP supports the planning and scheduling necessary for repetitive operations, such as the assembly lines at Harley-Davidson, Whirlpool, and a thousand other places. In these environments, the planning portion of MRP is combined with JIT execution. The JIT portion uses kanbans, visual signals, and reliable suppliers to pull the material through the facility. In these systems, execution is achieved by maintaining a carefully balanced flow of material to assembly areas with small lot sizes.

Supermarket Another technique that joins MRP and JIT is the use of a "supermarket." In many firms, subassemblies, their components, and hardware items are common to a variety of products. In such cases, releasing orders for these common items with traditional lead-time offset, as is done in an MRP system, is not necessary. The subassemblies, components, and hardware items can be maintained in a common area, sometimes called a **supermarket**, adjacent to the production areas where they are used. For instance, Ducati, Italy's high-performance motorcycle manufacturer, pulls "kits" with the materials needed for one engine or vehicle from the supermarket and delivers them to the assembly line on a JIT basis. Items in the supermarket are replenished by a JIT/kanban system.

Supermarket
An inventory area that holds common items that are replenished by a kanban system.

LOT-SIZING TECHNIQUES

AUTHOR COMMENT
Managers need to know how to group/order the "planned order releases."

An MRP system is an excellent way to determine production schedules and net requirements. However, whenever we have a net requirement, a decision must be made about *how much* to order. This decision is called a **lot-sizing decision**. There are a variety of ways to determine lot sizes in an MRP system; commercial MRP software usually includes the choice of several lot-sizing techniques. We now review a few of them.

Lot-sizing decision
The process of, or techniques used in, determining lot size.

Lot-for-Lot In Example 3, we used a lot-sizing technique known as **lot-for-lot**, which produced exactly what was required. This decision is consistent with the objective of an MRP system, which is to meet the requirements of *dependent* demand. Thus, an MRP system should produce units only as needed, with no safety stock and no anticipation of further orders. When frequent orders are economical and just-in-time inventory techniques implemented, lot-for-lot can be very efficient. However, when setup costs are significant or management has been unable to implement JIT, lot-for-lot can be expensive. Example 4 uses the lot-for-lot criteria and determines cost for 10 weeks of demand.

Lot-for-lot
A lot-sizing technique that generates exactly what is required to meet the plan.

EXAMPLE 4

Lot sizing with lot-for-lot

Speaker Kits, Inc., wants to compute its ordering and carrying cost of inventory on lot-for-lot criteria.

APPROACH ▶ With lot-for-lot, we order material only as it is needed. Once we have the cost of ordering (setting up), the cost of holding each unit for a given time period, and the production schedule, we can assign orders to our net requirements plan.

SOLUTION ▶ Speaker Kits has determined that, for the 12-inch speaker unit, setup cost is $100 and holding cost is $1 per period. The production schedule, as reflected in net requirements for assemblies, is as follows:

MRP Lot Sizing: Lot-for-Lot Technique*

		1	2	3	4	5	6	7	8	9	10
Gross requirements		35	30	40	0	10	40	30	0	30	55
Scheduled receipts											
Projected on hand	35	35	0	0	0	0	0	0	0	0	0
Net requirements		0	30	40	0	10	40	30	0	30	55
Planned order receipts			30	40		10	40	30		30	55
Planned order releases		30	40		10	40	30		30	55	

*Holding costs = $1/unit/week; setup cost = $100; gross requirements average per week = 27; lead time = 1 week.

The lot-sizing solution using the lot-for-lot technique is shown in the table. The holding cost is zero as there is never any inventory. (Inventory in the first period is used immediately and therefore has no holding cost.) But seven separate setups (one associated with each order) yield a total cost of $700. (Holding cost $= 0 \times 1 = 0$; ordering cost $= 7 \times 100 = 700$.)

INSIGHT ▶ When supply is reliable and frequent orders are inexpensive, but holding cost or obsolescence is high, lot-for-lot ordering can be very efficient.

LEARNING EXERCISE ▶ What is the impact on total cost if holding cost is $2 per period rather than $1? [Answer: Total holding cost remains zero, as no units are held from one period to the next with lot-for-lot.]

RELATED PROBLEMS ▶ 14.17, 14.20, 14.21, 14.22

LO4: Determine lot sizes for lot-for-lot, EOQ, and PPB

Economic Order Quantity EOQ can be used as a lot-sizing technique, but EOQ is preferable when *relatively constant* independent demand exists, not when we *know* the demand. EOQ is a statistical technique using averages (such as average demand for a year), whereas the MRP procedure assumes *known* (dependent) demand reflected in a master

John Russell/AP Wide World Photos

This Nissan line in Smyrna, Tennessee, has little inventory because Nissan schedules to a razor's edge. At Nissan, MRP helps reduce inventory to world-class standards. World-class automobile assembly requires that purchased parts have a turnover of slightly more than once a day and that overall turnover approaches 150 times per year.

production schedule. Operations managers should take advantage of demand information when it is known, rather than assuming a constant demand. EOQ is examined in Example 5.

EXAMPLE 5

Lot sizing with EOQ

With a setup cost of $100 and a holding cost per week of $1, Speaker Kits, Inc., wants to examine its cost with lot sizes based on an EOQ criteria.

APPROACH ▶ Using the same cost and production schedule as in Example 4, we determine net requirements and EOQ lot sizes.

SOLUTION ▶ Ten-week usage equals a gross requirement of 270 units; therefore, weekly usage equals 27, and 52 weeks (annual usage) equals 1,404 units. The EOQ model is:

$$Q^* = \sqrt{\frac{2DS}{H}}$$

where
D = annual usage = 1,404
S = setup cost = $100
H = holding (carrying) cost, on an annual basis per unit
= $1 × 52 weeks = $52

$$Q^* = 73 \text{ units}$$

MRP Lot Sizing: EOQ Technique*

		1	2	3	4	5	6	7	8	9	10
Gross requirements		35	30	40	0	10	40	30	0	30	55
Scheduled receipts											
Projected on hand	35	35	0	43	3	3	66	26	69	69	39
Net requirements		0	30	0	0	7	0	4	0	0	16
Planned order receipts			73			73		73			73
Planned order releases		73			73		73			73	

*Holding costs = $1/unit/week; setup cost = $100; gross requirements average per week = 27; lead time = 1 week.

$$\text{Setups} = 1{,}404/73 = 19 \text{ per year}$$
$$\text{Annual Setup cost} = 19 \times \$100 = \$1{,}900$$
$$\text{Annual Holding cost} = \tfrac{73}{2} \times (\$1 \times 52 \text{ weeks}) = \$1{,}898$$
$$\text{Annual Setup cost} + \text{Holding cost} = \$1{,}900 + 1{,}898 = \$3{,}798$$

The EOQ solution yields a computed 10-week cost of $730 [$3,798 × (10 weeks/52 weeks) = $730].

INSIGHT ▶ EOQ can be an effective lot-sizing technique when demand is relatively constant. However, notice that actual holding cost will vary from the computed $730, depending on the rate of actual usage. From the preceding table, we can see that in our 10-week example, costs really are $400 for four setups, plus a holding cost of 375 units (includes 57 remaining at the end of the period) at $1 per week for a total of $775. Because usage was not constant, the actual computed cost was in fact more than the theoretical EOQ ($730) and the lot-for-lot rule ($700). If any stockouts had occurred, these costs too would need to be added to our actual EOQ cost of $775.

LEARNING EXERCISE ▶ What is the impact on total cost if holding cost is $2 per period rather than $1? [Answer: The EOQ quantity becomes 52, the theoretical annual total cost becomes $5,404, and the 10-week cost is $1,039 ($5,404 × (10/52).]

RELATED PROBLEMS ▶ 14.18, 14.20, 14.21, 14.22

Part Period Balancing **Part period balancing (PPB)** is a more dynamic approach to balance setup and holding cost.[3] PPB uses additional information by changing the lot size to reflect requirements of the next lot size in the future. PPB attempts to balance setup and holding cost for

Part period balancing (PPB)
An inventory ordering technique that balances setup and holding costs by changing the lot size to reflect requirements of the next lot size in the future.

[3] J. J. DeMatteis, "An Economic Lot-Sizing Technique: The Part-Period Algorithms," *IBM Systems Journal* 7 (1968): 30–38.

Economic part period (EPP)
A period of time when the ratio of setup cost to holding cost is equal.

known demands. Part period balancing develops an **economic part period (EPP)**, which is the ratio of setup cost to holding cost. For our Speaker Kits example, EPP = \$100/\$1 = 100 units. Therefore, holding 100 units for one period would cost \$100, exactly the cost of one setup. Similarly, holding 50 units for two periods also costs \$100 (2 periods × \$1 × 50 units). PPB merely adds requirements until the number of part periods approximates the EPP—in this case, 100. Example 6 shows the application of part period balancing.

EXAMPLE 6 ▶ Lot sizing with part period balancing

Speaker Kits, Inc., wants to compute the costs associated with lot sizing using part period balancing. It will use a setup cost of \$100 and a \$1 holding cost.

APPROACH ▶ Using the same costs and production schedule as Examples 3 and 4, we develop a format that helps us compute the PPB quantity and apply that to our net requirements plan.

SOLUTION ▶ The procedure for computing the order releases of 80, 100, and 55 is shown in the following PPB calculation. In the second table, we apply the PPB order quantities to the net requirements plan.

PPB Calculations

Periods Combined	Trial Lot Size (cumulative net requirements)	Part Periods	Costs: Setup	Costs: Holding	Costs: Total
2	30	0	**40 units held for 1 period = \$40**		
2, 3	70	40 = 40 × 1	**10 units held for 3 periods = \$30**		
2, 3, 4	70	40			
2, 3, 4, 5	80	70 = **40 × 1** + **10 × 3**	100 +	70	= 170
2, 3, 4, 5, 6	120	230 = 40 × 1 + 10 × 3 + 40 × 4			
(Therefore, combine periods 2 through 5; 70 is as close to our EPP of 100 as we are going to get.)					
6	40	0			
6, 7	70	30 = 30 ×1			
6, 7, 8	70	30 = 30 × 1 + 0 × 2			
6, 7, 8, 9	100	120 = 30 × 1 + 30 × 3	100 +	120	= 220
(Therefore, combine periods 6 through 9; 120 is as close to our EPP of 100 as we are going to get.)					
10	55	0	100 +	0	= 100
			300 +	190	= 490

MRP Lot Sizing: PPB Technique*

		1	2	3	4	5	6	7	8	9	10
Gross requirements		35	30	40	0	10	40	30	0	30	55
Scheduled receipts											
Projected on hand	35	35	0	50	10	10	0	60	30	30	0
Net requirements		0	30	0	0	0	40	0	0	0	55
Planned order receipts			80				100				55
Planned order releases		80				100				55	

*Holding costs = \$1/unit/week; setup cost = \$100; gross requirements average per week = 27; lead time = 1 week.

EPP is 100 (setup cost divided by holding cost = \$100/\$1). The first lot is to cover periods 2, 3, 4, and 5 and is 80.

The total costs are \$490, with setup costs totaling \$300 and holding costs totaling \$190.

INSIGHT ▶ Both the EOQ and PPB approaches to lot sizing balance holding cost and ordering cost. But PPB places an order each time holding cost equals ordering cost, while EOQ takes a longer averaging approach.

LEARNING EXERCISE ▶ What is the impact on total cost if holding cost is \$2 per period rather than \$1? [Answer: With higher holding costs [PPB becomes 100/2 = 50], reorder points become more frequent, with orders now being placed for 70 units in period 1, 50 in period 4, 60 in period 6, and 55 in period 9.]

RELATED PROBLEMS ▶ 14.19, 14.20, 14.21, 14.22

Wagner-Whitin Algorithm The **Wagner-Whitin procedure** is a dynamic programming model that adds some complexity to the lot-size computation. It assumes a finite time horizon beyond which there are no additional net requirements. It does, however, provide good results.[4]

Wagner-Whitin procedure
A technique for lot-size computation that assumes a finite time horizon beyond which there are no additional net requirements to arrive at an ordering strategy.

Lot-Sizing Summary In the three Speaker Kits lot-sizing examples, we found the following costs:

Lot-for-lot	\$700
EOQ	\$730
Part period balancing	\$490

These examples should not, however, lead operations personnel to hasty conclusions about the preferred lot-sizing technique. In theory, new lot sizes should be computed whenever there is a schedule or lot-size change anywhere in the MRP hierarchy. However, in practice, such changes cause the instability and system nervousness referred to earlier in this chapter. Consequently, such frequent changes are not made. This means that all lot sizes are wrong because the production system cannot respond to frequent changes.

In general, the lot-for-lot approach should be used whenever low-cost deliveries can be achieved. Lot-for-lot is the goal. Lots can be modified as necessary for scrap allowances, process constraints (for example, a heat-treating process may require a lot of a given size), or raw material purchase lots (for example, a truckload of chemicals may be available in only one lot size). However, caution should be exercised prior to any modification of lot size because the modification can cause substantial distortion of actual requirements at lower levels in the MRP hierarchy. When setup costs are significant and demand is reasonably smooth, part period balancing (PPB), Wagner-Whitin, or even EOQ should provide satisfactory results. Too much concern with lot sizing yields false accuracy because of MRP dynamics. A correct lot size can be determined only after the fact, based on what actually happened in terms of requirements.

EXTENSIONS OF MRP

In this section, we review three extensions of MRP.

Material Requirements Planning II (MRP II)

Material requirements planning II is an extremely powerful technique. Once a firm has MRP in place, requirements data can be enriched by resources other than just components. When MRP is used this way, *resource* is usually substituted for *requirements,* and MRP becomes **MRP II**. It then stands for material *resource* planning.

Material requirements planning II (MRP II)
A system that allows, with MRP in place, inventory data to be augmented by other resource variables; in this case, MRP becomes *material resource planning.*

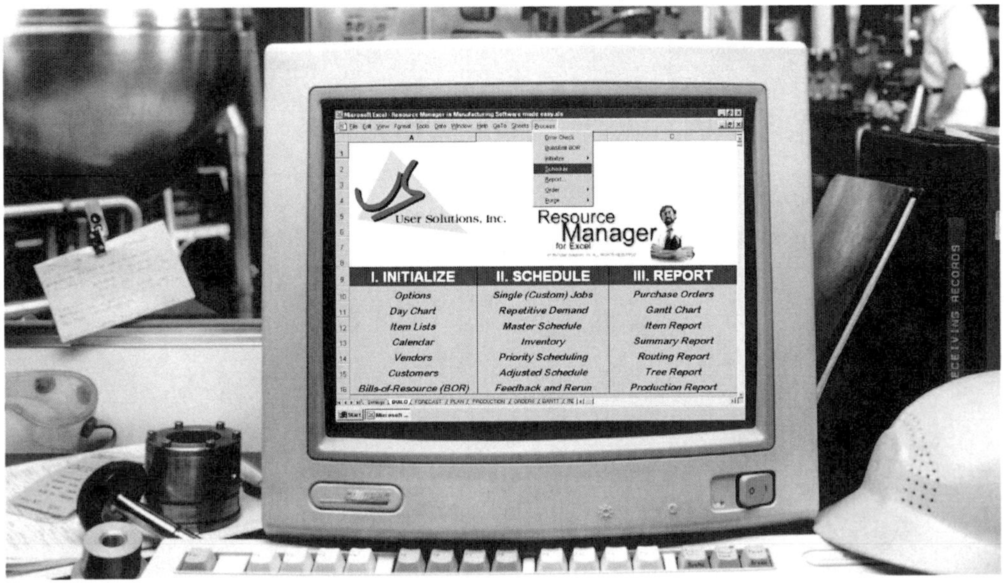

Courtesy of User Solutions, Inc.

Many MRP programs, such as *Resource Manager for Excel* and *DB*, are commercially available. *Resource Manager's* initial menu screen is shown here.

A demo program is available for student use at **www.usersolutions.com.**

[4] We leave discussion of the algorithm to mathematical programming texts. The Wagner-Whitin algorithm yields a cost of \$455 for the data in Examples 4, 5, and 6.

▶ **TABLE 4**
Material Resource Planning (MRP II)

By utilizing the logic of MRP, resources such as labor, machine-hours, scrap, and cost can be accurately determined and scheduled. Weekly demand for labor, machine-hours, scrap, and payables for 100 computers are shown.

	Lead Time	WEEKS 5	6	7	8
Computer	1				100
Labor-hours: .2 each					20
Machine-hours: .2 each					20
Scrap: 1 ounce fiberglass each					6.25 lbs
Payables: $0					$0
PC board (1 each)	2			100	
Labor-hours: .15 each				15	
Machine-hours: .1 each				10	
Scrap: .5 ounces copper each				3.125 lb	
Payables: raw material at $5 each				$500	
Processors (5 each)	4	500			
Labor-hours: .2 each		100			
Machine-hours: .2 each		100			
Scrap: .01 ounces of acid waste each		0.3125 lb			
Payables: processors at $10 each		$5,000			

LO5: Describe MRP II

So far in our discussion of MRP, we have scheduled products and their components. However, products require many resources, such as energy and money, beyond the product's tangible components. In addition to these resource inputs, *outputs* can be generated as well. Outputs can include such things as scrap, packaging waste, effluent, and carbon emissions. As OM becomes increasingly sensitive to the environmental and sustainability issues, identifying and managing byproducts becomes increasingly important. MRP II provides a vehicle for doing so. Table 4 provides an example of labor-hours, machine-hours, pounds of scrap, and cash, in the format of a gross requirements plan. With MRP II, management can identify both the inputs and outputs as well as the relevant schedule. MRP II provides another tool in OM's battle for sustainable operations.

MRP II systems are seldom stand-alone programs. Most are tied into other computer software that provide data to the MRP system or receive data from the MRP system. Purchasing, production scheduling, capacity planning, inventory, and warehouse management are a few examples of this data integration.

Closed-loop MRP system
A system that provides feedback to the capacity plan, master production schedule, and production plan so planning can be kept valid at all times.

LO6: Describe closed-loop MRP

Closed-Loop MRP

Closed-loop material requirements planning implies an MRP system that provides feedback to scheduling from the inventory control system. Specifically, a **closed-loop MRP system** provides information to the capacity plan, master production schedule, and ultimately to the production plan (as shown in Figure 8). Virtually all commercial MRP systems are closed-loop.

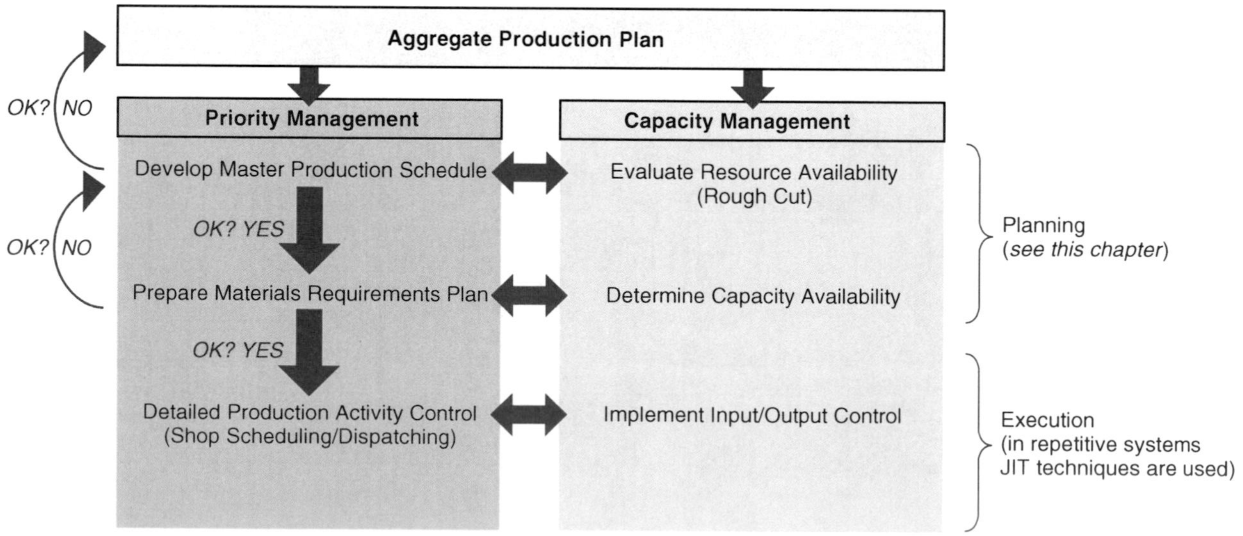

▲ **FIGURE 8** **Closed-Loop Material Requirements Planning**

Capacity Planning

In keeping with the definition of closed-loop MRP, feedback about workload is obtained from each work center. **Load reports** show the resource requirements in a work center for all work currently assigned to the work center, all work planned, and expected orders. Figure 9(a) shows that the initial load in the milling center exceeds capacity on days 2, 3, and 5. Closed-loop MRP systems allow production planners to move the work between time periods to smooth the load or at least bring it within capacity. (This is the "capacity planning" part of Figure 8.) The closed-loop MRP system can then reschedule all items in the net requirements plan (see Figure 9[b]).

Load report
A report for showing the resource requirements in a work center for all work currently assigned there as well as all planned and expected orders.

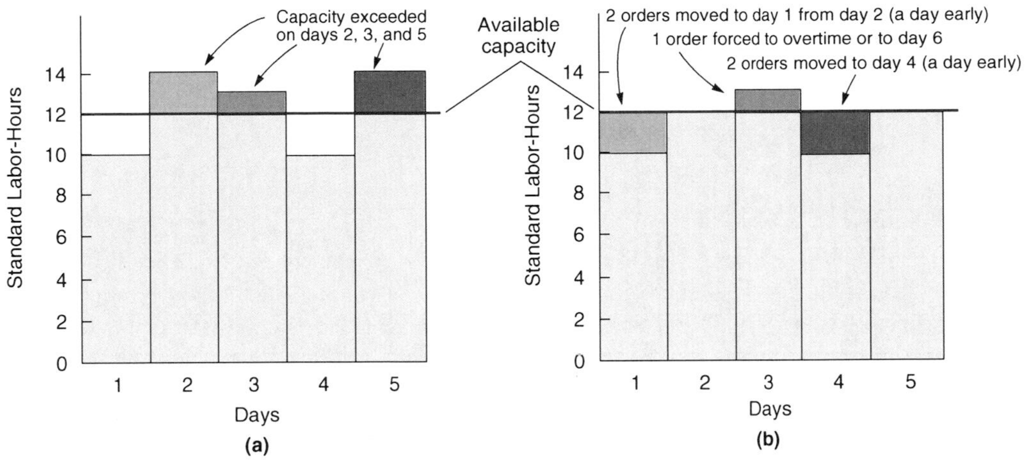

◀ **FIGURE 9**
(a) Initial Resource Requirements Profile for a Work Center (b) Smoothed Resource Requirements Profile for a Work Center

Tactics for smoothing the load and minimizing the impact of changed lead time include the following:

1. *Overlapping,* which reduces the lead time, sends pieces to the second operation before the entire lot is completed on the first operation.
2. *Operations splitting* sends the lot to two different machines for the same operation. This involves an additional setup, but results in shorter throughput times, because only part of the lot is processed on each machine.
3. *Order* or, *lot splitting,* involves breaking up the order and running part of it earlier (or later) in the schedule.

Example 7 shows a brief detailed capacity scheduling example using order splitting to improve utilization.

◀ **EXAMPLE 7**
Order splitting

Kevin Watson, the production planner at Wiz Products, needs to develop a capacity plan for a work center. He has the production orders shown below for the next 5 days. There are 12 hours available in the work cell each day. The parts being produced require 1 hour each.

Day	1	2	3	4	5
Orders	10	14	13	10	14

APPROACH ▶ Compute the time available in the work center and the time necessary to complete the production requirements.

SOLUTION ▶

Day	Units Ordered	Capacity Required (hours)	Capacity Available (hours)	Utilization: Over/ (Under) (hours)	Production Planner's Action	New Production Schedule
1	10	10	12	(2)		12
2	14	14	12	2	Split order: move 2 units to day 1	12
3	13	13	12	1	Split order: move 1 unit to day 6 or request overtime	13
4	10	10	12	(2)		12
5	14	14	12	2	Split order: move 2 units to day 4	12
	61					

INSIGHT ▶ By moving orders, the production planner is able to utilize capacity more effectively and still meet the order requirements, with only 1 order produced on overtime in day 3.

LEARNING EXERCISE ▶ If the units ordered for day 5 increase to 16, what are the production planner's options? [Answer: In addition to moving 2 units to day 4, move 2 units of production to day 6, or request overtime.]

RELATED PROBLEMS ▶ 14.23, 14.24

When the workload consistently exceeds work-center capacity, the tactics just discussed are not adequate. This may mean adding capacity. Options include adding capacity via personnel, machinery, overtime, or subcontracting.

MRP IN SERVICES

The demand for many services or service items is classified as dependent demand when it is directly related to or derived from the demand for other services. Such services often require product-structure trees, bills-of-material and labor, and scheduling. MRP can make a major contribution to operational performance in such services. Examples from restaurants, hospitals, and hotels follow.

Restaurants In restaurants, ingredients and side dishes (bread, vegetables, and condiments) are typically meal components. These components are dependent on the demand for meals. The meal is an end item in the master schedule. Figure 10 shows (a) a product-structure tree and (b) a bill of material for veal picante, a top-selling entrée in a New Orleans restaurant. Note that the various components of veal picante (that is, veal, sauce, spinach, and linguini) are prepared by different kitchen personnel (see part [a] of Figure 10). These preparations also require different amounts of time to complete. Figure 10(c) shows a bill-of-labor for the veal dish. It lists the operations to be performed, the order of operations, and the labor requirements for each operation (types of labor and labor-hours).

Hospitals MRP is also applied in hospitals, especially when dealing with surgeries that require known equipment, materials, and supplies. Houston's Park Plaza Hospital and many hospital suppliers, for example, use the technique to improve the scheduling and management of expensive surgical inventory.

Hotels Marriott develops a bill of material (BOM) and a bill of labor when it renovates each of its hotel rooms. Marriott managers explode the BOM to compute requirements for materials, furniture, and decorations. MRP then provides net requirements and a schedule for use by purchasing and contractors.

Distribution Resource Planning (DRP)

Distribution resource planning (DRP)
A time-phased stock-replenishment plan for all levels of a distribution network.

When dependent techniques are used in the supply chain, they are called distribution resource planning (DRP). **Distribution resource planning (DRP)** is a time-phased stock-replenishment plan for all levels of the supply chain.

DRP procedures and logic are analogous to MRP. With DRP, expected demand becomes gross requirements. Net requirements are determined by allocating available inventory to gross requirements. The DRP procedure starts with the forecast at the retail level (or the most distant point of the distribution network being supplied). All other levels are computed. As is the case with MRP, inventory is then reviewed with an aim to satisfying demand. So that stock will arrive when it is needed, net requirements are offset by the necessary lead time. A planned order release quantity becomes the gross requirement at the next level down the distribution chain.

DRP *pulls* inventory through the system. Pulls are initiated when the retail level orders more stock. Allocations are made to the retail level from available inventory and production after being adjusted to obtain shipping economies. Effective use of DRP requires an integrated information system to rapidly convey planned order releases from one level to the next. The goal of the DRP system is small and frequent replenishment within the bounds of economical ordering and shipping.

(a) PRODUCT STRUCTURE TREE

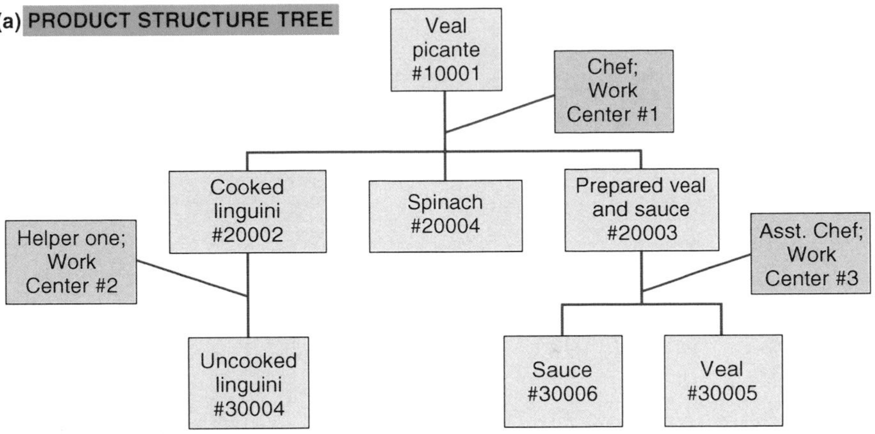

◄ **FIGURE 10**
Product Structure Tree, Bill-of-Material, and Bill-of-Labor for Veal Picante

Source: Adapted from John G. Wacker, "Effective Planning and Cost Control for Restaurants," *Production and Inventory Management* (Vol. 26, no. 1): 60. Reprinted by permission of American Production and Inventory Control Society.

(b) BILL OF MATERIALS

Part Number	Description	Quantity	Unit of Measure	Unit Cost
10001	Veal picante	1	Serving	—
20002	Cooked linguini	1	Serving	—
20003	Prepared veal and sauce	1	Serving	—
20004	Spinach	0.1	Bag	0.94
30004	Uncooked linguini	0.5	Pound	—
30005	Veal	1	Serving	2.15
30006	Sauce	1	Serving	0.80

(c) BILL OF LABOR FOR VEAL PICANTE

			Labor-Hours	
Work Center	Operation	Labor Type	Setup Time	Run Time
1	Assemble dish	Chef	.0069	.0041
2	Cook linguini	Helper one	.0005	.0022
3	Cook veal and sauce	Assistant chef	.0125	.0500

ENTERPRISE RESOURCE PLANNING (ERP)

AUTHOR COMMENT ERP tries to integrate all of a firm's information.

Advances in MRP II systems that tie customers and suppliers to MRP II have led to the development of enterprise resource planning (ERP) systems. **Enterprise resource planning (ERP)** is software that allows companies to (1) automate and integrate many of their business processes, (2) share a common database and business practices throughout the enterprise, and (3) produce information in real time. A schematic showing some of these relationships for a manufacturing firm appears in Figure 11.

Enterprise resource planning (ERP)
An information system for identifying and planning the enterprise-wide resources needed to take, make, ship, and account for customer orders.

The objective of an ERP system is to coordinate a firm's whole business, from supplier evaluation to customer invoicing. This objective is seldom achieved, but ERP systems are evolving as umbrella systems that tie together a variety of specialized systems. This is accomplished by using a centralized database to assist the flow of information among business functions. Exactly what is tied together, and how, varies on a case-by-case basis. In addition to the traditional components of MRP, ERP systems usually provide financial and human resource (HR) management information. ERP systems also include:

LO7: Describe ERP

- *Supply chain management (SCM)* software to support sophisticated vendor communication, e-commerce, and those activities necessary for efficient warehousing and logistics. The idea is to tie operations (MRP) to procurement, to materials management, and to suppliers, providing the tools necessary for effective management of all four areas.
- *Customer relationship management (CRM)* software for the incoming side of the business. CRM is designed to aid analysis of sales, target the most profitable customers, and manage the sales force.

In addition to data integration, ERP software promises reduced transaction costs and fast, accurate information. A strategic emphasis on just-in-time systems and supply chain integration

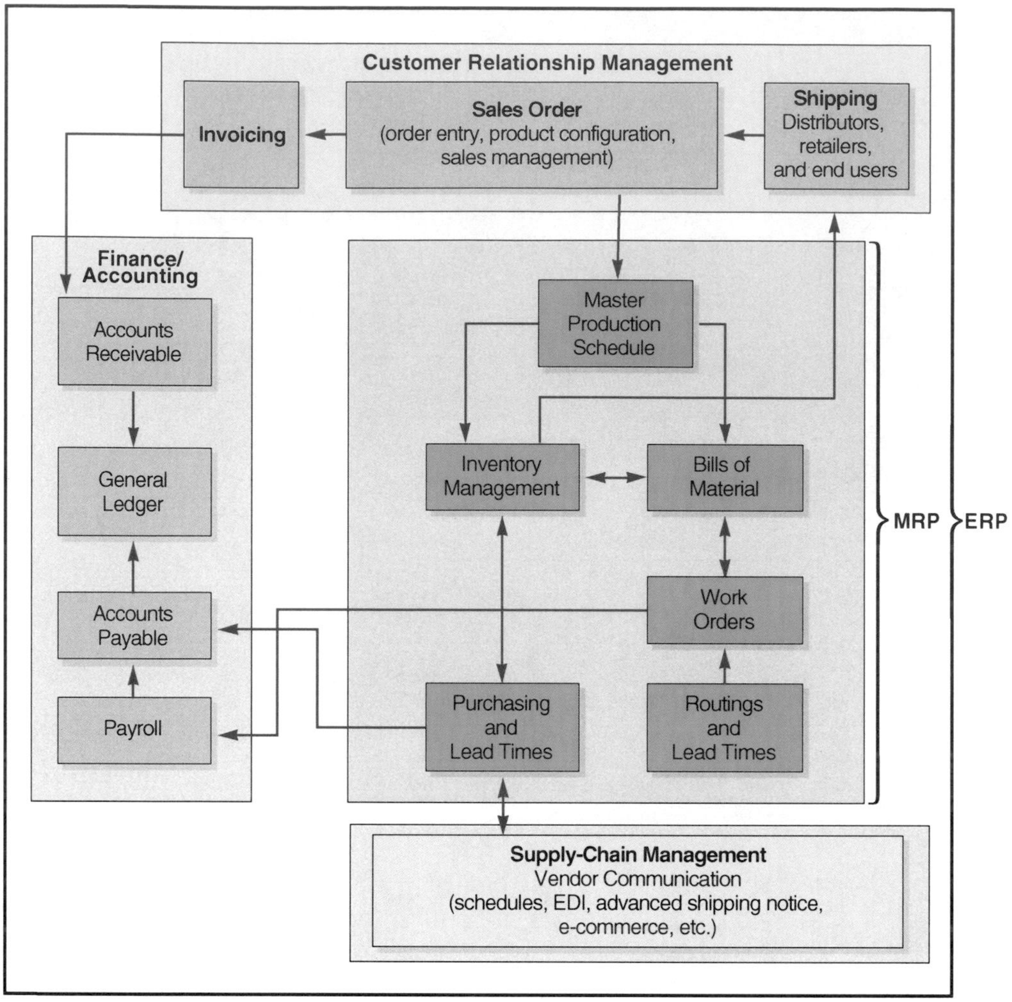

▶ **FIGURE 11**
MRP and ERP Information Flows, Showing Customer Relationship Management (CRM), Supply-Chain Management (SCM), and Finance/Accounting
Other functions such as human resources are often also included in ERP systems.

drives the desire for enterprise-wide software. The *OM in Action* box "Managing Benetton with ERP Software" provides an example of how ERP software helps integrate company operations.

OM in Action ▶ Managing Benetton with ERP Software

Thanks to ERP, the Italian sportswear company Benetton can probably claim to have the world's fastest factory and the most efficient distribution in the garment industry. Located in Ponzano, Italy, Benetton makes and ships 50 million pieces of clothing each year. That is 30,000 boxes every day—boxes that must be filled with exactly the items ordered going to the correct store of the 5,000 Benetton outlets in 60 countries. This highly automated distribution center uses only 19 people. Without ERP, hundreds of people would be needed.

Here is how ERP software works:

1. *Ordering:* A salesperson in the south Boston store finds that she is running out of a best-selling blue sweater. Using a laptop PC, her local Benetton sales agent taps into the ERP sales module.
2. *Availability:* ERP's inventory software simultaneously forwards the order to the mainframe in Italy and finds that half the order can be filled immediately from the Italian warehouse. The rest will be manufactured and shipped in 4 weeks.
3. *Production:* Because the blue sweater was originally created by computer-aided design (CAD), ERP manufacturing software passes the specifications to a knitting machine. The knitting machine makes the sweaters.
4. *Warehousing:* The blue sweaters are boxed with a radio frequency ID (RFID) tag addressed to the Boston store and placed in one of the 300,000 slots in the Italian warehouse. A robot flies by, reading RFID tags, picks out any and all boxes ready for the Boston store, and loads them for shipment.
5. *Order tracking:* The Boston salesperson logs onto the ERP system through the Internet and sees that the sweater (and other items) are completed and being shipped.
6. *Planning:* Based on data from ERP's forecasting and financial modules, Benetton's chief buyer decides that blue sweaters are in high demand and quite profitable. She decides to add three new hues.

Sources: The Wall Street Journal (April 10, 2007): B1; *Frontline Solutions* (April 2003): 54; and *MIT Sloan Management Review* (Fall 2001): 46–53.

In an ERP system, data are entered only once into a common, complete, and consistent database shared by all applications. For example, when a Nike salesperson enters an order into his ERP system for 20,000 pairs of sneakers for Foot Locker, the data are instantly available on the manufacturing floor. Production crews start filling the order if it is not in stock, accounting prints Foot Locker's invoice, and shipping notifies the Foot Locker of the future delivery date. The salesperson, or even the customer, can check the progress of the order at any point. This is all accomplished using the same data and common applications. To reach this consistency, however, the data fields must be defined identically across the entire enterprise. In Nike's case, this means integrating operations at production sites from Vietnam to China to Mexico, at business units across the globe, in many currencies, and with reports in a variety of languages.

Each ERP vendor produces unique products. The major vendors, SAP AG (a German firm), BEA (Canada), SSAGlobal, American Software, PeopleSoft/Oracle, CMS Software (all of the U.S.), sell software or modules designed for specific industries (a set of SAP's modules is shown in Figure 12). However, companies must determine if their way of doing business will fit the standard ERP module. If they determine that the product will not fit the standard ERP product, they can change the way they do business to accommodate the software. But such a change can have an adverse impact on their business process, reducing a competitive advantage. Alternatively, ERP software can be customized to meet their specific process requirements. Although the vendors build the software to keep the customization process simple, many companies spend up to five times the cost of the software to customize it. In addition to the expense, the major downside of customization is that when ERP vendors provide an upgrade or enhancement to the software, the customized part of the code must be rewritten to fit into the new version. ERP programs cost from a minimum of $300,000 for a small company to hundreds of millions of dollars for global giants like Ford and Coca-Cola. It is easy to see, then, that ERP systems are expensive, full of hidden issues, and time-consuming to install.

▼ **FIGURE 12** **SAP's Modules for ERP**

CASH TO CASH
Covers all financial related activity:
- Accounts receivable
- Accounts payable
- General ledger
- Treasury
- Cash management
- Asset management

PROMOTE TO DELIVER
Covers front-end customer-oriented activities:
- Marketing
- Quote and order processing
- Transportation
- Documentation and labeling
- After sales service
- Warranty and guarantees

DESIGN TO MANUFACTURE
Covers internal production activities:
- Design engineering
- Production engineering
- Plant maintenance
- Shop floor reporting
- Contract/project management
- Subcontractor management

RECRUIT TO RETIRE
Covers all HR- and payroll-oriented activity:
- Time and attendance
- Travel and expenses
- Payroll

PROCURE TO PAY
Covers sourcing activities:
- Vendor sourcing
- Purchase requisitioning
- Purchase ordering
- Purchase contracts
- Inbound logistics
- Supplier invoicing/matching
- Supplier payment/settlement
- Supplier performance

DOCK TO DISPATCH
Covers internal inventory management:
- Warehousing
- Distribution planning
- Forecasting
- Replenishment planning
- Physical inventory
- Material handling

Source: www.sap.com.

Advantages and Disadvantages of ERP Systems

We have alluded to some of the pluses and minuses of ERP. Here is a more complete list of both.

Advantages:

1. Provides integration of the supply chain, production, and administrative process.
2. Creates commonality of databases.
3. Can incorporate improved, reengineered, "best processes."
4. Increases communication and collaboration among business units and sites.
5. Has a software database that is off-the-shelf coding.
6. May provide a strategic advantage over competitors.

Disadvantages:

1. Is very expensive to purchase, and even more costly to customize.
2. Implementation may require major changes in the company and its processes.
3. Is so complex that many companies cannot adjust to it.
4. Involves an ongoing process for implementation, which may never be completed.
5. Expertise in ERP is limited, with staffing an ongoing problem.

ERP in the Service Sector

ERP vendors have developed a series of service modules for such markets as health care, government, retail stores, and financial services. Springer-Miller Systems, for example, has created an ERP package for the hotel market with software that handles all front- and back-office functions. This system integrates tasks such as maintaining guest histories, booking room and dinner reservations, scheduling golf tee times, and managing multiple properties in a chain. PeopleSoft/Oracle combines ERP with supply chain management to coordinate airline meal preparation. In the grocery industry, these supply chain systems are known as *efficient consumer response* (ECR) systems. As is the case in manufacturing, **efficient consumer response** systems tie sales to buying, to inventory, to logistics, and to production.

Efficient consumer response (ECR)
Supply chain management systems in the grocery industry that tie sales to buying, to inventory, to logistics, and to production.

CHAPTER SUMMARY

Material requirements planning (MRP) schedules production and inventory when demand is dependent. For MRP to work, management must have a master schedule, precise requirements for all components, accurate inventory and purchasing records, and accurate lead times.

Production should often be lot-for-lot in an MRP system. When properly implemented, MRP can contribute in a major way to reduction in inventory while improving customer service levels. MRP techniques allow the operations manager to schedule and replenish stock on a "need-to-order" basis rather than simply a "time-to-order" basis.

The continuing development of MRP systems has led to its use with lean manufacturing techniques. In addition, MRP can integrate production data with a variety of other activities, including the supply chain and sales. As a result, we now have integrated database-oriented enterprise resource planning (ERP) systems. These expensive and difficult-to-install ERP systems, when successful, support strategies of differentiation, response, and cost leadership.

Key Terms

Material requirements planning (MRP)
Master production schedule (MPS)
Bill of material (BOM)
Modular bills
Planning bills (or kits)
Phantom bills of material
Low-level coding
Lead time
Gross material requirements plan
Net material requirements
Planned order receipt
Planned order release
System nervousness
Time fences
Pegging
Buckets
Bucketless system
Back flush
Supermarket
Lot-sizing decision
Lot-for-lot
Part period balancing (PPB)
Economic part period (EPP)
Wagner-Whitin procedure
Material requirements planning II (MRP II)
Closed-loop MRP system
Load report
Distribution resource planning (DRP)
Enterprise resource planning (ERP)
Efficient consumer response (ECR)

Ethical Dilemma

For many months your prospective ERP customer has been analyzing the hundreds of assumptions built into the $900,000 ERP software you are selling. So far, you have knocked yourself out to try to make this sale. If the sale goes through, you will reach your yearly quota and get a nice bonus. On the other hand, loss of this sale may mean you start looking for other employment.

The accounting, human resource, supply chain, and marketing teams put together by the client have reviewed the specifications and finally recommended purchase of the software. However, as you looked over their shoulders and helped them through the evaluation process, you began to realize that their purchasing procedures—with much of the purchasing being done at hundreds of regional stores—were not a good fit for the software. At the very least, the customizing will add $250,000 to the implementation and training cost. The team is not aware of the issue, and you know that the necessary $250,000 is not in the budget.

What do you do?

Discussion Questions

1. What is the difference between a *gross* requirements plan and a *net* requirements plan?
2. Once a material requirements plan (MRP) has been established, what other managerial applications might be found for the technique?
3. What are the similarities between MRP and DRP?
4. How does MRP II differ from MRP?
5. Which is the best lot-sizing policy for manufacturing organizations?
6. What impact does ignoring carrying cost in the allocation of stock in a DRP system have on lot sizes?
7. MRP is more than an inventory system; what additional capabilities does MRP possess?
8. What are the options for the production planner who has:
   (a) scheduled more than capacity in a work center next week?
   (b) a consistent lack of capacity in that work center?
9. Master schedules are expressed in three different ways depending on whether the process is continuous, a job shop, or repetitive. What are these three ways?
10. What functions of the firm affect an MRP system? How?
11. What is the rationale for (a) a phantom bill of material, (b) a planning bill of material, and (c) a pseudo bill of material?
12. Identify five specific requirements of an effective MRP system.
13. What are the typical benefits of ERP?
14. What are the distinctions between MRP, DRP, and ERP?
15. As an approach to inventory management, how does MRP differ from the approach dealing with economic order quantities (EOQ)?
16. What are the disadvantages of ERP?
17. Use the Web or other sources to:
    (a) Find stories that highlight the advantages of an ERP system.
    (b) Find stories that highlight the difficulties of purchasing, installing, or failure of an ERP system.
18. Use the Web or other sources to identify what an ERP vendor (SAP, PeopleSoft/Oracle, American Software, etc.) includes in these software modules:
    (a) Customer relationship management.
    (b) Supply-chain management.
    (c) Product life cycle management.
19. The very structure of MRP systems suggests fixed lead times. However, many firms have moved toward JIT and kanban techniques. What are the techniques, issues, and impact of adding JIT inventory and purchasing techniques to an organization that has MRP?

Using Software to Solve MRP Problems

There are many commercial MRP software packages, for companies of all sizes. MRP software for small and medium-size companies includes User Solutions, Inc., a demo of which is available at **www.usersolutions.com,** and MAX, from Exact Software North America, Inc. Software for larger systems is available from SAP, CMS, BEA, Oracle, i2 Technologies, and many others. The Excel OM software that accompanies this text includes an MRP module, as does POM for Windows. The use of both is explained in the following sections.

Using Excel OM

Using Excel OM's MRP module requires the careful entry of several pieces of data. The initial MRP screen is where we enter (1) the total number of occurrences of items in the BOM (including the top item), (2) what we want the BOM items to be called (i.e., Item no., Part), (3) total number of periods to be scheduled, and (4) what we want the periods called (i.e., days, weeks).

Excel OM's second MRP screen provides the data entry for an indented bill of material. Here we enter (1) the name of each item in the BOM, (2) the quantity of that item in the assembly, and (3) the correct indent (i.e., parent/child relationship) for each item. The indentations are critical as they provide the logic for the BOM explosion. The indentations should follow the logic of the product structure tree with indents for each assembly item in that assembly.

Excel OM's third MRP screen repeats the indented BOM and provides the standard MRP tableau for entries. This is shown in Program 1 using the data from Examples 1, 2, and 3.

▶ PROGRAM 1
Using Excel OM's MRP Module to Solve Examples 1, 2, and 3

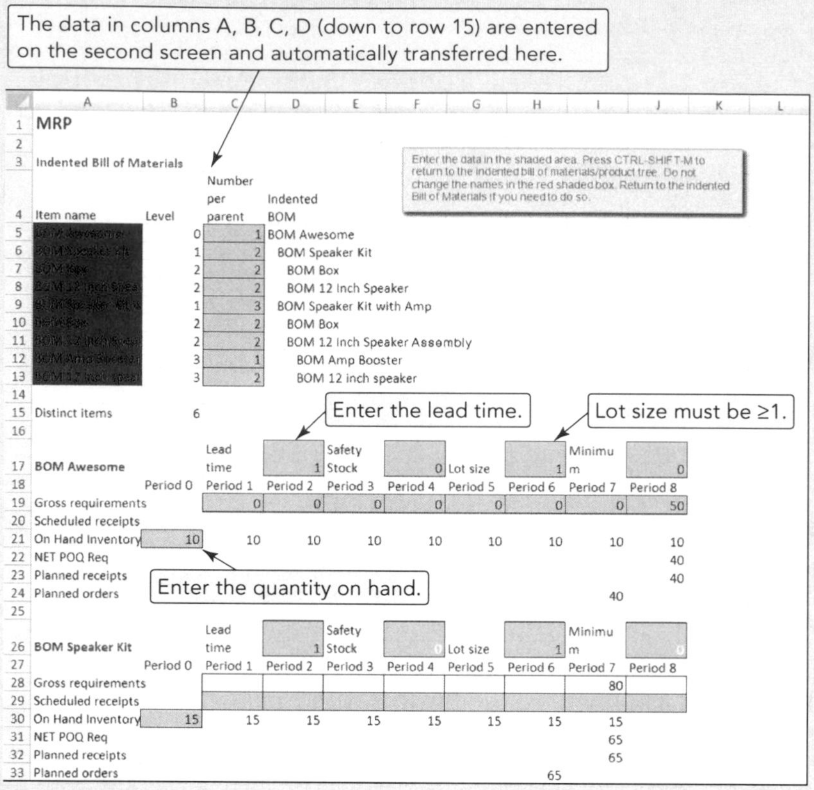

P Using POM for Windows

The POM for Windows MRP module can also solve Examples 1 to 3. Up to 18 periods can be analyzed. Here are the inputs required:

1. *Item names:* The item names are entered in the left column. The same item name will appear in more than one row if the item is used by two parent items. Each item must follow its parents.
2. *Item level:* The level in the indented BOM must be given here. The item *cannot* be placed at a level more than one below the item immediately above.
3. *Lead-time:* The lead time for an item is entered here. The default is 1 week.
4. *Number per parent:* The number of units of this subassembly needed for its parent is entered here. The default is 1.
5. *On hand:* List current inventory on hand once, even if the subassembly is listed twice.
6. *Lot size:* The lot size can be specified here. A 0 or 1 will perform lot-for-lot ordering. If another number is placed here, then all orders for that item will be in integer multiples of that number.
7. *Demands:* The demands are entered in the end item row in the period in which the items are demanded.
8. *Scheduled receipts:* If units are scheduled to be received in the future, they should be listed in the appropriate time period (column) and item (row). (An entry here in level 1 is a demand; all other levels are receipts.)

Further details regarding POM for Windows are seen in Using Excel OM and POM for Windows.

Solved Problems

Virtual Office Hours help is available at www.myomlab.com

▶ SOLVED PROBLEM 14.1

Determine the low-level coding and the quantity of each component necessary to produce 10 units of an assembly we will call Alpha. The product structure and quantities of each component needed for each assembly are noted in parentheses.

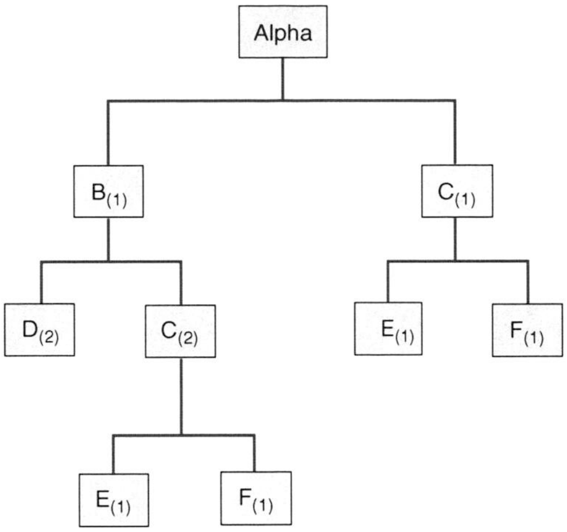

▶ SOLUTION

Redraw the product structure with low-level coding. Then multiply down the structure until the requirements of each branch are determined. Then add across the structure until the total for each is determined.

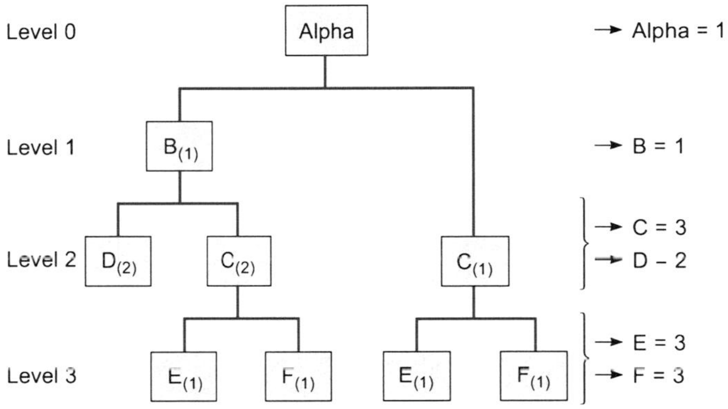

Es required for left branch:

$$(1_{\text{alpha}} \times 1_B \times 2_C \times 1_E) = 2 \text{ Es}$$

and Es required for right branch:

$$(1_{\text{alpha}} \times 1_C \times 1_E) = \underline{1 \text{ E}}$$

3 Es required in total

Then "explode" the requirement by multiplying each by 10, as shown in the table to the right:

Level	Item	Quantity per Unit	Total Requirements for 10 Alpha
0	Alpha	1	10
1	B	1	10
2	C	3	30
2	D	2	20
3	E	3	30
3	F	3	30

▶ SOLVED PROBLEM 14.2

Using the product structure for Alpha in Solved Problem 14.1, and the following lead times, quantity on hand, and master production schedule, prepare a net MRP table for Alphas.

Item	Lead Time	Quantity on Hand
Alpha	1	10
B	2	20
C	3	0
D	1	100
E	1	10
F	1	50

Master Production Schedule for Alpha

Period	6	7	8	9	10	11	12	13
Gross requirements			50			50		100

▼ SOLUTION

See the chart on following page.

Lot Size	Lead Time (# of Periods)	On Hand	Safety Stock	Allo-cated	Low-Level Code	Item ID			1	2	3	4	5	6	7	8	9	10	11	12	13
Lot-for-Lot	1	10	—	—	0	Alpha (A)	Gross Requirements									50			50		100
							Scheduled Receipts														
							Projected On Hand	10								10					
							Net Requirements									40			50		100
							Planned Order Receipts									40			50		
							Planned Order Releases								40			50		100	100
Lot-for-Lot	2	20	—	—	1	B	Gross Requirements								40(A)			50(A)		100(A)	
							Scheduled Receipts														
							Projected On Hand	20							20						
							Net Requirements								20			50		100	
							Planned Order Receipts								20			50		100	
							Planned Order Releases						20			50		100			
Lot-for-Lot	3	0	—	—	2	C	Gross Requirements						40(B)		40(A)	100(B)		200(B) + 50(A)		100(A)	
							Scheduled Receipts														
							Projected On Hand	0													
							Net Requirements						40		40	100		250		100	
							Planned Order Receipts						40		40	100		250		100	
							Planned Order Releases			40		40	100		250		100				
Lot-for-Lot	1	100	—	—	2	D	Gross Requirements						40(B)			100(B)		200(B)			
							Scheduled Receipts														
							Projected On Hand	100					100			60					
							Net Requirements						0			40		200			
							Planned Order Receipts						0			40		200			
							Planned Order Releases					0			40		200				
Lot-for-Lot	1	10	—	—	3	E	Gross Requirements			40(C)		40(C)	100(C)		250(C)		100(C)				
							Scheduled Receipts														
							Projected On Hand	10		10											
							Net Requirements			30		40	100		250		100				
							Planned Order Receipts			30		40	100		250		100				
							Planned Order Releases		30		40	100		250		100					
Lot-for-Lot	1	50	—	—	3	F	Gross Requirements			40(C)		40(C)	100(C)		250(C)		100(C)				
							Scheduled Receipts														
							Projected On Hand	50		50		10					—				
							Net Requirements			0		30	100		250		100				
							Planned Order Receipts					30	100		250		100				
							Planned Order Releases				30	100		250		100					

Net Material Requirements Planning Sheet for Alpha

The letter in parentheses (A) is the source of the demand.

Problems*

• **14.1** You have developed the following simple product structure of items needed for your gift bag for a rush party for prospective pledges in your organization. You forecast 200 attendees. Assume that there is no inventory on hand of any of the items. Explode the bill of material. (Subscripts indicate the number of units required.)

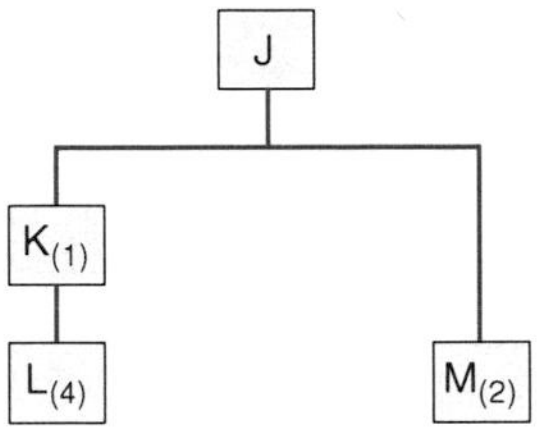

•• **14.2** You are expected to have the gift bags in Problem 14.1 ready at 5 P.M.. However, you need to personalize the items (monogrammed pens, note pads, literature from the printer, etc.). The lead time is 1 hour to assemble 200 Js once the other items are prepared. The other items will take a while as well. Given the volunteers you have, the other time estimates are item K (2 hours), item L (1 hour), and item M (4 hours). Develop a time-phased assembly plan to prepare the gift bags.

•• **14.3** The demand for subassembly S is 100 units in week 7. Each unit of S requires 1 unit of T and 2 units of U. Each unit of T requires 1 unit of V, 2 units of W, and 1 unit of X. Finally, each unit of U requires 2 units of Y and 3 units of Z. One firm manufactures all items. It takes 2 weeks to make S, 1 week to make T, 2 weeks to make U, 2 weeks to make V, 3 weeks to make W, 1 week to make X, 2 weeks to make Y, and 1 week to make Z.

a) Construct a product structure. Identify all levels, parents, and components.
b) Prepare a time-phased product structure.

•• **14.4** Using the information in Problem 14.3, construct a gross material requirements plan. Px

•• **14.5** Using the information in Problem 14.3, construct a net material requirements plan using the following on-hand inventory.

*Note: Px means the problem may be solved with POM for Windows and/or Excel OM. Many of the exercises in this chapter (14.1 through 14.16 and 14.23 through 14.27) can be done on *Resource Manager for Excel*, a commercial system made available by User Solutions, Inc. Access to a trial version of the software and a set of notes for the user is available at **www.usersolutions.com.**

Lot Size	Lead Time (# of periods)	On Hand	Safety Stock	Allo-cated	Low-Level Code	Itcm ID		Poriod (wook, day)							
								1	2	3	4	5	6	7	8
							Gross Requirements								
							Scheduled Receipts								
							Projected On Hand								
							Net Requirements								
							Planned Order Receipts								
							Planned Order Releases								
							Gross Requirements								
							Scheduled Receipts								
							Projected On Hand								
							Net Requirements								
							Planned Order Receipts								
							Planned Order Releases								
							Gross Requirements								
							Scheduled Receipts								
							Projected On Hand								
							Net Requirements								
							Planned Order Receipts								
							Planned Order Releases								
							Gross Requirements								
							Scheduled Receipts								
							Projected On Hand								
							Net Requirements								
							Planned Order Receipts								
							Planned Order Releases								
							Gross Requirements								
							Scheduled Receipts								
							Projected On Hand								
							Net Requirements								
							Planned Order Receipts								
							Planned Order Releases								

▲ **FIGURE 13 MRP Form for Homework Problems in this Chapter**
For several problems in this chapter, a copy of this form may be helpful.

Item	On-Hand Inventory	Item	On-Hand Inventory
S	20	W	30
T	20	X	25
U	40	Y	240
V	30	Z	40

•• **14.6** Refer again to Problems 14.3 and 14.4. In addition to 100 units of S, there is also a demand for 20 units of U, which is a component of S. The 20 units of U are needed for maintenance purposes. These units are needed in week 6. Modify the *gross material requirements plan* to reflect this change.

•• **14.7** Refer again to Problems 14.3 and 14.5. In addition to 100 units of S, there is also a demand for 20 units of U, which is a component of S. The 20 units of U are needed for maintenance purposes. These units are needed in week 6. Modify the *net material requirements plan* to reflect this change.

•• **14.8** As the production planner for Gerry Cook Products, Inc., you have been given a bill of material for a bracket that is made up of a base, two springs, and four clamps. The base is assembled from one clamp and two housings. Each clamp has one handle and one casting. Each housing has two bearings and one shaft. There is no inventory on hand.

a) Design a product structure noting the quantities for each item and show the low-level coding.
b) Determine the gross quantities needed of each item if you are to assemble 50 brackets.
c) Compute the net quantities needed if there are 25 of the base and 100 of the clamp in stock.

•• **14.9** Your boss at Gerry Cook Products, Inc., has just provided you with the schedule and lead times for the bracket in Problem 14.8. The unit is to be prepared in week 10. The lead times for the components are bracket (1 week), base (1 week), spring (1 week), clamp (1 week), housing (2 weeks), handle (1 week), casting (3 weeks), bearing (1 week), and shaft (1 week).

a) Prepare the time-phased product structure for the bracket.
b) In what week do you need to start the castings?

•• **14.10**

a) Given the product structure and master production schedule (Figure 14 below), develop a gross requirements plan for all items.
b) Given the preceding product structure, master production schedule, and inventory status (Figure 14), develop a net materials requirements (planned order release) for all items.

••• **14.11** Given the following product structure, master production schedule, and inventory status (Figure 15 on the next page) and assuming the requirements for each BOM item is 1: (a) develop a gross requirements plan for Item C; (b) develop a net requirements plan for Item C.

•••• **14.12** Based on the data in Figure 15, complete a net material requirements schedule for:

a) All items (10 schedules in all), assuming the requirement for each BOM item is 1.
b) All 10 items, assuming the requirement for all items is 1, except B, C, and F, which require *2 each.*

••• **14.13** Electro Fans has just received an order for one thousand 20-inch fans due week 7. Each fan consists of a housing assembly, two grills, a fan assembly, and an electrical unit. The housing assembly consists of a frame, two supports, and a handle. The fan assembly consists of a hub and five blades. The electrical unit consists of a motor, a switch, and a knob. The following table gives lead times, on-hand inventory, and scheduled receipts.

a) Construct a product structure.
b) Construct a time-phased product structure.
c) Prepare a net material requirements plan.

Data Table for Problem 14.13

Component	Lead Time	On Hand Inventory	Lot Size*	Scheduled Receipt
20″ Fan	1	100	—	
Housing	1	100	—	
Frame	2	—	—	
Supports (2)	1	50	100	
Handle	1	400	500	
Grills (2)	2	200	500	
Fan Assembly	3	150	—	
Hub	1	—	—	
Blades (5)	2	—	100	
Electrical Unit	1	—	—	
Motor	1	—	—	
Switch	1	20	12	
Knob	1	—	25	200 knobs in week 2

*Lot-for-lot unless otherwise noted

••• **14.14** A part structure, lead time (weeks), and on-hand quantities for product A are shown in Figure 16. From the information shown, generate

▼ **FIGURE 14 Information for Problem 14.10**

Master Production Schedule for X1

PERIOD	7	8	9	10	11	12
Gross requirements		50		20		100

ITEM	LEAD TIME	ON HAND	ITEM	LEAD TIME	ON HAND
X1	1	50	C	1	0
B1	2	20	D	1	0
B2	2	20	E	3	10
A1	1	5			

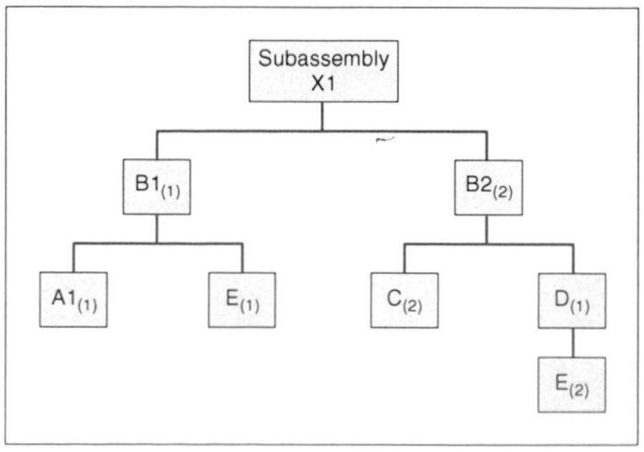

▶ **FIGURE 15**
Information for Problems 14.11 and 14.12

PERIOD	8	9	10	11	12
Gross requirements: A	100		50		150
Gross requirements: H		100		50	

ITEM	ON HAND	LEAD TIME	ITEM	ON HAND	LEAD TIME
A	0	1	F	75	2
B	100	2	G	75	1
C	50	2	H	0	1
D	50	1	J	100	2
E	75	2	K	100	2

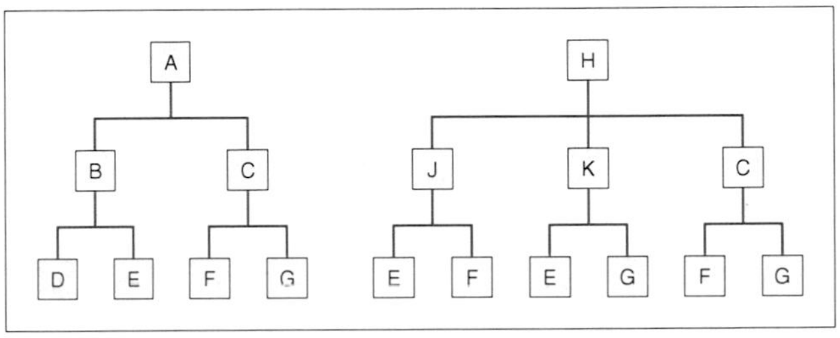

a) An indented bill of material for product A.
b) Net requirements for each part to produce 10 As in week 8 using lot-for-lot. Px

••• **14.15** You are product planner for product A (in Problem 14.14 and Figure 16). The field service manager, Al Trostel, has just called and told you that the requirements for B and F should each be increased by 10 units for his repair requirements in the field.

a) Prepare a list showing the quantity of each part required to produce the requirements for the service manager *and* the production request of 10 Bs and Fs.
b) Prepare a net requirement plan by date for the new requirements (for both production and field service), assuming that the field service manager wants his 10 units of B and F in week 6 and the 10 production units of A in week 8. Px

••• **14.16** You have just been notified via fax that the lead time for component G of product A (Problem 14.15 and Figure 16) has been increased to 4 weeks.

a) Which items have changed and why?
b) What are the implications for the production plan?
c) As production planner, what can you do? Px

Data Table for Problems 14.17 through 14.19*

Period	1	2	3	4	5	6	7	8	9	10	11	12
Gross requirements	30		40		30	70	20		10	80		50

*Holding cost = $2.50/unit/week; setup cost = $150; lead time = 1 week; beginning inventory = 40.

••• **14.17** Develop a lot-for-lot solution and calculate total relevant costs for the data in the preceding table. Px

••• **14.18** Develop an EOQ solution and calculate total relevant costs for the data in the preceding table. Stockout costs equal $10 per unit. Px

••• **14.19** Develop a PPB solution and calculate total relevant costs for the data in the preceding table. Px

••• **14.20** Using the gross requirements schedule in Examples 4, 5, and 6 in the text, prepare an alternative ordering system that always orders 100 units the week prior to a shortage (a fixed order quantity of 100) with the same costs as in the example (setup at $100 each, holding at $1 per unit per period). What is the cost of this ordering system? Px

▶ **FIGURE 16**
Information for Problems 14.14, 14.15 and 14.16

PART	INVENTORY ON HAND
A	0
B	2
C	10
D	5
E	4
F	5
G	1
H	10

PART STRUCTURE TREE

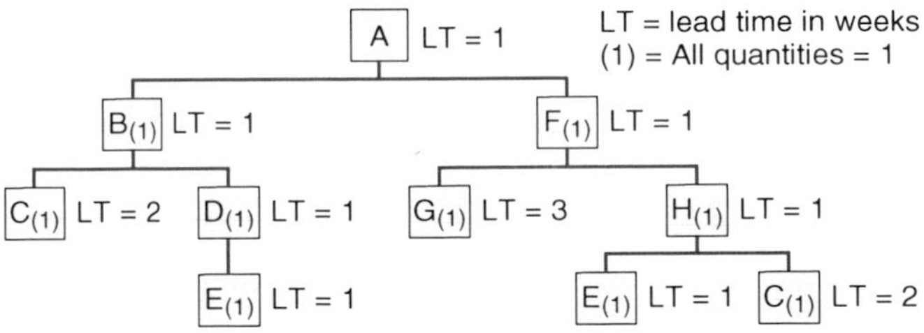

••• **14.21** Using the gross requirements schedule in Examples 4, 5, and 6 in the text, prepare an alternative ordering system that orders every 3 weeks for 3 weeks ahead (a periodic order quantity). Use the same costs as in the example (setup at $100 each, holding at $1 per unit per period). What is the cost of this ordering system? Px

••• **14.22** Using the gross requirements schedule in Examples 4, 5, and 6 in the text, prepare an alternative ordering system of your own design that uses the same cost as in the example (setup at $100 each, holding at $1 per unit per period). Can you do better than the costs shown in the text? What is the cost of your ordering system? Px

••• **14.23** Katharine Hepburn, Inc., has received the following orders:

Period	1	2	3	4	5	6	7	8	9	10
Order size	0	40	30	40	10	70	40	10	30	60

The entire fabrication for these units is scheduled on one machine. There are 2,250 usable minutes in a week, and each unit will take 65 minutes to complete. Develop a capacity plan, using lot splitting, for the 10-week time period.

••• **14.24** David Jurman, Ltd., has received the following orders:

Period	1	2	3	4	5	6	7	8	9	10
Order size	60	30	10	40	70	10	40	30	40	0

The entire fabrication for these units is scheduled on one machine. There are 2,250 usable minutes in a week, and each unit will take 65 minutes to complete. Develop a capacity plan, using lot splitting, for the 10-week time period.

•• **14.25** Heather Adams, production manager for a Colorado exercise equipment manufacturer, needs to schedule an order for 50 UltimaSteppers, which are to be shipped in week 8. Subscripts indicate quantity required for each parent. Assume lot-for-lot ordering. Below is information about the steppers:

Item	Lead time	On-Hand Inventory	Components
Stepper	2	20	$A_{(1)}, B_{(3)}, C_{(2)}$
A	1	10	$D_{(1)}, F_{(2)}$
B	2	30	$E_{(1)}, F_{(3)}$
C	3	10	$D_{(2)}, E_{(3)}$
D	1	15	
E	2	5	
F	2	20	

a) Develop a product structure for Heather.
b) Develop a time-phased structure.
c) Develop a net material requirements plan for F. Px

•••• **14.26** You are scheduling production of your popular Rustic Coffee Table. The table requires a top, four legs, $\frac{1}{8}$ gallon of stain, $\frac{1}{16}$ gallon of glue, 2 short braces between the legs and 2 long braces between the legs, and a brass cap that goes on the bottom of each leg. You have 100 gallons of glue in inventory, but none of the other components. All items except the brass caps, stain, and glue are ordered on a lot-for-lot basis. The caps are purchased in quantities of 1,000, stain and glue by the gallon. Lead time is 1 day for each item. Schedule the order releases necessary to produce 640 coffee tables on days 5 and 6, and 128 on days 7 and 8. Px

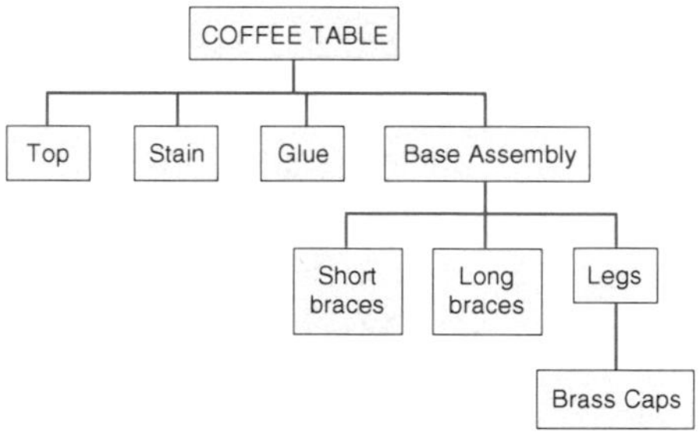

•••• **14.27** Using the data for the coffee table in Problem 14.26, build a labor schedule when the labor standard for each top is 2 labor hours; each leg including brass cap installation requires $\frac{1}{4}$ hour, as does each pair of braces. Base assembly requires 1 labor-hour, and final assembly requires 2 labor-hours. What is the total number of labor-hours required each day, and how many employees are needed each day at 8 hours per day?

► **Refer to myomlab for these additional homework problems: 14.28–14.32**

Case Studies

► Hill's Automotive, Inc.

Hill's Automotive, Inc., is an aftermarket producer and distributor of automotive replacement parts. Art Hill has slowly expanded the business, which began as a supplier of hard-to-get auto air-conditioning units for classic cars and hot rods. The firm has limited manufacturing capability, but a state-of-the-art MRP system and extensive inventory and assembly facilities. Components are purchased, assembled, and repackaged. Among its products are private-label air-conditioning, carburetors, and ignition kits. The downturn in the economy, particularly the company's discretionary segment, has put downward pressure on volume and margins. Profits have fallen considerably. In addition, customer service levels have declined, with late deliveries now exceeding 25% of orders. And to make matters worse, customer returns have been rising at a rate of 3% per month.

Wally Hopp, vice president of sales, claims that most of the problem lies with the assembly department. He says that although the firm has accurate bills of materials, indicating what goes into each product, it is not producing the proper mix of the product. He also believes the firm has poor quality control and low productivity, and as a result its costs are too high.

Melanie Thompson, treasurer, believes that problems are due to investing in the wrong inventories. She thinks that marketing has too many options and products. Melanie also thinks that purchasing department buyers have been hedging their inventories and requirements with excess purchasing commitments.

The assembly manager, Kalinga Jagoda, says, "The symptom is that we have a lot of parts in inventory, but no place to assemble them in the production schedule. When we have the right part, it is not very good, but we use it anyway to meet the schedule."

Marshall Fisher, manager of purchasing, has taken the stance that purchasing has not let Hill's Automotive down. He has stuck by his old suppliers, used historical data to determine requirements, maintained what he views as excellent prices from suppliers, and evaluated new sources of supply with a view toward lowering cost. Where possible, Marshall reacted to the increased pressure for profitability by emphasizing low cost and early delivery.

Discussion Question

1. Prepare a plan for Art Hill that gets the firm back on a course toward improved profitability. Be sure to identify the symptoms, the problems, and the specific changes you would implement.
2. Explain how MRP plays a role in this plan.

► MRP at Wheeled Coach

Video Case

Wheeled Coach, the world's largest manufacturer of ambulances, builds thousands of different and constantly changing configurations of its products. The custom nature of its business means lots of options and special designs—and a potential scheduling and inventory nightmare. Wheeled Coach addressed such problems, and succeeded in solving a lot of them, with an MRP system (described in the *Global Company Profile* that opens this chapter). As with most MRP installations, however, solving one set of problems uncovers a new set.

One of the new issues that had to be addressed by plant manager Lynn Whalen was newly discovered excess inventory. Managers discovered a substantial amount of inventory that was not called for in any finished products. Excess inventory was evident because of the new level of inventory accuracy required by the MRP system. The other reason was a new series of inventory reports generated by the IBM MAPICS MRP system purchased by Wheeled Coach. One of those reports indicates where items are used and is known as the "Where Used" report. Interestingly, many inventory items were not called out on bills-of-material (BOMs) for any current products. In some cases, the reason some parts were in the stockroom remained a mystery.

The discovery of this excess inventory led to renewed efforts to ensure that the BOMs were accurate. With substantial work, BOM accuracy increased and the number of engineering change notices (ECNs) decreased. Similarly, purchase-order accuracy, with regard to both part numbers and quantities ordered, was improved. Additionally, receiving department and stockroom accuracy went up, all helping to maintain schedule, costs, and ultimately, shipping dates and quality.

Eventually, Lynn Whalen concluded that the residual amounts of excess inventory were the result, at least in part, of rapid changes in ambulance design and technology. Another source was customer changes made after specifications had been determined and materials ordered. This latter excess occurs because, even though Wheeled Coach's own throughput time is only 17 days, many of the items that it purchases require much longer lead times.

Discussion Questions*

1. Why is accurate inventory such an important issue at Wheeled Coach?
2. Why does Wheeled Coach have excess inventory, and what kind of a plan would you suggest for dealing with it?
3. Be specific in your suggestions for reducing inventory and how to implement them.

*You may wish to view the video that accompanies this case before answering the questions.

►**Additional Case Study:** Visit **www.myomlab.com** or **www.pearsonhighered.com/heizer** for this free case study:
Ikon's attempt at ERP: The giant office technology firm faces hurdles with ERP implementation.

Bibliography

Barba-Gutierrez, Y., B. Adenso-Diaz, and S. M. Gupta. "Lot Sizing in Reverse MRP for Scheduling Disassembly." *International Journal of Production Economics* 111, no. 2 (February 2008): 741.

Bell, Steve. "Time Fence Secrets." *APICS* 16, no. 4 (April 2006): 44–48.

Bolander, Steven, and Sam G. Taylor. "Scheduling Techniques: A Comparison of Logic." *Production and Inventory Management Journal* 41, no. 1 (1st Quarter 2000): 1–5.

Crandall, Richard E. "The Epic Life of ERP." *APICS* 16, no. 2 (February 2006): 17–19.

Gattiker, Thomas "Anatomy of an ERP Implementation Gone Awry." *Production and Inventory Management* 43, nos. 3–4 (3rd/4th Quarter 2002): 96–105.

Kanet, J., and V. Sridharan. "The Value of Using Scheduling Information in Planning Material Requirements." *Decision Sciences* 29, no. 2 (Spring 1998): 479–498.

Koh, S. C. L., and S. M. Saad. "Managing Uncertainty in ERP-controlled Manufacturing Environments." *International Journal of Production Economics* 101, no. 1 (May 2006): 109.

Krupp, James A. G. "Integrating Kanban and MRP to Reduce Lead Time." *Production and Inventory Management Journal* 43, no. 3–4 (3rd/4th quarter 2002): 78–82.

Lawrence, Barry F., Daniel F. Jennings, and Brian E. Reynolds. *ERP in Distribution.* Florence, KY: Thomson South-Western, (2005).

Moncrief, Stephen. "Push and Pull." *APICS—The Performance Advantage* (June 2003): 46–51.

Norris, G. *E-Business & ERP.* New York: Wiley (2005).
O' Sullivan, Jill, and Gene Caiola. *Enterprise Resource Planning,* 2nd ed. New York: McGraw-Hill (2008).
Segerstedt, A. "Master Production Scheduling and a Comparison of MRP and Cover-Time Planning." *International Journal of Production Research* 44, no. 18–19 (September 2006): 3585.
Summer, M. *Enterprise Resource Planning.* Upper Saddle River, NJ: Prentice Hall (2005).
Wagner, H. M., and T. M. Whitin. "Dynamic Version of the Economic Lot Size Model." *Management Science* 5, no. 1 (1958): 89–96.
Wu, Jen-Hur, et al. "Using Multiple Variables Decision-Making Analysis for ERP Selection." *International Journal of Manufacturing Technology and Management* 18, no. 2 (2009): 228.

Rapid Review

Main Heading	Review Material	myomlab

DEPENDENT DEMAND

Demand for items is *dependent* when the relationship between the items can be determined. For any product, all components of that product are dependent demand items.

- **Material requirements planning (MRP)**—A dependent demand technique that uses a bill-of-material, inventory, expected receipts, and a master production schedule to determine material requirements.

VIDEO 14.1
MRP at Wheeled Coach Ambulances

DEPENDENT INVENTORY MODEL REQUIREMENTS

Dependent inventory models require that the operations manager know the:

(1) Master production schedule; (2) Specifications or bill of material; (3) Inventory availability; (4) Purchase orders outstanding; and (5) Lead times

- **Master production schedule (MPS)**—A timetable that specifies what is to be made and when.

The MPS is a statement of *what is to be produced*, not a forecast of demand.

- **Bill of material (BOM)**—A listing of the components, their description, and the quantity of each required to make one unit of a product.

Items above any level in a BOM are called *parents*; items below any level are called *components*, or *children*. The top level in a BOM is the 0 level.

- **Modular bills**—Bills of material organized by major subassemblies or by product options.
- **Planning bills (or kits)**—A material grouping created in order to assign an artificial parent to a bill of material; also called "pseudo" bills.
- **Phantom bills of material**—Bills of material for components, usually subassemblies, that exist only temporarily; they are never inventoried.
- **Low-level coding**—A number that identifies items at the lowest level at which they occur.
- **Lead time**—In purchasing systems, the time between recognition of the need for an order and receiving it; in production systems, it is the order, wait, move, queue, setup, and run times for each component.

When a bill of material is turned on its side and modified by adding lead times for each component, it is called a *time-phased product structure*.

Problems: 14.1, 14.3

Virtual Office Hours for Solved Problem: 14.1

MRP STRUCTURE

- **Gross material requirements plan**—A schedule that shows the total demand for an item (prior to subtraction of on-hand inventory and scheduled receipts) and (1) when it must be ordered from suppliers, or (2) when production must be started to meet its demand by a particular date.
- **Net material requirements**—The result of adjusting gross requirements for inventory on hand and scheduled receipts.
- **Planned order receipt**—The quantity planned to be received at a future date.
- **Planned order release**—The scheduled date for an order to be released.

$$\text{Net requirements} = \text{Gross requirements} + \text{Allocations} - (\text{On hand} + \text{Scheduled receipts})$$

Problems: 14.2, 14.4–14.8

Virtual Office Hours for Solved Problem: 14.2

ACTIVE MODEL 14.1

MRP MANAGEMENT

- **System nervousness**—Frequent changes in an MRP system.
- **Time fences**—A means for allowing a segment of the master schedule to be designated as "not to be rescheduled."
- **Pegging**—In material requirements planning systems, tracing upward the bill of material from the component to the parent item.

Four approaches for integrating MRP and JIT are (1) finite capacity scheduling, (2) small buckets, (3) balanced flow, and (4) supermarkets.

- **Buckets**—Time units in a material requirements planning system.

Finite capacity scheduling (FCS) considers department and machine capacity. FCS provides the precise scheduling needed for rapid material movement.

- **Bucketless system**—Time-phased data are referenced using dated records rather than defined time periods, or buckets.
- **Back flush**—A system to reduce inventory balances by deducting everything in the bill of material on completion of the unit.
- **Supermarket**—An inventory area that holds common items that are replenished by a kanban system.

LOT-SIZING TECHNIQUES

- **Lot-sizing decision**—The process of, or techniques used in, determining lot size.
- **Lot-for-lot**—A lot-sizing technique that generates exactly what is required to meet the plan.
- **Part period balancing (PPB)**—An inventory ordering technique that balances setup and holding costs by changing the lot size to reflect requirements of the next lot size in the future.

Problems: 14.17–14.22

Rapid Review *continued*

Main Heading	Review Material	myomlab
	■ **Economic part period (EPP)**—A period of time when the ratio of setup cost to holding cost is equal. ■ **Wagner-Whitin procedure**—A technique for lot-size computation that assumes a finite time horizon beyond which there are no additional net requirements to arrive at an ordering strategy. In general, the lot-for-lot approach should be used whenever low-cost deliveries can be achieved.	
EXTENSIONS OF MRP	■ **Material requirements planning II (MRP II)**—A system that allows, with MRP in place, inventory data to be augmented by other resource variables; in this case, MRP becomes *material resource planning.* ■ **Closed-loop MRP system**—A system that provides feedback to the capacity plan, master production schedule, and production plan so planning can be kept valid at all times. ■ **Load report**—A report for showing the resource requirements in a work center for all work currently assigned there as well as all planned and expected orders. Tactics for smoothing the load and minimizing the impact of changed lead time include: *Overlapping, Operations splitting,* and *Order,* or, *lot splitting.*	
MRP IN SERVICES	■ **Distribution resource planning (DRP)**—A time-phased stock-replenishment plan for all levels of a distribution network.	
ENTERPRISE RESOURCE PLANNING (ERP)	■ **Enterprise resource planning (ERP)**—An information system for identifying and planning the enterprise-wide resources needed to take, make, ship, and account for customer orders. In an ERP system, data are entered only once into a common, complete, and consistent database shared by all applications. ■ **Efficient consumer response (ECR)**—Supply-chain management systems in the grocery industry that tie sales to buying, to inventory, to logistics, and to production.	

Self Test

■ **Before taking the self-test,** refer to the learning objectives listed at the beginning of the chapter and the key terms listed at the end of the chapter.

LO1. In a product structure diagram:
- **a)** parents are found only at the top level of the diagram.
- **b)** parents are found at every level in the diagram.
- **c)** children are found at every level of the diagram except the top level.
- **d)** all items in the diagrams are both parents and children.
- **e)** all of the above.

LO2. The difference between a gross material requirements plan (gross MRP) and a net material requirements plan (net MRP) is:
- **a)** the gross MRP may not be computerized, but the net MRP must be computerized.
- **b)** the gross MRP includes consideration of the inventory on hand, whereas the net MRP doesn't include the inventory consideration.
- **c)** the net MRP includes consideration of the inventory on hand, whereas the gross MRP doesn't include the inventory consideration.
- **d)** the gross MRP doesn't take taxes into account, whereas the net MRP includes the tax considerations.
- **e)** the net MRP is only an estimate, whereas the gross MRP is used for actual production scheduling.

LO3. Net requirements =
- **a)** Gross requirements + Allocations − On-hand inventory + Scheduled receipts.
- **b)** Gross requirements − Allocations − On-hand inventory − Scheduled receipts.
- **c)** Gross requirements − Allocations − On-hand inventory + Scheduled receipts.
- **d)** Gross requirements + Allocations − On-hand inventory − Scheduled receipts.

LO4. A lot-sizing procedure that assumes a finite time horizon beyond which there are no additional net requirements is:
- **a)** Wagner-Whitin algorithm.
- **b)** part period balancing.
- **c)** economic order quantity.
- **d)** all of the above.

LO5. MRP II stands for:
- **a)** material resource planning.
- **b)** management requirements planning.
- **c)** management resource planning.
- **d)** material revenue planning.
- **e)** material risk planning.

LO6. A(n) ________ MRP system provides information to the capacity plan, to the master production schedule, and ultimately to the production plan.
- **a)** dynamic
- **b)** closed-loop
- **c)** continuous
- **d)** retrospective
- **e)** introspective

LO7. Which system extends MRP II to tie in customers and suppliers?
- **a)** MRP III
- **b)** JIT
- **c)** IRP
- **d)** ERP
- **e)** Enhanced MRP II

Answers: LO1. c; LO2. c; LO3. d; LO4. a; LO5. a; LO6. b; LO7. d.

Solutions to Even-Numbered Problems

14.2 The time-phased plan for the gift bags is:
Someone should start on item M by noon.

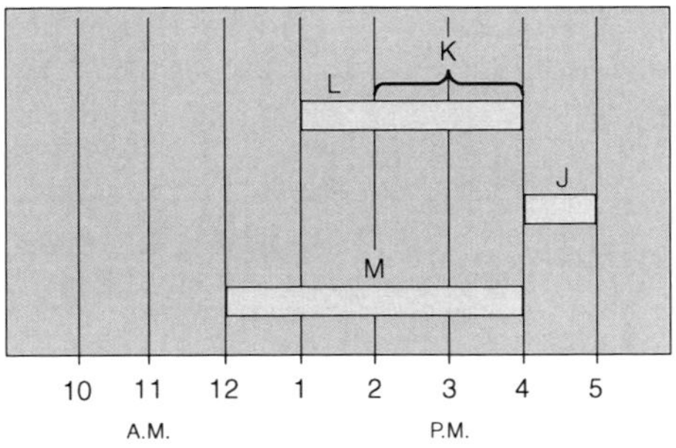

14.4 Gross material requirements plan:

Item		Week 1	2	3	4	5	6	7	8	Lead Time (wk.)
S	Gross req.							100		
	Order release					100				2
T	Gross req.					100				
	Order release				100					1
U	Gross req.					200				
	Order release			200						2
V	Gross req.				100					
	Order release		100							2
W	Gross req.				200					
	Order release	200								3
X	Gross req.				100					
	Order release			100						1
Y	Gross req.			400						
	Order release	400								2
Z	Gross req.			600						
	Order release		600							1

14.6 Gross material requirements plan, modified to include the 20 units of U required for maintenance purposes:

Item		Week 1	2	3	4	5	6	7	8	Lead Time (wk.)
S	Gross req.							100		
	Order release					100				2
T	Gross req.					100				
	Order release				100					1
U	Gross req.					200	20			
	Order release			200	20					2
V	Gross req.				100					
	Order release		100							2
W	Gross req.				200					
	Order release	200								3
X	Gross req.				100					
	Order release			100						1
Y	Gross req.			400	40					
	Order release	400	40							2
Z	Gross req.			600	60					
	Order release		600	60						1

14.8 (a)

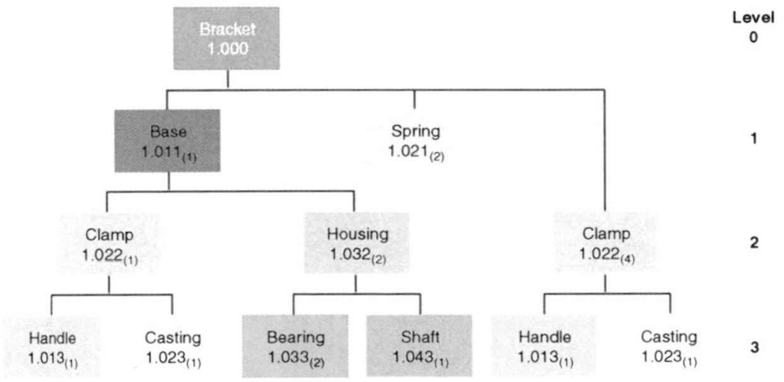

(b) For 50 brackets, the gross requirements are for 50 bases, 100 springs, 250 clamps, 250 handles, 250 castings, 100 housings, 200 bearings, and 100 shafts.

(c) For 50 brackets, net requirements are 25 bases, 100 springs, 125 clamps, 125 handles, 125 castings, 50 housings, 100 bearings, and 50 shafts.

14.10 **(a)** Gross material requirements plan for the first three items:

Item		1	2	3	4	5	6	7	8	9	10	11	12
X1	Gross req.								50		20		100
	Order release							50		20		100	
B1	Gross req.							50		20		100	
	Order release					50		20		100			
B2	Gross req.							100		40		200	
	Order release					100		40		200			

(b) The net materials requirement plan for the first two items:

Level: 0 Parent: Quantity:
Item: X1 Lead Time: Lot Size: L4L

Week No.	1	2	3	4	5	6	7	8	9	10	11	12
Gross Requirement								50		20		100
Scheduled Receipt												
On-hand Inventory								50		0		0
Net Requirement								0		20		100
Planned Order Receipt										20		100
Planned Order Release									20		100	

Level: 1 Parent: X1 Quantity: 1X
Item: B1 Lead Time: 2 Lot Size: L4L

Week No.	1	2	3	4	5	6	7	8	9	10	11	12
Gross Requirement									20		100	
Scheduled Receipt												
On-hand Inventory									20		0	
Net Requirement									0		100	
Planned Order Receipt											100	
Planned Order Release									100			

14.12 **(a)** Net material requirements schedule (only items A and H are shown):

	1	2	3	4	5	6	7	8	9	10	11	12
A Gross Required								100		50		150
On Hand								0		0		0
Net Required								100		50		150
Order Receipt								100		50		150
Order Release							100		50		150	
H Gross Required									100		50	
On Hand									0		0	
Net Required									100		50	
Order Receipt									100		50	
Order Release								100		50		

(b) Net material requirements schedule (only items B and C are shown; schedule for items A and H remains the same as in part a.)

		1	2	3	4	5	6	7	8	9	10	11	12	13
B Gross Requirements								200		100		300		
Scheduled Receipts														
Projected On Hand	100							100		0		0		
Net Requirements								100		100		300		
Planned Order Receipts								100		100		300		
Planned Order Releases						100		100		300				
C Gross Requirements								200	200	100	100	300		
Scheduled Receipts														
Projected On Hand	50							50		0		0		
Net Requirements								150	200	100	100	300		
Planned Order Receipts								150	200	100	100	300		
Planned Order Releases						150	200	100	100	300				

14.14 **(a)**

Level	Description	Qty
0	A	1
1	B	1
2	C	1
2	D	1
3	E	1
1	F	1
2	G	1
2	H	1
3	E	1
3	C	1

Note: with low-level coding "C" would be a level-3 code

14.14 **(b)** Solution for Items A, B, F (on next page):

Lot Size	Lead Time	On Hand	Safety Stock	Allo-cated	Low-Level Code	Item ID		1	2	3	4	5	6	7	8
								Period (week)							
Lot for Lot	1	0	—	—	0	A	Gross Requirement								10
							Scheduled Receipt								
							Projected On Hand								0
							Net Requirement								10
							Planned Receipt								10
							Planned Release							10	
Lot for Lot	1	2	—	—	1	B	Gross Requirement							10	
							Scheduled Receipt								
							Projected On Hand	2	2	2	2	2	2	2	0
							Net Requirement							8	
							Planned Receipt							8	
							Planned Release						8		
Lot for Lot	1	5	—	—	1	F	Gross Requirement							10	
							Scheduled Receipt								
							Projected On Hand	5	5	5	5	5	5	5	0
							Net Requirement							5	
							Planned Receipt							5	
							Planned Release						5		

14.16 **(a)** Only item G changes.
(b) Component F and 4 units of A will be delayed one week.
(c) Options include: delaying 4 units of A for 1 week; asking supplier of G to expedite production.

14.18 EOQ = 57; Total cost $ = $1,630

14.20 $650

14.22 $455

14.24 Selection for first 5 weeks:

Week	Units	Capacity Required (time)	Capacity Available (time)	Over/ (Under)	Production Scheduler's Action
1	60	3,900	2,250	1650	Lot split. Move 300 minutes (4.3 units) to week 2 and 1,350 minutes to week 3.
2	30	1,950	2,250	(300)	
3	10	650	2,250	(1,600)	
4	40	2,600	2,250	350	Lot split. Move 250 minutes to week 3. Operations split. Move 100 minutes to another machine, overtime, or subcontract.
5	70	4,550	2,250	2,300	Lot split. Move 1,600 minutes to week 6. Overlap operations to get product out door. Operations split. Move 700 minutes to another machine, overtime, or subcontract.

14.26 Here are the order releases for the table and the top:

Lot Size	Lead Time (# of periods)	On Hand	Safety Stock	Allo-cated	Low-Level Code	Item ID		1	2	3	4	5	6	7	8
								Period (day)							
Lot for Lot	1	—	—	—	0	Table	Gross Requirements					640	640	128	128
							Scheduled Receipts								
							Projected on Hand								
							Net Requirements					640	640	128	128
							Planned Order Receipts					640	640	128	128
							Planned Order Releases				640	640	128	128	
Lot for Lot	1	—	—	—	1	Top	Gross Requirements				640	640	128	128	
							Scheduled Receipts								
							Projected on Hand								
							Net Requirements				640	640	128	128	
							Planned Order Receipts				640	640	128	128	
							Planned Order Releases			640	640	128	128		

JIT and Lean Operations

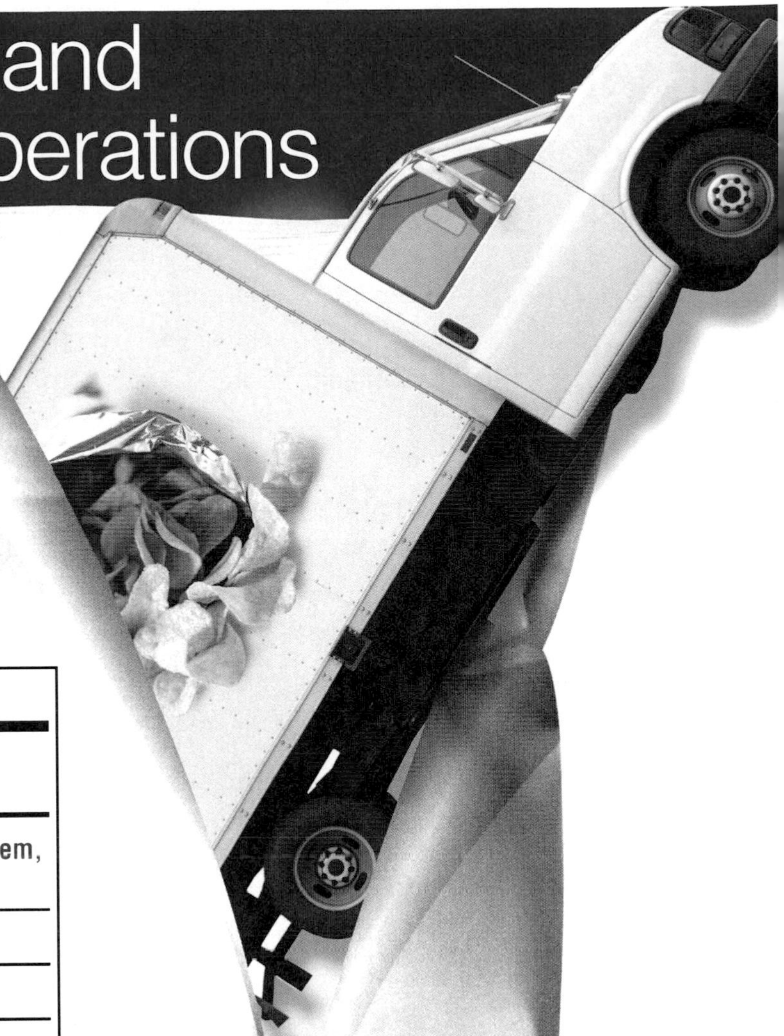

Chapter Outline

10

OM Strategy Decisions

- ► Design of Goods and Services
- ► Managing Quality
- ► Process Strategy
- ► Location Strategies
- ► Layout Strategies
- ► Human Resources
- ► Supply-Chain Management
- ► Inventory Management
  - Independent Demand
  - Dependent Demand
  - JIT and Lean Operations
- ► Scheduling
- ► Maintenance

ACHIEVING COMPETITIVE ADVANTAGE WITH LEAN OPERATIONS AT TOYOTA MOTOR CORPORATION

Toyota Motor Corporation, with annual sales of over 9 million cars and trucks, is the largest vehicle manufacturer in the world. Two techniques, just-in-time (JIT) and the Toyota Production System (TPS), have been instrumental in this post-WWII growth. Toyota, with a wide range of vehicles, competes head-to-head with successful long-established companies in Europe and the U.S. Taiichi Ohno, a former vice president of Toyota, created the basic framework for the world's most discussed systems for improving productivity, JIT and TPS. These two concepts provide much of the foundation for lean operations:

- Central to JIT is a philosophy of continued problem solving. In practice, JIT means making only what is needed, when it is needed. JIT provides an excellent vehicle for finding and eliminating problems because problems are easy to find in a system that has no slack. When excess inventory is eliminated, quality, layout, scheduling, and supplier issues become immediately evident—as does excess production.
- Central to TPS is employee learning and a continuing effort to create and produce products under ideal conditions. Ideal conditions exist only when facilities, machines, and people are brought

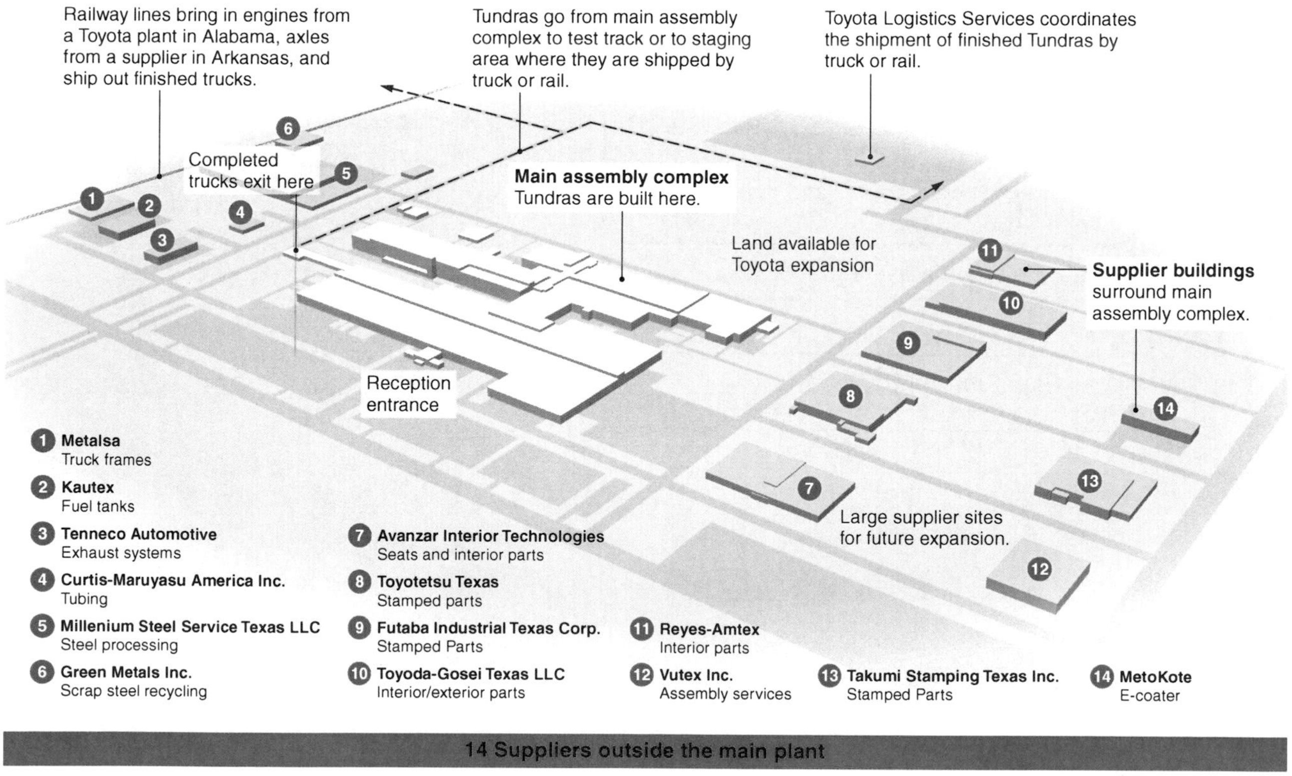

Outside: Toyota has a 2,000-acre site with 14 of the 21 onsite suppliers, adjacent rail lines, and near-by interstate highway. The site provides expansion space for both Toyota and for its suppliers — and provides an environment for Just-in-time.

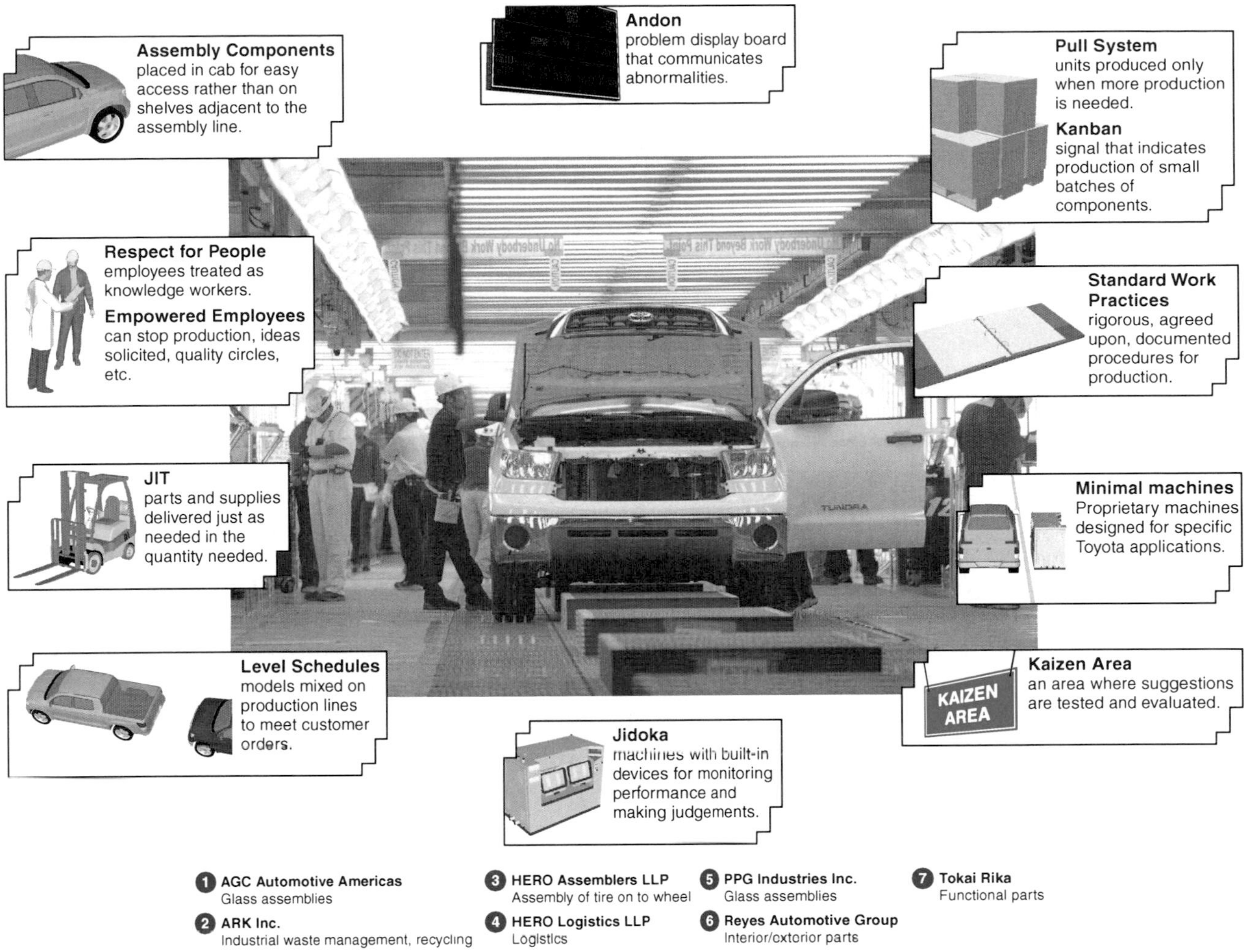

7 Suppliers inside the main plant

Toyota's San Antonio plant has about 2 million interior sq. ft., providing facilities within the final assembly building for 7 of the 21 onsite suppliers, and capacity to build 200,000 pick-up trucks annually. But most importantly, Toyota practices the world-class Toyota Production System and expects its suppliers to do the same thing wherever they are.

together, adding value without waste. Waste undermines productivity by diverting resources to excess inventory, unnecessary processing, and poor quality. Respect for people, extensive training, cross-training, and standard work practices of empowered employees focusing on driving out waste are fundamental to TPS.

Toyota's latest implementation of TPS and JIT is present at its new San Antonio plant, the largest Toyota land site for an automobile assembly plant in the U.S. Interestingly, despite its annual production capability of 200,000 Tundra pick-up trucks, the building itself is one of the smallest in the industry. Modern automobiles have 30,000 parts, but at Toyota, independent suppliers combine many of these parts into sub-assemblies. Twenty-one of these suppliers are on site at the San Antonio facility and transfer components to the assembly line on a JIT basis.

Operations such as these taking place in the new San Antonio plant are why Toyota continues to perform near the top in quality and maintain the lowest labor-hour assembly time in the industry. JIT, TPS, and lean operations work—and they provide a competitive advantage at Toyota Motor Corporation.

Learning Objectives

LO1: Define just-in-time, TPS, and lean operations

LO2: Define the seven wastes and the 5Ss

LO3: Explain JIT partnerships

LO4: Determine optimal setup time

LO5: Define kanban

LO6: Compute the required number of kanbans

LO7: Explain the principles of the Toyota Production System

AUTHOR COMMENT World-class firms everywhere are using these three techniques.

JUST-IN-TIME, THE TOYOTA PRODUCTION SYSTEM, AND LEAN OPERATIONS

LO1: Define just-in-time, TPS, and lean operations

Just-in-time (JIT)
Continuous and forced problem solving via a focus on throughput and reduced inventory.

Toyota Production System (TPS)
Focus on continuous improvement, respect for people, and standard work practices.

Lean operations
Eliminates waste through a focus on exactly what the customer wants.

As shown in the *Global Company Profile*, the Toyota Production System (TPS) contributes to a world-class operation at Toyota Motor Corporation. In this chapter, we discuss JIT, TPS, and lean operations as approaches to continuing improvement that drive out waste and lead to world-class organizations.

Just-in-time (JIT) is an approach of continuous and forced problem solving via a focus on throughput and reduced inventory. The **Toyota Production System (TPS)**, with its emphasis on continuous improvement, respect for people, and standard work practices, is particularly suited for assembly lines. **Lean operations** supplies the customer with exactly what the customer wants when the customer wants it, without waste, through continuous improvement. Lean operations are driven by workflow initiated by the "pull" of the customer's order. When implemented as a comprehensive manufacturing strategy, JIT, TPS, and lean systems sustain competitive advantage and result in increased overall returns.

If there is any distinction between JIT, TPS, and lean operations, it is that:

- JIT emphasizes forced problem solving.
- TPS emphasizes employee learning and empowerment in an assembly-line environment.
- Lean operations emphasize understanding the customer.

However, in practice, there is little difference, and the terms are often used interchangeably. Leading organizations use the approaches and techniques that make sense for them. In this chapter, we use the term *lean operations* to encompass all of the related approaches and techniques.

Regardless of the label put on operations improvement, good production systems require that managers address three issues that are pervasive and fundamental to operations management: eliminate waste, remove variability, and improve throughput. We first introduce these three issues and then discuss the major attributes of JIT, TPS, and lean operations. Finally, we look at lean operations applied to services.

LO2: Define the seven wastes and the 5Ss

Eliminate Waste

Traditional producers have limited goals—accepting, for instance, the production of some defective parts and some inventory. Lean producers set their sights on perfection; no bad parts, no inventory, only value-added activities, and no waste. Any activity that does not add value in the eyes of the customer is a waste. The customer defines product value. If the customer does not want to pay for it, it is a waste. Taiichi Ohno, noted for his work on the Toyota Production System, identified seven categories of waste. These categories have become popular in lean organizations and cover many of the ways organizations waste or lose money. Ohno's **seven wastes** are:

Seven wastes
Overproduction
Queues
Transportation
Inventory
Motion
Overprocessing
Defective product

- *Overproduction:* Producing more than the customer orders or producing early (before it is demanded) is waste. Inventory of any kind is usually a waste.
- *Queues:* Idle time, storage, and waiting are wastes (they add no value).
- *Transportation:* Moving material between plants or between work centers and handling more than once is waste.
- *Inventory:* Unnecessary raw material, work-in-process (WIP), finished goods, and excess operating supplies add no value and are wastes.

- *Motion:* Movement of equipment or people that adds no value is waste.
- *Overprocessing:* Work performed on the product that adds no value is waste.
- *Defective product:* Returns, warranty claims, rework, and scrap are a waste.

A broader perspective—one that goes beyond immediate production—suggests that other resources, such as energy, water, and air, are often wasted but should not be. Efficient, sustainable production minimizes inputs and maximizes outputs, wasting nothing.

For over a century, managers have pursued "housekeeping" for a neat, orderly, and efficient workplace and as a means of reducing waste. Operations managers have embellished "housekeeping" to include a checklist—now known as the 5Ss.[1] The Japanese developed the initial 5Ss. Not only are the 5Ss a good checklist for lean operations, they also provide an easy vehicle with which to assist the culture change that is often necessary to bring about lean operations. The **5Ss** follow:

5Ss
A lean production checklist:
Sort
Simplify
Shine
Standardize
Sustain

- *Sort/segregate:* Keep what is needed and remove everything else from the work area; when in doubt, throw it out. Identify non-value items and remove them. Getting rid of these items makes space available and usually improves work flow.
- *Simplify/straighten:* Arrange and use methods analysis tools to improve work flow and reduce wasted motion. Consider long-run and short-run ergonomic issues. Label and display for easy use only what is needed in the immediate work area.
- *Shine/sweep:* Clean daily; eliminate all forms of dirt, contamination, and clutter from the work area.
- *Standardize:* Remove variations from the process by developing standard operating procedures and checklists; good standards make the abnormal obvious. Standardize equipment and tooling so that cross-training time and cost are reduced. Train and retrain the work team so that when deviations occur, they are readily apparent to all.
- *Sustain/self-discipline:* Review periodically to recognize efforts and to motivate to sustain progress. Use visuals wherever possible to communicate and sustain progress.

U.S. managers often add two additional Ss that contribute to establishing and maintaining a lean workplace:

- *Safety:* Build good safety practices into the above five activities.
- *Support/maintenance:* Reduce variability, unplanned downtime, and costs. Integrate daily shine tasks with preventive maintenance.

The Ss provide a vehicle for continuous improvement with which all employees can identify. Operations managers need think only of the examples set by a well-run hospital emergency room or the spit-and-polish of a fire department for a benchmark. Offices and retail stores, as well as manufacturers, have successfully used the 5Ss in their respective efforts to eliminate waste and move to lean operations. A place for everything and everything in its place does make a difference in a well-run office. And retail stores successfully use the Ss to reduce misplaced merchandise and improve customer service. An orderly workplace reduces waste so that assets are released for other, more productive, purposes.

Remove Variability

Managers seek to remove variability caused by both internal and external factors. **Variability** is any deviation from the optimum process that delivers perfect product on time, every time. Variability is a polite word for problems. The less variability in a system, the less waste in the system. Most variability is caused by tolerating waste or by poor management. Among the many sources of variability are:

Variability
Any deviation from the optimum process that delivers perfect product on time, every time.

- Poor production processes that allow employees and suppliers to produce improper quantities or late or non-conforming units
- Unknown customer demands
- Incomplete or inaccurate drawings, specifications, and bills of material

[1]The term 5S comes from the Japanese words seiri (*sort* and clear out), seiton (*straighten* and configure), seiso (*scrub* and cleanup), seiketsu (maintain *sanitation* and cleanliness of self and workplace), and shitsuke (*self-discipline and standardization* of these practices).

Both JIT and inventory reduction are effective tools for identifying causes of variability. The precise timing of JIT makes variability evident, just as reducing inventory exposes variability. The removal of variability allows managers to move good materials on schedule, add value at each step of the production process, drive down costs, and win orders.

Improve Throughput

Throughput
The time required to move orders through the production process, from receipt to delivery.

Manufacturing cycle time
The time between the arrival of raw materials and the shipping of finished products.

Pull system
A concept that results in material being produced only when requested and moved to where it is needed just as it is needed.

Throughput is a measure (in units or time) that it takes to move an order from receipt to delivery. Each minute products remain on the books, costs accumulate and competitive advantage is lost. The time that an order is in the shop is called **manufacturing cycle time**. This is the time between the arrival of raw materials and the shipping of finished product. For example, phone-system manufacturer Northern Telecom now has materials pulled directly from qualified suppliers to the assembly line. This effort has reduced a segment of Northern's manufacturing cycle time from 3 weeks to just 4 hours, the incoming inspection staff from 47 to 24, and problems on the shop floor caused by defective materials by 97%. Driving down manufacturing cycle time can make a major improvement in throughput.

A technique for increasing throughput is a pull system. A **pull system** *pulls* a unit to where it is needed just as it is needed. Pull systems are a standard tool of JIT systems. Pull systems use signals to request production and delivery from supplying stations to stations that have production capacity available. The pull concept is used both within the immediate production process and with suppliers. By *pulling* material through the system in very small lots—just as it is needed—waste and inventory are removed. As inventory is removed, clutter is reduced, problems become evident, and continuous improvement is emphasized. Removing the cushion of inventory also reduces both investment in inventory and manufacturing cycle time. A push system dumps orders on the next downstream workstation, regardless of timeliness and resource availability. Push systems are the antithesis of JIT. Pulling material through a production process as it is needed rather than in a "push" mode typically lowers cost and improves schedule performance, enhancing customer satisfaction.

AUTHOR COMMENT
JIT places added demands on performance, but that is why it pays off.

JUST-IN-TIME (JIT)

With its forced problem solving via a focus on rapid throughput and reduced inventory, JIT provides a powerful strategy for improving operations. With JIT, materials arrive *where* they are needed only *when* they are needed. When good units do not arrive just as needed, a "problem" has been identified. By driving out waste and delay in this manner, JIT reduces costs associated with excess inventory, cuts variability and waste, and improves throughput. JIT is a key ingredient of lean operations and is particularly helpful in supporting strategies of rapid response and low cost.

Many services have adopted JIT techniques as a normal part of their business. Restaurants like Olive Garden and Red Lobster expect and receive JIT deliveries. Both buyer and supplier expect fresh, high-quality produce delivered without fail just when it is needed. The system doesn't work any other way.

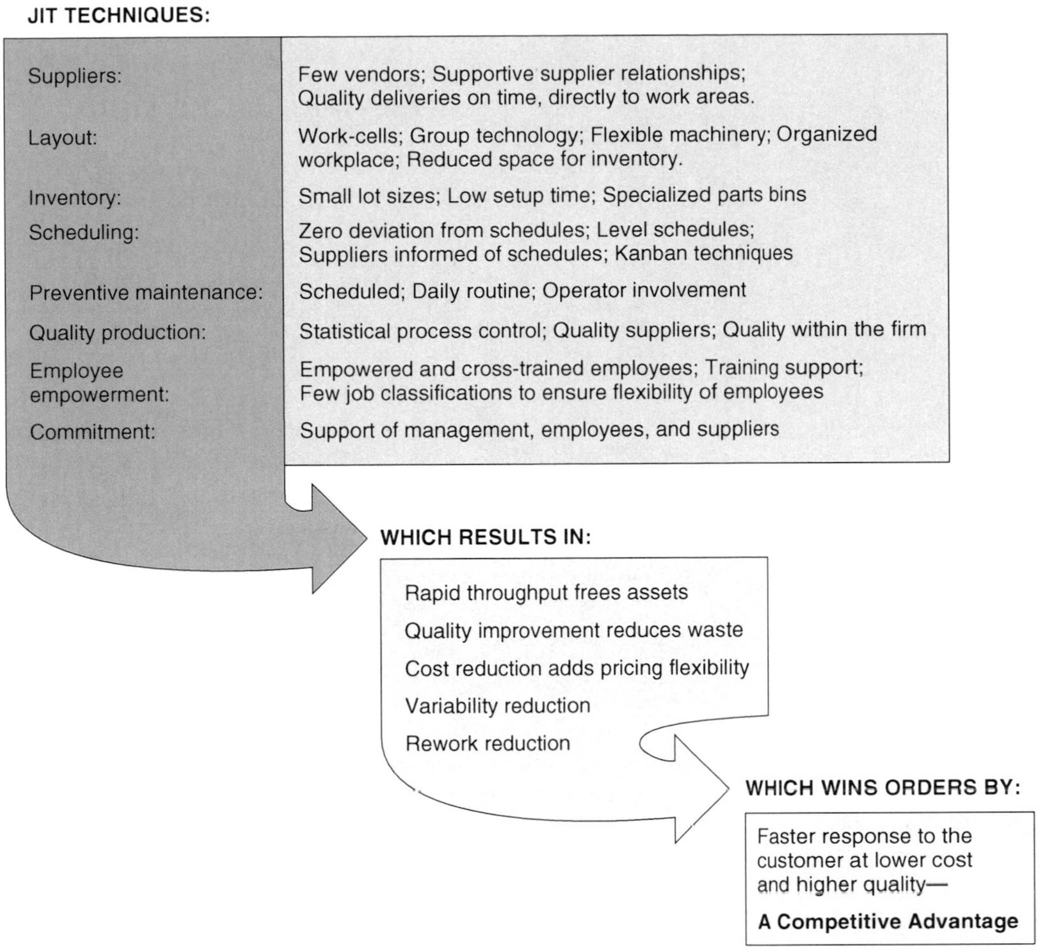

◀ **FIGURE 1**
JIT Contributes to Competitive Advantage

Every moment material is held, an activity that adds value should be occurring. Consequently, as Figure 1 suggests, JIT often yields a competitive advantage.

Effective JIT requires a meaningful buyer–supplier partnership.

JIT Partnerships

A **JIT partnership** exists when a supplier and a purchaser work together with open communication and a goal of removing waste and driving down costs. Close relationships and trust are critical to the success of JIT. Figure 2 shows the characteristics of JIT partnerships. Some specific goals of JIT partnerships are:

JIT partnerships
Partnerships of suppliers and purchasers that remove waste and drive down costs for mutual benefits.

- *Removal of unnecessary activities*, such as receiving, incoming inspection, and paperwork related to bidding, invoicing, and payment.
- *Removal of in-plant inventory* by delivery in small lots directly to the using department as needed.
- *Removal of in-transit inventory* by encouraging suppliers to locate nearby and provide frequent small shipments. The shorter the flow of material in the resource pipeline, the less inventory. Inventory can also be reduced through a technique known as *consignment*. **Consignment inventory** (see the *OM in Action* box "Lean Production at Cessna Aircraft"), a variation of vendor-managed inventory, means the supplier maintains the title to the inventory until it is used. For instance, an assembly plant may find a hardware supplier that is willing to locate its warehouse where the user currently has its stockroom. In this manner, when hardware is needed, it is no farther than the stockroom. Schedule and production information must be shared with the consignment supplier, or inventory holding costs will just be transferred from the buyer to the supplier, with no net cost reduction. Another option is to have the supplier ship to other, perhaps smaller, purchasers from the "stockroom."
- *Obtain improved quality and reliability* through long-term commitments, communication, and cooperation.

Consignment inventory
An arrangement in which the supplier maintains title to the inventory until it is used.

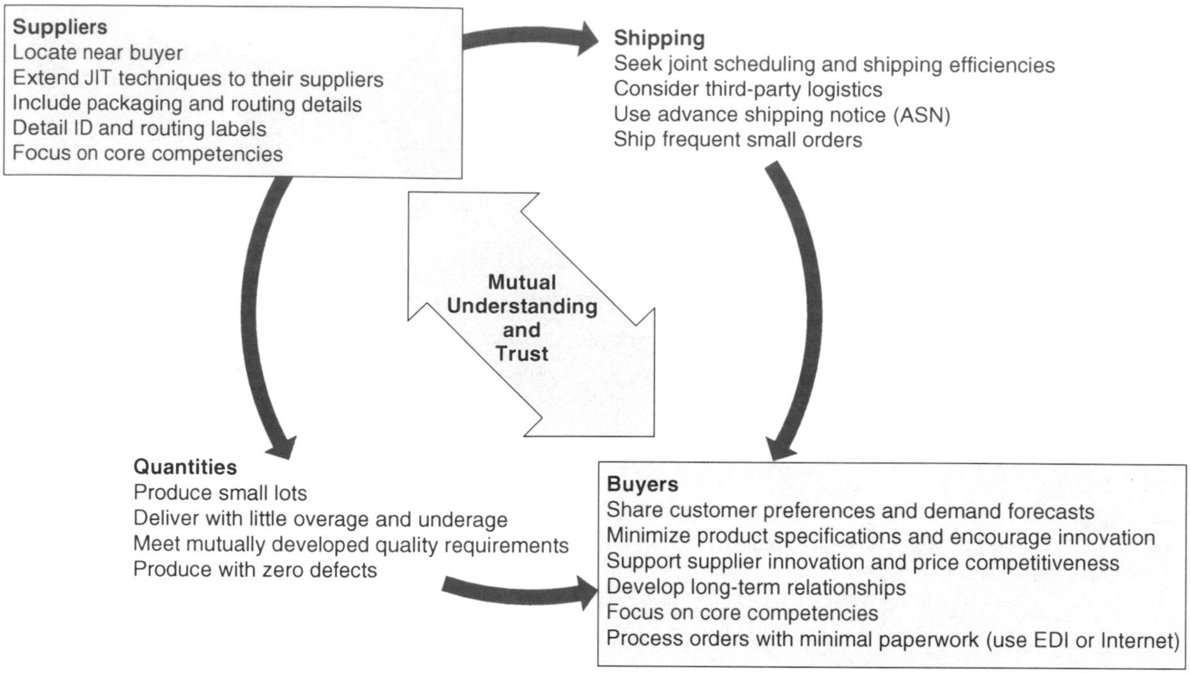

▲ **FIGURE 2** **Characteristics of JIT Partnerships**

Leading organizations view suppliers as extensions of their own organizations and expect suppliers to be fully committed to improvement. Such relationships require a high degree of respect by both supplier and purchaser. Supplier concerns can be significant; Harley-Davidson, for example, initially had difficulty implementing JIT because supplier issues outweighed the perceived benefits.

LO3: Explain JIT partnerships

Concerns of Suppliers

Successful JIT partnerships require that supplier concerns be addressed. These concerns include:

1. *Diversification:* Suppliers may not want to tie themselves to long-term contracts with one customer. The suppliers' perception is that they reduce their risk if they have a variety of customers.
2. *Scheduling:* Many suppliers have little faith in the purchaser's ability to produce orders to a smooth, coordinated schedule.

OM in Action ► Lean Production at Cessna Aircraft

When Cessna Aircraft opened its new plant in Independence, Kansas, it saw the opportunity to switch from a craftwork mentality producing small single-engine planes to a lean manufacturing system. In doing so, Cessna adopted three lean practices.

First, Cessna set up consignment- and vendor-managed inventories with several of its suppliers. Blanket purchase orders allow Honeywell, for example, to maintain a 30-day supply of avionic parts onsite. Other vendors were encouraged to use a nearby warehouse to keep parts that could then be delivered daily to the production line.

Second, Cessna managers committed to cross-training, in which team members learn the duties of other team members and can shift across assembly lines as needed. To develop these technical skills, Cessna brought in 60 retired assembly-line workers to mentor and teach new employees. Employees were taught to work as a team and to assume responsibility for their team's quality.

Cessna Aircraft Company

Third, the company used group technology and manufacturing cells to move away from a batch process that resulted in large inventories and unsold planes. Now, Cessna pulls product through its plant only when a specific order is placed.

These commitments to manufacturing efficiency are part of the lean operations that has made Cessna the world's largest manufacturer of single-engine aircraft.

Sources: **www.cessna.com** (2007); *Strategic Finance* (November 2002): 32; *Purchasing* (September 4, 2003): 25–30; and *Fortune* (May 1, 2000): 1222B.

3. *Lead time:* Engineering or specification changes can play havoc with JIT because of inadequate lead time for suppliers to implement the necessary changes.
4. *Quality:* Suppliers'capital budgets, processes, or technology may limit ability to respond to changes in product and quality.
5. *Lot sizes:* Suppliers may see frequent delivery in small lots as a way to transfer buyers' holding costs to suppliers.

JIT LAYOUT

JIT layouts reduce another kind of waste—movement. The movement of material on a factory floor (or paper in an office) does not add value. Consequently, managers want flexible layouts that reduce the movement of both people and material. JIT layouts place material directly in the location where needed. For instance, an assembly line should be designed with delivery points next to the line so material need not be delivered first to a receiving department and then moved again. This is what VF Corporation's Wrangler Division in Greensboro, North Carolina, did; denim is now delivered directly to the line. Toyota has gone one step farther and places hardware and components in the chassis of each vehicle moving down the assembly line. This is not only convenient, but it allows Toyota to save space and opens areas adjacent to the assembly line previously occupied by shelves. When a layout reduces distance, firms often save labor and space and may have the added bonus of eliminating potential areas for accumulation of unwanted inventory. Table 1 provides a list of JIT layout tactics.

▼ **TABLE 1**
JIT Layout Tactics

Build work cells for families of products
Include a large number of operations in a small area
Minimize distance
Design little space for inventory
Improve employee communication
Use poka-yoke devices
Build flexible or movable equipment
Cross-train workers to add flexibility

Distance Reduction

Reducing distance is a major contribution of work cells, work centers, and focused factories. The days of long production lines and huge economic lots, with goods passing through monumental, single-operation machines, are gone. Now firms use work cells, often arranged in a U shape, containing several machines performing different operations. These work cells are often based on group technology codes. Group technology codes help identify components with similar characteristics so we can group them into families. Once families are identified, work cells are built for them. The result can be thought of as a small product-oriented facility where the "product" is actually a group of similar products—a family of products. The cells produce one good unit at a time, and ideally they produce the units *only* after a customer orders them.

Increased Flexibility

Modern work cells are designed so they can be easily rearranged to adapt to changes in volume, product improvements, or even new designs. Almost nothing in these new departments is bolted down. This same concept of layout flexibility applies to office environments. Not only is most office furniture and equipment movable, but so are office walls, computer connections, and telecommunications. Equipment is modular. Layout flexibility aids the changes that result from product *and* process improvements that are inevitable with a philosophy of continuous improvement.

Impact on Employees

JIT layouts allow cross-trained employees to bring flexibility and efficiency to the work cell. Employees working together can tell each other about problems and opportunities for improvement. When layouts provide for sequential operations, feedback can be immediate. Defects are waste. When workers produce units one at a time, they test each product or component at each subsequent production stage. Machines in work cells with self-testing poka-yoke functions detect defects and stop automatically when they occur. Before JIT, defective products were replaced from inventory. Because surplus inventory is not kept in JIT facilities, there are no such buffers. Getting it right the first time is critical.

Reduced Space and Inventory

Because JIT layouts reduce travel distance, they also reduce inventory by removing space for inventory. When there is little space, inventory must be moved in very small lots or even single units. Units are always moving because there is no storage. For instance, each month Security

Pacific Corporation's focused facility sorts 7 million checks, processes 5 million statements, and mails 190,000 customer statements. With a JIT layout, mail processing time has been reduced by 33%, salary costs by tens of thousands of dollars per year, floor space by 50%, and in-process waiting lines by 75% to 90%. Storage, including shelves and drawers, has been removed.

AUTHOR COMMENT
Accountants book inventory as an asset, but operations managers know it is costly.

JIT INVENTORY

Just-in-time inventory
The minimum inventory necessary to keep a perfect system running.

"Inventory is evil."
S. Shingo

Inventories in production and distribution systems often exist "just in case" something goes wrong. That is, they are used just in case some variation from the production plan occurs. The "extra" inventory is then used to cover variations or problems. Effective inventory tactics require "just in time," not "just in case." **Just-in-time inventory** is the minimum inventory necessary to keep a perfect system running. With just-in-time inventory, the exact amount of goods arrives at the moment it is needed, not a minute before or a minute after. Some useful JIT inventory tactics are shown in Table 2 and discussed in more detail in the following sections.

Reduce Inventory and Variability

Operations managers move toward JIT by first removing inventory. The idea is to eliminate variability in the production system hidden by inventory. Reducing inventory uncovers the "rocks" in Figure 3(a) that represent the variability and problems currently being tolerated. With reduced inventory, management chips away at the exposed problems. After the lake is lowered, managers make additional cuts in inventory and continue to chip away at the next level of exposed problems (see Figure 3[b,c]). Ultimately, there will be virtually no inventory and no problems (variability).

Dell estimates that the rapid changes in technology costs $\frac{1}{2}$% to 2% of its inventory's value *each week*. Shigeo Shingo, co-developer of the Toyota JIT system, says, "Inventory is evil." He is not far from the truth. If inventory itself is not evil, it hides evil at great cost.

▼ **TABLE 2**
JIT Inventory Tactics

Use a pull system to move inventory
Reduce lot size
Develop just-in-time delivery systems with suppliers
Deliver directly to the point of use
Perform to schedule
Reduce setup time
Use group technology

Reduce Lot Sizes

Just-in-time has also come to mean elimination of waste by reducing investment in inventory. The key to JIT is producing good product in small lot sizes. Reducing the size of batches can be a major help in reducing inventory and inventory costs. When inventory usage is constant, the average inventory level is the sum of the maximum inventory plus the minimum inventory divided by 2. Figure 4 shows that lowering the order size increases the number of orders but drops inventory levels.

Ideally, in a JIT environment, order size is one and single units are being pulled from one adjacent process to another. More realistically, analysis of the process, transportation time, and containers used for transport are considered when determining lot size. Such analysis typically results in a small lot size but a lot size larger than one. Once a lot size has been determined, the

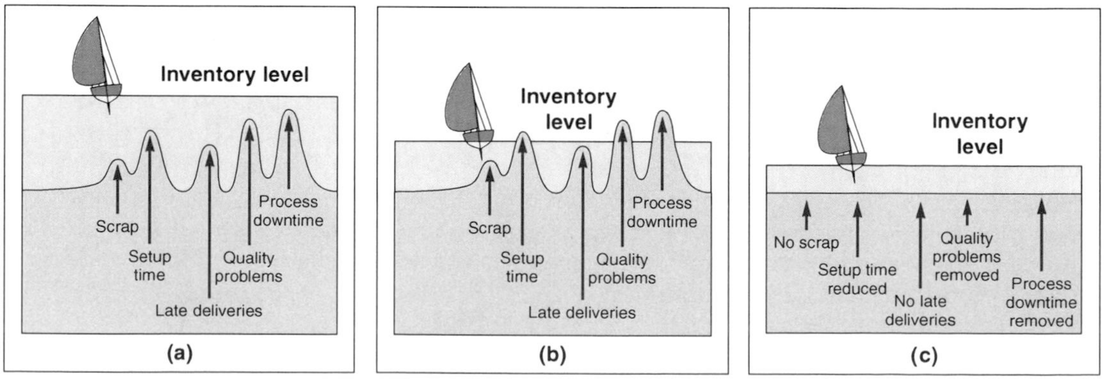

▲ **FIGURE 3** **High levels of inventory hide problems (a), but as we reduce inventory, problems are exposed (b), and finally after reducing inventory and removing problems we have lower inventory, lower costs, and smooth sailing (c).**

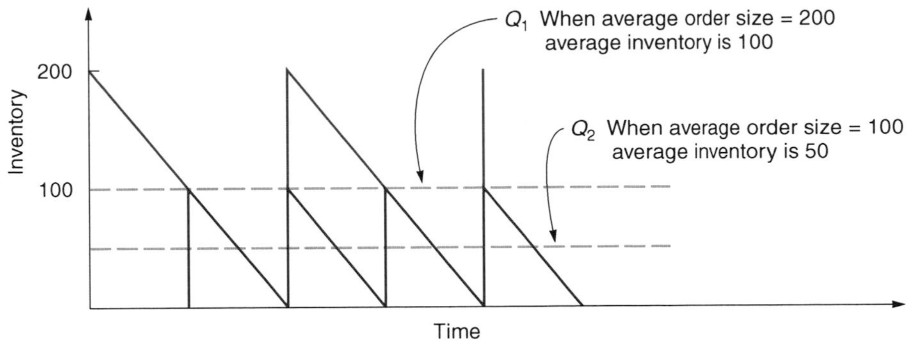

◀ **FIGURE 4**
Frequent Orders Reduce Average Inventory
A lower order size increases the number of orders and total ordering cost but reduces average inventory and total holding cost.

EOQ production order quantity model can be modified to determine the desired setup time. The production order quantity model takes the form:

$$Q^* = \sqrt{\frac{2DS}{H[1 - (d/p)]}} \qquad (1)$$

where D = Annual demand, S = Setup cost, H = Holding cost, d = Daily demand, p = Daily production

Example 1 shows how to determine the desired setup time.

EXAMPLE 1
Determining optimal setup time

Crate Furniture, Inc., a firm that produces rustic furniture, desires to move toward a reduced lot size. Crate Furniture's production analyst, Aleda Roth, determined that a 2-hour production cycle would be acceptable between two departments. Further, she concluded that a setup time that would accommodate the 2-hour cycle time should be achieved.

APPROACH ▶ Roth developed the following data and procedure to determine optimum setup time analytically:

D = Annual demand = 400,000 units
d = Daily demand = 400,000 per 250 days = 1,600 units per day
p = Daily production rate = 4,000 units per day
Q = EOQ desired = 400 (which is the 2-hour demand; that is, 1,600 per day per four 2-hour periods)
H = Holding cost = \$20 per unit per year
S = Setup cost (to be determined)

SOLUTION ▶ Roth determines that the cost, on an hourly basis, of setting up equipment is \$30. Further, she computes that the setup cost per setup should be:

LO4: Determine optimal setup time

$$Q = \sqrt{\frac{2DS}{H(1 - d/p)}}$$

$$Q^2 = \frac{2DS}{H(1 - d/p)}$$

$$S = \frac{(Q^2)(H)(1 - d/p)}{2D} \qquad (2)$$

$$= \frac{(400)^2(20)(1 - 1{,}600/4{,}000)}{2(400{,}000)}$$

$$= \frac{(3{,}200{,}000)(0.6)}{800{,}000} = \$2.40$$

$$\text{Setup time} = \$2.40/(\text{hourly labor rate})$$
$$= \$2.40/(\$30 \text{ per hour})$$
$$= 0.08 \text{ hour, or } 4.8 \text{ minutes}$$

INSIGHT ▶ Now, rather than produce components in large lots, Crate Furniture can produce in a 2-hour cycle with the advantage of an inventory turnover of four *per day*.

LEARNING EXERCISE ▶ If labor cost goes to $40 per hour, what should be the setup time? [Answer: .06 hour, or 3.6 minutes.]

RELATED PROBLEMS ▶ 16.8, 16.9, 16.10

Only two changes need to be made for small-lot material flow to work. First, material handling and work flow need to be improved. With short production cycles, there can be very little wait time. Improving material handling is usually easy and straightforward. The second change is more challenging, and that is a radical reduction in setup times. We discuss setup reduction next.

AUTHOR COMMENT Reduced lot sizes must be accompanied by reduced setup times.

Reduce Setup Costs

Both inventory and the cost of holding it go down as the inventory-reorder quantity and the maximum inventory level drop. However, because inventory requires incurring an ordering or setup cost that must be applied to the units produced, managers tend to purchase (or produce) large orders. With large orders, each unit purchased or ordered absorbs only a small part of the setup cost. Consequently, the way to drive down lot sizes *and* reduce average inventory is to reduce setup cost, which in turn lowers the optimum order size.

The effect of reduced setup costs on total cost and lot size is shown in Figure 5. Moreover, smaller lot sizes hide fewer problems. In many environments, setup cost is highly correlated with setup time. In a manufacturing facility, setups usually require a substantial amount of preparation. Much of the preparation required by a setup can be done prior to shutting down the machine or process. Setup times can be reduced substantially, as shown in Figure 6. For instance, in Kodak's Guadalajara, Mexico, plant a team reduced the setup time to change a bearing from 12 hours to 6 minutes! This is the kind of progress that is typical of world-class manufacturers.

Just as setup costs can be reduced at a machine in a factory, setup time can also be reduced during the process of getting the order ready. It does little good to drive down factory setup time from hours to minutes if orders are going to take 2 weeks to process or "set up" in the office. This is exactly what happens in organizations that forget that JIT concepts have applications in offices as well as in the factory. Reducing setup time (and cost) is an excellent way to reduce inventory investment and to improve productivity.

AUTHOR COMMENT Effective scheduling is required for effective use of capital and personnel.

JIT SCHEDULING

Effective schedules, communicated both within the organization and to outside suppliers, support JIT. Better scheduling also improves the ability to meet customer orders, drives down inventory by allowing smaller lot sizes, and reduces work-in-process. For instance, Ford

▶ FIGURE 5
Lower Setup Costs Will Lower Total Cost
More frequent orders require reducing setup costs; otherwise, inventory costs will rise. As the setup costs are lowered (from S_1 to S_2), total inventory costs also fall (from T_1 to T_2).

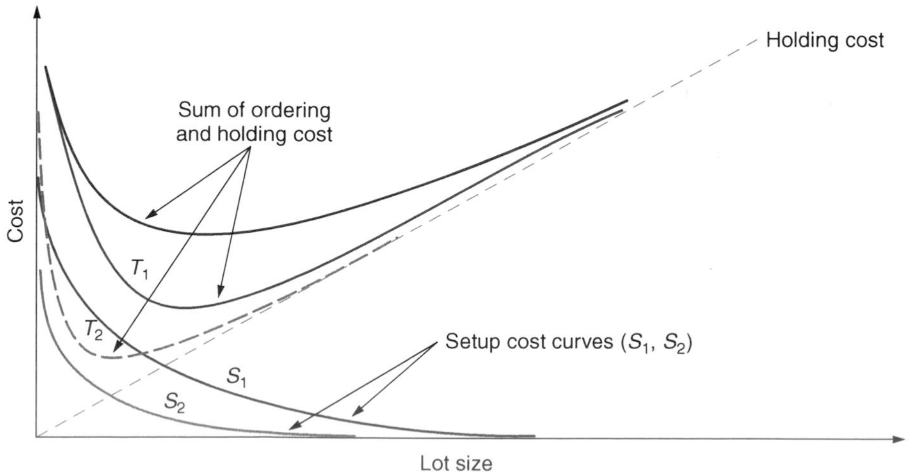

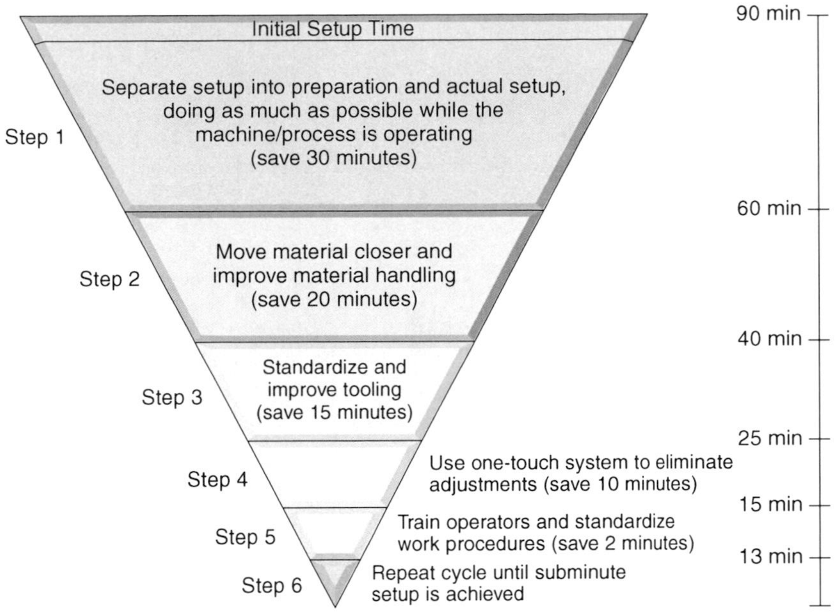

◀ **FIGURE 6**
Steps for Reducing Setup Times
Reduced setup times are a major JIT component.

▼ **TABLE 3**
JIT Scheduling Tactics

Communicate schedules to suppliers
Make level schedules
Freeze part of the schedule
Perform to schedule
Seek one-piece-make and one-piece-move
Eliminate waste
Produce in small lots
Use kanbans
Make each operation produce a perfect part

Motor Company now ties some suppliers to its final assembly schedule. Ford communicates its schedules to bumper manufacturer Polycon Industries from the Ford Oakville production control system. The scheduling system describes the style and color of the bumper needed for each vehicle moving down the final assembly line. The scheduling system transmits the information to portable terminals carried by Polycon warehouse personnel who load the bumpers onto conveyors leading to the loading dock. The bumpers are then trucked 50 miles to the Ford plant. Total time is 4 hours. However, as we saw in our opening *Global Company Profile*, Toyota has moved its seat supplier inside the new Tundra plant; this has driven down delivery time even further.

Table 3 suggests several items that can contribute to achieving these goals, but two techniques (in addition to communicating schedules) are paramount. They are *level schedules* and *kanban*.

Level Schedules

Level schedules process frequent small batches rather than a few large batches. Because this technique schedules many small lots that are always changing, it has on occasion been called "jelly bean" scheduling. Figure 7 contrasts a traditional large-lot approach using large batches with a JIT level schedule using many small batches. The operations manager's task is to make and move small lots so the level schedule is economical. This requires success with the issues discussed in this chapter that allow small lots. As lots get smaller, the constraints may change and become increasingly challenging. At some point, processing a unit or two may not be feasible.

Level schedules
Scheduling products so that each day's production meets the demand for that day.

▼ **FIGURE 7** **Scheduling Small Lots of Parts A, B, and C Increases Flexibility to Meet Customer Demand and Reduces Inventory**
The JIT approach to scheduling produces just as many of each model per time period as the large-lot approach, provided that setup times are lowered.

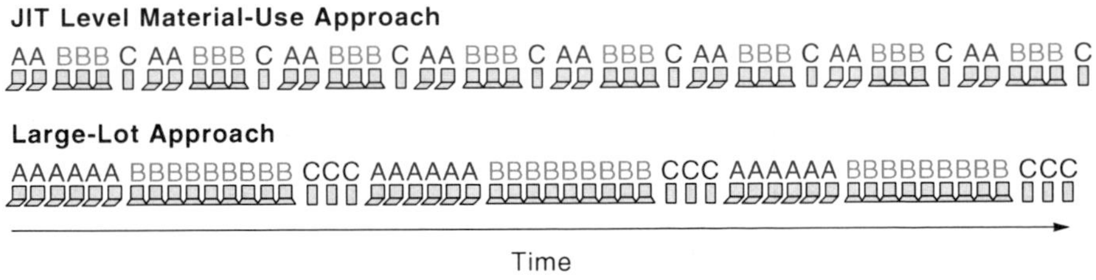

The constraint may be the way units are sold and shipped (four to a carton), or an expensive paint changeover (on an automobile assembly line), or the proper number of units in a sterilizer (for a food-canning line).

The scheduler may find that *freezing* the portion of the schedule closest to due dates allows the production system to function and the schedule to be met. Freezing means not allowing changes to be part of the schedule. Operations managers expect the schedule to be achieved with no deviations from the schedule.

Kanban

One way to achieve small lot sizes is to move inventory through the shop only as needed rather than *pushing* it on to the next workstation whether or not the personnel there are ready for it. As noted earlier, when inventory is moved only as needed, it is referred to as a *pull* system, and the ideal lot size is one. The Japanese call this system *kanban*. Kanbans allow arrivals at a work center to match (or nearly match) the processing time.

Kanban
The Japanese word for *card*, which has come to mean "signal"; a kanban system moves parts through production via a "pull" from a signal.

Kanban is a Japanese word for *card*. In their effort to reduce inventory, the Japanese use systems that "pull" inventory through work centers. They often use a "card" to signal the need for another container of material—hence the name *kanban. The card is the authorization for the next container of material to be produced.* Typically, a kanban signal exists for each container of items to be obtained. An order for the container is then initiated by each kanban and "pulled" from the producing department or supplier. A sequence of kanbans "pulls" the material through the plant.

The system has been modified in many facilities so that even though it is called a *kanban*, the card itself does not exist. In some cases, an empty position on the floor is sufficient indication that the next container is needed. In other cases, some sort of signal, such as a flag or rag (Figure 8) alerts that it is time for the next container.

When there is visual contact between producer and user, the process works like this:

LO5: Define kanban

1. The user removes a standard-size container of parts from a small storage area, as shown in Figure 8.
2. The signal at the storage area is seen by the producing department as authorization to replenish the using department or storage area. Because there is an optimum lot size, the producing department may make several containers at a time.

Figure 9 shows how a kanban works, pulling units as needed from production. This system is similar to the resupply that occurs in your neighborhood supermarket: The customer buys; the stock clerk observes the shelf or receives notice from the end-of-day sales list and restocks. When the limited supply, if any, in the store's storage is depleted, a "pull" signal is sent to the warehouse, distributor, or manufacturer for resupply, usually that night. The complicating factor in a manufacturing firm is the time needed for actual manufacturing (production) to take place.

A kanban need not be as formal as signal lights or empty carts. The cook in a fast-food restaurant knows that when six cars are in line, eight meat patties and six orders of french fries should be cooking.

Donna Shader

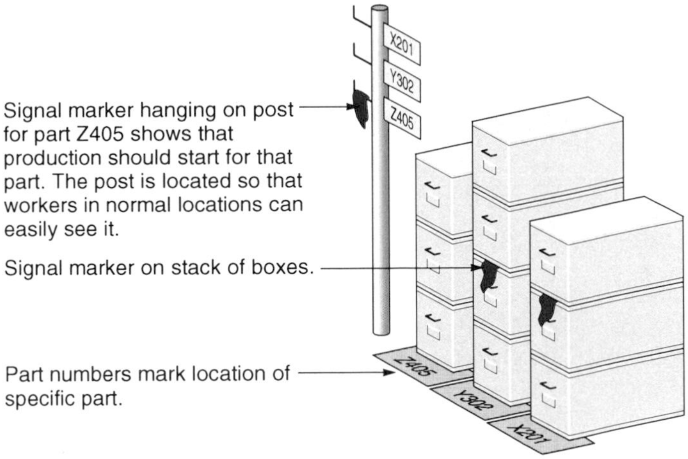

◀ **FIGURE 8**
Diagram of Outbound Stockpoint with Warning-Signal Marker

Several additional points regarding kanbans may be helpful:

- When the producer and user are not in visual contact, a card can be used; otherwise, a light or flag or empty spot on the floor may be adequate.
- Because a pull station may require several resupply components, several kanban pull techniques can be used for different products at the same pull station.
- Usually, each card controls a specific quantity of parts, although multiple card systems are used if the producing work cell produces several components or if the lot size is different from the move size.
- In an MRP system, the schedule can be thought of as a "build" authorization and the kanban as a type of "pull" system that initiates the actual production.
- The kanban cards provide a direct control (limit) on the amount of work-in-process between cells.
- If there is an immediate storage area, a two-card system may be used—one card circulates between user and storage area, and the other circulates between the storage area and the producing area.

Determining the Number of Kanban Cards or Containers The number of kanban cards, or containers, in a JIT system sets the amount of authorized inventory. To determine the number of containers moving back and forth between the using area and the producing areas, management first sets the size of each container. This is done by computing the lot size, using a

▼ **FIGURE 9 Kanban Signals "Pull" Material Through the Production Process**

As a customer "pulls" an order from finished goods, a signal (kanban card) is sent to the final assembly area. Final assembly produces and resupplies finished goods. When final assembly needs components, it sends a signal to *its* supplier, a work cell. The work cell, in turn, sends a signal to the material/parts supplier.

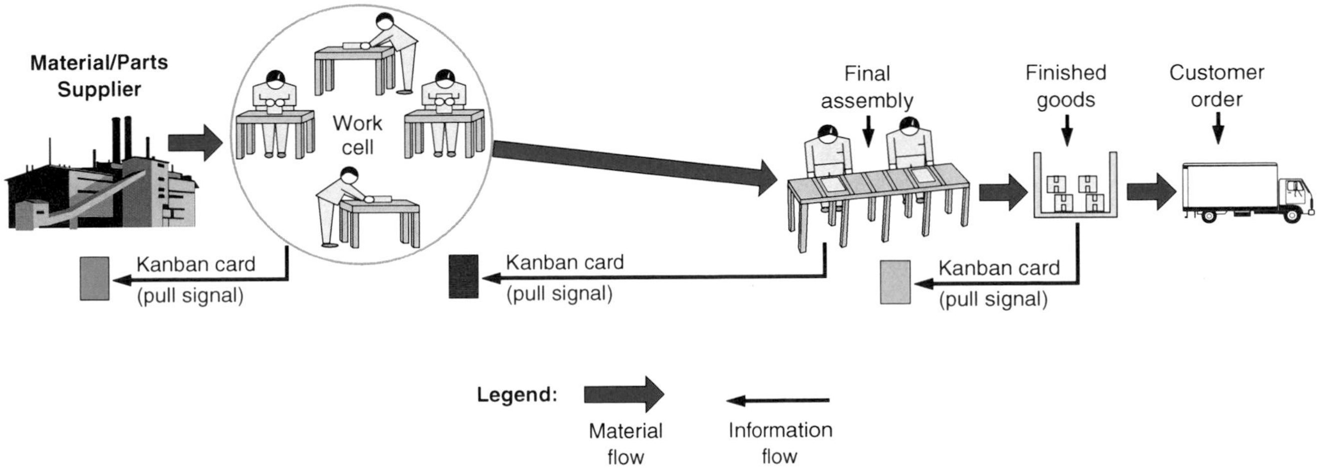

model such as the production order quantity model (shown in Equation [16–1]). Setting the number of containers involves knowing (1) lead time needed to produce a container of parts and (2) the amount of safety stock needed to account for variability or uncertainty in the system. The number of kanban cards is computed as follows:

$$\text{Number of kanbans (containers)} = \frac{\text{Demand during lead time} + \text{Safety stock}}{\text{Size of container}} \quad (3)$$

Example 2 illustrates how to calculate the number of kanbans needed.

EXAMPLE 2

Determining the number of kanban containers

Hobbs Bakery produces short runs of cakes that are shipped to grocery stores. The owner, Ken Hobbs, wants to try to reduce inventory by changing to a kanban system. He has developed the following data and asked you to finish the project.

Daily demand = 500 cakes

Production lead time = Wait time + Material handling time + Processing time = 2 days

Safety stock = $\frac{1}{2}$ day

Container size (determined on a production order size EOQ basis) = 250 cakes

APPROACH ▶ Having determined that the EOQ size is 250, we then determine the number of kanbans (containers) needed.

SOLUTION ▶ Demand during lead time =

Lead time × Daily demand = 2 days × 500 cakes = 1,000

Safety stock = 250

LO6: Compute the required number of kanbans

Number of kanbans (containers) needed =

$$\frac{\text{Demand during lead time} + \text{Safety stock}}{\text{Container size}} = \frac{1{,}000 + 250}{250} = 5$$

INSIGHT ▶ Once the reorder point is hit, five containers should be released.

LEARNING EXERCISE ▶ If lead time drops to 1 day, how many containers are needed? [Answer: 3.]

RELATED PROBLEMS ▶ 16.1, 16.2, 16.3, 16.4, 16.5, 16.6

Advantages of Kanban Containers are typically very small, usually a matter of a few hours' worth of production. Such a system requires tight schedules. Small quantities must be produced several times a day. The process must run smoothly with little variability in quality of lead time because any shortage has an almost immediate impact on the entire system. Kanban places added emphasis on meeting schedules, reducing the time and cost required by setups, and economical material handling.

Whether it is called kanban or something else, the advantages of small inventory and *pulling* material through the plant only when needed are significant. For instance, small batches allow only a very limited amount of faulty or delayed material. Problems are immediately evident. Numerous aspects of inventory are bad; only one aspect—availability—is good. Among the bad aspects are poor quality, obsolescence, damage, occupied space, committed assets, increased insurance, increased material handling, and increased accidents. Kanban systems put downward pressure on all these negative aspects of inventory.

In-plant kanban systems often use standardized, reusable containers that protect the specific quantities to be moved. Such containers are also desirable in the supply chain. Standardized containers reduce weight and disposal costs, generate less wasted space in trailers, and require less labor to pack, unpack, and prepare items.

AUTHOR COMMENT Good quality costs less.

JIT QUALITY

The relationship between JIT and quality is a strong one. They are related in three ways. First, JIT cuts the cost of obtaining good quality. This saving occurs because scrap, rework, inventory investment, and damage costs are buried in inventory. JIT forces down inventory; therefore, fewer bad units are produced and fewer units must be reworked. In short, whereas inventory *hides* bad quality, JIT immediately *exposes* it.

This auto plant, like most JIT facilities, empowers employees so they can stop the entire production line by pulling the overhead cord if any quality problems are spotted.

New United Motor Manufacturing, Inc. (NUMMI)

Second, JIT improves quality. As JIT shrinks queues and lead time, it keeps evidence of errors fresh and limits the number of potential sources of error. In effect, JIT creates an early warning system for quality problems so that fewer bad units are produced and feedback is immediate. This advantage can accrue both within the firm and with goods received from outside vendors.

Finally, better quality means fewer buffers are needed and, therefore, a better, easier-to-employ JIT system can exist. Often the purpose of keeping inventory is to protect against unreliable quality. If consistent quality exists, JIT allows firms to reduce all costs associated with inventory. Table 4 suggests some requirements for quality in a JIT environment.

▼ **TABLE 4**
JIT Quality Tactics

Use statistical process control
Empower employees
Build fail-safe methods (poka-yoke, checklists, etc.)
Expose poor quality with small lot JIT
Provide immediate feedback

TOYOTA PRODUCTION SYSTEM

AUTHOR COMMENT TPS brings the entire person to work.

Toyota Motor's Eiji Toyoda and Taiichi Ohno are given credit for the Toyota Production System (TPS) (see the *Global Company Profile* that opens this chapter). Three core components of TPS are continuous improvement, respect for people, and standard work practice.

Continuous Improvement

Continuous improvement under TPS means building an organizational culture and instilling in its people a value system stressing that processes can be improved—indeed, that improvement is an integral part of every employee's job. This process is formalized in TPS by **kaizen**, the Japanese word for change for the good, or what is more generally known as *continuous improvement*. In application, it means making a multitude of small or incremental changes as one seeks ellusive perfection. (See the *OM in Action Box* "Kaizen at Ducati."). Instilling the mantra of continuous improvement begins at recruiting and continues through extensive and continuing training. One of the reasons continuous improvement works at Toyota, we should note, is because of another core value at Toyota, Toyota's respect for people.

Kaizen
A focus on continuous improvement.

Respect for People

At Toyota, people are recruited, trained, and treated as knowledge workers. Aided by aggressive cross-training and few job classifications, TPS engages the mental as well as physical capacities of employees in the challenging task of improving operations. Employees are empowered. They are empowered to make improvements. They are empowered to stop machines and processes when quality problems exist. Indeed, empowered employees are a necessary part of TPS. This means that those tasks that have traditionally been assigned to staff are moved to employees. Toyota recognizes that employees know more about their jobs than anyone else. TPS respects employees by giving them the opportunity to enrich both their jobs and their lives.

Standard Work Practice

Standard work practice at Toyota includes these underlying principles:

- Work is completely specified as to content, sequence, timing, and outcome.
- Internal and external customer–supplier connections are direct, specifying personnel, methods, timing, and quantity.

LO7: Explain the principles of the Toyota Production System

OM in Action ► Kaizen at Ducati

Ducati Motor Holding SpA of Bologna, Italy, is a motorcycle racing company whose engineering department replicates its high-performance racing machines for street use. But the production department is more interested in replicating lean thinking and adapting the Toyota Production System to Ducati's culture. Ducati has trained everyone throughout the plant, not just assembly specialists, in lean thinking. One result is a total productive maintenance effort and improved material flow that has increased machine reliability 12% and cut hourly costs 23%.

Another successful approach to drive out waste was Ducati's 4-week workshop approach to kaizen. This is a longer commitment to kaizen teams than is typical, as kaizens are not designed for perfection on the first pass; progress, not perfection, is the objective. This approach provided an opportunity for incremental but significant changes. The kaizen workshops also provided the added advantage of bringing people together in cross-functional teams, which reinforces a culture of continuous improvement.

Gerardo Burgos Galindo/Shutterstock

The astounding results at Ducati would make Eiji Toyoda and Taiichi Ohno, founders of TPS, proud. Production costs are down by 25%, manufacturing cycle time has been reduced by 50%, and quality before delivery has been increased by 70%.

Sources: The Wall Street Journal (March 26, 2008): D1, D5; *Target* 27, no. 4 (2007): 10–15; and **www.oracle.com**.

- Product and service flows are to be simple and direct. Goods and services are directed to a specific person or machine.
- Improvements in the system must be made in accordance with the "scientific method," at the lowest possible level in the organization.[2]

TPS requires that activities, connections, and flows include built-in tests to automatically signal problems. Any gap between what is expected and what occurs becomes immediately evident. The education and training of Toyota's employees and the responsiveness of the system to problems make the seemingly rigid system flexible and adaptable to changing circumstances. The result is ongoing improvements in reliability, flexibility, safety, and efficiency.

AUTHOR COMMENT Lean drives out non-value-added activities.

LEAN OPERATIONS

Lean production can be thought of as the end result of a well-run OM function. While JIT and TPS tend to have an *internal* focus, lean production begins *externally* with a focus on the customer. Understanding what the customer wants and ensuring customer input and feedback are starting points for lean production. Lean operations means identifying customer value by analyzing all the activities required to produce the product and then optimizing the entire process from the customer's perspective.

Building a Lean Organization

The transition to lean production is difficult. Building an organizational culture where learning, empowerment, and continuous improvement are the norm is a challenge. However, organizations that focus on JIT, quality, and employee empowerment are often lean producers. Such firms drive out activities that do not add value in the eyes of the customer: they include leaders like United Parcel Service, Harley-Davidson, and, of course, Toyota. Even traditionally craft-oriented organizations such as Louis Vuitton (see the *OM in Action* box) find improved productivity with lean operations. Lean operations adopt a philosophy of minimizing waste by striving for perfection through continuous learning, creativity, and teamwork. They tend to share the following attributes:

- *Use JIT techniques* to eliminate virtually all inventory.
- *Build systems that help employees* produce a perfect part every time.
- *Reduce space requirements* by minimizing travel distance.

[2]Adopted from Steven J. Spear, "Learning to Lead at Toyota," *Harvard Business Review* 82, no. 5 (May 2004): 78–86; and Steven Spear and H. Kent Bowen, "Decoding the DNA of the Toyota Production System," *Harvard Business Review* 77, no. 5 (September–October 1999): 97–106.

OM in Action ► Going Lean at Louis Vuitton

LVMH Moet Hennessy Louis Vuitton is the world's largest luxury-goods company. Its Louis Vuitton unit, responsible for half of the company's profit, makes very upscale handbags and enjoys a rich markup on sales of about $5 billion. The return-on-investment is excellent, but sales could be even better: the firm often can't match production to the sales pace of a successful new product. In the high fashion business that is all about speed-to-market, this is bad news; a massive overhaul was in order.

Changes on the factory floor were key to the overhaul. The traditional approach to manufacturing at Louis Vuitton was batch production: craftsmen, working on partially completed handbags, performed specialized tasks such as cutting, gluing, sewing, and assembly. Carts moved batches of semi-finished handbags on to the next workstation. It took 20 to 30 workers 8 days to make a handbag. And defects were high. Lean manufacturing looked like the way to go.

Craftsmen were retrained to do multiple tasks in small U-shaped work cells. Each work cell now contains 6 to 12 cross-trained workers and the necessary sewing machines and work tables. Consistent with one-piece flow, the work is passed through the cell from worker to worker. The system reduces inventory and allows workers to detect flaws earlier. Rework under the old system was sometimes as high as 50% and internal losses as high as 4%. Returns are down by two-thirds. The system has not only improved productivity and quality, it also allows Louis Vuitton to respond to the market faster—with daily scheduling as opposed to weekly scheduling.

Colin Young-Wolff/PhotoEdit Inc.

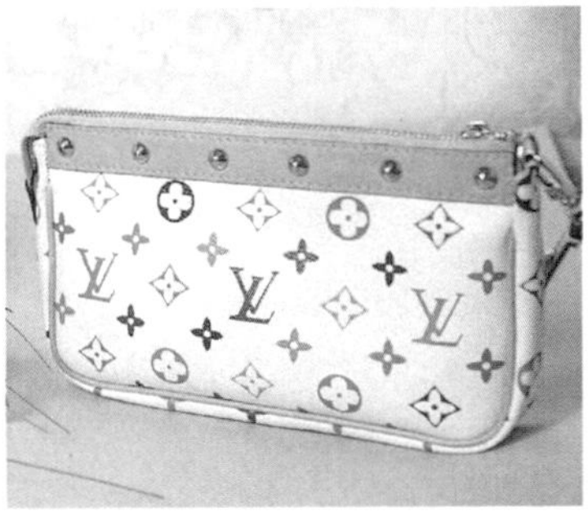

Sources: The Wall Street Journal (October 9, 2006): A1, A15 and (January 31, 2006): A1, A13.

- *Develop partnerships with suppliers*, helping them to understand the needs of the ultimate customer.
- *Educate suppliers* to accept responsibility for satisfying end customer needs.
- *Eliminate all but value-added activities.* Material handling, inspection, inventory, and rework are the likely targets because these do not add value to the product.
- *Develop employees* by constantly improving job design, training, employee commitment, teamwork, and empowerment.
- *Make jobs challenging*, pushing responsibility to the lowest level possible.
- *Build worker flexibility* through cross-training and reducing job classifications.

Success requires the full commitment and involvement of managers, employees, and suppliers. The rewards that lean producers reap are spectacular. Lean producers often become benchmark performers.

LEAN OPERATIONS IN SERVICES

AUTHOR COMMENT JIT, TPS, and lean began in factories but are now also used in services throughout the world.

The features of lean operations apply to services just as they do in other sectors. (See the *OM in Action* box "Toyota University Teaches Lean Thinking.") Here are some examples applied to suppliers, layout, inventory, and scheduling in the service sector.

Suppliers As we have noted, virtually every restaurant deals with its suppliers on a JIT basis. Those that do not are usually unsuccessful. The waste is too evident—food spoils, and customers complain or get sick.

Layouts Lean layouts are required in restaurant kitchens, where cold food must be served cold and hot food hot. McDonald's, for example, has reconfigured its kitchen layout at great expense to drive seconds out of the production process, thereby speeding delivery to customers. With the new process, McDonald's can produce made-to-order hamburgers in 45 seconds. Layouts also make a difference in airline baggage claim, where customers expect their bags just-in-time.

Inventory Stockbrokers drive inventory down to nearly zero every day. Most sell and buy orders occur on an immediate basis because an unexecuted sell or buy order is not acceptable to the client. A broker may be in serious trouble if left holding an unexecuted trade. Similarly, McDonald's reduces inventory waste by maintaining a finished-goods inventory of only 10 minutes; after that, it is thrown away. Hospitals, such as Arnold Palmer (described in this chapter's

VIDEO 16.1 JIT at Arnold Palmer Hospital

Lean operations take on an unusual form in an operating room. McKesson-General, Baxter International, and many other hospital suppliers provide surgical supplies for hospitals on a JIT basis. (1) They deliver prepackaged surgical supplies based on hospital operating schedules, and (2) the surgical packages themselves are prepared so supplies are available in the sequence in which they will be used during surgery.

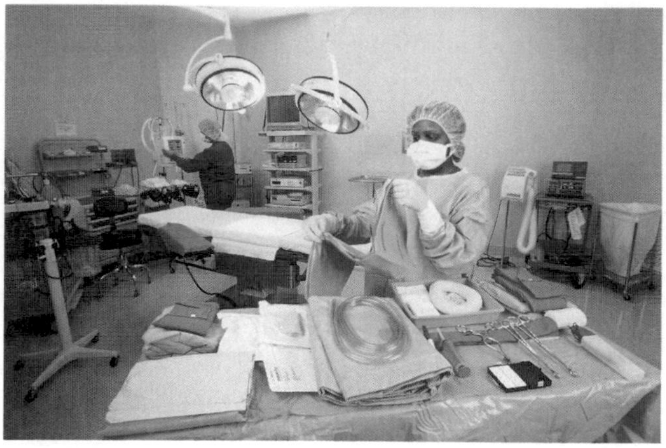

Courtesy of Cardinal Health, Inc.

Video Case Study), manage JIT inventory and low safety stocks for many items. Even critical supplies such as pharmaceuticals may be held to low levels by developing community networks as backup systems. In this manner, if one pharmacy runs out of a needed drug, another member of the network can supply it until the next day's shipment arrives.

Scheduling At airline ticket counters, the focus of the system is on adjusting to customer demand. But rather than being accommodated by inventory availability, demand is satisfied by personnel. Through elaborate scheduling, ticket counter personnel show up just-in-time to cover peaks in customer demand. In other words, rather than "things" inventoried, personnel are scheduled. At a salon, the focus is only slightly different: the *customer* and the staff are scheduled to assure prompt service. At McDonald's and Walmart, scheduling of personnel is down to 15-minute increments, based on precise forecasting of demand. Additionally, at McDonald's, production is done in small lots to ensure that fresh, hot hamburgers are delivered just-in-time. In short, both personnel and production are scheduled to meet specific demand. Notice that in all three of these lean organizations—the airline ticket counter, the salon, and McDonald's—scheduling is a key ingredient. Excellent forecasts drive those schedules. Those forecasts may be very elaborate, with seasonal, daily, and even hourly components in the case of the airline ticket counter (holiday sales, flight time, etc.), seasonal and weekly components at the salon (holidays and Fridays create special problems), and down to a few minutes (to respond to the daily meal cycle) at McDonald's.

To deliver goods and services to customers under continuously changing demand, suppliers need to be reliable, inventories lean, cycle times short, and schedules nimble. A lean focus engages and empowers employees to create and deliver the customer's perception of value, eliminating whatever does not contribute to this goal. Lean operations are currently being developed with great success in many firms, regardless of their products. Lean techniques are widely used in both goods-producing and service-producing firms; they just look different.

OM in Action ► Toyota University Teaches Lean Thinking

Based in Gardenia, California, Toyota University teaches its employees the Toyota Production System. But Toyota has also opened its door to others. As a public service, Toyota has been teaching lean thinking classes to the Los Angeles Police Department and the U.S. military. Classes begin, as one might expect, with a car-building exercise. Using model cars and desks as workstations and delivery areas, students begin with a focus on fast throughput and high production goals. This results in a "push" system, with lots of work-in-process piling up, lots of defects to be reworked, and too many of the wrong kind of cars on the "dealer's" lot.

The exercise is then revised, and students are taught to respond to orders and to form *kaizen* (continuous improvement) teams. The revised exercise then uses a "pull" system that responds to orders and fixes even the most minor problems immediately. With a focus only on filling orders and "pulling" demand through the production process with no defects, a faster, more efficient production line is formed.

Instructor Matthew May's observation about adapting lean methods beyond the factory: "If you can do it with LAPD, you can do it anywhere."

Sources: The Wall Street Journal (March 5, 2007): B1, B4; and **www.isosupport.com**.

CHAPTER SUMMARY

JIT, TPS, and lean operations are philosophies of continuous improvement. Lean operations focus on customer desires, TPS focuses on respect for people and standard work practices, and JIT focuses on driving out waste by reducing inventory. But all three approaches reduce waste in the production process. And because waste is found in anything that does not add value, organizations that implement these techniques are adding value more efficiently than other firms. The expectation of these systems is that empowered employees work with committed management to build systems that respond to customers with ever-lower cost and higher quality.

Key Terms

Just-in-time (JIT)
Toyota Production System (TPS)
Lean operations
Seven wastes
5Ss
Variability
Throughput
Manufacturing cycle time
Pull system
JIT partnerships
Consignment inventory
Just-in-time inventory
Level schedules
Kanban
Kaizen

Ethical Dilemma

In this lean operations world, in an effort to lower handling costs, speed delivery, and reduce inventory, retailers are forcing their suppliers to do more and more in the way of preparing their merchandise for their cross-docking warehouses, shipment to specific stores, and shelf presentation. Your company, a small manufacturer of aquarium decorations, is in a tough position. First, Mega-Mart wanted you to develop bar-code technology, then special packaging, then small individual shipments bar coded for each store (this way when the merchandise hits the warehouse it is cross-docked immediately to the correct truck and store and is ready for shelf placement). And now Mega-Mart wants you to develop RFID—immediately. Mega-Mart has made it clear that suppliers that cannot keep up with the technology will be dropped.

Earlier, when you didn't have the expertise for bar codes, you had to borrow money and hire an outside firm to do the development, purchase the technology, and train your shipping clerk. Then, meeting the special packaging requirement drove you into a loss for several months, resulting in a loss for last year. Now it appears that the RFID request is impossible. Your business, under the best of conditions, is marginally profitable, and the bank may not be willing to bail you out again. Over the years, Mega-Mart has slowly become your major customer and without them, you are probably out of business. What are the ethical issues and what do you do?

Discussion Questions

1. What is JIT?
2. What is a lean producer?
3. What is TPS?
4. What is level scheduling?
5. JIT attempts to remove delays, which do not add value. How then does JIT cope with weather and its impact on crop harvest and transportation times?
6. What are three ways in which JIT and quality are related?
7. How does TPS contribute to competitive advantage?
8. What are the characteristics of just-in-time partnerships with respect to suppliers?
9. Discuss how the Japanese word for *card* has application in the study of JIT.
10. Standardized, reusable containers have fairly obvious benefits for shipping. What is the purpose of these devices within the plant?
11. Does lean production work in the service sector? Provide an illustration.
12. Which lean techniques work in both the manufacturing *and* service sectors?

Solved Problems **Virtual Office Hours help is available at www.myomlab.com**

▼ SOLVED PROBLEM 16.1

Krupp Refrigeration, Inc., is trying to reduce inventory and wants you to install a kanban system for compressors on one of its assembly lines. Determine the size of the kanban and the number of kanbans (containers) needed.

Setup cost = \$10
Annual holding cost per compressor = \$100
Daily production = 200 compressors
Annual usage = 25,000 (50 weeks × 5 days each × daily usage of 100 compressors)
Lead time = 3 days
Safety stock = $\frac{1}{2}$ day's production of compressors

▼ SOLUTION

First, we must determine kanban container size. To do this, we determine the production order quantity (see Equation [1]), which determines the kanban size:

$$Q_p^* = \sqrt{\frac{2DS}{H\left(1 - \frac{d}{p}\right)}} = \sqrt{\frac{2(25{,}000)(10)}{H\left(1 - \frac{d}{p}\right)}} = \sqrt{\frac{500{,}000}{100\left(1 - \frac{100}{200}\right)}} = \sqrt{\frac{500{,}000}{50}}$$

$= \sqrt{10{,}000} = 100$ compressors. So the production order size and the size of the kanban container $= 100$.

Then we determine the number of kanbans:

$$\text{Demand during lead time} = 300\ (= 3 \text{ days} \times \text{daily usage of } 100)$$

$$\text{Safety stock} = 100\ (= \tfrac{1}{2} \times \text{daily production of } 200)$$

$$\text{Number of kanbans} = \frac{\text{Demand during lead time} + \text{Safety stock}}{\text{Size of container}}$$

$$= \frac{300 + 100}{100} = \frac{400}{100} = 4 \text{ containers}$$

Problems*

• **16.1** Leblanc Electronics, Inc., in Nashville, produces short runs of custom airwave scanners for the defense industry. You have been asked by the owner, Larry Leblanc, to reduce inventory by introducing a kanban system. After several hours of analysis, you develop the following data for scanner connectors used in one work cell. How many kanbans do you need for this connector?

Daily demand	1,000 connectors
Lead time	2 days
Safety stock	$\frac{1}{2}$ day
Kanban size	500 connectors

• **16.2** Chip Gillikin's company wants to establish kanbans to feed a newly established work cell. The following data have been provided. How many kanbans are needed?

Daily demand	250 units
Production lead time	$\frac{1}{2}$ day
Safety stock	$\frac{1}{4}$ day
Kanban size	50 units

•• **16.3** Chris Millikan Manufacturing, Inc., is moving to kanbans to support its telephone switching-board assembly lines. Determine the size of the kanban for subassemblies and the number of kanbans needed.

Setup cost = \$30
Annual holding cost = \$120 per subassembly
Daily production = 20 subassemblies
Annual usage = 2,500 (50 weeks × 5 days each × daily usage of 10 subassemblies)
Lead time = 16 days
Safety stock = 4 days' production of subassemblies. PX

*Note: PX means the problem may be solved with POM for Windows and/or Excel OM.

•• **16.4** Maggie Moylan Motorcycle Corp. uses kanbans to support its transmission assembly line. Determine the size of the kanban for the mainshaft assembly and the number of kanbans needed.

Setup cost = \$20
Annual holding cost of mainshaft assembly = \$250 per unit
Daily production = 300 mainshafts
Annual usage = 20,000 (= 50 weeks × 5 days each × daily usage of 80 mainshafts)
Lead time = 3 days
Safety stock = $\frac{1}{2}$ day's production of mainshafts PX

Green Gear Cycling, Inc.

• **16.5** Discount-Mart, a major East Coast retailer, wants to determine the economic order quantity for its halogen lamps. It currently buys all halogen lamps from Specialty Lighting Manufacturers, in Atlanta. Annual demand is 2,000 lamps, ordering cost per order is $30, annual carrying cost per lamp is $12.

a) What is the EOQ?
b) What are the total annual costs of holding and ordering (managing) this inventory?
c) How many orders should Discount-Mart place with Specialty Lighting per year? Px

••• **16.6** Discount-Mart (see Problem 16.5), as part of its new JIT program, has signed a long-term contract with Specialty Lighting and will place orders electronically for its halogen lamps. Ordering costs will drop to $.50 per order, but Discount-Mart also reassessed its carrying costs and raised them to $20 per lamp.

a) What is the new economic order quantity?
b) How many orders will now be placed?
c) What is the total annual cost of managing the inventory with this policy? Px

•• **16.7** How do your answers to Problems 16.5 and 16.6 provide insight into a JIT purchasing strategy?

••• **16.8** Bill Penny has a repetitive manufacturing plant producing trailer hitches in Arlington, Texas. The plant has an average inventory turnover of only 12 times per year. He has therefore determined that he will reduce his component lot sizes. He has developed the following data for one component, the safety chain clip:

Annual demand = 31,200 units
Daily demand = 120 units
Daily production (in 8 hours) = 960 units
Desired lot size (1 hour of production) = 120 units
Holding cost per unit per year = $12
Setup labor cost per hour = $20

How many minutes of setup time should he have his plant manager aim for regarding this component?

••• **16.9** Given the following information about a product, at Phyllis Simon's firm, what is the appropriate setup time?

Annual demand = 39,000 units
Daily demand = 150 units
Daily production = 1,000 units
Desired lot size = 150 units
Holding cost per unit per year = $10
Setup labor cost per hour = $40

••• **16.10** Rick Wing has a repetitive manufacturing plant producing automobile steering wheels. Use the following data to prepare for a reduced lot size. The firm uses a work year of 305 days.

Annual demand for steering wheels	30,500
Daily demand	100
Daily production (8 hours)	800
Desired lot size (2 hours of production)	200
Holding cost per unit per year	$10

a) What is the setup cost, based on the desired lot size?
b) What is the setup time, based on $40 per hour setup labor?

▶ **Refer to myomlab for these additional homework problems: 16.11–16.12**

Case Studies

▶ Mutual Insurance Company of Iowa

Mutual Insurance Company of Iowa (MICI) has a major insurance office facility located in Des Moines, Iowa. The Des Moines office is responsible for processing all of MICI's insurance claims for the entire nation. The company's sales have experienced rapid growth during the last year, and as expected, record levels in claims followed. Over 2,500 forms for claims a day are now flowing into the office for processing. Unfortunately, fewer than 2,500 forms a day are flowing out. The total time to process a claim, from the time it arrives to the time a check is mailed, has increased from 10 days to 10 weeks. As a result, some customers are threatening legal action. Sally Cook, the manager of Claims Processing, is particularly distressed, as she knows that a claim seldom requires more than 3 hours of actual work. Under the current administrative procedures, human resources limitations, and facility constraints, there appear to be no easy fixes for the problem. But clearly, something must be done, as the workload has overwhelmed the existing system.

MICI management wants aggressive, but economical, action taken to fix the problem. Ms. Cook has decided to try a JIT approach to claim processing. With support from her bosses, and as a temporary fix, Cook has brought in part-time personnel from MICI sales divisions across the country to help. They are to work down the claims backlog while a new JIT system is installed.

Meanwhile, Claims Processing managers and employees are to be trained in JIT principles. With JIT principles firmly in mind, managers will redesign jobs to move responsibilities for quality control activities to each employee, holding them responsible for quality work and any necessary corrections. Cook will also initiate worker-training programs that explain the entire claim processing flow, as well as provide comprehensive training on each step in the process. Data-entry skills will also be taught to both employees and managers in an effort to fix responsibility for data accuracy on the processor rather than on data entry clerks. Additionally, cross-training will be emphasized to enable workers within departments to process a variety of customer claim applications in their entirety.

Cook and her supervisors are also reexamining the insurance and claim forms currently in use. They want to see if standardization of forms will cut processing time, reduce data-entry time, and cut work-in-process.

They hope the changes will also save training time. Making changes in work methods and worker skills leads logically to a need for change in the layout of the Claims Processing Department. This potential change represents a major move from the departmental layout of the past, and will be a costly step. To help ensure the successful implementation of this phase of the

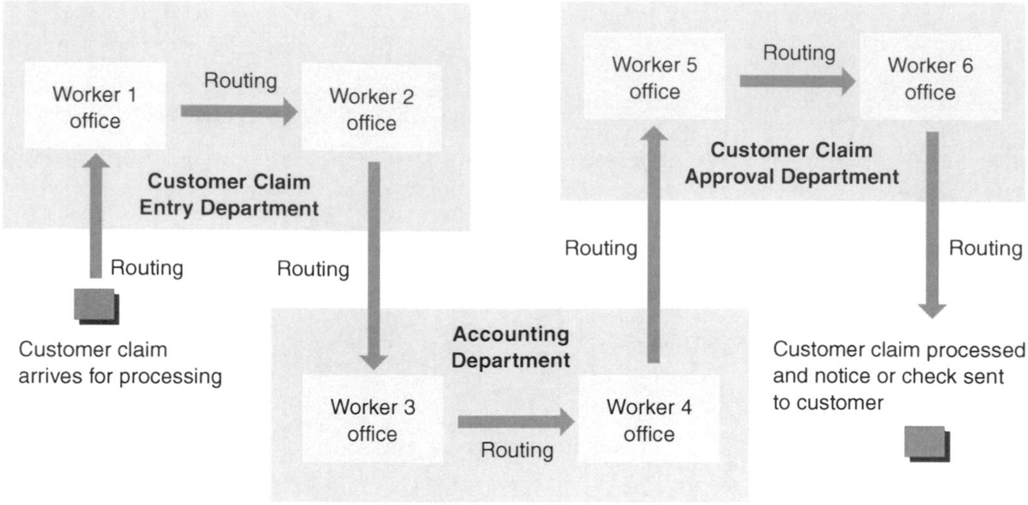

▲ **FIGURE 10** **Claims Processing Department Layout**

changeover, Cook established a team made up of supervisors, employees, and an outside office layout consultant. She also had the team visit the Kawasaki motorcycle plant in Lincoln, Nebraska, to observe their use of work cells to aid JIT.

The team concluded that a change in the office facilities was necessary to successfully implement and integrate JIT concepts at MICI. The team believes it should revise the layout of the operation and work methods to bring them in line with "group technology cell" layouts. An example of the current departmental layout and claim processing flow pattern is presented in Figure 10. As can be seen in this figure, customer claims arrive for processing at the facility and flow through a series of offices and departments to eventually complete the claim process. Although the arrangement of the offices and workers in Figure 10 is typical, the entire facility actually operates 20 additional flows, each consisting of the same three departments. However, not all of the 20 flows are configured the same. The number of employees, for example, varies depending on the claim form requirements (larger claims have to be approved by more people). So while all forms must pass through the same three departments (Customer Claim Entry, Accounting, and Customer Claim Approval), the number of workers for each claim may vary from two to four. For this reason, the MICI facility currently maintains a staff of over 180 office workers just to process and route claims. All these people work for Ms. Cook.

Discussion Questions

1. Identify the attributes you would expect the Claims Processing Department at MICI to have once the new JIT system is in place.
2. What will the restructured cell layout for claim processing in Figure 10 look like? Draw it.
3. What assumptions are you making about personnel and equipment in the new group technology cell layout?
4. How will the new JIT oriented system benefit the MICI operation? Explain.

Source: Adapted from Marc J. Schniederjans, *Topics in Just-in-Time Management*, pp. 283–285. Reprinted by permission of Pearson Education, Inc., Upper Saddle River, NJ.

► JIT after a Catastrophe

You name the catastrophe, and JIT has been through it and survived. Toyota Motor Corporation has had its world-renowned JIT system tested by fire. The massive fire incinerated the main source of crucial brake valves that Toyota buys from the Aisin Seiki plant in Kariya, Japan, and uses in most of its cars. The impact was the loss of 70,000 cars not produced while Toyota got the supply chain repaired. Then an earthquake destroyed Toyota's transmission supplier, Riken, shutting down production in a dozen factories. Chrysler and many others had their JIT systems tested on September 11, 2001, when the terrorists attacks shut down their state-of-the-art air delivery systems. And on February 5, 2008, during the second shift at Caterpillar's high-pressure couplings plant in Oxford, Mississippi, a tornado all but destroyed the facility. Despite these catastrophes, managers at these firms, like other executives all over the world, are still cutting costs by consolidating production, reducing inventory, and implementing JIT.

Consistent with JIT practice, these firms maintain minimal inventory of components and tight supply chains. There are very few components in these closely knit networks that constitute their respective supply chains. Without critical components, production comes to a rapid halt. And in Caterpillar's case, the Oxford plant is the only plant in the world that makes this unique coupling. The couplings link hydraulic hoses on *every* piece of machinery Caterpillar makes. Depending on a single source and holding little inventory is a risk, but it also keeps firms lean and costs low.

The morning after the tornado tore apart the Oxford plant, Greg Folley, who runs Caterpillar's parts division, toured the plant. Much of the roof, including 10-ton heating and air-conditioning units, had fallen onto three critical metal stamping machines. The first piece of equipment was up and running in 2 weeks; getting production back to normal would take 6 months. But the Oxford plant had been making over 1 million of the critical couplings each month; this left a huge hole in Caterpillar's supply line.

Discussion Questions

1. If you are Mr. Folley, looking over the devastation at the Oxford plant, what do you do to keep Caterpillar's worldwide production running?
2. Given the inherent risk in JIT and the trauma that the companies have experienced, why has JIT survived?
3. What do these experiences, and the continuing popularity of JIT, tell you about just-in-time?
4. What actions or changes in policy do you suggest for Caterpillar?

Sources: Case is based on material in: *The Wall Street Journal* (May 19, 2008): B1, B2; (July 20, 2007): B1; **www.USAToday.com/money/world/2007-07-18-toyota-quake**; and *Harvard Business Review* (September–October 1999): 97–106.

▶ JIT at Arnold Palmer Hospital

Video Case

Orlando's Arnold Palmer Hospital, founded in 1989, specializes in treatment of women and children and is renowned for its high-quality rankings (top 10% of 2000 benchmarked hospitals), its labor and delivery volume (more than 16,000 births per year, and growing), and its neonatal intensive care unit (one of the highest survival rates in the nation). But quality medical practices and high patient satisfaction require costly inventory—some $30 million per year and thousands of SKUs.* With pressure on medical care to manage and reduce costs, Arnold Palmer Hospital has turned toward controlling its inventory with just-in-time (JIT) techniques.

Within the hospital, for example, drugs are now distributed at nursing workstations via dispensing machines (almost like vending machines) that electronically track patient usage and post the related charge to each patient. The dispensing stations are refilled each night, based on patient demand and prescriptions written by doctors.

To address JIT issues externally, Arnold Palmer Hospital turned toward a major distribution partner, McKesson General Medical, which as a first-tier supplier provides the hospital with about one quarter of all its medical/surgical inventory. McKesson supplies sponges, basins, towels, mayo stand covers, syringes, and hundreds of other medical/surgical items. To ensure coordinated daily delivery of inventory purchased from McKesson, an account executive has been assigned to the hospital on a full-time basis, as well as two other individuals who address customer service and product issues. The result has been a drop in Central Supply average daily inventory from $400,000 to $114,000 since JIT.

JIT success has also been achieved in the area of *custom surgical packs*. Custom surgical packs are the sterile coverings, disposable plastic trays, gauze, and the like, specialized to each type of surgical procedure. Arnold Palmer Hospital uses 10 different custom packs for various surgical procedures. "Over 50,000 packs are used each year, for a total cost of about $1.5 million," says George DeLong, head of Supply-Chain Management.

The packs are not only delivered in a JIT manner but packed that way as well. That is, they are packed in the reverse order they are used so each item comes out of the pack in the sequence it is needed. The packs are bulky, expensive, and must remain sterile. Reducing the inventory and handling while maintaining an assured sterile supply for scheduled surgeries presents a challenge to hospitals.

Here is how the supply chain works: Custom packs are *assembled* by a packing company with *components supplied* primarily from manufacturers selected by the hospital, and *delivered* by McKesson from its local warehouse. Arnold Palmer Hospital works with its own surgical staff (through the Medical Economics Outcome Committee) to identify and standardize the custom packs to reduce the number of custom pack SKUs. With this integrated system, pack safety stock inventory has been cut to one day.

The procedure to drive the custom surgical pack JIT system begins with a "pull" from the doctors' daily surgical schedule. Then, Arnold Palmer Hospital initiates an electronic order to McKesson between 1:00 and 2:00 P.M. daily. At 4:00 A.M. the next day, McKesson delivers the packs. Hospital personnel arrive at 7:00 A.M. and stock the shelves for scheduled surgeries. McKesson then reorders from the packing company, which in turn "pulls" necessary inventory for the quantity of packs needed from the manufacturers.

Arnold Palmer Hospital's JIT system reduces inventory investment, expensive traditional ordering, and bulky storage, and supports quality with a sterile delivery.

Discussion Questions**

1. What do you recommend be done when an error is found in a pack as it is opened for an operation?
2. How might the procedure for custom surgical packs described here be improved?
3. When discussing JIT in services, the text notes that suppliers, layout, inventory, and scheduling are all used. Provide an example of each of these at Arnold Palmer Hospital.
4. When a doctor proposes a new surgical procedure, how do you recommend the SKU for a new custom pack be entered into the hospital's supply-chain system?

*SKU = stock keeping unit

**You may wish to view the video that accompanies this case before answering these questions.

Bibliography

Burke, Robert, and Gregg Messel. "From Simulation to Implementation: Cardinal Health's Lean Journey." *Target: Innovation at Work* 19, no. 2 (2nd Quarter 2003): 27–32.

Flinchbauh, Jamie. *The Hitchhiker's Guide to Lean*, Dearborn, MI: Society of Manufacturing Engineers (2006).

Graban, Mark. *Lean Hospitals*. New York: CRC Press (2009).

Hall, Robert W. "'Lean' and the Toyota Production System." *Target* 20, no. 3 (3rd Issue 2004): 22–27.

Keyte, Beau, and Drew Locher. *The Complete Lean Enterprise*. University Park, IL: Productivity Press (2004).

Morgan, James M., and Jeffrey K. Liker. *The Toyota Product Development System*. New York: Productivity Press (2007).

Nelson-Peterson, Dana L., and Carol J. Leppa, "Creating an Environment of Caring Using Lean Principles of the Virginia Mason Production System, "*Journal of Nursing Administration* 37 (2007): 289.

Parks, Charles M. "The Bare Necessities of Lean." *Industrial Engineer* 35, no. 8 (August 2003): 39.

Schonberger, Richard J. "Lean Extended." *Industrial Engineer* (December 2005): 26–31.

van Veen-Dirks, Paula. "Management Control and the Production Environment." *International Journal of Production Economics* 93 (January 8, 2005): 263.

Womack, James P., and Daniel T. Jones. "Lean Consumption." *Harvard Business Review* 83 (March 2005): 58–68.

Womack, James P., and Daniel T. Jones. *Lean Solutions: How Companies and Customers Can Create Value and Wealth Together.* New York: The Free Press (2005).

Rapid Review

myomlab

Main Heading	Review Material
JUST-IN-TIME, THE TOYOTA PRODUCTION SYSTEM, AND LEAN OPERATIONS	▪ **Just-in-time (JIT)**—Continuous and forced problem solving via a focus on throughput and reduced inventory. ▪ **Toyota Production System (TPS)**—Focus on continuous improvement, respect for people, and standard work practices. ▪ **Lean operations**—Eliminates waste through a focus on exactly what the customer wants. *When implemented as a comprehensive manufacturing strategy, JIT, TPS, and lean systems sustain competitive advantage and result in increased overall returns.* ▪ **Seven wastes**—Overproduction, queues, transportation, inventory, motion, overprocessing, and defective product. ▪ **5Ss**—A lean production checklist: sort, simplify, shine, standardize, and sustain. U.S. managers often add two additional *S*s to the 5 original ones: *safety* and *support/maintenance*. ▪ **Variability**—Any deviation from the optimum process that delivers perfect product on time, every time. Both JIT and inventory reduction are effective tools for identifying causes of variability. ▪ **Throughput**—The time required to move orders through the production process, from receipt to delivery. ▪ **Manufacturing cycle time**—The time between the arrival of raw materials and the shipping of finished products. ▪ **Pull system**—A concept that results in material being produced only when requested and moved to where it is needed just as it is needed. Pull systems use signals to request production and delivery from supplying stations to stations that have production capacity available.
JUST-IN-TIME (JIT)	▪ **JIT partnerships**—Partnerships of suppliers and purchasers that remove waste and drive down costs for mutual benefits. Some specific goals of JIT partnerships are: *removal of unnecessary activities, removal of in-plant inventory*; *removal of in-transit inventory*; and *obtain improved quality and reliability*. ▪ **Consignment inventory**—An arrangement in which the supplier maintains title to the inventory until it is used. Concerns of suppliers in JIT partnerships include: (1) *diversification*; (2) *scheduling*; (3) *lead time*; (4) *quality*; and (5) *lot sizes*.
JIT LAYOUT	JIT layout tactics include building work cells for families of products, include a large number of operations in a small area, minimizing distance, designing little space for inventory, improving employee communication, using poka-yoke devices, building flexible or movable equipment, and cross-training workers to add flexibility.
JIT INVENTORY	▪ **Just-in-time inventory**—The minimum inventory necessary to keep a perfect system running. The idea behind JIT is to eliminate inventory that hides variability in the production system. JIT inventory tactics include using a pull system to move inventory, reducing lot size, developing just-in-time delivery systems with suppliers, delivering directly to the point of use, performing to schedule, reducing setup time, and using group technology. $$Q^* = \sqrt{\frac{2DS}{H[1 - (d/p)]}} \quad (1)$$ Using (16–1), for a given desired lot size, Q, we can solve for the optimal setup cost, S: $$S = \frac{(Q^2)(H)(1 - d/p)}{2D} \quad (2)$$

Problems: 16.8–16.10

Rapid Review *continued*

Main Heading	Review Material	myomlab
JIT SCHEDULING	JIT scheduling tactics include: communicate schedules to suppliers, make level schedules, freeze part of the schedule, perform to schedule, seek one-piece-make and one-piece-move, eliminate waste, produce in small lots, use kanbans, and make each operation produce a perfect part. ■ **Level schedules**—Scheduling products so that each day's production meets the demand for that day. ■ **Kanban**—The Japanese word for *card*, which has come to mean "signal"; a kanban system moves parts through production via a "pull" from a signal: $\text{Number of Kanbans (containers)} = \frac{\text{Demand during lead time} + \text{Safety stock}}{\text{Size of container}}$ (3)	Problems: 16.1–16.6 Virtual Office Hours for Solved Problem: 16.1
JIT QUALITY	Whereas inventory *hides* bad quality, JIT immediately *exposes* it. JIT quality tactics include using statistical process control, empowering employees, building fail-safe methods (poka-yoke, checklists, etc.), exposing poor quality with small lot JIT, and providing immediate feedback.	
TOYOTA PRODUCTION SYSTEM	■ **Kaizen**—A focus on continuous improvement. At Toyota, people are recruited, trained, and treated as knowledge workers. They are empowered. TPS employs aggressive cross-training and few job classifications.	
LEAN OPERATIONS	Lean operations tend to share the following attributes: *use JIT techniques* to eliminate virtually all inventory; *build systems that help employees* produce a perfect part every time; *reduce space requirements* by minimizing travel distance; *develop partnerships with suppliers*, helping them to understand the needs of the ultimate customer; *educate suppliers* to accept responsibility for satisfying end customer needs; *eliminate all but value-added activities*; *develop employees* by constantly improving job design, training, employee commitment, teamwork, and empowerment; *make jobs challenging*, pushing responsibility to the lowest level possible; and *build worker flexibility* through cross-training and reducing job classifications.	
LEAN OPERATIONS IN SERVICES	The features of lean operations apply to services just as they do in other sectors. Forecasts in services may be very elaborate, with seasonal, daily, hourly, or even shorter components.	**VIDEO 16.1** JIT at Arnold Palmer Hospital

Self Test

■ **Before taking the self-test,** refer to the learning objectives listed at the beginning of the chapter and the key terms listed at the end of the chapter.

LO1. Continuous improvement and forced problem solving via a focus on throughput and reduced inventory is a reasonable definition of:
- **a)** lean operations.
- **b)** expedited management.
- **c)** the 5*S*s of housekeeping.
- **d)** just-in-time.
- **e)** Toyota Production System.

LO2. The 5*S*s for lean production are _______, _______, _______, _______, and _______.

LO3. Concerns of suppliers when moving to JIT include:
- **a)** small lots sometimes seeming economically prohibitive.
- **b)** realistic quality demands.
- **c)** changes without adequate lead time.
- **d)** erratic schedules.
- **e)** all of the above.

LO4. What is the formula for optimal setup time?
- **a)** $\sqrt{2DQ/[H(1 - d/p)]}$
- **b)** $\sqrt{Q^2H(1 - d/p)/(2D)}$
- **c)** $QH(1 - d/p)/(2D)$
- **d)** $Q^2H(1 - d/p)/(2D)$
- **e)** $H(1 - d/p)$

LO5. Kanban is the Japanese word for:
- **a)** car.
- **b)** pull.
- **c)** card.
- **d)** continuous improvement.
- **e)** level schedule.

LO6. The required number of kanbans equals:
- **a)** 1.
- **b)** Demand during lead time/Q
- **c)** Size of container.
- **d)** Demand during lead time.
- **e)** (Demand during lead time + safety stock)/Size of container.

LO7. TPS's standard work practices include:
- **a)** completely specified work.
- **b)** "pull" systems.
- **c)** level scheduling.
- **d)** kanbans.
- **e)** JIT techniques.

Answers: LO1. d; LO2. sort, simplify, shine, standardize, sustain; LO3. e; LO4. d; LO5. c; LO6. e; LO7. a.

Solutions to Even-Numbered Problems

16.2 3.75, or 4 kanbans

16.4 Size of kanban = 66; number of kanbans = 5.9, or 6

16.6 **(a)** EOQ = 10 lamps
(b) 200 orders/yr.
(c) $200

16.8 7.26 min.

16.10 **(a)** Setup cost = $5.74
(b) Setup time = 8.61 min.

Maintenance and Reliability

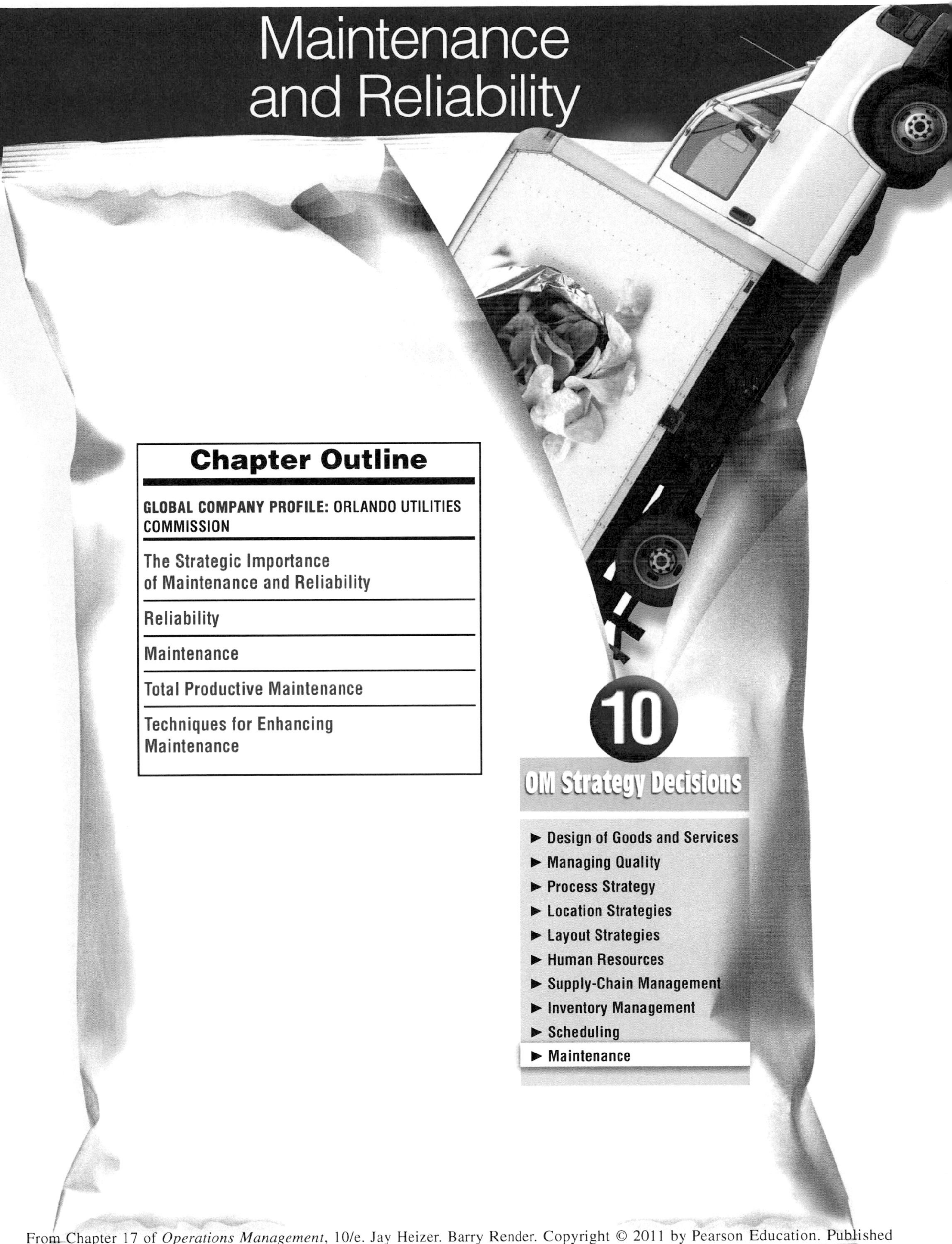

Chapter Outline

10

OM Strategy Decisions

- Design of Goods and Services
- Managing Quality
- Process Strategy
- Location Strategies
- Layout Strategies
- Human Resources
- Supply-Chain Management
- Inventory Management
- Scheduling
- **Maintenance**

MAINTENANCE PROVIDES A COMPETITIVE ADVANTAGE FOR ORLANDO UTILITIES COMMISSION

The Orlando Utilities Commission (OUC) owns and operates power plants that supply power to two central Florida counties. Every year, OUC takes each one of its power-generating units off-line for 1 to 3 weeks to perform maintenance work.

Additionally, each unit is also taken off-line every 3 years for a complete overhaul and turbine generator inspection. Overhauls are scheduled for spring and fall, when the weather is mildest and demand for power is low. These overhauls last from 6 to 8 weeks.

Units at OUC's Stanton Energy Center require that maintenance personnel perform approximately 12,000 repair and preventive maintenance tasks a year. To accomplish these tasks efficiently, many of these jobs are scheduled daily via a computerized maintenance management program. The computer generates preventive maintenance work orders and lists of required materials.

Every day that a plant is down for maintenance costs OUC about $110,000 extra for the replacement cost of power that must be generated elsewhere. However, these costs pale beside the costs associated with a forced outage. An unexpected outage could cost OUC an additional $350,000 to $600,000 each day!

Scheduled overhauls are not easy; each one has 1,800 distinct tasks and requires 72,000 labor-hours. But the value of preventive maintenance was illustrated by the first overhaul of a new turbine generator. Workers discovered a cracked rotor blade, which could have destroyed a $27 million piece of equipment. To find such cracks, which are invisible to the naked eye, metals are examined using dye tests, X-rays, and ultrasound.

At OUC, preventive maintenance is worth its weight in gold. As a result, OUC's electric distribution system has been ranked number one in the Southeast U.S. by PA Consulting Group—a leading consulting firm. Effective maintenance provides a competitive advantage for the Orlando Utilities Commission.

Orlando Utilities Commission

The Stanton Energy Center in Orlando.

◀ Two employees are on scaffolding near the top of Stanton Energy Center's 23-story high boiler, checking and repairing super heaters.

▲ This inspector is examining a low-pressure section of turbine. The tips of these turbine blades will travel at supersonic speeds of 1,300 miles per hour when the plant is in operation. A crack in one of the blades can cause catastrophic failure.

Orlando Utilities Commission

▲ Maintenance of capital-intensive facilities requires good planning to minimize downtime. Here, turbine overhaul is under way. Organizing the thousands of parts and pieces necessary for a shutdown is a major effort.

Learning Objectives

LO1: Describe how to improve system reliability

LO2: Determine system reliability

LO3: Determine mean time between failures (MTBF)

LO4: Distinguish between preventive and breakdown maintenance

LO5: Describe how to improve maintenance

LO6: Compare preventive and breakdown maintenance costs

LO7: Define autonomous maintenance

AUTHOR COMMENT If the system is not reliable, everything else is more difficult.

THE STRATEGIC IMPORTANCE OF MAINTENANCE AND RELIABILITY

VIDEO 17.1 Maintenance Drives Profits at Frito-Lay

Managers at Orlando Utilities Commission (OUC), the subject of the chapter-opening *Global Company Profile*, fight for reliability to avoid the undesirable results of equipment failure. At OUC, a generator failure is very expensive for both the company and its customers. Power outages are instantaneous, with potentially devastating consequences. Similarly, managers at Frito-Lay, Walt Disney Company, and United Parcel Service (UPS) are intolerant of failures or breakdowns. Maintenance is critical at Frito-Lay to achieve high plant utilization and excellent sanitation. At Disney, sparkling-clean facilities and safe rides are necessary to retain its standing as one of the most popular vacation destinations in the world. Likewise, UPS's famed maintenance strategy keeps its delivery vehicles operating and looking as good as new for 20 years or more.

These companies, like most others, know that poor maintenance can be disruptive, inconvenient, wasteful, and expensive in dollars and even in lives. As Figure 1 illustrates, the interdependency of operator, machine, and mechanic is a hallmark of successful maintenance and reliability. Good maintenance and reliability management enhances a firm's performance and protects its investment.

The objective of maintenance and reliability is to maintain the capability of the system. Good maintenance removes variability. Systems must be designed and maintained to reach expected performance and quality standards. **Maintenance** includes all activities involved in keeping a system's equipment in working order. **Reliability** is the probability that a machine part or product will function properly for a specified time under stated conditions.

Maintenance
The activities involved in keeping a system's equipment in working order.

Reliability
The probability that a machine part or product will function properly for a specified time under stated conditions.

In this chapter, we examine four important tactics for improving the reliability and maintenance not only of products and equipment but also of the systems that produce them. The four tactics are organized around reliability and maintenance.

The reliability tactics are:

1. Improving individual components
2. Providing redundancy

AUTHOR COMMENT Employee commitment makes a big difference.

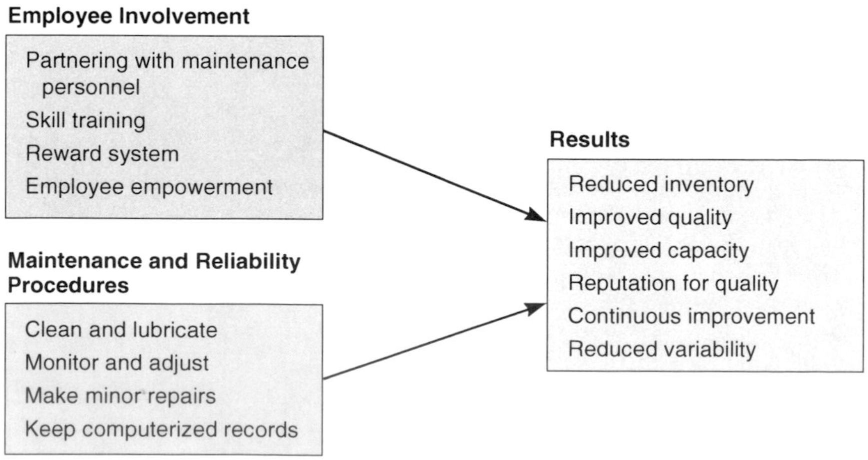

► **FIGURE 1** **Good Maintenance and Reliability Management Requires Employee Involvement and Good Procedures**

The maintenance tactics are:

1. Implementing or improving preventive maintenance
2. Increasing repair capabilities or speed

Variability corrupts processes and creates waste. The operations manager must drive out variability: Designing for reliability and managing for maintenance are crucial ingredients for doing so.

RELIABILITY

AUTHOR COMMENT
Designing for reliability is an excellent place to start reducing variability.

Systems are composed of a series of individual interrelated components, each performing a specific job. If any *one* component fails to perform, for whatever reason, the overall system (for example, an airplane or machine) can fail. First, we discuss improving individual components, and then we discuss providing redundancy.

LO1: Describe how to improve system reliability

Improving Individual Components

Because failures do occur in the real world, understanding their occurrence is an important reliability concept. We now examine the impact of failure in a series. Figure 2 shows that as the number of components in a *series* increases, the reliability of the whole system declines very quickly. A system of $n = 50$ interacting parts, each of which has a 99.5% reliability, has an overall reliability of 78%. If the system or machine has 100 interacting parts, each with an individual reliability of 99.5%, the overall reliability will be only about 60%!

To measure reliability in a system in which each individual part or component may have its own unique rate of reliability, we cannot use the reliability curve in Figure 2. However, the method of computing system reliability (R_s) is simple. It consists of finding the product of individual reliabilities as follows:

$$R_s = R_1 \times R_2 \times R_3 \times \ldots \times R_n \tag{1}$$

where R_1 = reliability of component 1
R_2 = reliability of component 2

and so on.

Equation (1) assumes that the reliability of an individual component does not depend on the reliability of other components (that is, each component is independent). Additionally, in this equation as in most reliability discussions, reliabilities are presented as *probabilities*. Thus, a .90 reliability means that the unit will perform as intended 90% of the time. It also means that it will fail $1 - .90 = .10 = 10\%$ of the time. We can use this method to evaluate the reliability of a service or a product, such as the one we examine in Example 1.

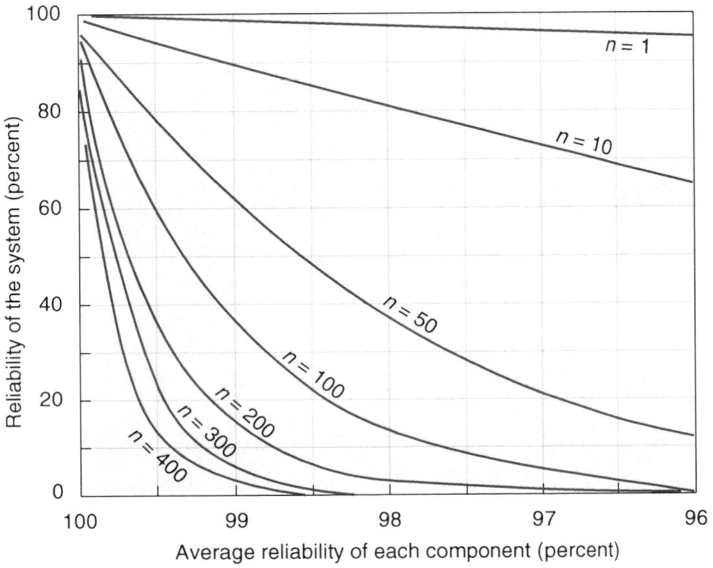

◄ **FIGURE 2**
Overall System Reliability as a Function of Number of *n* Components (Each with the Same Reliability) and Component Reliability with Components in a Series

EXAMPLE 1

Reliability in a series

The National Bank of Greeley, Colorado, processes loan applications through three clerks set up in series, with reliabilities of .90, .80, and .99. It wants to find the system reliability.

APPROACH ▶ Apply Equation (1) to solve for R_s.

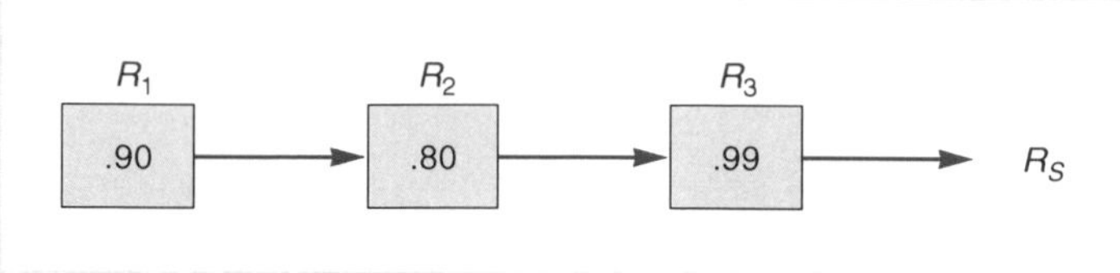

SOLUTION ▶ The reliability of the loan process is:

$$R_s = R_1 \times R_2 \times R_3 = (.90)(.80)(.99) = .713, \text{ or } 71.3\%$$

LO2: Determine system reliability

INSIGHT ▶ Because each clerk in the series is less than perfect, the error probabilities are cumulative and the resulting reliability for this series is .713, which is less than any one clerk.

LEARNING EXERCISE ▶ If the lowest-performing clerk (.80) is replaced by a clerk performing at .95 reliability, what is the new expected reliability? [Answer: .846.]

RELATED PROBLEMS ▶ 17.1, 17.2, 17.5, 17.11

ACTIVE MODEL 17.1 This example is further illustrated in Active Model 17.1 at **www.pearsonhighered.com/heizer**.

Component reliability is often a design or specification issue for which engineering design personnel may be responsible. However, supply-chain personnel may be able to improve components of systems by staying abreast of suppliers' products and research efforts. Supply-chain personnel can also contribute directly to the evaluation of supplier performance.

The basic unit of measure for reliability is the *product failure rate* (FR). Firms producing high-technology equipment often provide failure-rate data on their products. As shown in Equations (2) and (3), the failure rate measures the percent of failures among the total number of products tested, FR(%), or a number of failures during a period of time, FR(N):

$$\text{FR}(\%) = \frac{\text{Number of failures}}{\text{Number of units tested}} \times 100\% \qquad (2)$$

$$\text{FR}(N) = \frac{\text{Number of failures}}{\text{Number of unit-hours of operation time}} \qquad (3)$$

Mean time between failures (MTBF)
The expected time between a repair and the next failure of a component, machine, process, or product.

Perhaps the most common term in reliability analysis is the **mean time between failures (MTBF)**, which is the reciprocal of FR(N):

$$\text{MTBF} = \frac{1}{\text{FR}(N)} \qquad (4)$$

In Example 2, we compute the percentage of failure FR(%), number of failures FR(N), and mean time between failures (MTBF).

EXAMPLE 2

Determining mean time between failures

Twenty air-conditioning systems designed for use by astronauts in NASA's space shuttles were operated for 1,000 hours at NASA's Huntsville, Alabama, test facility. Two of the systems failed during the test—one after 200 hours and the other after 600 hours.

APPROACH ▶ To determine the percent of failures [FR(%)], the number of failures per unit of time [FR(N)], and the mean time between failures (MTBF), we use Equations (2), (3), and (4), respectively.

SOLUTION ▶ Percentage of failures:

$$FR(\%) = \frac{\text{Number of failures}}{\text{Number of units tested}} = \frac{2}{20}(100\%) = 10\%$$

Number of failures per operating hour:

$$FR(N) = \frac{\text{Number of failures}}{\text{Operating time}}$$

where Total time = (1,000 hr)(20 units)
= 20,000 unit-hour

Nonoperating time = 800 hr for 1st failure + 400 hr for 2nd failure
= 1,200 unit-hour

Operating time = Total time − Nonoperating time

$$FR(N) = \frac{2}{20{,}000 - 1{,}200} = \frac{2}{18{,}800}$$

$$= .000106 \text{ failure/unit-hour}$$

Because $\text{MTBF} = \frac{1}{FR(N)}$

$$\text{MTBF} = \frac{1}{.000106} = 9{,}434 \text{ hr}$$

LO3: Determine mean time between failures (MTBF)

If the typical space shuttle trip lasts 6 days, NASA may be interested in the failure rate per trip:

$$\text{Failure rate} = (\text{Failures/unit-hr})(24 \text{ hr/day})(6 \text{ days/trip})$$
$$= (.000106)(24)(6)$$
$$= .0153 \text{ failure/trip}$$

INSIGHT ▶ Mean time between failures (MTBF) is the standard means of stating reliability.

LEARNING EXERCISE ▶ If non-operating time drops to 800, what is the new MTBF? [Answer: 9,606 hr.]

RELATED PROBLEMS ▶ 17.6, 17.7

If the failure rate recorded in Example 2 is too high, NASA will have to either increase the reliability of individual components, and thus of the system, or install several backup air-conditioning units on each space shuttle. Backup units provide redundancy.

Providing Redundancy

Redundancy
The use of components in parallel to raise reliability.

To increase the reliability of systems, **redundancy** is added. The technique here is to "back up" components with additional components. This is known as putting units in parallel and is a standard operations management tactic. Redundancy is provided to ensure that if one component fails, the system has recourse to another. For instance, say that reliability of a component is .80 and we back it up with another component with reliability of .80. The resulting reliability is the probability of the first component working plus the probability of the backup (or parallel) component working multiplied by the probability of needing the backup component (1 − .8 = .2). Therefore:

$$\begin{pmatrix}\text{Probability}\\ \text{of first}\\ \text{component}\\ \text{working}\end{pmatrix} + \left[\begin{pmatrix}\text{Probability}\\ \text{of second}\\ \text{component}\\ \text{working}\end{pmatrix} \times \begin{pmatrix}\text{Probability}\\ \text{of needing}\\ \text{second}\\ \text{component}\end{pmatrix}\right] =$$

$$(.8) + [(.8) \times (1 - .8)] = .8 + .16 = .96$$

Example 3 shows how redundancy can improve the reliability of the loan process presented in Example 1.

EXAMPLE 3

Reliability with a parallel process

The National Bank is disturbed that its loan-application process has a reliability of only .713 (see Example 1) and would like to improve this situation.

APPROACH ▶ The bank decides to provide redundancy for the two least reliable clerks.

SOLUTION ▶ This procedure results in the following system:

R_1	R_2	R_3
0.90	0.80	
↓	↓	
0.90 →	0.80 →	0.99

$$= [.9 + .9(1 - .9)] \times [.8 + .8(1 - .8)] \times .99$$
$$= [.9 + (.9)(.1)] \times [.8 + (.8)(.2)] \times .99$$
$$= .99 \times .96 \times .99 = .94$$

INSIGHT ▶ By providing redundancy for two clerks, National Bank has increased reliability of the loan process from .713 to .94.

LEARNING EXERCISE ▶ What happens when the bank replaces both R_2 clerks with one new clerk who has a reliability of .90. [Answer: $R_s = .88$.]

RELATED PROBLEMS ▶ 17.8, 17.9, 17.10, 17.12, 17.13, 17.14, 17.16, 17.18

ACTIVE MODEL 17.2 This example is further illustrated in Active Model 17.2 at **www.pearsonhighered.com/heizer**.

AUTHOR COMMENT Even the most reliable systems require maintenance.

MAINTENANCE

There are two types of maintenance: preventive maintenance and breakdown maintenance. **Preventive maintenance** involves performing routine inspections and servicing and keeping facilities in good repair. These activities are intended to build a system that will find potential failures and make changes or repairs that will prevent failure. Preventive maintenance is much more than just keeping machinery and equipment running. It also involves designing technical and human systems that will keep the productive process working within tolerance; it allows the system to perform. The emphasis of preventive maintenance is on understanding the process and keeping it working without interruption. **Breakdown maintenance** occurs when equipment fails and must be repaired on an emergency or priority basis.

Preventive maintenance
A plan that involves routine inspections, servicing, and keeping facilities in good repair to prevent failure.

Breakdown maintenance
Remedial maintenance that occurs when equipment fails and must be repaired on an emergency or priority basis.

Infant mortality
The failure rate early in the life of a product or process.

Implementing Preventive Maintenance

Preventive maintenance implies that we can determine when a system needs service or will need repair. Therefore, to perform preventive maintenance, we must know when a system requires service or when it is likely to fail. Failures occur at different rates during the life of a product. A high initial failure rate, known as **infant mortality**, may exist for many products.[1] This is why many electronic firms "burn in" their products prior to shipment: That is to say, they execute a variety of tests (such as a full wash cycle at Whirlpool) to detect "startup" problems prior to shipment. Firms may also provide 90-day warranties. We should note that many infant mortality failures are not product failures per se, but rather failure due to improper use. This fact points up the importance in many industries of operations management's building an after-sales service system that includes installing and training.

Once the product, machine, or process "settles in," a study can be made of the MTBF (mean time between failures) distribution. Such distributions often follow a normal curve. When these distributions exhibit small standard deviations, then we know we have a candidate for preventive maintenance, even if the maintenance is expensive.

LO4: Distinguish between preventive and breakdown maintenance

[1]Infant mortality failures often follow a negative exponential distribution.

Once our firm has a candidate for preventive maintenance, we want to determine *when* preventive maintenance is economical. Typically, the more expensive the maintenance, the narrower must be the MTBF distribution (that is, have a small standard deviation). In addition, if the process is no more expensive to repair when it breaks down than the cost of preventive maintenance, perhaps we should let the process break down and then do the repair. However, the consequence of the breakdown must be fully considered. Even some relatively minor breakdowns have catastrophic consequences. (See the *OM in Action* box "Preventive Maintenance Saves Lives" on the next page). At the other extreme, preventive maintenance costs may be so incidental that preventive maintenance is appropriate even if the MTBF distribution is rather flat (that is, it has a large standard deviation). In any event, consistent with job enrichment practices, machine operators must be held responsible for preventive maintenance of their own equipment and tools.

LO5: Describe how to improve maintenance

With good reporting techniques, firms can maintain records of individual processes, machines, or equipment. Such records can provide a profile of both the kinds of maintenance required and the timing of maintenance needed. Maintaining equipment history is an important part of a preventive maintenance system, as is a record of the time and cost to make the repair. Such records can also provide information about the family of equipment and suppliers.

Reliability and maintenance are of such importance that most systems are now computerized. Figure 3 shows the major components of such a system with files to be maintained on the left and reports generated on the right.

Both Boeing and General Motors are pursuing competitive advantage via their reliability and maintenance information systems. Boeing can now monitor the health of an airplane in flight and relay relevant information in real time to the ground, providing a head start on reliability and maintenance issues. Similarly, General Motors, with its On Star wireless satellite service, alerts car owners to 1,600 possible diagnostic failures, such as faulty airbags sensor or even the need for an oil change. For GM, the service provides immediate data that its engineers can use to jump on quality issues before customers even notice a problem. This has saved the firm an estimated $100 million in warranty costs by catching problems early.

Figure 4(a) shows a traditional view of the relationship between preventive maintenance and breakdown maintenance. In this view, operations managers consider a *balance* between the two costs. Allocating more resources to preventive maintenance will reduce the number of breakdowns. At some point, however, the decrease in breakdown maintenance costs may be less than the increase in preventive maintenance costs. At this point, the total cost curve begins to rise. Beyond this optimal point, the firm will be better off waiting for breakdowns to occur and repairing them when they do.

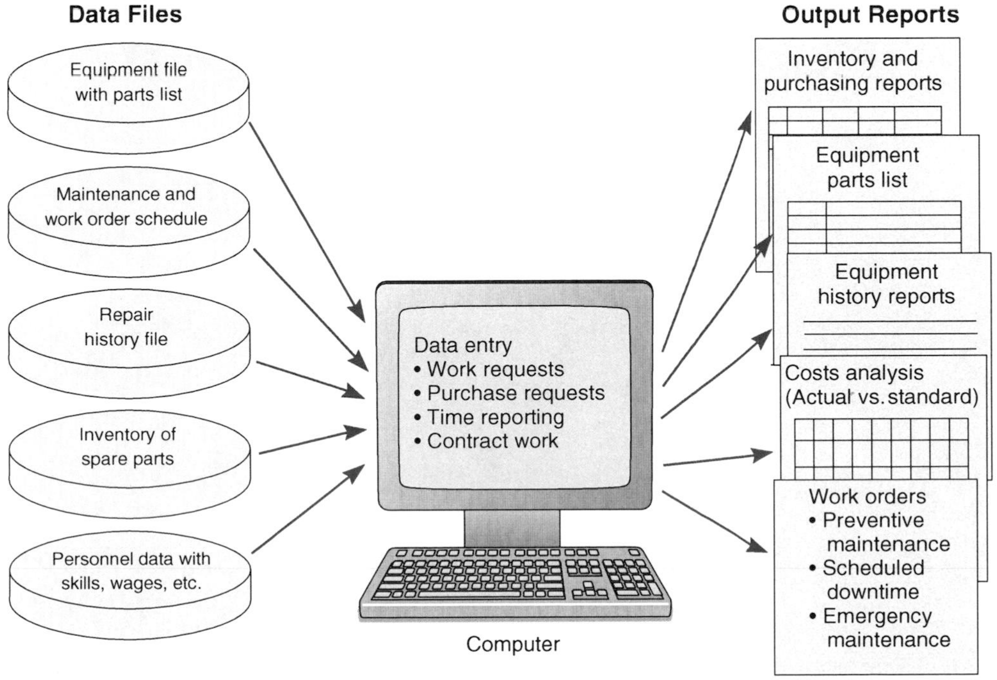

◄ **FIGURE 3**
A Computerized Maintenance System

OM in Action ▶ Preventive Maintenance Saves Lives

Flight 5481's trip was short. It lasted 70 seconds. The flight left the Charlotte Airport, bound for Greenville/Spartanburg, but seconds after lift-off, the nose of the aircraft pitched upward, the plane rolled, and, moments later, slammed into the corner of a maintenance facility at the airport. The Beech 1900D commuter plane carried 21 people to their death. The following are selected comments from the final moments of the flight:

8:47:02—Co-pilot Jonathan Gibbs: "Wuh."
8:47:03—Capt. Katie Leslie: "Help me. . . . You got it?"
8:47:05—Gibbs: "Oh (expletive). Push down."
8:47:12—Leslie: "Push the nose down."
8:47:14—Leslie: "Oh my God."
8:47:16—Leslie (calling to controllers): "We have an emergency for Air Midwest fifty-four eighty-one."
8:47:18—Faint voice from passenger area: "Daddy."
8:47:26—Leslie: "Oh my God, ahh."
8:47:26—Gibbs: "Uh, uh, God, ahh (expletive)."
8:47:28 End of recording

The National Transportation Safety Board's focus in this situation is a preventive maintenance error made two days prior to the crash. The mechanic and a supervisor skipped at least 12 steps required in the maintenance of the tension of the pitch-control cables during the *Detail 6* check that include the pitch of the control cable tension. Data show that the control column position changed during the maintenance and the plane lost about two-thirds down-elevator capability. Investigators believe that the aircraft would have been flyable with fully functioning controls had it been given proper preventive maintenance. Maintenance can improve quality, reduce costs, and win orders. It can also be a matter of life and death.

Sources: Aviation Week and Space Technology (May 26, 2003): 52; *USA Today* (May 21, 2003): 8A; and *The Wall Street Journal* (May 21, 2003): D3 and (May 20, 2003): D1, D3.

Unfortunately, cost curves such as in Figure 4(a) seldom consider the *full costs of a breakdown*. Many costs are ignored because they are not *directly* related to the immediate breakdown. For instance, the cost of inventory maintained to compensate for downtime is not typically considered. Moreover, downtime can have a devastating effect on safety and morale. Employees may also begin to believe that performance to standard and maintaining equipment are not important. Finally, downtime adversely affects delivery schedules, destroying customer relations and future sales. When the full impact of breakdowns is considered, Figure 4(b) may be a better representation of maintenance costs. In Figure 4(b), total costs are at a minimum when the system does not break down.

Assuming that all potential costs associated with downtime have been identified, the operations staff can compute the optimal level of maintenance activity on a theoretical basis. Such analysis, of course, also requires accurate historical data on maintenance costs, breakdown probabilities,

AUTHOR COMMENT
When all breakdown costs are considered, much more maintenance may be advantageous.

▼ FIGURE 4 **Maintenance Costs**

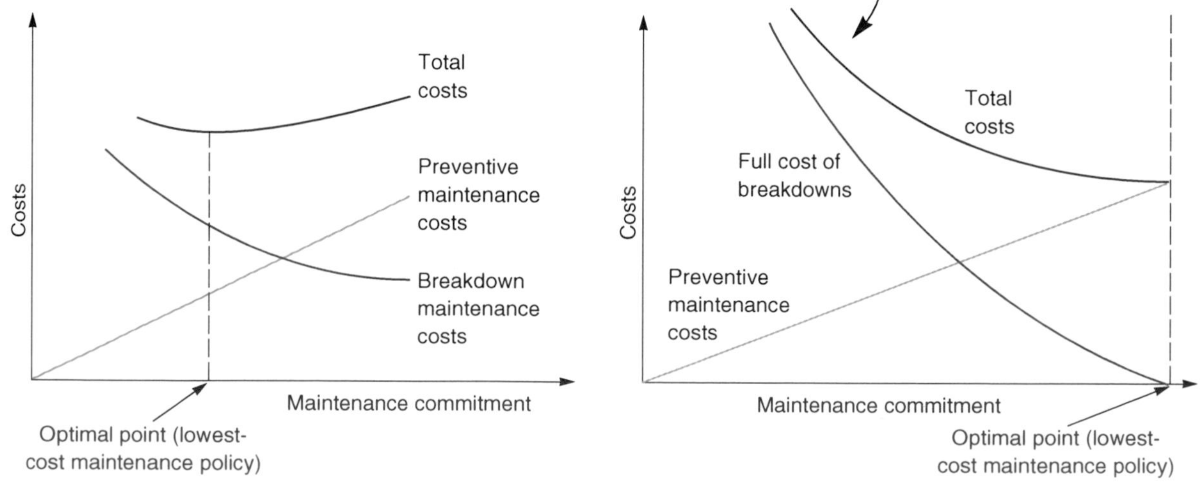

(a) Traditional View of Maintenance **(b) Full Cost View of Maintenance**

and repair times. Example 4 shows how to compare preventive and breakdown maintenance costs to select the least expensive maintenance policy.

EXAMPLE 4

Comparing preventive and breakdown maintenance costs

Farlen & Halikman is a CPA firm specializing in payroll preparation. The firm has been successful in automating much of its work, using high-speed printers for check processing and report preparation. The computerized approach, however, has problems. Over the past 20 months, the printers have broken down at the rate indicated in the following table:

Number of Breakdowns	Number of Months That Breakdowns Occurred
0	2
1	8
2	6
3	4
	Total: 20

Each time the printers break down, Farlen & Halikman estimates that it loses an average of $300 in production time and service expenses. One alternative is to purchase a service contract for preventive maintenance. Even if Farlen & Halikman contracts for preventive maintenance, there will still be breakdowns, *averaging* one breakdown per month. The price for this service is $150 per month.

APPROACH ▶ To determine if the CPA firm should follow a "run until breakdown" policy or contract for preventive maintenance, we follow a 4-step process:

LO6: Compare preventive and breakdown maintenance costs

STEP 1. Compute the *expected number* of breakdowns (based on past history) if the firm continues as is, without the service contract.
STEP 2. Compute the expected breakdown cost per month with no preventive maintenance contract.
STEP 3. Compute the cost of preventive maintenance.
STEP 4. Compare the two options and select the one that will cost less.

SOLUTION ▶

STEP 1.

Number of Breakdowns	Frequency	Number of Breakdowns	Frequency
0	2/20 = .1	2	6/20 = 0.3
1	8/20 = .4	3	4/20 = 0.2

$$\begin{aligned}\begin{pmatrix}\text{Expected number}\\\text{of breakdowns}\end{pmatrix} &= \sum\left[\begin{pmatrix}\text{Number of}\\\text{breakdowns}\end{pmatrix}\times\begin{pmatrix}\text{Corresponding}\\\text{frequency}\end{pmatrix}\right]\\ &= (0)(.1) + (1)(.4) + (2)(.3) + (3)(.2)\\ &= 0 + .4 + .6 + .6\\ &= 1.6 \text{ breakdowns/month}\end{aligned}$$

STEP 2.

$$\begin{aligned}\text{Expected breakdown cost} &= \begin{pmatrix}\text{Expected number}\\\text{of breakdowns}\end{pmatrix}\times\begin{pmatrix}\text{Cost per}\\\text{breakdown}\end{pmatrix}\\ &= (1.6)(\$300)\\ &= \$480/\text{month}\end{aligned}$$

STEP 3.

$$\begin{aligned}\begin{pmatrix}\text{Preventive}\\\text{maintenance cost}\end{pmatrix} &= \begin{pmatrix}\text{Cost of expected}\\\text{breakdowns if service}\\\text{contract signed}\end{pmatrix} + \begin{pmatrix}\text{Cost of}\\\text{service contract}\end{pmatrix}\\ &= (1\text{ breakdown/month})(\$300) + \$150/\text{month}\\ &= \$450/\text{month}\end{aligned}$$

STEP 4. Because it is less expensive overall to hire a maintenance service firm ($450) than to not do so ($480), Farlen & Halikman should hire the service firm.

INSIGHT ▶ Determining the expected number of breakdowns for each option is crucial to making a good decision. This typically requires good maintenance records.

LEARNING EXERCISE ▶ What is the best decision if the preventive maintenance contract cost increases to $195 per month? [Answer: At $495(= $300 + $195) per month, "run until breakdown" becomes less expensive (assuming that all costs are included in the $300 per breakdown cost).]

RELATED PROBLEMS ▶ 17.3, 17.4, 17.17

Using variations of the technique shown in Example 4, operations managers can examine maintenance policies.

Increasing Repair Capabilities

Because reliability and preventive maintenance are seldom perfect, most firms opt for some level of repair capability. Enlarging or improving repair facilities can get the system back in operation faster. A good maintenance facility should have these six features:

1. Well-trained personnel
2. Adequate resources
3. Ability to establish a repair plan and priorities[2]
4. Ability and authority to do material planning
5. Ability to identify the cause of breakdowns
6. Ability to design ways to extend MTBF

However, not all repairs can be done in the firm's facility. Managers must, therefore, decide where repairs are to be performed. Figure 5 provides a continuum of options and how they rate in terms of speed, cost, and competence. Moving to the right in Figure 5 may improve the competence of the repair work, but at the same time it increases costs and replacement time.

LO7: Define autonomous maintenance

Autonomous Maintenance

Autonomous maintenance
Operators partner with maintenance personnel to observe, check, adjust, clean, and notify.

Preventive maintenance policies and techniques must include an emphasis on employees accepting responsibility for the "observe, check, adjust, clean, and notify" type of equipment maintenance. Such policies are consistent with the advantages of employee empowerment. This approach is known as **autonomous maintenance**. Employees can predict failures, prevent breakdowns, and prolong equipment life. With autonomous maintenance, the manager is making a step toward both employee empowerment and maintaining system performance.

AUTHOR COMMENT
Maintenance improves productivity.

TOTAL PRODUCTIVE MAINTENANCE

Many firms have moved to bring total quality management concepts to the practice of preventive maintenance with an approach known as **total productive maintenance (TPM)**. It involves the concept of reducing variability through autonomous maintenance and excellent maintenance practices. Total productive maintenance includes:

Total productive maintenance (TPM)
Combines total quality management with a strategic view of maintenance from process and equipment design to preventive maintenance.

- Designing machines that are reliable, easy to operate, and easy to maintain
- Emphasizing total cost of ownership when purchasing machines, so that service and maintenance are included in the cost
- Developing preventive maintenance plans that utilize the best practices of operators, maintenance departments, and depot service
- Training for autonomous maintenance so operators maintain their own machines and partner with maintenance personnel

[2]You may recall from our discussion of network planning that DuPont developed the critical path method (CPM) to improve the scheduling of maintenance projects.

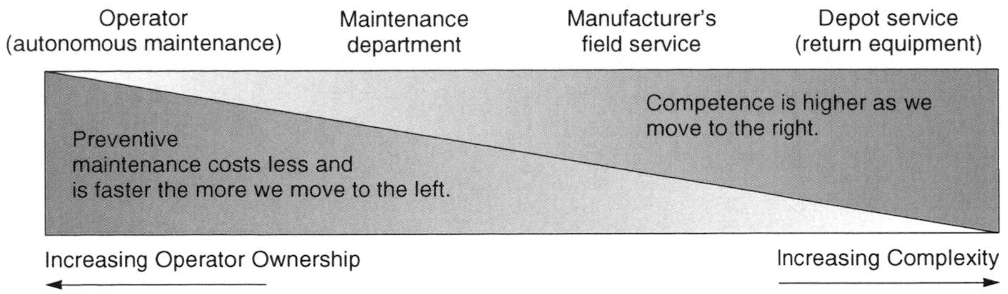

◄ **FIGURE 5**
The Operations Manager Determines How Maintenance Will Be Performed

High utilization of facilities, tight scheduling, low inventory, and consistent quality demand reliability. Total productive maintenance is the key to reducing variability and improving reliability.

TECHNIQUES FOR ENHANCING MAINTENANCE

AUTHOR COMMENT
Both OM techniques and the physical sciences can improve maintenance.

Three techniques have proven beneficial to effective maintenance: simulation, expert systems, and sensors.

Simulation Because of the complexity of some maintenance decisions, computer simulation is a good tool for evaluating the impact of various policies. For instance, operations personnel can decide whether to add more staff by determining the trade-offs between machine reliability and the costs of additional labor. Management can also simulate the replacement of parts that have not yet failed as a way of preventing future breakdowns. Simulation via physical models can also be useful. For example, a physical model can vibrate an airplane to simulate thousands of hours of flight time to evaluate maintenance needs.

Expert Systems OM managers use expert systems (that is, computer programs that mimic human logic) to assist staff in isolating and repairing various faults in machinery and equipment. For instance, General Electric's DELTA system asks a series of detailed questions that aid the user in identifying a problem. DuPont uses expert systems to monitor equipment and to train repair personnel.

Automated Sensors Sensors warn when production machinery is about to fail or is becoming damaged by heat, vibration, or fluid leaks. The goal of such procedures is not only to avoid failures but also to perform preventive maintenance before machines are damaged.

CHAPTER SUMMARY

Operations managers focus on design improvements and backup components to improve reliability. Reliability improvements also can be obtained through the use of preventive maintenance and excellent repair facilities.

Firms give employees "ownership" of their equipment. When workers repair or do preventive maintenance on their own machines, breakdowns are less common. Well-trained and empowered employees ensure reliable systems through preventive maintenance. In turn, reliable, well-maintained equipment not only provides higher utilization but also improves quality and performance to schedule. Top firms build and maintain systems that drive out variability so that customers can rely on products and services to be produced to specifications and on time.

Key Terms

Maintenance
Reliability
Mean time between failures (MTBF)
Redundancy
Preventive maintenance
Breakdown maintenance
Infant mortality
Autonomous maintenance
Total productive maintenance (TPM)

Ethical Dilemma

The Space Shuttle *Columbia* disintegrated over Texas on its 2003 return to Earth. The *Challenger* exploded shortly after launch in 1986. An *Apollo 1* spacecraft imploded in fire on the launch pad in 1967. In each case, the lives of all crew members were lost. The hugely complex shuttle may look a bit like an airplane, but it is very different. In reality, its overall statistical reliability is such that about 1 out of every 50 flights will have a major malfunction. In fact, there have been almost 130 shuttle flights to date.

NASA has cut safety inspections by more than 50% since 1989. Employees often face a cumbersome process for bringing safety issues to management. And the agency continues to face pressure to launch the shuttle on missions to the space station and elsewhere. Of course, as one aerospace manager has stated "you can be perfectly safe and never get off the ground."

Given the huge reliability and maintenance issues NASA faces (e.g., seals cracking in cold weather, heat shielding tiles falling off), should astronauts be allowed to fly? (In earlier *Atlas* rockets, men were inserted not out of necessity but because test pilots and politicians thought they should be there.) What are the pros and cons of manned space exploration from an ethical perspective? Should the U.S. spend billions of dollars to return an astronaut to the moon?

Discussion Questions

1. What is the objective of maintenance and reliability?
2. How does one identify a candidate for preventive maintenance?
3. Explain the notion of "infant mortality" in the context of product reliability.
4. Why is simulation often an appropriate technique for maintenance problems?
5. What is the trade-off between operator-performed maintenance versus supplier-performed maintenance?
6. How can a manager evaluate the effectiveness of the maintenance function?
7. How does machine design contribute to either increasing or alleviating the maintenance problem?
8. What roles can information technology play in the maintenance function?
9. During an argument as to the merits of preventive maintenance at Windsor Printers, the company owner asked, "Why fix it before it breaks?" How would you, as the director of maintenance, respond?
10. Will preventive maintenance eliminate *all* breakdowns?

Using Software to Solve Reliability Problems

Excel OM and POM for Windows may be used to solve reliability problems. The reliability module allow us to enter (1) number of systems (components) in the series (1 through 10); (2) number of backup, or parallel, components (1 through 12); and (3) component reliability for both series and parallel data.

Solved Problems

Virtual Office Hours help is available at www.myomlab.com

▼ SOLVED PROBLEM 17.1

The semiconductor used in the Sullivan Wrist Calculator has five circuits, each of which has its own reliability rate. Component 1 has a reliability of .90; component 2, .95; component 3, .98; component 4, .90; and component 5, .99. What is the reliability of one semiconductor?

▼ SOLUTION

Semiconductor reliability, $R_s = R_1 \times R_2 \times R_3 \times R_4 \times R_5$

$= (.90)(.95)(.98)(.90)(.99)$

$= .7466$

▼ SOLVED PROBLEM 17.2

A recent engineering change at Sullivan Wrist Calculator places a backup component in each of the two least reliable transistor circuits. The new circuits will look like the following:

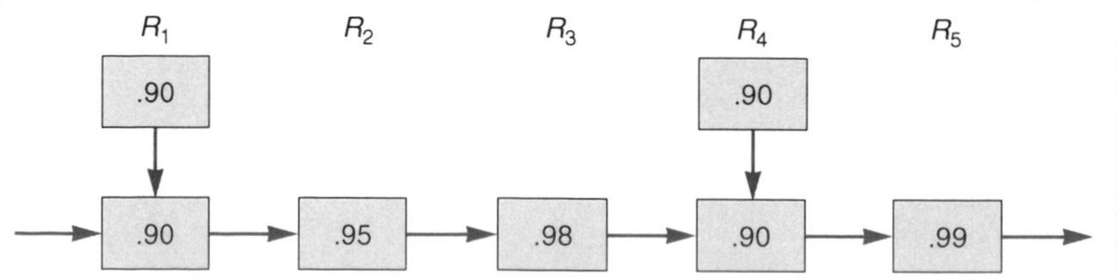

What is the reliability of the new system?

▼ SOLUTION

$$\begin{aligned}\text{Reliability} &= [.9 + (1 - .9) \times .9] \times .95 \times .98 \times [.9 + (1 - .9) \times .9] \times .99 \\ &= [.9 + .09] \times .95 \times .98 \times [.9 + .09] \times .99 \\ &= .99 \times .95 \times .98 \times .99 \times .99 \\ &= .903\end{aligned}$$

Problems*

• **17.1** The Beta II computer's electronic processing unit contains 50 components in series. The average reliability of each component is 99.0%. Using Figure 2, determine the overall reliability of the processing unit.

• **17.2** A testing process at Boeing Aircraft has 400 components in series. The average reliability of each component is 99.5%. Use Figure 2 to find the overall reliability of the whole testing process.

• **17.3** What are the *expected* number of yearly breakdowns for the power generator at Orlando Utilities that has exhibited the following data over the past 20 years? Px

Number of breakdowns	0	1	2	3	4	5	6
Number of years in which breakdown occurred	2	2	5	4	5	2	0

• **17.4** Each breakdown of a graphic plotter table at Airbus Industries costs $50. Find the expected daily breakdown cost, given the following data: Px

Number of breakdowns	0	1	2	3	4
Daily breakdown probability	.1	.2	.4	.2	.1

•• **17.5** A new aircraft control system is being designed that must be 98% reliable. This system consists of three components in series. If all three of the components are to have the same level of reliability, what level of reliability is required? Px

•• **17.6** Robert Klassan Manufacturing, a medical equipment manufacturer, subjected 100 heart pacemakers to 5,000 hours of testing. Halfway through the testing, 5 pacemakers failed. What was the failure rate in terms of the following:

a) Percentage of failures?
b) Number of failures per unit-hour?
c) Number of failures per unit-year?
d) If 1,100 people receive pacemaker implants, how many units can we expect to fail during the following year?

**Note:* Px means the problem may be solved with POM for Windows and/or Excel OM.

PHT/Photo Researchers, Inc.

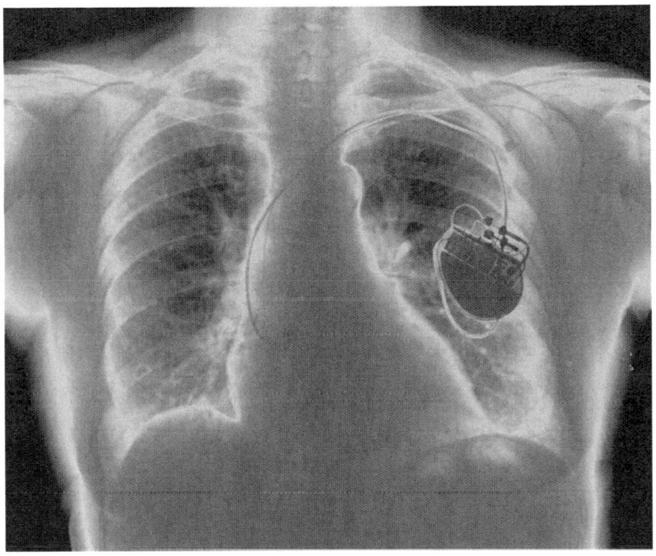

•• **17.7** A manufacturer of disk drives for notebook computers wants a MTBF of at least 50,000 hours. Recent test results for 10 units were one failure at 10,000 hrs, another at 25,000 hrs, and two more at 45,000 hrs. The remaining units were still running at 60,000 hours. Determine the following:

a) Percent of failures.
b) Number of failures per unit-hour
c) MTBF at this point in the testing

•• **17.8** What is the reliability of the following production process? $R_1 = 0.95$, $R_2 = 0.90$, $R_3 = 0.98$.

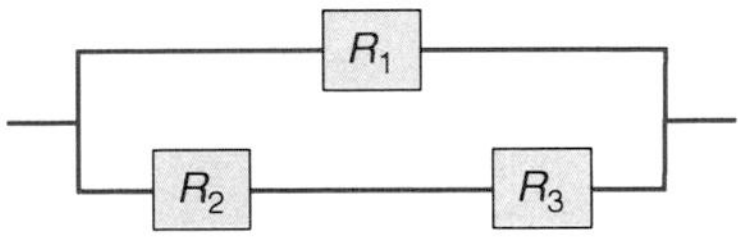

Px

•• **17.9** What is the reliability that bank loans will be processed accurately if each of the 5 clerks shown in the chart has the reliability shown?

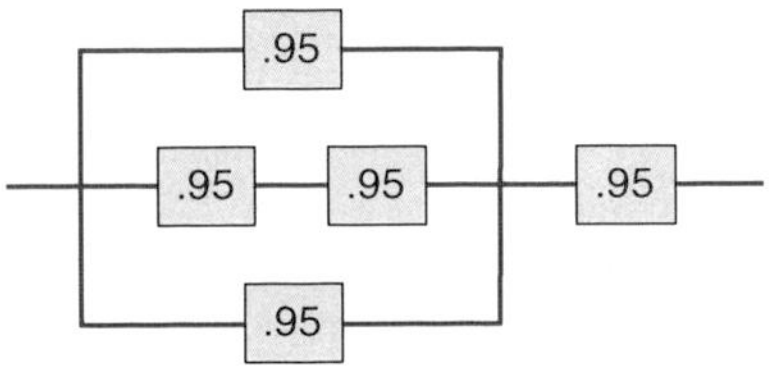

Px

•• **17.10** Merrill Kim Sharp has a system composed of three components in parallel. The components have the following reliabilities:

$$R_1 = 0.90, \quad R_2 = 0.95, \quad R_3 = 0.85$$

What is the reliability of the system? (*Hint:* See Example 3.)

• **17.11** A medical control system has three components in series with individual reliabilities (R_1, R_2, R_3) as shown:

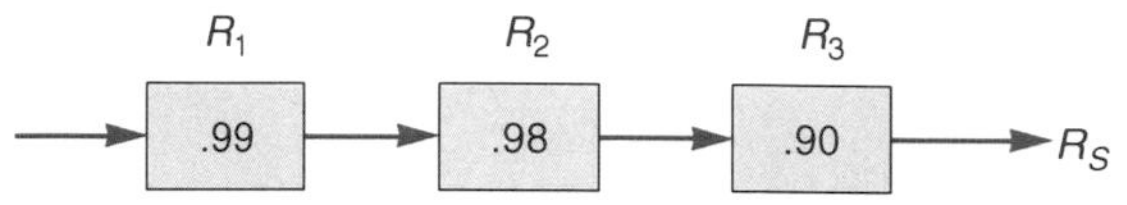

What is the reliability of the system?

•• **17.12** a) What is the reliability of the system shown?

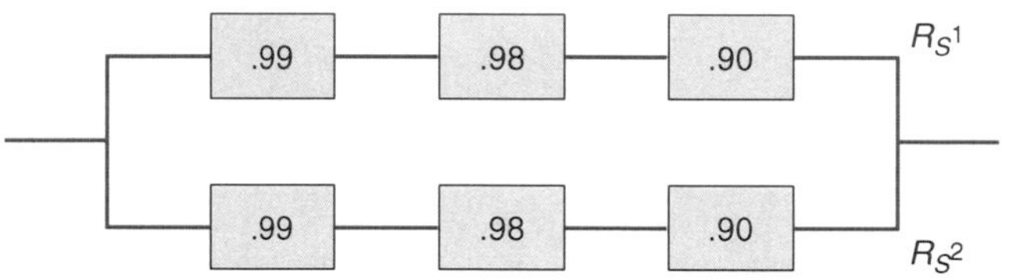

b) How much did reliability improve if the medical control system shown in Problem 17.11 changed to the redundant parallel system shown here?

••• **17.13** Assume that for cardiac bypass surgery, 85% of patients survive the surgery, 95% survive the recovery period after surgery, 80% are able to make the lifestyle changes needed to extend their survival to 1 year or more, and only 10% of those who do not make the lifestyle changes survive more than a year. What is the likelihood that a given patient will survive more than a year?

•• **17.14** Elizabeth Irwin's design team has proposed the following system with component reliabilities as indicated:

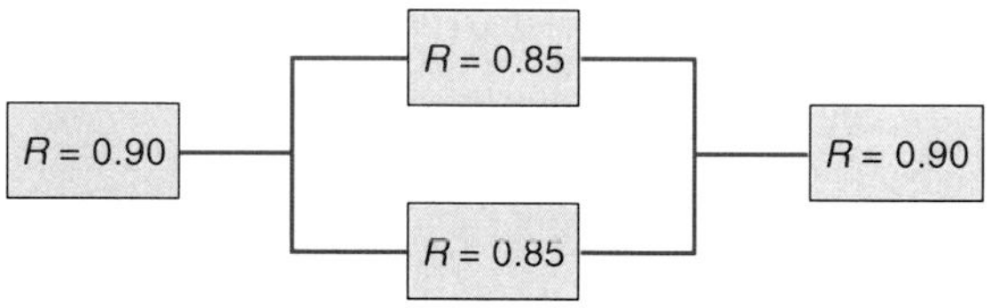

What is the reliability of the system?

•• **17.15** The maintenance department at Mechanical Dynamics has presented you with the following failure curve. What does it suggest?

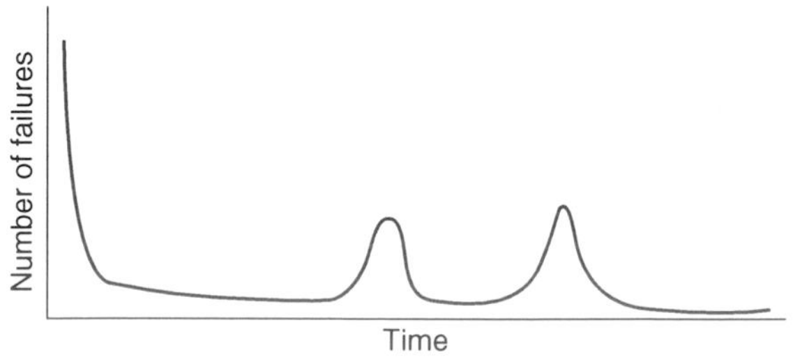

•• **17.16** Rick Wing, salesperson for Wave Soldering Systems, Inc. (WSSI), has provided you with a proposal for improving the temperature control on your present machine. The machine uses a hot-air knife to cleanly remove excess solder from printed circuit boards; this is a great concept, but the hot-air temperature control lacks reliability. According to Wing, engineers at WSSI have improved the reliability of the critical temperature controls. The new system still has the four sensitive integrated circuits controlling the temperature, but the new machine has a backup for each. The four integrated circuits have reliabilities of .90, .92, .94, and .96. The four backup circuits all have a reliability of .90.

a) What is the reliability of the new temperature controller?
b) If you pay a premium, Wing says he can improve all four of the backup units to .93. What is the reliability of this option?

••• **17.17** The fire department has a number of failures with its oxygen masks and is evaluating the possibility of outsourcing preventive maintenance to the manufacturer. Because of the risk associated with a failure, the cost of each failure is estimated at $2,000. The current maintenance policy (with station employees performing maintenance) has yielded the following history:

Number of breakdowns	0	1	2	3	4	5
Number of years in which breakdowns occurred	4	3	1	5	5	0

This manufacturer will guarantee repairs on any and all failures as part of a service contract. The cost of this service is $5,000 per year.

a) What is the expected number of breakdowns per year with station employees performing maintenance?
b) What is the cost of the current maintenance policy?
c) What is the more economical policy?

••• **17.18** As VP for operations at Brian Normoyle Engineering, you must decide which product design, A or B, has the higher reliability. B is designed with backup units for components R_3 and R_4. What is the reliability of each design?

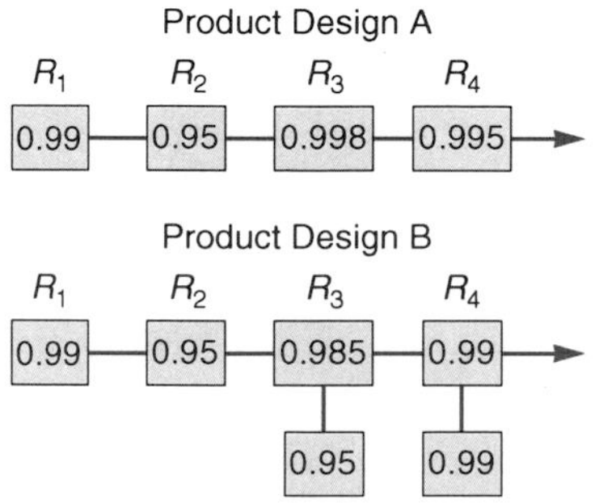

•••• **17.19** A typical retail transaction consists of several smaller steps, which can be considered components subject to failure. A list of such components might include:

Component	Description	Definition of Failure
1	Find product in proper size, color, etc.	Can't find product
2	Enter cashier line	No lines open; lines too long; line experiencing difficulty
3	Scan product UPC for name, price, etc.	Won't scan; item not on file; scans incorrect name or price
4	Calculate purchase total	Wrong weight; wrong extension; wrong data entry; wrong tax
5	Make payment	Customer lacks cash; check not acceptable; credit card refused
6	Make change	Makes change incorrectly
7	Bag merchandise	Damages merchandise while bagging; bag splits
8	Conclude transaction and exit	No receipt; unfriendly, rude, or aloof clerk

Let the eight probabilities of success be .92, .94, .99, .99, .98, .97, .95, and .96. What is the reliability of the system, that is, the probability that there will be a satisfied customer? If you were the store manager, what do you think should be an acceptable value for this probability? Which components would be good candidates for backup, which for redesign?

▶ **Refer to myomlab for these additional homework problems: 17.20–17.24**

Case Studies

▶ Maintenance Drives Profits at Frito-Lay

Video Case Study

Frito-Lay, the multi-billion-dollar subsidiary of food and beverage giant PepsiCo, maintains 36 plants in the U.S. and Canada. These facilities produce dozen of snacks, including the well-known Lay's, Fritos, Cheetos, Doritos, Ruffles, and Tostitos brands, each of which sells over $1 billion per year.

Frito-Lay plants produce in the high-volume, low-variety process model common to commercial baked goods, steel, glass, and beer industries. In this environment, preventive maintenance of equipment takes a major role by avoiding costly downtime. Tom Rao, Vice President for Florida operations, estimates that each 1% of downtime has a negative annual profit impact of $200,000. He is proud of the $1\frac{1}{2}\%$ unscheduled downtime his plant is able to reach—well below the 2% that is considered the "world-class" benchmark. This excellent performance is possible because the maintenance department takes an active role in setting the parameters for preventive maintenance. This is done with weekly input to the production schedule.

Maintenance policy impacts energy use as well. The Florida plant's technical manager, Jim Wentzel, states, "By reducing production interruptions, we create an opportunity to bring energy and utility use under control. Equipment maintenance and a solid production schedule are keys to utility efficiency. With every production interruption, there is substantial waste."

As a part of its total productive maintenance (TPM) program,* Frito-Lay empowers employees with what it calls the "Run Right" system. Run Right teaches employees to "identify and do." This means each shift is responsible for identifying problems and making the necessary corrections, when possible. This is accomplished through (1) a "power walk" at the beginning of the shift to ensure that equipment and process settings are performing to standard, (2) mid-shift and post-shift reviews of standards and performance, and (3) posting of any issues on a large whiteboard in the shift office. Items remain on the whiteboard until corrected, which is seldom more than a shift or two.

With good manpower scheduling and tight labor control to hold down variable costs, making time for training is challenging. But supervisors, including the plant manager, are available to fill in on the production line when that is necessary to free an employee for training.

The 30 maintenance personnel hired to cover 24/7 operations at the Florida plant all come with multi-craft skills (e.g., welding, electrical, plumbing). "Multi-craft maintenance personnel are harder to find and cost more," says Wentzel, "but they more than pay for themselves."

Discussion Questions**

1. What might be done to help take Frito-Lay to the next level of outstanding maintenance? Consider factors such as sophisticated software.
2. What are the advantages and disadvantages of giving more responsibility for machine maintenance to the operator?
3. Discuss the pros and cons of hiring multi-craft maintenance personnel.

*At Frito-Lay preventive maintenance, autonomous maintenance, and total productive maintenance are part of a Frito-Lay program known as total productive manufacturing.

**You may wish to view the video that accompanies this case before answering these questions.

Source: Professors Barry Render (Rollins College), Jay Heizer (Texas Lutheran University), and Beverly Amer (Northern Arizona University).

▶**Additional Case Studies:** Visit **www.myomlab.com** or **www.pearsonhighered.com/heizer** for these free case studies:
Cartak's Department Store: Requires the evaluation of the impact of an additional invoice verifier.
Worldwide Chemical Company: The maintenance department in this company is in turmoil.

Bibliography

Bauer, Eric, X. Zhang, and D. A. Kimber. *Practical System Reliability*. New York: Wiley (2009).

Blank, Ronald. *The Basics of Reliability*. University Park, IL: Productivity Press (2004).

Cua, K. O., K. E. McKone, and R. G. Schroeder. "Relationships between Implementation of TQM, JIT, and TPM and Manufacturing Performance." *Journal of Operations Management* 19, no. 6 (November 2001): 675–694.

Finigen, Tim, and Jim Humphries. "Maintenance Gets Lean." *IE Industrial Systems* 38, no. 10 (October 2006): 26–31.

Sova, Roger, and Lea A. P. Tonkin. "Total Productive Maintenance at Crown International." *Target: Innovation at Work* 19, no. 1 (1st Quarter 2003): 41–44.

Stephens, M. P. *Productivity and Reliability-Based Maintenance Management*. Upper Saddle River, NJ: Prentice Hall (2004).

Weil, Marty. "Beyond Preventive Maintenance." *APICS* 16, no. 4 (April 2006): 40–43.

Rapid Review

Main Heading	Review Material	myomlab
THE STRATEGIC IMPORTANCE OF MAINTENANCE AND RELIABILITY	Poor maintenance can be disruptive, inconvenient, wasteful, and expensive in dollars and even in lives. The interdependency of operator, machine, and mechanic is a hallmark of successful maintenance and reliability. Good maintenance and reliability management requires employee involvement and good procedures; it enhances a firm's performance and protects its investment. *The objective of maintenance and reliability is to maintain the capability of the system.* ▪ **Maintenance**—All activities involved in keeping a system's equipment in working order. ▪ **Reliability**—The probability that a machine part or product will function properly for a specified time under stated conditions. The two main tactics for improving reliability are: 1. Improving individual components 2. Providing redundancy The two main tactics for improving maintenance are: 1. Implementing or improving preventive maintenance 2. Increasing repair capabilities or speed	**VIDEO 17.1** Maintenance Drives Profits at Frito-Lay
RELIABILITY	A system is composed of a series of individual interrelated components, each performing a specific job. If any *one* component fails to perform, the overall system can fail. As the number of components in a *series* increases, the reliability of the whole system declines very quickly: $R_s = R_1 \times R_2 \times R_3 \times \ldots \times R_n$ (1) where R_1 = reliability of component 1, R_2 = reliability of component 2, and so on Equation (1) assumes that the reliability of an individual component does not depend on the reliability of other components. A .90 reliability means that the unit will perform as intended 90% of the time, and it will fail 10% of the time. The basic unit of measure for reliability is the *product failure rate* (FR). FR(*N*) is the number of failures during a period of time: $\text{FR}(\%) = \frac{\text{Number of failures}}{\text{Number of units tested}} \times 100\%$ (2) $\text{FR}(N) = \frac{\text{Number of failures}}{\text{Number of unit-hours of operation time}}$ (3) ▪ **Mean time between failures (MTBF)**—The expected time between a repair and the next failure of a component, machine, process, or product. $\text{MTBF} = \frac{1}{\text{FR}(N)}$ (4) ▪ **Redundancy**—The use of components in parallel to raise reliability. The reliability of a component along with its backup equals: (Probability that 1st component works) + [(Prob. that backup works) × (Prob. that 1st fails)]	Problems: 17.1–17.2, 17.5–17.14, 17.16, 17.18, 17.19 Virtual Office Hours for Solved Problems: 17.1, 17.2 **ACTIVE MODEL 17.1**
MAINTENANCE	▪ **Preventive maintenance**—Involves routine inspections, servicing, and keeping facilities in good repair to prevent failure. ▪ **Breakdown maintenance**—Remedial maintenance that occurs when equipment fails and must be repaired on an emergency or priority basis. ▪ **Infant mortality**—The failure rate early in the life of a product or process. Consistent with job enrichment practices, machine operators must be held responsible for preventive maintenance of their own equipment and tools.	Problems: 17.3, 17.4, 17.15, 17.17

Main Heading	Review Material
	Reliability and maintenance are of such importance that most maintenance systems are now computerized. Costs of a breakdown that may get ignored include: • The cost of inventory maintained to compensate for downtime • Downtime, which can have a devastating effect on safety and morale and which adversely affects delivery schedules, destroying customer relations and future sales ■ **Autonomous maintenance**—Partners operators with maintenance personnel to observe, check, adjust, clean, and notify. Employees can predict failures, prevent breakdowns, and prolong equipment life. With autonomous maintenance, the manager is making a step toward both employee empowerment and maintaining system performance.
TOTAL PRODUCTIVE MAINTENANCE	■ **Total productive maintenance (TPM)**—Combines total quality management with a strategic view of maintenance from process and equipment design to preventive maintenance. Total productive maintenance includes: • Designing machines that are reliable, easy to operate, and easy to maintain • Emphasizing total cost of ownership when purchasing machines, so that service and maintenance are included in the cost • Developing preventive maintenance plans that utilize the best practices of operators, maintenance departments, and depot service • Training for autonomous maintenance so operators maintain their own machines and partner with maintenance personnel
TECHNIQUES FOR ENHANCING MAINTENANCE	Three techniques that have proven beneficial to effective maintenance are simulation, expert systems, and sensors. Computer simulation is a good tool for evaluating the impact of various policies. Expert systems are computer programs that mimic human logic. Automatic sensors warn when production machinery is about to fail or is becoming damaged by heat, vibration, or fluid leaks.

Self Test

■ **Before taking the self-test,** refer to the learning objectives listed at the beginning of the chapter and the key terms listed at the end of the chapter.

LO1. The two main tactics for improving reliability are _________ and _________.

LO2. The reliability of a system with n independent components equals:
- **a)** the sum of the individual reliabilities.
- **b)** the minimum reliability among all components.
- **c)** the maximum reliability among all components.
- **d)** the product of the individual reliabilities.
- **e)** the average of the individual reliabilities.

LO3. What is the formula for the mean time between failures?
- **a)** Number of failures ÷ Number of unit-hours of operation time
- **b)** Number of unit-hours of operation time ÷ Number of failures
- **c)** (Number of failures ÷ Number of units tested) × 100%
- **d)** (Number of units tested ÷ Number of failures) × 100%
- **e)** 1 ÷ FR(%)

LO4. The process that is intended to find potential failures and make changes or repairs is known as:
- **a)** breakdown maintenance.
- **b)** failure maintenance.
- **c)** preventive maintenance.
- **d)** all of the above.

LO5. The two main tactics for improving maintenance are _________ and _________.

LO6. The appropriate maintenance policy is developed by balancing preventive maintenance costs with breakdown maintenance costs. The problem is that:
- **a)** preventive maintenance costs are very difficult to identify.
- **b)** full breakdown costs are seldom considered.
- **c)** preventive maintenance should be performed, regardless of the cost.
- **d)** breakdown maintenance must be performed, regardless of the cost.

LO7. _________ maintenance partners operators with maintenance personnel to observe, check, adjust, clean, and notify.
- **a)** Partnering
- **b)** Operator
- **c)** Breakdown
- **d)** Six Sigma
- **e)** Autonomous

Answers: LO1. improving individual components, providing redundancy; LO2. d; LO3. b; LO4. c; LO5. implementing or improving preventive maintenance, increasing repair capabilities or speed; LO6. b; LO7. e.

Solutions to Even-Numbered Problems

17.2 From Figure 2, about 13% overall reliability.
17.4 Expected daily breakdowns = 2.0
Expected cost = $100 daily
17.6 **(a)** 5.0%
(b) .00001026 failures/unit-hr.
(c) .08985
(d) 98.83
17.8 $R_s = .9941$
17.10 $R_p = .99925$
17.12 **(a)** $R_p = .984$
(b) Increase by 11.1%.
17.14 $R = .7918$
17.16 **(a)** .972
(b) .980
17.18 System B is slightly higher, at .9397.

ıdex

ɟe references followed by "f" indicate illustrated
ıres or photographs; followed by "t" indicates a
ıe.